Lecture Notes in Compu'

Commenced Publication in 1973
Founding and Former Series Editors:
Gerhard Goos, Juris Hartmanis, and Jan va

Springer
Berlin
Heidelberg
New York
Hong Kong
London
Milan
Paris
Tokyo

Maurice Bruynooghe   Kung-Kiu Lau (Eds.)

Program Development in Computational Logic

A Decade of Research Advances
in Logic-Based Program Development

Springer

Volume Editors

Maurice Bruynooghe
Katholieke Universiteit Leuven
Department of Computer Science
Celestijnenlaan 200A, 3001 Heverlee, Belgium
E-mail: Maurice.Bruynooghe@cs.kuleuven.ac.be

Kung-Kiu Lau
University of Manchester
Department of Computer Science
Manchester M13 9PL, United Kingdom
E-mail: kung-kiu@cs.man.ac.uk

Library of Congress Control Number: 2004107507

CR Subject Classification (1998): F.3.1, D.1.1, D.1.6, I.2.2, F.4.1, D.2, D.3

ISSN 0302-9743
ISBN 3-540-22152-2 Springer-Verlag Berlin Heidelberg New York

Springer-Verlag is a part of Springer Science+Business Media

springeronline.com

© Springer-Verlag Berlin Heidelberg 2004
Printed in Germany

Typesetting: Camera-ready by author, data conversion by Boller Mediendesign
Printed on acid-free paper   SPIN: 11012061   06/3142   5 4 3 2 1 0

Preface

The tenth anniversary of the LOPSTR[1] symposium provided the incentive for this volume. LOPSTR started in 1991 as a workshop on logic program synthesis and transformation, but later it broadened its scope to logic-based program development in general, that is, program development in computational logic, and hence the title of this volume.

The motivating force behind LOPSTR has been the belief that declarative paradigms such as logic programming are better suited to program development tasks than traditional non-declarative ones such as the imperative paradigm. Specification, synthesis, transformation or specialization, analysis, debugging and verification can all be given logical foundations, thus providing a unifying framework for the whole development process.

In the past 10 years or so, such a theoretical framework has indeed begun to emerge. Even tools have been implemented for analysis, verification and specialization.

However, it is fair to say that so far the focus has largely been on programming-in-the-small. So the future challenge is to apply or extend these techniques to programming-in-the-large, in order to tackle software engineering in the real world.

Returning to this volume, our aim is to present a collection of papers that reflect significant research efforts over the past 10 years. These papers cover the whole development process: specification, synthesis, analysis, transformation and specialization, as well as semantics and systems.

We would like to thank all the authors for their valuable contributions that made this volume possible. We also thank the reviewers for performing their arduous task meticulously and professionally: Annalisa Bossi, Nicoletta Cocco, Bart Demoen, Danny De Schreye, Yves Deville, Sandro Etalle, Pierre Flener, John Gallagher, Samir Genaim, Gopal Gupta, Ian Hayes, Patricia Hill, Andy King, Vitaly Lagoon, Michael Leuschel, Naomi Lindenstrauss, Nancy Mazur, Mario Ornaghi, Dino Pedreschi, Alberto Pettorossi, Maurizio Proietti, CR Ramakrishnan, Sabina Rossi, Abhik Roychoudhury, Salvatore Ruggieri, Tom Schrijvers, Alexander Serebrenik, Jan-Georg Smaus, Wim Vanhoof and Sofie Verbaeten.

April 2004   Maurice Bruynooghe and Kung-Kiu Lau

---

[1] http://www.cs.man.ac.uk/~kung-kiu/lopstr/

Table of Contents

Specification and Synthesis

Semantics

Analysis

Transformation and Specialisation

Termination

Systems

Specifying Compositional Units for Correct Program Development in Computational Logic

Kung-Kiu Lau[1] and Mario Ornaghi[2]

[1] Department of Computer Science, University of Manchester
Manchester M13 9PL, United Kingdom
kung-kiu@cs.man.ac.uk
[2] Dipartimento di Scienze dell'Informazione, Universita' degli studi di Milano
Via Comelico 39/41, 20135 Milano, Italy
ornaghi@dsi.unimi.it

Abstract. In order to provide a formalism for defining program correctness and to reason about program development in Computational Logic, we believe that it is better to distinguish between specifications and programs. To this end, we have developed a general approach to specification that is based on a model-theoretic semantics. In our previous work, we have shown how to define specifications and program correctness for open logic programs. In particular we have defined a notion of correctness called *steadfastness*, that captures at once modularity, reusability and correctness. In this paper, we review our past work and we show how it can be used to define compositional units that can be correctly reused in modular or component-based software development.

1 Introduction

In software engineering, requirements analysis, design and implementation are distinctly separate phases of the development process [18], as they employ different methods and produce different artefacts. In requirements analysis and design, *specifications* play a central role, as a frame of reference capturing the requirements and the design decisions. By contrast, data and programs only appear in the implementation phase, towards the end of the development process. There is therefore a clear distinction between specifications and programs.

In Computational Logic, however, this distinction is usually not maintained. This is because there is a widely held view that logic programs are executable specifications and therefore there is no need to produce specifications before the implementation phase of the development process. We believe that undervaluing specifications in this manner is not an ideal platform for program development. If programs are indistinguishable from specifications, then how do we define program correctness, and how do we reason about program development? We hold the view that the meaning of correctness must be defined in terms of something other than logic programs themselves. We are not alone in this, see e.g., [17, p. 410]. In our view, the specification should axiomatise all our relevant knowledge of the problem context and the necessary data types, whereas,

M. Bruynooghe and K.-K. Lau (Eds.): Program Development in CL, LNCS 3049, pp. 1–29, 2004.
© Springer-Verlag Berlin Heidelberg 2004

for complexity reasons, programs rightly capture only what is strictly necessary for computing. In the process of extracting programs from specifications, a lot of knowledge is lost, making programs much weaker axiomatisations. This suggests that specifying and programming are different activities, involving different methodological aspects. Thus, we take the view that specifications should be clearly distinguished from programs, especially for the purpose of program development. Indeed, we have shown (in [28,29]) that in Computational Logic, not only can we maintain this distinction, but we can also define various kinds of specifications for different purposes. Moreover, we can also define correctness with respect to these specifications.

Our semantics for specification and correctness is model-theoretic. The declarative nature of such a semantics allows us to define *steadfastness* [34], a notion of correctness that captures at once modularity, reusability and correctness. *Open* programs are incomplete pieces of code that can be (re)used in many different *admissible* situations, by *closing* them (by adding the missing code) in many different ways. *Steadfastness* of an open program P is pre-proved correctness of the various closures of P, with respect to the different meanings that the specification of P assumes in the admissible situations. For correct reuse, we need to know when a situation is admissible. This knowledge is given by the *problem context*. We have formalised problem context as a *specification framework* [27], namely, a first-order theory that axiomatises the problem context, characterises the admissible situations as its (intended) models, and is used to write specifications and to reason about them.

In this paper, we review our work in *specification* and *correctness* of logic programs, including steadfastness. Our purpose is to discuss the role of steadfastness for correct software development. In particular, we are interested in modularity and reuse, which are key aspects of software development. Our work is centred on the notion of a *compositional unit*. A compositional unit is a *software component*, which is commonly defined as a unit of composition with contractually specified interfaces and context dependencies only [46]. The interfaces declare the imported and exported operations, and the context dependencies specify the constraints that must be satisfied in order to correctly (re)use them. Throughout the paper, we will not refer to compositional units as software components, however, for the simple reason that as yet there is no standard definition for the latter (although the one we used above [46] is widely accepted). So we prefer to avoid any unnecessary confusion. In our compositional units, the interfaces and the context dependencies are declaratively specified in the context of the specification framework $\mathcal{F}$ axiomatising the problem context. $\mathcal{F}$ gives a precise semantics to specifications and allows us to reason about the *correctness* of programs, as well as their *correct reuse*. Thus, in our formalisation, a compositional unit has a three-tier structure, with separate levels for framework, specifications and programs.

We introduce compositional units in Section 2, and consider the three levels separately. We focus on model-theoretic semantics of frameworks and specifications, and on steadfastness (i.e., open program correctness).

In Section 3, we show how the proposed formalisation of compositional units can be used to support correct reuse. Our aim is to highlight the aspects related to specifications, so we consider only the aspects related to the framework and the specification levels, while assuming the possibility of deriving (synthesising) steadfast programs from specifications.

At the end of each section we briefly discuss and compare our results with related work, and finally in the conclusion we comment on future developments.

2 Compositional Units

In our approach, compositional units represent correctly reusable units of *specifications and correct open programs*. Our view is that specifications and programs are not stand-alone entities, but are always to be considered in the light of a problem context. The latter plays a central role: it is the *semantic context* in which specifications and program correctness assume their appropriate meaning, and it contains the necessary knowledge for *reasoning* about correctness and correct reuse. This is reflected in the three-tier structure (with model-theoretic semantics) of a compositional unit, as illustrated in Figure 1.

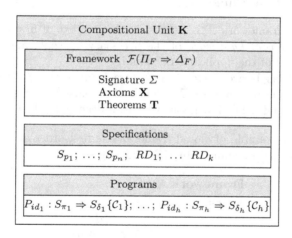

Fig. 1. A three-tier formalism.

At the top level of a compositional unit **K**, we have a *specification framework* $\mathcal{F}$, or *framework* for short, that embodies an axiomatisation of the problem context. $\mathcal{F}$ has a signature Σ, a set **X** of *axioms*, a set **T** of *theorems*, a list Π_F of *open symbols*, and a list Δ_F of *defined symbols*. The syntax $\Pi_F \Rightarrow \Delta_F$ indicates that the axioms of $\mathcal{F}$ fix (the meaning of) the symbols Δ_F whenever $\mathcal{F}$ is composed with frameworks that fix Π_F. The defined and open symbols belong to the signature Σ, which may also contain *closed symbols*, namely symbols defined completely by the axioms (i.e., independently from Π_F). Frameworks are explained in Section 2.1, and framework composition is explained in Section 3.1.

In the middle, we have the *specification section*. Its role is to bridge the gap between the framework $\mathcal{F}$ and the chosen *programming language*. So far, we have considered only logic programs, and the corresponding specification formalism is explained in Section 2.2. The specification section contains the specifications $S_{p_1}, \ldots, S_{p_n}$ of the program predicates occurring in the program section. It may also contain a set of *specification reduction theorems* theorems $RD_1, \ldots, RD_k$, that are useful to reason about correct reuse. Specification reduction is explained in Section 3.2.

At the bottom, we have the *program section*. Programs are open logic (or constraint logic) programs. An open program $P_{id_i} : S_{\pi_i} \Rightarrow S_{\delta_i} \{C_i\}$ ($1 \leq i \leq h$) has an identifier id_i, an *interface specification* $S_{\pi_i} \Rightarrow S_{\delta_i}$ and a set $\{C_i\}$ of *implementation clauses*. S_{π_i} and S_{δ_i} are lists of specifications defined in the specification section. An interface specification contains all the information needed to *correctly* reuse a *correct* program. Programs and correctness are explained in Section 2.3. Correct reuse is explained in Section 3.3.

2.1 Specification Frameworks

A specification framework $\mathcal{F}$ is defined in the context of first-order logic, and contains the *relevant knowledge* of the necessary concepts and data types for building a model of the application at hand.

We distinguish between *closed* and *open* frameworks. A *closed framework* $\mathcal{F} = \langle \Sigma, \mathbf{X}, \mathbf{T} \rangle$ has a signature Σ, a set $\mathbf{X}$ of axioms, and a set $\mathbf{T}$ of theorems. It has no open and defined symbols, that is, all the symbols of Σ are closed.

Example 1. An example of closed framework is first-order arithmetic $\mathcal{NAT} = \langle \Sigma_{Nat}, \mathbf{X}_{Nat}, \mathbf{T}_{Nat} \rangle$, introduced by the following syntax:[3]

$$\textbf{Framework } \mathcal{NAT};$$

DECLS: $Nat : sort$;
          $0 : [\,] \rightarrow Nat$;
          $s : [Nat] \rightarrow Nat$;
          $\_+\_, \_*\_ : [Nat, Nat] \rightarrow Nat$;
AXS: $Nat : construct(0, s : Nat)$;
$+ :$ $i + 0 = i$;
          $i + s(j) = s(i + j)$;
$\;\;:$ $i * 0 = 0$;
          $i * s(j) = i * j + i$;
THMS: $i + j = j + i$;
          $\ldots$

---

[3] In all the examples, we will omit the outermost universal quantifiers, but their omnipresence should be implicitly understood.

The signature Σ_{Nat}, introduced in the declaration section DECLS, is the signature of Peano's arithmetic. The axioms $\mathbf{X}_{Nat}$, introduced in the AXS section, are the usual ones of first-order arithmetic. 0 and s are the *constructors* of *Nat* and their axioms, which we call the *constructor axioms* for *Nat*, are collectively indicated by $construct(0, s : Nat)$. The latter contains Clark's equality theory [35] for 0 and s, as well as all the instances of the first-order induction schema. $\mathcal{N\!AT}$ has been widely studied, and there are a lot of known theorems (in section THMS), including for example the associative, commutative and distributive laws.

Theorems are an important part of a framework. However, they are not relevant in the definitions that follow, so we will not refer to them explicitly here.

For closed frameworks we adopt isoinitial semantics, that is, we choose the intended model of $\mathcal{F} = \langle \Sigma, \mathbf{X} \rangle$ to be a *reachable isoinitial model*, defined as follows:

Definition 1 (Reachable Isoinitial Model [5]). *Let* $\mathbf{X}$ *be a set of* Σ*-axioms. A* Σ*-structure* I *is an* isoinitial *model of* $\mathbf{X}$ *iff, for every model* M *of* $\mathbf{X}$*, there is a unique isomorphic embedding* $i : \text{I} \rightarrow \text{M}$.

A model I *is* reachable *if its elements can be represented by ground terms.*

Definition 2 (Adequate Closed Frameworks [30]). *A closed framework* $\mathcal{F} = \langle \Sigma, \mathbf{X} \rangle$ *is* adequate *iff there is a reachable isoinitial model* I *of* $\mathbf{X}$ *that we call 'the' intended model of* $\mathcal{F}$.

In fact I is one of many intended models of $\mathcal{F}$, all of which are isomorphic. So I is unique up to isomorphism, and hence our (ab)use of 'the'.

As shown in [5], adequacy entails the computability of the operations and predicates of the signature.

Example 2. $\mathcal{N\!AT}$ is an adequate closed framework. Its intended model is the standard structure $\mathcal{N}$ of natural numbers ($\mathcal{N}$ is a reachable isoinitial model of $\mathbf{X}_{Nat}$). $\mathcal{N}$ interprets *Nat* as the *set of natural numbers*, and $s, +$ and $*$ as the *successor, sum* and *product* function, respectively.

The adequacy of a closed framework is not a decidable property. We have the following useful proof-theoretic characterisation, which can be seen as a "richness requirement" implicit in isoinitial semantics [31]:

Definition 3 (Atomic Completeness). *A framework* $\mathcal{F} = \langle \Sigma, \mathbf{X} \rangle$ *is* atomically complete *iff, for every ground atomic formula A, either* $\mathbf{X} \vdash A$ *or* $\mathbf{X} \vdash \neg A$.

Theorem 1 (Adequacy Condition [38]). *A closed framework* $\mathcal{F} = \langle \Sigma, \mathbf{X} \rangle$ *is adequate iff it has at least one reachable model and is atomically complete.*

Closed adequate frameworks can be built incrementally, starting from a closed adequate kernel, by means of *adequate extensions*.

Definition 4 (Adequate Extensions [30]). *An* adequate extension *of an adequate closed framework* $\mathcal{F} = \langle \Sigma, \mathbf{X} \rangle$ *is an adequate closed framework* $\mathcal{F}_\delta = \langle \Sigma \cup \delta, \mathbf{X} \cup D_\delta \rangle$ *such that:*

a) D_δ *is a set of* $(\Sigma \cup \delta)$-*axioms, axiomatising a set of* new *(i.e., not in* Σ*) symbols* δ;
b) *the* Σ-*reduct* $\text{I}|\Sigma$ *of the intended model* I *of* $\mathcal{F}_\delta$ *is the intended model of* $\mathcal{F}$.

The notions of *reduct* and *expansion* are standard in logic [4]. The Σ-reduct $\text{I}' = \text{I}|\Sigma$ forgets the interpretation of the symbols not in Σ, in our case the new symbols δ. Conversely, I is said to be a $(\Sigma \cup \delta)$-*expansion* of I', that is, a $(\Sigma \cup \delta)$-expansion is a $(\Sigma \cup \delta)$-interpretation that preserves the meaning of the old Σ-symbols, and interprets the new δ arbitrarily.

In Definition 4, by b), the intended model I of an adequate extension is an expansion of the old intended model, that is, adequacy entails that the meaning of the old symbols is preserved.

If the axioms D_δ of an *adequate* extension are explicit definitions, we say that they are *adequate explicit definitions*. Since they are important in our approach, we briefly recall them.

An explicit definition of a new relation r has the form $\forall \underline{x} \bullet r(\underline{x}) \leftrightarrow R(\underline{x})$, where $\underline{x}$ indicates a tuple of variables and (as usual) "$\bullet$" extends the scope of a quantifier to the longest subformula next to it. The explicit definition of a new function f has the form $\forall \underline{x} \bullet F(\underline{x}, f(\underline{x}))$, where $R(\underline{x})$ and $F(\underline{x}, y)$ are formulas of the framework that contain free only the indicated variables. The explicit definition of f has the *proof obligation* $\mathbf{X} \vdash \forall \underline{x} \bullet \exists! y \bullet F(\underline{x}, y)$, where $\mathbf{X}$ are the framework axioms (as usual, $\exists! y$ means unique existence). $R(\underline{x})$ is called the *definens* (or *defining formula*) of r, and $F(\underline{x}, y)$ the *definiens* (or *defining formula*) of f.

Explicit definitions have nice properties. They are *purely* declarative, in the following sense: they define the new symbols *purely in terms of the old ones*, that is, in a *non-recursive* way. This declarative character is reflected by the following *eliminability* property, where Σ is the signature of the framework and δ are the new explicitly defined symbols: the extension is conservative (i.e., no new Σ-theorem is added) and every formula of $\Sigma + \delta$ is provably equivalent to a corresponding formula of the old signature Σ. Moreover, if we start from a sufficiently expressive kernel, most of the relevant relations and functions can be explicitly defined. Finally, we can prove:

Proposition 1. *If the definiens of an explicit definition is quantifier-free, then the definition is adequate.*

If the definiens is not quantifier-free, adequacy must be checked. To state the adequacy of closed frameworks and of explicit definitions, we can apply proof methods based on logic program synthesis [26,27] or constructive logic [38].

Example 3. The kernel $\mathcal{NAT}$ of Example 1 is sufficiently expressive in the following sense. Every recursively enumerable relation r can be introduced by an explicit definition.[4] For example, we can define the ordering relations $\leq$ and $<$ by the explicit definitions:

$$D_\leq : i \leq j \leftrightarrow \exists k \bullet i + k = j;$$
$$D_< : i < j \leftrightarrow i \leq j \wedge \neg i = j.$$

Since the outermost universal quantifiers are implicitly present, $D_\leq$ is the closed formula $\forall i, j \bullet i \leq j \leftrightarrow \exists k \bullet i + k = j$ (similarly, $D_<$ is understood to be universally closed).

Since the definiens $\exists k \bullet i + k = j$ of $\leq$ is quantified, adequacy of $D_\leq$ must be checked. It can be proved by logic program synthesis, as follows.

(a) We derive the following clauses in $\mathcal{NAT} + D_\leq$:

$$P_\leq : \qquad 0 \leq i \leftarrow$$
$$s(i) \leq s(j) \leftarrow i \leq j.$$

(b) In $\mathcal{NAT} + D_\leq$ we prove the *only-if part* of the completed definition [35] of $\leq$ in $P_\leq$ (the *if part* is guaranteed by a)).
(c) Finally, we prove that $P_\leq$ existentially terminates, i.e., for every ground atom A, the goal $\leftarrow A$ finitely fails or has at least one successful derivation (with program $P_\leq$).

By (a), (b) and (c) we get ([27], Theorem 11) that the extension by $D_\leq$ is adequate. By the way, adequacy entails that the new predicate $\leq$ is computable. We do not have to check the adequacy of $D_<$, because its definiens is quantifier free. $D_<$ uses $\leq$. However, an explicit definition of $<$ and a proof of its adequacy can be given directly in $\mathcal{NAT}$, by the eliminability of explicit definitions. Thus we could define $<$ first, prove its adequacy, and then define $\leq$ on top of $<$. That is, the order of explicit definitions is not relevant.

We can explicitly define functions, for example the integer square root *sqrt*:

$$D_{sqrt} : sqrt(i) * sqrt(i) \leq i \wedge i < s(sqrt(i)) * s(sqrt(i)).$$

The *proof obligation* $\forall i \bullet \exists! j \bullet j * j \leq i \wedge i < s(j) * s(j)$ can be proved in $\mathcal{NAT}$ by induction. Adequacy follows from the fact that the definiens $j * j \leq i \wedge i < s(j) * s(j)$ is quantifier free.

An *open framework* $\mathcal{F}(\Pi \Rightarrow \Delta) = \langle \Sigma, \mathbf{X} \rangle$ represents an incomplete axiomatisation. It has a non-empty import list Π, containing the symbols left *open* by the axioms, and a (possibly empty) disjoint export list Δ, containing the symbols that are *defined* by the axioms, in terms of the open ones. The *closed* symbols are the symbols of the signature that are not in $\Pi \cup \Delta$, and their meaning is fixed in a unique way by the axioms. We distinguish three sets of axioms, where Σ_K is the sub-signature of the closed symbols:

---

[4] Every recursively enumerable relation is Diophantine (Matijacevic theorem [37]).

- the *kernel axioms* $\mathbf{X}_K = \mathbf{X}|\Sigma_K$ $(\dots|\Sigma_K$ is the subset of the axioms with symbols from Σ_k); the kernel axioms axiomatise the closed symbols, that is, $\mathcal{F}_K = \langle \Sigma_K, \mathbf{X}_K \rangle$ must be an adequate closed framework, that we call the *closed kernel*;
- the *constraints* $\mathbf{X}_C = (\mathbf{X}|(\Sigma_K \cup \Pi)) \setminus \mathbf{X}_K$, which constrain the possible interpretations of the open symbols Π;
- and the *definition axioms* $\mathbf{X}_D = \mathbf{X} \setminus (\mathbf{X}_K \cup \mathbf{X}_C)$, which fix the meaning of the defined symbols Δ, in terms of the open and closed symbols.

Example 4. The following open framework axiomatises lists with generic elements X and a generic total ordering $\lhd$ on X. From now on, in the examples, the variables of sort X will begin with x, y, z, w, those of sort *Nat* with i, j, h, k, and those of sort *ListX* with l, m, n, o.

> **Framework** $\mathcal{LIST}(X, \lhd \Rightarrow ListX, nil, ., @, nocc)$;
>
> KERNEL: $\mathcal{NAT}$;
>
> DECLS: $X : sort$;
> $ListX : sort$;
> $\_ \lhd \_ : [X, X]$;
> $nil : [\,] \to ListX$;
> $\_.\_ : [X, ListX] \to ListX$;
> $\_@(\_,\_) : [X, Nat, ListX]$;
> $nocc : [X, ListX] \to Nat$;
>
> DEFAXS: $ListX : construct(nil, . : ListX)$;
> $@ :$ $x@(0, l) \leftrightarrow \exists y, m \bullet l = y.m \wedge x = y$;
> $x@(s(i), l) \leftrightarrow \exists y, m \bullet l = y.m \wedge x@(i, m)$;
> $nocc :$ $nocc(x, nil) = 0$;
> $x = y \to nocc(x, y.l) = nocc(x, l) + 1$;
> $\neg x = y \to nocc(x, y.l) = nocc(x, l)$;
>
> CONSTRS: $\lhd : TotalOrdering(\lhd)$.

The signature Σ_{Nat}, the axioms $\mathbf{X}_{Nat}$ and the theorems $\mathbf{T}_{Nat}$ of the imported *kernel* $\mathcal{NAT}$ are automatically included. In the *definition axioms* DEFAXS, *nil* and "." are the *list constructors*, as indicated by $construct(nil, . : ListX)$, which contains Clark's equality theory and structural induction on constructors; $x@(i, l)$ means that the element x occurs at position i in the list l, where positions start from 0; $nocc(x, l)$ is the number of occurrences of the element x in the list l; by the *constraint axioms* CONSTRS, $\lhd$ is a total ordering relation.

To specify the basic operations on the ADT of lists, the closed kernel $\mathcal{NAT}$ is not necessary. We have imported it for specification and reasoning purposes. Indeed, by using natural numbers we can introduce @ and *nocc*. The resulting language and axiomatic system give a rich starting framework, which allows us to explicitly define the usual operations on lists and ordered lists, and to reason about them (see Example 6).

An open framework $\mathcal{F}$ has a class of not necessarily isomorphic intended models, since $\mathbf{X}_K \cup \mathbf{X}_C$ allows many $(\varSigma_K \cup \varPi)$-interpretations, that we call *pre-models*. The semantics considered here is a variant of the one presented in [30]. A pre-model is an expansion of the intended model of the kernel that satisfies the constraints $\mathbf{X}_C$. For every pre-model P, the axioms of $\mathcal{F}$ fix a corresponding intended P-model Ip, defined as follows.

A P-model of $\mathcal{F}$ is a $\varSigma$-model M of $\mathbf{X}$ such that $\text{M}|(\varSigma_K \cup \varPi) = \text{P}$, that is, M coincides with P over the closed and open symbols. Since $\varPi$ may contain open sorts, we consider $\varPi$-reachable models, where $\varPi$-reachability is reachability in an expansion containing a new constant for each element of each open sort.

Definition 5 (P-isoinitial Models). *A* P-*model* I *is a* P-isoinitial model of $\mathcal{F}$ *iff, for every* P-*model* M, *there is a unique isomorphic embedding* $i : \text{I} \to \text{M}$ *such that* i *is the identity over the open sorts.*

Definition 6 (Adequate Open Frameworks and Intended Models). *An open framework $\mathcal{F}$ is* adequate *iff, for every pre-model* P *of $\mathcal{F}$, there is a $\varPi$-reachable* P-*isoinitial model* Ip, *that we call the intended* P-*model of $\mathcal{F}$.*

M *is an* intended model *of $\mathcal{F}$ iff there is a pre-model* P *of $\mathcal{F}$ such that* M *is the intended* P-*model of $\mathcal{F}$.*

For every pre-model P, the intended P-model is unique up to isomorphism. Intended models with non-isomorphic pre-models are, of course, non-isomorphic. We consider closed frameworks as a limiting case, where the kernel coincides with the whole framework and the unique intended model coincides with the unique pre-model.

Example 5. $\mathcal{LIST}$ is an adequate open framework. In it, a pre-model P coincides with $\mathcal{N}$ for the kernel signature $\varSigma_{Nat}$ and interprets X as any set with a total ordering $\lhd$. The intended P-model of $\mathcal{LIST}$ interprets $ListX$ as the set of the finite lists with elements from X, and the other defined symbols in the way already explained in Example 4.

Adequate open frameworks can be built incrementally, by *adequate extensions*, where the intended models of an adequate extension $\mathcal{F}'$ of a framework $\mathcal{F}$ are expansions of intended models of $\mathcal{F}$.

Definition 7 (Adequate Extensions). *A framework $\mathcal{F}'$ is an* adequate extension *of an adequate open framework $\mathcal{F}$ iff $\mathcal{F}'$ is an adequate open or closed framework, the signature and the axioms of $\mathcal{F}'$ contain those of $\mathcal{F}$, the kernel signature of $\mathcal{F}'$ contains the kernel signature of $\mathcal{F}$, and for every intended model* I' *of $\mathcal{F}'$, the reduct* $\text{I}'|\varSigma$ *is an intended model of $\mathcal{F}$.*

In the limiting case, an adequate extension $\mathcal{F}'$ of an open framework $\mathcal{F}$ may be a closed framework. In this case, we say that $\mathcal{F}'$ is an *instance* of $\mathcal{F}$, and the axioms that "instantiate" (i.e., close) the open symbols are called *closure axioms*. A set of closure axioms is called a *closure*. Closures will be considered in Section 3.1, together with other framework operations.

In general, the adequacy of an extension is not decidable, but we may have different kinds of extensions, with different adequacy conditions. In particular, we distinguish:

- Parameter extensions. In this case new parameters and/or new constraints are added. Parameter extensions are adequate iff, adding new constraints, consistency is preserved.
- Defined symbol extensions. In this case new defined symbols, together with the corresponding definition axioms, are added. Adequate explicit definitions are still useful for introducing new defined symbols, and adequacy can be stated in a way similar to those mentioned before for closed framework extensions (by program synthesis or constructive logic [27,38]). Proposition 1 still holds.
- Kernel extensions. In this case the closed kernel is extended by new closed symbols, as already shown for closed frameworks.

Example 6. The framework $\mathcal{LIST}(X, \lhd \Rightarrow ListX, nil, ., @, nocc)$ can be obtained by extending the framework $\mathcal{LIST}(X \Rightarrow ListX, nil, ., @, nocc)$, without $\lhd$ and without constraint axioms, by the *parameter* $\lhd : [X, X]$ constrained by $TotalOrdering(\lhd)$. The *kernel* $\mathcal{NAT}$ can be extended by explicitly defining the most useful operations and predicates on natural numbers. The *defined symbols* can be extended by the relevant operations on lists, by means of explicit definitions. For example, the definitions of list membership, length, concatenation and permutation are:[5]

$$
\begin{aligned}
D_{\in} \quad &: x \in l \leftrightarrow nocc(x, l) > 0 \\
D_{len} \quad &: \forall i \bullet (\exists x \bullet x@(i, l)) \leftrightarrow i < len(l) \\
D_{|} \quad &: \forall i, x \bullet (i < len(l) \rightarrow (x@(i, l) \leftrightarrow x@(i, l|m))) \quad \wedge \\
& \qquad (len(l) \leq i \rightarrow (x@(i, m) \leftrightarrow x@(i + len(l), l|m))) \\
D_{perm} &: perm(l, m) \leftrightarrow \forall x \bullet nocc(x, l) = nocc(x, m)
\end{aligned}
$$

$D_{\in}$ gives rise to an adequate extension, because its definiens is quantifier free. The definiens of D_{len} is $\forall i \bullet (\exists x \bullet x@(i, l)) \leftrightarrow i < k$ and the proof obligation requires a proof of $\forall l \bullet \exists! k \bullet \forall i \bullet (\exists x \bullet x@(i, l)) \leftrightarrow i < k$. Since the definiens is quantified, adequacy must be checked (and can be proved), by constructive proofs or by program synthesis. Adequacy must be checked (and can be proved) also for $D_{|}$ and D_{perm}.

Using $\lhd : [X, X]$, we can also define operations on ordered lists, like $l \lhd_L m$ (lexicographic ordering on lists), $ord(l)$ (l is an ordered list), and so on. Their properties can be proved using the total ordering constraints. For example, we can prove that the lexicographic ordering $\lhd_L$ is, in turn, a total ordering.

2.2   Specifications

In a compositional unit **K**, specifications assume their proper meaning only in the context of the framework $\mathcal{F}$. In this section we define formally what we

---

[5] In D_{len} and $D_{|}$, the universal quantifiers of the definiens have not been omitted.

mean by specifications in $\mathcal{F}$ and we show some examples. We maintain a strict distinction between specification frameworks and (program) specifications and, to distinguish the function and relation symbols of the framework from those computed by programs, the latter will be called (program) *operations*.

Definition 8 (Specifications and S-expansions). *Let $\mathcal{F}(\Pi \Rightarrow \Delta) = \langle \Sigma, \mathbf{X} \rangle$ be a framework. A specification S_ω in (the context of) $\mathcal{F}$ is a set of closed $(\Sigma + \omega)$-formulas, that define a set of operations ω in terms of $\mathcal{F}$.*

An S_ω-expansion of a model M of $\mathcal{F}$ is a $(\Sigma + \omega)$-expansion M' of M such that $\mathrm{M}' \models S_\omega$.

That is, S_ω can be interpreted as an *expansion operator* that associates with every intended model of $\mathcal{F}$ the corresponding S_ω-expansions, namely the expansions that interpret the specified operations according to S_ω.

Definition 9 (Strict Specifications). *A specification S_ω is strict in a framework $\mathcal{F}$, if, for every model M of $\mathcal{F}$, there is only one S_ω-expansion. It is non-strict otherwise.*

Now we list different kinds of strict and non-strict specifications considered in [28], essentially based on explicit definitions. The specification formalism considered here is tailored to logic programs with definite clauses in a many-sorted signature. Program semantics is based on *minimum Herbrand models*, where *program data* (those used in programs) coincide with ground terms. We assume that the signature Σ_D of program data is *pre-defined* by the framework $\mathcal{F}$, and that, for every closed or defined sort s of Σ_D, $\mathcal{F}$ contains the axioms $construct(c_1, \ldots, c_n : s)$, where $c_1, \ldots, c_n$ are the constructors of s. They are the unique operations of sort s that can be used in logic programs. This assumption concerns Herbrand models of standard logic programs, where $construct(\ldots)$ holds, but our treatment readily extends to the specification formalism for constraint logic programs by assuming that Σ_D is the constraint signature, and is pre-defined by the framework.

Since in logic programs only *program predicates* are not pre-defined, we have to specify only them. There are different forms of specifications.

If-and-Only-if Specifications. An *if-and-only-if specification* in a framework $\mathcal{F}$ is an explicit definition of a new predicate r:

$$S_r : \quad \forall \underline{x} \bullet r(\underline{x}) \leftrightarrow R(\underline{x})$$

By the well known properties of explicit definitions, for every model M of the framework $\mathcal{F}$, there is only one S_r-expansion of M, that is, S_r is strict.

Example 7. In $\mathcal{NAT}$ we can specify, for example, the following predicates:

$$\begin{aligned} S_{div} \quad &: div(i,j,h,k) \leftrightarrow i = j * h + k \wedge k < j; \\ S_{divides} \quad &: divides(i,j) \leftrightarrow \exists h \bullet div(j,i,h,0); \\ S_{prime} \quad &: prime(i) \leftrightarrow \forall j \bullet divides(j,i) \rightarrow j = 1 \vee j = i; \end{aligned}$$

Super-and-sub Specifications. A *super-and-sub specification* in a framework $\mathcal{F}$ is of the form

$$S_r: \quad \forall \underline{x} \bullet (R_{sub}(\underline{x}) \to r(\underline{x})) \wedge (r(\underline{x}) \to R_{super}(\underline{x}))$$

where $R_{sub}(\underline{x})$ and $R_{super}(\underline{x})$ are two formulas of $\mathcal{F}$ such that $\mathcal{F} \vdash \forall \underline{x} \bullet R_{sub}(\underline{x}) \to R_{super}(\underline{x})$.

The implication $\forall \underline{x} \bullet R_{sub}(\underline{x}) \to R_{super}(\underline{x})$ is satisfied by the models of $\mathcal{F}$. Therefore, in every intended model I, the relation R_{sub} in I, i.e., the set of values $\mathbf{x}$ such that $I \models R_{sub}(\mathbf{x})$, is a sub-relation of the relation R_{super}, and the specified relation r is any relation that is a super-relation of R_{sub} but is a sub-relation of R_{super}.

Conditional Specifications. A *conditional specification* of a new relation r in a framework $\mathcal{F}$ has the form:

$$\forall \underline{x}, \underline{y} \bullet IC(\underline{x}) \to (r(\underline{x}, \underline{y}) \leftrightarrow R(\underline{x}, \underline{y})) \tag{1}$$

where $IC(\underline{x})$ is the *input condition*, and $R(\underline{x}, \underline{y})$ is the *input-output condition*. Both $IC(\underline{x})$ and $R(\underline{x}, \underline{y})$ are formulas of $\mathcal{F}$. (1) specifies $r(\underline{x}, \underline{y})$ only when the input condition $IC(\underline{x})$ is true, while nothing is required if the input condition is false. That is, $IC(\underline{x})$ states that $r(\underline{x}, \underline{y})$ is to be called *only* in contexts that make it true. This fact allows us to assume $IC(\underline{x})$ when reasoning about correct reuse, as shown in Section 3.2.

(1) is equivalent to the following super-and-sub specification, which allows us to apply the results of [34] in correctness proofs:

$$\forall \underline{x}, \underline{y} \bullet (IC(\underline{x}) \wedge R(\underline{x}, \underline{y}) \to r(\underline{x}, \underline{y})) \wedge (r(\underline{x}, \underline{y}) \to \neg IC(\underline{x}) \vee R(\underline{x}, \underline{y}))$$

Example 8. In the open framework $\mathcal{LIST}(X, \lhd \Rightarrow ListX, nil, ., @, nocc)$, we have for example the following specification:

$$
\begin{aligned}
S_{sort} \quad &: sort(l, m) \leftrightarrow perm(l, m) \wedge ord(m); \\
S_{merge} &: ord(l) \wedge ord(m) \to (merge(l, m, o) \leftrightarrow ord(o) \wedge perm(l|m, o)); \\
S_{split} \quad &: (len(l) > 1 \wedge split(l, m, n) \to perm(l, m|n) \wedge len(m) < len(l) \wedge \\
&\quad len(n) < len(l)) \ \wedge \ (len(l) > 1 \to \exists m, n \bullet split(l, m, n));
\end{aligned}
$$

S_{sort} is an if-and-only-if specification, S_{merge} is a conditional specification. By the input condition, $merge(l, m)$ is to be called only in contexts where the input lists are ordered. If they are not, o is not required to be ordered. S_{split} is an example of another form of non-strict specification (called a *selector specification*) that we do not discuss here (see [28]).

2.3   Interface Specifications, Programs, and Correctness

Here we consider correctness of (logic) programs with respect to interface specifications. In Section 3.2, we will consider the role of interface specifications in correct reuse. We start by introducing some terminology.

The *signature* Σ_P of a program P contains the declarations of its predicate, constant and function symbols, and the sorts occurring in such declarations. The *data signature* of P is the subsignature of its sort, constant and function symbols. According to the previous section, the data signature belongs to the framework signature. We will distinguish *open* and *closed* programs, as follows.

The *defined predicates* of a program P are those that occur in the head of at least one clause of P, while the (possible) *open predicates* of P are those that occur only in the body. A program P is *open* if its signature contains at least one open sort or predicate. It is *closed* if no open symbol belongs to its signature.

A *interface specification* for an *open* program P is of the form $S_\pi \Rightarrow S_\delta$, where S_π are specifications of a set π of predicates that includes all the open predicates of P, and S_δ are specifications of a set δ of predicates that are included in the defined predicates of P. We will write $P : S_\pi \Rightarrow S_\delta$ to indicate that P has specification $S_\pi \Rightarrow S_\delta$. If P has no open predicates, then S_π will be empty. In this case, we write $P : \Rightarrow S_\delta$.

Example 9. In a compositional unit with open framework $\mathcal{LIST}$, we can declare the following open sorting program (where S_{split}, S_{merge} and S_{sort} are as shown in Example 8):

$$\text{Program } P_{sort} : S_{split}, S_{merge} \Rightarrow S_{sort}$$
$$\{$$
$$sort(nil, nil) \leftarrow$$
$$sort(x.nil, x.nil) \leftarrow$$
$$sort(x.y.l, o) \leftarrow split(x.y.l), m, n),$$
$$sort(m, m_1), sort(n, n_1),$$
$$merge(m_1, n_1, o).$$
$$\}$$

Programs may be open independently from the framework, i.e., closed frameworks may contain open programs. For example, in the closed framework $\mathcal{NAT}$, we can declare:

$$\text{Program } P_{prod} : S_{sum} \Rightarrow S_{prod}$$
$$\{$$
$$prod(i, 0, 0) \quad \leftarrow$$
$$prod(i, s(j), h) \leftarrow prod(i, j, k), sum(k, i, h). \}$$
$$\{$$

where:

$$S_{sum} : sum(x, y, z) \leftrightarrow z = x + y;$$
$$S_{prod} : prod(x, y, z) \leftrightarrow z = x \cdot y.$$

Now we can define program correctness. We will first explain the correctness of closed programs in closed frameworks, because it is simpler and more intuitive. Then we introduce correctness of open programs.

Correctness of Closed Programs. A closed program P has only defined predicates, and an interface specification of P is of the form $\Rightarrow S_\delta$. For simplicity, we will consider the case of interface specifications $\Rightarrow S_r$ with one defined predicate r (the extension to $\Rightarrow S_{r_1}, \ldots, S_{r_k}$, with $k > 1$, is immediate). We define program correctness in a closed framework as follows:

Definition 10 (Correctness of Closed Programs). *Let $\mathcal{F}$ be a closed framework with intended model* I. *Let S_r be a specification of a predicate r, P be a program that computes r, and* H *be the minimum Herbrand of P. P is correct with respect to the interface specification $\Rightarrow S_r$ iff the interpretation of r in* H *coincides with the interpretation of r in one of the S_r-expansions of* I.

For conciseness, we will say that $P : \Rightarrow S_r$ is correct, to indicate that P is correct with respect to $\Rightarrow S_r$.

For a strict specification S_r, there is only one S_r-expansion of I, that is, the new symbol r defined by S_r has a unique interpretation in I, and one in H. Correctness of $P : \Rightarrow S_r$ means that the two interpretations of r coincide, or, at least, are isomorphic. This is illustrated in Figure 2.

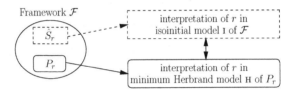

Fig. 2. Strict specifications.

If S_r is not strict, then r has many interpretations with respect to I. Correctness of $P : \Rightarrow S_r$ in this case means that the interpretation of r in H coincides with one of the interpretations of r with respect to I. This is illustrated in Figure 3.

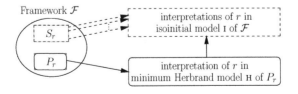

Fig. 3. Non-strict specifications.

Steadfastness: Correctness of Open Programs. Now we consider open programs in open frameworks, and we discuss the associated notion of correctness. An open program is correct if it behaves as expected in all the circumstances. We called this property *steadfastness* [34].

The correctness relation between an interface specification $S_\pi \Rightarrow S_\delta$ and an open program P cannot be defined as in Definition 10, because open frameworks may have many intended models and we cannot use minimum Herbrand models as the semantics of open programs, since in the minimum Herbrand models, open relations are assumed to be empty, and therefore cannot play the role of parameters. So in [34] we introduced *minimum J-models*, together with the notion of *steadfastness*, to serve as the basis for a model and proof theory of the correctness of open programs.

Here we first recall the definition of steadfastness informally, and then define correctness of open programs, and give its relevant properties. A *pre-signature* for an open program P is a signature Ω that contains the data signature and the open predicates of P, but *not* the defined predicates of P. A *pre-interpretation in Ω* is an Ω-interpretation. That is, symbols of Ω are considered to be open, and a pre-interpretation J interprets them arbitrarily. In contrast, the intended meaning of the defined predicates of P is stated by its clauses, in terms of J.

Let P be a program with defined predicates δ. To define the intended meaning of δ in a pre-interpretation J, we introduce J-models. A J-model of P is a model M of P, such that $M \mid \Omega = J$, i.e., M coincides with J over Ω. Since two distinct J-models M and N differ only for the interpretation of δ, we can compare them by looking at δ: we say that M is contained in N, written $M \subseteq_\delta N$, iff the interpretation of (the predicates of) δ in M is contained in that of δ in N. We can show that a minimum J-model (with respect to $\subseteq_\delta$) exists. The minimum J-model of P will be indicated by J^P, and it represents the interpretation of δ stated by the program P, in the pre-interpretation J.

Using minimum J-models, steadfastness in an interpretation can be defined as follows.

Definition 11 (Steadfastness). *Let P be an open program, Ω be a pre-signature for P, and r be a predicate defined by P. P is steadfast for r in a $(\Omega + r)$-interpretation I if and only if the interpretation of r in its minimum $I \mid \Omega$-model coincides with the interpretation of r in I.*

More intuitively, steadfastness in I for r means that the interpretation of r in I coincides with the interpretation of r stated by P, when the open symbols Ω are interpreted as in I (i.e., when the pre-interpretation is $I \mid \Omega$). Consider for example the open program P in the context of $\mathcal{NAT}$:

$$r(x) \leftarrow p(z, x)$$

where x and z are of sort Nat. $\Sigma_{Nat} \cup \{p : [Nat, Nat]\}$ is a pre-signature for this program. Consider the interpretation I_1 where Σ_{Nat} is interpreted as in $\mathcal{NAT}$, $r(x)$ means "x is even", and $p(z, x)$ means "$z + z = x$". If we interpret p as in I_1, we can easily see that the interpretation of $r(x)$ in the corresponding minimum model of P coincides with the interpretation of $r(x)$ in I_1, i.e., P is steadfast in I_1. Similarly, if we consider I_2 that interprets $p(z, x)$ as "$z * z = x$", to get steadfastness I_2 has to interpret $r(x)$ as "x is a perfect square".

Correctness is steadfastness in the expansions of the intended models stated by the interface specification:

Definition 12 (Correctness of Open Programs). *Let $\mathcal{F}$ be an open framework, and $P : S_\pi \Rightarrow S_\delta$ be an open program. $P : S_\pi \Rightarrow S_\delta$ is correct in $\mathcal{F}$ iff for every intended model I of $\mathcal{F}$ and every S_π-expansion I_π of I, there is a S_δ-expansion $I_{\pi,\delta}$ of I_π, such that P is steadfast in $I_{\pi,\delta}$ for the predicate symbols of δ.*

The intuitive meaning of the previous definition is the following: $\Sigma + \pi$ is a pre-signature for P, and I_π is a pre-interpretation that interprets the data signature according to $\mathcal{F}$ and the open symbols according to S_π, i.e., I_π represents a legal parameter passing. Steadfastness of P in $I_{\pi,\delta}$ means that the interpretation of δ stated by P for the parameter passing I_π is correct with respect to S_δ.

The following important properties of correct reusability hold (see [34]):

Proposition 2 (Inheritance). *Let $\mathcal{F}'$ be an adequate extension of an adequate (open) framework $\mathcal{F}$. If $P : S_\pi \Rightarrow S_\delta$ is correct in $\mathcal{F}$, then it is correct in $\mathcal{F}'$.*

As we will show in Section 3, framework composition can be treated in terms of extension. Therefore inheritance yields a first level of correct reusability, namely reusability of correct programs through framework composition, extension and instantiation. This level of correct reusability would not be important, however, if we could not guarantee the correctness of the composition of the inherited open programs. This second, important level of correct reusability will be called *compositionality*. In compositionality, interface specifications play a central role, as shown by the following theorems:

Theorem 2 (Compositionality). *If $P : S_{\pi_1}, S_{\delta_2} \Rightarrow S_{\delta_1}$ and $Q : S_{\pi_2} \Rightarrow S_{\delta_2}$ are correct in a framework $\mathcal{F}$ and are not mutually recursive, then $P \cup Q : S_{\pi_1}, S_{\pi_2} \Rightarrow S_{\delta_1}, S_{\delta_2}$ is correct in $\mathcal{F}$.*

As we can see, interface specifications indicate how programs can be composed to correctly interact. Theorem 2 can be extended to mutually recursive programs, but in this case we have to check that open termination [34] is preserved. By inheritance and compositionality we get reusability, as shown by the following example.

Example 10. We can show that the open program $P : S_{split}, S_{merge} \Rightarrow S_{sort}$ in Example 9 is correct in the open framework $\mathcal{LIST}$. This means that, in every instance of $\mathcal{LIST}$, $P : S_{split}, S_{merge} \Rightarrow S_{sort}$ is always correct with respect to the specification $\Rightarrow S_{sort}$, provided that it is composed with closed correct programs $Q_{merge} : \Rightarrow S_{merge}$ and $Q_{split} : \Rightarrow S_{split}$.

This example shows that compositionality corresponds to *a priori* correctness of open programs in a framework. It thus corresponds to correctness of open modules in a library. It is to be contrasted with *a posteriori* correctness, i.e., correctness established by verification after program composition.

2.4 Related Work

Specification frameworks are similar to Abstract Data Types (ADT's). ADT's became popular in the 80's and have been widely studied [47]. In general, they are based on the initial algebra approach, that is, intended models are initial models. Parametric ADT's have also been studied. These are similar to our open frameworks, even though they are technically defined in a different way. A detailed treatment of algebraic ADT's, including the parametric case, can be found, for example, in [13].

The initial algebra approach is adequate for ADT specification, where the purpose is to give the minimal signature and axioms that are needed to characterise the desired data and operations. Initial models generalise the idea of minimum Herbrand models, and always exist for algebraic ADT's and consistent Horn theories [21]. The existence of an initial model allows us to axiomatise only positive knowledge and to use (consistently) negation as failure: a fact is false if we do not have evidence of its truth. This allows for very compact axiomatisations.

In contrast, our purpose is "knowledge representation", that is, we are looking for an expressive signature and a rich set of axioms, to obtain a framework that represents our overall knowledge of a problem domain and allows us to reason about it. Isoinitial semantics requires stronger axiomatisations, and better meets our "richness requirement", compared to initial semantics. It was introduced in [5], with the purpose of giving a model-theoretic characterisation of computable ADT's.

Finally, our approach is different from the algebraic approach in the three-level architecture of our compositional units, and in the role that frameworks play in it. In this regard, we are closer to the two-tiered specification style of Larch [20], where specifications have two components: the first one is written in the Larch Shared Language LSL, and the second one in a Larch Interface Language, which is oriented to the programming language and is used to specify the interfaces between program components, i.e., the way they communicate.

We consider non-recursive definitions, like explicit or conditional definitions, to be an important tool for both extending frameworks and specifying programs. In this regard, our work is similar to [36]. At the program and specification levels, our approach is in the tradition of logic program synthesis and correctness. Our notion of correctness for closed programs is similar to the one introduced in [22]. Correctness of open programs with respect to specifications similar to our interface specifications is considered in [10]. A conditional specification is like a pre-post-condition style of specification as in VDM [24], Z [45], and B [1], except that it is declarative. Declarative conditional specifications for logic programs were introduced in [8].

3 Operations on Compositional Units

In this section we consider compositional units as building blocks for program development, that is, we focus on operations on compositional units that allow their correct reuse in the process of developing an application. This process starts from pre-existing compositional units, and iteratively extends them either directly, by inserting domain specific knowledge, or by reusing, i.e., incorporating, other compositional units. Reuse can, in turn, be factorised into *composition* and *extension*, which are the basic operations considered in this section. Such operations involve the framework, the specification and the program levels. We will consider the different levels separately.

3.1   Framework Reuse

To compose two units C_1 and C_2, first we compose and/or extend their frameworks $\mathcal{F}_1$ and $\mathcal{F}_2$ into a common extension $\mathcal{F}$, and then use the specifications and programs in this richer $\mathcal{F}$. Thus, in general, the framework level is the first level to be involved in operations on compositional units. Here we consider the basic operations needed at this level.

Framework Morphisms. Operations like renaming or identifying different symbols may be needed for framework reuse. This kind of operation is formalised by framework morphisms. Before introducing framework morphisms, we briefly recall signature and theory morphisms [19,13].

A *signature morphism* $\mu : \Sigma_1 \to \Sigma_2$ is a map from the symbols of Σ_1 to those of Σ_2 that preserves the declarations. Σ_2 extends Σ_1, in the following sense:

- Σ_2 contains the μ-image of Σ_1;
- every Σ_1-formula F translates into a Σ_2-formula $\mu(F)$;
- instead of Σ_1-reducts we have μ-reducts: the μ-reduct of a Σ_2-interpretation M is the Σ_1-interpretation M$|\mu$ that interprets every symbol σ of Σ_1 as M interprets the image $\mu(\sigma)$.

A *theory morphism* $\mu : \langle \Sigma_1, \mathbf{X}_1 \rangle \to \langle \Sigma_2, \mathbf{X}_2 \rangle$ is a signature morphism $\mu : \Sigma_1 \to \Sigma_2$ such that $\mu(\mathbf{X}_1)^* \subseteq \mathbf{X}_2^*$, where * denotes the proof-theoretic closure. μ works as a generalised extension, in the sense that Σ_2 contains (the μ-image of) Σ_1 and the theorems of $\mathbf{X}_2$ contain (the μ-translation of) those of $\mathbf{X}_1$.

Framework morphisms are defined as follows:

Definition 13 (Framework Morphism). *Let* $\mathcal{F}(\Pi \Rightarrow \Delta) = \langle \Sigma, \mathbf{X} \rangle$ *and* $\mathcal{F}'(\Pi' \Rightarrow \Delta') = \langle \Sigma', \mathbf{X}' \rangle$ *be two frameworks. A framework morphism* $\epsilon : \mathcal{F} \to \mathcal{F}'$ *is a theory morphism* $\epsilon : \langle \Sigma, \mathbf{X} \rangle \to \langle \Sigma', \mathbf{X}' \rangle$ *such that the kernel signature of* $\mathcal{F}'$ *contains the* ϵ-image of the kernel signature of $\mathcal{F}$.

$\mathcal{F}'$ can be considered as a generalised extension of $\mathcal{F}$. We say that it is the extension generated by the morphism $\epsilon : \mathcal{F} \to \mathcal{F}'$. Let $\mathcal{F}$ be adequate. We say that $\mathcal{F}'$ is an *adequate extension* of $\mathcal{F}$ if $\mathcal{F}'$ is adequate and, for every intended model I$'$ of $\mathcal{F}'$, the ϵ-reduct I$'|\epsilon$ is an intended model of $\mathcal{F}$.

Framework extensions considered in the previous section, that simply introduce new symbols and axioms, are a particular case. They correspond to *inclusion morphisms* ϵ that map each symbol σ into σ itself.

Example 11. A (generalised) adequate extension of $\mathcal{LIST}$ is:

> **Framework** $\mathcal{LIST}_1(\lhd \Rightarrow ListNat, nil, ., @, nocc)$
> EXTENDS $\mathcal{LIST}$;
> CLOSE: X BY Nat;
> RENAME: $ListX$ BY $ListNat$;

It is generated by the morphism ϵ defined by the clauses CLOSE and RENAME. ϵ
maps the sort symbol X into Nat, the sort symbol $ListX$ into $ListNat$, and leaves
the other symbols unchanged. Of course, arities and sorts in relation, function
and constant declarations are translated by replacing X and $ListX$ by Nat and
$ListNat$. For example, now we have $nil : [\,] \to ListNat$ and $. : [Nat, ListNat] \to$
$ListNat$.

In $\mathcal{LIST}_1$, $ListNat$ is closed (its intended meaning is the set of finite lists of
natural numbers) and the only open symbol is $\lhd : [Nat, Nat]$. A closed adequate
extension can be obtained by closing $\lhd$ by

$$D_\lhd : \quad x \lhd y \leftrightarrow x \le y$$

In this case, we have simply added the new axiom $D_\lhd$, that is, we have an
inclusion morphism of $\mathcal{LIST}_1$ into a closed framework, that we will indicate by
$\mathcal{LISTNAT}$.

The morphisms considered in this example are at the basis of the closure
operations that we consider next.

Closure. A closure is an extension that closes the meaning of some symbols.
Here, we consider closure by *internalisation*, as defined in [30]. As shown in [30],
internalisation can be used to implement constrained parameter passing, as well
as to introduce *objects* as the closures of suitable open frameworks that represent
classes.

Let $\mathcal{F}(\Pi \Rightarrow \Delta) = \langle \Sigma, \mathbf{X} \rangle$ be an open framework. An *internalisation* of an
open symbol is one of the following operations:

- *Sort closure.* The closure: CLOSE S BY s
  renames the open *sort* S by a sort s of the signature Σ_K of the closed kernel.
  No axioms are added.
- *Relation closure.* The operation: CLOSE r BY $\forall \underline{x} \bullet r(\underline{x}) \leftrightarrow R(\underline{x})$
  closes r by the new *closure axiom* $\forall x \bullet r(\underline{x}) \leftrightarrow R(\underline{x})$. The declaration of r may
  contain only sorts of Σ_K, and the defining formula $R(\underline{x})$ is a Σ_K-formula.
- *Function closure.* The operation: CLOSE f BY $\forall \underline{x} \bullet F(\underline{x}, f(\underline{x}))$
  closes f by the new *closure axiom* $\forall \underline{x} \bullet F(\underline{x}, f(\underline{x}))$. The declaration of f may
  contain only sorts of Σ_K, and the defining formula $F(\underline{x}, y)$ is a Σ_K-formula
  such that $\mathbf{X}_K \vdash \forall \underline{x} \bullet \exists! y \bullet F(\underline{x}, y)$.

Let $\mathcal{F}(\Pi \Rightarrow \Delta) = \langle \Sigma, \mathbf{X} \rangle$ be an open framework. A *closure by internalisation*
is an internalisation that closes all the open sorts by closed sorts and all the open

relation and function symbols by a set D_Π of closure axioms, and satisfies the following *constraint satisfaction* condition:

$$\mathbf{X}_K \cup D_\Pi \vdash \mathbf{X}_C \tag{2}$$

It produces the framework $\mathcal{F}' = \langle \Sigma', (\mathbf{X}\backslash\mathbf{X}_C)\cup D_\Pi, \mathbf{T}\cup\mathbf{X}_C\rangle$ where Σ' is obtained by replacing in Σ each open sort s with the sort s' closing s, D_Π are the closure axioms of the open functions and relations, and, by (2), the constraints $\mathbf{X}_C$ have been deleted from the axioms and added to the theorems.

Example 12. $\mathcal{LISTNAT}$ of Example 11 is a closure of $\mathcal{LIST}$. It has been obtained by a sort closure and a relation closure, by the definition $D_\lhd$. Constraints are satisfied because

$$\mathbf{X}_{Nat} \cup D_\lhd \vdash TotalOrdering(\lhd)$$

Now the total ordering axioms $TotalOrdering(\lhd)$ are no longer constraints, but theorems.

A different closure could be obtained, e.g., by closing $\lhd$ by the reverse ordering $x \lhd y \leftrightarrow y \leq x$.

A closure of a framework $\mathcal{F}$ should be an adequate closed extension of $\mathcal{F}$. We can prove:

Theorem 3 (Closure). *Let $\mathcal{F}(\Pi \Rightarrow \Delta) = \langle \Sigma, \mathbf{X} \rangle$ be an adequate framework, and $\mathcal{F}' = \langle \Sigma', (\mathbf{X} \setminus \mathbf{X}_C) \cup D_\Pi, \mathbf{T} \cup \mathbf{X}_C \rangle$ be the result of a closure. Then $\mathcal{F}'$ is an adequate closed extension of $\mathcal{F}$ iff $\mathcal{F}'$ is* consistent *and* atomically complete.

The relation and function closures preserve consistency because D_Π are explicit definitions in the kernel and, by the constraint satisfaction condition, $\mathbf{X}_C$ become theorems. Thus *consistency* is preserved if sort closures preserve the consistency of $\mathbf{X} \setminus \mathbf{X}_C$. A sufficient condition to preserve consistency is that no cardinality restrictions are imposed on the open sorts, as is commonly the case (like, e.g., the open sort X in generic lists).

Concerning *atomic completeness*, let $\mathcal{K}$ be the extension of the closed kernel of $\mathcal{F}$ by the closure axioms D_Π. Atomic completeness may be not guaranteed for two reasons: (a) $\mathcal{K}$ is not atomically complete because D_Π are not adequate explicit definitions in the kernel, or (b) the atomic completeness of $\mathcal{K}$ is not sufficient to obtain the atomic completeness for the defined symbols, because stronger properties are required by the definition axioms. To avoid (a), D_Π must be adequate explicit definitions in the kernel. With quantifier free defining formulas, adequacy is guaranteed by Proposition 1. An example of (b) is the definition axiom $r(x) \leftrightarrow \exists y \bullet p(x, y)$, where p is a parameter; in this case, $\mathcal{K}$ should prove $\exists y \bullet p(\mathbf{x}, y)$ or $\neg\exists y \bullet p(\mathbf{x}, y)$ for every ground $\mathbf{x}$, i.e., atomic completeness of $\mathcal{K}$ does not suffice. However, in general it is reasonable to look for definition axioms that close the defined symbols whenever the open ones become closed, i.e., case (b) should be the exception. Thus, if we do not use quantified defining formulas, closures by internalisation are, in general, adequate.

Closure may also be performed incrementally, step by step. A partial closure is called a *specialisation*, because it does not close all the open symbols. Besides partial closure, we may have other kinds of specialisation. For example: adding constraints, using open symbols in the defining formulas, mapping open sorts into non-closed sorts, and so on. All these operations can be formalised by extension morphisms, but we will omit relevant details.

Example 13. The framework $\mathcal{LIST}_1$ of Example 11 is a specialisation of $\mathcal{LIST}$, obtained by the partial closure of X.

Framework Composition. Framework composition essentially coincides with framework union. The simplest case is disjoint union. However, it may happen that we want to preserve a common part, for example natural numbers. Here we consider the composition of two frameworks $\mathcal{F}_1$ and $\mathcal{F}_2$ that have a common subframework $\mathcal{G}$ containing their closed kernel, and have disjoint signatures for the symbols not in $\mathcal{G}$. In this case, composition preserving $\mathcal{G}$ can be defined as the operation $+_\mathcal{G}$ that builds the composite $\mathcal{F}_1 +_\mathcal{G} \mathcal{F}_2$ simply by making the union of signatures, open and closed symbols, and axioms. If $\mathcal{F}_1$ and $\mathcal{F}_2$ share symbols not in $\mathcal{G}$, then we rename such symbols, to make them different before performing the union.

$+_\mathcal{G}$ is syntactic composition. Its semantic counterpart is amalgamation. Two intended models I_1 of $\mathcal{F}_1$ and I_2 of $\mathcal{F}_2$ are amalgamable if they coincide over the common signature. Their amalgamation is the interpretation $\mathsf{I}_1 + \mathsf{I}_2$ that coincides with I_1 over the signature of $\mathcal{F}_1$ and with I_2 over the signature of $\mathcal{F}_2$ (the definition is consistent, because I_1 and I_2 coincide over the common signature). The intended models of $\mathcal{F}_1 +_\mathcal{G} \mathcal{F}_2$ are the amalgamations of the pairs of amalgamable intended models of $\mathcal{F}_1$ and $\mathcal{F}_2$.

This kind of composition has been formalised in ADT's using *pushouts* (see e.g., [13]), and the pushout approach also works for frameworks, and it allows us to generalise the operation $+_\mathcal{G}$. We do not consider the general case here for conciseness.

Example 14. Let $\mathcal{BOOL}$ be a framework defining booleans in the usual way. Lists of booleans with open ordering $\lhd : [Bool, Bool]$ can be defined starting from the disjoint union $\mathcal{LIST} + \mathcal{BOOL}$, as follows:

> **Framework** $\mathcal{LIST}_2(\lhd \Rightarrow ListBool, nil, ., @, nocc)$
> EXTENDS $\mathcal{LIST} + \mathcal{BOOL}$;
> CLOSE: X BY $Bool$;
> RENAME: $ListX$ BY $ListBool$;

We can compose lists of booleans $\mathcal{LIST}_2$ and lists of natural numbers $\mathcal{LIST}_1$ (see Example 11). To avoid duplicating the kernel of natural numbers, we perform the composition with common subframework $\mathcal{NAT}$:

$$\mathcal{LIST}_1 \ +_{\mathcal{NAT}} \ \mathcal{LIST}_2$$

To distinguish the non-common symbols, the composition renames them. Since we allow overloading, only sort and constant renaming may be needed. For example, we have $nil_1 : [] \rightarrow ListNat$, $] nil_2 : [] \rightarrow ListBool$, overloaded $. : [Nat, ListNat] \rightarrow ListNat$ and $. : [Nat, ListBool] \rightarrow ListBool$, and so on.

3.2   Specification Reuse

Specifications are used in two ways. Before composition or extension, they are used as a guide to search for possible compositional units that specify a desired context and set of operations. For example, if we need list sorting, we look for compositional units that contain the framework for lists with totally ordered elements, a specification S_{sort} of a *sort* operation, and a program $P : \ldots \Rightarrow S_{sort}, \ldots$. After composition or extension, the compositional units guide program composition, according to Theorem 2.

Reusability after composition or extension is enhanced by *specification reduction*, as considered in [15]. Indeed, after extension or composition, we have a richer framework, where new properties have been added. It may happen that a specification can be reduced to a new specification, that is, in the new context the new specification can replace the old one.

Informally, an "old" specification S reduces to a "new" specification S' if correctness with respect to the new S' entails correctness with respect to the old S. Formally, we give the following definition:

Definition 14 (Specification Reduction). *Let $\mathcal{F}$ be a framework, and S_{ω}, $S'_{\omega'}$ be two sets of specifications in $\mathcal{F}$. We say that S_{ω} reduces to $S'_{\omega'}$ iff $\omega \subseteq \omega'$ and $\mathcal{F} \vdash S'_{\omega'} \rightarrow S_{\omega}$.*

For two interface specifications $S_{\pi_1} \Rightarrow S_{\delta_1}$, $S_{\pi_2} \Rightarrow S_{\delta_2}$, we say that $S_{\pi_1} \Rightarrow S_{\delta_1}$ reduces $S_{\pi_2} \Rightarrow S_{\delta_2}$ iff S_{π_2} reduces to S_{π_1} and S_{δ_1} reduces to S_{δ_2}.

Reduction is transitive and reflexive. Its meaning is made clear by Theorem 4:

Theorem 4. *Let $\mathcal{F}$ be a framework, and $S_{\pi_1} \Rightarrow S_{\delta_1}$ and $S_{\pi_2} \Rightarrow S_{\delta_2}$ be two interface specifications. If $S_{\pi_1} \Rightarrow S_{\delta_1}$ reduces to $S_{\pi_2} \Rightarrow S_{\delta_2}$ in $\mathcal{F}$, then every program P that is correct with respect to $S_{\pi_2} \Rightarrow S_{\delta_2}$ is also correct with respect to $S_{\pi_1} \Rightarrow S_{\delta_1}$ (in $\mathcal{F}$).*

Example 15. Let **K** be a compositional unit with open framework $\mathcal{LIST}$, and let S_{lhd} be the strict specification $S_{lhd} : lhd(x, y) \leftrightarrow x \lhd y$. In the extension $\mathcal{LISTNAT}$ of $\mathcal{LIST}$, $S'_{lhd} : lhd(x, y) \leftrightarrow x \leq y$ reduces to S_{lhd} (we prove $S_{lhd} \rightarrow S'_{lhd}$ by the closure axiom $x \lhd y \leftrightarrow x \leq y$). Thus $S_{lhd} \Rightarrow S_{merge}$ (where S_{merge} is defined in Example 8) reduces to $S'_{lhd} \Rightarrow S_{merge}$, and we can use S'_{lhd} when deriving correct *merge* programs. For example, we could write a correct program $P_{merge'} : S'_{lhd} \Rightarrow S_{merge}$ which avoids comparisons with 0, since 0 is the minimum natural number; $P_{merge'}$ would correctly override a (possibly) inherited $P_{merge} : S_{lhd} \Rightarrow S_{merge}$.

In the reduction of conditional specifications [15], we can take into account the *call context*. This is shown in the following example.

Example 16. In the open framework $\mathcal{LIST}$ we can give the following specifications:

$$S'_{merge} : \quad l = x.nil \wedge ord(m) \rightarrow (merge(l, m, o) \leftrightarrow ord(o) \wedge perm(x.m, o));$$
$$S'_{split} : \quad split(x.l, m, n) \leftrightarrow m = x.nil \wedge n = l.$$

S_{split} of Example 8 reduces to S'_{split} ($S'_{split} \rightarrow S_{split}$ can be proved in $\mathcal{LIST}$). S_{merge} of Example 8 reduces to S'_{merge} in a *call context* where the input condition $l = x.nil \wedge ord(m)$ of S'_{merge} holds for the lists l and m to be merged. Indeed, in such a context, S'_{merge} corresponds to $merge(x.nil, m, o) \leftrightarrow ord(o) \wedge perm(x.m, o)$, S_{merge} to $merge(x.nil, m, o) \leftrightarrow ord(o) \wedge perm(x.nil|m, o)$, and they are equivalent. We will say that S_{merge} *contextually reduces* to S'_{merge}.

Contextual reduction implies *contextual reuse*, that is, S_{merge} correctly reduces to S'_{merge} only when the input condition of S'_{merge} is true. As a consequence, we cannot replace S_{merge} by S'_{merge} in isolation, but we have to consider the call context. In contrast, we can replace S_{split} by S'_{split} in isolation, because the corresponding reduction is not contextual.

As we will see in Example 17, S'_{merge} and S'_{split} are tailored to the insertion sort algorithm. In a similar way, we can specialise S_{merge} and S_{split} to obtain specifications tailored to different sorting algorithms, like merge sort, quick sort, and so on.

In general, it is useful to list proven reduction theorems in the specification section of a compositional unit. Such a list would allow us to automatically search for families of program compositions, giving rise to families of implementations. It is for this reason that we have put $RD_1, ... RD_k$ in Fig. 1.

3.3   Program Reuse

Like specifications, programs in compositional units can be used before and after unit composition.

We use programs before composition when we look for existing compositional units containing *specific algorithms*. Otherwise, reuse is after unit composition, when we use the inherited programs to solve the problem in question. The operation that allows us to reuse the inherited programs is program composition. It is strongly guided by specifications. Specification reduction is important for program reusability, since it allows us to use the richer knowledge obtained after framework composition and extension to solve the puzzle of composing the inherited open programs into a correct solution of the problem at hand.

Example 17. Let **K** be a compositional unit with framework $\mathcal{LIST}$, and let us assume that it already contains the correct program $P_{insert} : S_{lhd} \Rightarrow S_{insert}$, where P_{insert} implements the usual algorithm for inserting an element into its correct position in an ordered list, S_{lhd} is the specification shown in Example 15, and S_{insert} is:

$$S_{insert}: \quad ord(l) \rightarrow (insert(x,l,m) \leftrightarrow (ord(m) \wedge perm(x.l,m))).$$

We show how reductions of Example 16 can be used to solve the puzzle of obtaining a correct sorting program $Q_{sort} : S_{lhd} \Rightarrow S_{sort}$. If we compose P_{insert} with the correct one-clause programs

$$P_{split} :\Rightarrow S'_{split} \qquad\qquad split(x.l, x.nil, l) \leftarrow$$
$$P_{link} : S_{insert} \Rightarrow S'_{merge} \qquad merge(x.nil, l, o) \leftarrow insert(x, l, o)$$

we get a correct program $Q_{aux} : S_{lhd} \Rightarrow S'_{split}, S'_{merge}$. By the specification reductions of Example 16, the interface specification $S'_{split}, S'_{merge} \Rightarrow S_{sort}$ *contextually* reduces to $S_{split}, S_{merge} \Rightarrow S_{sort}$. Thus, the program $P_{sort} : S_{split}, S_{merge} \Rightarrow S_{sort}$ of Example 9 is also correct with respect to $S'_{split}, S'_{merge} \Rightarrow S_{sort}$, because the input condition of S'_{merge} is satisfied in the call context of $merge$, as required. By composing P_{sort} and Q_{aux}, we get a correct $Q_{sort} : S_{lhd} \Rightarrow S_{sort}$.

Q_{sort} can be closed in the instances that close lhd. For example, S_{lhd} reduces to S'_{lhd} in a compositional unit with framework $\mathcal{LISTNAT}$, as shown in Example 15. Suppose that our compositional unit already contains a correct program $P_{leq} :\Rightarrow S_{leq}$. If we compose it with the correct one-clause program

$$P_{lhd} : S_{leq} \Rightarrow S'_{lhd} \qquad\qquad lhd(x,y) \leftarrow leq(x,y)$$

we get a closed correct program $Q_{lhd} :\Rightarrow S_{lhd}$. By specification reduction we get that $Q_{lhd} : \Rightarrow S'_{lhd}$ is also correct. Then the closed program $Q_{lhd} \cup Q_{sort} :\Rightarrow S_{sort}$ is correct in $\mathcal{LISTNAT}$.

3.4   Related Work

At the framework level, our approach to modularity and reuse is in the tradition of algebraic ADT's [2,13,47]. We can apply the techniques developed there, based on theory morphisms. Our *specification frameworks* should not be confused with the *specification frames* introduced in [25]. The latter, like institutions [19], are general frames for the composition and reuse of formal theories. With respect to modularity and compositionality, our frameworks with open symbols and defined symbols are similar, for example, to modules with import and export interfaces, as introduced in [14].

In [25], a distinction between parameterised specifications and parameterised data types is introduced, following [42]. In [42], programs and specifications are considered as different entities, involved in different phases and different methodological aspects of program development, and a distinction between parameterised specifications and specifications of parameterised programs is introduced. In this, [42] is very close to our general view, but our approach is different. Our three-level architecture of compositional units is closer to Larch [20]. Like Larch, our specifications state precisely how open programs interact, and allow us to compose them correctly. However, unlike Larch, we have a further specification level, which is intermediate between the framework level and the interface specification level. This yields a further level of correct reuse, through the specification reduction theorems.

With regard to modularity in logic programming, there are approaches based on ideas similar to our J-models (see [7]), while the approach proposed in [39] relates to specification frames [25]. However, all these approaches do not distinguish between specifications and programs. A distinction between programs and specifications is made in [40], where modular Prolog programs (as proposed in [44]) are derived from first-order specifications (based on Extended ML [43]). However, in [40], the role of specifications is different from ours, and there is no counterpart of specification frameworks.

Finally, in the area of object-oriented analysis and design, component-based development methods [12,3] have emerged, where components and reuse are two of the main aspects of the software development process. In this area, a software component is a unit of composition with contractually specified interfaces and context dependencies only [46]. Our compositional units broadly fit this characterisation, considering interface specifications $S_\pi \Rightarrow S_\delta$ as interfaces, and specifications and their reducibility relation in the context of the framework as context dependencies.

4   Conclusion

In this paper we have essentially collected our previous work on program specification and synthesis, and we have organised it by introducing compositional units, which are a more complete and refined version of correct schemas [16]. Then we have illustrated the basic operations for extending and correctly reusing (composing) compositional units.

A compositional unit is a unit of reuse that contains both a formalisation of the problem domain, at the framework level, and a collection of open programs, correct with respect to their specifications, at the specification and program levels. The framework level specifies, by the constraint axioms, when and how a compositional unit can be correctly reused. The specification and program levels support program reuse and development. The examples of Section 3 have been mainly devoted to illustrating the role of specifications in the correct reuse of compositional units for program development. In particular, specifications are a guide for program composition, and specification reduction allows us to deal with the problem of adapting the inherited open programs to the specific context of reuse.

In this paper, we have not considered program synthesis, because we concentrated on specifications and their role in the reuse of compositional units and correct open programs. However, there is a strong relationship to logic program synthesis [11], and indeed our research started in this area. An interesting fact is the possibility of using logic program synthesis as a way for expanding frameworks in an adequate way [27].

The distinct levels for specifications and programs distinguish our approach. At these levels, we have integrated our research on steadfast open programs and specifications. As we have shown, specifications and steadfast programs yield a further level of reuse, through specification reduction and program composition. We believe that this is an important feature of our approach, especially in the context of so-called software components [46]. Our future work will be devoted to the study of the applicability of our approach to the development of correct component-based software.

On the one hand, we want to develop the approach further, based on logic programs, along the following two lines: (a) We will extend our approach to other kinds of logic programs. For constraint logic programs and those normal programs that have one intended model, the extension of our results is almost immediate. (b) We will study methods for deriving steadfast programs from their interface specifications, based on our compositional units and on the results of [34] and the ideas exposed in [16]. To this end, tools would be necessary for developing an interactive environment where we can define and compose specification frameworks, specifications and programs, and use a proof assistant for developing the necessary proofs. We are looking at logical frameworks like Isabelle [23] as possible candidates.

On the other hand, we want to consider the extension of our approach to different programming paradigms. This can be done in two ways. The first choice is to define, on top of specification frameworks, different specification formalisms, oriented to different program languages. Such formalisms would provide different interface specification languages, in a way similar to Larch [20]. The second choice is to use our compositional units as meta-level declarative specifications of systems implemented in possibly imperative programming languages.

So far, we have considered only the second choice. We began a study of object-oriented systems, with the aim of testing the versatility of our model and, hopefully, of obtaining a formalisation of object-oriented compositional units that could be used as software components. In [32], we introduced a static model of object-oriented systems, suitable for formalising states and queries. Our static approach shares similarities with [6,36], and allows us to formalise UML class and object diagrams [41], queries and OCL constraints [9]. The introduction of time in our object-oriented systems is work in progress.

Our final goal is to obtain a methodology for the specification and the development of correct component-based software, where programs are developed together with the formal proof of their correctness. This methodology should allow the development of correct compositional units to be used as software components, that is, units of composition that can be deployed independently and are subject to composition by third parties [46].

Acknowledgements

We are very grateful to the referees for their valuable suggestions and comments. This paper has been radically improved as a result of their efforts.

References

1. J.R. Abrial. *The B-Book: Assigning Programs to Meanings.* Cambridge University Press, 1996.
2. E. Astesiano, H.-J. Kreowski, and B. Krieg-Brückner, editors. *Algebraic Foundations of Systems Specifications.* Springer, 1999.
3. C. Atkinson *et al. Component-based Product Line Engineering with UML.* Addison-Wesley, 2001.
4. J. Barwise, editor. *Handbook of Mathematical Logic.* North Holland, 1977.
5. A. Bertoni, G. Mauri, and P. Miglioli. On the power of model theory in specifying abstract data types and in capturing their recursiveness. *Fundamenta Informaticae,* VI(2):127–170, 1983.
6. R.H. Bourdeau and B. H.C. Cheng. A formal semantics for object model diagrams. *IEEE Trans. Soft. Eng.,* 21(10):799–821, 1995.
7. M. Bugliesi, E. Lamma, and P. Mello. Modularity in logic programming. *J. Logic Programming,* 19,20:443–502, 1994. Special issue: Ten years of logic programming.
8. K.L. Clark. *Predicate Logic as a Computational Formalism.* Report 79/59, Imperial College of Science and Technology, University of London, 1979.
9. S. Cook, A. Kleppe, R. Mitchell, B. Rumpe, J. Warmer, and A. Wills. The Amsterdam manifesto on OCL. In T. Clark and J. Warmer, editors, *Object Modeling with the OCL: The Rationale behind the Object Constraint Language, LNCS 2263,* pages 115–149. Springer, 2002.
10. Y. Deville. *Logic Programming. Systematic Program Development.* Addison-Wesley, 1990.
11. Y. Deville and K.-K. Lau. Logic program synthesis. *J. Logic Programming,* 19,20:321–350, 1994. Special Issue: Ten Years of Logic Programming.
12. D.F. D'Souza and A.C. Wills. *Objects, Components, and Frameworks with UML: The Catalysis Approach.* Addison-Wesley, 1999.
13. H. Ehrig and B. Mahr. *Fundamentals of Algebraic Specification 1.* Springer-Verlag, 1987.
14. H. Ehrig and B. Mahr. *Fundamentals of Algebraic Specification 2.* Springer-Verlag, 1989.
15. P. Flener, K.-K. Lau, and M. Ornaghi. On correct program schemas. In N. Fuchs, editor, *Proc. LOPSTR 97, Lecture Notes in Computer Science 1463,* pages 124–143. Springer-Verlag, 1998.
16. P. Flener, K.-K. Lau, M. Ornaghi, and J. Richardson. An abstract formalisation of correct schemas for program synthesis. *Journal of Symbolic Computation,* 30(1):93–127, July 2000.
17. J.H. Gallier. *Logic for Computer Science: Foundations for Automatic Theorem Proving.* Harper and Row, 1986.
18. C. Ghezzi, M. Jazayeri, and D.Mandrioli. *Fundamentals of Software Engineering.* Prentice Hall, second edition, 2003.
19. J.A. Goguen and R.M. Burstall. Institutions: Abstract model theory for specification and programming. *J. ACM,* 39(1):95–146, 1992.
20. J.V. Guttag and J.J. Horning. *Larch: Languages and Tools for Formal Specification.* Springer-Verlag, 1993.
21. W. Hodges. Logical Features of Horn Clauses. In D.M. Gabbay, C.J. Hogger, and J.A. Robinson, editors, *Handbook of Logic in Artificial Intelligence and Logic Programming, Volume 1*:449–503, Oxford University Press, 1993.
22. C.J. Hogger. *Derivation of Logic Programs. J. ACM,* 28(2):372–392, 1981.

23. Isabelle: www.cl.cam.ac.uk/Research/HVG/Isabelle

24. C.B. Jones. *Systematic Software Development Using VDM*. Prentice Hall, second edition, 1990.

25. R.M. Jimenez, F. Orejas, and H. Ehrig. Compositionality and Compatibility of Parametrization and Parameter Passing in Specification Languages. *Math. Struct. in Computer Science*, 5:283–314, 1995.

26. C. Kreitz, K.-K. Lau, and M. Ornaghi. Formal reasoning about modules, reuse and their correctness. In D.M. Gabbay and H.J. Ohlbach, editors, *Proc. Int. Conf. on Formal and Applied Practical Reasoning, Lecture Notes in Artificial Intelligence 1085*, pages 384–399. Springer-Verlag, 1996.

27. K.-K. Lau and M. Ornaghi. On specification frameworks and deductive synthesis of logic programs. In L. Fribourg and F. Turini, editors, *Proc. LOPSTR 94 and META 94, Lecture Notes in Computer Science 883*, pages 104–121. Springer-Verlag, 1994.

28. K.-K. Lau and M. Ornaghi. Forms of logic specifications: A preliminary study. In J. Gallagher, editor, *Proc. LOPSTR 96, Lecture Notes in Computer Science 1207*, pages 295–312. Springer-Verlag, 1997.

29. K.-K. Lau and M. Ornaghi. The relationship between logic programs and specifications — the subset example revisited. *J. Logic Programming*, 30(3):239–257, March 1997.

30. K.-K. Lau and M. Ornaghi. OOD frameworks in component-based software development in computational logic. In P. Flener, editor, *Proc. LOPSTR 98, Lecture Notes in Computer Science 1559*, pages 101–123. Springer-Verlag, 1999.

31. K.-K. Lau and M. Ornaghi. Isoinitial semantics for logic programs. In J.W. Lloyd *et al*, editor, *Proc. 1st Int. Conf. on Computational Logic, Lecture Notes in Artificial Intelligence 1861*, pages 223–238. Springer-Verlag, 2000.

32. K.-K. Lau and M. Ornaghi. Correct object-oriented systems in computational logic. In A. Pettorossi, editor, *Proc. LOPSTR 01, Lecture Notes in Computer Science 2372*, pages 168–190. Springer-Verlag, 2002.

33. K.-K. Lau and M. Ornaghi. Specifying object-oriented systems in computational logic. In M. Bruynooghe, editor, *Pre-Proceedings of LOPSTR 03*, pages 49–64, 2003. Report CW 365, Dept. of Computer Science, Katholieke Universiteit Leuven, Belgium.

34. K.-K. Lau, M. Ornaghi, and S.-Å. Tärnlund. Steadfast logic programs. *J. Logic Programming*, 38(3):259–294, March 1999.

35. J.W. Lloyd. *Foundations of Logic Programming*. 2nd edn., Springer-Verlag, 1987.

36. T. Maibaum. Conservative extensions, interpretations between theories and all that. In M. Bidoit and M. Dauchet, editors, *Proc. TAPSOFT '97: Theory and Practice of Software Developement*, pages 40–67. Springer-Verlag, 1997. LNCS 1214.

37. Yu.V. Matijacevic. Recursively enumerable sets are Diophantine. *Dokl. Akad. Nauk SSSR*, 191:279–282, 1970.

38. P. Miglioli, U.Moscato, and M. Ornaghi. Abstract parametric classes and abstract data types defined by classical and constructive logical methods. *J. Symbolic Computation*, 18:41–81, 1994.

39. P. Miglioli, U.Moscato, and M. Ornaghi. An algebraic framework for the definition of compositional semantics of normal logic programs. *The Journal of Logic Programming*, 40:89–123, 1999.

40. M.G. Read and E.A. Kazmierczak. Formal program development in modular Prolog: A case study. In T.P. Clement and K.-K. Lau, editors, *Proc. LOPSTR 91*, pages 69–93. Springer-Verlag, 1992.

41. J. Rumbaugh, I. Jacobson, and G. Booch. *The Unified Modeling Language Reference Manual.* Addison-Wesley, 1999.

42. D. Sannella, S. Sokolowski, and A. Tarlecki. Toward formal development of programs from algebraic specifications: parametrisation revisited. *Acta Informatica,* 29(8):689–736, 1992.

43. D. Sannella and A. Tarlecki. Extended ML: past, present and future. In *Proc. 7th workshop on specification of abstract data types,* LNCS 534, pages 297–322. Springer-Verlag, 1991.

44. D. Sannella and L.A. Wallen. A calculus for the construction of mdular prolog programs. In *IEEE 4th Symposium on Logic Programming,* IEEE, 1987.

45. J.M. Spivey. *The Z Notation: A Reference Manual.* Prentice Hall, second edition, 1992.

46. C. Szyperski, D. Gruntz, and S. Murer. *Component Software: Beyond Object-Oriented Programming.* Addison-Wesley, second edition, 2002.

47. M. Wirsing. Algebraic specification. In J. Van Leeuwen, editor, *Handbook of Theoretical Computer Science,* pages 675–788. Elsevier, 1990.

Synthesis of Programs in Computational Logic

David Basin[1], Yves Deville[2], Pierre Flener[3], Andreas Hamfelt[4], and
Jørgen Fischer Nilsson[5]

[1] Department of Computer Science
ETH Zurich
Zürich Switzerland
`basin@inf.ethz.ch`
[2] Department of Computing Science and Engineering
Université catholique de Louvain,
Pl. Ste Barbe 2, B-1348 Louvain-la-Neuve, Belgium
`yde@info.ucl.ac.be`
[3] Computing Science Division,
Department of Information Technology
Uppsala University, Box 337, S-751 05 Uppsala, Sweden
`Pierre.Flener@it.uu.se`
[4] Computer Science Division,
Department of Information Science
Uppsala University, Box 513, S-751 20 Uppsala, Sweden
`Andreas.Hamfelt@dis.uu.se`
[5] Informatics and Mathematical Modelling
Technical University of Denmark
DK-2800 Lyngby, Denmark
`jfn@it.dtu.dk`

Abstract. Since the early days of programming and automated reasoning, researchers have developed methods for systematically constructing programs from their specifications. Especially the last decade has seen a flurry of activities including the advent of specialized conferences, such as LOPSTR, covering the synthesis of programs in computational logic. In this paper we analyze and compare three state-of-the-art methods for synthesizing recursive programs in computational logic. The three approaches are constructive/deductive synthesis, schema-guided synthesis, and inductive synthesis. Our comparison is carried out in a systematic way where, for each approach, we describe the key ideas and synthesize a common running example. In doing so, we explore the synergies between the approaches, which we believe are necessary in order to achieve progress over the next decade in this field.

1 Introduction

Program synthesis is concerned with the following question: Given a not necessarily executable specification, how can an executable program satisfying the specification be developed? The notions of "specification" and "executable" are

M. Bruynooghe and K.-K. Lau (Eds.): Program Development in CL, LNCS 3049, pp. 30–65, 2004.

here interpreted broadly. The objective of program synthesis is to develop methods and tools to mechanize or automate (part of) this process.

In the last 30 years, program synthesis has been an active research area; see e.g. [14,4,40,13,26,29] for a description of major achievements. The starting point of program synthesis is usually a formal specification, that is an expression in some formal language (a language having a syntax, a semantics, and usually a proof theory). Program synthesis thus has many relationships with *formal specification* [69]. As the end product is a verified correct program, program synthesis is also related to *formal methods* in the development of computer systems [22], and to *automated software engineering*. All of these disciplines share the goal of improving the quality of software.

PROGRAM SYNTHESIS IN COMPUTATIONAL LOGIC. It is generally recognized that a good starting point for program synthesis is to use declarative formalisms such as functional programming or computational logic, where one specifies *what* a program should do instead of *how*. We focus here on the synthesis of recursive programs in *computational logic*, which provides an expressive and uniform framework for program synthesis. On the one hand, the specification, the resulting program, and their relationship, can all be expressed in the same logic. On the other hand, logic specifications can describe complete specifications as well as incomplete ones, such as examples or properties of the relation that is to be computed. Since all this information can be expressed in the same language, it can be treated uniformly in a synthesis process.

There exist many different approaches to program synthesis in computational logic and different ways of viewing and categorizing them. For example, one can distinguish constructive from deductive synthesis. In *constructive* synthesis, a conjecture based on the specification is constructively proved, and from this proof a program is extracted. In the *deductive* approach, a program is deduced directly from the specification by suitably transforming it. As will be shown in this paper, these two approaches can profitably be viewed together and expressed in a uniform framework. In a different approach, called *schema-based* synthesis, the idea is to use program schemas, that is some abstraction of a class of actual programs, to guide and enhance the synthesis process. Another approach is *inductive* synthesis, where a program is induced from an incomplete specification.

OBJECTIVES. Our intent in this paper is to analyze and compare three state-of-the-art methods for synthesizing recursive programs in computational logic. The chosen approaches are constructive/deductive synthesis, schema-guided synthesis, and inductive synthesis. We perform our comparison in a systematic way: we first identify common, generic features of all approaches and afterwards we use a common example to explain these features for each approach. This analysis forms the basis for an in-depth comparison. We show, for example, that from an appropriately abstract viewpoint, there are a number of synergies between the approaches that can be exploited. For example, by identifying rules with schemas, all three methods have a common, underlying synthesis mechanism and it becomes easier to see how the methods can be fruitfully combined, or differentiated. Overall, we hope that our comparison will deepen the communities understanding of the approaches — their relationships, synergies, where they excel, and why — and thereby contribute to achieving progress in this field.

We see this paper as complementary to surveys of program synthesis in computational logic (or more precisely in logic programming), in particular [26,29]. Rather than a making a broad survey, we focus on the analysis and in-depth comparison of the different approaches and we also consider schema-guided synthesis. Due to lack of space and to comply with our objectives, some technical details are omitted. Here, the reader may rely on his or her intuitive understanding of relevant concepts or follow pointers to references in the literature.

ORGANIZATION. Section 2 presents the different elements that will be used to present and compare the chosen synthesis approaches. These elements include general features of program synthesis approaches as well as the example that will be used for their comparison. Sections 3 through 5 describe the three chosen approaches: constructive/deductive synthesis, schema-guided synthesis, and inductive synthesis. To facilitate a systematic analysis and comparison of the methods, each section has a similar structure. Section 6 compares the three approaches. Finally, Section 7 draws conclusions and presents perspectives for future developments.

2   Elements of Comparison

In the subsequent sections, we will present three synthesis approaches. For each approach, one representative method is described. However, before describing them, we first present their general features. These features are developed in the context of each particular method and serve both to facilitate our analysis and systematize our comparison. We also introduce our example.

2.1   General Features

SPECIFICATION. The starting point for program synthesis is a specification expressed in some language. For each synthesis method, we must fix the specification language and the form of the specification (e.g., a formula or a set of examples).

MECHANISM. Program synthesis methods are based on calculi and procedures prescribing how program are synthesized from specifications. Although the underlying mechanisms of the various systems differ, there are, in some cases, similar underlying concepts.

HEURISTICS. Program synthesis is search intensive and heuristics are required in practice to guide the synthesis process. Are the heuristics specific to a synthesis method or are there common heuristics? How effective are the heuristics in the different methods and to what extent do different methods structure and restrict the search space?

BACKGROUND KNOWLEDGE. Usually, non-trivial specifications refer to background knowledge that formalizes information about the properties of objects used in the specification, e.g., theories about the relevant data types.

HUMAN INTERACTION. Human interaction involves two different issues. First, how much can a human be automatically assisted? Second, what is the nature of human-computer interaction in synthesis? How can the human step in and, for example, give key steps rather than leave the matter to blind search? Allowing input at critical points requires appropriate system support.

TOOL SUPPORT. What kind of tool support is needed for turning a synthesis method into a viable system?

SCALABILITY. Scalability is a major concern in program synthesis. Synthesis systems should not only be able to synthesize small simple programs, but they should also be able to tackle large or complex programs that solve real-life problems.

2.2   The Chosen Example

The same example will be used throughout the paper to facilitate a comparison of the different methods. We have chosen a problem simple enough to present in full, but complex enough to illustrate the main issues associated with each approach.

Specification 21 *Let L be a list, I a natural number, and E a term. The relation $atpos(L, I, E)$ holds iff E is the element of L at position I. By convention, the first element of a list is at position 0. The atpos relation can be formally specified as follows:*

$$atpos(L, I, E) \leftrightarrow \exists P, S \,.\, append(P, E \cdot S, L) \wedge length(P, I)$$

where append and length have their usual meaning, and are assumed to be defined in the background theory.

   In the formula above, and in the rest of the paper, free variables are assumed to be universally quantified over the entire formula. As list notation, we use *nil* to represent the empty list, and $H \cdot T$ for the list with head H and tail T.

3   Constructive and Deductive Synthesis

We will now look at two approaches to synthesizing programs that are often grouped together: constructive and deductive synthesis. We shall highlight their similarities by viewing both from the same perspective: In both cases, deduction can be used to synthesize programs by solving for unknowns during the application of rules.

3.1   Background

For historical reasons, and because the ideas are simplest to present there, we begin by considering synthesis of functional programs in constructive type theory.

Constructive type theories are logics used for reasoning about functional programs. The simplest example is the simply typed λ-calculus [5,48], which we briefly review here. Programs in the simply typed λ-calculus are terms in the λ-calculus, which are built from variables, application, and abstraction. Types are built from a set of base types, closed under the function space constructor $\rightarrow$. One reasons about judgments that assert that a term t has a type T, relative to a sequence of bindings Γ, of the form $x_1 : A_1, \ldots, x_n : A_n$, which associate variables to types. The valid judgments are inductively defined by the following rules:

$$\frac{x : A \in \Gamma}{\Gamma \vdash x : A} \; hyp \qquad \frac{\Gamma, x : A \vdash M : B}{\Gamma \vdash (\lambda x. M) : (A \rightarrow B)} \; abst$$

$$\frac{\Gamma \vdash M : A \rightarrow B \quad \Gamma \vdash N : A}{\Gamma \vdash (MN) : B} \; appl$$

These rules comprise a deduction system for proving that a program t has a type T. Under the *propositions-as-types* interpretation, this type may also be understood as a logical proposition (reading '$\rightarrow$' as intuitionistic implication) that specifies t's properties. Of course, the specification language is quite weak, so it is difficult to specify many interesting properties. In stronger type theories, such as [24,56], types correspond to propositions in richer logics and one can, for example, specify sorting as

$$\vdash t : (\forall x : int\ list\ .\ \exists y : int\ list\ .\ perm(x, y) \land ord(y)) . \tag{1}$$

This asserts that the program t is a function that, on input x, returns an ordered permutation y.

The given deduction system can be used for *program verification*: given a program t and a specification T, prove $\vdash t : T$. For example, for p and q types, we can verify that the program $\lambda x. \lambda y. x$ satisfies the specification $p \rightarrow (q \rightarrow p)$:

$$\frac{\dfrac{\dfrac{x : p \in x : p,\ y : q}{x : p,\ y : q \vdash x : p}\;hyp}{x : p \vdash \lambda y. x : q \rightarrow p}\;abst}{\vdash \lambda x. \lambda y. x : p \rightarrow (q \rightarrow p)}\;abst \tag{2}$$

Perhaps less obviously, the same rules can be used for *program synthesis*: given a specification T, construct a program t such that $\vdash t : T$. This can be done by

1. Reversing the direction in which rules are applied and proofs are constructed. That is, build the proof in a goal-directed, "refinement style" way by starting with the goal and working towards the axioms.

2. Leaving the program t as an unknown, or *metavariable*, which is solved during proof.

Let's try this out in the example above. Using capital letters to indicate metavariables, we begin with

$$\vdash R : p \rightarrow (q \rightarrow p)\,.$$

Resolving this with the (conclusion of the) *abst* rule yields the new goal

$$x : p \vdash R_1(x) : (q \rightarrow p)\,,$$

where R is unified with $\lambda x.\, R_1(x)$. Applying *abst* again results in

$$x : p,\, y : q \vdash R_2(x, y) : p\,,$$

where $R_1(x) = \lambda y.\, R_2(x, y)$. Finally, applying *hyp* unifies the assumption $x : p$ with $R_2(x, y) : p$, instantiating $R_2(x, y)$ to x and completing the proof. Composing the substitutions yields the previously verified program $t = \lambda x.\, \lambda y.\, x$.

The account above is complicated by the fact that the abstraction operator λ binds variables and, to work properly, higher-order unification is required when applying rules. The rules constitute clauses in a higher-order (meta-)language and proofs are constructed by higher-order resolution. A higher-order logic programming language or logical framework based on higher-order resolution like λ-Prolog [27], ELF [61], or Isabelle [59] would support this kind of proof.

There are two conclusions we would like to draw. First, verification and synthesis are closely related activities. In fact, when rules are applied using (higher-order) resolution, they are essentially identical. The only difference is whether unification is between ground or non-ground terms, i.e., whether or not an answer substitution is built. This conclusion should not be surprising to those working in logic programming: the same sequence of resolution steps can be used to establish a ground query $p(t)$ or a non-ground one $p(X)$, generating the substitution $X = t$.

Second, constructive synthesis is of a deductive nature and the line between the two can be fine. As the analogy with Prolog shows, proofs construct objects. In type theory, the objects are programs. Indeed, the idea of proofs synthesizing programs, sometimes called *proofs-as-programs*, can be decomposed into

$$proofs\text{-}as\text{-}programs = proofs\text{-}as\text{-}objects + objects\text{-}as\text{-}programs.$$

In our example, unification, not the constructivity of the logic, is responsible for constructing an object. Constructivity does not play a role in the *synthesis* of objects, but rather in their *execution* and *meaning*. That is, because the logic is constructive, the synthesized terms can be executed and their evaluation behavior agrees with the semantics of the type theory. In contrast, [49], for example, presents a classical type theory where programs correspond to (non-computable) oracles that cannot be executed. There one might say that the line is crossed from constructive (and deductive) program synthesis to deductive object synthesis.

The use of unification is at the heart of deductive and constructive synthesis. Unification is driven by resolution, to synthesize, or solve for, programs during proofs. This idea goes back to work in the 1960s on using first-order resolution to construct terms that represent plans or, more generally, programs [19,42]. In the logical framework community, the use of higher-order metalogics to represent rules and the use of higher-order unification to apply them is now standard, e.g., [2,8,9,23]. For example, the Isabelle distribution [59] comes with encodings of a number of type theories, where programs can be synthesized as described here.

The vast majority of approaches for synthesizing logic programs are based on first-order reasoning, e.g., equivalence preserving transformations. There have been many proposed methods and [26] contains a good survey. They differ in the form of their axioms (Horn clauses, *iff*-definitions, etc.), exact notion of equivalence used (and there are many, see e.g., [55]), and ease of automation. Many of these, for example unfold-fold based transformations [60], can be recast as synthesis by resolution using rules like those presented here [7,10].

3.2   Overview

SPECIFICATIONS. In type theory, programs and specifications belong to different languages. When synthesizing logic programs, the specification language is typically the language of a first-order theory and the programming language is some suitable, executable subset thereof. By sharing the same language, logic programs are well suited for deductive synthesis where specifications are manipulated, using equivalence preserving transformations, until a formula with some desired form or property is reached.

MECHANISM. The mechanism for synthesizing logic programs during proofs is essentially the same as what we have just seen for type theory. However, what is proved (i.e., the form of the theorem to be proven), and the proof rules used to establish it, are of course different. Namely, we will prove theorems about equivalences between specifications and programs and we will prove these theorems using rules suitable for establishing such equivalences.

For our example, we will employ the following rules:

$$\frac{}{A \leftrightarrow A} \leftrightarrow\!\!-refl \qquad \frac{A_1 \leftrightarrow B_1 \quad A_2 \leftrightarrow B_2}{(A_1 \vee A_2) \leftrightarrow (B_1 \vee B_2)} \vee\!\!-split$$

In addition, for building recursive programs that recurse over lists we employ the rule schema

$$\frac{A_1 \quad A_2 \quad A_3}{\forall L, \overline{X} . \, P(L, \overline{X}) \leftrightarrow Q(L, \overline{X})} \ ind \, ,$$

where L is a variable ranging over lists, $\overline{X}$ denotes sequences of zero or more variables of any type, and the assumptions A_i are:

$$A_1 \equiv \forall L, \overline{X} . \, Q(L, \overline{X}) \leftrightarrow (L = nil \wedge B(\overline{X}))$$
$$\vee \exists H, T . \, L = H \cdot T \wedge S(H, T, \overline{X})$$

$$A_2 \equiv \forall \overline{X} . \ P(nil, \overline{X}) \leftrightarrow B(\overline{X})$$
$$A_3 \equiv \forall T . \ (\forall \overline{X} . \ P(T, \overline{X}) \leftrightarrow Q(T, \overline{X})) \rightarrow \forall H, \overline{X} . \ P(H \cdot T, \overline{X})$$
$$\leftrightarrow S(H, T, \overline{X})$$

This rule, which can be derived by induction on the list L, states the equivalence between predicates P and Q (which are metavariables). For the purpose of synthesis, we can take A_1 as the definition of Q, and A_2 and A_3 constrain (and will be used to define) Q's base and recursive cases. In A_3, we are allowed to use the existence of Q, when defining Q, but only on smaller arguments.

We will show below how, by applying these rules (using higher-order resolution), we can construct R while proving its equivalence to *atpos*.

HEURISTICS AND HUMAN INTERACTION. Proof rules, like those given above, can be applied interactively, semi-interactively, or even automatically. The use of a tactic based theorem prover [41], which allows users to write programs that construct proofs, leaves open the degree of automation.

[50,51], for example, show how to completely automate the construction of such synthesis proofs in a tactic based setting. In this work, the most important tactic implements the rippling heuristic of [17,12]. This heuristic automates the application of rewrite or equivalence preserving transformation rules in a way that minimizes differences between terms or formulas. Rippling is typically used in inductive theorem proving to enable the use of the induction hypothesis in simplifying the induction conclusion and it can be used in a similar way during program synthesis where rules that introduce recursion (like *ind*) produce induction-like proof obligations. Rippling has been used to automate completely the synthesis of a number of non-trivial logic programs. However, it should be noted that some interaction with the user is often desirable since the application of proof rules, in particular rules that build recursive programs, determines the efficiency of the synthesized program.

BACKGROUND KNOWLEDGE. The approach we present here for synthesizing logic programs involves two kinds of rules. The first kind are rules, like $\leftrightarrow$-*refl* and $\vee$-*split*, which are derived rules of first-order logic. These derived rules are not, strictly speaking, necessary (provided we are working in a complete axiomatization of first-order logic), but their addition makes it easier to construct synthesis proofs by reasoning about equivalences. The second kind of rules are theory specific rules, e.g., rules about inductively defined data types like numbers and lists. The rule *ind* given above is an example of such a rule. It is derivable in a theory that axiomatizes lists and formalizes induction over lists.

TOOL SUPPORT. For synthesizing the *atpos* example, we have used the Isabelle system. Isabelle's basic mechanism for proof construction is top-down proof by higher-order resolution, which is precisely what we require. Moreover, as a logical framework, Isabelle supports the derivation of new rules, so we can formally derive, and thus insure the correctness of, the specialized rules needed for synthesis; in our example, we derive the rules just presented in a standard first-order theory of lists. Finally, tactics can be used to partially, or entirely, automate proof construction. The Isabelle distribution comes with simplifiers and decision procedures that we used to semi-automate synthesis.

SCALABILITY. The search space in most approaches to deductive synthesis is quite large. In practice, building non-trivial programs requires an environment that supports heuristics for automating simple proof steps, e.g., by the application of tactics. It is also important that the user can safely augment a synthesis system with derived rules. As we will later observe, schemas, for schema guided synthesis, can be seen as derived rules specialized for synthesizing programs of a particular form, and their integration with deductive synthesis approaches can help with large scale developments. Examples of this are provided in [1].

3.3   Example

Let us illustrate our synthesis method on the *atpos* example. We wish to construct a logic program equivalent to the specification 21. As with synthesis in the type theory, we use a metavariable, R, to stand in for the desired program. Hence we start with

$$\vdash \forall L, I, E \,.\, atpos(L, I, E) \leftrightarrow R(L, I, E) \,. \tag{3}$$

Working backwards, resolving (using higher-order unification) this conclusion with the conclusion of the *ind* rule yields the three subgoals

$$\forall L, I, E \,.\, R(L, I, E) \leftrightarrow (L = nil \wedge B(I, E))$$
$$\vee \exists H, T \,.\, L = H \cdot T \wedge S(H, T, I, E)$$
$$\forall I, E \,.\, atpos(nil, I, E) \leftrightarrow B(I, E)$$
$$\forall T \,.\, (\forall I, E \,.\, atpos(T, I, E) \leftrightarrow$$
$$R(T, I, E) \rightarrow \forall H, I, E \,.\, atpos(H \cdot T, I, E) \leftrightarrow S(H, T, I, E)$$

and Q is unified with R.

The first subgoal constitutes a program template, which will later be filled out by solving the other subgoals. In the second subgoal, expanding the definition of *atpos* results in

$$\vdash \forall I, E \,.\, (\exists P, S \,.\, append(P, E \cdot S, nil) \wedge length(P, I)) \leftrightarrow B(I, E) \,.$$

Let I and E be arbitrary. To show

$$\vdash (\exists P, S \,.\, append(P, E \cdot S, nil) \wedge length(P, I)) \leftrightarrow B(I, E) \,,$$

observe that there are no values for P or S for which $append(P, E \cdot S, nil)$ is true. Hence this subgoal is equivalent to

$$\vdash false \leftrightarrow B(I, E) \,.$$

We can complete the proof with $\leftrightarrow$-*refl*, which unifies $B(I, E)$ with *false*.

For the third subgoal, we assume the existence of an arbitrary list T and the antecedent of the implication (which amounts to an induction hypothesis) and must prove the consequent (the induction conclusion). Hence, expanding the definition of *atpos*, we assume

$$\forall I, E \, . \, (\exists P, S \, . \, append(P, E \cdot S, T) \wedge length(P, I)) \leftrightarrow R(T, I, E)$$

and we must prove, for some arbitrary H, I, and E,

$$\vdash (\exists P, S \, . \, append(P, E \cdot S, H \cdot T) \wedge length(P, I)) \leftrightarrow S(H, T, I, E).$$

Now, since P ranges over lists, for any formula $\phi(l)$, $\exists P.\phi(P)$ is equivalent (by case analysis) to $\phi(nil) \vee \exists H, T \, . \, \phi(H \cdot T)$. Hence, the above is equivalent to

$$\vdash ((\exists S \, . \, append(nil, E \cdot S, H \cdot T) \wedge length(nil, I)) \\ \vee (\exists H', T', S.append(H' \cdot T', E \cdot S, H \cdot T) \wedge length(H' \cdot T', I))) \\ \leftrightarrow S(H, T, I, E).$$

We proceed by decomposing the disjunction on the left-hand side by resolving with $\vee$–*split*. Doing so builds a disjunction for S, by instantiating $S(H, T, I, E)$ with $S_1(H, T, I, E) \vee S_2(H, T, I, E)$, and yields the two subgoals:

$$\vdash \exists S \, . \, append(nil, E \cdot S, H \cdot T) \wedge length(nil, I) \leftrightarrow S_1(H, T, I, E)$$
$$\vdash \exists H', T', S \, . \, append(H' \cdot T', E \cdot S, H \cdot T) \\ \wedge length(H' \cdot T', I) \leftrightarrow S_2(H, T, I, E)$$

For the first, the left-hand side is true whenever $\exists S \, . \, E = H \wedge S = T \wedge I = 0$. Hence, setting S to T, this subgoal is equivalent to

$$\vdash (E = H \wedge I = 0) \leftrightarrow S_1(H, T, I, E).$$

We can again discharge this using $\leftrightarrow$–*refl*, which unifies $S_1(H, T, I, E)$ with $E = H \wedge I = 0$. Now, under the standard definition of *append* and *length*, the second subgoal is equivalent to

$$\vdash (\exists I'.s(I') = I \wedge (\exists T', S.append(T', E \cdot S, T) \wedge length(T', I'))) \\ \leftrightarrow S_2(H, T, I, E)$$

where $s(I')$ represents the successor of I'. We can now simplify this using the antecedent (induction hypothesis), which yields

$$(\exists I'.s(I') = I \wedge R(T, I', E)) \leftrightarrow S_2(H, T, I, E).$$

We complete the proof with $\leftrightarrow$–*refl*, unifying $S_2(H, T, I, E)$ with $\exists I'.s(I') = I \wedge R(T, I', E)$.

We are done! If we apply the accumulated substitutions to the remaining assumption A_1 we have

$$\forall L, I, E \, . \, R(L, I, E) \\ \leftrightarrow (L = nil \wedge false) \\ \vee \exists H, T \, . \, L = H \cdot T \wedge ((E = H \wedge I = 0) \\ \vee \exists I' \, . \, s(I') = I \wedge R(T, I', E)).$$

and we have proved the equivalence of (3) under this definition, i.e., $atpos(L, I, E)$ is equivalent to the synthesized instance of $R(L, I, E)$.

The alert reader may have wondered why we did not complete the proof earlier by resolving with $\leftrightarrow$–*refl*. In this example, our goal was to transform *atpos* so that the result falls within a particular subset of first-order formulae, sometimes called *pure logic programs* [16] or *logic descriptions* [25], that define logic programs. These formulae can be easily translated to Horn clauses or run directly in a language like Gödel [47]. In this case, we get the clauses:

$$atpos(nil, I, E) \leftarrow false$$
$$atpos(H \cdot T, I, E) \leftarrow E = H, I = 0$$
$$atpos(H \cdot T, I, E) \leftarrow s(I') = I, atpos(T, I', E)$$

which can be simplified to

$$atpos(E \cdot \_, 0, E) \leftarrow$$
$$atpos(\_ \cdot T, s(I'), E) \leftarrow atpos(T, I', E)$$

3.4   Analysis

Overall, when cast in this way, the deductive synthesis of logic programs is quite similar to the previous constructive/deductive synthesis of functional programs. In both cases, we leave the program as an unknown, and solve for it, by unification, during proof. Of course, the metatheoretic properties of the programs produced are quite different. In the case of logic program synthesis, the rules, as they are given, do not enforce that the object constructed has any special syntactic properties (e.g., is a pure logic program); we only know that it is an equivalent formula. Moreover, we do not *a priori* know anything about its termination behavior (although it is not difficult to show that the induction rule builds predicates that terminate when the first argument is ground).

This kind of development, as with most approaches to logic program synthesis, is best described as deductive synthesis. They are constructive only in the weak sense that, at the metalevel (or metalogic, if one is carrying out the proof in a logical framework), one is essentially proving a theorem of the form

$$\exists R \,.\, \forall L, I, E \,. atpos(L, I, E) \leftrightarrow R(L, I, E)$$

and building a witness (in this case, a predicate definition) for R. (For more on this notion of constructivity and the proof theory behind it, see [11].) Many proposed methods for the constructive synthesis of logic programs can also be explained in this way. For example, the Whelk Calculus of [71], which is motivated by experiments in synthesizing relations in a constructive type theory, can be recast as this kind of synthesis [6].

4   Schema-Guided Synthesis

We here outline Flener, Lau, Ornaghi, and Richardson's definition, representation, and semantics of program schemas: see [33] for details.

4.1   Background

Intuitively, a program schema is an abstraction of a class of actual programs, in the sense that it represents their data-flow and control-flow, but neither contains all their actual computations nor all their actual data structures. Program schemas have been shown to be useful in a variety of applications. In synthesis, the main idea is to simplify the proof obligations by taking the difficult ones offline, so that they are proven once and for all at schema design time. Also, the reuse of existing programs is made the main synthesis mechanism.

A symbol occurring in a theory T is *open* [52] in T if it is neither defined in T, nor a predefined symbol. A non-open symbol in T is *closed* in T. A theory with at least one open symbol is an *open* theory; otherwise it is *closed*. This terminology applies to formal specifications and logic programs. An (open) program for a relation r is *steadfast* [25,53] with respect to its specification if it is correct with respect to its specification whenever composed with programs that are correct with respect to the specifications of its (open) relations other than r.

Among the many possible forms of programs, there are the *divide-and-conquer programs* with one recursive call: if a distinguished formal parameter, called the *induction parameter*, say X, has a minimal value, then one can directly solve for a corresponding other formal parameter, called the *result parameter*, say Y; otherwise, X is decomposed into a "smaller" value T (under some well-founded relation $\prec$) by splitting off a quantity H, so that a sub-result V corresponding to T can be computed by a recursive call, and an overall result Y can be composed from H and V. A third formal parameter, called the *passive parameter*, say Z, participates unchanged in these operations. Formally, this *problem-independent* dataflow and control-flow can be captured in the following open program for r:

$$r(X, Y, Z) \leftarrow min(X, Z), solve(X, Y, Z)$$
$$r(X, Y, Z) \leftarrow \neg min(X, Z), dec(X, Z, H, T), \qquad (DC)$$
$$r(T, V, Z), comp(H, Z, V, Y)$$

The relations $min, solve, dec, comp$ are open. When I is the induction parameter, L the result, and E the passive parameter, so that $atpos(L, I, E) \leftrightarrow r(I, L, E)$, a closed program for $atpos$ is the instance of DC under the program substitution

$$min(X, Z) \leftarrow X = 0 \qquad\qquad solve(X, Y, Z) \leftarrow Y = Z \cdot S$$
$$dec(X, Z, H, T) \leftarrow X = s(T) \qquad comp(H, Z, V, Y) \leftarrow Y = F \cdot V \qquad (\phi_1)$$

This substitution captures the *problem-dependent* computations of that program.

But programs by themselves are syntactic entities, hence some programs are undesired instances of open programs. For instance, the generate-and-test program $r(X, Y, Z) \leftarrow g(X, Y, Z)$, $t(Y, Z)$ is an instance of DC under the substitution

$$min(X, Z) \leftarrow true \qquad solve(X, Y, Z) \leftarrow g(X, Y, Z),\ t(Y, Z)$$
$$dec(X, Z, H, T) \leftarrow true \qquad comp(H, Z, V, Y) \leftarrow true$$

An open program such as DC thus has no fixed meaning. The knowledge captured by an open program is not completely formalized, and the domain knowledge and underlying language are still implicit. In order for such open programs to be useful for guiding synthesis, such undesired instances need to be prevented and some semantic considerations need to be explicitly added.

A *program schema* [33] has a name, a set of formal sort and relation parameters, a signature with sorted relation and function declarations, a set of axioms defining the declared symbols, a set of constraints restricting the actual parameters, an open program T called the *template*, and specifications S of the relations in T, such that T is steadfast with respect to S in that axiomatization.

The schema $\mathcal{DC}$ can be abduced, as in [32], from our informal account of how divide-and-conquer programs work. The parameters SX, SY, SZ, SH are sorts; they are used in the signatures of the other parameters, which are relations. There are no axioms because the signature declares no other symbols than the parameters. The template is the open program DC, which defines the relation r and has min, $solve$, dec, $comp$ as open relations. The closed relation r is specified by S_r, and the open relations have S_{min}, S_{solve}, S_{dec}, S_{comp} as specifications. The conditional specification S_r exhibits i_r, o_r as the input/output conditions of r, while S_{dec} exhibits i_{dec}, o_{dec} as the input/output conditions of dec. The input/output conditions of the remaining open relations are also expressed in terms of the parameters i_r, i_{dec}, o_r, o_{dec}. The constraints restrict dec to succeed at least once if its input condition holds, and then to yield a value that satisfies the input condition of r (so that a recursive call to r is "legal") and that is smaller than X according to $\prec$, which must be a well-founded relation (so that recursion terminates). The open program DC is steadfast with respect to S_r, within the given axiomatization.

In the schema $\mathcal{REUSE}$, the parameters SX, SY, SZ are sorts; they are used in the signatures of the other parameters, which are relations. There are no axioms because the signature declares no other symbols than the parameters. The template is the open program $\{r(X, Y, Z) \leftarrow q(X, Y, Z)\}$, which defines the relation r and has q as the open relation. The relation r is specified by S_r, and the relation q has the same input/output conditions as r. There are no constraints on the parameters. This schema provides for the reuse of a program for q when starting from a specification for r. The open program $Reuse$ is steadfast with respect to S_r, within the given axiomatization.

4.2   Overview

Let us now examine the specifications, mechanism, heuristics, background knowledge, human interaction, tool support, and scalability of schema-guided synthesis.

Schema $\mathcal{DC}(\mathsf{SX}, \mathsf{SY}, \mathsf{SZ}, \mathsf{SH}, \prec, i_r, o_r, i_{dec}, o_{dec})$

SORTS: $\mathsf{SX}, \mathsf{SY}, \mathsf{SZ}, \mathsf{SH}$

RELATIONS: $i_r, i_{dec} : (\mathsf{SX}, \mathsf{SZ})$ $\prec$: $(\mathsf{SX}, \mathsf{SX})$
o_r : $(\mathsf{SX}, \mathsf{SY}, \mathsf{SZ})$ $o_{dec} : (\mathsf{SX}, \mathsf{SZ}, \mathsf{SH}, \mathsf{SX})$

AXIOMS: (none)

CONSTRS: $i_{dec}(X, Z) \rightarrow \exists H : \mathsf{SH} . \exists T : \mathsf{SX} . o_{dec}(X, Z, H, T)$ $\hspace{2em}(C_1)$
$i_{dec}(X, Z) \wedge o_{dec}(X, Z, H, T) \rightarrow i_r(T, Z) \wedge T \prec X$ $\hspace{1em}(C_2)$
$wellFounded(\prec)$ $\hspace{13em}(C_3)$

SPECIFS: $i_r(X, Z) \rightarrow (r(X, Y, Z) \leftrightarrow o_r(X, Y, Z))$ $\hspace{4em}(S_r)$
$i_r(X, Z) \rightarrow (min(X, Z) \leftrightarrow \neg i_{dec}(X, Z))$ $\hspace{3.5em}(S_{min})$
$i_r(X, Z) \wedge \neg i_{dec}(X, Z) \rightarrow (solve(X, Y, Z) \leftrightarrow o_r(X, Y, Z))$ $\hspace{0.5em}(S_{solve})$
$i_{dec}(X, Z) \rightarrow (dec(X, Z, H, T) \leftrightarrow o_{dec}(X, Z, H, T))$ $\hspace{1.5em}(S_{dec})$
$o_{dec}(X, Z, H, T) \wedge o_r(T, V, Z) \rightarrow$
$\hspace{4em}(comp(H, Z, V, Y) \leftrightarrow o_r(X, Y, Z))$ $\hspace{2em}(S_{comp})$

TEMPLATE: $r(X, Y, Z) \leftarrow min(X, Z), solve(X, Y, Z)$
$r(X, Y, Z) \leftarrow \neg min(X, Z), dec(X, Z, H, T),$ $\hspace{5em}(DC)$
$\hspace{4em}r(T, V, Z), comp(H, Z, V, Y)$

Schema $\mathcal{REUSE}(\mathsf{SX}, \mathsf{SY}, \mathsf{SZ}, i_r, o_r)$

SORTS: $\mathsf{SX}, \mathsf{SY}, \mathsf{SZ}$

RELATIONS: $i_r : (\mathsf{SX}, \mathsf{SZ})$ $o_r : (\mathsf{SX}, \mathsf{SY}, \mathsf{SZ})$

AXIOMS: (none)

CONSTRAINTS: (none)

SPECIFICATIONS: $i_r(X, Z) \rightarrow (r(X, Y, Z) \leftrightarrow o_r(X, Y, Z))$ $\hspace{2em}(S_r)$
$i_r(X, Z) \rightarrow (q(X, Y, Z) \leftrightarrow o_r(X, Y, Z))$ $\hspace{2em}(S_q)$

TEMPLATE: $r(X, Y, Z) \leftarrow q(X, Y, Z)$ $\hspace{5em}(Reuse)$

SPECIFICATIONS. Among the many possible forms of specifications, there are the classical *conditional specifications*: under some input condition i_r on inputs X, Z, a program for relation r succeeds iff some output condition o_r on X, Z and output Y holds. Formally, this gives rise to the following open specification of r:

$$\forall X : \mathsf{SX} . \forall Y : \mathsf{SY} . \forall Z : \mathsf{SZ} . \hspace{4em} (Cond)$$
$$i_r(X, Z) \rightarrow (r(X, Y, Z) \leftrightarrow o_r(X, Y, Z))$$

The open symbols are the relations i_r, o_r and the sorts SX, SY, SZ. Other forms of specification can also be handled.

MECHANISM. *Schema-guided synthesis* from a specification S_0 is a tree construction process consisting of 5 steps, where the initial tree has just one node, namely S_0:

1. Choose a specification S_i that has not been handled yet.
2. Choose a program schema with parameters P, axioms A, constraints C, template T, and specifications S.

3. Infer a substitution θ_1 under which S_i is an instance of the specification (available in S) of the defined relation in template T. This instantiates some (if not all) of the parameters P.
4. Choose a substitution θ_2 that instantiates the remaining (if any) parameters in P, such that the constraints C hold (i.e., such that $\theta_1 \cup \theta_2 \vdash C$) and such that one can reuse existing programs P_Q for some (if not all) of the now fully instantiated specifications $S \cup \theta_1 \cup \theta_2$ of the open relations in template T. Simplify the remaining (if any) specifications in $S \cup \theta_1 \cup \theta_2$, yielding S_G.
5. Add $T \cup P_Q$ — called the *reused program* — to the node with S_i and add the elements of S_G to the unhandled specifications, as children of S_i.

These steps are iterated until all specifications have been handled; the overall result program P_0 for S_0 is then assembled by conjoining, at each node, the reused programs. If any of these steps fails, synthesis backtracks to its last choice point. Schema-guided program synthesis is thus a recursive specification (problem) decomposition process followed by a recursive program (solution) composition process.

The $\mathcal{REUSE}$ schema can be chosen at Step 2; it forces the reuse at Step 4 of a program for q, because q is its only open relation. *Every* schema leads to some reuse at Step 4; for instance, $\mathcal{DC}$ results in the reuse of a program for *dec*.

HEURISTICS. Many choice points reside in schema-guided synthesis, so heuristics are needed to make good decisions, possibly by looking ahead into the synthesis.

Some heuristics can be applied when designing a schema. For instance, a *synthesis strategy* is the choice at Step 4 of the open relations for which programs are reused. All templates envisaged by us so far have only a few meaningful strategies, hence it is best to hardwire these. For instance, template DC has only two interesting strategies: when starting with *dec*, the divide-and-conquer schema is as above; when starting with *comp*, it would have to be reexpressed in terms of the input/output conditions of r and *comp*, giving rise to another schema, with the same template.

Other heuristics can be expressed as applicability conditions. For instance, the question arises of *what* program schema to apply at Step 2. An implicit heuristic can be achieved by ordering the schemas; putting $\mathcal{REUSE}$ first would enforce our emphasis on reuse. There also is the question of *how* to apply a chosen program schema at Step 3. For instance, with $\mathcal{DC}$, one of the formal parameters in the given specification S_r has to be the induction parameter, and another the result parameter. This can be done based on the sort information in S_r: only a parameter of an inductively defined sort can be the induction parameter. One can also augment specifications with mode information, because parameters declared to be ground at call-time are particularly good induction parameters [25].

BACKGROUND KNOWLEDGE. Step 2 assumes a base of program schemas, capturing a range of program classes. Also, Step 4 relies on a base of reusable programs. For instance, for the $\mathcal{DC}$ schema, a base of specifications and programs for *dec* programs and $\prec$ well-founded relations needs to be available.

HUMAN INTERACTION. Schema-guided synthesis can be fully automated, as demonstrated with CYPRESS [65], KIDS [66], DESIGNWARE [67], and PLANWARE [15]. However, interactive synthesis is preferable, with the human programmer taking the creative, high-level, heuristic design decisions, and the synthesizer doing the more clerical work. The design issues are intelligible to humans because the very objective of program schemas is to capture recognized, useful, human-designed programming strategies and program classes.

TOOL SUPPORT. An implementation of schema-guided synthesis can be made on top of any existing proof planner, exploiting the fact that program schemas can be seen as proof methods [35]. This provides support for the necessary higher-order matching and discharging of proof obligations.

SCALABILITY. The search space of schema-guided synthesis is much smaller than for deductive synthesis. First, schema-guided synthesis by definition bottoms out in reuse, both of the template itself and of existing programs. One can significantly reduce the number of reuse queries by applying heuristics detecting that an *ad hoc* program can be trivially built from the specification. Second, the proof obligations of Steps 3 and 4 are quite lightweight. Schema-guided synthesis thus scales up to real-life synthesis tasks, especially if coupled with a powerful program optimization workbench and sufficient domain knowledge. For instance, Smith [67] has successfully deployed his tools on real-life problems, such as transportation scheduling.

4.3   Example

Let us synthesize a program from the following specification, open in sort ST:

$$\forall L : list(\mathsf{ST}) . \ \forall I : nat . \ \forall E : \mathsf{ST} . \ true \ \rightarrow$$
$$(\ atpos(L, I, E) \qquad\qquad\qquad (S_{atpos})$$
$$\leftrightarrow \exists P, S : list(\mathsf{ST}) . \ append(P, E \cdot S, L) \wedge length(P, I))$$

The first iteration of synthesis proceeds as follows. At Step 1, the specification S_{atpos} is chosen because it is the only unhandled specification. At Step 2, suppose schema $\mathcal{DC}$ is chosen, after a failed attempt to apply schema $\mathcal{REUSE}$. At Step 3, the specification S_{atpos} is inferred to be an instance of S_r, when $atpos(L, I, E)$ is seen as $r(I, L, E)$, under the substitution

$$\langle \mathsf{SX}, \mathsf{SY}, \mathsf{SZ} \rangle = \langle nat, list(\mathsf{ST}), \mathsf{ST} \rangle$$
$$i_r(X, Z) \leftrightarrow true$$
$$o_r(X, Y, Z) \leftrightarrow \exists P, S : list(\mathsf{ST}) . \ append(P, Z \cdot S, Y) \qquad (\phi_2)$$
$$\wedge length(P, X)$$

So far, 5 of the 9 parameters of $\mathcal{DC}$ have been instantiated. At Step 4, suppose the following substitution is chosen:

$$\mathsf{SH} = nat \qquad\qquad A \prec B \leftrightarrow B = s(A)$$
$$i_{dec}(X, Z) \leftrightarrow \neg X = 0 \qquad o_{dec}(X, Z, H, T) \leftrightarrow X = s(T)$$

This instantiates the remaining 4 parameters of $\mathcal{DC}$ in a way that the constraints C_1, C_2, C_3 hold and that the program $P_{dec} = \{dec(X, Z, H, T) \leftarrow X = s(T)\}$ can be reused to meet the now fully instantiated specification S_{dec}. The specifications of the remaining open relations in template DC are now also fully instantiated:

$$true \rightarrow (\ min(X, Z) \leftrightarrow \neg\neg X = 0\ ) \qquad (S_{min})$$

$$true \wedge \neg\neg X = 0 \rightarrow$$
$$(solve(X, Y, Z) \leftrightarrow \exists P, S\ .\ append(P, Z \cdot S, Y) \wedge length(P, X))\ (S_{solve})$$

$$X = s(T) \wedge \exists P, S\ .\ append(P, Z \cdot S, V) \wedge length(P, T) \rightarrow$$
$$(\ comp(H, Z, V, Y) \leftrightarrow \exists P', S'\ .\ append(P', Z \cdot S', Y) \qquad (S_{comp})$$
$$\wedge length(P', X)\ )$$

They can be simplified into the following specifications:

$$min(X, Z) \leftrightarrow X = 0 \qquad (S'_{min})$$
$$X = 0 \rightarrow (\ solve(X, Y, Z) \leftrightarrow \exists S : list(\mathsf{ST})\ .\ Y = Z \cdot S\ ) \qquad (S'_{solve})$$
$$X = s(T) \wedge \exists P, S\ .\ append(P, Z \cdot S, V) \wedge length(P, T) \rightarrow \qquad (S'_{comp})$$
$$(comp(H, Z, V, Y) \leftrightarrow \exists F : \mathsf{ST}\ .\ Y = F \cdot V)$$

At Step 5, the program $DC \cup P_{dec}$ becomes the reused program for S_{atpos}, while S'_{min}, S'_{solve}, and S'_{comp} are added to the now empty list of unhandled specifications.

The next iterations of synthesis proceed as follows. When S'_{min}, S'_{solve}, and S'_{comp} are chosen, suppose applications of some suitable variants of $\mathcal{REUSE}$ succeed through the *ad hoc* building of the programs $P_{min} = \{min(X, Z) \leftarrow X = 0\}$, $P_{solve} = \{solve(X, Y, Z) \leftarrow Y = Z \cdot S\}$, and $P_{comp} = \{comp(H, Z, V, Y) \leftarrow Y = F \cdot V\}$. Since no new specifications were created, the synthesis is completed and has discovered the substitution ϕ_1. For call-mode $atpos(+, -, +)$, say, the corresponding logic program

$$atpos(L, I, E) \leftarrow I = 0,\ L = E \cdot S$$
$$atpos(L, I, E) \leftarrow \neg I = 0,\ I = s(T),\ atpos(V, T, E),\ L = F \cdot V$$

can be implemented [25], say by the Mercury compiler [68], into the following steadfast program:

$$atpos(E \cdot S, 0, E) \leftarrow$$
$$atpos(F \cdot V, s(T), E) \leftarrow atpos(V, T, E)$$

The *comp* operator had to be moved in front of the recursive call to achieve this. (Prolog cannot do this, so mode-specific implementation is left as a manual task to the Prolog programmer.)

This example illustrated a relatively simple use of the $\mathcal{DC}$ schema. In [31], a quicksort program is synthesized, using a variant of the divide-and-conquer schema $\mathcal{DC}$ with two recursive calls.

4.4   Analysis

Schema-guided synthesis captures recognized, useful, human-designed programming strategies and program classes in program schemas. In doing so, it takes the hardest proof obligations offline, preventing their repeated proof across various syntheses and making reuse of existing programs the central mechanism for synthesizing programs. In the presence of powerful program optimization tools and sufficient domain knowledge, it thus naturally scales up, without any limitations on specification forms or program forms, due to the modular nature of the various forms of background knowledge. Heuristic guidance issues are still best tackled by humans, so schema-guided synthesis is best carried out interactively.

A unified view of schema-guided synthesis and proof planning has been proposed [35], revealing potential new aspects of program schemas, such as applicability conditions capturing heuristics, as well as the possibility of formulating program schemas as proof methods and thereby reusing an existing proof planner as a homogeneous implementation platform for both the schema applications and the proof obligations of schema-guided synthesis.

Our future work includes redoing the constraint abduction process for more general divide-and-conquer templates, where some $nonMinimal(X, Z)$ is not necessarily $\neg min(X, Z)$, and crafting the corresponding strategies, in order to allow the synthesis of a larger class of programs. Other design methodologies need to be captured in logic programming schemas; for instance, a global search schema has been proposed for the synthesis of constraint logic programs [37].

5   Inductive Synthesis

Following a brief introduction to inductive generalization, we present a particular approach to induction of recursive logic program called compositional inductive synthesis, which is described in detail in [46].

5.1   Background

The inductive approach to program synthesis originates in inductive logic. Inductive logic is concerned with the construction of logical theories T explaining available observations or events. This means that, given evidence in the form of atomic formulas $a_1, a_2, \ldots, a_s$, the logical induction approach is to devise an appropriate logical theory T so that

$$T \vdash a_1 \wedge a_2 \wedge \ldots \wedge a_s.$$

A major concern is to constrain T so as to rule out trivial solutions, such as T being inconsistent (thus supporting any evidence), or T being identical to the conjunction of available evidence. In the more traditional application of logical theories of induction in artificial intelligence, the quest is for a theory T taking the form of general rules, e.g., scientific rules, supporting the given evidence. In the context of induction of logic programs addressed here, the "observations" are intended sample program input-output results in the form of atomic formulas, and the theory T is to be a definite clause logic program. Thus the consistency of T is guaranteed, but computational properties such as termination and computational tractability of the synthesized program have to be separately considered.

So the goal of inductive logic programming (ILP) is to obtain a collection of clauses with universally quantified variables, which subsumes the given finite list of intended program results. The main approach to achieve this goal is syntactic generalization of the given examples. Consider atoms $p(a, a \cdot b \cdot nil)$ and $p(b, b \cdot nil)$. These two unit clauses generalize to the clause program $p(X, X \cdot Y) \leftarrow$. This rests on the existence of a dual of the most general unifier of two atoms known as the least general generalization (LGG) [63,62]. In this simple case, the LGG yields the intended program as a unit clause witness, $p(X, X \cdot Y) \vdash p(a, a \cdot b \cdot nil) \wedge p(b, b \cdot nil)$.

The syntactical generalization of terms has been extended to a notion of generalized subsumption of clauses [18,63] and further to a method known as inverse resolution, see e.g., [58]. This method has proven useful for concept formation, deductive databases and data mining. However, it is too weak for induction of recursive logic programs. Consider examples of list concatenation, e.g., $p(nil, a \cdot nil, a \cdot nil)$ and $p(a \cdot nil, b \cdot nil, a \cdot b \cdot nil)$. The least general generalization yields the clause $p(X, Y \cdot nil, a \cdot Z) \leftarrow$, which fails to capture the recursive definition of concatenation. Providing more examples eventually leads to an overly general clause: the universal predicate $p(X, Y, Z)$, which subsumes all concatenation examples though it blatantly fails to capture concatenation of lists. A general remedy for over-generalization is to include negative examples, which are understood as examples in the complement set of the intended result set of atoms. In general, the key problem in synthesizing such programs is the invention and introduction of appropriate recursive forms of clauses.

Compositional inductive synthesis employs a compositional logical language for computing relations in analogy to functional programming languages intended for composing and computing functions. The method does not apply the above generalization mechanisms. A program takes the form of a variable-free predicate expression φ encompassing elementary predicates and operators for combining relations and producing new resulting relations.

Let $\varphi \vdash e$ mean that the tuple (of terms) e is deducible from the program predicate expression φ. The computational semantics of the language can then be explained by means of inference rules of the form

$$\frac{\varphi_1 \vdash e_1 \quad \cdots \quad \varphi_n \vdash e_n}{op(\varphi_1, \ldots, \varphi_n) \vdash e},$$

where e depends on op and $e_1, \ldots, e_n$, as explicated in the concrete rules below. Let $\varphi \vdash e_1 + \ldots + e_n$ mean $\varphi \vdash e_i$ for $i = 1..n$, so that $+$ combines result tuples. Thus, $\varphi \vdash e_1 + e_2 + \ldots$ expresses that the tuples e_i of the term form $\langle t_1, t_2, \ldots, t_n \rangle$ are computable from the n-ary predicate expression φ.

In the language COMBILOG employed here, the given elementary predicates are constant formation, identity and list construction defined by the inference rules:

$$\frac{}{const_c \vdash \langle c \rangle} \qquad \frac{}{id \; \vdash \; \langle t, t \rangle} \qquad \frac{}{cons \; \vdash \; \langle h, t, h \cdot t \rangle}$$

In addition to the elementary predicates, there is a collection of operators, which map argument relations to relations. The three fundamental operators are here defined by:

$$\frac{\varphi \vdash \langle t_1, t_2, \ldots, t_n \rangle}{make_{\mu_1, \mu_2, \ldots, \mu_m}(\varphi) \vdash \langle t_{\mu_1}, t_{\mu_2}, \ldots, t_{\mu_m} \rangle} \; (make)$$

$$\frac{\varphi_1 \vdash e + e' \quad \varphi_2 \vdash e + e''}{and(\varphi_1, \varphi_2) \vdash e} \; (and) \qquad \frac{\varphi_1 \vdash e_1 \quad \varphi_2 \vdash e_2}{or(\varphi_1, \varphi_2) \vdash e_1 + e_2} \; (or)$$

The *make* operator is a generalized unary projection operator carrying an auxiliary vector of indices $\mu_1, \ldots, \mu_m$ serving to reorder arguments and introduce don't cares. As described in [46], COMBILOG possesses a compositional semantics in which *and* is set intersection and *or* is set union, which motivates the inference rules for the *and* and *or* operators. These operators reflect, respectively, logical conjunctions in clause bodies and multiple defining clauses.

This operator language becomes as expressive as ordinary clause programs if the language is extended with facilities for naming predicate expressions and using these names recursively in program predicate definitions. However, in the present form the language does not introduce predicate names in a program. Instead, the defined predicates are anonymous and in order to accommodate recursive formulations e.g., for list processing, the iteration operators *foldr* and *foldl* are introduced. These operators are akin to the *fold* operators in functional programming and with theoretical underpinning in the theory of primitive recursive functions as discussed in [45,46], The associated rules are:

$$\frac{\psi \vdash \langle t_1, t_3 \rangle}{foldr(\varphi, \psi) \vdash \langle t_1, nil, t_3 \rangle} \; (foldr \; 0)$$

$$\frac{foldr(\varphi, \psi) \vdash \langle t_1, t_2, z \rangle \quad \varphi \vdash \langle h, z, t_3 \rangle}{foldr(\varphi, \psi) \vdash \langle t_1, h \cdot t_2, t_3 \rangle} \; (foldr > 0)$$

$$\frac{\psi \vdash \langle t_1, t_3 \rangle}{foldl(\varphi, \psi) \vdash \langle t_1, nil, t_3 \rangle} \; (foldl \; 0)$$

$$\frac{\varphi \vdash \langle h, t_1, z \rangle \quad foldl(\varphi, \psi) \vdash \langle z, t_2, t_3 \rangle}{foldl(\varphi, \psi) \vdash \langle t_1, h \cdot t_2, t_3 \rangle} \; (foldl > 0)$$

For instance, with *foldr* available, the well-known *append* concatenation predicate is $make_{2,1,3}(foldr(cons, id))$, where the *make* operator swaps the two first arguments.

Below we illustrate the application of the rules using the append program, proving $make_{2,1,3}(foldr(cons, id)) \vdash \langle a \cdot nil, b \cdot nil, a \cdot b \cdot nil\rangle$:

$$\cfrac{\cfrac{\cfrac{id \vdash \langle b \cdot nil, b \cdot nil\rangle}{foldr(cons, id) \vdash \langle b \cdot nil, nil, b \cdot nil\rangle}\ (foldr\ 0) \qquad cons \vdash \langle a, b \cdot nil, a \cdot b \cdot nil\rangle}{foldr(cons, id) \vdash \langle b \cdot nil, a \cdot nil, a \cdot b \cdot nil\rangle}\ (foldr > 0)}{make_{2,1,3}(foldr(cons, id)) \vdash \langle a \cdot nil, b \cdot nil, a \cdot b \cdot nil\rangle}\ (make)$$

When the inference rules are used to compute result tuples, these tuples are unknown parameters to be determined in the course of the execution. In contrast, in the compositional inductive synthesis method, the result tuples are given initially, as a contribution to the result, whereas $\varphi_1, \ldots, \varphi_n$ are (partly) unknown program constituents to be determined recursively in the course of the synthesis. These inference rules are used in the way described in Section 3.1 for building proofs in a goal directed manner where the program constructs are unknowns, given as metavariables, and instantiated during proof. This facilitates understanding of the induction process as a stepwise, principled, program composition process.

5.2   Overview

Let us now present compositional inductive synthesis in terms of its generic features.

SPECIFICATIONS. In inductive synthesis, specifications are partial extensional definitions of the programs to be induced, i.e., a set of atoms or tuples constituting sample program results. No other problem specific specifications need be employed.

MECHANISM. The operators are similar to schemas in the schema guided approach to synthesis. In the present method, the program is synthesized in a strict recursive divide-and-conquer process by tentatively selecting an operator and then recursively attempting synthesis of constituent parameter programs.

Our synthesis takes advantage of the metainterpreter outlined below for compositional programs and does not rely on generalization mechanisms. The approach can be characterized as the top-down stepwise composition and specialization of a COMBILOG program intended as a solution in the sense that the program subsumes the program examples. The search involved in choosing between operators is taken care of by the back-tracking mechanism in the synthesizer.

In principle, our synthesis proceeds by introducing meta-variables for the left operand predicate expressions of $\vdash$ in the proof construction, and then successively instantiating these variables in the course of the goal-driven proof construction; in doing so, we also appeal to the rule

$$\frac{\varphi \vdash e_1 \quad \varphi \vdash e_2}{\varphi \vdash e_1 + e_2},$$

which is used for goal splitting on the program examples. Thus the above proof may be conceived of as a trace of a sample inductive synthesis proof.

In our metainterpreter system, the relationship $\varphi \vdash e$ is realized as a binary predicate *syn*, which simultaneously serves as metainterpreter and synthesizer. The key principle of our synthesis method is the inverted use of our metainterpreter so that the first argument program predicate is to be instantiated in the course of synthesizing a program.

Thus the heart of the synthesizer is clauses of the following, general, divide-and-conquer form for the available operators:

$$syn(comb(P_1, \ldots, P_m), Ex) \leftarrow apply\_comb(Ex, Ex_1, \ldots, Ex_m)$$
$$\wedge\ syn(P_1, Ex_1) \wedge \ldots \wedge syn(P_m, Ex_m).$$

Programs consisting of an elementary predicate are trivially synthesized without recursive invocation of *syn*. Let us consider the synthesis of a basic predicate expression for the *head* predicate yielding the head of a non-empty list, given say the two examples $\langle a \cdot b \cdot nil, a \rangle$ and $\langle a \cdot nil, a \rangle$. Synthesis of *head* is initiated with a goal clause

$$\leftarrow syn(P, [[a, b], a]) \wedge syn(P,\ [[a], a]).$$

A successful proof instantiates P with the synthesized expression $make_{3,1}(cons)$.

HEURISTICS. A detailed description of the synthesizer is found in [46]. To prevent the synthesizer from running astray in the infinite space of possible program hypotheses, the search is conducted as an iterative deepening. To avoid unwanted trivial program solutions, further constraints are imposed on the synthesizer. Consider, for instance, synthesis of the *append* predicate. An overly general solution is obtained as the universal predicate, say, with the expression $make_{2,3,4}(const_c)$ corresponding to the clause $p(X_1, X_2, X_3)$. As mentioned, such unwanted solutions might be ruled out by the use of negative examples. However in our synthesizer we have chosen to enforce well-modedness constraints on the synthesized programs thus suppressing the above solution in favor of the recursive

$$P = make_{2,1,3}(foldr(cons, id)),$$

which is obtained as the syntactically smallest solution given the two sample results $\langle nil, nil, nil \rangle$ and $\langle a \cdot nil, b \cdot nil, a \cdot b \cdot nil \rangle$ and the mode pattern $[+, +, -]$, and complying with the usual clauses for *append*. The synthesis proceeds as a goal-driven proof construction of the sample proof shown in the above section.

BACKGROUND KNOWLEDGE. The elementary predicates and the operators determine the admissible forms of programs and thereby constitute a form of background knowledge. No problem-specific background knowledge is provided but a search bias may be imposed by providing additional auxiliary predicates.

TOOL SUPPORT. For synthesizing the *at_pos* program, a system called COM-BINDUCE was used, which is based on the method outlined above and described in detail in [46].

HUMAN INTERACTION AND SCALABILITY. The current experimental system conducts the inductive synthesis automatically. The computational search costs limit the size of inducible programs to around 6 predicates and operators.

However, we envisage integration of the COMBIINDUCE principles into a semi-automatic compositional development system. In this system, the programmer can offer assistance by proposing appropriate auxiliary predicates within the pertinent data type. The imposition of data types will also serve to constrain further the search space of well-moded program candidates. Recursion (fold) over lists will be generalized to other data types later.

5.3   Example

Since at this stage, the synthesis system supports list as the only data type we represent the number n as a list of length n with constants i, where i can be any constant. Synthesis of the *atpos* program from the single sample $\langle a \cdot b \cdot nil, i \cdot nil, b \rangle$ yields the solution

$$atpos = foldl(make_{4,3,2}(cons), make_{3,1}(cons)))$$

as illustrated by the following trace:

$$
\cfrac{
make_{4,3,2}(cons) \vdash \atop
\langle \_, a \cdot b \cdot nil, b \cdot nil \rangle
\qquad
\cfrac{
make_{3,1}(cons) \vdash \langle b \cdot nil, b \rangle
}{
\begin{array}{c} foldl(make_{4,3,2}(cons), make_{3,1}(cons)) \vdash \\ \langle b \cdot nil, nil, b \rangle \end{array}
} \; (foldl\ 0)
}{
foldl(make_{4,3,2}(cons), make_{3,1}(cons)) \vdash \langle a \cdot b \cdot nil, i \cdot nil, b \rangle
} \; (foldl > 0)
$$

The synthesized program is the COMBILOG form of the definite clause program

$$atpos(L, I, E) \leftarrow syn(foldl(tail', head), [L, I, E])$$
$$syn(tail', [\_, F \cdot T, T]) \leftarrow$$
$$syn(head, [F \cdot T, F]) \leftarrow$$

Synthesis with the *foldr* operator is not possible. However, swapping the two subgoals of *foldr* yields the operator *foldrrev* allowing the following variant program to be synthesized

$$atpos = make_{3,2,1}(foldrrev(cons, make_{1,3}(cons))).$$

The relationship between such a pair of variant programs is theoretically established by a duality theorem stated and proved in [44].

In order to facilitate the comparison of the synthesis approaches, let us transform the first COMBILOG form of the *atpos* definite clause program into a recursive *atpos* program. We first unfold the *atpos* clause:

$$atpos(L, nil, E) \leftarrow head(L, E)$$
$$atpos(L, X \cdot T, E) \leftarrow tail'(X, L, Z), syn(foldl(tail', head), [Z, T, E])$$

Now, unfolding *head* and *tail*, and folding back the second literal with *atpos*, we obtain the following logic program.

$$atpos(L, nil, E) \leftarrow L = E \cdot T$$
$$atpos(L, X \cdot T, E) \leftarrow L = F \cdot Z, atpos(Z, T, E)$$

5.4   Analysis

Check that meaning is preserved! Designing a metainterpreter for COMBILOG is simplified by the variable-free form of COMBILOG programs, the separation of predicate expressions and terms in separate arguments, and the elimination of introduced predicate names. These simplifications substantially reduce search and allow us to effectively use the metainterpreter as the backbone of our ILP method by reversing the provability metalogic programming *demo* predicate as examined e.g., in [43] and in [21] for ordinary definite clauses.

In [46] we compare with other inductive synthesis systems and report results on successful automatic synthesis of a number of textbook programs including non-naive as well as naive reversal of lists. The latter program makes calls for the auxiliary predicate *append*, which is recursively induced. This predicate invention, which is generally considered problematic in ILP, is handled smoothly in our compositional method since explicit predicate names are not introduced.

The outlined compositional method facilitates a program development methodology where customized domain specific operators are added to the general purpose ones. Moreover, it seems that the compositional method surpasses more traditional ILP methods with respect to predicate invention and termination of induced programs within the considered class of primitive recursive relations delineated by the available recursive operators.

6   Comparison

In this section, the synthesis approaches are compared from different points of view. First, we compare the synthesized *atpos* programs. Afterwards, we contrast the general features of the different approaches. Finally, we conclude by analyzing how schemas are used, implicitly or explicitly, in program synthesis and we suggest that they play a central role in understanding different synthesis methods. In the following, we will refer to *inductive synthesis*, *deductive synthesis*, and *schema-guided synthesis* to denote the particular synthesis methods presented in this paper.

6.1   The *atpos(L,I,E)* Program

All three methods yielded the same program. This was the case even though they differ in which variable they choose as an induction parameter: both *inductive synthesis* and *schema-guided synthesis* choose I as the induction parameter, while *deductive synthesis* chooses L. In the case of *deductive synthesis*, we could just as well have carried out induction on I. However, for *schema-guided synthesis*, switching would require a separate schema with a different template, namely with an additional non-recursive clause for the non-minimal case. The same holds for *inductive synthesis* where a fold combinator over numbers and an associated rule would be required.

In general, the choice of the induction parameter will affect the form of the resulting program and even its complexity [25]. In this regard, *deductive synthesis* offers more flexibility, as one can perform induction over any well-founded relation, and development (hence program construction) proceeds in smaller steps. Of course, in *schema-guided synthesis* and *inductive synthesis*, one can always introduce new schemas, respectively operators, corresponding to new ways of building programs, as the need arises.

6.2   Specification

The forms of the specifications in *deductive synthesis* and *schema-guided synthesis* are similar. Both are first-order formulas asserting a possibly conditional equivalence. In *inductive synthesis*, the specification is a finite set of examples (a subset of the extensional definition of the relation), which is by nature incomplete (when the extensional definition is infinite). Specifications in *inductive synthesis* may also include negative examples or properties [28,36], but in general they remain incomplete. This incompleteness is a significant difference and, as we will see, it has far-reaching consequences. Indeed, it will play a key role in differentiating *inductive synthesis* from the other two approaches with respect to the other generic features.

For the *deductive synthesis* and *schema-guided synthesis* approaches, in contrast to *inductive synthesis*, it is important for non-trivial applications to be able to construct complex specifications and this requires ways of parameterizing and combining specifications. In our work on *deductive synthesis*, we achieve this, in practice, by using logical frameworks like Isabelle [59], which provide support for structured theory presentations. In *schema-guided synthesis*, [33] express program schemas as extensions of specification frameworks [52], which support parameterized specifications and their composition.

Of course, the use of first-order logic as a specification language has its limitations. For example, in *schema-guided synthesis*, we needed the well-foundedness of a relation $\prec$ as a constraint in the $\mathcal{DC}$ schema. However, a formalization of well-foundedness generally falls outside of first-order logic, unless one formalizes, e.g., set-theory. A work-around is to assume that some fixed collection of relations is declared to be well-founded. The alternative is to use a stronger (higher-order) logic or theory [1] where concepts such as well-foundedness can be defined and well-founded relations can be constructed. Stronger logics, of course, have their own drawbacks; in particular it is more difficult to automate deduction.

6.3   Mechanism

As presented, the mechanisms used in the three methods appear quite dissimilar. *Deductive synthesis* is oriented around derivations, *schema-guided synthesis* was described using an algorithm for applying schemas, and *inductive synthesis* uses a meta-interpreter to build programs. Yet it is possible to recast all three so that the central mechanism is the same: *a top-down application of rules is used to incrementally construct a program, during a derivation, in a correctness-preserving way.* In *deductive synthesis*, derived rules are applied top-down, using higher-order unification to build programs as a "side-effect" of proof construction. Although the mechanism for applying schemas has been presented in an algorithmic fashion, it is possible to recast *schema-guided synthesis* as the application of rules in a deductive system [1]; namely, a schema constitutes a (derivable) rule whose premises are given by the schema's constraints and (the completion of its) template and the conclusion is given by the schema's specifications. Viewed in this way, *schema-guided synthesis*, like *deductive synthesis*, constructs programs, during proofs, by the higher-order application of rules. The main distinction between the two methods boils down to the rules, granularity of steps, and heuristics/interaction for constructing proofs. Finally, in *inductive synthesis*, rules are also given for constructing COMBILOG programs. There, the rules are automatically applied by a Prolog meta-interpreter.

Although they differ in form, the rules employed by the different methods have a similar nature. Not surprisingly, in all cases, mathematical induction plays a key role in program synthesis, as it is necessary for constructing iterative or recursive programs. In *deductive synthesis*, induction principles can be derived from induction principles for data types or even the inductive (least-fixedpoint) semantics of logic programs [1]. The induction principles (perhaps in a reformulated form, e.g., the *ind* rule of Section 3.2) are then explicitly applied and their application constructs a template for a recursive program. In *schema-guided synthesis*, the correctness of schemas for synthesizing recursive programs is also justified by inductive arguments. Indeed, complex schemas can be seen as kinds of complex macro-development steps that precompile many micro steps, including induction. One might say that induction is implicitly applied when using a schema to construct recursive programs. In *inductive synthesis*, programs are iterative, instead of recursive, and programs that iterate over lists (or, more generally, other inductively defined data types) are built using *fold* rules. Again, mathematical induction principles play a role, behind-the-scenes, in justifying the correctness of iteration rules, and rule application can be seen as an implicit use of induction. There is, of course, a tradeoff. By compiling induction into specialized rules, *schema-guided synthesis* and *inductive synthesis* can take larger steps than *deductive synthesis*; however, they are more specialized. In particular, by building only iterative programs, the *inductive synthesis* method presented can sharply reduce the search space, but at the price of limited expressibility.

The underlying mechanisms are, in some respects, fundamentally different. Although all three methods are based on first-order logic, any system implementing *deductive synthesis* (respectively *schema-guided synthesis*) will require higher-order unification (respectively higher-order matching). This is necessary to construct substitution instances for variables in rules and schemas that range over functions, relations, and more generally, contexts (terms with holes); the downside is that higher-order matching and unification are more difficult than their first-order counterparts, and the existence of multiple unifiers (respectively matchers) can lead to large branching points in the synthesis search space. The operator form of COMBILOG means that rules in *inductive synthesis* manipulate only first-order terms. Moreover, all complications concerning object language variables are eliminated. This simplifies the metainterpreter and reduces the synthesis to search in the space of operator combinations subjected to well-modedness constraints.

Finally, the differing nature of the specifications, in particular, complete versus incomplete information, makes a substantial difference in the underlying semantics of the different methods and the relationship of the synthesized program to its specification. As presented here, both *deductive synthesis* and *schema-guided synthesis* construct programs that are (possibly under conditions) equivalent to some initial specification. In the case of *inductive synthesis*, equivalence is weakened to implication or entailment. This changes, of course, the semantics of the rules. Moreover it has a significant impact on extra-logical considerations, i.e., considerations that are not formalized in the synthesis logic (e.g., the program synthesized should have a particular syntactic form or complexity). In *inductive synthesis* these considerations (in particular, having a syntactically small recursive program that entails the examples) become central to the synthesis process and it is important to use a well-specified strategy, embodied in a metainterpreter, to ensure them.

6.4   Heuristics

Each of the methods presented has an infinite search space. However, the spaces are differently structured and different heuristics may be employed in searching them.

In *deductive synthesis*, one proceeds in a top-down fashion, employing induction and simplification. The search space has both infinite branching points associated with the application of higher-order unification (as there may be infinitely many unifiers) and branches of unbounded length (as induction may be applied infinitely often and simplification may not necessarily terminate). In practice, an effective heuristic is to follow an induction step by eager simplification; here, rippling can be used to control the simplification process and guarantee its termination. Moreover, with the exception of applying induction, unification problems are usually of a restricted form, involving "second-order patterns," which can be easily solved [51]. Hence, it is possible, in some cases, to use heuristics to reduce the search space to the point where synthesis can be completely automated.

Schema-guided synthesis uses a strict recursive divide-and-conquer strategy in the selection of operators and the synthesis of the parameter programs. It also employs a stepwise composition/specialization of programs where the objective is to reuse existing code. Analogous to *deductive synthesis*, critical branch-points include schema selection and selection of a substitution (higher-order matching is required as the same schema can be used in different ways). Search can be conducted as an iterative deepening search employing heuristics. Although *schema-guided synthesis* also has an infinite search space, it is fair to say that when a program is in the search space, one is likely to find it more quickly than with *deductive synthesis* since the steps in *schema-guided synthesis* are larger, and hence the program is at a shallower ply in the search tree.

The search space in *inductive synthesis* is more difficult to navigate than in the other two methods because of the additional extra-logical concerns mentioned previously. Here a strict control (dictated by a metainterpreter) is required to generate candidate programs in a particular order. To make automated search practical, the search space is restricted, a priori, by restrictions in the method. For example, the programs synthesizable are restricted to those involving iteration, instead of general recursion, and the use of combinators ensures that first-order (Prolog) unification suffices for program construction. In addition there is the well-modedness requirement and, to reduce explosive branching, the use of *or* is restricted. It is an interesting question as to whether any of these pruning measures could be profitably used in the other approaches.

6.5   Background Knowledge

The three approaches formalize background knowledge in different ways. For *deductive synthesis*, background knowledge about data types is given by a standard first-order theory augmented with appropriately reformulated (for synthesis) induction schemas (e.g., *ind*). For *schema-guided synthesis*, background knowledge must be formalized in terms of a base of program schemas, capturing a range of program classes, which may (or may not) directly incorporate information about data types, as well as a database of reusable programs and information about well-founded relations (typically associated with data types). Here, more work is usually required to formalize background knowledge, but the payoff is that this work is done once and for all and the resulting schemas can be used to reduce search and guide development to specialized classes of programs. For *inductive synthesis*, the background knowledge is basically the elementary operators (*const, id, cons,* etc.), which encode knowledge about iterative programs operating over lists. As with the other approaches, this knowledge is domain-dependent, and synthesizing programs operating over other data types would require additional rules.

6.6   Human Interaction and Scalability

The *deductive synthesis* proof presented was constructed interactively. There, within a first-order formalization of list theory, specialized rules for synthesis were derived, and interactively applied. However, proof search can also be automated using tactics and one can adjust the size of proof steps by deriving new proof rules (analogous to complex program schemas). This process of writing tactics and deriving new rules is open, leads to a customizable approach, and can, at least in theory, scale arbitrarily. The use of tactics also makes it possible to arbitrarily mix automation with human interaction.

Conversely, the *schema-guided synthesis* method was presented as fully automatable, although a human could be used to drive the selection of schemas and substitution instances. Indeed, as with *deductive synthesis*, this is often preferable, as it provides a way of influencing extra-logical concerns, such as the complexity of the synthesized program. The approach scales well as specialized schemas can be tuned to particular classes of problems (divide and conquer, global search, etc.). Moreover, there is a natural mechanism for the reuse of programs.

For the moment, there is no human interaction in the presented method for *inductive synthesis*. It is not clear either how feasible this is, given the importance that extra-logical concerns play in the synthesis process. How would a human know, for example, that steps suggested will generate the simplest possible program? The reuse of existing programs also is not handled.

It is not clear how the inductive synthesis approach can be scaled up to synthesize more complex programs with recursion or iteration. For complex examples, the incomplete nature of the input specification makes the program space so intractable that human interaction, heuristics, support for reuse, and "more complete" specification information, such as properties [30,28], appear necessary. But even with these extensions, the purely inductive approach to the synthesis of programs with recursion or iteration remains very hard, and it seems doubtful whether this approach will ever scale up to the synthesis of complex, real-life programs.

When the synthesized program does *not* feature recursion or iteration (and methods for this are outside the scope of this paper) then the inductive synthesis approach *can* usefully scale. This is witnessed by recent progress in ILP, on problems in domains, such as face recognition [54], where only (large) sets of input/output examples are available as humans have difficulty writing a formal, complete specification [34].

6.7   Tool Support

For *deductive synthesis*, we used Isabelle [59], a generic logical framework, for our implementation. For *schema-guided synthesis*, the higher-order proof planning system $\lambda Clam$ can be used, upon reformulation of the program schemas as proof planning methods [35]; this has the nice side-effect that the proof obligations of *schema-guided synthesis* can also be discharged using the same theorem proving machinery. For *inductive synthesis*, a specialized Prolog implementation was used.

It is interesting to speculate on whether generic logical frameworks, like Isabelle, could be effectively used for all three approaches. And could the approaches even be profitably combined?

Our discussion at the top of Section 6.3 suggests that a generic logical framework can effectively be used for *schema-guided synthesis*. Of course, there are some potential drawbacks. First, a logical framework requires recasting any synthesis method as one based on theorem proving; for instance, *schema-guided synthesis* was not cast this way in Section 4. This may require some contortions; see [9] for an example of this. Second, the logical framework will impose its own discipline for presenting and structuring theories, and this may deviate from that desired by a particular synthesis method; e.g., specification frameworks [52] provide more structuring possibilities than those possible using the Isabelle system. Finally, a hand-coded synthesis system will probably be more efficient. Although it is easy to write a Prolog interpreter (to realize *inductive synthesis*) as a tactic in a logical framework, this involves a layer of metainterpretation and a corresponding slow-down in execution time. The price may be too high when substantial search is involved.

As to the question whether the approaches could be profitably combined, the answer is a clear 'yes' for *deductive synthesis* and *schema-guided synthesis*, and we will develop this point in the next sub-section. Combining *inductive synthesis* with the other approaches raises the question of how to deal with the ensuing redundancy in the overall specification, as the incomplete part supposedly is a logical consequence of the complete one. To a human programmer, examples attached to a specification that is intended to be complete often facilitate the understanding of the task. But an automated synthesizer probably does not need such help. Should there be a contradiction between the complete specification and the examples, then the overall specification is almost certainly wrong. In the absence of such a contradiction, one knows nothing about the quality of the overall specification and thus has to forge ahead. The question then arises of how to exploit the redundancy. A convincing proposal was made by Minton [57]: to cope with the instance sensitivity of the heuristics used to efficiently solve ubiquitous, NP-hard, constraint satisfaction problems, industry-strength solver synthesizers should use training instances (i.e., the input parts of examples) in addition to the specification of the problem, so that the most suitable heuristics can be empirically determined during synthesis. As long as the actual runs of the synthesised program are on instances within the distribution of the training instances, a good performance can be guaranteed.

6.8   Implicit *versus* Explicit Use of Schema

A central part of our comparison has been that the boundaries between *deductive synthesis*, *schema-guided synthesis*, and *inductive synthesis* are somewhat fluid with respect to the use of schemas. In particular, from the appropriate viewpoint, the difference between *deductive synthesis* and *schema-guided synthesis* is vanishingly small. We would like to close the comparison by driving these points home.

The derived rules in *deductive synthesis* for reasoning about equivalences are rule schemas, i.e., rules with metavariables ranging over predicates. These are metavariables from the view of a metalogic, but they also can be viewed as uninterpreted relations in the object logic and play the same role as the open relation symbols in *schema-guided synthesis*. Viewed this way, if the background theory of *deductive synthesis* is formalized as a specification framework, then the inference rules are a variation of the program schemas in *schema-guided synthesis*.

For example, the *ind* rule with its assumptions A_1–A_3 presented here in *deductive synthesis* is similar (although not equivalent) to the $\mathcal{DC}$ schema developed in *schema-guided synthesis*. In particular:

- *ind* commits to an induction parameter of type list, whereas $\mathcal{DC}$ has an open sort SX for the induction parameter;
- *ind* commits to one-step, head-tail decomposition of the induction parameter, whereas $\mathcal{DC}$ has an open relation *dec* for this;
- $\mathcal{DC}$ commits to always one recursive call in the step case, whereas *ind* is flexible (there can be any number of recursive calls);
- the assumption A_1 of *ind* plays the same role as the template DC in $\mathcal{DC}$, but they differ in content;
- the predicate variable B of *ind* plays the same role as the open relation *solve* in $\mathcal{DC}$;
- the assumption A_2 of *ind* plays the same role as the specification S_{solve} in $\mathcal{DC}$;
- the predicate variable S of *ind* does not play the same role as the open relation *comp* in $\mathcal{DC}$; indeed, an instance of S may include recursive call(s), whereas recursion is dictated by the template DC and is thus not considered when instantiating *comp*;
- the assumption A_3 of *ind* plays the same role as the specification S_{comp} in $\mathcal{DC}$, but they differ in content;
- there is no explicit equivalent of the constraints C_1, C_2, and C_3 and the specifications S_{min} and S_{dec} of $\mathcal{DC}$ in *ind*.

The differences here are not due to the underlying synthesis mechanism, but are an artifact of the particular implicit schema used (for reasons of simplicity) in this presentation of *deductive synthesis*. More elaborate rules and schemas, neither committed to a particular type nor a well-founded relation, have been developed in *deductive synthesis*, as presented in, e.g., [1,3].

A similar comparison can be made between the *foldr* and *foldl* operators in *inductive synthesis*, and the $\mathcal{DC}$ schema in *schema-guided synthesis*. The *foldr* and *foldl* operators can also be seen as implicit program schemas. More elaborate rules could also be used to build COMBILOG programs in larger steps.

Program schemas are thus used (implicitly or explicitly) in the different synthesis approaches. In the literature, program schemas are often reduced to templates, formalized as higher-order expressions, and applied using higher-order unification. As shown in *schema-guided synthesis*, such templates must be enhanced with semantic information, expressed for instance through axioms, constraints, and specifications. Viewing such schemas as derivation rules, and schema application as logical inference, the distinction vanishes between the schema-guided and deductive/constructive approaches. For instance, in [1] it is shown how schemas for transformational development can be formalized as derived rules and combined with other kinds of verification and synthesis. In [30,28], a $\mathcal{DC}$-like schema is used in the context of inductive synthesis.

7   Conclusion

In this paper, we have analyzed and compared representative methods of three approaches to program synthesis in computational logic. Despite their differences, we established strong similarities. In particular, program schemas are used (implicitly or explicitly) in each of the methods and are central in driving the synthesis process and exploiting synergies. We would therefore like to conclude by discussing some limitations of schemas and open issues.

Despite their central role, schemas have their limitations. Schemas are usually expressed in some logical language, but any given language has syntactical restrictions that in turn restrict what can be expressed as a schema. For example, a first-order language fixes the arity of predicates and functions, their associated types, etc. There is no way to capture certain simple kinds of generalization or extra-logical annotations, for example to employ term or atom ellipses $t_1, \ldots, t_n$ of variable length n. As an example of this limitation, consider the *ind* rule of Section 3.2. There we used $\overline{X}$ to denote a sequence of zero or more variables and hence the induction rule given cannot be captured by a single schema, but rather requires a family of schemas, one for each n. Extensions here are possible; [64,28,70,39,20] provide notions of *schema patterns* that describe such families and can be specialized as needed before, or during, synthesis.

Schemas are here defined as abstractions of classes of programs. At the same time, they formalize particular design strategies, such as *divide-and-conquer* or *global search*; part of the associated strategy can also be specified by associated tactics, which choose induction parameters, find appropriate well-founded relations, and so on. However, in their present form, schemas cannot handle more sophisticated design strategies, namely strategies abstracting a class of programs that cannot be obtained by instantiation with formulae. Typical examples are so-called *design patterns* [38], which aim at the description of software design solutions and architectures (typically described by UML diagrams and text). How to extend schemas to handle such strategies is an open problem in program synthesis.

Overall, by examining the relationships and differences between the chosen synthesis methods, we have sought to bring out synergies and possibilities for cross-fertilization, as well as limitations. The primary synergies involve a common mechanism: a notion of schematic rule and the use of unification to apply rules in a top-down way that incrementally construct a program, during a derivation that demonstrates its correctness. The primary differences concern the nature of the specifications, in particular the information present; this also manifests itself in different semantics and radically different search spaces for the different methods. As it is, the purely inductive approach to the synthesis of programs with recursion or iteration remains very hard, and it seems doubtful whether this approach will ever scale up to the synthesis of complex, real-life programs. Fortunately, fruitful combinations of these synthesis approaches exist.

In the end, we believe that progress in this field will be based on exploiting the identified synergies and possibilities for cross-fertilization, as well as supporting an enhanced, flexible use of schemas. We hope, with this paper, to have made a constructive analysis of the last decade of research, thereby showing a possible path for the next decade.

Acknowledgements

We would like to thank the anonymous referees for their feedback and our co-investigators on research related to this paper.

References

1. P. Anderson and D. Basin. Program development schemata as derived rules. *Journal of Symbolic Computation*, 30(1):5–36, 2000.
2. A. Ayari and D. Basin. Generic system support for deductive program development. In T. Margaria and B. Steffen, editors, *Proc. of TACAS'96*, volume 1055 of *LNCS*, pages 313–328. Springer-Verlag, 1996.
3. A. Ayari and D. Basin. A higher-order interpretation of deductive tableau. *Journal of Symbolic Computation*, 2002. To Appear.
4. R. Balzer. A 15 year perspective on automatic programming. *IEEE Transactions on Software Engineering*, 11(11):1257–1268, 1985.
5. H.P. Barendregt. *The Lambda Calculus: Its Syntax and Semantics*, volume 103 of *Studies in Logic*. North-Holland, second, revised edition, 1984.
6. D. Basin. IsaWhelk: Whelk interpreted in Isabelle. In P. Van Hentenryck, editor, *Proc. of ICLP'94*, page 741. The MIT Press, 1994.
7. D. Basin. Logic frameworks for logic programs. In L. Fribourg and F. Turini, editors, *Proc. of LOPSTR'94 and META'94*, volume 883 of *LNCS*, pages 1–16. Springer-Verlag, 1994.
8. D. Basin. Logical-framework-based program development. *ACM Computing Surveys*, 30(3es):1–4, 1998.
9. D. Basin and S. Friedrich. Modeling a hardware synthesis methodology in Isabelle. *Formal Methods in Systems Design*, 15(2):99–122, September 1999.
10. D. Basin and B. Krieg-Brückner. Formalization of the development process. In E. Astesiano, H.-J. Kreowski, and B. Krieg-Brückner, editors, *Algebraic Foundations of System Specification*, pages 521–562. Springer-Verlag, 1998.
11. D. Basin and S. Matthews. Adding metatheoretic facilities to first-order theories. *Journal of Logic and Computation*, 6(6):835–849, 1996.
12. D. Basin and T. Walsh. Annotated rewriting in inductive theorem proving. *Journal of Automated Reasoning*, 16(1–2):147–180, 1996.
13. A.W. Biermann. Automatic programming. In S.C. Shapiro, editor, *Encyclopedia of Artificial Intelligence*, pages 59–83. John Wiley, second, extended edition, 1992.
14. A.W. Biermann, G. Guiho, and Y. Kodratoff, editors. *Automatic Program Construction Techniques*. Macmillan, 1984.
15. L. Blaine, L. Gilham, J. Liu, D.R. Smith, and S. Westfold. PlanWare: Domain-specific synthesis of high-performance schedulers. In *Proc. of ASE'98*, pages 270–279. IEEE Computer Society Press, 1998.
16. A. Bundy, A. Smaill, and G.A. Wiggins. The synthesis of logic programs from inductive proofs. In J.W. Lloyd, editor, *Computational Logic*, Esprit Basic Research Series, pages 135–149. Springer-Verlag, 1990.

17. A. Bundy, A. Stevens, F. van Harmelen, A. Ireland, and A. Smaill. Rippling: A heuristic for guiding inductive proofs. *Artificial Intelligence*, 62(2):185–253, 1993.

18. W. Buntine. Generalized subsumption and its application to induction and redundancy. *Artificial Intelligence*, 36(2):375–399, 1988.

19. C.-L. Chang and R.C.-T. Lee. *Symbolic Logic and Mechanical Theorem Proving*. Academic Press, 1973.

20. E. Chasseur and Y. Deville. Logic program schemas, constraints and semiunification. In N.E. Fuchs, editor, *Proc. of LOPSTR'97*, volume 1463 of *LNCS*, pages 69–89. Springer-Verlag, 1998.

21. H. Christiansen. Implicit program synthesis by a reversible metainterpreter. In N.E. Fuchs, editor, *Proc. of LOPSTR'97*, volume 1463 of *LNCS*, pages 90–110. Springer-Verlag, 1998.

22. E.M. Clarke and J.M. Wing. Formal methods: State of the art and future directions. *ACM Computing Surveys*, 28(4):626–643, 1996.

23. M.D. Coen. Interactive program derivation. Technical Report 272, Cambridge University Computer Laboratory, UK, 1992.

24. T. Coquand and G. Huet. The calculus of constructions. *Information and Computation*, pages 95–120, 1988.

25. Y. Deville. *Logic Programming: Systematic Program Development*. International Series in Logic Programming. Addison-Wesley, 1990.

26. Y. Deville and K.-K. Lau. Logic program synthesis. *Journal of Logic Programming*, 19–20:321–350, 1994.

27. A. Felty and D. Miller. Specifying theorem provers in a higher-order logic programming language. In E.L. Lusk and R.A. Overbeek, editors, *Proc. of CADE'88*, volume 310 of *LNCS*, pages 61–80. Springer-Verlag, 1988.

28. P. Flener. *Logic Program Synthesis from Incomplete Information*. Kluwer Academic Publishers, 1995.

29. P. Flener. Achievements and prospects of program synthesis. In A.C. Kakas and F. Sadri, editors, *Computational Logic: Logic Programming and Beyond; Essays in Honour of Robert A. Kowalski*, volume 2407 of *Lecture Notes in Artificial Intelligence*, pages 310–346. Springer-Verlag, 2002.

30. P. Flener and Y. Deville. Logic program synthesis from incomplete specifications. *Journal of Symbolic Computation*, 15(5–6):775–805, 1993.

31. P. Flener, K.-K. Lau, and M. Ornaghi. Correct-schema-guided synthesis of steadfast programs. In *Proc. of ASE'97*, pages 153–160. IEEE Computer Society Press, 1997.

32. P. Flener, K.-K. Lau, and M. Ornaghi. On correct program schemas. In N.E. Fuchs, editor, *Proc. of LOPSTR'97*, volume 1463 of *LNCS*, pages 124–143. Springer-Verlag, 1998.

33. P. Flener, K.-K. Lau, M. Ornaghi, and J.D.C. Richardson. An abstract formalisation of correct schemas for program synthesis. *Journal of Symbolic Computation*, 30(1):93–127, 2000.

34. P. Flener and D. Partridge. Inductive programming. *Automated Software Engineering*, 8(2):131–137, 2001.

35. P. Flener and J.D.C. Richardson. A unified view of programming schemas and proof methods. In A. Bossi, editor, *Proc. of LOPSTR'99*, pages 75–82. Tech. rept. CS-99-16, Univ. of Venice, Italy, 1999. Also see Technical Report 2003-008 at the Department of Information Technology, Uppsala University, Sweden, 2003.

36. P. Flener and S. Yılmaz. Inductive synthesis of recursive logic programs: Achievements and prospects. *Journal of Logic Programming*, 41(2–3):141–195, 1999.

37. P. Flener, H. Zidoum, and B. Hnich. Schema-guided synthesis of CLP programs. In *Proc. of ASE'98*, pages 168–176. IEEE Computer Society Press, 1998.

38. E. Gamma, R. Helm, R. Johnson, and J. Vlissides. *Design Patterns: Elements of Reusable Object-Oriented Software*. Addison-Wesley, 1995.

39. T.S. Gegg-Harrison. Extensible logic program schemata. In J. Gallagher, editor, *Proc. of LOPSTR'96*, volume 1207 of *LNCS*, pages 256–274. Springer-Verlag, 1997.

40. A.T. Goldberg. Knowledge-based programming: A survey of program design and construction techniques. *IEEE Transactions on Software Engineering*, 12(7):752–768, 1986.

41. M.J. Gordon, R. Milner, and C.P. Wadsworth. *Edinburgh LCF: A Mechanized Logic of Computation*, volume 78 of *Lecture Notes in Computer Science*. Springer-Verlag, 1979.

42. C. Green. Application of theorem proving to problem solving. In *Proc. of IJCAI'69*, pages 219–239. Morgan Kaufmann, 1969.

43. A. Hamfelt and J. Fischer Nilsson. Inductive metalogic programming. In S. Wrobel, editor, *Proc. of ILP'94*, volume 237 of *GMD-Studien*, pages 85–96, 1994.

44. A. Hamfelt and J. Fischer Nilsson. Declarative logic programming with primitive recursive relations on lists. In M.J. Maher, editor, *Proc. of JICSLP'96*, pages 230–243. The MIT Press, 1996.

45. A. Hamfelt and J. Fischer Nilsson. Towards a logic programming methodology based on higher-order predicates. *New Generation Computing*, 15(4):421–448, 1997.

46. A. Hamfelt, J. Fischer Nilsson, and N. Oldager. Logic program synthesis as problem reduction using combining forms. *Automated Software Engineering*, 8(2):167–193, 2001.

47. P. Hill and J.W. Lloyd. *The Gödel Programming Language*. The MIT Press, 1994.

48. J.R. Hindley and J.P. Seldin. *Introduction to Combinators and the λ-Calculus*. Cambridge University Press, 1986.

49. D.J. Howe. On computational open-endedness in Martin-Löf's type theory. In *Proc. of LICS'91*, pages 162–172. IEEE Computer Society Press, 1991.

50. I. Kraan, D. Basin, and A. Bundy. Logic program synthesis via proof planning. In K.-K. Lau and T. Clement, editors, *Proc. of LOPSTR'92*, Workshops in Computing Series, pages 1–14. Springer-Verlag, 1993.

51. I. Kraan, D. Basin, and A. Bundy. Middle-out reasoning for synthesis and induction. *Journal of Automated Reasoning*, 16(1–2):113–145, 1996.

52. K.-K. Lau and M. Ornaghi. On specification frameworks and deductive synthesis of logic programs. In L. Fribourg and F. Turini, editors, *Proc. of LOPSTR'94 and META'94*, volume 883 of *LNCS*, pages 104–121. Springer-Verlag, 1994.

53. K.-K. Lau, M. Ornaghi, and S.-Å. Tärnlund. Steadfast logic programs. *Journal of Logic Programming*, 38(3):259–294, 1999.

54. C.L. Lisett and D.E Rumelhart. Facial recognition using a neural network. In *Proc. of the 11th International Florida AI Research Symposium FLAIRS-98*, pages 328–332, 1998.

55. M.J. Maher. Equivalences of logic programs. In J. Minker, editor, *Foundations of Deductive Databases and Logic Programming*. Morgan Kaufmann, 1987.

56. P. Martin-Löf. Constructive mathematics and computer programming. In *Proc. of the Sixth International Congress for Logic, Methodology, and Philosophy of Science*, pages 153–175. North-Holland, 1982.

57. S. Minton. Automatically configuring constraint satisfaction programs: A case study. *Constraints*, 1(1–2):7–43, 1996.

58. S. Muggleton. Inverse entailment and Progol. *New Generation Computing*, 13(3–4):245–286, 1995.

59. L.C. Paulson. *Isabelle: A Generic Theorem Prover*, volume 828 of *LNCS*. Springer-Verlag, 1994.

60. A. Pettorossi and M. Proietti. Transformation of logic programs. In D.M. Gabbay, C.J. Hogger, and J.A. Robinson, editors, *Handbook of Logic in Artificial Intelligence and Logic Programming*. Clarendon Press, 1998.

61. F. Pfenning. Logic programming in the LF logical framework. In *Logical Frameworks*, pages 149–181. Cambridge University Press, 1991.

62. G.D. Plotkin. A note on inductive generalization. In B. Meltzer and D. Michie, editors, *Machine Intelligence 5*, pages 153–163. Edinburgh University Press, 1970.

63. J.C. Reynolds. Transformational systems and the algebraic structure of atomic formulas. In B. Meltzer and D. Michie, editors, *Machine Intelligence 5*, pages 135–151. Edinburgh University Press, 1970.

64. D.R. Smith. The structure of divide and conquer algorithms. Technical Report 52-83-002, Naval Postgraduate School, Monterey, California, USA, 1983.

65. D.R. Smith. Top-down synthesis of divide-and-conquer algorithms. *Artificial Intelligence*, 27(1):43–96, 1985.

66. D.R. Smith. KIDS: A semiautomatic program development system. *IEEE Transactions on Software Engineering*, 16(9):1024–1043, 1990.

67. D.R. Smith. Toward a classification approach to design. In M. Wirsing and M. Nivat, editors, *Proc. of AMAST'96*, volume 1101 of *LNCS*, pages 62–84. Springer-Verlag, 1996.

68. Z. Somogyi, F. Henderson, and T. Conway. The execution algorithm of Mercury: An efficient purely declarative logic programming language. *Journal of Logic Programming*, 29(1–3):17–64, 1996.

69. A. van Lamsweerde. Formal specification: A roadmap. In A. Finkelstein, editor, *The Future of Software Engineering*, pages 147–159. ACM Press, 2000.

70. W.W. Vasconcelos and N.E. Fuchs. An opportunistic approach for logic program analysis and optimisation using enhanced schema-based transformations. In M. Proietti, editor, *Proc. of LOPSTR'95*, volume 1048 of *LNCS*, pages 174–188. Springer-Verlag, 1996.

71. G.A. Wiggins. Synthesis and transformation of logic programs in the Whelk proof development system. In K.R. Apt, editor, *Proc. of JICSLP'92*, pages 351–365. The MIT Press, 1992.

Developing Logic Programs from Specifications Using Stepwise Refinement

Robert Colvin[2], Lindsay Groves[2], Ian J. Hayes[1], David Hemer[1], Ray Nickson[2], and Paul Strooper[1]

[1] School of Information Technology and Electrical Engineering,
University of Queensland, Brisbane, Australia
`ianh@itee.uq.edu.au`, `hemer@itee.uq.edu.au`, `pstroop@itee.uq.edu.au`
[2] School of Mathematical and Computing Sciences,
Victoria University of Wellington, New Zealand
`robert@itee.uq.edu.au`, `lindsay@comp.vuw.ac.nz`, `nickson@mcs.vuw.ac.nz`

Abstract. In this paper we demonstrate a refinement calculus for logic programs, which is a framework for developing logic programs from specifications. The paper is written in a tutorial-style, using a running example to illustrate how the refinement calculus is used to develop logic programs. The paper also presents an overview of some of the advanced features of the calculus, including the introduction of higher-order procedures and the refinement of abstract data types.

1 Introduction

The aim of this paper is to present an overview of a refinement calculus for logic programs. The calculus provides a framework for the stepwise refinement of logic programs from specifications. As with other refinement calculi, such as the imperative refinement calculus of Back [2], we make use of a wide-spectrum programming language that includes both specification constructs and a subset that corresponds to executable code. This allows one to transform a specification to code within a single notational framework. The specification constructs include a *specification* command that allows the effect of a program to be specified in terms of a general predicate, and an *assumption* command that defines the range of values for which a program is expected to work. A semantics for the refinement calculus has been given which models commands (both specifications and code) as partial functions from sets of bindings of program variables to subsets of those bindings [12]. A tool has been developed to support the refinement calculus [15], based on the Isabelle/HOL theorem prover.

To enhance the expressive power of the language, it has been augmented with both higher-order procedures [7] and a module mechanism with local (abstract) data types [6]. Higher-order procedures allow generic procedures to be written that apply a parameter procedure in a systematic manner. For example, the procedure *map* relates two (equal-length) lists of values by relating their corresponding elements according to a procedure given as a parameter to *map*.

M. Bruynooghe and K.-K. Lau (Eds.): Program Development in CL, LNCS 3049, pp. 66–89, 2004.
© Springer-Verlag Berlin Heidelberg 2004

Modules allow an (abstract) data type to be associated with a set of procedures for manipulating values of that type. Programs can then be developed using higher-level data types that may be specified in terms of mathematical structures, such as (multi-)sets and relations, that may not be directly available in the implementation language. By suitably restricting the structure of programs using such a module, the module may be replaced by a module of a similar structure that uses an implementable or a more efficient representation of the data type.

We give an overview of the refinement calculus by presenting the refinement of a program, *applyInst*, that applies instantiations to a meta-expression to give an expression. The example is derived from an algorithm for adapting reusable library components in a software development system [13].

In Sect. 2 we introduce the wide-spectrum language. In Sect. 3 we give a specification of the *applyInst* procedure. In Sect. 4 we introduce the notion of refinement, present some refinement laws, and begin the refinement of *applyInst*. In Sect. 5 we further refine *applyInst* by introducing higher-order procedure calls. The refinement is completed in Sect. 6, where we replace an abstract specification type with an implementation type. Sect. 7 discusses aspects of the refinement calculus project that distinguish it from other logic program derivations schemes.

2   The Wide-Spectrum Language

In our wide-spectrum language we can write both specifications and executable programs. This has the benefit of allowing stepwise refinement within a single notational framework.

A *program* in our language is a collection of parameterised *procedures*. Each procedure has a body which is a *command* whose only free variables are the parameters of the procedure. As well as commands that correspond to programming language constructs, the wide-spectrum language contains two commands that are not necessarily executable: the *specification* command, that constrains its free variables; and the *assumption* command, that can be used to define the context in which a command is required to work correctly. Commands may also be formed by using disjunction, parallel conjunction, sequential conjunction, existential and universal quantification, and recursion.

A specification command is of the form $\langle P \rangle$, where P is formula of predicate logic. The specification $\langle X = 1 \rangle$ may be understood as binding X to 1 in states where X is unbound; it succeeds in states where X is bound to 1, and fails if X is bound to something other that 1. In our semantics we model the meaning of specification command, and any command in general, as a function from sets of *bindings* to sets of bindings, where a binding maps variables to values [12]. A binding represents an answer, providing a (single) value for every free variable. A variable X is unbound in a set of bindings, or *state*, if X is mapped to every possible value by the bindings. Using this functional meaning for commands, the behaviour of a command S is to constrain the set of answers to only those that satisfy S; alternatively, S eliminates those answers that do not satisfy S.

The meaning function, e, of any command in our language satisfies the property $e(s) \subseteq s$ for a set of bindings s; this models the constraining nature of logic programs (command execution cannot decrease "groundedness"). We provide further examples below.

The following is a definition of the procedure *foo*, that constrains its parameter X to be either 0 or 1, and Y to be one greater than X.

$$foo \mathrel{\widehat{=}} (\lambda\, X, Y : \mathbb{N} \bullet \langle (X = 0 \vee X = 1) \wedge Y = X + 1 \rangle)$$

The name *foo* is defined ($\widehat{=}$) as a procedure whose parameters are natural numbers X and Y, and whose body is a specification command that constrains the possible values for X and Y. During the refinement process high-level procedure specifications are broken down into components that can be executed directly in an implementation language such as Prolog or Mercury [24]. This typically involves turning logical connectives in the specification into corresponding connectives in the programming language. For example, *foo* may be implemented as the procedure:

$$(\lambda\, X, Y : \mathbb{N} \bullet (\langle X = 0 \rangle \vee \langle X = 1 \rangle), \langle Y = X + 1 \rangle) \tag{2.1}$$

Here we have replaced the logical connectives '$\wedge$' and '$\vee$' by the corresponding program connectives ',' and '$\vee$'. We use the symbols '$\wedge$' and '$\vee$' for the logical operators conjunction and disjunction as well as the program operators for parallel conjunction and disjunction, respectively. Similarly we use the symbols '$\exists$' and '$\forall$' for both logical and program quantification. This does not lead to confusion within programs because the logical operators and quantifications can only appear inside specification and assumption commands. A summary of the operators and quantifiers of the language is shown in Fig. 1. We use S and T to stand for commands and X to stand for program variables.

		Example
$\vee$	disjunction	$S \vee T$
$\wedge$	parallel conj.	$S \wedge T$
,	sequential conj.	S, T
$\exists$	existential quant.	$(\exists\, X : \mathbb{Z} \bullet S)$
$\forall$	universal quant.	$(\forall\, X : \mathbb{Z} \bullet S)$

Fig. 1. Summary of operators in the wide-spectrum language

The meaning function of a disjunction $S \vee T$ constrains the set of answers to those that satisfy either S or T; similarly, the meaning function of a conjunction $S \wedge T$ restricts the set of answers to those that satisfy both S and T. For instance, $\langle X = 0 \rangle \vee \langle X = 1 \rangle$ constrains the set of answers to those that either bind X to 0 or 1. The program $\langle X = 0 \rangle \wedge \langle X = 1 \rangle$ constrains the set of answers to those that bind X to both 0 and 1, i.e., the empty set. A command that returns an empty set of answers acts as Prolog's `fail` command - it is equivalent to $\langle false \rangle$.

The meaning function of a sequential conjunction (S, T) is more interesting. It imposes an ordering on the execution; semantically, the answers satisfying S are passed as the input to the meaning function of T. Hence, T may assume that S is satisfied before it executes. For instance, in (2.1), the program connective ',' ensures that X is bound before the equality involving Y. This ordering allows the final equality to be implemented using the 'is' built-in of Prolog.

Our wide-spectrum language has an executable subset we refer to as *code*. A procedure is code if it has a straightforward translation into a logic programming language such as Prolog or Mercury [24]. This means the procedure uses the operators sequential and parallel conjunction, disjunction, and existential quantification, and may be recursive. Furthermore, the specification commands must contain predicates that have counterparts in the implementation language, e.g., equality, and procedure calls are only allowed on procedures that have also been refined to code. The procedure *foo* (2.1) satisfies these constraints - the corresponding Prolog syntax for the procedure *foo* is:

```
foo(X, Y) :- (X = 0; X = 1), Y is X + 1.
```

When defining procedures we often require some properties of its parameters. For instance, the following procedure *member* has an assumption command that its second parameter, L, is bound to a list of natural numbers; this is represented by the assumption command $\{L \in list(\mathbb{N})\}$. It also has a specification command that constrains its first parameter, E, to be an element in the range of (set of elements in) L, i.e., in our notation $E \in \mathrm{ran}(L)$.

$$member \ \hat{=} \ (\lambda E : \mathbb{N}, L : list(\mathbb{N}) \bullet \{L \in list(\mathbb{N})\}, \langle E \in \mathrm{ran}(L) \rangle) \qquad (2.2)$$

We make no assumption about whether E is bound or unbound. If E is bound, the procedure checks whether E is an element of L, failing if it is not. If E is unbound, it becomes bound to each element of L. In this paper we use "bound" to refer to a variable for which we have an assumption (command) that it is bound to a value of its type. Semantically, the meaning function of an assumption $\{A\}$ is a *partial* function that is defined for only those states that satisfy A. An assumption does not constrain the set of answers. Hence, the behaviour of the command $\{L \in list(\mathbb{N})\}$ is undefined for states in which L is not bound to a list of natural numbers, and does not restrict the set of answers if L is bound appropriately. The worst possible program in our language is $\{false\}$, which we call **abort**. Its behaviour is undefined for any input: it may do anything, including not terminating, halting abnormally, failing (returning an empty answer set), or succeeding with arbitrary answers.

As another example of the use of assumption commands, consider the following procedure:

$$divide \ \hat{=} \ (\lambda X, Y, Z : \mathbb{N} \bullet \{X \in \mathbb{N} \land Y \in \mathbb{N} \land Y \neq 0\}, \langle Z = X \ \mathrm{div} \ Y \rangle)$$

This procedure assumes that the variables X and Y are bound to natural numbers, and that Y is non-zero, and establishes the relation that Z is the integer quotient of the division of X by Y. It is not required to do anything when Y is zero. Assumptions are often needed to justify refinement steps, for example to ensure that the primitive predicates will be executed correctly when translated into the implementation language.

We may implement the specification of $member$ (2.2) as a recursive procedure. A natural number E is a member of a nonempty list $[H \mid T]$ if either $E = H$ or E is a member of T.

$$\mu\, mem \bullet (\lambda\, E : \mathbb{N}, L : list(\mathbb{N}) \bullet \{L \in list(\mathbb{N})\},$$
$$(\exists\, H : \mathbb{N}, T : list(\mathbb{N}) \bullet \langle L = [H \mid T]\rangle, (\langle E = H\rangle \vee mem(E, T))))$$

The notation $(\mu\, mem \bullet body)$ defines mem to be the least fixed point solution for mem of the (recursive) equation $mem = body$. A least fixed point always exists for our recursive programs [9], though for non-terminating recursions the fixed point is the worst possible program, **abort**. The refinement rule for introducing recursion prevents us from deriving non-terminating recursions in our refinements [12].

3   An Example: Applying Instantiations

In many computing applications it is necessary to define a mechanism for systematically replacing occurrences of certain syntactic constructs by other constructs. For example, in macro languages such as TEX, M4, and the language defined by the C preprocessor, parameterised macros are replaced by structures in the object language. A similar process may also be used to obtain partial evaluations of logic (and other) programs: schematic variables are consistently instantiated by other expressions.

In this section we present a specification of a program that performs such a replacement. This particular example is based on an algorithm used for adapting reusable library components in the CARE language [13]. In CARE, library components can be parameterised over *metavariables*. Components are used by instantiating their metavariables by expressions. The CARE tool includes an algorithm, based on higher-order pattern matching, for finding an instantiation that maps the metavariables occurring in library components (the source) to their corresponding object expressions. To simplify the presentation, we have chosen the easier task of applying a given instantiation to a component (source) to obtain the object.

Expressions (the results of applying instantiations) are constructed from variables (with names taken from the given set *VName*) and functors (with names in *FName*) applied to lists of expressions. Constants are viewed as nullary functors.

$$E \in Expr \Leftrightarrow$$
$$(\exists\, X : VName \bullet E = var(X)) \vee \qquad (3.1)$$
$$(\exists\, F : FName, L : list(Expr) \bullet E = fn(F, L))$$

Meta-expressions are a generalization of expressions which may contain meta-variables applied to some parameters; we call such applications *schemas*. Meta-expressions are transformed by instantiating their metavariables to give an expression. The constructors *var* and *fn* are as for expressions (except that the arguments of a function are themselves meta-expressions); in addition, there is a constructor for schemas, whose names are drawn from the given set *MVar*.

$$M \in MetaExpr \Leftrightarrow$$
$$(\exists X : VName \bullet M = var(X)) \vee$$
$$(\exists F : FName, L : list(MetaExpr) \bullet M = fn(F, L)) \vee \qquad (3.2)$$
$$(\exists V : MVar, L : list(MetaExpr) \bullet M = schema(V, L))$$

Instantiations map occurrences of metavariables to *patterns*. Patterns may contain *place holders* of the form $ph(i)$, where i is a natural number. Place holders give the position of the corresponding parameter in the schema arguments. Patterns are another generalization of expressions: as well as variables and functors, patterns may contain these placeholders.

$$P \in Pattern \Leftrightarrow$$
$$(\exists X : VName \bullet P = var(X)) \vee$$
$$(\exists F : FName, L : list(Pattern) \bullet P = fn(F, L)) \vee \qquad (3.3)$$
$$(\exists N : \mathbb{N} \bullet P = ph(N))$$

Instantiations are thus partial functions ($\rightarrowtail$) from metavariables to patterns:

$$Inst \,\widehat{=}\, MVar \rightarrowtail Pattern$$

For example, let f be a binary function, p and q be metavariables, and g and h be nullary functions. Consider an instantiation I that maps p to g and q to h.

$$I(p) = fn(g, [\,])$$
$$I(q) = fn(h, [\,])$$

Applying I to the meta-expression $f(p, q)$ results in the expression $f(g, h)$. For readability purposes we use conventional notation to write (meta-)expressions, though formally the meta-expression $f(p, q)$ and the expression $f(g, h)$ are represented by $fn(f, [schema(p, [\,]), schema(q, [\,])])$ and $fn(f, [fn(g, [\,]), fn(h, [\,])])$, respectively.

Instantiations may also map metavariables to patterns involving placeholders. For example, the instantiation I' below defines a metavariable p that accepts two parameters, denoted by place holders $ph(1)$ and $ph(2)$, and yields an expression which might be interpreted as the difference between the second and double the first:

$$I'(p) = fn('-', [ph(2), fn('*', [ph(1), fn(2, [\,])])])$$

Applying I' to the meta-expression $p(a, b)$ results in the expression $b - a * 2$. The expanded representation of the two expressions are $schema(p, [fn(a, [\,]), fn(b, [\,])])$ and $fn('-', [fn(b, [\,]), fn('\times', [fn(a, [\,]), fn(2, [\,])])])$, respectively.

Elements of $Inst$ are partial as they need not have a mapping for every metavariable. The range of $Inst$ is restricted to patterns, which themselves contain no schemas, therefore we only need to consider one level of instantiation application.

We now give three properties of a relation applyInst for applying an instantiation to a meta-expression. For all $I \in Inst$ and $Q \in Expr$:

$$(\forall X : VName \bullet \mathsf{applyInst}(I, var(X), var(X))) \tag{3.4}$$

$$(\forall F : FName, L : list(MetaExpr) \bullet \mathsf{applyInst}(I, fn(F, L), Q) \Leftrightarrow$$
$$(\exists L' : list(Expr) \bullet \#L = \#L' \wedge$$
$$(\forall i : 1..\#L \bullet \mathsf{applyInst}(I, L(i), L'(i))) \wedge$$
$$Q = fn(F, L'))) \tag{3.5}$$

$$(\forall V : MVar, L : list(MetaExpr) \bullet \mathsf{applyInst}(I, schema(V, L), Q) \Leftrightarrow$$
$$(\exists L' : list(Expr) \bullet \#L = \#L' \wedge$$
$$(\forall i : 1..\#L \bullet \mathsf{applyInst}(I, L(i), L'(i))) \wedge$$
$$V \in dom(I) \wedge \mathsf{substph}(L', I(V), Q))) \tag{3.6}$$

Property (3.4) states that applying an instantiation to a variable has no effect. Property (3.5) states that the result of applying I to $fn(F, L)$ is $fn(F, L')$, where the length of L, $\#L$, is the same as the length of L', and L' is the result of applying I to each element of L. To determine the result of applying I to $schema(V, L)$, property (3.6), we again construct the list L' which is the result of applying I to the elements of L. We extract the definition of V from I, $I(V)$, and use the relation substph to substitute place holders in $I(V)$ with expressions from the parameters list L'. The result of this, Q, is the instantiation of $schema(V, L)$ via I. Note that if V is not in the domain of I, $\mathsf{applyInst}(I, schema(V, L), Q)$ is false.

We define the result of substituting place holders with corresponding values from a list of expressions by introducing a relation substph. It is defined by the following three properties, one for each of the three forms of patterns. For all $Params \in list(Expr)$ and $Out \in Expr$:

$$(\forall X : VName \bullet \mathsf{substph}(Params, var(X), var(X))) \tag{3.7}$$

$$(\forall N : \mathbb{N} \bullet \mathsf{substph}(Params, ph(N), Out) \Leftrightarrow$$
$$N \in 1..\#Params \wedge Out = Params(N)) \tag{3.8}$$

$$(\forall F : FName, L : list(Pattern) \bullet \mathsf{substph}(Params, fn(F, L), Out) \Leftrightarrow$$
$$(\exists L' : list(Expr) \bullet \#L = \#L' \wedge$$
$$(\forall i : 1..\#L \bullet \mathsf{substph}(Params, L(i), L'(i))) \wedge$$
$$Out = fn(F, L'))) \tag{3.9}$$

Property (3.7) states that substituting place holders has no effect on a variable. Property (3.8) replaces a place holder $ph(N)$ with the Nth element from the list *Params*, provided N is a valid index into *Params*. If the input is a functor (3.9), we recursively apply substph to each of its parameters to obtain a value for *Out*.

We now specify our top-level program, *applyInst*, in terms of the relation applyInst(I, M, Q).

$$applyInst \mathrel{\widehat{=}} (\lambda\, I : Inst, M : MetaExpr, Q : Expr \bullet$$
$$\{I \in Inst \wedge M \in MetaExpr\}, \langle\mathsf{applyInst}(I, M, Q)\rangle)$$

Since we are applying an instantiation to a meta-expression, we make the assumption that the instantiation I and the meta-expression M are already bound to values of the appropriate types. Any program that calls *applyInst* must ensure that the assumption is satisfied. We refine *applyInst* in subsequent sections.

4   Refinement

Specifications are transformed into code via a sequence of correctness-preserving steps; this process is known as refinement. We say a command S *is refined by* a command T, written $S \sqsubseteq T$, if T terminates normally for all inputs for which S terminates normally (with respect to its *assumptions*) and T computes the same set of answers as S whenever S terminates. Each step in a refinement is justified by the use of a refinement law, which has been proved correct with respect to the underlying semantics. Below we present some refinement laws, and then illustrate their use by beginning the refinement of the procedure *applyInst* from Sect. 3.

4.1   Refinement Laws

We present a selection of refinement laws below. Where a law is divided into two parts by a horizontal line, the part above the line is the proof obligation that must be satisfied for the refinement below the line to be valid. A predicate equivalence, $P \equiv Q$, states that P and Q are equivalent for all possible values of their free variables. Similarly, $P \Rightarrow Q$ states that P implies Q for all possible values of their free variables. The symbols $\Leftrightarrow$ and $\Rightarrow$ are the usual equivalence and implication of predicates, which may or may not be true for given values of their free variables. We use A, P and Q for predicates, and S and T for commands.

Law 1 *Weaken assumption*   **Law 2** *Equivalent specifications*

$$\frac{P \Rightarrow Q}{\{P\} \sqsubseteq \{Q\}} \qquad\qquad \frac{P \equiv Q}{\langle P \rangle \sqsubseteq \langle Q \rangle}$$

We can refine an assumption command by transforming its predicate under logical implication using Law 1. We can refine a specification command by transforming its predicate under logical equivalence using Law 2. These laws correspond to weakening assumptions and maintaining the effect on free variables, respectively.

Law 3 *Assumption in context*

$$\frac{A \Rightarrow (P \Leftrightarrow Q)}{\{A\}, \langle P \rangle \sqsubseteq \{A\}, \langle Q \rangle}$$

Law 4 *Propagate assumption*

$$\langle P \rangle, S \sqsubseteq \langle P \rangle, (\{P\}, S)$$

Law 3 generalises Law 2, in that we may make use of the assumption predicate A in proving the equivalence of predicates P and Q. Assumptions may be *propagated* through sequential conjunction using Law 4. We use this law to pass contextual information around a program.

Law 5 *Parallel to sequential*

$$S \wedge T \sqsubseteq S, T$$

Law 6 *Lift disjunction*

$$\langle P \vee Q \rangle \sqsubseteq \langle P \rangle \vee \langle Q \rangle$$

A parallel conjunction can be refined to a sequential conjunction using Law 5. The second component of a sequential conjunction, T, may assume properties established by the first component, S, using Law 4. Law 6 allows a predicate disjunction inside a specification command to be lifted to its corresponding wide-spectrum program operator. Similar laws hold for parallel conjunction and the quantifiers.

Law 7 *Monotonicity of parallel conjunction*

$$\frac{S \sqsubseteq S' \wedge T \sqsubseteq T'}{S \wedge T \sqsubseteq S' \wedge T'}$$

Monotonicity laws state that the result of replacing a component of a program by its refinement refines the entire program. In this case, if S' refines S and T' refines T then the parallel conjunction $S' \wedge T'$ refines $S \wedge T$. Monotonicity holds for all the operators and both quantifiers in the wide-spectrum language. We use monotonicity laws implicitly in refinements.

4.2 Example: Initial Steps

In this section we begin the refinement of the procedure *applyInst* from Sect. 3. The initial stages of the refinement presented below follow the structure of applyInst. However, care needs to be exercised when introducing recursion to ensure the resulting procedures terminate. Some parts of the refinement require additional techniques which are introduced in later sections.

We begin with the specification as given in Sect. 3:

$$applyInst \mathrel{\widehat{=}} (\lambda\, I : Inst, M : MetaExpr, Q : Expr \bullet$$
$$\{I \in Inst \wedge M \in MetaExpr\}, \langle \mathsf{applyInst}(I, M, Q) \rangle)) \tag{4.1}$$

Since the definition of applyInst is recursive, we develop a recursive implementation of *applyInst*, using the principle of well-founded induction. Let $S(X)$ be a specification involving a parameter X of type σ, $\prec$ be a well-founded order on σ, and *id* be a fresh name. As is usual for a recursive procedure with parameter X, when developing the code for the procedure we may assume that the procedure satisfies its specification for values smaller than X. That is, we assume the inductive hypothesis $S(Y) \sqsubseteq id(Y)$ for all $Y \prec X$ when refining $S(X)$. If under that assumption we can refine $S(X)$ to P, then $S \sqsubseteq \mu\, id \bullet (\lambda X : \sigma \bullet P)$.

For the *applyInst* example, the parameter X is the triple (I, M, Q), whose type σ is *Inst* × *MetaExpr* × *Expr*. The well-founded ordering $(I', M', Q') \prec (I, M, Q)$ is satisfied when M' is a subexpression of M. Finally, we choose the name *apply* as our *id*. The inductive hypothesis is that for all $I' : Inst$, $M' : MetaExpr$, $Q' : Expr$:

$$\{I' \in Inst \land M' \in MetaExpr \land M' \prec M\}, \langle \mathsf{applyInst}(I', M', Q') \rangle$$
$$\sqsubseteq \hspace{6cm} (4.2)$$
$$apply(I', M', Q')$$

We can use the inductive hypothesis to introduce recursive calls to *apply* within procedure *applyInst*. We will then have refined *applyInst* to the recursive procedure $\mu\, apply \bullet (\lambda I : Inst, M : MetaExpr, Q : Expr \bullet \ldots apply(\ldots) \ldots)$.

We begin the refinement of the body *applyInst* (4.1). Initially our goal is to manipulate the body so that recursive calls may be introduced using (4.2). Using Law 3 (*assumption in context*) with the assumption $M \in MetaExpr$ allows us to refine $\langle \mathsf{applyInst}(I, M, Q) \rangle$ to the following.

$$\langle M \in MetaExpr \land \mathsf{applyInst}(I, M, Q) \rangle$$

The following proof obligation was required to apply Law 3:

$$I \in Inst \land M \in MetaExpr \Rightarrow$$
$$(\mathsf{applyInst}(I, M, Q) \Leftrightarrow (M \in MetaExpr \land \mathsf{applyInst}(I, M, Q)))$$

Continuing with the refinement, we expand the predicate $M \in MetaExpr$ using (3.2), and distribute the resulting disjunction over $\mathsf{applyInst}(I, M, Q)$ using Law 2 (*equivalent specifications*). We lift the resulting disjuncts using Law 6 (*lift disjunction*) and expand the scope of the quantifications and then lift them. In addition, we lift the conjunctions and refine them by sequential conjunctions using Law 5 (*parallel to sequential*). The body of *applyInst* is now:

$$(\exists X : VName \bullet$$
$$\langle M = var(X) \rangle, \langle \mathsf{applyInst}(I, M, Q) \rangle) \lor \hspace{2cm} (4.3)$$
$$(\exists F : FName, L : list(MetaExpr) \bullet$$
$$\langle M = fn(F, L) \rangle, \langle \mathsf{applyInst}(I, M, Q) \rangle) \lor \hspace{2cm} (4.4)$$
$$(\exists V : MVar, L : list(MetaExpr) \bullet$$
$$\langle M = schema(V, L) \rangle, \langle \mathsf{applyInst}(I, M, Q) \rangle) \hspace{2cm} (4.5)$$

Note that for each of the three branches, the structural form of M, established by the first specification command in each branch, e.g., $\langle M = var(X) \rangle$, can be assumed when refining the second specification command, $\langle \mathsf{applyInst}(I, M, Q) \rangle$. We now refine each branch in turn. The first branch (4.3), where M is a variable, may be refined by using Law 2 (*equivalent specifications*) with (3.4) on the second conjunct. The resulting code is:

$$(\exists\, X : VName \bullet \langle M = var(X) \rangle, \langle Q = var(X) \rangle)$$

The second branch (4.4), where M is a function application, may be refined using (3.5). We lift the resulting conjunctions and quantifiers, giving:

$$
\begin{aligned}
&(\exists\, F : FName, L : list(MetaExpr) \bullet \langle M = fn(F, L) \rangle, \\
&\quad (\exists\, L' : list(Expr) \bullet \langle \#L = \#L' \rangle \wedge \\
&\quad\quad (\forall\, i : 1..\#L \bullet \langle \mathsf{applyInst}(I, L(i), L'(i)) \rangle) \wedge \\
&\quad\quad \langle Q = fn(F, L') \rangle)))
\end{aligned}
$$

Noting the presence of the specification command $\langle \mathsf{applyInst}(I, L(i), L'(i)) \rangle$, we can introduce a recursive call using (4.2) provided we can establish the assumption $\{I \in Inst \wedge L(i) \in MetaExpr \wedge L(i) \prec M\}$. We note that we are in a context in which I and M are assumed to be bound variables of type $Inst$ and $MetaExpr$ respectively. Since M is bound, and $M = fn(F, L)$ is established earlier in a sequential conjunction, it follows that L must be bound also, and therefore each element of L is bound. Furthermore, $L(i) \prec M$ holds since $L(i)$ is a subexpression of L, which is a subexpression of M. We introduce the assumption $\{I \in Inst \wedge L(i) \in MetaExpr \wedge L(i) \prec M\}$ and propagate it into the second branch to syntactically match (part of) our program with the left-hand side of the refinement in the inductive hypothesis (4.2).

$$
\begin{aligned}
&(\exists\, F : FName, L : list(MetaExpr) \bullet \langle M = fn(F, L) \rangle, \\
&\quad (\exists\, L' : list(Expr) \bullet \langle \#L = \#L' \rangle \wedge \\
&\quad\quad (\forall\, i : 1..\#L \bullet \\
&\quad\quad\quad \{I \in Inst \wedge L(i) \in MetaExpr \wedge L(i) \prec M\}, \\
&\quad\quad\quad \langle \mathsf{applyInst}(I, L(i), L'(i)) \rangle) \wedge \\
&\quad\quad \langle Q = fn(F, L') \rangle)))
\end{aligned}
$$

We can now refine lines four and five to a recursive call, using (4.2).

$$
\begin{aligned}
&(\exists\, F : FName, L : list(MetaExpr) \bullet \langle M = fn(F, L) \rangle, \\
&\quad (\exists\, L' : list(Expr) \bullet \langle \#L = \#L' \rangle \wedge \\
&\quad\quad (\forall\, i : 1..\#L \bullet apply(I, L(i), L'(i))) \wedge \\
&\quad\quad \langle Q = fn(F, L') \rangle)))
\end{aligned}
\tag{4.6}
$$

The universal quantification will be eliminated in Sect. 5.1.

The third branch (4.5), where M is a schema, may be refined using (3.6). We lift the resulting conjunctions and quantifiers, giving:

$$(\exists\, V : MVar, L : list(MetaExpr) \bullet \langle M = schema(V, L)\rangle,$$
$$(\exists\, L' : list(Expr) \bullet \langle \#L = \#L'\rangle \wedge$$
$$(\forall\, i : 1..\#L \bullet \langle \mathsf{applyInst}(I, L(i), L'(i))\rangle) \wedge$$
$$\langle V \in \mathrm{dom}(I)\rangle \wedge \langle \mathsf{substph}(L', I(V), Q)\rangle)))$$

We again introduce a recursive call within the universal quantification, after introducing the assumption $\{I \in Inst \wedge L(i) \in MetaExpr \wedge L(i) \prec M\}$ as in the refinement of (4.4).

$$(\exists\, V : MVar, L : list(MetaExpr) \bullet \langle M = schema(V, L)\rangle,$$
$$(\exists\, L' : list(Expr) \bullet \langle \#L = \#L'\rangle \wedge$$
$$(\forall\, i : 1..\#L \bullet apply(I, L(i), L'(i))) \wedge \tag{4.7}$$
$$\langle V \in \mathrm{dom}(I)\rangle \wedge \langle \mathsf{substph}(L', I(V), Q)\rangle)))$$

The universal quantification will be eliminated in Sect. 5.1. The last line includes the expression $I(V)$, which is not directly executable. We show how to develop code for this situation in Sect. 6. First, in Sect. 4.3, we refine the last line to a call on a procedure that implements the relation substph.

4.3   Example: Substituting Parameters for Place Holders

We define a procedure that implements the relation substph under the assumption that its first two parameters are bound. Any program that calls *substph*, such as *applyInst*, must ensure the assumptions are satisfied.

$$substph \,\widehat{=}\, (\lambda\, Params : list(Expr), In : Pattern, Out : Expr \bullet$$
$$\{Params \in list(Expr) \wedge In \in Pattern\},$$
$$\langle \mathsf{substph}(Params, In, Out)\rangle)$$

To implement the specification command $\langle \mathsf{substph}(L', I(V), Q)\rangle$ from (4.7) as a procedure call $substph(L', I(V), Q)$, we must establish the assumption $\{L' \in list(Expr) \wedge I(V) \in Pattern\}$. $L' \in list(Expr)$ follows from the recursive calls $apply(I, L(i), L'(i))$. We refine the parallel conjunction involving $apply(I, L(i), L'(i))$ to sequential conjunction (Law 5), and then use Law 4 to establish $L' \in list(Expr)$ as an assumption before $\langle \mathsf{substph}(L', I(V), Q)\rangle$. $I(V) \in Pattern$ follows from $I \in Inst$ and $V \in \mathrm{dom}(I)$, therefore we similarly refine the parallel conjunction involving $V \in \mathrm{dom}(I)$ to sequential conjunction and propagate the assumption $I(V) \in Pattern$. The code for *applyInst* so far is:

$applyInst \sqsubseteq$
$\mu\, apply \bullet (\lambda\, I : Inst, M : MetaExpr, Q : Expr \bullet \{I \in Inst \land M \in MetaExpr\},$
$\quad (\exists\, X : VName \bullet \langle M = var(X)\rangle, \langle Q = var(X)\rangle) \lor$
$\quad (\exists\, F : FName, L : list(MetaExpr) \bullet \langle M = fn(F, L)\rangle,$
$\quad\quad (\exists\, L' : list(Expr) \bullet \langle \#L = \#L'\rangle \land$
$\quad\quad\quad (\forall\, i : 1..\#L \bullet apply(I, L(i), L'(i))) \land$
$\quad\quad\quad \langle Q = fn(F, L')\rangle)) \lor$
$\quad (\exists\, V : MVar, L : list(MetaExpr) \bullet \langle M = schema(V, L)\rangle,$
$\quad\quad (\exists\, L' : list(Expr) \bullet \langle \#L = \#L'\rangle \land$
$\quad\quad\quad (\forall\, i : 1..\#L \bullet apply(I, L(i), L'(i))),$
$\quad\quad\quad \langle V \in \mathrm{dom}(I)\rangle, substph(L', I(V), Q))))$

We refine the body of *substph* following a similar pattern to that of *applyInst*. We introduce a case analysis on the type of *In*, apply the properties (3.7), (3.8) and (3.9) as appropriate, and lift the predicate operators to their wide-spectrum counterparts. As with *applyInst*, we refine the conjunctions occurring in the pattern $\langle In = \ldots\rangle \land \ldots$ by sequential conjunctions. This allows us to satisfy assumptions for the recursive calls that are introduced as part of the refinement.

$(\exists\, X : VName \bullet \langle In = var(X)\rangle, \langle Out = var(X)\rangle) \lor$
$(\exists\, N : \mathbb{N} \bullet \langle In = ph(N)\rangle, \langle N \in 1..\#Params\rangle \land \langle Out = Params(N)\rangle) \lor$
$(\exists\, F : FName, L : list(Pattern) \bullet \langle In = fn(F, L)\rangle,$
$\quad (\exists\, L' : list(Expr) \bullet \langle \#L = \#L'\rangle \land$
$\quad\quad (\forall\, i : 1..\#L \bullet \langle substph(Params, L(i), L'(i))\rangle) \land$
$\quad\quad \langle Out = fn(F, L')\rangle))$

The first disjunct is already code. The second disjunct involves an array-like access of a list. We may refine this to a call on a recursive procedure that traverses the list and returns the Nth element, or fails if N is not a valid index. For brevity we omit the refinement and assume procedure $elemi(L, I, E)$, that implements $\langle I \in 1..\#L \land E = L(I)\rangle$ exists in our target implementation language. The refinements of similar list processing procedures are presented in [9]. In the third disjunct we introduce a recursive call in a similar manner as for *applyInst*. The universal quantification is eliminated in Sect. 5.1. Collecting the refinement of *substph* gives:

$substph \sqsubseteq$
$\mu\, sub \bullet (\lambda\, Params : list(Expr), In : Pattern, Out : Expr \bullet$
$\quad \{Params \in list(Expr) \land In \in Pattern\},$
$\quad (\exists\, X : VName \bullet \langle In = var(X)\rangle, \langle Out = var(X)\rangle) \lor$
$\quad (\exists\, N : \mathbb{N} \bullet \langle In = ph(N)\rangle, elemi(Params, N, Out)) \lor$
$\quad (\exists\, F : FName, L : list(Pattern) \bullet \langle In = fn(F, L)\rangle,$
$\quad\quad (\exists\, L' : list(Expr) \bullet \langle \#L = \#L'\rangle \land$
$\quad\quad\quad (\forall\, i : 1..\#L \bullet sub(Params, L(i), L'(i))) \land$
$\quad\quad\quad \langle Out = fn(F, L')\rangle))))$

To refine this program to code, we eliminate the universal quantifications in Sect. 5 and refine the last line of *applyInst* in Sect. 6.5.

5   Higher-Order Procedures

In this section we continue the refinement of the *applyInst* example to illustrate the use of higher-order procedures. A higher-order procedure is one that takes a procedure as a parameter. For example, consider the following specification of the standard higher-order procedure *map*, which applies a procedure P to all the elements in a list L, returning the list L'.

$$map \mathrel{\widehat{=}} \lambda\, P : \sigma \to \tau \to Cmd, L : list(\sigma), L' : list(\tau) \bullet$$
$$\{L \in list(\sigma)\}, \qquad\qquad\qquad\qquad\qquad\qquad (5.1)$$
$$\langle \#L = \#L'\rangle \wedge (\forall\, i : 1..\#L \bullet P(L(i), L'(i)))$$

The higher-order parameter, P, is a procedure that takes two parameters, of (generic) types σ and τ, respectively, and provides a command (type Cmd) that defines the relation between these parameters. The *map* procedure then relates two equal length lists, L and L', provided every element of L is related to the corresponding element of L' by P. In [7] we show how *map* may be refined to recursive code.

From the definition of *map* we may deduce the following refinement law.

Law 8 *Introduce map. For all L and L' of type $list(\sigma)$ and $list(\tau)$, respectively, and all procedures P that take two parameters of type σ and τ,*

$$\{L \in list(\sigma)\},$$
$$\langle \#L = \#L'\rangle \wedge (\forall\, i : 1..\#L \bullet P(L(i), L'(i))) \qquad \sqsubseteq \quad map(P, L, L')$$

5.1   Example: Introducing *map*

Recall the second case of *applyInst*, where the input pattern is a functor (4.6):

$$(\exists\, F : FName, L : list(MetaExpr) \bullet \langle M = fn(F, L)\rangle,$$
$$(\exists\, L' : list(Expr) \bullet \langle \#L = \#L'\rangle \wedge$$
$$(\forall\, i : 1..\#L \bullet apply(I, L(i), L'(i))) \wedge$$
$$\langle Q = fn(F, L')\rangle)))$$

Note that the second and third lines almost match the definition of *map* (5.1). From the assumption $M \in MetaExpr$ in *applyInst* we can introduce the assumption $L \in list(MetaExpr)$, which implies L is bound.

$$(\exists\, F : FName, L : list(MetaExpr) \bullet \langle M = fn(F, L)\rangle,$$
$$(\exists\, L' : list(Expr) \bullet$$
$$\{L \in list(MetaExpr)\},$$
$$\langle \#L = \#L'\rangle \wedge (\forall\, i : 1..\#L \bullet apply(I, L(i), L'(i))) \wedge$$
$$\langle Q = fn(F, L')\rangle)))$$

The third and fourth lines now match (5.1), except that *apply* takes three parameters instead of the two expected by *map*. To match fully with the definition of *map*, we use a partial application of *apply*, *apply*(I). In our language all procedures are curried (though for brevity of presentation we have not shown them as such). Hence, $apply(I)$ is a function which takes two parameters, as required by the signature of map, and we may write $apply(I, L(i), L'(i))$ as $apply(I)(L(i), L'(i))$. We use Law 8 (*introduce map*) with $apply(I)$ as the first parameter to map, giving:

$$(\exists F : FName, L : list(MetaExpr) \bullet \langle M = fn(F, L)\rangle,$$
$$(\exists L' : list(Expr) \bullet map(apply(I), L, L') \wedge \langle Q = fn(F, L')\rangle)))$$

The procedure $apply$ with instantiation I is applied to each element of L, resulting in the list L'. Given a target language that implements a map function and supports partial application of procedure calls, such as Mercury [24], the above command can be translated to executable code.

Using similar refinements to those above, we may replace the universal quantifications appearing elsewhere in $applyInst$ and $substph$ by calls to map. Collecting the refinement of $applyInst$ and $substph$ gives:

$$applyInst \sqsubseteq$$
$$\mu\, apply \bullet (\lambda\, I : Inst, M : MetaExpr, Q : Expr \bullet \{I \in Inst \wedge M \in MetaExpr\},$$
$$(\exists X : VName \bullet \langle M = var(X)\rangle, \langle Q = var(X)\rangle) \vee$$
$$(\exists F : FName, L : list(MetaExpr) \bullet \langle M = fn(F, L)\rangle,$$
$$(\exists L' : list(Expr) \bullet map(apply(I), L, L') \wedge \langle Q = fn(F, L')\rangle)) \vee$$
$$(\exists V : MVar, L : list(MetaExpr) \bullet \langle M = schema(V, L)\rangle,$$
$$(\exists L' : list(Expr) \bullet map(apply(I), L, L'),$$
$$\langle V \in dom(I)\rangle, substph(L', I(V), Q)))))$$

$$substph \sqsubseteq$$
$$\mu\, sub \bullet (\lambda\, Params : list(Expr), In : Pattern, Out : Expr \bullet$$
$$\{Params \in list(Expr) \wedge In \in Pattern\},$$
$$(\exists X : VName \bullet \langle In = var(V)\rangle, \langle Out = var(V)\rangle) \vee$$
$$(\exists N : \mathbb{N} \bullet \langle In = ph(N)\rangle, elemi(Params, N, Out)) \vee$$
$$(\exists F : FName, L : list(Pattern) \bullet \langle In = fn(F, L)\rangle,$$
$$(\exists L' : list(Expr) \bullet map(sub(Params), L, L') \wedge \langle Out = fn(F, L')\rangle))))$$

Only the last line of $applyInst$ is not code; we present the refinement of this line in Sect. 6.5.

6   Modular Logic Program Refinement

In this section we outline a technique for module *data refinement* [6], where a program is refined by changing the type of some of its variables. We assume a type and operations on that type are encapsulated in a module. By making some assumptions about the way in which such modules are used, we can develop efficient implementations of abstract modules. We use module refinement to complete the refinement of the $applyInst$ procedure.

6.1 Modules

A module is a collection of procedures that operate on values of a given data type. We refer to variables of the given type as *opaque*. For instance, consider the module *AbstractInst* that operates on values of the abstract partial function type for *Inst*.

Module *AbstractInst*
Type $Inst \mathrel{\widehat{=}} MVar \nrightarrow Expr$

$$init \mathrel{\widehat{=}} (\lambda\, I : Inst \bullet \langle I = \varnothing \rangle)$$
$$lookup \mathrel{\widehat{=}} (\lambda\, I : Inst, K : MVar, V : Expr \bullet$$
$$\{I \in Inst \wedge K \in MVar\}, \langle (K, V) \in I \rangle)$$
$$update \mathrel{\widehat{=}} (\lambda\, I : Inst, K : MVar, V : Expr, I' : Inst \bullet \ldots)$$
End

The procedure *init* establishes I as the empty function, $\varnothing$, while *lookup* establishes V as the value of $I(K)$, or fails if K is not in the domain of I. The procedure *update*, the details of which we omit for brevity, may be used to construct a nonempty value I' of type *Inst*. The *AbstractInst* module could be generalised to implement a partial function with any types for the domain and range; for simplicity we use the above instance where the partial function is from *MVar* to *Expr*.

For encapsulation purposes, a program that uses the abstract *Inst* type should make use of that type only through the procedures of the *AbstractInst* module. A program that uses *AbstractInst* must also respect its intended modes, which can be determined by looking at the assumptions for each procedure. If a parameter is assumed to be of the opaque type, that parameter is called an *input* to the procedure; if there is no such type assumption the parameter is called an *output*.

Since partial functions are not directly implemented in most languages, we would like to replace all the references to the abstract module with references to a concrete module that faithfully implements the abstract procedures using an implementation language data type.

6.2 Module Refinement

In general we say a module $\mathcal{M}$ is *module-refined* by module $\mathcal{M}'$ under the following condition: all programs P are refined by replacing calls to the procedures of the module $\mathcal{M}$ by calls to the corresponding procedures in the module $\mathcal{M}'$. While this definition is the most general, by restricting the class of programs P for which the module refinement must hold we can simplify some of the reasoning. Furthermore, by assuming that calls to a module occur in a certain order (imposed by sequential conjunction), we can allow efficient representations to be used that would not be possible in the more general case. Consider the following program that uses the procedures from *AbstractInst*:

$$(\exists\, I : Inst \bullet init(I), \ldots, (\exists\, I' : Inst \bullet update(I, X, Y, I'), \ldots,$$
$$lookup(I', K, V)))$$

There is a strict order on the calls to *init*, *update*, and *lookup*, though within the
... there may be arbitrary commands that do not use the module or variables
of its type. Suppose we have a module *ConcreteInst* that is a module refinement
of *AbstractInst*, providing procedures $init^+$, $lookup^+$ and $update^+$ using an implementable type, $Inst^+$, to represent the instantiation. Since *ConcreteInst* is a
module refinement of *AbstractInst*, we may refine the above program to

$$(\exists\, I^+ : Inst^+ \bullet init^+(I^+), \ldots, (\exists\, I'^+ : Inst^+ \bullet update^+(I^+, X, Y, I'^+), \ldots,$$
$$lookup^+(I'^+, K, V))$$

Note, however, that it is not the case that $init \sqsubseteq init^+$. Indeed, because they
operate on different types (*Inst* and $Inst^+$), one could not possibly refine the
other since they provide different sets of answers for their parameters.

To prove that a module $\mathcal{M}$ is refined by a module $\mathcal{M}'$ we use a *coupling
invariant*, which is a relation between variables of the abstract and concrete type.
Each pair of corresponding procedures from the modules are checked against
the conditions for module refinement, given in [6], using the particular coupling
invariant chosen. However, in many situations it is possible to automatically
calculate a concrete module, given an abstract module and a coupling invariant.
Using the calculation process to derive the concrete module guarantees that the
conditions for module refinement will be met. In Sect. 6.3 we refine *applyInst*
to use a call on *lookup* from the *AbstractInst* module. In Sect. 6.4 we introduce
module calculation, and in Sect. 6.5 we show how it may be applied to the *lookup*
procedure.

6.3   Example: Introducing *lookup*

In the third case of *applyInst*, where M is a *schema*, we need a refinement of
the command:

$$\langle V \in \mathrm{dom}(I) \rangle, substph(L', I(V), Q)$$

This is the only part of the *applyInst* program that makes direct use of the
instantiation I. However we are not able to refine this directly to code because
the expression $I(V)$ is not directly implementable in most logic programming
languages. Below we refine the above program fragment to make use of the
procedure *lookup* from the *AbstractInst* module.

We separate $I(V)$ from the use of its value (sometimes called *flattening*). We
introduce an existential variable *FDefn* that has the value $I(V)$, using Law 2
(*equivalent specifications*).

$$\langle (\exists\, FDefn : Expr \bullet V \in \mathrm{dom}(I) \wedge FDefn = I(V)) \rangle, substph(L', I(V), Q)$$

Treating the abstract partial function representation of an instantiation, I, as
a set of pairs, we rewrite $V \in \mathrm{dom}(I) \wedge FDefn = I(V)$ as $(V, FDefn) \in I$.
Now we lift the existential quantifier, expand its scope to encompass the call to
substph, and replace $I(V)$ with *FDefn* in the call to *substph*.

$$(\exists\, FDefn : Expr \bullet \langle (V, FDefn) \in I \rangle, substph(L', FDefn, Q))$$

The command $\langle (V, FDefn) \in I \rangle$ is refined by a call to *lookup*, since $I \in Inst$ and $V \in MVar$ are guaranteed by the context.

$$(\exists FDefn : Expr \bullet lookup(I, V, FDefn), substph(L', FDefn, Q)) \tag{6.1}$$

Thus the only non-trivial reference to the instantiation I in the *applyInst* procedure occurs in a call on module *AbstractInst*.

6.4 Module Calculation

A technique for deriving, or calculating, a concrete module from an abstract module has been developed [9]. Consider an abstract procedure of the form $(\lambda I : \sigma, V : \tau \bullet \{A\}, \langle P \rangle)$, having no opaque output parameters, and in which V is not of the opaque type (V is referred to as a *regular* parameter). Given a coupling invariant $CI(I, L)$ relating a variable I of the abstract type σ with a variable L of the concrete type σ^+, we may calculate the corresponding concrete procedure as:

$$(\lambda L : \sigma^+, V : \tau \bullet$$
$$\{(\exists I : \sigma \bullet CI(I, L) \wedge A)\}, \tag{6.2}$$
$$\langle (\forall I : \sigma \bullet CI(I, L) \wedge A \Rightarrow P) \rangle)$$

The assumption may be understood as a constraint on L that there exists some abstract instantiation I which satisfies the abstract assumption A and to which L is related via the coupling invariant. Similarly, the specification command can be understood as specifying that, for all abstract instantiations I related to L and satisfying the assumption A, the abstract specification P must hold. Once a procedure has been calculated in the above form, the developer then simplifies the assumption and specification to eliminate references to the abstract type σ. In many cases, depending on the form of the coupling invariant, this can be done via applications of the one-point laws. In the next section we use the above result to calculate the concrete procedure for *lookup*.

The calculation technique may also be applied to abstract procedures with opaque output parameters, but for brevity we do not present the general form of the corresponding concrete procedure here (see [9] for details).

6.5 Example: Calculation

We can calculate the corresponding concrete procedure for *lookup* after choosing an appropriate concrete representation and relating it to the abstract type via a coupling invariant. We choose to concretely represent the partial function by a list whose elements are pairs of *MVars* and *Exprs*. We relate a variable I of the abstract (partial function) type with a variable L of the concrete (list) type using the coupling invariant $I = \mathrm{ran}(L)$. This coupling invariant states that the abstract instantiation I contains all of the pairs in the list L. The relationship is straightforward since a partial function can be thought of as a set of pairs, the first elements of which form the domain of the function, with the second elements being the corresponding values for the members of the domain. Hence, the range of the list $[(x, g), (y, h)]$ forms the set $\{(x, g), (y, h)\}$, which is a partial function which maps x to g and y to h.

Using the general form of (6.2) with the coupling invariant $I = \mathrm{ran}(L)$, noting that the type σ is $Inst$ and K and V are regular variables, generates the concrete procedure $lookup^+$:

$$lookup^+ \mathrel{\widehat{=}} (\lambda\, L : list(MVar \times Expr), K : MVar, V : Expr \bullet$$
$$\{(\exists\, I : Inst \bullet I = \mathrm{ran}(L) \wedge I \in Inst \wedge K \in MVar)\},$$
$$\langle(\forall\, I : Inst \bullet I = \mathrm{ran}(L) \wedge I \in Inst \wedge K \in MVar \Rightarrow (K, V) \in I)\rangle))$$

This is a valid module refinement of $lookup$ using a list of pairs to represent the abstract partial function. However, it is rather complex and not directly executable at this stage, since it still uses the abstract type (though such references are scoped by quantifications).

We refine the procedure body to code. The assumption and specification commands may be simplified using the one-point rules for existential and universal quantification, respectively, and the resulting redundant antecedent in the specification command may be removed using Law 3 (*assumption in context*), giving:

$$\{\mathrm{ran}(L) \in Inst \wedge K \in MVar\}, \langle(K, V) \in \mathrm{ran}(L)\rangle$$

We simplify the assumption using Law 1 (*weaken assumption*) since

$$\mathrm{ran}(L) \in Inst \Rightarrow L \in list(MVar \times Expr)$$

However we must still refine the specification $\langle(K, V) \in \mathrm{ran}(L)\rangle$ to code. This is a membership test in the list L. We omit the details of the refinement for brevity, and assume that our target implementation language has an appropriate procedure $member$, similar to that presented in Sect. 2.

After applying the calculation technique to the $init$ and $update$ procedures (each of which contains output parameters, and therefore require slightly different calculations to that of $lookup$ [9]), we have the full concrete module. We use $Inst^+$ as the name of the concrete type $list(MVar \times Expr)$.

> **Module** *ConcreteInst*
> **Type** $Inst^+ \mathrel{\widehat{=}} list(MVar \times Expr)$
> $\qquad init^+ \mathrel{\widehat{=}} (\lambda\, L : Inst^+ \bullet \langle L = [\,]\rangle)$
> $\qquad lookup^+ \mathrel{\widehat{=}} (\lambda\, L : Inst^+, K : MVar, V : Expr \bullet$
> $\qquad\qquad \{L \in Inst^+ \wedge K \in MVar\}, member((K, V), L))$
> $\qquad update^+ \mathrel{\widehat{=}} \ldots$
> **End**

Since we have followed the calculation process, we may refine a program that uses *AbstractInst* – provided the program satisfies the structural restrictions discussed in Sect. 6.2 – by replacing each of its calls to procedures of module *AbstractInst* with calls to the corresponding procedures of module *ConcreteInst*.

Collecting the refinements from each section gives us the complete program. It uses the type $Inst^+$ and procedure $lookup^+$ from the *ConcreteInst* module. We use the the symbol $\sqsubseteq_D$ to indicate that the refinement of *applyInst* is a data refinement, since we data refined the original instantiation type (partial function) to a list of pairs.

$applyInst \sqsubseteq_D$
$\mu\, apply \bullet (\lambda\, I : Inst^+, M : MetaExpr, Q : Expr \bullet \{I \in Inst^+ \wedge M \in MetaExpr\},$
$\qquad (\exists\, X : VName \bullet \langle M = var(X)\rangle, \langle Q = var(X)\rangle) \vee$
$\qquad (\exists\, F : FName, L : list(MetaExpr) \bullet \langle M = fn(F, L)\rangle,$
$\qquad\qquad (\exists\, L' : list(Expr) \bullet map(apply(I), L, L') \wedge \langle Q = fn(F, L')\rangle)) \vee$
$\qquad (\exists\, V : MVar, L : list(MetaExpr) \bullet \langle M = schema(V, L)\rangle,$
$\qquad\qquad (\exists\, L' : list(Expr) \bullet map(apply(I), L, L'),$
$\qquad\qquad\qquad (\exists\, FDefn : Expr \bullet lookup^+(I, V, FDefn),$
$\qquad\qquad\qquad\quad substph(L', FDefn, Q)))))$

$substph \sqsubseteq$
$\mu\, sub \bullet (\lambda\, Params : list(Expr), In : Pattern, Out : Expr \bullet$
$\qquad \{Params \in list(Expr) \wedge In \in Pattern\},$
$\qquad (\exists\, X : VName \bullet \langle In = var(V)\rangle, \langle Out = var(V)\rangle) \vee$
$\qquad (\exists\, N : \mathbb{N} \bullet \langle In = ph(N)\rangle, elemi(Params, N, Out)) \vee$
$\qquad (\exists\, F : FName, L : list(Pattern) \bullet \langle In = fn(F, L)\rangle,$
$\qquad\qquad (\exists\, L' : list(Expr) \bullet map(sub(Params), L, L') \wedge \langle Out = fn(F, L')\rangle))))$

7   Conclusions

In this paper we have presented a refinement calculus for logic programming, and illustrated how it can be used by developing a small, but non-trivial, logic program from its specification. Our refinement calculus is similar in style to deductive logic program synthesis (surveys of which can be found in [3, 11]). At the most fundamental level, logic program development is the manipulation of predicates from general logic to a subset that corresponds to code, and developing a logic program in either the refinement calculus or synthesis style will require similar manipulation. We compare our approach to other logic program development schemes in the next section.

A distinguishing feature of the refinement calculus approach is its rich specification language. In particular, a program (fragment) has an associated assumption component, similar to the precondition component of a program specification in an imperative programming formalism. This allows one to partially specify procedures, in the sense that their operation is not defined if the assumptions do not hold. We make use of this when developing recursive procedures by requiring that recursive calls satisfy an assumption that their arguments are bound to values that are strictly less than those of the enclosing call according to some well-founded relation. For instance, if the *member* procedure given in

Sect. 2 is passed an unbound parameter for formal parameter L, then the tail of L, T, will also be unbound. This will result in infinite recursion. In the refinement calculus framework, the conditions for introducing recursion require a well-founded ordering to be maintained. To satisfy this condition, the recursive parameter must be bound. In this paper we have introduced recursion somewhat informally, but a more formal approach based the use of a refinement law for introducing recursion may be found in [12].

The translation to actual logic program code is not as straightforward as for an imperative language. The translation is not just a matter of turning conjunctions into commas and using defined language primitives – the order of conjuncts in a procedure goal must also be considered. At the logic level, conjunction is commutative, and therefore does not provide any guide to ordering its conjuncts. Knowledge of the execution mechanism of the implementation language is required to correctly order the conjuncts in a goal. In the calculus framework, assumptions and sequential conjunction partially bridge this gap. In Sect. 4.3 we saw that parallel conjunctions needed to be refined to sequential conjunctions so that the assumptions of the second operand of the conjunction (which was refined to a procedure call to *substph*) were established by the first operand (these assumptions are required to ensure the recursion of *substph* terminates). This ordering is precisely that required in a real (Prolog) implementation to ensure termination. The order of remaining parallel conjunctions is irrelevant to the satisfaction of procedure call assumptions, and termination of recursion (the order may be relevant, however, to performance issues – in this case, knowledge of the execution mechanism is required). Related to the issue of ordering conjuncts (goals) is the ordering of disjuncts (clauses). Given our total-correctness requirement, recursive procedures developed using the recursion introduction refinement law will terminate regardless of the ordering of disjuncts, assuming that assumptions are met. For this reason, the wide-spectrum language does not have a sequential disjunction operator.

The refinement calculus approach as described in [12] has been extended in several directions. One of these is *data refinement* [8, 6], where the type of a program variable is refined to some other type, usually for implementation purposes, as illustrated in Sect. 6. The specification language has been extended to include higher-order constructs [7]. The introduction of higher-order constructs simplifies some refinements by the use of powerful higher-order procedures, as illustrated in Sect. 5. The specification language has also been extended to include demonic non-determinism [14], although we did not make use of it in this paper. Demonic, or "don't care" non-determinism allows one to choose between sets of possible answers that a program must return; normally an implementation must return exactly the same set of answers as the specification. The set of answers associated with a demonic choice between two programs S and T, written $S \sqcap T$, is either the set of answers that S returns or the set of answers T returns. This is in contrast to the set of answers associated with a disjunction $S \vee T$, which is the union of the set of answers for S and T.

A tool has been developed to support the refinement calculus [15], based on the Isabelle/HOL theorem prover. By using facilities provided by the theorem prover it is possible to automatically discharge many proof obligations associated with refinement law applications, though the user of the tool guides the refinement by selecting which rules to apply. A code generation tool has also been developed [5]. It takes output from the refinement tool and generates executable code for the Mercury language [24]. This involves the deduction of intended (Mercury) mode information from the assumptions a procedure makes about its parameters. The full semantics of the calculus and more details on some of the above topics can be found in [9].

7.1 Related Work

Traditionally, the refinement calculus has been used to develop imperative programs from specifications [1, 21, 22, 20]. The increase in expressive power of logic programming languages, when compared with imperative languages, leads to a reduced conceptual gap between a problem and its solution, which means that fewer development steps are required during refinement. An additional advantage of logic programming languages over procedural languages is their simpler, cleaner semantics, which leads to simpler proofs of the refinement steps. Finally, the higher expressive level of logic programming languages means that the individual refinement steps typically achieve more.

There have been several proposals for the constructive development of logic programs, for example in Jacquet [17]. Much of this work has focused on program transformations or equivalence transformations from a first-order logic specification [4, 16]. Read and Kazmierczak [23] propose a stepwise development of modular logic programs from first-order specifications, based on three refinement steps that are much coarser than the refinement steps proposed in this paper. This leaves most of the work to be done in discharging the proof obligations for the refinement steps, for which they provide little guidance. Another approach to constructing logic programs is through *schemata* [19]. A logic program is designed through the application of common algorithmic structures. The designer chooses which program structure is most suitable to a task based on the data types in question. As such, the focus of this method is to aid the design of large programs. The refinement steps and corresponding verification proofs are therefore much larger.

Deductive logic program synthesis [3, 11] is probably the most similar to the refinement calculus approach. In deductive synthesis, a specification is successively transformed using synthesis laws proven in an underlying framework (typically first-order logic). As mentioned earlier, the main difference between most deductive synthesis approaches and logic program refinement is the inclusion of assumptions in the wide-spectrum language, acting as preconditions. However, Lau and Ornaghi [18] have the concept of a *conditional* specification, which includes an input relation for a procedure (e.g., types, modes) with respect to which the synthesis of the procedure can take place. The refinement calculus generalises this by allowing an assumption (input relation) for any arbitrary program fragment. Another aspect of deductive synthesis is that the deduction rules are derived with the SLD computation rule in mind. Thus aspects of termination, completeness etc., have to be dealt with during the synthesis process. The refinement approach leaves clause ordering and computational termination as part of the translation from wide-spectrum language to code.

Deville [10] introduces a systematic program development method for Prolog that incorporates assumptions and types similar to ours. The main difference is that Deville's approach to program development is mostly informal, whereas our approach is fully formal. A second distinction is that Deville's approach concentrates on the development of individual procedures. By using a wide-spectrum language, our approach blurs the distinction between a logic description and a logic program. For example, general predicates may appear anywhere within a program, and the refinement rules allow them to be transformed within that context. Similarly, programming language constructs may be used and transformed at any point.

References

[1] R.-J. Back. Correctness preserving program refinements: Proof theory and applications. Tract 131, Mathematisch Centrum, Amsterdam, 1980.

[2] R. J. R. Back. A calculus of refinements for program derivations. *Acta Informatica*, 25:593–624, 1988.

[3] David Basin, Yves Deville, Pierre Flener, Andreas Hamfelt, and Jorgen Fischer Nilsson. Synthesis of programs in computational logic. *Ten years of LOPSTR*, 2004.

[4] K. Clark. The synthesis and verification of logic programs. Research report, Imperial College, 1978.

[5] R. Colvin, I. Hayes, D. Hemer, and P. Strooper. Translating refined logic programs to Mercury. In Michael Oudshoorn, editor, *Proceedings of the Twenty-Fifth Australasian Computer Science Conference*, volume 4 of *Conferences in Research and Practice in Information Technology*, pages 33–40. Australian Computer Society, January 2002.

[6] R. Colvin, I. Hayes, and P. Strooper. A technique for modular logic program refinement. In K.-K. Lau, editor, *Logic Based Program Synthesis and Transformation (LOPSTR 2000), Selected Papers*, volume 2402 of *LNCS*, pages 38–56. Springer, 2001.

[7] R. Colvin, I. J. Hayes, D. Hemer, and P.A. Strooper. Refinement of higher-order logic programs. In M. Leuschel, editor, *Proceedings of the International Workshop on Logic-based Program Synthesis and Transformation (LOPSTR 2002)*, volume 2664 of *Lecture Notes in Computer Science*, pages 126–143. Springer, 2003.

[8] R. Colvin, I. J. Hayes, and P. Strooper. Data refining logic programs. In Jim Grundy, Martin Schwenke, and Trevor Vickers, editors, *International Refinement Workshop and Formal Methods Pacific 1998*, Discrete Mathematics and Theoretical Computer Science, pages 100–116. Springer-Verlag, 1998.

[9] Robert Colvin. *Contextual and Data Refinement for the Refinement Calculus for Logic Programs*. PhD thesis, School of Information Technology and Electrical Engineering, University of Queensland, August 2002.

[10] Y. Deville. *Logic Programming: Systematic Program Development*. Addison-Wesley, 1990.

[11] Y. Deville and K.-K. Lau. Logic program synthesis. *Journal of Logic Programming*, 19,20:321–350, 1994. Special Issue: Ten Years of Logic Programming.

[12] I. J. Hayes, R. Colvin, D. Hemer, R. Nickson, and P. A. Strooper. A refinement calculus for logic programs. *Theory and Practice of Logic Programming*, 2(4–5):425–460, July–September 2002.

[13] D. Hemer. An algorithm for pattern-matching mathematical expressions. In Lindsay Groves and Steve Reeves, editors, *Proc. Formal Methods Pacific (FMP'97)*, Discrete Mathematics and Theoretical Computer Science, pages 103–123. Springer Verlag, July 1997.

[14] D. Hemer, R. Colvin, I. Hayes, and P. Strooper. Don't care non-determinism in logic program refinement. In James Harland, editor, *Proceeding of Computing: the Australasian Theory Symposium*, volume 61 of *Electronic Notes in Computer Science (ENTCS)*. Elsevier Science, January 2002. http://www.elsevier.nl/locate/entcs/volume61.html.

[15] D. Hemer, I. Hayes, and P. Strooper. Refinement Calculus for Logic Programming in Isabelle/HOL. In R. Boulton and P. Jackson, editors, *Theorem Proving in Higher Order Logics, 14th International Conference, TPHOLs 2001*, volume 2152 of *LNCS*, pages 249–264. Springer, September 2001.

[16] C.J. Hogger. Derivation of logic programs. *Journal of the ACM*, 28(2):372–392, 1981.

[17] J.-M. Jacquet, editor. *Constructing Logic Programs*. Wiley Professional Computing, 1993.

[18] K.-K. Lau and M. Ornaghi. The relationship between logic programs and specifications — the subset example revisited. *J. Logic Programming*, 30(3):239–257, March 1997.

[19] Emmanouil I. Marakakis. *Logic Program Development Based on Typed Moded Schemata and Data Types*. PhD thesis, Department of Computer Science, University of Bristol, February 1997.

[20] C. C. Morgan. *Programming from Specifications*. Prentice Hall, second edition, 1994.

[21] C. C. Morgan and K.A. Robinson. Specification statements and refinement. *IBM Journal of Research and Development*, 31(5), September 1987.

[22] J.M. Morris. A theoretical basis for stepwise refinement and the programming calculus. *Science of Computer Programming*, 9(3):287–306, December 1987.

[23] M.G. Read and E.A. Kazmierczak. Formal program development in Modular Prolog: A case study. In T.P. Clement and K.-K. Lau, editors, *Proc. of LOPSTR'91*, Workshops in Computing, pages 69–93. Springer Verlag, 1991.

[24] Z. Somogyi, F.J. Henderson, and T.C. Conway. Mercury, an efficient purely declarative logic programming language. In R. Kotagiri, editor, *Proceedings of the Eighteenth Australasian Computer Science Conference*, pages 499–512, Glenelg, South Australia, 1995. Australian Computer Science Communications.

Declarative Semantics of
Input Consuming Logic Programs

Annalisa Bossi[1], Nicoletta Cocco[1], Sandro Etalle[2,3], and Sabina Rossi[1]

[1] Università di Venezia, via Torino 155, 30172 Venezia, Italy
{bossi,cocco,srossi}@dsi.unive.it
[2] University of Twente, P.O. Box 616, 6200 MD Maastricht, The Netherlands
s.etalle@utwente.nl
[3] CWI, Kruislaan 413, P.O. Box 94079, 1090 GB Amsterdam, The Netherlands

Abstract. Most logic programming languages actually provide some kind of *dynamic scheduling* to increase the expressive power and to control execution. *Input consuming* derivations have been introduced to describe dynamic scheduling while abstracting from the technical details. In this paper we review and compare the different proposals given in [9], [10] and [12] for denotational semantics of programs with input consuming derivations. We also show how they can be applied to termination analysis.

1 Introduction

1.1 Dynamic Scheduling in Logic Programming

In logic programming the *selection rule* determines which atom in a query is selected at each derivation step. The standard selection rule is the left-to-right one of Prolog, which is simple to implement, but which can cause problems both with termination and with negation when selected atoms are not fully instantiated. Moreover there are situations – like in the context of parallel executions or generate-and-test patterns – that require a more flexible control mechanism (*dynamic scheduling*) in which the atom to be selected is determined at runtime.

Dynamic scheduling is achieved by using a *dynamic selection rule* and this increases the expressive power of the language and allows for a finer control of the execution. In practical systems, dynamic selection rules are implemented by means of constructs such as *delay declarations* (as in Gödel [26] and ECLiPSe [27]) or *block declarations* (as in SICStus Prolog [28] – block declarations are actually a special kind of delay declarations). Alternatively, in concurrent logic languages such as GHC [43], programs are augmented with *guards* controlling the selection of atoms dynamically. For example Moded Flat GHC [45] uses conditions based on modes and instantiation constraints imposed on individual clauses.

Delay declarations, advocated by van Emden and de Lucena [46], were introduced explicitly in logic programming by Naish [37,34]. By associating conditions to predicate symbols, delay declarations indicate when an atom can be selected

M. Bruynooghe and K.-K. Lau (Eds.): Program Development in CL, LNCS 3049, pp. 90–114, 2004.
© Springer-Verlag Berlin Heidelberg 2004

for resolution. Such conditions are based on instantiation: typical delay declarations are `ground(X)` or `nonvar(X)` which specify that the associated atom can be selected for evaluation only if its argument X is respectively a ground term or a non-variable term. Delay declarations can be also combined together by means of logical operators, allowing for more complex control.

To see how delay declarations can enforce dynamic scheduling, consider the following programs APPEND and IN_ORDER:

```
%    append(Xs,Ys,Zs)  ← Zs is the concatenation of the lists Xs and Ys
     append([H|Xs],Ys,[H|Zs])  ← append(Xs,Ys,Zs).
     append([],Ys,Ys).
```

```
%    in_order(Tree,List)  ← List is an ordered list of the nodes of Tree
     in_order(tree(Label,Left,Right),Xs)  ←
         in_order(Left,Ls),
         in_order(Right,Rs),
         append(Ls,[Label|Rs],Xs).
     in_order(void,[]).
```

together with the query

Q : read_tree(Tree), in_order(Tree,List), write_list(List).

where read_tree and write_list are defined elsewhere. If read_tree cannot read the whole tree at once – say, it receives the input from a stream – it would be nice to be able to run the "processes" in_order and write_list on the available input. This can be done properly only if one uses a dynamic selection rule. Prolog's rule would call in_order only after read_tree has finished, while other fixed rules would immediately diverge. For instance, the fixed rule that selects always the second atom in a clause body, and that selects the first one only when the body contains only one atom can lead to nontermination, as the query in_order(Tree,List) can easily diverge. The same applies to the rule that always selects the rightmost atom in a query, with the extra problem that write_list(List) would be called with a non-instantiated argument: if write_list is non-backtrackable (as many IO predicates are) this would imply that this selection rule yields a wrong output. In the above program, in order to avoid nontermination one can declare that predicates in_order, append and write_list can be selected only if their first argument is not just a variable. Formally,

```
    delay in_order(T,_) until nonvar(T).
    delay append(Ls,_,_) until nonvar(Ls).
    delay write_list(Ls,_) until nonvar(Ls).
```

These declarations prevent in_order, append and write_list from being selected "too early", i.e., when their arguments are not "sufficiently instantiated". Note that instead of having interleaving "processes", one can also select several atoms in *parallel*, as long as the delay declarations are respected. This approach to parallelism has been first proposed by Naish [36] and – as observed by Apt and Luitjes [5] – "has an important advantage over the ones proposed in the literature in that it allows us to parallelize programs written in a large subset of Prolog by merely adding to them delay declarations, so *without modifying* the original program".

Compared to other mechanisms for user-defined control, e.g., using the cut operator in connection with built-in predicates that test for the instantiation of a variable (var or ground), delay declarations are more compatible with the declarative character of logic programming. Nevertheless, many important declarative properties that have been proven for logic programs do not apply to programs with delay declarations. This is mainly due to the fact that delay declarations can cause *deadlock* situations, in which no atom in the query respects its delay declaration and therefore no atom is selectable. Because of this the well-known equivalence between model-theoretic and operational semantics does not hold. As an example, consider the query append(X,Y,Z) with the execution mechanism described above: it does not succeed (it *deadlocks*) and this is in contrast with the fact that (infinitely many) instances of append(X,Y,Z) are contained in the least Herbrand model of APPEND.

1.2   Semantics of Logic Programs with Dynamic Scheduling

By introducing dynamic scheduling we obtain more powerful and flexible programs but we are faced with the problem of finding new techniques for ensuring correctness and termination of such programs and more generally for analyzing them. The standard semantics and properties are no longer valid when an atom can be delayed under some condition. In particular the standard semantics cannot capture the possibility of floundering when no atom in the goal can be selected. Hence it is not surprising that only relatively few proposals have been given for a semantics for logic programs with dynamic scheduling despite of their practical importance.

The first proposal of an *operational semantics for dynamic scheduling* in the form of coroutining was given by Naish [35]. He defined *SLDF resolution*, which is a straightforward generalization of SLD resolution, where execution of atoms may be suspended indefinitely. He also considered termination of such programs and observed that if the set of callable atoms is closed under instantiation, the termination behaviour is more amenable to analysis. Moreover Naish stressed the importance of mode information for reasoning about termination of such programs. An operational semantics for constraint logic programs (CLP) with dynamic scheduling has been given also by Debray *et al.* [19].

Falaschi *et al.* [24,33,23] have defined *a denotational semantics for CLP programs with dynamic scheduling* where the semantics of a query is given by a set of closure operators (each operator corresponds to a sequence of rule choices). They start from an operational semantics for constraint logic programs with dynamic scheduling given in terms of derivations from the goals, which is similar to the one in [19] and in [32]. Then they give a semantics in terms of and-trees, which captures the structure of a derivation in a compositional way. An and-tree can be seen as a function mapping an initial constraint to its answer. The denotation of a sequence of atoms is then a set of closure operators, corresponding to the and-trees which have this sequence as root. Their denotational semantics is the analogue of the bottom-up S-semantics [13] for usual logic programs, where atoms are mapped to their set of answers.

Such a denotational semantics can be used as a basis for the *analysis of logic programs with dynamic scheduling*, since closure operators can be abstracted by descriptions that capture their behaviour. This idea was followed by Marriott *et al.* in [32] where a framework for global dataflow analysis for logic programming languages with dynamic scheduling is developed. Its main use is to give information on calling patterns. In [17] the analysis is further improved both in precision and in efficiency. From such proposals also optimization techniques for logic programs with dynamic scheduling have been derived, such as in [38].

A very elegant definition of *an algebraic and logical semantics for constraint logic languages with dynamic scheduling* has been given by Marriott in [31]. It corresponds to an operational semantics based on the one given by Naish in [35] generalized to arbitrary constraints. Delayed atoms are considered as constraints and then the soundness and completeness results for success and finite failure for CLP are extended to CLP with dynamic scheduling.

In spite of these proposals some problems remained open. Dynamic scheduling is often introduced to ensure the termination of the program, preventing possible diverging derivations. Nevertheless, while for pure Prolog programs (i.e., logic programs employing the fixed leftmost selection rule) there exist results characterizing when a program is terminating such as in [7,18,14] no such a characterization was derived for programs with dynamic scheduling from these semantics.

1.3   Semantics of Input Consuming Derivations

In order to provide a characterization of dynamic scheduling that is reasonably abstract and amenable to termination analysis, Smaus introduced in [40] *input consuming derivations*. The definition of input consuming program relies on the concept of *mode*. A *moded program* is a program in which each atom's arguments are partitioned into *input* and *output* ones. Output arguments are those produced by the atom during the computation process, while input arguments are consumed. Roughly speaking, in an input consuming program only atoms whose input arguments are not instantiated through the unification step are allowed to be selected.

We believe that – in many cases – the adoption of "natural" delay declarations is equivalent to considering only input consuming derivations [11]. This is the case, for instance, of the programs mentioned in the example above together with their natural mode where the first position of in_order is considered in input, while the second one is in output. In fact under normal circumstances, the adoption of the stated delay declarations enforces nothing but a restriction to input consuming derivations. Moreover also other control mechanisms, such

as the one in Moded Flat GHC, are similar to requiring input consuming derivations: the resolution of an atom with a definition must not instantiate the input
arguments of the resolved atom.

Input consuming programs allow for simpler definitions of denotational semantics and have nice properties regarding termination. Henceforth they seem
to be a resonable and safe approximation to programs with general dynamic
scheduling. In this paper we review and compare the different proposals given
for denotational semantics of programs with input consuming derivations. We
also show how they can be applied to termination analysis. Our review is based
on [9], [10] and [12].

1.4   Structure of the Paper

The paper is organized as follows. Section 2 contains some preliminary notations
and definitions including input consuming programs. Section 3 introduces a first
denotational semantics capturing computed answer substitutions of successful
derivations. This semantics applies to well and nicely moded input consuming
programs. In Section 4 a second denotational semantics for simply moded input
consuming programs is presented which is able to model also intermediate results of partial derivations. Section 5 shows how these semantics have been used
to characterize termination properties of input consuming programs. Section 6
concludes the paper.

2   Preliminaries

The reader is assumed to be familiar with the terminology and the basic results
of logic programs and their semantics [1,2,29]. In this section we introduce few
notions that will be used in the sequel.

2.1   Terms and Substitutions

Let $\mathcal{T}$ be the set of terms built on a finite set of *data constructors* $\mathcal{C}$ and a
denumerable set of *variable symbols* $\mathcal{V}$. For any syntactic object o, we denote
by $Var(o)$ the set of variables occurring in o. A syntactic object is linear if every variable occurs in it at most once. A *substitution* θ is a mapping from $\mathcal{V}$
to $\mathcal{T}$. Given a *substitution* $\sigma = \{x_1/t_1, \ldots, x_n/t_n\}$, we say that $\{x_1, \ldots, x_n\}$ is
its *domain* (denoted by $Dom(\sigma)$), and $Var(\{t_1, \ldots, t_n\})$ is its *range* (denoted
by $Ran(\sigma)$). Note that $Var(\sigma) = Dom(\sigma) \cup Ran(\sigma)$. We denote by ϵ the empty
substitution: $Dom(\epsilon) = Ran(\epsilon) = \emptyset$. The result of the application of a substitution θ to a term t is said an *instance* of t and it is denoted by $t\theta$. Given a
substitution σ and a syntactic object E, we denote by $\sigma_{|E}$ the restriction of σ to
the variables in $Var(E)$, i.e., $\sigma_{|E}(x) = \sigma(x)$ if $x \in Var(E)$, otherwise $\sigma_{|E}(x) = x$.
If $t_1, \ldots, t_n$ is a permutation of $x_1, \ldots, x_n$ then we say that σ is a *renaming*. The
composition of substitutions is denoted by juxtaposition, i.e., $x\theta\sigma$. We say that
t is a *variant* of t', written $t \approx t'$, if t and t' are instances of each other. In this

case there exists a renaming θ such that $t' = t\theta$. A substitution θ is a *unifier* of terms t and t' if $t\theta = t'\theta$. We denote by $mgu(t,t')$ any *most general unifier* (*mgu*, in short) of t and t'.

2.2   Programs and Derivations

Let $\mathcal{P}$ be a finite set of *predicate symbols*. An *atom* is an object of the form $p(t_1,\ldots,t_n)$ where $p \in \mathcal{P}$ is an n-ary predicate symbol and $t_1,\ldots,t_n \in \mathcal{T}$. Given an atom A, we denote by $Rel(A)$ the predicate symbol of A. A *query* is a finite, possibly empty, sequence of atoms $A_1,\ldots,A_m$. The empty query is denoted by $\square$. Following the convention adopted in [2], we use bold characters to denote sequences of objects: so, for instance, $\mathbf{t}$ denotes a sequence of terms, while $\mathbf{B}$ is a query (i.e., a possibly empty sequence of atoms). A *(definite) clause* is a formula $H \leftarrow \mathbf{B}$ where H is an atom (the *head*) and $\mathbf{B}$ is a query (the *body*). When $\mathbf{B}$ is empty, $H \leftarrow \mathbf{B}$ is written $H \leftarrow$ and is called a *unit clause*. A *(definite) program* is a finite set of clauses. We denote atoms by $A, B, H, \ldots$, queries by $Q, \mathbf{A}, \mathbf{B}, \mathbf{C}, \ldots$, clauses by $c, d, \ldots$, and programs by P.

Computations are constructed as sequences of "basic" steps. Consider a non-empty query $\mathbf{A}, B, \mathbf{C}$ and a clause c. Let $H \leftarrow \mathbf{B}$ be a variant of c variable disjoint from $\mathbf{A}, B, \mathbf{C}$ and assume that B and H unify with mgu θ. The query $(\mathbf{A}, \mathbf{B}, \mathbf{C})\theta$ is called a *resolvent of* $\mathbf{A}, B, \mathbf{C}$ *and c with selected atom B and mgu θ*. A *derivation step* is denoted by $\mathbf{A}, B, \mathbf{C} \overset{\theta}{\Longrightarrow}_{P,c} (\mathbf{A}, \mathbf{B}, \mathbf{C})\theta$. The clause $H \leftarrow \mathbf{B}$ is called its *input clause*. The atom B is called the *selected atom* of $\mathbf{A}, B, \mathbf{C}$.

If P is clear from the context or c is irrelevant then we drop the reference to them. A derivation is obtained by iterating derivation steps. A maximal sequence

$$\delta : Q_0 \overset{\theta_1}{\Longrightarrow}_{P,c_1} Q_1 \overset{\theta_2}{\Longrightarrow}_{P,c_2} \cdots Q_n \overset{\theta_{n+1}}{\Longrightarrow}_{P,c_{n+1}} Q_{n+1} \cdots$$

is called a *derivation of $P \cup \{Q_0\}$* provided that for every step the standardization apart condition holds, i.e., the input clause employed is variable disjoint from the initial query Q_0 and from the substitutions and the input clauses used at earlier steps.

Derivations can be finite or infinite. If $\delta : Q_0 \overset{\theta_1}{\Longrightarrow}_{P,c_1} \cdots \overset{\theta_n}{\Longrightarrow}_{P,c_n} Q_n$ is a finite prefix of a derivation, also denoted by $\delta : Q_0 \overset{\theta}{\longrightarrow} Q_n$ with $\theta = \theta_1 \cdots \theta_n$, we say that δ is a *partial derivation* and θ is a *partial computed answer substitution* of $P \cup \{Q_0\}$. If δ is maximal and ends with the empty query, then θ is called *computed answer substitution* (*c.a.s.*, for short). In this case we say that the derivation is *successful*. The length of a (partial) derivation δ, denoted by $len(\delta)$, is the number of derivation steps in δ.

2.3   Modes and Input Consuming Programs

Modes are a common tool for verification. A *mode* is a function that labels as *input* or *output* the positions of each predicate in order to indicate how the arguments of such a predicate should be used.

Definition 1 (Mode). *A mode for a predicate symbol p of arity n, is a function* m_p *from* $\{1, \ldots, n\}$ *to* $\{I, O\}$.

We call moded atom (clause, program, query), *any atom (clause, program, query) which has a mode associated to its predicate symbols.*

If $m_p(i) = I$ (resp. O), we say that i is an *input* (resp. *output*) *position of* p (with respect to m_p). In the examples, we often indicate the mode by writing the atom $p(m_p(1), \ldots, m_p(n))$, e.g., $\texttt{append}(I, I, O)$.

We assume that each predicate symbol has a unique mode associated to it; multiple modes may be obtained by simply renaming the predicates. We denote by $In(Q)$ (resp. $Out(Q)$) the sequence of terms filling in the input (resp. output) positions of predicates in Q. Moreover, when writing an atom as $p(\mathbf{s}, \mathbf{t})$, we are indicating that $\mathbf{s}$ is the sequence of terms filling in its input positions and $\mathbf{t}$ is the sequence of terms filling in its output positions.

The notion of input consuming derivation was introduced in [40] as a formalism for describing dynamic scheduling in an abstract way.

Definition 2 (Input Consuming Derivation).

- *A derivation step* $\mathbf{A}, B, \mathbf{C} \xRightarrow{\theta} (\mathbf{A}, \mathbf{B}, \mathbf{C})\theta$ *is input consuming if* $In(B)\theta = In(B)$.
- *A derivation is* input consuming *if all its derivation steps are input consuming.*

In the following sometimes we use *ic-derivation* for input consuming derivation and we call *input consuming program* (*ic-program*) a program when considered with respect to input consuming derivations only.

Example 3. Consider the program REVERSE with accumulator and the following modes: $\texttt{reverse}(I, O)$ and $\texttt{reverse\_acc}(I, O, I)$.

```
reverse(Xs,Ys)  ← reverse_acc(Xs,Ys,[]).
reverse_acc([],Ys,Ys).
reverse_acc([X|Xs],Ys,Zs)  ← reverse_acc(Xs,Ys,[X|Zs]).
```

The following derivation δ of REVERSE $\cup$ {reverse([X1,X2],Zs)} is input consuming.

δ: reverse([X1,X2],Zs) $\Rightarrow$ reverse_acc([X1,X2],Zs,[]) $\Rightarrow$
    reverse_acc([X2],Zs,[X1]) $\Rightarrow$ reverse_acc([],Zs,[X2,X1]) $\Rightarrow \square$.

Allowing only input consuming derivations is a form of dynamic scheduling, since whether or not an atom can be selected depends on its degree of instantiation at runtime. Given a non-empty query, if no atom is resolvable via an input consuming derivation step and no failure arises, then we say that the query *deadlocks*. Therefore, an ic-derivation can either be successful or finitely failing or infinite or deadlock. Each ic-derivation which is not a deadlock is also an SLD derivation.

2.4   Classes of Moded Programs

In the sequel we are going to refer to classes of programs that in some way behave well with respect to the given mode. In particular, we are going to use the concepts of well moded program (Dembinski and Maluszynski [20]), of nicely moded program (Chadha and Plaisted [15]) and of simply moded program (Apt and Etalle [4]).

Definition 4 (Well, Nicely and Simply Moded Program).

- **Well Moded.** A clause $p(t_0, s_{n+1}) \leftarrow p_1(s_1, t_1), \ldots, p_n(s_n, t_n)$ is well moded *if for all* $i \in [1, n+1]$

$$Var(s_i) \subseteq \bigcup_{j=0}^{i-1} Var(t_j).$$

If we call *producing* positions the input positions of the head and the output positions of the body and *consuming* positions the other ones, then we can intuitively say that a clause is well moded if every variable in a consuming position occurs also in an *earlier* (w.r.t. the indices, which have been deliberately chosen in this way) producing position.

- **Nicely Moded.** A clause $p(t_0, s_{n+1}) \leftarrow p_1(s_1, t_1), \ldots, p_n(s_n, t_n)$ is nicely moded *if* $t_1, \ldots, t_n$ *is a linear sequence of terms,* $Var(t_0) \cap Var(t_1, \ldots, t_n) = \emptyset$, *and for all* $i \in [1, n]$

$$Var(s_i) \cap \bigcup_{j=i}^{n} Var(t_j) = \emptyset.$$

Intuitively a clause is nicely moded if there are no conflicts among producing positions, (a variable may appear in at most one producing position with one exception: a variable may appear twice in a producing position of the head), and a variable may not be consumed before it is produced.

- **Simply Moded.** A clause $p(t_0, s_{n+1}) \leftarrow p_1(s_1, t_1), \ldots, p_n(s_n, t_n)$ is simply moded *if it is nicely moded and* $t_1, \ldots, t_n$ *is a linear sequence of variables.*
- A query **Q** is well (resp. nicely, simply) moded, if the clause $q \leftarrow$ **Q** is well (resp. nicely, simply) moded, where q is a variable-free atom.
  Note that an atomic query $p(s, t)$ is well moded if **s** is a sequence of ground terms and it is nicely moded if **t** is linear and $Var(s) \cap Var(t) = \emptyset$.
- A program is well (resp. nicely, simply) moded, if all of its clauses are well (resp. nicely, simply) moded.

Hence the class of simply moded programs is a subclass of nicely moded ones and it includes both some well moded and some non-well moded programs.

In [42] *permutation well (nicely) moded* programs and queries are also defined, i.e., programs and queries which would be well (nicely) moded after a permutation of the atoms respectively in the bodies and in the queries.

Example 5.

- The program APPEND of the introduction in the mode append(I, I, O) is well nicely and simply moded.
- REVERSE with accumulator of Example 3 is well and simply moded.
- Furthermore, consider the following program PALINDROME

     palindrome(Xs) ← reverse(Xs,Xs).

  in the mode palindrome(I), together with the program REVERSE with the modes reverse(I, O). This program is well moded but not nicely moded (since Xs occurs both in an input and in an output position of the same body atom). However, since the program REVERSE is used here for checking whether a list is a palindrome, its natural modes are reverse(I, I) and reverse_acc(I, I, I). With these modes, the program PALINDROME is both well moded and simply moded.

Most programs are simply moded (see the mini-survey at the end of [4]) and often programs that are not simply moded can naturally be transformed into simply moded ones (see [10]).

The above notions of well, nicely and simply moded are "persistent" with respect to input consuming derivations. The following lemma is a straightforward extension of [5, Lemma 30].

Lemma 6. *In a input consuming derivation, every resolvent of a well (resp. nicely, simply) moded query and a well (resp. nicely, simply) moded clause is well (resp. nicely, simply) moded.*

Notice that in the case of nicely and simply moded programs the above lemma depends on the fact that only input consuming derivations are considered. Indeed, when "normal" SLD derivations are considered persistence holds only when the leftmost selection rule is used. Otherwise, speculative bindings might destroy the property of being nicely moded.

On the other hand, for well moded programs, any SLD resolvent of a well moded query with a well moded clause is well moded ([2]).

Finally, it is worth reminding that, when considering nicely (respectively simply) moded, input consuming programs, half of the famous switching lemma still applies. The following Left-Switching Lemma that has been proven in [10].

Lemma 7. (Left-Switching) *Let the program P and the query Q_0 be nicely moded. Let δ be a (partial) input consuming derivation of $P \cup \{Q_0\}$ of the form*

$$\delta : Q_0 \stackrel{\theta_1}{\Longrightarrow}_{c_1} Q_1 \cdots Q_n \stackrel{\theta_{n+1}}{\Longrightarrow}_{c_{n+1}} Q_{n+1} \stackrel{\theta_{n+2}}{\Longrightarrow}_{c_{n+2}} Q_{n+2}$$

where

- Q_n *is a query of the form* $\mathbf{A}, A, \mathbf{B}, B, \mathbf{C}$,
- Q_{n+1} *is a resolvent of Q_n and c_{n+1} w.r.t. B,*
- Q_{n+2} *is a resolvent of Q_{n+1} and c_{n+2} w.r.t. $A\theta_{n+1}$.*

Then, there exist Q'_{n+1}, θ'_{n+1}, θ'_{n+2} and a derivation δ' such that

$$\theta_{n+1}\theta_{n+2} = \theta'_{n+1}\theta'_{n+2}$$

and

$$\delta' : Q_0 \xrightarrow{\theta_1}_{c_1} Q_1 \cdots Q_n \xrightarrow{\theta'_{n+1}}_{c_{n+2}} Q'_{n+1} \xrightarrow{\theta'_{n+2}}_{c_{n+1}} Q_{n+2}$$

where δ' is input consuming and

- *δ and δ' coincide up to the resolvent Q_n,*
- *Q'_{n+1} is a resolvent of Q_n and c_{n+2} w.r.t. A,*
- *Q_{n+2} is a resolvent of Q'_{n+1} and c_{n+1} w.r.t. $B\theta'_{n+1}$,*
- *δ and δ' coincide after the resolvent Q_{n+2}.*

2.5 The $\mathcal{S}$-semantics

The aim of the $\mathcal{S}$-semantics approach (see [13]) is modeling the observable behaviors for a variety of logic programming languages. The observable we consider here is the *computed answer substitutions*. The semantics is defined as follows:

$$\mathcal{S}(P) = \{ \, p(x_1, \ldots, x_n)\theta \mid x_1, \ldots, x_n \text{ are distinct variables and}$$
$$p(x_1, \ldots, x_n) \xrightarrow{\theta}_P \square \text{ is an SLD derivation}\}.$$

This semantics enjoys all the valuable properties of the least Herbrand model as summarized below in the following. To present the main results on the $\mathcal{S}$-semantics we need to introduce two further concepts: Let P be a program, and I be a set of atoms closed under variance.

- The immediate consequence operator for the $\mathcal{S}$-semantics is defined as:

$$T_P^{\mathcal{S}}(I) = \{ \, H\theta \mid \exists \, H \leftarrow \mathbf{B} \text{ variant of a clause of } P$$
$$\exists \, \mathbf{C} \in I, \text{renamed apart}^4 \text{ w.r.t. } H, \mathbf{B}$$
$$\theta = mgu(\mathbf{B}, \mathbf{C})\}.$$

- I is called an $\mathcal{S}$-*model* of P if $T_P^{\mathcal{S}}(I) \subseteq I$.

Falaschi et al. [25] showed that $T_P^{\mathcal{S}}$ is continuous on the lattice of term interpretations, that is sets of possibly non-ground atoms, with the subset-ordering. Powers of the operator $T_P^{\mathcal{S}}$ are defined in the standard way as follows: $T_P^{\mathcal{S}} \uparrow 0(I) = I$, $T_P^{\mathcal{S}} \uparrow (i+1)(I) = T_P^{\mathcal{S}}(T_P^{\mathcal{S}} \uparrow i(I))$, and $T_P^{\mathcal{S}} \uparrow \omega(I) = \bigcup_{i=0}^{\infty} T_P^{\mathcal{S}} \uparrow i(I)$. We abbreviate $T_P^{\mathcal{S}} \uparrow \omega(\emptyset)$ to $T_P^{\mathcal{S}} \uparrow \omega$. In [25] they proved the following:

- $\mathcal{S}(P) = $ least $\mathcal{S}$-model of $P = T_P^{\mathcal{S}} \uparrow \omega$.

---

[4] Here and in the sequel, when we write "$\mathbf{C} \in I$, renamed apart w.r.t. some expression e", we naturally mean that I contains the atoms $C_1^{\square}, \ldots, C_n^{\square}$, and that $\mathbf{C}$ is a renaming of $C_1^{\square}, \ldots, C_n^{\square}$ such that $\mathbf{C}$ shares no variable with e and that two distinct atoms of $\mathbf{C}$ share no variables with each other.

Therefore, the $\mathcal{S}$-semantics enjoys a declarative interpretation and a bottom-up construction, just like the Herbrand one. In addition, we have that the $\mathcal{S}$-semantics reflects the observable behavior in terms of computed answer substitutions, as shown by the following well-known result.

Theorem 8 ([25]). *Let P be a program, $\mathbf{A}$ be a query. The following statements are equivalent:*

- *there exists an SLD derivation $\mathbf{A} \xrightarrow{\vartheta}_P \square$,*
- *there exists $\mathbf{A}' \in \mathcal{S}(P)$ (renamed apart w.r.t. $\mathbf{A}$), such that $\sigma = mgu(\mathbf{A}, \mathbf{A}')$,*

where $\mathbf{A}\sigma \approx \mathbf{A}\vartheta$.

Example 9. Let us see this semantics applied to the programs APPEND and REVERSE so far encountered.

- $\mathcal{S}(\text{APPEND}) = \{$ append([],X,X),
                     append([X1],X,[X1|X]),
                     append([X1,X2],X,[X1,X2|X]),... $\}$.
- $\mathcal{S}(\text{REVERSE}) = \{$ reverse([],[]),
                     reverse([X1],[X1]),
                     reverse([X1,X2],[X2,X1]),   ...

                     reverse_acc([],X,X),
                     reverse_acc([X1],X,[X1|X]),
                     reverse_acc([X1,X2],X,[X2,X1|X]),... $\}$.

2.6 Semantics of Input Consuming Programs

In Sections 3 and 4 we present two semantics for input consuming programs which are related to $\mathcal{S}$-semantics. To define such semantics, the observables we focus on are the *computed answer substitutions*. First, we consider a semantics given by the computed answer substitutions of *successful* derivations. This corresponds to the $\mathcal{S}$-semantics of logic programming [13] when restricted to a particular set of queries. Given a program P and a set of queries C, this semantics can be defined formally as

$$\mathcal{O}_s^{ic}(P,C) = \{\mathbf{A}\theta|\ \mathbf{A} \in C \text{ and there exists an ic-derivation } \mathbf{A} \xrightarrow{\theta}_P \square\}.$$

While this semantics appears very natural, it can be unsuitable for modelling the reactive nature of input consuming programs. In fact, as we mentioned in the introduction, input consuming derivations can be used to model dynamic scheduling and parallelism, and in this context it is very important to model the results of partial computations. Indeed, the standard semantics for concurrent logic languages such as ccp [39,22] and GHC [44] often capture such intermediate results, or in any case, also the results of non-successful computations [16]. In fact, the (partial) result of a computation may trigger another computation by instantiating sufficiently the input positions of another atom so that it becomes resolvable. Because of this, when one wants to characterize for instance termination, the adoption of a semantics which is able to model intermediate results becomes essential, as shown in Section 5. Thus we also consider a semantics capturing the results of partial input consuming derivations. Given a program P and a set of queries C, this semantics can be defined formally as

$$\mathcal{O}_p^{ic}(P, C) = \{\mathbf{A}\theta|\ \mathbf{A} \in C \text{ and there exists an ic-derivation } \mathbf{A} \xrightarrow{\theta}_P \mathbf{B}\}.$$

where $\mathbf{B}$ is any query.

3   Semantics of Well Moded Input Consuming Programs

To characterize our two semantics for ic-programs, we start from the simplest case: when one is interested only in the successful derivations. Then – if one does not restrict to ic-derivations – the observables (given by successful derivations) can be captured by the $\mathcal{S}$-semantics of classical logic programs.

In this section we show that *the standard $\mathcal{S}$-semantics is compositional and correct also for input consuming programs, provided that the programs are well and nicely moded and that only nicely moded queries are considered.* The results reported in this section are proved in [9].

Proposition 10. *Let P be a well and nicely moded program, A be a nicely moded atomic query. The following statements are equivalent:*

(i) there exists an input consuming derivation $A \xrightarrow{\vartheta}_P \square$,
(ii) there exists $A' \in \mathcal{S}(P)$ (renamed apart w.r.t. A), and $\sigma = mgu(A, A')$ such that $In(A)\sigma \approx In(A)$,

where $A\sigma \approx A\vartheta$.

To extend Proposition 10 to arbitrary (non-atomic) queries we need the following definition.

Definition 11. *Let $\mathbf{A} = p_1(\mathbf{s}_1, \mathbf{t}_1), \dots, p_n(\mathbf{s}_n, \mathbf{t}_n)$ be a query. We define*

$$VIn^*(\mathbf{A}) := \bigcup_{i=1}^{n} \{x|\ x \in Var(\mathbf{s}_i) \text{ and } x \notin \bigcup_{j=1}^{i-1} Var(\mathbf{t}_j)\}.$$

$VIn^*(\mathbf{A})$ denotes the set of variables occurring in an input position of an atom of $\mathbf{A}$ but not occurring in an output position of an earlier atom. Note that if $\mathbf{A}$ is well moded then $VIn^*(\mathbf{A}) = \emptyset$.

Theorem 12. *Let P be a well and nicely moded program, $\mathbf{A}$ be a nicely moded query and NM be the class of nicely moded queries. The following statements are equivalent:*

(i) there exists $\mathbf{A}\vartheta \in \mathcal{O}_s^{ic}(P, NM)$,
(ii) there exists $\mathbf{A}' \in \mathcal{S}(P)$ (renamed apart w.r.t. $\mathbf{A}$), and $\sigma = mgu(\mathbf{A}, \mathbf{A}')$ such
*   that $\mathbf{A}\sigma_{|VIn^*(\mathbf{A})} \approx \mathbf{A}$,*

where $\mathbf{A}\sigma \approx \mathbf{A}\vartheta$.

The condition $\mathbf{A}\sigma_{|VIn^*(\mathbf{A})} \approx \mathbf{A}$ above says that the substitution σ just renames the variables occurring in an input position of $\mathbf{A}$ but not occurring in an output position of an earlier atom. In case of an atomic query $\mathbf{A} := A$, we might substitute this condition with the somewhat more attractive condition $In(A)\sigma \approx In(A)$ of Proposition 10.

   Theorem 12 shows thus that $\mathcal{S}(P)$ is *compositional* and *correct* for input consuming programs, provided that programs are well and nicely moded and that queries are nicely moded. In other words, given the restrictions on programs and queries, the $\mathcal{S}$-semantics is correct with respect to the observables given by the computed answer substitutions of successful ic-derivations.

Example 13. Consider the program APPEND of the introduction with the mode append(I, I, O). $\mathcal{S}(\text{APPEND})$, reported in Example 9, allows us to draw a number of conclusions:

- append([X,b],Y,Z) has an input consuming successful derivation.
   In particular, it has an input consuming derivation with c.a.s. $\{Z/[X, b|Y]\}$. This can be derived by just looking at $\mathcal{S}(\text{APPEND})$, from the fact that $A = $ append([X1,X2],X3,[X1,X2|X3]) $\in \mathcal{S}(P)$ and that append([X,b],Y,Z) is
   - in its input positions - an instance of A.
- append(Y,[X,b],Z) has no input consuming successful derivations.
   This is because there is no $A \in \mathcal{S}(P)$ such that append(Y, [X, b], Z) is an instance of A in the input positions.
- Observe that the query append(Y,[X,b],Z) has infinitely many successful SLD derivations and no failures. Therefore it does not fail also when we consider ic-derivations. Since, as noted above, the query has no input consuming successful derivations, this implies that – in presence of input consuming derivations – append(Y,[X,b],Z) will eventually either deadlock or run into an infinite derivation.

   The previous results hold also in case the programs are *permutation well and nicely moded* and queries are *permutation nicely moded* [42].
   While in the context of SLD (not input consuming) derivations the $\mathcal{S}$-semantics is also *fully abstract*, when considering input consuming program this is not so. Consider the following two trivial programs:

```
P1  = { c1:  p(X).
          c2:  p(a).    }

P2  = {       p(X).    }
```

In both programs the mode is $p(I)$. These two programs, despite being different, yield exactly the same computed answer substitutions for all queries when ic-derivations are considered. In fact the extra clause c2 in P1 can resolve an atom

A only if A contains the term a in its input position, but in this case c2 behaves exactly as c1 does[5]. Nevertheless, the $\mathcal{S}(\texttt{P1}) = \{\texttt{p(X)}, \texttt{p(a)}\} \neq \{\texttt{p(X)}\} = \mathcal{S}(\texttt{P2})$, demonstrating that the $\mathcal{S}$-semantics is not fully abstract when considering ic-derivations. In the next section we present a more complex semantics, which is also fully abstract for ic-derivations.

4   Semantics of Simply Moded Input Consuming Programs

The semantics presented in the previous section applies only when we are interested in the computed answer substitutions of *successful* derivations. As we discussed before, there are many situations in which we also want to model the (intermediate) results of partial derivations. For instance, this will be the case when – in the next section – we study the termination of input consuming programs.

   In this section we define a somewhat more complex denotational semantics which has the advantage of modelling the observables given by both successful and partial derivations in a rather symmetric way. The two semantics we are going to introduce are *compositional, correct and fully abstract* with respect to the operational semantics of input consuming simply moded programs and queries, i.e., $\mathcal{O}_s^{ic}(P, SM)$ and $\mathcal{O}_p^{ic}(P, SM)$, where SM is the class of simply moded queries. As in the standard $\mathcal{S}$-semantics, this is a denotational semantics that can be built by means of a bottom-up construction.

4.1   Simply Local Substitutions and Simply Local Models

When input consuming derivations are applied to simply moded programs and queries, important properties follow from the way clauses become instantiated along the derivations. The notion of *simply local* substitution is introduced in [12] to reflect this instantiation mechanism. A clause $c = H \leftarrow B_1, \ldots, B_n$ becomes instantiated by its "caller" (the atom that is resolved using c) and its "callees" (the clauses used to resolve the body atoms of c). Thus, a simply local substitution is defined as the composition of several substitutions, $\sigma_0, \sigma_1 \ldots, \sigma_n$, one for each atom in the given clause, such that σ_0 binds the input variables of the head of the clause, and each σ_i $(i > 0)$ creates a binding from the output variables to input terms of $B_i \sigma_0, \ldots, \sigma_{i-1}$.

Definition 14 (Simply Local Substitution). *Let θ be a substitution. We say that θ is simply local w.r.t. the clause $H \leftarrow B_1, \ldots, B_n$ if there exist substitutions $\sigma_0, \sigma_1 \ldots, \sigma_n$ and disjoint sets of fresh (w.r.t. c) variables $v_0, v_1, \ldots, v_n$ such that $\theta = \sigma_0 \sigma_1 \cdots \sigma_n$ where*

---

[5] The only observable difference between **P1** and **P2** lies in the *multiplicity* of the answers: the query q(a) succeeds twice in **P1** and only once in **P2**, but answer multiplicity is not an observable we consider here.

- $Dom(\sigma_0) \subseteq Var(In(H))$ *and* $Ran(\sigma_0) \subseteq v_0$,
- *for* $i \in [1..n]$,
  $Dom(\sigma_i) \subseteq Var(Out(B_i))$ *and* $Ran(\sigma_i) \subseteq Var(In(B_i)\sigma_0\sigma_1 \cdots \sigma_{i-1}) \cup v_i$.

The substitution θ is simply local *w.r.t. a query* $\mathbf{B}$ *if θ is simply local w.r.t. the clause* $q \leftarrow \mathbf{B}$ *where q is any variable-free atom.*

Example 15. Consider the program APPEND together with the mode append(I, I, O) and its recursive clause

$\quad c:$ append($[H|Xs]$, Ys, $[H|Zs]$) $\leftarrow$ append(Xs, Ys, Zs).

The substitution $\theta = \{Xs/[\,], Ys/W, Zs/W\}$ is simply local w.r.t. c. In fact $\theta = \sigma_0\sigma_1$ where $\sigma_0 = \{Xs/[\,], Ys/W\}$ and $\sigma_1 = \{Zs/W\}$. Consider now the query

$\quad Q:$ append($[a, X, c]$, Ys, Zs), append(Zs, $[b]$, Ls).

The substitution $\theta = \{Zs/[a, X, c\,|\,Ys]\}$ is simply local w.r.t. Q. In fact $\theta = \sigma_1\sigma_2$ where $\sigma_1 = \{Zs/[a, X, c\,|\,Ys]\}$ and σ_2 is the empty substitution.

The denotational semantics we are about to define is based on a restricted notion of model. Here and in the sequel interpretations are *sets of moded atoms* closed under variance.

Definition 16 (Simply Local Model). *Let M be a set of moded atoms. We say that M is a* simply local model *of a clause $c: H \leftarrow B_1, \ldots, B_n$ if for every substitution θ simply local w.r.t. c,*

$$\text{if } B_1\theta, \ldots, B_n\theta \in M \text{ then } H\theta \in M. \tag{1}$$

M is a simply local model *of a program P if it is a simply local model of each clause of it.*

Clearly a simply local model is not necessarily a model in the classical sense, since the substitution θ in (1) is required to be simply local. For example, given the program $\{q(1)., p(X) \leftarrow q(X).\}$ with modes $q(I)$, $p(O)$, a model must contain the atom $p(1)$, whereas a simply local model does not necessarily contain $p(1)$, since $\{X/1\}$ is not simply local w.r.t. $p(X) \leftarrow q(X)$.

A minimal simply local model exists and it is bottom-up computable by applying the following operator [12].

Definition 17. *Given a program P and a set of moded atoms I, we define*

$$T_P^{SL}(I) = I \cup \{H\theta \mid \exists\, c: H \leftarrow \mathbf{B} \text{ variant of a clause of } P,$$
$$\theta \text{ is simply local w.r.t. } c,$$
$$\mathbf{B}\theta \in I\}$$

T_P^{SL} is monotonic and continuous on the lattice where sets of moded atoms are ordered by set inclusion.

In the following we denote by SM_P the set of all simply moded atoms of the extended Herbrand universe of P. In [12] it is proven that if P is simply moded and $I \subseteq SM_P$ then

$$T_P^{SL} \uparrow \omega(I) \text{ is the least simply local model of } P \text{ containing } I \qquad (2)$$

This allows us to define our models.

Definition 18. *Let P be a program. We define*

- M_P^{SL} *is the least simply local model of P,*
- PM_P^{SL} *is the least simply local model of P containing SM_P.*

The existence of these models is guaranteed by (2), in fact (2) also shows how to construct them, as it implies that

$$M_P^{SL} = T_P^{SL} \uparrow \omega(\emptyset), \text{ and } PM_P^{SL} = T_P^{SL} \uparrow \omega(SM_P) \qquad (3)$$

4.2   Relation among Denotational and Operational Semantics

To relate the M_P^{SL} and PM_P^{SL} to $\mathcal{O}_s^{ic}(P, SM)$ and $\mathcal{O}_p^{ic}(P, SM)$ we need to relate T_P^{SL} to the results of input consuming derivations; this is achieved in the following lemma, proved in [12].

Lemma 19. *Let the program P and the query $\mathbf{A}$ be simply moded and $I \subseteq SM_P$ be a set of moded atoms. The following statements are equivalent:*

(i) there exists an input consuming derivation $\mathbf{A} \xrightarrow{\vartheta}_P \mathbf{C}$ with $\mathbf{C} \subseteq I$,
(ii) there exists a substitution θ simply local w.r.t. $\mathbf{A}$, such that $\mathbf{A}\theta \subseteq T_P^{SL} \uparrow \omega(I)$,

where $\mathbf{A}\vartheta \approx \mathbf{A}\theta$.

We can now prove that M_P^{SL} and PM_P^{SL} fully characterize the semantics of ic-derivations for simply moded programs and queries, namely they are equal to $\mathcal{O}_s^{ic}(P, SM)$ and $\mathcal{O}_p^{ic}(P, SM)$, respectively.

Theorem 20. *Let P be simply moded. Then*

(i) $M_P^{SL} = \mathcal{O}_s^{ic}(P, SM)$.
(ii) $PM_P^{SL} = \mathcal{O}_p^{ic}(P, SM)$.

Proof.   Immediate by (3), Lemma 19 and the definitions of $\mathcal{O}_s^{ic}(P, SM)$ and $\mathcal{O}_p^{ic}(P, SM)$.

An example follows.

Example 21. Let us consider again the program APPEND.

1. First let us consider its *successful* ic-derivations. Hence we have to build M_{APPEND}^{SL}

$$M_{\text{APPEND}}^{SL} = \{\text{append}([t_1,\ldots,t_n], s, [t_1,\ldots,t_n|s]) \mid n \in [0..\infty],$$
$$\text{and } t_1,\ldots,t_n, s \text{ are any terms}\}.$$

   Notice that this model is different from $\mathcal{S}(\text{APPEND})$, reported in Example 9. We are going to relate $\mathcal{S}(P)$ and M_P^{SL} later in this section.
2. Now let us consider the results of *partial* derivations. Recall that PM_{APPEND}^{SL} is obtained by repeatedly applying T_P^{SL} to each simply moded atom. Simply moded atoms are $\text{append}(s, t, x)$ where s and t are arbitrary terms but x is a variable not occurring in s or in t. We obtain

$$PM_{\text{APPEND}}^{SL} = M_{\text{APPEND}}^{SL}$$
$$\cup \{\text{append}(s, t, x) \mid x \text{ is a fresh variable }\}$$
$$\cup \{\text{append}([t_1,\ldots,t_m|s], t, [t_1,\ldots,t_m|x]) \mid x \text{ is a fresh variable}\}$$

where $s, t, t_1,\ldots,t_m$ are arbitrary terms.

Consider now the query $\text{append}([a, b, c|X], Y, Z)$. It is straightforward to check that the substitution $\theta = \{Z/[a, b|Z']\}$ is simply local w.r.t. it, and that $\text{append}([a, b, c|X], Y, Z)\theta \in PM_{\text{APPEND}}^{SL}$. Therefore, by using Theorem 20, we can conclude that there exists a partial derivation starting in $\text{append}([a, b, c|X], Y, Z)$, with computed answer θ. Following the same reasoning, one can also conclude that the query has a partial derivation with computed answer $\theta' = \{Z/[a|Z']\}$.

4.3   Relation between $\mathcal{S}$-semantics and Denotational Semantics for IC-programs

In this section we compare the denotational semantics M_P^{SL} with the $\mathcal{S}$-semantics $\mathcal{S}(P)$ of simply moded programs.

First, we need a new definition: let I be a set of moded atoms, the *input closure* of I is defined as:

$$InCl(I) = \{A\theta \mid A \in I \text{ and } Var(A) \cap Var(\theta) \subseteq Var(In(A))\}$$

So the input closure of an atom is obtained by instantiating its input positions in all possible ways, provided that no new links are created between the input and the output positions.

Theorem 22. *Let P be a well and simply moded program, then*

$$M_P^{\text{SL}} = InCl(\mathcal{S}(P))$$

Proof. First observe that the class of simply moded programs is contained in the class of nicely moded programs, hence Theorem 12 is applicable also when we consider well and simply moded programs and simply moded queries.

- $M_P^{SL} \subseteq InCl(\mathcal{S}(P))$. Let A be simply moded and assume $A\vartheta \in M_P^{SL}$. Then, by Theorem 20, $A\vartheta \in \mathcal{O}_s^{ic}(P, SM)$. By Theorem 12 there exists $A' \in \mathcal{S}(P)$ (renamed apart w.r.t. A), and $\sigma = mgu(A, A')$ such that $In(A)\sigma \approx In(A)$ and $A\sigma \approx A\vartheta$. Since A is simply moded, we can choose σ such that $Dom(\sigma) \cap Var(A') \subseteq Var(In(A'))$. Therefore $A\vartheta \approx A\sigma = A'\sigma \in InCl(\mathcal{S}(P))$.

- $M_P^{SL} \supseteq InCl(\mathcal{S}(P))$. Let $A\theta \in InCl(\mathcal{S}(P))$ and $A = p(\mathbf{s}, \mathbf{t}) \in \mathcal{S}(P)$. There exist a simply moded atom $A' = p(\mathbf{s}', \mathbf{z})$, renamed apart w.r.t. A, and a substitution σ such that $\sigma = mgu(A, A')$, $In(A')\sigma = In(A')$ and $A'\sigma = A\sigma \approx A\theta$. By Theorem 12 there exists ϑ such that $A'\vartheta \in \mathcal{O}_s^{ic}(P, SM)$ and $A'\vartheta \approx A'\sigma \approx A\theta$. Hence, by Theorem 20, $A\theta \in M_P^{SL}$.

5   Semantic-Based Verification of Termination

There have been only few proposals which tackled the specific problem of verifying the termination of logic programs with dynamic scheduling, namely by Apt and Luitjes [5], Marchiori and Teusink [30] and Smaus. Input consuming derivations were indeed introduced by Smaus in [40] to simplify the study of program properties which depend on selection rules and in [41] he started to study in particular the problem of termination of input consuming derivations.

In [10] and [12] we study two classes of programs terminating with respect to input consuming derivations and well-formed queries. The two classes differ in various aspects. First of all, two different classes of well-formed queries are considered: nicely moded queries in [10], simply moded queries in [12]. To give an uniform presentation, in [12] we consider a parametric class of programs in which all input consuming derivations terminate. The parameter is a given class C of queries.

Definition 23 (Input Termination w.r.t. a class C of queries). *Let C be a class of queries. A program is called* input terminating with respect to C *if all its input consuming derivations started in a query in C are finite.*

The second difference among the two classes of terminating programs in [10] and [12] is in the termination proof techniques. The first class follows the style of [3,8] and it uses a simple (syntactic) termination condition, but it is also a rather restrictive class. The second class follows the style of [6,7], that is based on a more complex model theoretic approach, and it uses the semantics introduced in Section 4; this is a significantly larger class of programs.

Let us consider first the more restrictive and simple class introduced in [10]: The class of nicely moded *quasi recurrent* programs. Its definition is based on the notion of well moded level mapping, first introduced in [21]. Here we use well moded level mappings extended to all the terms on $\mathcal{B}_P^{\mathcal{E}}$ as in [10]. $\mathcal{B}_P^{\mathcal{E}}$, the extended Herbrand base of P, is the set of equivalence classes of all (possibly non-ground) atoms, modulo renaming, whose predicate symbols appear in P.

Definition 24 (Moded Level Mapping). *Let P be a program and $\mathcal{B}_P^{\mathcal{E}}$ be the extended Herbrand base for the language associated with P. A function $|\ |$ is a moded level mapping for P if:*

- *it is a function $|\ | : \mathcal{B}_P^{\mathcal{E}} \to \mathbf{N}$ from atoms to natural numbers;*
- *for any $\mathbf{t}$ and $\mathbf{u}$, $|p(\mathbf{s},\mathbf{t})| = |p(\mathbf{s},\mathbf{u})|$.*

For $A \in \mathcal{B}_P^{\mathcal{E}}$, $|A|$ is the level *of A.*

Definition 25 (Quasi Recurrency). *Let P be a program.*

- *A clause of P is called* quasi recurrent with respect to a moded level mapping $|\ |$ *if for every instance $H \leftarrow \mathbf{A}, B, \mathbf{C}$ of it,*

$$\text{if } Rel(H) \simeq Rel(B) \text{ then } |H| > |B|.^6$$

- *P is called* quasi recurrent with respect to $|\ |$ *if all its clauses are. P is called* quasi recurrent *if it is quasi recurrent with respect to some moded level mapping $|\ | : \mathcal{B}_P^{\mathcal{E}} \to \mathbf{N}$.*

Theorem 26. *Let P be a nicely moded program. If P is quasi recurrent then P is input terminating with respect to the class of nicely moded queries.*

The proof of this theorem can be found in [10].

Thus, the quasi recurrent condition is a sufficient condition for input termination of nicely moded programs and nicely moded queries. But it is not a necessary condition: there are nicely moded programs input terminating on all nicely moded queries which are not quasi recurrent as shown by the following simple example taken from [10].

Example 27. Consider the following program with moding $p(I, O)$.

```
p(X,a)  ←p(X,b).
p(X,b).
```

This program is clearly input terminating, however it is not quasi recurrent. For the first clause to be quasi recurrent it would have to be the case that $|p(X,a)| > |p(X,b)|$, for some moded level mapping $|\ |$. On the other hand, since $p(X,a)$ and $p(X,b)$ differ only for the terms filling in their output positions, by definition of moded level mapping, $|p(X,a)| = |p(X,b)|$. Hence, we have a contradiction.

A full characterization can be obtained only by further restricting the class of programs, passing from nicely moded to simply moded and *input-recursive* programs.

---

[6] Given two predicate symbols defined in a program P we denote by $p \simeq q$ the fact that the definitions of the two predicates are mutually recursive.

Definition 28 (Input-Recursive Program). *Let P be a program.*

- *A clause H ← **A**, B, **C** of P is called* input-recursive *if*

    if Rel(H) ≃ Rel(B) then Var(In(B)) ⊆ Var(In(H)).

- *A program P is called* input-recursive *if all its clauses are.*

Input-recursive is a syntactic condition on a clause requiring that the set of variables occurring in the arguments filling in the input positions of each recursive call in the clause body is a subset of the set of variables occurring in the arguments filling in the input positions of the clause head. The class of input-recursive programs has strong similarities with the class of primitive recursive functions and recurrent logic programs. It does not include programs whose termination depend on the so-called *inter-argument relations* such as `quicksort`.

Quasi recurrency fully characterizes input termination of simply moded and input-recursive programs with respect to nicely moded queries.

Theorem 29. *Let P be a simply moded and input-recursive program. P is quasi recurrent if and only if P is input terminating with respect to the class of nicely moded queries.*

The proof of this theorem can be found in [10].

To consider a larger class of input terminating programs we can follow the same approach pursued by Apt and Pedreschi in defining acceptable programs and use a model to capture the inter-argument relations between the atoms in a query. Intuitively, the model represents all the possible contexts in which a specific atom in a query can be called. Standard models suffice when standard left-to-right derivations are considered, that is when the contexts depends only on the computed answers of the atoms occurring on the left of the considered one. When input consuming derivations are considered, the description of all the possible contexts is much more complex since there may be atoms in the query which are only partially computed when the considered atom is selected. Hence a computed answer semantics does not provide enough information, which is why we need to capture partial computed answers of input consuming derivations.

The semantics defined in [12] and the concept of simply local model give us the right tools and allow us to identify a large class of input terminating programs which includes also programs employing a non-trivial recursion scheme such as `quicksort`, `permute`, `transpose`. In fact, based on the notion of simply local models, in [12] we introduced the notion of simply acceptable programs which corresponds to the notion of acceptable programs introduced in [6].

Definition 30 (Simply Acceptable Program). *Let P be a program and M a simply local model of P containing SM$_P$.*

- *A clause c of P is* simply acceptable *with respect to a moded level mapping | | and M if for every variant H ← **A**, B, **C** of c and every substitution θ simply local with respect to c,*

    *if **A**θ ∈ M and Rel(H) ≃ Rel(B) then |Hθ| > |Bθ|.*

- *P is* simply acceptable with respect to *M if there exists a moded level map-ping* | | *such that each clause of P is simply acceptable with respect to* | | *and M. We also say that P is* simply acceptable *if it is simply acceptable with respect to some M and moded level mapping* | |.

Simple acceptability fully characterizes input termination of simply moded programs with respect to simply moded queries.

Theorem 31. *Let P be a simply moded program. P is simply acceptable if and only if it is input terminating with respect to simply moded queries.*

The following example shows how we can use the above theorem to reason about termination of a program.

Example 32. Consider the following PERMUTE program

```
permute([X|Xs],Ys)  ← insert(Zs,X,Ys), permute(Xs,Zs).
permute([],[]).

insert([],X,[X]).
insert([U|Xs],X,[U|Zs])  ← insert(Xs,X,Zs).
```

We consider it with two different modes.

1. First, consider the mode permute(O, I), insert(O, O, I).
   Notice that the program is not input terminating in this mode: by repeatedly selecting the rightmost atom, the query permute(Xs,Ys) generates an infinite input consuming derivation. By Theorem 31, we can prove it by showing that PERMUTE in this mode cannot be simply acceptable with respect to PM_{PERMUTE}^{SL} and a moded level mapping which is invariant under renaming. First note that PM_{PERMUTE}^{SL} contains every atom of the form insert(Us,U,t) where Us and U are disjoint from t, i.e., every simply moded atom whose predicate is insert. Therefore, in particular, insert(Us,U,Vs) $\in PM_{\text{PERMUTE}}^{SL}$. The substitution $\theta = \{$Ys/Vs, Zs/Us, X/U$\}$ is simply local w.r.t. the first clause. Therefore, for this clause to be simply acceptable, by Theorem 31, there would have to be a moded level mapping, invariant under renaming, such that |permute([U|Xs],Vs)| > |permute(Xs,Us)|. This is a contradiction since a *moded* level mapping depends only on the input arguments (the second argument of permute) and we are considering a level mapping invariant under renaming.
   Thus Theorem 31 can be used to diagnose a program, in that we can pinpoint why it does not input terminate.
2. Now consider the program PERMUTE together with the mode permute(I, O), insert(I, I, O).
   In this case, in order to make the program simply moded we have to permute the two body atoms of the first permute clause[7]. I.e., permute is redefined as

---

[7] Actually, everything we state applies to the class of *permutation* simply moded programs, i.e., those programs and queries that are simply moded possibly after a permutation of body atoms. For the sake of notation simplicity, we avoid to refer to this in a structural way.

```
permute([X|Xs],Ys) ← permute(Xs,Zs), insert(Zs,X,Ys).
permute([],[]).
```

Notice that the program is now input terminating with respect to simply moded queries. This is in fact the *natural* mode of the PERMUTE program. To demonstrate the termination one can apply Theorem 31 using *any* simply local model containing SM_P together with the following moded level mapping:

$$|\texttt{permute}(l, \_)| = len(l),$$
$$|\texttt{insert}(l, \_, \_)| = len(l).$$

6 Conclusion

In this paper, we have illustrated two denotational semantics proposed in [9], [10] and in [12] for input consuming derivation in logic programs and we have shown how these semantics have been used for studying termination properties of such programs.

While the first semantics (introduced in [9]) models exclusively the results of successful derivations and requires programs to be *well moded* and *nicely moded*, the second one (introduced in [12]) models also the results of incomplete derivations and requires programs and queries to be simply moded.

As mentioned in the introduction, in the context of parallel and concurrent programs, one can have derivations that never *succeed*, and yet compute substitutions [36]. Thus we have provided a denotational semantics also for such programs, which goes beyond the usual success-based SLD resolution mechanism of logic programming.

Input consuming derivations bear a certain resemblance with derivations in the language of *Moded (Flat) GHC* [45]. Actually, input consuming programs can be seen as a simplified version of moded (F)GHC. We want to note however that Moded (F)GHC is a full-fledged programming paradigm, while input consuming programs are meant for abstraction purposes.

As a concluding remark, we want to stress the relation between ic-programs and programs that use delay declarations. A significant class of programs with delay declarations whose derivations are input consuming derivations has been identified in [11].

References

1. K. R. Apt. Logic Programming. In J. van Leeuwen, editor, *Handbook of Theoretical Computer Science*, volume B: Formal Models and Semantics, pages 495–574. Elsevier and The MIT Press, Amsterdam and Cambridge, MA, 1990.
2. K. R. Apt. *From Logic Programming to Prolog*. Prentice Hall, London, 1997.
3. K. R. Apt and M. Bezem. Acyclic programs. *New Generation Computing*, 9(3&4):335–363, 1991.

4. K. R. Apt and S. Etalle. On the unification free Prolog programs. In A. Borzyszkowski and S. Sokolowski, editors, *Proceedings of the Conference on Mathematical Foundations of Computer Science (MFCS'93)*, volume 711 of *Lecture Notes in Computer Science*, pages 1–19, Berlin, Germany, 1993. Springer-Verlag.

5. K. R. Apt and I. Luitjes. Verification of logic programs with delay declarations. In A. Borzyszkowski and S. Sokolowski, editors, *Proceedings of the Fourth International Conference on Algebraic Methodology and Software Technology, (AMAST'95)*, volume 936 of *Lecture Notes in Computer Science*, pages 1–19, Berlin, Germany, 1995. Springer-Verlag.

6. K. R. Apt and D. Pedreschi. Proving termination of general Prolog programs. In T. Ito and A. Meyer, editors, *Proceedings of the International Conference on Theoretical Aspects of Computer Software*, Lecture Notes in Computer Science 526, pages 265–289, Berlin, Germany, 1991. Springer-Verlag.

7. K. R. Apt and D. Pedreschi. Reasoning about termination of pure Prolog programs. *Information and Computation*, 106(1):109–157, 1993.

8. M. Bezem. Strong termination of logic programs. *Journal of Logic Programming*, 15(1&2):79–97, 1993.

9. A. Bossi, S. Etalle, and S. Rossi. Semantics of well-moded input-consuming logic programs. *Computer Languages*, 26(1):1–25, 2000.

10. A. Bossi, S. Etalle, and S. Rossi. Properties of input-consuming derivations. *Theory and Practice of Logic Programming*, 2(2):125–154, 2002.

11. A. Bossi, S. Etalle, S. Rossi, and J.-G. Smaus. Semantics and termination of simply-moded logic programs with dynamic scheduling. In D. Sands, editor, *Proceedings of the European Symposium on Programming*, volume 2028 of *Lecture Notes in Computer Science*, pages 402–416, Genova, Italy, 2001. Springer-Verlag.

12. A. Bossi, S. Etalle, S. Rossi, and J.-G. Smaus. Termination of simply-moded logic programs with dynamic scheduling. *ACM Transactions on Computational Logic (TOCL)*, 2004. To appear.

13. A. Bossi, M. Gabrielli, G. Levi, and M. Martelli. The S-semantics approach: Theory and applications. *The Journal of Logic Programming*, 19 & 20:149–198, May 1994.

14. A. Bossi, S. Etalle N. Cocco, and S. Rossi. On Modular Termination Proofs of General Logic Programs. *Theory and Practice of Logic Programming*, 2(3):263–291, 2002.

15. R. Chadha and D.A. Plaisted. Correctness of unification without occur check in Prolog. Technical report, Department of Computer Science, University of North Carolina, Chapel Hill, N.C., 1991.

16. F.S. de Boer and C. Palamidessi. A fully abstract model for concurrent constraint programming. In S. Abramsky and T.S.E. Maibaum, editors, *Proc. of the International Joint Conference on Theory and Practice of Software Development, (TAPSOFT/CAAP)*, volume 493 of *Lecture Notes in Computer Science*, pages 296–319, Brighton, UK, 1991. Springer-Verlag.

17. M. Garcia de la Banda, K. Marriott, and P. Stuckey. Efficient analysis of logic programs with dynamic scheduling. In J. Lloyd, editor, *Proc. Twelfth International Logic Programming Symposium*, pages 417–431. The MIT Press, 1995.

18. D. De Schreye and S. Decorte. Termination of logic programs: the never-ending story. *Journal of Logic Programming*, 19-20:199–260, 1994.

19. S. Debray, D. Gudemann, and P. Bigot. Detection and optimization of suspension-free logic programs. In M. Bruynooghe, editor, *Proc. Eleventh International Logic Programming Symposium*, pages 487–504. The MIT Press, 1994.

20. P. Dembinski and J. Maluszynski. AND-parallelism with intelligent backtracking for annotated logic programs. In *Proceedings of the International Symposium on Logic Programming*, pages 29–38, Boston, 1985.

21. S. Etalle, A. Bossi, and N. Cocco. Termination of well-moded programs. *Journal of Logic Programming*, 38(2):243–257, 1999.

22. S. Etalle, M. Gabbrielli, and M. C. Meo. Transformations of CCP programs. *ACM Transactions on Programming Languages and Systems*, 23(3):304–395, 2002.

23. M. Falaschi, M. Gabbrielli, K. Marriott, and C. Palamidessi. Constraint logic programming with dynamic scheduling: a semantics based on closure operators. *Information and Computation*, 137(1):41–67, 1997.

24. M. Falaschi, M. Gabrielli, K. Marriott, and C. Palamidessi. Compositional analysis for concurrent constraint programming. In *Proceedings of the IEEE Symposium on Logic in Computer Science*. IEEE, 1993.

25. M. Falaschi, G. Levi, M. Martelli, and C. Palamidessi. Declarative modeling of the operational behavior of logic languages. *Theoretical Computer Science*, 69(3):289–318, 1989.

26. P. M. Hill and J. W. Lloyd. *The Gödel programming language*. The MIT Press, 1994.

27. IC Parck, Imperial College London. *The ECLiPSe Constraint Logic Programming System*, 2003. http://www-icparc.doc.ic.ac.uk/eclipse/.

28. Intelligent Systems Laboratory, Swedish Institute of Computer Science, PO Box 1263, S-164 29 Kista, Sweden. *SICStus Prolog Page*, 2003. http://www.sics.se/sicstus/.

29. J. W. Lloyd. *Foundations of Logic Programming*. Symbolic Computation – Artificial Intelligence. Springer-Verlag, Berlin, Berlin, Germany, 1987. Second edition.

30. E. Marchiori and F. Teusink. Termination of logic programs with delay declarations. *Journal of Logic Programming*, 39(1–3):95–124, 1999.

31. K. Marriott. Algebraic and logical semantics for CLP languages with dynamic scheduling. *Journal of Logic Programming*, 32(1):71–84, 1997.

32. K. Marriott, M. Garcia de la Banda, and M. Hermenegildo. Analyzing logic programs with dynamic scheduling. In *Proc. 21st Annual ACM Symp. on Principles of Programming Languages*, pages 240–253. ACM Press, 1994.

33. K. Marriott, M. Falaschi, M. Gabrielli, and C. Palamidessi. A simple semantics for logic programming languages with delay. In *Proceedings of the Eighteenth Australian Computer Science Conference*, 1995.

34. L. Naish. *Negation and control in Prolog*, volume 238 of *Lecture Notes in Computer Science*. Springer-Verlag, New York, 1986.

35. L. Naish. Coroutining and the construction of terminating logic programs. *Australian Computer Science Communications*, 15(1):181–190, 1993.

36. L. Naish. Parallelizing NU-Prolog. In K. A. Bowen and R. A. Kowalski, editors, *Proceedings of the Fifth International Conference/Symposium on Logic Programming*, pages 1546–1564, Seattle, Washington, August 1988. The MIT Press.

37. L. Naish. An introduction to MU-Prolog. Technical Report 82/2, Department of Computer Science, University of Melbourne, Melbourne, Australia, March 1982 (Revised July 1983).

38. G. Puebla, M. Garcia de la Banda, K. Marriott, and P. Stuckey. Optimization of logic programs with dynamic scheduling. In *ICLP 1997*, pages 93–107, 1997.

39. V. A. Saraswat and M. Rinard. Concurrent constraint programming. In *Proc. of the Seventeenth ACM Symposium on Principles of Programming Languages*, pages 232–245, San Francisco, California, 1990. ACM, New York.

40. J.-G. Smaus. *Modes and Types in Logic Programming*. PhD thesis, University of Kent at Canterbury, 1999. Available from `http://www.cs.ukc.ac.uk/pubs/1999/986/`.

41. J.-G. Smaus. Proving termination of input-consuming logic programs. In D. De Schreye, editor, *Proceedings of the 16th International Conference on Logic Programming*, pages 335–349, Las Cruces, New Mexico, USA, 1999. The MIT Press.

42. J.-G. Smaus, P. M. Hill, and A. M. King. Termination of logic programs with `block` declarations running in several modes. In C. Palamidessi, editor, *Proceedings of the 10th Symposium on Programming Language Implementations and Logic Programming*, volume 1490 of *Lecture Notes in Computer Science*, pages 73–88, Pisa, Italy, 1998. Springer-Verlag.

43. K. Ueda. Guarded Horn Clauses, a parallel logic programming language with the concept of a guard. In M. Nivat and K. Fuchi, editors, *Programming of Future Generation Computers*, pages 441–456. North Holland, Amsterdam, 1988.

44. K. Ueda and K. Furukawa. Transformation rules for GHC Programs. In *Proc. of the International Conference on Fifth Generation Computer Systems*, pages 582–591, Tokyo, Japan, 1988. Institute for New Generation Computer Technology, Tokyo, OHMSHA Ltd. Tokyo and Springer-Verlag.

45. K. Ueda and M. Morita. Moded flat GHC and its message-oriented implementation technique. *New Generation Computing*, 13(1):3–43, 1994.

46. M. H. van Emden and G. J. de Lucena. Predicate logic as a language for parallel programming. In K.L. Clark and S.-A. Tärnlund, editors, *Logic Programming*, London, 1982. Academic Press.

On the Semantics of Logic Program Composition

Antonio Brogi

Department of Computer Science, University of Pisa, Italy
brogi@di.unipi.it

Abstract. This paper aims at offering an insightful synthesis of different compositional semantics for logic program composition which have been developed in the literature. In particular, we will analyse the notions of program equivalence, compositionality, and full abstraction for logic programs. We will show how the notion of *supported interpretation* provides a unifying compositional model-theoretic characterisation both of positive programs and of programs containing negation.

1 Introduction

Building complex software systems by combining existing components is a standard methodology of modern software development. The effectiveness of the program composition approach depends on the possibility of reasoning on the composition process itself. The availability of well-founded characterisations of programs and program compositions is needed to perform transformation, analysis and verification.

One of the most important relations between programs (in any programming language) is *program equivalence*. This relation is at the basis of most, if not all, programming methodologies. Each method of giving a semantics to programs induces an equivalence relation on programs. It is therefore essential to understand how these equivalences are related.

As pointed out in [30], different formulations that define identical equivalences offer different frameworks in which to reason about programs. Moreover, stronger equivalence relations may be used to reason about programs and ensure that the programs are equivalent in a weaker sense, which might not be as suitable for reasoning. Reasoning about programs concerns also the correctness of source-to-source transformations such as those occurring in program development [35].

The properties of *compositionality* and *full abstraction* play a crucial role in the study of the semantics of programming languages. Simply stated, a semantics is compositional (or homomorphic) if the meaning of a program can be obtained from the meaning of its components. If a semantics is compositional with respect to some composition operations then the induced equivalence relation is a congruence for those operations. This property establishes a firm foundation for reasoning about programs and program transformations. Suppose that a program P consists of two parts, Q and R say, suitably composed together. Suppose also that R' is a more efficient version of R, obtained for instance by

M. Bruynooghe and K.-K. Lau (Eds.): Program Development in CL, LNCS 3049, pp. 115–151, 2004.
© Springer-Verlag Berlin Heidelberg 2004

applying some program transformation technique to R. If R' is equivalent to R in the chosen semantics then the property of compositionality ensures that the substitution of R' for R will not affect the meaning of the whole program P.

Often the semantics $\mathcal{O}$ describing the observable behaviour of programs is not compositional. In these cases it is then necessary to consider a more distinguishing (or finer) semantics $\mathcal{S}$ which preserves $\mathcal{O}$ and which is a congruence for the set of compositions considered. The compositionality of $\mathcal{S}$ ensures that programs (or program parts) which are $\mathcal{S}$-equivalent can be replaced with one another without affecting the intended semantics $\mathcal{O}$ of the whole system. The property of full abstraction establishes that the equivalence relation induced by $\mathcal{S}$ is the largest equivalence relation that can be used to substitute programs (or program parts) without affecting the intended semantics of the whole system.

In this paper we analyse the properties of compositionality and full abstraction in the context of logic programming. Indeed, because of the declarative programming style it features, logic programming can be fruitfully employed as the specification language of software components. Logic programming supports a wealth of programming styles developed in algorithmic programming, database programming, and artificial intelligence programming via a small number of powerful features (unification, recursion, and nondeterminism). On the other hand, logic programming has firm foundations in mathematical logic. The availability of different equivalent characterisations of programs offers the ground to perform sound semantics-based transformation, analysis and verification.

In this paper, we focus on the most basic composition operation over logic programs, the *union* of programs, and we analyse and compare different semantics that have been proposed in the literature. In the perspective of providing an insightful synthesis of these semantics, we will show how the notion of *supported interpretation* provides a unifying characterisation of both positive programs and of programs containing negation. Notice that the aim of this paper is not to provide a comprehensive survey of the compositional semantics for logic programs which have been proposed in the last ten years. (The interested reader may refer to [10] for a survey which covers also different modular extensions of logic programming.)

The rest of the paper is organised as follows.

Section 2 introduces some background material, namely some logic programming terminology, the notions of compositionality and full abstraction, and a hierarchy of logic program equivalences.

Section 3 is devoted to analyse compositional semantics of definite programs. We first analyse three equivalence relations considered in [30]: Subsumption equivalence, weak subsumption equivalence and logical equivalence. We show that while they are all compositional, logical equivalence is *the* fully abstract relation. We then consider a different model-theoretic characterisation, based on the notion of *admissible model* presented in [10]. The relation between admissible models and the other semantics is illustrated, and a fully abstract refinement of admissible models is presented here for the first time. The section is concluded by introducing the notion of *supported interpretation* which provides an alternative characterisation of logical equivalence and which will be used also to characterise normal programs. The results presented in this section are summarised in Figure 2 which contains a hierarchy of compositional semantics for definite programs.

Section 4 is devoted to analyse compositional semantics for normal programs, that is, programs containing negation. Two main problems arise here: (1) the existence of many "intended" semantics for normal programs, and (2) the orthogonality of non-monotonicity and compositionality. We will show that the notion of supported interpretation introduced in Section 3 provides a unifying characterisation of a number of "intended" semantics for normal programs. A general full abstraction result will be also presented here for the first time.

Finally, Section 5 briefly discusses other forms of program compositions, while Section 6 contains some concluding remarks.

To simplify the reading, all proofs are reported in the Appendix.

2   Preliminaries

2.1   Logic Programming

We will use the standard definitions and terminology of logic programming, as reported for instance in [2,29]. A *definite logic program* is a finite set of clauses of the form $A \leftarrow B_1, \ldots, B_n$ $(n \geq 0)$, where $A, B_1, \ldots, B_n$ are atoms. A *normal logic program* is a finite set of clauses of the form $A \leftarrow B_1, \ldots, B_n$ $(n \geq 0)$, where A is an atom and where $B_1, \ldots, B_n$ are possibly negated atoms.

Clauses without premise part, i.e., of the form $A \leftarrow$, will be called *extensional* (or unit) clauses, and programs containing only extensional clauses will be called *extensional programs*. We will also denote by $Defs(P)$ the set of predicates defined in a program P.

We will use the standard notions of Herbrand interpretations and Herbrand models, and we will denote by $LHM(P)$ the least Herbrand model of a program P. We will also use the definition of the standard immediate consequence operator $T(P)$:

$$T(P)(I) = \{A \mid \exists \overline{B} : A \leftarrow \overline{B} \in ground(P) \wedge \overline{B} \subseteq I\}$$

where P is a definite program, $\overline{B}$ denotes a (possibly empty) conjunction of atoms, and $ground(P)$ denotes the set of ground instances of clauses of P.

2.2   Compositionality and Full Abstraction

A semantics for a programming language provides meanings for programs or, more generally, program parts. Moreover, each method of giving semantics to a programming language induces an equivalence relation on programs. Namely, two programs are equivalent if and only if they have the same meaning in the chosen semantics.

An equivalence relation $\equiv_1$ is finer than another equivalence relation $\equiv_2$ ($\equiv_1 \subseteq \equiv_2$) if and only if whenever $P \equiv_1 Q$ then $P \equiv_2 Q$. Furthermore $\equiv_1$ is strictly finer than $\equiv_2$ ($\equiv_1 \subset \equiv_2$) if and only if $\equiv_1$ is finer than $\equiv_2$ and $\equiv_2$ is not finer than $\equiv_1$.

The properties of *compositionality* and *full abstraction* have been recognised as two fundamental concepts in the studies on the semantics of programming languages [32,36]. Informally, a semantics is compositional if equivalent programs (or program parts) are indistinguishable, that is, if they exhibit equal observable behaviour in all possible context. On the other hand, a semantics is fully abstract if indistinguishable programs (or program parts) are equivalent.

The formal definition of these properties relies on the notion of observable behaviour of a program and on the notion of program composition. The former can be represented by a mapping $\mathcal{O}$ which associates with every program P an object $\mathcal{O}(P)$ denoting the observable behaviour of P. The latter can be represented by a set Com of (possibly partial) functions over programs.

A semantics is *compositional* if the induced equivalence is compositional for the pair $(\mathcal{O}, Com)$, that is, if it preserves the observables and is a congruence for the set of compositions. Formally, an equivalence relation $\equiv$ is *compositional* for $(\mathcal{O}, Com)$ if and only if:

1. $\equiv$ *preserves* $\mathcal{O}$, that is $\forall P, Q : P \equiv Q \implies \mathcal{O}(P) = \mathcal{O}(Q)$.
2. $\equiv$ *is a congruence* for Com, that is $\forall \mathcal{F} \in Com, \forall P_1, \ldots, P_n, Q_1, \ldots, Q_n$:
   $P_i \equiv Q_i \ (i = 1, \ldots, n) \implies \mathcal{F}(P_1, \ldots, P_n) \equiv \mathcal{F}(Q_1, \ldots, Q_n)$.

There is always a coarsest congruence for $(\mathcal{O}, Com)$, which is intuitively the "indistinguishability relation". A semantics is fully abstract if the induced equivalence includes this largest congruence. A semantics is both compositional and fully abstract if it coincides with it. Two programs P and Q are *distinguishable* under $(\mathcal{O}, Com)$ if there exists a context $\mathcal{C}[.]$ (defined via Com) in which the substitution of P with Q changes the external behaviour (defined via $\mathcal{O}$) of the context. Formally, P and Q are *distinguishable* iff $\exists \mathcal{C}[.] : \mathcal{O}(\mathcal{C}[P]) \neq \mathcal{O}(\mathcal{C}[Q])$. We put:

$$P \cong Q \iff P \text{ and } Q \text{ are not distinguishable under } (\mathcal{O}, Com).$$

Then an equivalence relation $\equiv$ is *fully abstract* for $(\mathcal{O}, Com)$ if and only if:

$$\forall P, Q : P \cong Q \implies P \equiv Q.$$

In this paper, we consider both definite and normal programs, and we assume that the language (or vocabulary) in which programs are written is fixed. Namely, the Herbrand base $\mathcal{B}$ we refer to is determined by a set of function and predicate symbols that include all function and predicate symbols used in the programs being considered. We will consider (set-theoretic) union of programs (denoted by $\cup$) as the only composition operation. The observable behaviour of a logic program may be defined in different ways, depending on which aspects of the computation one is interested in looking at. In the case of definite logic programs, a natural choice of the observables is the *success set* of a program [2,29,40]. The success set $SS(P)$ of a program P is the set of ground atoms A such that $P \cup \{\leftarrow A\}$ has a SLD-refutation. Therefore we put:

$$\mathcal{O}(P) = SS(P).$$

2.3   Equivalence of Definite Logic Programs

A number of different equivalence relations for logic programs were studied and compared with one another in [30].

The equivalence relation induced by the immediate consequence operator $T(P)$ is one of these equivalences. Namely two programs are equivalent if and only if they have the same $T(P)$, that is, their immediate consequence operators coincide on every Herbrand interpretation. In [30] a syntactic notion of equivalence, *subsumption equivalence* was also introduced, and it was shown to coincide with the equality of $T(P)$ functions on programs. Let C_1 and C_2 be the definite clauses $A \leftarrow \bar{B}$ and $D \leftarrow \bar{E}$, respectively. C_1 is subsumed by C_2 if there is a substitution ϑ such that $A = D\vartheta$ and $\bar{E}\vartheta \subseteq \bar{B}$. Two logic programs P and Q are subsumption equivalent if every clause of P is subsumed by some clause of Q and vice-versa. Existing algorithms [25] can be therefore exploited to determine whether two programs are $T(P)$ equivalent.

Another equivalence relation considered in [30] is a refinement of subsumption equivalence, named *weak subsumption equivalence*. Namely two programs are weakly subsumption equivalent if and only if the two programs without tautologies are subsumption equivalent. As for the previous case, an equivalent formulation is given in terms of a refinement of the $T(P)$ semantics, defined by means of a $T(P) + Id$ function.

Furthermore, logical equivalence ($\models P \longleftrightarrow Q$) and the corresponding equivalence when only Herbrand models are considered ($M(P) = M(Q)$) are studied. It is also shown that these two equivalent relations can be equivalently formulated in terms of the functional semantics defined in [27].

Finally, the standard equivalence relation induced by the operational semantics of logic programs is considered, which identifies programs with same success set ($SS(P) = SS(Q)$), and the latter coincides with the least Herbrand model semantics [40].

Different formulations of equivalence are also compared in terms of their relative strength. In addition to the previously mentioned correspondences, it is shown that subsumption equivalence is strictly finer than weak subsumption equivalence, which is in turn strictly finer than logical equivalence, which is in turn strictly finer than operational equivalence.

Some of the results presented in [30] are summarised in Figure 1, where an arrow from $\equiv_1$ to $\equiv_2$ denotes that $\equiv_1$ is strictly finer than $\equiv_2$ (viz., $\equiv_1 \subset \equiv_2$).

3   Composition of Definite Programs

The union of programs is the most basic composition operation over logic programs. Actually, every logic program consists of the union of all its clauses.

$$P \text{ s-e } Q \quad \longleftrightarrow \quad T(P) = T(Q)$$
$$\downarrow$$
$$P \text{ w s-e } Q \quad \longleftrightarrow \quad T(P) + Id = T(Q) + Id$$
$$\downarrow$$
$$\models P \leftrightarrow Q \quad \longleftrightarrow \quad M(P) = M(Q)$$
$$\downarrow$$
$$SS(P) = SS(Q) \longleftrightarrow LHM(P) = LHM(Q)$$

Fig. 1. Equivalence hierarchy for logic programs.

The starting point of our analysis is the observation that the standard (model-theoretic, fixpoint or operational) semantics of logic programs is not compositional w.r.t. the union of programs.

The least Herbrand model is usually taken as the the intended meaning of a definite logic program. Unfortunately, the least Herbrand model of the union of two programs cannot always be determined from the least Herbrand models of the separate programs.

Example 1. For instance the program:

$$fallible(x) \leftarrow human(x)$$

is equivalent to the empty program, as the empty set is the least model of both programs. On the other hand, if these programs are composed with the program:

$$human(socrates) \leftarrow$$

we obtain two programs which have different least models ($\{human(socrates), fallible(socrates)\}$ and $\{human(socrates)\}$, respectively). $\Diamond$

The above example shows that the least Herbrand model semantics is not compositional w.r.t. the union of programs. The same observation applies to the standard least fixpoint and to the standard operational semantics, as these three semantics are all equivalent for definite programs [40].

A number of different compositional denotational semantics for logic programs have been proposed. In the next sections we will present some of those semantics, and analyse the existing relations among them.

3.1   Subsumption Equivalence

One of the first compositional semantics for logic programs was presented in [31]. Intuitively speaking, the idea of [31] is to adopt a higher-order semantics in order to achieve a compositional denotation of programs. Simply stated, a program P is denoted by its immediate consequence operator $T(P)$ rather than by the least fixpoint of $T(P)$, as done in the standard least fixpoint semantics of logic programs.

Indeed, the immediate consequences of the union of two programs can be determined by the immediate consequences of the two programs in the following way [31]:

$$T(P \cup Q)(I) = T(P)(I) \cup T(Q)(I)$$

(where abusing notation the $\cup$ on the left-hand side denotes program union while the $\cup$ on the right-hand side denotes set-theoretic union).

Let us denote by $\equiv_T$ the equivalence relation induced by the $T(P)$ semantics:

$$P \equiv_T Q \iff T(P) = T(Q).$$

Namely two programs are equivalent if and only if their immediate consequence operators coincide on every Herbrand interpretation. The equivalence relation $\equiv_T$ is a congruence for the union of programs (as well as for several other interesting composition operations, as shown for instance in [7]). Moreover, the equivalence relation $\equiv_T$ preserves the observables since:

$$\mathcal{O}(P) = SS(P) = LHM(P) = T^\omega(P)(\emptyset).$$

The equivalence relation $\equiv_T$ is hence a congruence for $(\mathcal{O}, \{\cup\})$. It is however easy to observe that $\equiv_T$ is not fully abstract for $(\mathcal{O}, \{\cup\})$. Indeed there are programs which are not subsumption equivalent, though they cannot be distinguished operationally.

Example 2. Consider for instance the programs:

P	Q
$a \leftarrow$	$a \leftarrow b$
$b \leftarrow$	$b \leftarrow$

We see that P and Q are indistinguishable under $(\mathcal{O}, \{\cup\})$ though they are not subsumption equivalent — since $T(P)(\emptyset) = \{a, b\}$ while $T(Q)(\emptyset) = \{b\}$. $\Diamond$

3.2   Weak Subsumption Equivalence

The weak subsumption equivalence relation was introduced in [30] as a refinement of subsumption equivalence. Two programs are weakly subsumption equivalent if and only if the two programs without tautologies are subsumption equivalent.

Weak subsumption equivalence can be characterised in terms of the function $T(P)$ by introducing a new operator $(T(P) + Id)$ defined as follows:

$$(T(P) + Id)(I) \;=\; I \cup T(P)(I)$$

and then by proving that [30]:

P *is weakly subsumption equivalent to* Q $\iff$ $(T(P) + Id = T(Q) + Id).$

Let us denote by $\equiv_{T+Id}$ the equivalence relation induced by $T(P) + Id$, that is:

$$P \equiv_{T+Id} Q \iff (T(P) + Id = T(Q) + Id).$$

As shown in [12], $\equiv_{T+Id}$ is a congruence for the union of programs. Indeed, for any interpretation I:

$$(T(P_1 \cup P_2) + Id)(I) = I \cup T(P_1 \cup P_2)(I) = I \cup T(P_1)(I) \cup T(P_2)(I).$$

Therefore, if $P_1 \equiv_{T+Id} Q_1$ and $P_2 \equiv_{T+Id} Q_2$ then for all I:

$$(T(P_1 \cup P_2) + Id)(I) = (T(Q_1 \cup Q_2) + Id)(I).$$

Since the equivalence relation $\equiv_{T+Id}$ preserves $\mathcal{O}$ [30] it is hence compositional for $(\mathcal{O}, \{\cup\})$. Weak subsumption equivalence is coarser than subsumption equivalence, that is $\equiv_{T+Id}$ distinguishes less programs than $\equiv_T$.

Example 3. For instance $\equiv_T$ distinguishes the programs:

$$
\begin{array}{ll}
P & Q \\
a \leftarrow b & a \leftarrow b \\
 & b \leftarrow b
\end{array}
$$

(since $T(P)(\{b\}) \subset T(Q)(\{b\})$) while they are equivalent under $\equiv_{T+Id}$. Indeed programs P and Q are identical up to tautologies and for each I:

$$(T(P) + Id)(I) = (T(Q) + Id)(I) = \begin{cases} I & \text{if } b \notin I \\ I \cup \{a\} & \text{if } b \in I \end{cases}$$

$\Diamond$

As for the case of $\equiv_T$, we can however observe that $\equiv_{T+Id}$ is not fully abstract for $(\mathcal{O}, \{\cup\})$. For instance, programs P and Q of Example 2 are indistinguishable under $(\mathcal{O}, \{\cup\})$ though they are not weak subsumption equivalent since $(T(P) + Id)(\{\}) = \{a, b\}$ and $(T(Q) + Id)(\{\}) = \{b\}$.

3.3 Logical Equivalence

While subsumption equivalence and weak subsumption equivalence are both compositional for $(\mathcal{O}, \{\cup\})$, they are not fully abstract for $(\mathcal{O}, \{\cup\})$ since they both distinguish programs that are instead operationally indistinguishable. If we look for a fully abstract denotation of programs, we must then consider some weaker equivalence relation over programs. The natural next candidate to examine, following the hierarchy of Figure 1, is logical equivalence.

In the case of logic programs, logical equivalence coincides with the equivalence induced by the set of (all) Herbrand models of a program. Two definite programs are logically equivalent if and only if they have the same Herbrand models. If we denote by $M(P)$ the set of Herbrand models of a program P:

$$M(P) = \{I \mid I \models P\}$$

then logical equivalence can be denoted as follows:

$$P \equiv_M Q \iff M(P) = M(Q).$$

The reason why the least Herbrand model semantics does not properly cope with program composition derives from the underlying Closed World Assumption (CWA) [39]. According to the CWA, and to the corresponding completion semantics [15], a logic program is interpreted as a complete knowledge specification. Such an interpretation does not reflect the implicit assumption underlying program composition, that is, that a program is an incomplete chunk of knowledge to be possibly completed with other knowledge. As a consequence, each program cannot be simply denoted by its least Herbrand model, where only provable formulae are considered. Also non-minimal Herbrand models of a program must be considered, including formulae not provable in the program, but which can possibly become provable after some program composition.

In this perspective, a compositional semantics of logic programs was defined in [11] by denoting a program with the set of *all* its Herbrand models. Indeed the Herbrand models of the union of two programs can be determined by the Herbrand models of the separate programs, as shown by the following observation.

Observation 1 *Let P and Q be definite programs. Then:*

$$I \in M(P \cup Q) \iff I \in M(P) \wedge I \in M(Q).$$

Namely an interpretation I is a model of the union of two programs if and only if I is a model of both programs. Therefore the set of models of the union of two programs coincides with the intersection of the set of models of the two programs, that is:

$$M(P \cup Q) = M(P) \cap M(Q)$$

and the least Herbrand model of the union of two programs is hence the least Herbrand interpretation which is a model of both programs.

Logical equivalence preserves the least Herbrand models semantics $\equiv_{LHM}$, since $\mathcal{O}(P) = \bigcap \{I \mid I \in M(P)\}$, and hence logical equivalence is compositional for $(\mathcal{O}, \{\cup\})$. This means that if two programs are logically equivalent then they are also operationally indistinguishable, that is, they exhibit the same observable behaviour in all possible contexts.

Differently from subsumption equivalence and weak subsumption equivalence, logical equivalence is fully abstract for $(\mathcal{O}, \{\cup\})$. Indeed, as proved in [12], programs which are indistinguishable w.r.t. $(\mathcal{O}, \{\cup\})$ are also logically equivalent. It is perhaps worth recalling here a sketch of the proof of the full abstraction of logical equivalence reported in [12].

> *The proof shows that if two programs P and Q are not logically equivalent, then there exists a context in which they exhibit different observational behaviour. By definition of logical equivalence, if $P \not\equiv_M Q$ then there exists an interpretation I such that $I \in M(P)$ and $I \notin M(Q)$. By definition of Herbrand model [29], this means that $T(P)(I) \subseteq I$ and $T(Q)(I) \not\subseteq I$. This implies that there exists a finite subset F of I such that $A \in T(Q)(F)$ while $A \notin F$, for some atom A. The proof is finally concluded by considering the program $R = \{B \leftarrow \mid B \in F\}$ and by showing that $A \notin \mathcal{O}(P \cup R)$ while $A \in \mathcal{O}(Q \cup R)$.*

Example 4. Consider for instance the programs:

$$P \qquad Q$$
$$a(x) \leftarrow c(x) \qquad a(x) \leftarrow b(x)$$
$$b(x) \leftarrow c(x) \qquad b(x) \leftarrow c(x)$$

Any interpretation of the form:

$$I = \{a(t) \mid t \in T\} \cup \{b(u) \mid u \in U\}$$

(where T and U are —possibly infinite— sets of ground terms such that $T \subset U$) is a model for P and not for Q. Following the above proof sketch, we observe that there exists a finite subset F of I (for instance $F = \{b(k)\}$ for any $k \in U - T$) such that $a(k) \in T(Q)(F)$ and $a(k) \notin F$. If we then consider the program:

$$R$$
$$b(k) \leftarrow$$

we see that $a(k) \notin \mathcal{O}(P \cup R)$ while $a(k) \in \mathcal{O}(Q \cup R)$. $\lozenge$

The results proved in [12] establish that logical equivalence is *the* fully abstract compositional equivalence relation for $(\mathcal{O}, \{\cup\})$. This means that Herbrand models induce the coarsest equivalence relation on programs w.r.t. $(\mathcal{O}, \{\cup\})$, in that any other denotation of programs one may choose must induce the same equivalence relation to be compositional and fully abstract.

3.4   Admissible Models

Before the full abstraction of logical equivalence was established, a different compositional model-theoretic semantics for definite programs was presented in [10]. The idea of [10] was to model the composition of definite programs by denoting each program with a subset of its Herbrand models, called the *admissible* Herbrand models. Intuitively speaking, a model is considered to be admissible if it is "supported" by a set of hypotheses which all occur in the bodies of the program clauses. The intuition behind the admissible model semantics is to consider only those Herbrand models which somehow denote the effects of the possible compositions of a program with other programs.

It is worth observing that each Herbrand model is "supported" by the assumption of a set of hypotheses.

Lemma 1. *Let P be a program and let $I \subseteq \mathcal{B}$. Then:*

$$I \in M(P) \quad \Longleftrightarrow \quad \exists H \subseteq \mathcal{B} : I = LHM(P \cup H).$$

Following [10], a set of admissible hypotheses is formally defined as follows:

A set $H \subseteq \mathcal{B}$ is an admissible set of hypotheses *for a program P if and only if for all $h \in H$ there exists a ground instance $A \leftarrow \overline{B}$ of a clause in P such that $h \in \overline{B}$.*

The set possible admissible hypotheses for a program P is hence defined as follows:

$$AH(P) = \{h \mid h \in \mathcal{B} \wedge \exists A, \overline{B} : (A \leftarrow \overline{B} \in ground(P) \wedge h \in \overline{B})\}.$$

The notion of admissible model is then defined as follows:

> Let P be a program, let $I \subseteq \mathcal{B}$, and let $H \subseteq AH(P)$. Then I is an admissible model *for* P *under the hypotheses* H *if and only if* $I = LHM(P \cup H)$.

A model I that is admissible under the set of hypotheses H is denoted by $I(H)$ to explicitly record the set of hypotheses supporting it. The set of admissible models $AM(P)$ for a program P is hence defined as follows:

$$AM(P) = \{I(H) \mid I \subseteq \mathcal{B} \wedge H \subseteq AH(P) \wedge I = LHM(P \cup H)\}.$$

It is easy to observe that the least Herbrand model is always an admissible model (under the empty set of hypotheses).

Example 5. Consider for instance the program P:

$$P$$
$$a \leftarrow b$$
$$c \leftarrow$$

which has three Herbrand models: $\{c\}$, $\{a, c\}$, and $\{a, b, c\}$. Since b is the only admissible hypothesis for P, there are only two admissible models for P: $\{c\}$ — admissible under the empty set of interpretations — and $\{a, b, c\}$ — admissible under the set of interpretations $\{b\}$. The model $\{a, c\}$ is instead considered not admissible since there is no admissible set of hypotheses supporting it.   ◊

As shown in [10], admissible models define a compositional semantics for logic programs. Indeed the admissible models of the union of two programs can be determined by composing the admissible models of the separate programs. Such composition is defined in [10] by means of a $\mathcal{T}(S)$ operator which, given a set S of admissible models, maps Herbrand interpretations into Herbrand interpretations. Intuitively, the definition of $\mathcal{T}(S)$ lifts the definition of $T(P)$ from program clauses to program (admissible) models. Namely, $T(P)(I)$ yields the union of all the atoms A such that P contains an implication "A if B" whose premise B is true in the interpretation I. Similarly, $\mathcal{T}(S)(I)$ yields the union of all the conclusions J such that $J(H)$ is an admissible model whose premise H is true in I.

The equivalence induced by the admissible models semantics is defined as follows:

$$P \equiv_{AM} Q \iff AM(P) = AM(Q).$$

Namely $P \equiv_{AM} Q$ if and only if the set of pairs $\langle I, H \rangle$ such that $I(H)$ is an admissible model is the same for both programs. It is easy to observe that the equivalence relation $\equiv_{AM}$ preserves the observables $\mathcal{O}$ since

$$LHM(P) = \bigcap \{I \mid I(H) \in AM(P)\}$$

and hence $\equiv_{AM}$ is compositional for $(\mathcal{O}, \{\cup\})$.

We can however observe that $\equiv_{AM}$ is not fully abstract for $(\mathcal{O}, \{\cup\})$. Indeed there are programs which do not have the same set of admissible models, although they cannot be distinguished operationally.

Example 6. For instance the programs:

$$
\begin{array}{ll}
P & Q \\
a \leftarrow b & a \leftarrow \\
b \leftarrow & b \leftarrow a
\end{array}
$$

are indistinguishable under $(\mathcal{O}, \{\cup\})$ though they do not have the same set of admissible models. Indeed P has two admissible models, $\{a, b\}(\emptyset)$ and $\{a, b\}(\{b\})$, while Q has the admissible models $\{a, b\}(\emptyset)$ and $\{a, b\}(\{a\})$.   ◇

The above example also highlights that programs having the same Herbrand models may have different sets of admissible models. Indeed this *per se* shows the non-fully abstractness of $\equiv_{AM}$ once the full abstraction of logical equivalence has been established.

3.5   Minimal Admissible Models

In Section 3.3 we have shown that the set of Herbrand models induces a fully abstract compositional equivalence relation (viz., logical equivalence $\equiv_M$). In the previous section we have shown that the idea of considering only *admissible* Herbrand models yields a compositional equivalence relation (viz., $\equiv_{AM}$) which is however not fully abstract.

An intriguing question is whether it is possible to refine the notion of admissible Herbrand model so as to restrict the set of admissible models of a program and to obtain a fully abstract denotation of programs.

Example 6 reported at the end of the previous section shows that the set of admissible models of a program includes models that are somehow "redundant" in view of possible program compositions.

Example 7. Consider again program P of Example 6:

$$
\begin{array}{l}
P \\
a \leftarrow b \\
b \leftarrow
\end{array}
$$

We observe that the inclusion of the admissible model $\{a, b\}(\{b\})$ does not really add much information to the program denotation, given the presence of the model $\{a, b\}(\emptyset)$. Intuitively speaking, the possible effects of the hypothesis b becoming true (because of some program composition) are already denoted by the admissible model $\{a, b\}(\emptyset)$.   ◇

Following the above observation, the definition of admissible model may hence be refined so as to exclude the somehow "redundant" models. Intuitively speaking, we might consider $I(H)$ to be a "minimal" admissible model only if H is the minimal set of hypotheses needed to derive the set of conclusions I, that is, only if:

$$\forall K \subset H : LHM(P \cup K) \subset LHM(P \cup H)$$

This constraint would eliminate some redundant admissible models —e.g., the indistinguishable programs P and Q of Example 6 would now have $\{a, b\}(\emptyset)$ as the only admissible model.

A stronger constraint is however needed to avoid all redundant models.

Example 8. For instance the program:

P

$a \leftarrow a$

would still have two admissible models ($\emptyset(\emptyset)$ and $\{a\}(\{a\})$) while being operationally indistinguishable from the empty program. Intuitively speaking, the information contained in the model $\{a\}(\{a\})$ for P is somehow already contained in the model $\emptyset(\emptyset)$, since the addition of the new hypothesis a does not add any other conclusion besides itself.   ◇

We therefore say that an admissible model $I(K \cup \Delta)$ is not redundant w.r.t. another admissible model $J(K)$ only if the extra hypotheses Δ add some other conclusions besides themselves, that is, only if $(I - J) \supset \Delta$. Formally, we define the set of minimal admissible models for a program P as follows:

$$\mu AM(P) = \{I(H) \mid I \subseteq \mathcal{B} \wedge H \subseteq AH(P) \wedge I = LHM(P \cup H)$$
$$\wedge \forall K \subset H : LHM(P \cup H) - LHM(P \cup K) \supset H - K\}.$$

Let us consider a simple example in order to better illustrate the way in which minimal admissible models restrict admissible models.

Example 9. Consider the program:

P

$a \leftarrow b, c$

$b \leftarrow$

$c \leftarrow d, c$

which has eight admissible models:

$\{b\}(\emptyset)$	$\{a, b, c\}(\{c\})$
$\{b\}(\{b\})$	$\{a, b, c\}(\{b, c\})$
$\{b, d\}(\{d\})$	$\{a, b, c, d\}(\{c, d\})$
$\{b, d\}(\{b, d\})$	$\{a, b, c, d\}(\{b, c, d\})$

Remarkably only two of such models are minimal admissible models, that is:

$$\mu AM(P) = \{\{b\}(\emptyset), \{a, b, c\}(\{c\})\}.$$

Indeed the model $\{b\}(\{b\})$ is redundant w.r.t. $\{b\}(\emptyset)$ since $LHM(P \cup \{b\}) = LHM(P)$. In other words the addition of the hypothesis b does not add any new conclusion. The models $\{b,d\}(\{d\})$ and $\{b,d\}(\{b,d\})$ are redundant w.r.t. $\{b\}(\emptyset)$ too, since in both cases $LHM(P\cup H)-LHM(P)=\{d\}\not\supseteq\{d\}$. Again, the addition of the set of hypotheses $\{d\}$ or $\{b,d\}$ does not add any other conclusion besides the hypotheses themselves. Similar considerations apply to the other non-minimal admissible models $\{a,b,c\}(\{b,c\})$, $\{a,b,c,d\}(\{c,d\})$, and $\{a,b,c,d\}(\{b,c,d\})$ which are all redundant w.r.t. $\{a,b,c\}(\{c\})$. $\Diamond$

The following proposition shows that for each admissible model $I(H)$ there exists a minimal admissible model $J(K)$ supported by a smaller set of hypotheses and such that $LHM(P\cup H)=LHM(P\cup K)\cup(H-K)$.

Proposition 1. *Let P be a program, let $I\subseteq B$ and let $H\subseteq B$.*

$$I(H)\in AM(P) \implies \exists K,J:(K\subseteq H \wedge J(K)\in \mu AM(P) \wedge I=J\cup(H-K)).$$

We finally prove that the equivalence relation $\equiv_{\mu AM}$, induced by the set of minimal admissible models of a program, does coincide with the fully abstract equivalence relation $\equiv_M$. To simplify the equivalence proof, we first provide the following alternative characterization of logical equivalence.

Lemma 2. *Let P and Q be two programs. Then:*

$$P\equiv_M Q \iff \forall H\subseteq B:LHM(P\cup H)=LHM(Q\cup H).$$

We are now ready to establish that the equivalence relations $\equiv_{\mu AM}$ and $\equiv_M$ coincide.

Proposition 2. $\equiv_M = \equiv_{\mu AM}$.

To conclude our analysis of admissible models, let us reconsider Example 9 to illustrate the relation between Herbrand and (minimal) admissible models.

Example 10. Consider again the program:

$$P$$
$$a\leftarrow b,c$$
$$b\leftarrow$$
$$c\leftarrow d,c$$

If $B=\{a,b,c,d\}$ then the set of Herbrand, admissible and minimal admissible models of program P are, respectively:

$HM(P)$	$AM(P)$	$\mu AM(P)$
$\{b\}$	$\{b\}(\emptyset)$	$\{b\}(\emptyset)$
	$\{b\}(\{b\})$	
$\{a,b\}$		
$\{b,d\}$	$\{b,d\}(\{d\})$	
	$\{b,d\}(\{b,d\})$	
$\{a,b,c\}$	$\{a,b,c\}(\{c\})$	$\{a,b,c\}(\{c\})$
	$\{a,b,c\}(\{b,c\})$	
$\{a,b,d\}$		
$\{a,b,c,d\}$	$\{a,b,c,d\}(\{c,d\})$	
	$\{a,b,c,d\}(\{b,c,d\})$	

It is worth noting that since $\mu AM(P) = \{\{b\}(\emptyset), \{a, b, c\}(\{c\})\}$ then the minimal admissible model semantics (correctly) identifies the above program P for instance with the program:

Q
$a \leftarrow c$
$b \leftarrow$

whose Herbrand, admissible, and minimal admissible models are, respectively:

$HM(Q)$	$AM(Q)$	$\mu AM(Q)$
$\{b\}$	$\{b\}(\emptyset)$	$\{b\}(\emptyset)$
$\{a, b\}$		
$\{b, d\}$		
$\{a, b, c\}$	$\{a, b, c\}(\{c\})$	$\{a, b, c\}(\{c\})$
$\{a, b, d\}$		
$\{a, b, c, d\}$		

We see that while the admissible model semantics distinguishes P and Q, the two programs are identified both by the minimal admissible model semantics ($\mu AM(P) = \mu AM(Q)$) and by logical equivalence ($HM(P) = HM(Q)$). $\Diamond$

3.6   Supported Interpretations

We finally introduce an alternative characterization of logical equivalence, which is defined by means of the notion of *supported interpretation* originally introduced in [9].

Besides providing another equivalent formulation of logical equivalence, the notion of supported interpretation will be exploited in the following sections to define a compositional semantics for extended logic programs, such as programs containing negation.

Intuitively speaking, a (Herbrand) interpretation I for a program P is supported by a set of hypotheses H if I is the least Herbrand model of the program P extended with H. More precisely, I is an interpretation for P supported by H if and only if I is the least Herbrand model of the program $P \cup H$, where $P \cup H$ stands for $P \cup \{h \leftarrow | h \in H\}$.

If the sets of hypotheses to be considered are arbitrary subsets of the Herbrand base $\mathcal{B}$, we obtain the following definition of supported interpretation:

Let P be a program, and let $I \subseteq \mathcal{B}$, $H \subseteq \mathcal{B}$. Then I is an interpretation for P supported by H if and only if $I = LHM(P \cup H)$.

An interpretation I supported by a set of hypotheses H is denoted by $I(H)$ to explicitly record the set of hypotheses supporting it.

The set of supported interpretations for a program P is then defined as follows:

$$SI(P, \mathcal{B}) = \{I(H) \mid H \subseteq \mathcal{B} \wedge I = LHM(P \cup H)\}.$$

As pointed out in [9], the above notion of supportedness properly extends the notion of admissibility introduced in Section 3.4. Namely the admissible models of a program are in general a subset of its supported interpretations, that is, $AM(P) \subseteq SI(P, \mathcal{B})$.

Lemma 1 shows that there is a direct correspondence between the supported interpretations and the Herbrand models of a program. Namely for each program P:

$$I \in M(P) \iff \exists H : I(H) \in SI(P, \mathcal{B}).$$

Let us denote by $\equiv_{SI(\mathcal{B})}$ the equivalence relation induced by the set of supported interpretations of a program, that is:

$$P \equiv_{SI(\mathcal{B})} Q \iff SI(P, \mathcal{B}) = SI(Q, \mathcal{B}).$$

We now establish that the equivalence relation $\equiv_{SI(\mathcal{B})}$ coincides with logical equivalence $\equiv_M$.

Proposition 3. $\equiv_M \; = \; \equiv_{SI(\mathcal{B})}$.

In the following sections, we will use a more general definition of supported interpretation by considering a set $\mathcal{H}$ of *assumable hypotheses*, where $\mathcal{H}$ is some pre-defined subset of the Herbrand base $\mathcal{B}$ (viz., $\mathcal{H} \subseteq \mathcal{B}$). Namely the set of supported interpretations of a program P w.r.t. a set of assumable hypotheses $\mathcal{H}$ is defined as follows:

$$SI(P, \mathcal{H}) \; = \; \{I(H) \mid H \subseteq \mathcal{H} \wedge I = LHM(P \cup H)\}.$$

Notice that the choice of the set of assumable hypotheses affects the induced equivalence relations as pointed out by the following proposition.

Proposition 4. *Let* $\mathcal{H} \subseteq \mathcal{B}$, $\mathcal{K} \subseteq \mathcal{B}$ *be two sets of assumable hypotheses. Then:*

(1) $\mathcal{H} \subseteq \mathcal{K} \implies \equiv_{SI(\mathcal{K})} \subseteq \equiv_{SI(\mathcal{H})}$
(2) $\mathcal{H} \subset \mathcal{K} \implies \equiv_{SI(\mathcal{K})} \subset \equiv_{SI(\mathcal{H})}$

3.7   Summary

In the previous sections, we analysed different compositional semantics for definite logic programs that have been proposed in the literature. The relations between the semantics considered are summarized in Figure 2.

We have first considered three equivalence relations analyzed in [30]: subsumption equivalence ($\equiv_T$), weak subsumption equivalence ($\equiv_{T+Id}$), and logical equivalence ($\equiv_M$). We have shown that they are all compositional w.r.t. $(\mathcal{O}, \{\cup\})$, and while the first two semantics are not fully abstract w.r.t. $(\mathcal{O}, \{\cup\})$, logical equivalence is the fully abstract compositional equivalence w.r.t. $(\mathcal{O}, \{\cup\})$.

We have then considered a different equivalence relation ($\equiv_{AM}$) defined in terms of the admissible Herbrand models of a program. We have shown that while admissible models induce a compositional denotation of programs, the corresponding equivalence relation is not fully abstract w.r.t. $(\mathcal{O}, \{\cup\})$. We have then shown how the notion of admissible model can be suitably constrained so as to obtain a fully abstract denotation of programs. The new equivalence relation $\equiv_{\mu AM}$, induced by the so-called minimal admissible models of a program, coincides with the fully abstract equivalence relation $\equiv_M$.

Finally, we have introduced the notion of supported interpretation that will be used in the following sections. We have shown that supported interpretations provide an alternative definition of logical equivalence, that is, the induced equivalence relation $\equiv_{SI(\mathcal{B})}$ coincides with the fully abstract compositional equivalence relation $\equiv_M$.

The relations between the semantics considered are summarized in Figure 2, where a double arrow from $\equiv_A$ to $\equiv_B$ denotes that $\equiv_A$ coincides with $\equiv_B$, while a single arrow from $\equiv_A$ to $\equiv_B$ denotes that $\equiv_A$ is strictly finer than $\equiv_B$, that is, $\equiv_A \subseteq \equiv_B$.

$$T(P) = T(Q)$$
$$\downarrow$$
$$T(P) + Id = T(Q) + Id) \qquad AM(P) = AM(Q)$$
$$\downarrow \qquad\qquad\qquad \downarrow$$
$$SI(P,\mathcal{B}) = SI(Q,\mathcal{B}) \longleftrightarrow \quad M(P) = M(Q) \quad \longleftrightarrow \mu AM(P) = \mu AM(Q)$$
$$\downarrow$$
$$LHM(P) = LHM(Q)$$

Fig. 2. The new equivalence hierarchy.

The chain of inclusions $\equiv_T \subset \equiv_{T+Id} \subset \equiv_M \subset \equiv_{LHM}$ was established in [30].

The strict inclusion $\equiv_{AM} \subset \equiv \mu AM$ has been established in Section 3.5. Indeed the minimal admissible models $\mu AM(P)$ of a program P are obtained from the admissible models $AM(P)$ of P. It is hence easy to show that $\equiv_{AM} \subseteq \equiv_{\mu AM}$, that is, if $P \equiv_{AM} Q$ then $P \equiv_{\mu AM} Q$. Moreover, as shown in Section 3.5, $\equiv_{\mu AM} \not\subseteq \equiv_{AM}$, that is, there exist programs that have the same set of minimal admissible models, while they have different sets of admissible models. For instance the empty program and the program P of Example 8 are distinguished by the admissible models semantics, since $AM(P) = \{\emptyset(\emptyset), \{a\}(\{a\})\}$, while $\emptyset(\emptyset)$ is the only admissible model for the empty program. On the other hand the two programs are identified by the minimal admissible model semantics in that $\emptyset(\emptyset)$ is the only minimal admissible model for both programs.

It is worth noting that while $\equiv_{AM}$ is strictly finer than $\equiv_{\mu AM}$ (and hence than $\equiv_M$ and $\equiv_{SI(\mathcal{B})}$), $\equiv_{AM}$ is not comparable with either $\equiv_T$ or $\equiv_{T+Id}$. Indeed there are programs which are (weak) subsumption equivalent and not admissible interpretations equivalent, and vice-versa.

Example 11. For instance consider the programs:

$$
\begin{array}{ll}
P & Q \\
a \leftarrow & a \leftarrow \\
 & a \leftarrow a
\end{array}
$$

We observe that $P \equiv_T Q$ (since $\forall I \colon T(P)(I) = \{a\} = T(Q)(I)$) and $P \equiv_{T+Id} Q$ (since $\forall I \colon (T + Id)(P)(I) = \{a\} \cup I = (T + Id)(Q)(I)$), while $P \not\equiv_{AM} Q$ since $\{a\}(\{a\}) \in AM(Q) - AM(P)$. On the other hand, if we consider the programs:

$$
\begin{array}{ll}
P & Q \\
a \leftarrow & a \leftarrow b \\
b \leftarrow & b \leftarrow \\
c \leftarrow b & c \leftarrow b
\end{array}
$$

we see that $P \equiv_{AM} Q$ since $AM(P) = AM(Q) = \{\{a,b,c\}(\emptyset), \{a,b,c\}(\{b\})\}$, while $P \not\equiv_T Q$ and $P \not\equiv_{T+Id} Q$ (since $T(P)(\emptyset) = \{a,b\}$ and $T(Q)(\emptyset) = \{b\}$). ◊

In this section, we have examined a number of compositional semantics for definite programs. However, as already anticipated in the Introduction, our analysis is not intended to be exhaustive. Other semantics have been proposed in the literature, such as [27,33] which were then extended by [31]. A survey describing these and other modular extensions of logic programming can be found in [14].

Moreover, our analysis focusses on standard Herbrand interpretations [2,29]. Many efforts have been devoted to define compositional semantics by using extended interpretations containing possibly non-ground atoms (e.g., see [6,22]). The relation between these semantics and the semantics based on standard Herbrand interpretations is summarised in [1].

4   Composition of Normal Programs

The need of extending definite programs to deal with forms of non-monotonic reasoning was recognized since the early years of logic programming. Negation as failure was introduced in [15] to express negative information, and it has been shown to support various forms of non-monotonic reasoning. A number of other extensions have been then proposed to further enrich the expressive power of logic programming as a general formalism for knowledge representation (see [4] for a survey).

The formalization of these extensions has called for new semantics capable to capture their "intended" meaning. Even for the case of negation as failure, many different characterizations have been defined from different perspectives, most of them inspired by an interpretation of negation as failure as a more general notion of negation by default (e.g., [19]). A survey of the semantics of logic programs with negation (by default) is reported in [3].

Something similar happened for other extensions such as abductive logic programming (e.g., [17,19,26]) and logic programming with a second form of negation in addition to negation by default (e.g., [24,34,38]).

For each extension there is no general agreement on what its semantics should be. Formal comparisons among different semantics are hard to be drawn, mainly because they are often based on different grounds. Furthermore, many proposals are based on a proof-theoretic approach rather than on a model-theoretic approach, and this constitutes a further obstacle for the study of formal properties, and hence formal comparisons, of different proposals.

On these premises, analysing compositionality issues in extended logic programs seems to be a quite difficult enterprise since:

- Many semantics have been proposed for different extensions of logic programming, and there is no general agreement on the intended meaning of each extension.
- Non-monotonic reasoning and compositionality are intuitively orthogonal issues that do not seem easy to be reconciled. Indeed the semantics for extended logic programs are typically non-compositional w.r.t. program union.

Consider for instance the case of normal logic programs, that is, logic programs with negation as default. It is easy to show, for instance, that the stable model semantics [23] is not compositional with respect to the union of programs.

Example 12. Consider for instance the programs:

P $\qquad\qquad$ Q
$a \leftarrow$ $\qquad\qquad$ $a \leftarrow not\ b$

which have the same (unique) stable model $\{a\}$. If these programs are extended with the program:

R
$b \leftarrow$

we obtain two programs which have different stable models ($\{a, b\}$ and $\{b\}$, respectively). Therefore it is not possible, in general, to determine the stable models of a program from the stable models of its clauses. $\qquad\qquad \Diamond$

A unifying view of different extensions of logic programming was presented in [9], where it is shown how the meaning of various extensions of logic programming can be expressed by means of the supported interpretations of a program. Many extensions are considered in [9], including negation-by-default, other forms of negation and abduction.

The approach can be summarised as follows:

1. Given an extended logic program, construct its *"positive"* version.
2. Consider the set of supported interpretations of (the positive version of) the program.
3. Select among the supported interpretations the *complete* models which characterise the intended meaning of a program.

The interest of complete models derives from their correspondence relation with other models proposed in the literature. Such a correspondence makes the supported interpretation approach a general framework for characterising and comparing different semantics of various extensions of logic programming.

In this paper we will focus only on one of these extensions, negation-by-default, and on the corresponding class of normal programs.

4.1   Positive Version of a Normal Program

A *normal program* P is a set of clauses of the form

$$A \leftarrow L_1, \ldots, L_n   (n \geq 0)$$

where A is an atom and $L_1, \ldots, L_n$ are literals. Negated literals in clause bodies have the form *not B*, where B is an atom. In the following, without loss of generality, we will consider only (possibly infinite) propositional programs. A non-propositional program is then understood as a shorthand for the (possibly infinite) set of ground clauses obtained by instantiating the original rules in all possible ways over the Herbrand universe.

Following [18,38], the *positive version* P^+ of a normal program P is the definite program obtained by replacing in P each negated atom *not A* by a new positive atom *not_A*. The Herbrand base $\mathcal{B}^+$ associated with P^+ is then the set obtained by extending the Herbrand base $\mathcal{B}$ of P with the new set of atoms:

$$not\_\mathcal{B} = \{not\_A \mid A \in \mathcal{B}\}$$

that is:

$$\mathcal{B}^+ = (\mathcal{B} \cup not\_\mathcal{B}).$$

The intended meaning of P will be defined by suitably restricting the Herbrand models of P^+, which are subsets of the extended Herbrand base.

From now onward, we will not distinguish any further between a normal program P and its positive version P^+, that is we will denote P directly by its positive version.

4.2   Supported Interpretations for Normal Programs

Let us take the negative part $not\_\mathcal{B}$ of the extended Herbrand base $\mathcal{B}^+$ as the set of assumable hypotheses. We get the following definition of supported interpretations of a program P:

$$SI(P, not\_\mathcal{B}) = \{I(H) \mid H \subseteq not\_\mathcal{B} \wedge I = LHM(P \cup H)\}.$$

As shown in [9], the set of supported interpretations can be suitably restricted in a step-wise way so as to identify the set of complete models of a program.

Such a step-wise process can be summarised as follows:

- A supported interpretation $I(H)$ of a program P is a supported *model* of P if I is consistent (i.e., $\not\exists A : A \in I \wedge not\_A \in I$).
- A supported interpretation $J(K)$ is a *conservative extension* of a supported model $I(H)$ if and only if $K \supseteq H$ and ($\not\exists A : not\_A \in K \wedge A \in I$).
- A supported model $I(H)$ is a *complete model* of P if and only if $\forall a \in \mathcal{B}$:

$$not\_a \in H \iff (a \notin J \text{ for each conservative extension } J(K) \text{ of } I(H)).$$

- Each normal programs has at least one complete model.

Example 13. Consider for instance the program:

$$P$$
$$a \leftarrow not\ b$$

and suppose for the sake of simplicity that $\mathcal{B} = \{a, b\}$. Then the supported interpretations $SI(P, not\_\mathcal{B})$ are:

$$\emptyset \ (\emptyset)$$
$$\{not\_a\} \ (\{not\_a\})$$
$$\{a, not\_b\} \ (\{not\_b\})$$
$$\{a, not\_a, not\_b\} \ (\{not\_a, not\_b\})$$

It is easy to observe that each supported interpretation of P is a conservative extension of the model supported by the empty set of hypotheses. On the other hand, there is no conservative extension of the model $\{a, not\_b\}(\{not\_b\})$ since its only extension $\{a, not\_a, not\_b\}(\{not\_a, not\_b\})$ is not conservative with it (viz., not_a is an hypothesis of the latter while a belongs to the model of the former). We can therefore observe that $\{a, not\_b\}(\{not\_b\})$ is the only complete model for P. ◇

Notably these complete models have a tight relation with other models proposed in the literature. In the case of normal programs, complete models have been shown in [9] to correspond to:

- stable models semantics [23],
- well-founded semantics [41],
- stationary semantics [38], and
- preferential semantics [17].

For instance, in [9], it is shown that:

Let P be a normal program and let $M \subseteq \mathcal{B}$. Then M is a stable model of P if and only if $M \cup \{not\_A \mid A \notin M\}$ is a total complete model for P. (An interpretation M is total iff for each $A \in \mathcal{B}$: $A \in M$ or $not\_A \in M$.)

Similar correspondences are established with well-founded models [41], with stationary expansions [38], and with complete scenaria [17].

These correspondences can be equivalently described in the following way. For each semantics S considered, there exists a suitable *projection* function ψ_S which, given the set of supported interpretations $SI(P^+, not\_B)$ of (the positive version of) a program P, yields the models $\mathcal{S}(P)$ of the corresponding semantics $\mathcal{S}$

$$\psi_{\mathcal{S}} : SI(P^+, not\_B) \to \mathcal{S}(P).$$

In terms of program equivalence, this means that the supported interpretations semantics preserves all the semantics which have been considered in [9]. Indeed for any such semantics $\mathcal{S}$:

$$P^+ \equiv_{SI(not\_B)} Q^+ \implies P \equiv_{\mathcal{S}} Q.$$

4.3   Compositionality

As the supported interpretations semantics preserves many different meanings of programs, the compositionality of the induced equivalence relation $\equiv_{SI(not\_B)}$ would be of major importance. Indeed it would allow the substitution of parts of normal programs without affecting the meaning of the whole program, for *any* meaning considered.

Unfortunately, the equivalence relation $\equiv_{SI(not\_B)}$ is not a congruence w.r.t. the union of programs.

Example 14. Consider for instance the program

$$P$$
$$a \leftarrow b$$

and let Q be the empty program. While $P \equiv_{SI(not\_B)} Q$ there exists a program R such that $P \cup R \not\equiv_{SI(not\_B)} Q \cup R$. For instance, consider the program

$$R$$
$$b \leftarrow not\ c$$

It is easy to see that $SI(P \cup R, not\_B) \neq SI(Q \cup R, not\_B)$ since the supported interpretations $\{a, b, not\_c\}(\{not\_c\})$ belongs to the former and not the latter. $\Diamond$

By exploiting Proposition 4 it is however possible to establish a compositionality result for normal programs. Indeed since $not\_B \subset B^+$ we have that:

$$\equiv_{SI(B^+)}\ \subseteq\ \equiv_{SI(not\_B)}$$

and by the compositionality of logical equivalence we obtain the following result.

Proposition 5. $\equiv_{SI(B^+)}$ *is compositional for* $(\equiv_{SI(not\_B)}, \{\cup\})$.

Since the supported interpretations equivalence relation $\equiv_{SI(not\_B)}$ preserves all the semantics for normal programs considered in [9], we have that if (the positive versions of) two programs are logically equivalent then they have the same meaning $\mathcal{S}$ for each $\mathcal{S}$ considered in [9], that is they have the same complete scenaria [17], the same stationary expansions [38], the same stable models [23], and the same well-founded model [41].

Corollary 1. $\equiv_{SI(B^+)}$ *is compositional for* $(\equiv_{\mathcal{S}}, \{\cup\})$*, for all $\mathcal{S}$ considered in [9].*

4.4   Full Abstraction

The compositionality of logical equivalence for $(\equiv_{SI(not\_B)}, \{\cup\})$ states that *if* (the positive version of) two programs R and R' are logically equivalent then they can be exchanged with one another without affecting the meaning S of the context in which they occur.

An intriguing question is whether or not this is the largest class of programs which can be substituted one another without affecting the intended meaning S of the context in which they occur.

As the equivalence relation $\equiv_{SI(not\_B)}$ preserves several semantics for normal programs, it is interesting to determine whether logical equivalence is fully abstract for $(\equiv_{SI(not\_B)}, \{\cup\})$. This is exactly what we establish here for the first time with the following proposition.

Proposition 6. $\equiv_{SI(B+)}$ *is fully abstract for* $(\equiv_{SI(not\_B)}, \{\cup\})$.

It is worth noting that the above result states that logical equivalence defines the largest class of programs which can be substituted one another without affecting the set of negatively supported interpretations of the context in which they occur. The full abstraction result is hence relative to the equivalence relation $\equiv_{SI(not\_B)}$, and its importance is due to the fact that $\equiv_{SI(not\_B)}$ preserves a number of different intended semantics for normal programs. On the other hand, Proposition 6 does not imply that logical equivalence is fully abstract for every intended meaning of normal programs. For instance, an equivalence relation coarser than logical equivalence (of the positive versions) may be fully abstract for the stable model semantics of normal programs.

4.5   Summary

In the previous sections, we have discussed the issue of compositionality for the case of normal logic programs. As we observed at the beginning of Section 4, the two main problems of designing of a tour for analyzing compositionality issues in normal logic programs were:

(1) the existence of many different semantics for normal programs (no universal agreement on the intended meaning of a normal program, as it happens instead for the case for definite programs), and

(2) the orthogonality of negation and compositionality (existing semantics for normal programs are typically not compositional).

Following the steps of [9], we have observed that supported interpretations provide a unifying model-theoretic characterizations of a number of semantics for normal programs. The idea is to consider the positive version of programs and to take not_B as the universe of assumable hypotheses. The induced equivalence relation $\equiv_{SI(not\_B)}$ then preserves the stable models semantics [23], the well-founded semantics [41], the preferential semantics [17], and the stationary semantics [38]. While $\equiv_{SI(not\_B)}$ is not a congruence for the union of programs, the equivalence relation $\equiv_{SI(B+)}$ is compositional for $(\equiv_{SI(not\_B)}, \{\cup\})$, and hence $\equiv_{SI(\mathcal{B}^+)}$ is compositional for $(\equiv_{\mathcal{S}_i}, \{\cup\})$, for each semantics $\mathcal{S}_i$ preserved by $\equiv_{SI(not\_\mathcal{B})}$. Finally, as a new result, we have shown that $\equiv_{SI(\mathcal{B}^+)}$ is the fully abstract equivalence relation for $(\equiv_{SI(not\_\mathcal{B})}, \{\cup\})$. The relations between the semantics considered in this section are summarised in Figure 3.

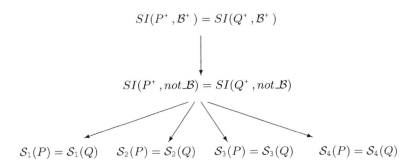

$$SI(P^+, \mathcal{B}^+) = SI(Q^+, \mathcal{B}^+)$$

$$SI(P^+, not\_\mathcal{B}) = SI(Q^+, not\_\mathcal{B})$$

$$\mathcal{S}_1(P) = \mathcal{S}_1(Q) \quad \mathcal{S}_2(P) = \mathcal{S}_2(Q) \quad \mathcal{S}_3(P) = \mathcal{S}_3(Q) \quad \mathcal{S}_4(P) = \mathcal{S}_4(Q)$$

Fig. 3. The equivalence hierarchy for normal programs, where $\mathcal{S}_1$—$\mathcal{S}_4$ are the semantics for normal programs considered in [9].

It is worth observing that the notion of supported interpretation can be exploited to provide a compositional characterization of other extensions of logic programming, besides negation-by-default. Two main classes of extensions of logic programming are considered in [9]:

 – *Other forms of negation* — such as explicit negation [34], answer set semantics [24], and 3-valued stable semantics [37];
 – *Abduction* — as modeled for instance in [16] and in [26].

As shown in [9], all these extensions can be provided with a uniform characterization by means of supported interpretations by considering different universes of assumable hypotheses. Lack of space forces us to invite the reader to refer to [9] for more details.

Several other efforts have been devoted to investigate the composition of normal logic programs.

The *splitting* of a logic program into parts was investigated in [28] in the context of the answer set semantics [24]. The basic idea is that, in many cases, a program can be divided into a "bottom" part and a "top" part, such that the former does not refer to predicates defined in the latter. In [28] it is shown that computing the answer sets for a program can be simplified when the program is split into parts. It is also shown that the idea of splitting can be applied for proving properties of simple program compositions, like a conservative extension property for a program P extended by rules whose heads do not occur in P.

The problem of defining compositional semantics for normal logic programs was studied in [20] and in [42]. [20] defines a compositional semantics for normal programs by means of a first-order unfolding operator. Such a semantics is applied for composing "open" normal programs by considering the union of programs as the only composition operation. [42] presents several results on the compositionality of normal logic programs by generalising the well-founded semantics of logic programming. More precisely, they identify some conditions under which the class of extended well-founded models of the union of two normal programs coincides with the intersection of the classes of extended well-founded models of the two programs. Another difference between the approaches presented in [20,42] and ours is the restrictive naming policy imposed on the predicate names of the programs to be composed. Namely, in contrast with our naming policy, predicate definitions cannot be spread over different programs.

An even more restrictive naming policy is considered in [13] for defining a compositional model-theory for definite and disjunctive programs. The author investigates the usability of minimal logic for modeling the meaning of extended logic programs by allowing "local" inconsistencies. The compositionality results are however restricted to pairs of programs which define disjoint sets of predicates and which do not interact with each other.

A compositional semantics for normal programs was also defined in [8], where a family of program composition operations is considered. The semantics of programs and program compositions is defined in terms of three-valued logic by extending the three-valued immediate consequence operator for logic programs proposed in [21].

Finally, a related work is [5], where a set of operations for composing logic programs are studied in the context of *intensional negation*. Negation is handled in a constructive way by transforming normal programs into pairs of definite programs and by defining the composition operations on such pairs.

5   Other Forms of Program Compositions

5.1   Program Extension

The operation of union between programs can be employed to combine programs that fully cooperate in the deduction process. Namely one program may exploit partial conclusions of the other, and vice-versa.

Such a symmetric composition-by-union is not however the only form of program composition employed in program development. For instance, programs often import the functionalities of some existing module or library, where the latter does not in turn rely on the former for its computation [28].

A typical example comes from deductive databases, where a set of (recursive) rules R is composed with an extensional database D defining the values of a set of relations and typically consisting of extensional clauses. An intriguing question is when R can be substituted with a different, possibly more efficient, set of rules R' without affecting the meaning of the whole system.

Let us then consider here this form of program composition, that we call *program extension* to distinguish it from the composition-by-union considered in the previous sections. Formally, rather than considering arbitrary expressions of the form:

$$Exp \; ::== \; P \; | \; Exp \cup Exp$$

where P is a definite program, we now consider restricted compositions of the form:

$$Exp \; ::== \; P \; | \; Exp \cup_\pi D$$

where D is an *extension*, that is, an extensional program consisting of unit clauses only. We may also assume that the predicates defined by extensions are all members of a pre-fixed set of predicates π. The symbol $\cup_\pi$ is hence both to record the set π and to distinguish program extension from the general composition-by-union considered in the previous sections. According to the above syntax, we therefore consider expressions of the form:

$$P, \quad P \cup_\pi D_1, \quad (P \cup_\pi D_1) \cup_\pi D_2, \quad ((P \cup_\pi D_1) \cup_\pi D_2) \cup_\pi D_3, \quad \ldots$$

and so on and so forth. Notice that instead of introducing the new symbol $\cup_\pi$ we may simply consider the union operation $\cup$ as a partial composition function which is defined only when its second argument is an extension.

We now show that supported interpretations can be naturally employed to obtain a compositional denotation of programs also for this new form of composition-by-extension. Consider as the set of assumable hypotheses the following set:

$$\mathcal{B}_\pi \; = \; \{A \mid A \in \mathcal{B} \wedge pred(A) \in \pi\}.$$

where $pred(A)$ denotes the predicate symbol of the atom A. Namely $\mathcal{B}_\pi$ is the set of atoms in the Herbrand base with predicates in the set π. The corresponding set of supported interpretations therefore is:

$$SI(P, \mathcal{B}_\pi) \; = \; \{I(H) \mid H \subseteq \mathcal{B}_\pi \wedge I = LHM(P \cup H)\}$$

and the induced equivalence relation is:

$$P \equiv_{SI(\mathcal{B}_\pi)} Q \quad \Longleftrightarrow \quad SI(P, \mathcal{B}_\pi) = SI(Q, \mathcal{B}_\pi).$$

We observe that the equivalence relation $\equiv_{SI(\mathcal{B}_\pi)}$ is strictly coarser than $\equiv_{SI(\mathcal{B})}$ and strictly finer than $\equiv_{LHM}$.

Proposition 7. $\equiv_{SI(\mathcal{B})} \subset \equiv_{SI(\mathcal{B}_\pi)} \subset \equiv_{LHM}.$

Moreover, the equivalence relation $\equiv_{SI(\mathcal{B}_\pi)}$ is compositional for $(\mathcal{O}, \{\cup_\pi\})$, as stated by the following proposition.

Proposition 8. $\equiv_{SI(\mathcal{B}_\pi)}$ *is compositional w.r.t* $(\mathcal{O}, \{\cup_\pi\}).$

It is perhaps even more interesting to observe that supported interpretations can be employed to define a compositional characterisation of program extension also in the case of *normal* programs.

Indeed, consider expressions of the form:

$$Exp ::= P \mid Exp \cup_\pi D$$

where P is a normal program and D is an extension, that is, an extensional program consisting of unit clauses only.

Then we simply consider as the set of assumable hypotheses the set:

$$\mathcal{B}_\pi \cup not\_\mathcal{B}$$

The corresponding set of supported interpretations therefore is:

$$SI(P, \mathcal{B}_\pi \cup not\_\mathcal{B}) = \{I(H) \mid H \subseteq (\mathcal{B}_\pi \cup not\_\mathcal{B}) \wedge I = LHM(P \cup H)\}$$

and the induced equivalence relation is:

$$P \equiv_{SI(\mathcal{B}_\pi \cup not\_\mathcal{B})} Q \iff SI(P, \mathcal{B}_\pi \cup not\_\mathcal{B}) = SI(Q, \mathcal{B}_\pi \cup not\_\mathcal{B}).$$

It is easy to observe that $\equiv_{SI(\mathcal{B}_\pi \cup not\_\mathcal{B})}$ is strictly coarser than $\equiv_{SI(\mathcal{B}+)}$ and strictly finer than $\equiv_{SI(not\_\mathcal{B})}$.

Proposition 9. $\equiv_{SI(\mathcal{B}+)} \subseteq \equiv_{SI(\mathcal{B}_\pi \cup not\_\mathcal{B})} \subseteq \equiv_{SI(not\_\mathcal{B})}$.

Moreover the equivalence relation $\equiv_{SI(\mathcal{B}_\pi \cup not\_\mathcal{B})}$ is compositional for $(\equiv_{SI(not\_\mathcal{B})}, \{\cup_\pi\})$, as proved by the following proposition.

Proposition 10. $\equiv_{SI(\mathcal{B}_\pi \cup not\_HB)}$ *is compositional for* $(\equiv_{SI(not\_\mathcal{B})}, \{\cup_\pi\})$.

5.2   A Family of Program Composition Operations

A family of program composition operations has been studied in [7]. Besides the union operation, other three main composition operations have been considered: *intersection* ($\cap$), *encapsulation* ($*$), and *import* ($\triangleleft$). These operations are defined in a semantics-driven style, following the observation that if the meaning of a program P is denoted by the corresponding immediate consequence operator $T(P)$, then such a meaning is a homomorphism for several interesting operations on programs. The formal semantics of the operations is defined as follows:

$$T(P \cap Q)(I) = T(P)(I) \cap T(Q)(I)$$
$$T(P^*)(I) = T^\omega(P)(\emptyset)$$
$$T(P \triangleleft Q)(I) = T(P)(I \cup T^\omega(Q)(\emptyset))$$

Such a set of basic composition operations forms an algebra of logic programs with interesting properties for reasoning about programs and program compositions. From a programming perspective, the operations enhance the expressive power of logic programming by supporting a wealth of programming techniques, ranging from software engineering to artificial intelligence applications.

A thorough discussion of the family of composition operations is outside the scope of the present paper. It is however worth mentioning here that [12] showed that the chain of equivalence relations $\equiv_T \subset \equiv_{T+Id} \subset \equiv_M \subset \equiv_{LHM}$ (see Figure 2) coincides with the chain of fully abstract compositional equivalence relations for subsets of a family of program composition operations, as summarized in Figure 4.

	$\{*, \cup, \cap, \lhd\}$	$\{*, \cup, \cap\}$	$\{*, \cup\}$	$\{*\}$
$\equiv_T$	FAC	C	C	C
$\equiv_{T+Id}$	-	FAC	C	C
$\equiv_M$	-	-	FAC	C
$\equiv_{LHM}$	-	-	-	FAC

Fig. 4. The chain of fully abstract compositional equivalence relations. ("C" stands for compositional, "FAC" for fully abstract and compositional, while "-" stands for non-compositional.)

6   Concluding Remarks

As we already mentioned in the Introduction, our analysis of compositional semantics for logic programs was not intended to be exhaustive, in the sense of analysing all the (many) different proposals that have been developed over the last ten years.

We have rather tried to guide the reader across different compositional semantics for logic programs by highlighting the existing relations among them, and by establishing new relations and results on our way.

During our tour, the notion of supported interpretation has been shown to provide a general and unifying mechanism for obtaining compositional denotations of both definite and normal programs, also in the case of asymmetric compositions.

Acknowledgements

I would like to thank here all the persons with whom I have had the pleasure of sharing many stimulating discussions on these topics. In particular, I would like to thank Simone Contiero, Evelina Lamma, Paolo Mancarella, Paola Mello, Dino Pedreschi, and Franco Turini, with whom I have had the pleasure of working together for many years.

References

1. K. Apt, M. Gabbrielli, and D. Pedreschi. A closer look to declarative interpretations. *Journal of Logic Programming*, 28(2):147–180, 1996.

2. K. R. Apt. Logic programming. In J. van Leeuwen, editor, *Handbook of Theoretical Computer Science*, pages 493–574. Elsevier, 1990. Vol. B.

3. K. R. Apt and R. Bol. Logic Programming and Negation: A Survey. *Journal of Logic Programming*, 19-20:9–71, 1994.

4. C. Baral and M. Gelfond. Logic programming and knowledge representation. *Journal of Logic Programming*, 19-20:73–148, 1994.

5. R. Barbuti, P. Mancarella, D. Pedreschi, and F. Turini. A Transformational Approach to Negation in Logic Programming. *Journal of Logic Programming*, 8:201–228, 1990.

6. A. Bossi, M. Gabbrielli, G. Levi, and M. Martelli. The s-semantics approach: Theory and applications. *Journal of Logic Programming*, 19-20:149–197, 1994.

7. A. Brogi. *Program Construction in Computational Logic*. PhD thesis, Department of Computer Science, University of Pisa, 1993.

8. A. Brogi, S. Contiero, and F. Turini. Programming by composing general logic programs. *Journal of Logic and Computation*, 9(1):7–24, 1999.

9. A. Brogi, E. Lamma, P. Mancarella, and P. Mello. A unifying view for logic programming with non-monotonic reasoning. *Theoretical Computer Science*, 184(1):1–59, 1997.

10. A. Brogi, E. Lamma, and P. Mello. Compositional Model-theoretic Semantics for Logic Programs. *New Generation Computing*, 11(1):1–21, 1992.

11. A. Brogi, P. Mancarella, D. Pedreschi, and F. Turini. Composition Operators for Logic Theories. In J.W. Lloyd, editor, *Computational Logic, Symposium Proceedings*, pages 117–134. Springer-Verlag, 1990.

12. A. Brogi and F. Turini. Fully abstract compositional semantics for an algebra of logic programs. *Theoretical Computer Science*, 149(2):201–229, 1995.

13. F. Bry. A Compositional Semantics for Logic Programs and Deductive Databases. In M. Maher, editor, *Proc. of the Joint International Conference and Symposium on Logic Programming*, pages 453–467, 1996.

14. M. Bugliesi, E. Lamma, and P. Mello. Modularity in logic programming. *Journal of Logic Programming*, 19,20:443–502, 1994.

15. K. Clark. Negation as failure. In H. Gallaire and J. Minker, editors, *Logic and Data Bases*, pages 293–322. Plenum, 1978.

16. C.V. Damasio and L.M. Pereira. Abduction over 3-valued extended logic programs. In *Proc. 3rd Int. Workshop on Logic Programming and Non Monotonic Reasoning*, pages 29–42. Springer-Verlag, 1995.

17. P.M. Dung. Negation as hypothesis: An abductive foundation for logic programming. In K. Furukawa, editor, *Proc. 8th Int. Conf. on Logic Programming ICLP91*, pages 3–17. The MIT Press, 1991.

18. P.M. Dung and P. Ruamviboonsuk. Well-founded reasoning with classical negation. In *Proc. 1st Int. Workshop on Logic Programming and Non-Monotonic Reasoning*, pages 120–132. The MIT Press, 1991.

19. K. Eshghi and R.A. Kowalski. Abduction compared with negation by failure. In G. Levi and M. Martelli, editors, *Proc. 6th Int. Conf. on Logic Programming ICLP89*, pages 234–254. The MIT Press, 1989.

20. S. Etalle and F. Teusink. A Compositional Semantics for Normal Open Programs. In M. Maher, editor, *JICSLP 96 Proceedings of the Joint International Conference and Symposium on Logic Programming*, pages 468–482, 1996.

21. M. Fitting. A Kriple-Kleene semantics for general logic programs. *Journal of Logic Programming*, 4:295–312, 1985.

22. M. Gabbrielli, G. Levi, and M. C. Meo. Observable behaviors and equivalences of logic programs. *Information and Computation*, pages 1–29, 1995.

23. M. Gelfond and V. Lifschitz. The stable model semantics for logic programming. In R. A. Kowalski and K. A. Bowen, editors, *Proceedings of the Fifth International Conference and Symposium on Logic Programming, Seattle, 1988*, pages 1070–1080. The MIT Press, 1988.

24. M. Gelfond and V. Lifschitz. Logic programs with classical negation. In D.H.D. Warren and P. Szeredi, editors, *Proceedings of the Seventh International Conference and Symposium on Logic Programming*, pages 579–597. The MIT Press, 1990.

25. G. Gottlob and A. Leitsch. On the efficiency of subsumption algorithms. *Journal of the ACM*, 32(2):280–295, 1985.

26. A.C. Kakas and P. Mancarella. Generalized stable models: a semantics for abduction. In *Proceedings of 9th European Conference on Artificial Intelligence ECAI90*, pages 385–391. Pitman Publishing, 1990.

27. J.L. Lassez and M.J. Maher. Closures and fairness in the semantics of logic programming. *Theoretical Computer Science*, 29:167–184, 1984.

28. V. Lifschitz and H. Turner. Splitting a logic program. In P. Van Entenryck, editor, *Proc. 11th International Conference on Logic Programming*, pages 23–37. The MIT Press, 1994.

29. J.W. Lloyd. *Foundations of logic programming*. Springer-Verlag, second edition, 1987.

30. M.J. Maher. Equivalences of logic programs. In J. Minker, editor, *Deductive databases and logic programming*, pages 627–658. Morgan Kaufmann, 1988.

31. P. Mancarella and D. Pedreschi. An algebra of logic programs. In R. A. Kowalski and K. A. Bowen, editors, *Proceedings Fifth International Conference on Logic Programming*, pages 1006–1023. The MIT Press, 1988.

32. R. Milner. Fully abstract models for typed λ-calculi. *Theoretical Computer Science*, 4:1–23, 1977.

33. R. O'Keefe. Towards an algebra for constructing logic programs. In J. Cohen and J. Conery, editors, *Proceedings of IEEE Symposium on Logic Programming*, pages 152–160. IEEE Computer Society Press, 1985.

34. L.M. Pereira and J.J. Alferes. Well founded semantics for logic programs with explicit negation. In *Proc. ECAI92*, pages 102–106. John Wiley and Sons, 1992.

35. A. Pettorossi and M. Proietti. Transformations of logic programs: Foundations and techniques. *Journal of Logic Programming*, 19 & 20:261–320, 1994.

36. G.D. Plotkin. LCF considered as a programming language. *Theoretical Computer Science*, 5:223–256, 1977.

37. T. Przymusinski. Extended stable semantics for normal and disjunctive programs. In D.H.D. Warren and P. Szeredi, editors, *Proceedings of the Seventh International Conference and Symposium on Logic Programming*, pages 459–477. The MIT Press, 1990.

38. T. Przymusinski. Stationary semantics for normal and disjunctive logic programs. In C. Delobel, M. Kifer, and Y. Masunagar, editors, *Proceedings of DOOD'91*. Springer-Verlag, 1991.

39. R. Reiter. On closed world data bases. In H. Gallaire and J. Minker, editors, *Logic and Data Bases*, pages 153–173. Plenum, 1978.

40. M. H. van Emden and R. A. Kowalski. The semantics of predicate logic as a programming language. *Journal of the ACM*, 23(4):733–742, 1976.

41. A. van Gelder, K. Ross, and J. Schlipf. The well-founded semantics for general logic programs. *Journal of the ACM*, 38(3):620–650, 1991.

42. S. Verbaeten, M. Denecker, and D. De Schreye. Compositionality of normal open logic programs. *Journal of Logic Programming*, 41(3):151–183, 2000.

Appendix

This Appendix contains the proofs of the propositions and lemmas stated in the paper. To simplify the proofs, we will sometimes abuse notation and denote with the same symbol, I say, both an interpretation I and the program $\{h \leftarrow | h \in I\}$.

Lemma 1
Let P be a program and let $I \subseteq \mathcal{B}$. Then:

$$I \in M(P) \quad \Longleftrightarrow \quad \exists H \subseteq \mathcal{B} : I = LHM(P \cup H).$$

Proof. (*if part*) If $I = LHM(P \cup H)$ then, by definition of least Herbrand model, $I \in M(P \cup H)$ and, by Observation 1, $I \in M(P)$.
(*only-if part*) We observe that if $I \in M(P)$ then $I = LHM(P \cup I)$. By definition of least Herbrand model and by Observation 1, we have that:
   $LHM(P \cup I) = min \ \{J \mid J \in M(P) \wedge J \in M(I)\}$.
Then since $I \in M(P)$ and since $I = LHM(I)$, we have that: $LHM(P \cup I) = I$.

Lemma 2
Let P and Q be two programs. Then:

$$P \equiv_M Q \quad \Longleftrightarrow \quad \forall H \subseteq \mathcal{B} : LHM(P \cup H) = LHM(Q \cup H)$$

Proof. (*if part*) If $I \in M(P)$ then by Lemma 1 there exists $H \subseteq \mathcal{B} : I = LHM(P \cup H)$. By hypothesis this implies that $I = LHM(Q \cup H)$ and hence, by Lemma 1, that $I \in M(Q)$.
(*only-if part*) By definition of least Herbrand model and by Observation 1:
   $LHM(P \cup H) = min\{I \mid I \in M(P) \wedge I \in M(H)\}$.
Hence, since $M(P) = M(Q)$ by hypothesis, we have that $LHM(P \cup H) = LHM(Q \cup H)$ for any $H \subseteq \mathcal{B}$.

We now introduce the following two lemmas, which will be used in the proofs of Propositions 1 and 2, respectively.

Lemma 3. *Let P be a program, let $K \subset H \subseteq \mathcal{B}$. Then:*

$$LHM(P \cup H) - LHM(P \cup K) \supset H - K \quad \Longleftrightarrow \quad H \cap (LHM(P \cup K) - K) = \emptyset.$$

Proof. (*if* part) Suppose that $LHM(P \cup H) - LHM(P \cup K) \not\supset H - K$, that is, suppose that there exists x such that: $x \in (H - K) \wedge x \notin (LHM(P \cup H) - LHM(P \cup K))$. Since $H \subseteq LHM(P \cup H)$ this means that: $x \in (H - K) \wedge x \in LHM(P \cup K)$. Hence we have that there exists x: $x \in (H \cap (LHM(P \cup K) - K))$. Contradiction.
(*only-if* part) Suppose that there exists x such that: $x \in H \wedge x \in LHM(P \cup K) \wedge x \notin K$. Then: $x \in (H - K) \wedge x \notin (LHM(P \cup H) - LHM(P \cup K))$. Contradiction.

Lemma 4. *Let P and Q be definite programs. Then:*

$$LHM(P \cup Q) \supseteq LHM(P) \cup LHM(Q).$$

Proof. This corollary descends immediately from Observation 1. For instance: $LHM(P \cup Q) = min\{I \mid I \in M(P \cup Q)\} = min\{I \mid I \in M(P) \wedge I \in M(Q)\} \supseteq min\{I \mid I \in M(P)\} = LHM(P)$.

Proposition 1
Let P be a program, let $I \subseteq \mathcal{B}$ and let $H \subseteq \mathcal{B}$.

$$I(H) \in AM(P) \implies \exists K, J : (K \subseteq H \wedge J(K) \in \mu AM(P) \wedge I = J \cup (H - K)).$$

Proof. (case a) If $I(H) \in \mu AM(P)$ then the assertion trivially holds (just take $K = H$).

(case b) If $I(H) \notin \mu AM(P)$ then, by definition of minimal admissible model:
$\quad \exists K \subset H : LHM(P \cup H) - LHM(P \cup K) \not\supseteq H - K$.
By Lemma 3, this means that:
$\quad \exists K \subset H : H \cap (LHM(P \cup K) - K) \neq \emptyset$
Let $x \in H \cap (LHM(P \cup K) - K)$. We now show that:
$\quad LHM(P \cup H) = LHM(P \cup H - \{x\}) \cup \{x\}$.
Since $x \in LHM(P \cup K)$ then by Observation 1 we have that $x \in LHM(P \cup K \cup \Delta)$ for any $\Delta \subseteq \mathcal{B}$. Therefore we have that $x \in LHM(P \cup K \cup (H - \{x\}))$, that is, since $x \notin K$, $x \in LHM(P \cup (H - \{x\}))$. Now if $x \in LHM(P \cup (H - \{x\}))$ then $LHM(P \cup H) = LHM(P \cup H - \{x\})$ and hence $LHM(P \cup H) = LHM(P \cup H - \{x\}) \cup \{x\}$.

Let now $J = LHM(P \cup H - \{x\})$. If $J(H - \{x\}) \in \mu AM(P)$ then the statement is proved. Otherwise we repeatedly apply the reasoning of (case b) to obtain a decreasing chain of sets of hypotheses $K_0 \supset K_1 \supset K_2 \supset \dots$ where $K_0 = H$ and where for each K_i:
    - $J_i(K_i) \in AM(P)$, where $J_i = LHM(P \cup K_i)$, and
    - $J_i = J_{i+1} \cup (K_i - K_{i+1})$.
Such a chain has a greatest lower bound $\overline{K} = \bigcap_i K_i$ such that $\overline{J}(\overline{K}) \in \mu AM(P)$, in the worst case $\overline{K}$ being the empty set. We therefore have that: $LHM(P \cup H) = LHM(P \cup \overline{K}) \cup (H - \overline{K})$.

Proposition 2
$\equiv_M = \equiv_{\mu AM}$.

Proof. ($\subseteq$) We first show that:
$\quad P \equiv_M Q \implies P \equiv_{\mu AM} Q$.
    Suppose that:
$\quad \exists P, Q : P \equiv_M Q \wedge P \not\equiv_{\mu AM} Q$,
    namely
$\quad \exists I, H : I(H) \in \mu AM(P) \wedge I(H) \notin \mu AM(Q)$.
(The other case is analogous.)

(i) Suppose that $H \subseteq AH(Q)$. Since $I(H) \in \mu AM(P)$ then:
$$\forall K \subset H: \ LHM(P \cup H) - LHM(P \cup K) \supset H - K.$$
Since $P \equiv_M Q$ then, by Lemma 2:
$$\forall K \subset H: \ LHM(Q \cup H) - LHM(Q \cup K) \supset H - K.$$
Therefore we have that $I(H) \in \mu AM(Q)$. Contradiction.

(ii) Suppose that $H \nsubseteq AH(Q)$.
Then $\exists n: \ n \in H \wedge n \notin AH(Q)$. Let $K = H - \{n\}$.
- If $n \in LHM(Q \cup K)$ then
$$LHM(Q \cup K \cup \{n\}) = LHM(Q \cup K),$$
that is,
$$LHM(Q \cup H) = LHM(Q \cup K).$$
Therefore, since $P \equiv_M Q$, by Lemma 2:
$$\exists K \subset H : LHM(P \cup H) - LHM(P \cup K) = \emptyset.$$
Therefore $I(H) \notin \mu AM(P)$. Contradiction.
- Suppose instead that $n \notin LHM(Q \cup K)$. Since $n \notin AH(Q)$:
$$LHM(Q \cup H) = LHM(Q \cup K) \cup \{n\}.$$
Then, since $n \notin LHM(Q \cup K)$:
$$LHM(Q \cup H) - LHM(Q \cup K) = \{n\}.$$
Therefore since $P \equiv_M Q$ and by Lemma 2:
$$\exists K \subset H : LHM(P \cup H) - LHM(P \cup K) \not\supset H - K.$$
Hence $I(H) \notin \mu AM(P)$. Contradiction.

($\supseteq$) We now show that:
$$P \equiv_{\mu AM} Q \Longrightarrow P \equiv_M Q.$$
Suppose that:
$$\exists P, Q: \ P \equiv_{\mu AM} Q \ \wedge \ P \not\equiv_M Q$$
that is:
$$\exists I: \ I \in M(P) \ \wedge \ I \notin M(Q).$$
(The other case is analogous.)
Observe that
$$LHM(P \cup I) = I$$
since, by Observation 1, $LHM(P \cup I) = min\{J \mid J \in M(P) \wedge J \in M(I)\}$
and since $I = LHM(I)$ and $I \in M(P)$. Moreover:
$$LHM(Q \cup I) \supset I$$
since, by Observation 1, if $J \in M(Q \cup I)$ then $J \supseteq I$ and since $I \notin M(Q)$.
Let now $I_{AQ} = I \cap AH(Q)$ and let $I_{NQ} = I - I_{AQ}$. Then:
$$LHM(Q \cup I) = LHM(Q \cup I_{AQ}) \cup I_{NQ}.$$
Since, by Lemma 4:
$$I = LHM(P \cup I) \supseteq LHM(P \cup I_{AQ}) \cup LHM(I_{NQ}) = LHM(P \cup I_{AQ}) \cup I_{NQ}$$
we observe that:
$$LHM(P \cup I_{AQ}) \subseteq I \text{ and } I_{NQ} \subseteq I.$$
Therefore, since $LHM(Q \cup I) \supset I$ and $LHM(Q \cup I) = LHM(Q \cup I_{AQ}) \cup I_{NQ}$
and $I_{NQ} \subseteq I$, we observe that:
$$LHM(Q \cup I_{AQ}) \nsubseteq I.$$
Consider now $N = LHM(Q \cup I_{AQ})$. Since $N(I_{AQ}) \in AM(Q)$ then, by
Proposition 1, $\exists K, J$:

$K \subseteq I_{AQ} \ \wedge \ J(K) \in \mu AM(Q) \ \wedge \ LHM(Q \cup I_{AQ}) = LHM(Q \cup K) \cup (I_{AQ} - K)$.

Since $LHM(Q \cup I_{AQ}) \not\subseteq I$ and since $I_{AQ} \subseteq I$, this implies that:

$LHM(Q \cup K) \not\subseteq I$.

Since $J(K) \in \mu AM(Q)$ and since $P \equiv_{\mu AM} Q$ then $J(K) \in \mu AM(P)$ and hence:

$LHM(P \cup K) \not\subseteq I$.

On the other hand, since $K \subseteq I_{AQ}$:

$I \supseteq LHM(P \cup I_{AQ}) \cup I_{NQ} \supseteq LHM(P \cup I_{AQ}) \supseteq LHM(P \cup K)$.

Contradiction.

Proposition 3

$\equiv_M \ = \ \equiv_{SI(\mathcal{B})}$.

Proof. ($\subseteq$) If $P \equiv_M Q$ then, by Lemma 2:

$\forall H \subseteq \mathcal{B} : LHM(P \cup H) = LHM(Q \cup H)$.

Hence:

$\{I(H) \mid H \subseteq \mathcal{B} \wedge I = LHM(P \cup H)\} \ = \ \{I(H) \mid H \subseteq \mathcal{B} \wedge I = LHM(Q \cup H)\}$

that is:

$P \equiv_{SI(\mathcal{B})} Q$.

($\supseteq$) By Lemma 1, if $I \in M(P)$ then $\exists H : I(H) \in SI(P)$. Since $SI(P) = SI(Q)$ by hypothesis, then $I(H) \in SI(Q)$ and hence $I \in M(Q)$ by Lemma 1.

Proposition 4

Let $\mathcal{H} \subseteq \mathcal{B}$, $\mathcal{K} \subseteq \mathcal{B}$ be two sets of assumable hypotheses. Then:

(1) $\mathcal{H} \subseteq \mathcal{K} \ \Longrightarrow \ \equiv_{SI(\mathcal{K})} \ \subseteq \ \equiv_{SI(\mathcal{H})}$
(2) $\mathcal{H} \subset \mathcal{K} \ \Longrightarrow \ \equiv_{SI(\mathcal{K})} \ \subset \ \equiv_{SI(\mathcal{H})}$

Proof. (1) We show that if $\mathcal{H} \subseteq \mathcal{K}$ then $(P \equiv_{SI(\mathcal{K})} Q \ \Longrightarrow \ P \equiv_{SI(\mathcal{H})} Q)$. Indeed if $I(H)$ belongs to the set $SI(P, \mathcal{H})$ then it also belongs to $SI(P, \mathcal{K})$ since $\mathcal{H} \subseteq \mathcal{K}$. Since $P \equiv_{SI(\mathcal{K})} Q$ by hypothesis, $I(H)$ also belongs to $SI(Q, \mathcal{K})$, as well as to $SI(Q, \mathcal{H})$ since $\mathcal{H} \subseteq \mathcal{K}$.

(2) We now show that if $\mathcal{H} \subset \mathcal{K}$ then $\equiv_{SI(\mathcal{K})} \subset \equiv_{SI(\mathcal{H})}$. Since we know from (1) that $\equiv_{SI(\mathcal{K})} \subseteq \equiv_{SI(\mathcal{H})}$, we just have to show that there exist two programs P and Q such that $P \not\equiv_{SI(\mathcal{K})} Q$ and $P \equiv_{SI(\mathcal{H})} Q$.

Let $b \in \mathcal{K}$ and $b \notin \mathcal{H}$. Consider the program

$$P$$
$$a \leftarrow b$$

and let Q be the empty program. It is easy to see that $P \equiv_{SI(\mathcal{H})} Q$ since:

$SI(P, \mathcal{H}) = SI(Q, \mathcal{H}) = \{I(I) \mid I \subseteq \mathcal{H}\}$.

On the other hand $P \not\equiv_{SI(\mathcal{K})} Q$ since $\{a, b\}(\{b\}) \in SI(P, \mathcal{K})$ while $\{a, b\}(\{b\}) \notin SI(Q, \mathcal{K})$.

Proposition 5

$\equiv_{SI(\mathcal{B}+)}$ *is compositional for* $(\equiv_{SI(not\_\mathcal{B})}, \{\cup\})$.

Proof. Since $not\_\mathcal{B} \subset \mathcal{B}^+$ we have, by Proposition 4, that $\equiv_{SI(\mathcal{B}+)} \subseteq \equiv_{SI(not\_\mathcal{B})}$, that is $\equiv_{SI(\mathcal{B}+)}$ preserves $\equiv_{SI(not\_\mathcal{B})}$.

Moreover $\equiv_{SI(\mathcal{B}+)}$ is a congruence for $\{\cup\}$ since $\equiv_M$ is a congruence for $\{\cup\}$ and since $\equiv_M = \equiv_{SI(\mathcal{B}+)}$ by Proposition 3.

Proposition 6

$\equiv_{SI(\mathcal{B}+)}$ *is fully abstract for* $(\equiv_{SI(not\_\mathcal{B})}, \{\cup\})$.

Proof. By counter-positive, we show that if $P \not\equiv_{SI(\mathcal{B}+)} Q$ then there is a context in which the substitution of P with Q does modify the set of negatively supported interpretations. Let P and Q be two programs such that $P \not\equiv_{SI(\mathcal{B}+)} Q$.

(1) We first show that there exists a finite program R such that:
$$LHM(P \cup R) \neq LHM(Q \cup R).$$
Since we are considering positive versions of programs, P and Q are definite programs and hence, by Proposition 3:
$$P \not\equiv_{SI(\mathcal{B}+)} Q \Longrightarrow P \not\equiv_M Q$$
This means that:
$$\exists I \subseteq \mathcal{B}^+ : I \in M(P) \wedge I \notin M(Q).$$
(The other case is analogous.) That is, by definition of Herbrand model:
$$\exists I \subseteq \mathcal{B}^+ : T(P)(I) \subseteq I \wedge T(Q)(I) \not\subseteq I.$$
Therefore, by definition of $T(Q)$:
$$\exists F, A : F \subseteq I \wedge F \text{ finite } \wedge A \in T(Q)(F) \wedge A \notin F.$$
Consider now the program:
$$R = \{B \leftarrow \mid B \in F\}.$$

- We now show that $A \notin LHM(P \cup R)$, that is, $A \notin T^\omega(P \cup R)(\emptyset)$.
  We first show, by induction on n, that:
  $$\forall n : T^n(P \cup R)(\emptyset) \subseteq I.$$
  Indeed $T^0(P \cup R)(\emptyset) = \emptyset$. Assume now that $T^n(P \cup R)(\emptyset) \subseteq I$. By definition of powers of T:
  $$T^{n+1}(P \cup R)(\emptyset) = T(P \cup R)(T^n(P \cup R)(\emptyset)).$$
  By inductive hypothesis and by the monotonicity of T:
  $$T^{n+1}(P \cup R)(\emptyset) \subseteq T(P \cup R)(I).$$
  Then by definition of $\cup$:
  $$T^{n+1}(P \cup R)(\emptyset) \subseteq T(P)(I) \cup T(R)(I).$$
  Since $T(P)(I) \subseteq I$ and since $F \subseteq I$, we then have that:
  $$T^{n+1}(P \cup R)(\emptyset) \subseteq I.$$
  Therefore, by the continuity of T:
  $$T^\omega(P \cup R)(\emptyset) \subseteq I$$
  and hence, since $A \notin I$, we conclude that:
  $$A \notin LHM(P \cup R).$$

- We now show that: $A \in LHM(Q \cup R)$, that is, $A \in T^{\omega}(Q \cup R)(\emptyset)$. Indeed:
  $$A \in T(Q)(F) \subseteq T(Q)(T(R)(\emptyset))$$
  By definition of $\cup$ and by monotonicity of T:
  $$T(Q)(T(R)(\emptyset)) \subseteq T(Q)(T(Q \cup R)(\emptyset)) \subseteq T(Q \cup R)(T(Q \cup R)(\emptyset))$$
  hence
  $$A \in T^2(Q \cup R)(\emptyset) \subseteq T^{\omega}(Q \cup R)(\emptyset)$$
  by continuity of T.

(2) We have therefore shown that if $P \not\equiv_{SI(\mathcal{B}+)} Q$ then
  $$\exists R : \ LHM(P \cup R) \neq LHM(Q \cup R).$$
  Notice that, since we are considering positive versions of programs, R can be a finite program of the form:
  $$R = \{B \leftarrow | \ B \in F\}$$
  where $F \subseteq (\mathcal{B} \cup not\_\mathcal{B})$. Namely R may be a finite program of the form:

  $$R$$
  $$C_1 \leftarrow$$
  $$\ldots$$
  $$C_m \leftarrow$$
  $$not\_D_1 \leftarrow$$
  $$\ldots$$
  $$not\_D_n \leftarrow$$

  Let now $R^+ = \{C \leftarrow | \ C \in F \cap \mathcal{B}\}$ and $R^- = \{not\_D \leftarrow | \ not\_D \in F \cap not\_\mathcal{B}\}$.
  - We now observe that if $LHM(P \cup R^+) \neq LHM(Q \cup R^+)$ then:
    $$\exists I, J : \ I(\emptyset) \in SI(P \cup R^+, not\_\mathcal{B}) \wedge J(\emptyset) \in SI(Q \cup R^+, not\_\mathcal{B}) \wedge I \neq J.$$
    This means that there exists a normal program R^+ such that:
    $$P \cup R^+ \not\equiv_{SI(not\_\mathcal{B})} Q \cup R^+$$
    and hence concludes the proof.
  - If instead $LHM(P \cup R^+) = LHM(Q \cup R^+)$ then, since $LHM(P \cup R) \neq LHM(Q \cup R)$, we observe that:
    $$LHM(P \cup R^+ \cup R^-) \neq LHM(Q \cup R^+ \cup R^-).$$
    Let $F^- = \{not\_D \ | \ not\_D \leftarrow \in R^-\}$. Then:
    $$\exists I, J : \ I(F^-) \in SI(P \cup R^+, not\_\mathcal{B}) \ \wedge \ J(F^-) \in SI(Q \cup R^+, not\_\mathcal{B})$$
    $$\wedge \ I \neq J.$$
    That is, there exists a normal program R^+ such that:
    $$P \cup R^+ \not\equiv_{SI(not\_\mathcal{B})} Q \cup R^+.$$

Proposition 7

$$\equiv_{SI(\mathcal{B})} \ \subset \ \equiv_{SI(\mathcal{B}_\pi)} \ \subset \ \equiv_{LHM}.$$

Proof. By Proposition 4 we know that if $\mathcal{B}_\pi \subset \mathcal{B}$ then $\equiv_{SI(\mathcal{B})} \subset \equiv_{SI(\mathcal{B}_\pi)}$. Moreover if $P \equiv_{SI(\mathcal{B}_\pi)} Q$ then $LHM(P) = LHM(Q)$, that is, $\equiv_{SI(\mathcal{B}_\pi)} \subseteq \equiv_{LHM}$. To show that $\equiv_{SI(\mathcal{B}_\pi)} \neq \equiv_{LHM}$, consider the programs

$$P \qquad\qquad Q$$
$$a \leftarrow b \qquad\quad a \leftarrow c$$

where $\{b, c\} \subseteq \mathcal{B}_\pi$. It is easy to observe that $P \equiv_{LHM} Q$ while $P \not\equiv_{SI(\mathcal{B}_\pi)} Q$ since for instance $\{a, b\}(\{b\}) \in SI(P, \mathcal{B}_\pi) - SI(Q, \mathcal{B}_\pi)$.

Proposition 8

$\equiv_{SI(\mathcal{B}_\pi)}$ is compositional w.r.t $(\mathcal{O}, \{\cup_\pi\})$.

Proof. Indeed $\equiv_{SI(\mathcal{B}_\pi)}$ preserves $\mathcal{O}$ by Prop. 7.

   Moreover $\equiv_{SI(\mathcal{B}_\pi)}$ is a congruence for $\cup_\pi$, namely $\forall P, Q$:
$$P \equiv_{SI(\mathcal{B}_\pi)} Q \implies P \cup_\pi D \equiv_{SI(\mathcal{B}_\pi)} Q \cup_\pi D$$
for any extension D.

   Let $H \subseteq \mathcal{B}_\pi$. We observe that, since both D and H are extensional programs:
$$LHM((P \cup_\pi D) \cup H) = LHM(P \cup_\pi LHM(D \cup H)).$$
Therefore, since $defs(D \cup H) \subseteq \pi$ and since $P \equiv_{SI(\mathcal{B}_\pi)} Q$:
$$LHM(P \cup_\pi LHM(D \cup H)) = LHM(Q \cup_\pi LHM(D \cup H))$$
and hence
$$LHM((P \cup_\pi D) \cup H) = LHM((Q \cup_\pi D) \cup H).$$

Proposition 9

$\equiv_{SI(\mathcal{B}+)} \subset \equiv_{SI(\mathcal{B}_\pi \cup not\_\mathcal{B})} \subset \equiv_{SI(not\_\mathcal{B})}.$

Proof. Immediate by Proposition 4, whenever $\pi \neq \emptyset$ (and $\mathcal{B}_\pi \subset \mathcal{B}$).

Proposition 10

$\equiv_{SI(\mathcal{B}_\pi \cup not\_\mathcal{B})}$ is compositional for $(\equiv_{SI(not\_\mathcal{B})}, \{\cup_\pi\})$.

Proof. The proof is analogous to the proof of Proposition 8.

Analysing Logic Programs by Reasoning Backwards

Jacob M. Howe[1], Andy King[2], and Lunjin Lu[3]

[1] City University, London, EC1V 0HB, UK
jacob@soi.city.ac.uk
[2] University of Kent, Canterbury, CT2 7NF, UK
A.M.King@ukc.ac.uk
[3] Oakland University, Rochester, MI 48309, USA
l2lu@oakland.edu

Abstract. One recent advance in program development has been the application of abstract interpretation to verify the partial correctness of a (constraint) logic program. Traditionally forwards analysis has been applied that starts with an initial goal and traces the execution in the direction of the control-flow to approximate the program state at each program point. This is often enough to verify assertions that a property holds. The dual approach is to apply backwards analysis to propagate properties of the allowable states against the control-flow to infer queries for which the program will not violate any assertion. Backwards analysis also underpins other program development tasks such as verifying the termination of a logic program or proving that a logic program with a delay mechanism cannot reduce to a state that contains sub-goals which suspend indefinitely. This paper reviews various backwards analyses that have been proposed for logic programs, identifying common threads in these techniques. The analyses are explained through a series of worked examples. The paper concludes with some suggestions for research in backwards analysis for logic program development.

1 Introduction

Abstract interpretation has an important rôle in program development and specifically the verification and debugging of (constraint) logic programs, as recently demonstrated in [12,42,57]. In this context, programmers are typically equipped with an annotation language in which they encode properties of the program state at various program points [56,64]. One approach to verification of logic programs is to trace the program state in the direction of control-flow from an initial goal (forwards analysis), using abstract interpretation to finitely represent and track the state. The program is deemed to be correct if all the assertions are satisfied whenever they are encountered during the execution of the program; otherwise the program is potentially buggy. The dual approach is to trace execution against the control-flow (backwards analysis) to infer those queries which ensure that the assertions are satisfied should they be encountered

M. Bruynooghe and K.-K. Lau (Eds.): Program Development in CL, LNCS 3049, pp. 152–188, 2004.
© Springer-Verlag Berlin Heidelberg 2004

[39,44]. If the class of initial queries does not conform to those expected by the programmer, then the program is potentially buggy.

Many program properties cannot be simply verified by checking (an abstraction of) the program store – they are properties of sequences of program states. For example, termination checking of logic programs attempts to verify that a logic program left-terminates for a given query [10,53]. This amounts to checking that sequences of program states are necessarily finite. Suspension analysis of concurrent logic programs [8,11,17] also reasons about sequences of states. It aims to verify that a given state cannot lead to another which possesses a subgoal that suspends indefinitely. These classic analyses are inherently forwards since they trace sequences of states in the direction of control-flow. Nevertheless these forwards analysis problems (and various related analyses) have corresponding backwards analysis problems, tracing requirements against the control-flow (specifying the backwards analysis will be referred to as reversal). The reversal of termination checking is termination inference which infers initial queries under which a logic program left-terminates [24,53]. The reversal of suspension analysis is suspension inference [26] which infers a class of goals that will not lead to suspended (floundering) sub-goals. It has been observed [24] that the "missing link" between termination inference and termination checking is the backwards analysis of [39]. Likewise suspension inference [26] relies on ideas inherited from backwards analysis [39].

The unifying idea behind these various backwards analyses [24,26,39,40,44] is reasoning about reverse information flow. In abstract interpretation, information is represented, albeit in an approximate way, with an abstract domain which is a lattice $\langle D, \trianglelefteq, \oplus, \otimes \rangle$. The ordering $\trianglelefteq$ expresses the relative precision of two domain elements; the join $\oplus$ models the merging of computation paths whereas meet $\otimes$ models the conjunction of constraints. To propagate information against the control-flow, the analyses of [24,26,39,40] (but notably not that of [44]) require the abstract domain D to be relatively pseudo-complemented, that is, the relative pseudo-complement of two domain elements uniquely exists. The pseudo-complement of d_1 relative to d_2, denoted $d_1 \rightarrow d_2$, delivers the weakest element of D whose conjunction with d_1 implies d_2, or more exactly, $d_1 \rightarrow d_2 = \oplus\{d \in D \mid d \otimes d_1 \trianglelefteq d_2\}$. The rôle of relative pseudo-complement is that if d_2 expresses a set of requirements that must hold after a constraint is added to the store, and d_1 models the constraint itself, then $d_1 \rightarrow d_2$ expresses the requirements that must hold on the store before the constraint. Relative pseudo-complement is central to many backwards analyses.

Not all domains come equipped with a relative pseudo-complement, but it turns out that it is always possible to synthesise a domain for backwards analysis for some given downward closed property by applying Heyting completion [30]. Heyting completion enriches a domain with new elements so that the relative pseudo-complement is well-defined. All domains that are condensing possess a relative pseudo-complement. Examples of condensing domains include the class of positive Boolean functions [37,46], the relational type domain of [9], and the domain of directional types [1,30]. The requirement for a domain to be relatively pseudo-complemented is one the major restrictions of backwards analysis. Despite this limitation, backwards analysis still offers two key advantages over forwards analysis for program development problems. These advantages are summarised below:

- Backwards analysis generalises forwards analysis in that a single application of backwards analysis can subsume many applications of a forwards analysis. Another advantage that relates to ease of use is that backwards analysis is not dependent on the programmer (or the module system) for providing a top-level goal. This is because backwards analysis is goal-independent.
- In terms of implementation, backwards analysis strikes a good balance between generality and simplicity. Moreover, backwards analysis does not necessarily incur a performance penalty over forwards analysis.

Both of these two points are multi-faceted and therefore they require some unpacking. Returning to the first point – the issue of generality – forwards analysis is driven from a top-level goal. Forwards analysis then verifies that the goal (and those goals it recursively calls) satisfy a set of requirements. Conversely, backwards analysis infers a class of goals all of which are guaranteed to satisfy the requirements. Under certain algebraic conditions this class is maximal with respect to forwards analysis [40]; it describes all those goals that can be verified with forwards analysis. For example, consider the problem of understanding how to re-use code developed by a third party. In the context of logic programming, part of this problem reduces to figuring out how to query a program. If the logic program does not come with any documentation, then the programmer is forced to experiment with queries in an *ad hoc* fashion. More systematically, forwards analysis could be repeatedly applied to discover queries which are consistent with the called builtins in that the calls do not generate any instantiation errors. By way of contrast the backwards analysis framework when instantiated with a domain for tracking groundness dependencies [37,46] yields an analysis for mode inference which would discover (in a single application) all queries that will not generate any instantiation errors. This recovered mode information then provides valuable insight into behaviour of the program.

Expanding the second point – the issue of implementation – the analyses presented in [26,39,40] reduce to two simple bottom-up fixpoint computations: a least fixpoint (lfp) and a greatest fixpoint (gfp). The lfp and the gfp calculations can be ordered and thus de-coupled. This significantly simplifies the tracking of dependencies which is the main source of complexity in an efficient fixpoint engine. Moreover, although few forwards analyses have been compared experimentally against backwards analyses, the notable exception is in termination inference. In this context, the speed of inference appears to at least match that of checking [24]. In fact the total analysis time for checking and inference can be broken down into *Joint* – the time spent on activities common to both checking and inference and *Inf* and *Check* – the time spent on activities specific to inference and checking respectively. *Joint* dominates both *Inf* and *Check* but *Inf* is typically smaller than *Check* [24]. Therefore the generality of inference does not necessarily incur a performance penalty.

Backwards analysis has been applied extensively in functional programming in, among other things, projection analysis [65], stream strictness analysis [31], inverse image analysis [18]. Furthermore, backwards reasoning on imperative programs dates back to the early days of static analysis [14]. In contrast, backwards analysis has until very recently [19,22,24,26,40,44,49] been rarely applied in logic programming. The aim of this paper is thus to promote the use of backwards analysis especially within the context of logic program development. To this end, the paper explains the key ideas behind backwards analyses for mode inference, termination inference, suspension inference and type inference. These analyses are each described in an informal way through a series of worked examples in sections 2, 3, 4 and 5 respectively. Each of these sections includes its own related work section. Section 6 then reviews directions for future work on backwards analysis for program development and section 7 concludes.

2   Backwards Mode Inference

The objective of backwards analysis is to infer queries for which the program is guaranteed to either not violate any assertion or satisfy some operational requirement. To realise this objective, backwards analyses propagate requirements of the allowable states against the control-flow. This tactic essentially reinterprets the calculation of weakest pre-conditions [35] for logic programming using abstract interpretation techniques. To illustrate these ideas, consider the problem of mode inference [39]. In mode inference, the problem is to deduce moding properties which, if satisfied by the initial query, ensure that the resulting derivations cannot encounter an instantiation error. Instantiation errors arise when a builtin is called with insufficiently instantiated arguments. For example, the Prolog builtins `tab` and `put` require their first (and only) argument to be bound to a ground term otherwise they error. Conversely, the builtin `is` requires its last argument to be ground. Other builtins such as the arithmetic tests `=:=`, `<`, `>`, etc require both arguments to be ground. These grounding requirements can be expressed with the domain of positive Boolean functions, Pos, which is traditionally used to track groundness dependencies [37,46]. Pos is the set of functions $f : \{true, false\}^n \rightarrow \{true, false\}$ such that $f(true, \ldots, true) = true$. For example, $X \wedge (Y \leftarrow Z) \in Pos$ since $true \wedge (true \leftarrow true) = true$. The formula describes states in which X is ground and Y is ground whenever Z is ground. Observe that this grounding property is closed under instantiation: if $X \wedge (Y \leftarrow Z)$ describes the state of the store, then both X and $Y \leftarrow Z$ still hold whenever the store is conjoined with additional constraints. When augmented with $false$, Pos forms the lattice $\langle Pos, \models, \vee, \wedge \rangle$ where $\models$ denotes the entailment ordering, $\wedge$ is logical conjunction and $\vee$ is logical disjunction. The top and bottom elements of the lattice are $true$ and $false$ respectively.

The assertions that are used in mode inference are Pos abstractions that express grounding requirements which ensure that instantiation errors are avoided. Specifically, an assertion is added to the program for each call to a builtin. The assertion itself precedes the call [39]. It is important to appreciate that the assertions only codify sufficient conditions; necessary conditions for the absence of instantiation errors cannot always be expressed within *Pos*. For example, the assertion $X \vee (Y \wedge Z)$ describes states for which the builtin functor(X, Y, Z) will not produce an instantiation error. Observe, however, that the same call will not generate an instantiation error if X is bound to a non-variable (non-ground) term such as [W|Ws], hence $X \vee (Y \wedge Z)$ is not a *necessary* condition for avoiding an instantiation error. Observe too that $X \vee (Y \wedge Z)$ only ensures that the call will not generate an *instantiation* error. For instance, a *domain* error will be thrown whenever functor(X, Y, Z) is called with Z is instantiated to a negative integer. However a richer domain, such as the numeric power domain introduced in [40], could express this positivity requirement on the variable Z. (The subtlety of reasoning about builtins is not confined to backwards analysis. In fact correctly and precisely encoding the behaviour of the builtins is often the most difficult part of any analysis [33,36].)

2.1   Worked Example on Mode Inference

To appreciate how the assertions and lattice operations $\vee$ and $\wedge$ fit together and why the domain is required to be relatively pseudo-complemented, it is helpful to consider a worked example. Thus consider the quicksort program listed in Figure 1 and the problem of computing those queries that avoid instantiation errors. The quicksort program is coded in Prolog and therefore the comma operator denotes sequential (rather than parallel) goal composition. A difference list is used to amortise the cost of appending the two lists produced by the goals qs(L, S, [M | R]) and qs(H, R, T).

```
qs([], S, S) :- true.
qs([M | Xs], S, T) :- pt(Xs, M, L, H), qs(L, S, [M | R]), qs(H, R, T).

pt([], _, [], []) :- true.
pt([X | Xs], M, [X | L], H) :- M ≤ X, pt(Xs, M, L, H).
pt([X | Xs], M, L, [X | H]) :- M > X, pt(Xs, M, L, H).
```

Fig. 1. quicksort program in expressed in Prolog

The backwards analysis consists of two computational steps. The first is a least fixpoint (lfp) calculation and the second is a greatest fixpoint (gfp) computation. The lfp is an analysis on its own right. It infers success patterns that are required for the gfp computation. The success pattern for a given predicate characterises the bindings made by the predicate whenever it succeeds; in this context the success patterns are described as groundness dependencies. Specifically, the lfp is a set of calls paired with groundness dependencies which describe how a call to each predicate in the program can succeed. The gfp is an analysis for input modes (the objective of the backwards analysis). To simplify both steps, the program is put into a form in which the arguments of head and body atoms are distinct variables. This gives the normalised program listed in the first column of Figure 2. To clearly differentiate assertions from the (Herbrand) constraints that occur within the program, the program is expressed in the concurrent constraint style [60] using ask to denote an assertion and tell to indicate a conventional store write. This notation (correctly) suggests that an assertion reads and checks a property of the store. Empty conjunctions of atoms are denoted by true. The process of normalisation does not introduce any assertions and therefore the program in the first column of Figure 2 includes only tell constraints. Note that each clause contains a single tell constraint which appears immediately before the (normalised) atoms that constitute the body of the clause.

After normalisation, the program is abstracted by replacing each tell constraint $x = f(x_1, \ldots, x_n)$ with a formula $x \leftrightarrow \bigwedge_{i=1}^{n} x_i$ that describes its groundness dependencies. This gives the abstract program listed in the second column of Figure 2. Builtins that are called from the program, such as the tests $\leq$ and $>$, are handled by augmenting the abstract program with fresh predicates, $\leq'$ and $>'$, which capture the grounding behaviour of the builtins. Assertions are introduced immediately after the head of these fresh clauses which specify a mode that is sufficient for the builtin not to generate an instantiation error. For example, the ask formula in the $\leq'$ clause asserts that the $\leq$ test will not error if its first two arguments are ground, whereas the tell formula describes the state that holds if the test succeeds. For uniformity, all clauses contain both an ask and a tell. This normal form simplifies the presentation of the theory and well as the structure of the abstract interpretation itself. In practise, the ask of most clauses are true and thus vacuous. In the case of quicksort, the only non-trivial assertions arise from builtins. This would change if the programmer introduced assertions for purposes of verification [56].

2.2   Least Fixpoint Calculation

An iterative algorithm is used to compute the lfp and thereby characterise the success patterns of the program. A success pattern is a pair consisting of an atom with distinct variables for arguments paired with a *Pos* formula over those variables which describes the groundness dependencies between the arguments. Renaming and equality of formulae induce an equivalence between success patterns which is needed to detect the fixpoint. The patterns $\langle p(u, w, v), u \wedge (w \leftrightarrow v) \rangle$ and $\langle p(x_1, x_2, x_3), (x_3 \leftrightarrow x_2) \wedge x_1 \rangle$, for example, are considered to be identical: both express the same inter-argument groundness dependencies. Each iteration produces a set of success patterns: at most one pair for each predicate in the program.

Upper Approximation of Success Patterns   A success pattern records an inter-argument groundness dependency that describes the binding effects of executing a predicate. If $\langle p(x), f \rangle$ correctly describes the predicate p, and g holds whenever f holds, then $\langle p(x), g \rangle$ also correctly describes p. Note that

```
qs(T1, S, T2) :-                      qs(T1, S, T2) :-
    tell(T1 = [], T2 = S),                ask(true),
    true.                                 tell(T1 ∧ (T2 ↔ S),
qs(T1, S, T3) :-                          true.
    tell(T1 = [M|Xs], T3 = [M|R]),    qs(T1, S, T3) :-
    pt(Xs, M, L, H),                      ask(true),
    qs(L, S, T3),                         tell(T1 ↔ (M ∧ Xs) ∧ T3 ↔ (M ∧ R)),
    qs(H, R, T).                          pt(Xs, M, L, H),
                                          qs(L, S, T3),
pt(T1, _, T2, T3) :-                      qs(H, R, T).
    tell(T1=[], T2=[], T3=[]),
    true.                             pt(T1, _, T2, T3) :-
pt(T1, M, T2, H) :-                       ask(true),
    tell(T1 = [X|Xs], T2 = [X|L]),        tell(T1 ∧ T2 ∧ T3),
    M ≤ X,                                true.
    pt(Xs, M, L, H).                  pt(T1, M, T2, H) :-
pt(T1, M, 1, T2) :-                       ask(true),
    tell(T1 = [X|Xs], T2 = [X|H]),        tell(T1 ↔ (X ∧ Xs) ∧ T2 ↔ (X ∧ L)),
    M > X,                                ≤'(M, X),
    pt(Xs, M, L, H).                      pt(Xs, M, L, H).
                                      pt(T1, M, L, T2) :-
                                          ask(true),
                                          tell(T1 ↔ (X ∧ Xs) ∧ T2 ↔ (X ∧ H)),
                                          >'(M, X),
                                          pt(Xs, M, L, H).

                                      ≤'(M, X) :-
                                          ask(M ∧ X), tell(M ∧ X), true.

                                      >'(M, X) :-
                                          ask(M ∧ X), tell(M ∧ X), true.
```

Fig. 2. quicksort program with assertions and as a *Pos* abstraction

here and henceforth x denotes a vector of distinct variables. Success patterns can thus be approximated from *above* without compromising correctness. Iteration is performed in a bottom-up fashion, T_P-style, [28] and commences with $F_0 = \{\langle p(x), false \rangle \mid p \in \Pi\}$ where Π is the set of predicates occurring in the program. F_0 is the bottom element of the lattice of success patterns; the top element is $\{\langle p(x), true \rangle \mid p \in \Pi\}$. F_{j+1} is computed from F_j by considering each clause $p(x) :- \mathsf{ask}(d), \mathsf{tell}(f), p_1(x_1), \ldots, p_n(x_n)$ in turn. It is at this stage that the lattice structure of *Pos* comes into play. Meet (the operator ∧ which is also known as greatest lower bound) provides a way of conjoining information from different body atoms, while join (the operator ∨ which is also known as least upper bound) is used to combine the information from different clauses. More exactly, the success pattern formulae f_i for the n body atoms $p_1(\boldsymbol{x}_1), \ldots, p_n(\boldsymbol{x}_n)$ are conjoined with f to obtain $g = f \wedge (\wedge_{i=1}^n f_i)$. Variables not present in $p(\boldsymbol{x})$, Y say, are then eliminated from g. The Schröder elimination principle provides a way of eliminating a variable from a given formula. It enables a projection operator $\exists_x$ to be defined by $\exists_x(f) = f[x \mapsto true] \vee f[x \mapsto false]$ which eliminates x from f. Since $f \models \exists_x(f)$, computing $g' = \exists_Y(g)$ where $\exists_{\{y_1 \ldots y_n\}}(g) = \exists_{y_1}(\ldots \exists_{y_n}(g))$ weakens g. Weakening g does not compromise correctness because success patterns can be safely approximated from above.

Weakening Upper Approximations The pattern $\langle p(\boldsymbol{x}), g'' \rangle$ where g'' is the current *Pos* abstraction is then replaced with $\langle p(\boldsymbol{x}), g' \vee g'' \rangle$ where g' is computed as above. Thus the success patterns become progressively weaker (or at least not stronger) on each iteration. Again, correctness is preserved because success patterns can be safely approximated from above.

Least Fixpoint Calculation for Quicksort The lfp for the abstracted quicksort program is obtained (and checked) in the following 3 iterations:

$$F_1 = \left\{ \begin{array}{l} \langle \mathsf{qs}(x_1, x_2, x_3), x_1 \wedge (x_2 \leftrightarrow x_3) \rangle \\ \langle \mathsf{pt}(x_1, x_2, x_3, x_4), x_1 \wedge x_3 \wedge x_4 \rangle \\ \langle =<'(x_1, x_2), x_1 \wedge x_2 \rangle \\ \langle >'(x_1, x_2), x_1 \wedge x_2 \rangle \end{array} \right\}$$

$$F_2 = \left\{ \begin{array}{l} \langle \mathsf{qs}(x_1, x_2, x_3), x_2 \leftrightarrow (x_1 \wedge x_3) \rangle \\ \langle \mathsf{pt}(x_1, x_2, x_3, x_4), x_1 \wedge x_3 \wedge x_4 \rangle \\ \langle =<'(x_1, x_2), x_1 \wedge x_2 \rangle \\ \langle >'(x_1, x_2), x_1 \wedge x_2 \rangle \end{array} \right\}$$

Finally, $F_3 = F_2$. The space of success patterns forms a complete lattice which ensures that a lfp exists. The iterative process will always terminate since the space is finite and hence the number of times each success pattern can be updated is also finite. Moreover, it will converge onto the lfp since (so-called Kleene) iteration commences with the bottom element F_0.

Observe that F_2, the lfp, faithfully describes the grounding behaviour of quicksort: a qs goal will ground its second argument if it is called with its first and third arguments already ground and *vice versa*. Note that assertions are not considered in the lfp calculation.

2.3 Greatest Fixpoint Calculation

A bottom-up strategy is used to compute a gfp and thereby characterise the safe call patterns of the program. A safe call pattern describes queries that do not lead to violation of the assertions. A call pattern has the same form as a success pattern (so there is one call pattern per predicate rather than one per clause). The analysis starts by checking that no call causes an error by reasoning backwards over all clauses. If an assertion is violated, the set of safe call patterns for the involved predicate is strengthened (made smaller), and the whole process is repeated until the assumptions turn out to be valid (the gfp is reached).

Lower Approximation of Safe Call Patterns Iteration commences with the top element $D_0 = \{\langle p(\boldsymbol{x}), true \rangle \mid p \in \Pi\}$. An iterative algorithm incrementally *strengthens* the call pattern formulae until they only describe queries which lead to computations that satisfy the assertions. Note that call patterns describe a subset, rather than a superset, of those queries which are safe. Call patterns are thus lower approximations, in contrast to success patterns which are upper approximations. Put another way, if $\langle p(\boldsymbol{x}), g \rangle$ correctly describes some safe call patterns of p, and g holds whenever f holds, then $\langle p(\boldsymbol{x}), f \rangle$ also correctly describes some safe call patterns of p. Call patterns can thus be approximated from *below* without compromising correctness (but not from above). D_{k+1} is computed from D_k by applying each $p(\boldsymbol{x})$:- $\mathsf{ask}(d), \mathsf{tell}(f), p_1(\boldsymbol{x}_1), \ldots, p_n(\boldsymbol{x}_n)$ in turn and calculating a formula that characterises its safe calling modes. A safe calling mode is calculated by propagating moding requirements right-to-left by repeated application of the logical operator $\rightarrow$. More exactly, let f_i denote the success pattern formula for $p_i(\boldsymbol{x}_i)$ in the previously computed lfp and let d_i denote the call pattern formula for $p_i(\boldsymbol{x}_i)$ in D_k. Set $e_{n+1} = true$ and then compute $e_i = d_i \wedge (f_i \rightarrow e_{i+1})$ for $1 \leq i \leq n$. Each e_i describes a safe calling mode for the compound goal $p_i(\boldsymbol{x}_i), \ldots, p_n(\boldsymbol{x}_n)$.

Intuition and Explanation The intuition behind the symbolism is that d_i represents the demand that is already known in order for $p_i(\boldsymbol{x}_i)$ not to error whereas e_i is d_i possibly strengthened with extra demand so as to ensure that the sub-goal $p_{i+1}(\boldsymbol{x}_{i+1}), \ldots, p_n(\boldsymbol{x}_n)$ also does not error when executed immediately after $p_i(\boldsymbol{x}_i)$. Put another way, anything larger than d_i may possibly cause an error when executing $p_i(\boldsymbol{x}_i)$ and anything larger than e_i may possibly cause an error when executing $p_i(\boldsymbol{x}_i), \ldots, p_n(\boldsymbol{x}_n)$.

The basic inductive step in the analysis is to compute an e_i which ensures that $p_i(\boldsymbol{x}_i), \ldots, p_n(\boldsymbol{x}_n)$ does not error, given d_i and e_{i+1} which respectively ensure that $p_i(\boldsymbol{x}_i)$ and $p_{i+1}(\boldsymbol{x}_{i+1}), \ldots, p_n(\boldsymbol{x}_n)$ do not error. This step propagates a demand after the call to $p_i(\boldsymbol{x}_i)$ into a demand before the call to $p_i(\boldsymbol{x}_i)$. The tactic is to set $e_{n+1} = true$ and then compute $e_i = d_i \wedge (f_i \rightarrow e_{i+1})$ for $i \leq n$. This tactic is best explained by unfolding the definitions of e_n, then e_{n-1}, then e_{n-2}, and so on. This reverse ordering reflects the order in which the e_i are computed; the e_i are computed whilst walking backwards across the clause. Any calling mode is safe for the empty goal and hence $e_{n+1} = true$. Note that $e_n = d_n \wedge (f_n \rightarrow e_{n+1}) = d_n \wedge (\neg f_n \vee true) = d_n$. Hence e_n represents a safe calling mode for the goal $p_n(\boldsymbol{x}_n)$.

Observe that e_i should not be larger than d_i, otherwise an error may occur while executing $p_i(\boldsymbol{x}_i)$. Observe too that if $p_i(\boldsymbol{x}_i), \ldots, p_n(\boldsymbol{x}_n)$ is called with a mode described by d_i, then $p_{i+1}(\boldsymbol{x}_{i+1}), \ldots, p_n(\boldsymbol{x}_n)$ is called with a mode described by $(d_i \wedge f_i)$, since f_i describes the success patterns of $p_i(\boldsymbol{x}_i)$. The mode $(d_i \wedge f_i)$ may satisfy the e_{i+1} demand. If it does not, then the minimal extra demand is added to $(d_i \wedge f_i)$ so as to satisfy e_{i+1}. This minimal extra demand is $((d_i \wedge f_i) \to e_{i+1})$ – the *weakest* mode that, in conjunction with $(d_i \wedge f_i)$, ensures that e_{i+1} holds. Put another way, $((d_i \wedge f_i) \to e_{i+1}) = \vee\{f \in Pos \mid (d_i \wedge f_i) \wedge f \models e_{i+1}\}$. Combining the requirements to satisfy $p_i(\boldsymbol{x}_i)$ and then $p_{i+1}(\boldsymbol{x}_{i+1}), \ldots, p_n(\boldsymbol{x}_n)$, gives $e_i = d_i \wedge ((d_i \wedge f_i) \to e_{i+1})$ which reduces to $e_i = d_i \wedge (f_i \to e_{i+1})$ because of algebraic properties of condensing domains [30] and yields the tactic used in the basic inductive step.

---

less_than_one(X, Flag) :- X ¡ 1, Flag = 1.
less_than_one(X, Flag) :- 1 =¡ X, Flag = 0.

less_than(X, Y) :- X ¡ Y.

Fig. 3. The less_than_one and less_than predicates

To illustrate how requirements are combined for compound queries, consider the predicates less_than_one and less_than given in figure 3. The first predicate uses a flag to indicate whether its first argument is less than one; the second predicate is a test which succeeds if and only if its first argument is less than its second. In particular consider the (artificial) compound query less_than_one(X, Flag), less_than(X, Flag) which also succeeds whenever X is less than one. Observe that the query less_than_one(X, Flag) will not admit an instantiation error if the query is called with X sufficiently instantiated, that is, if X is ground. It is natural for this property also to hold for the compound query, since declaratively it encodes the same behaviour (albeit with some redundancy). However, reasoning about the instantiation requirements for less_than_one(X, Flag), less_than(X, Flag) is more subtle because the first sub-goal instantiates Flag thereby partially discharging the instantiation requirements of the second sub-goal. Moreover, the requirement that X is ground for the first sub-goal ensures that the same requirement is satisfied in the second sub-goal. Observe that this interaction is faithfully modelled by $e_i = d_i \wedge (f_i \to e_{i+1})$. Specifically, with $p_1(\boldsymbol{x}_1) = $ less_than_one(X, Flag) and $p_2(\boldsymbol{x}_2) = $ less_than(X, Flag), the demand and success patterns for $p_1(\boldsymbol{x}_1)$ and $p_2(\boldsymbol{x}_2)$ are as follows $d_1 = \text{X}$ and $f_1 = \text{X} \wedge \text{Flag}$ and $d_2 = \text{X} \wedge \text{Flag}$ and $f_2 = \text{X} \wedge \text{Flag}$. Then

$$e_3 = true$$
$$e_2 = d_2 \wedge (f_2 \to e_3) = (\text{X} \wedge \text{Flag}) \wedge ((\text{X} \wedge \text{Flag}) \to true) = (\text{X} \wedge \text{Flag})$$
$$e_1 = d_1 \wedge (f_1 \to e_2) = (\text{X}) \wedge ((\text{X} \wedge \text{Flag}) \to (\text{X} \wedge \text{Flag})) = \text{X}$$

Thus it is sufficient to ground X in order to avoid an instantiation error in the compound goal.

Pseudo-complement This step of calculating the *weakest* mode that when conjoined with $d_i \wedge f_i$ implies e_{i+1}, is the very heart of the analysis. Setting $e_i = false$ would trivially achieve safety, but e_i should be as weak as possible to maximise the class of safe queries inferred. For *Pos*, computing the weakest e_i reduces to applying the $\to$ operator, but more generally this step amounts to applying the relative pseudo-complement. This operation (if it exists for a given abstract domain) takes, as input, two abstractions and returns, as output, the *weakest* abstraction whose conjunction with the first input abstraction is at least as strong as the second input abstraction. If the domain does not possess a relative pseudo-complement, then there is not always a *unique* weakest abstraction (whose conjunction with one given abstraction is at least as strong as another given abstraction).

To see this, consider the domain Def [2,38] which does not possess a relative pseudo-complement. Def is the sub-class of *Pos* that is definite [2,38]. This means that Def has the special property that each of its Boolean functions can be expressed as a (possibly empty) conjunction of propositional Horn clauses. As with *Pos*, Def is assumed to be augmented with the bottom element $false$. Def can thus represent the groundness dependencies $x \wedge y$, x, $x \leftrightarrow y$, y, $x \leftarrow y$, $x \to y$, $false$ and $true$ but *not* $x \vee y$. Suppose that $d_i \wedge f_i = (x \leftrightarrow y)$ and $e_{i+1} = (x \wedge y)$. Then conjoining x with $d_i \wedge f_i$ would be at least as strong as e_{i+1} and symmetrically conjoining y with $d_i \wedge f_i$ would be at least as strong as e_{i+1}. However, Def does not contain a Boolean function strictly weaker than both x and y, namely $x \vee y$, whose conjunction with $d_i \wedge f_i$ is at least as strong as e_{i+1}. Thus setting $e_i = x$ or $e_i = y$ would be safe but setting $e_i = (x \vee y)$ is prohibited because $x \vee y$ falls outside Def. Moreover, setting $e_i = false$ would lose an unacceptable degree of precision. A choice would thus have to be made between setting $e_i = x$ and $e_i = y$ in some arbitrary fashion, so there would be no clear tactic for maximising precision.

Returning to the compound goal $p_i(\boldsymbol{x}_i), \ldots, p_n(\boldsymbol{x}_n)$, a call described by the mode $d_i \wedge ((d_i \wedge f_i) \to e_{i+1})$ is thus sufficient to ensure that neither $p_i(\boldsymbol{x}_i)$ nor the sub-goal $p_{i+1}(\boldsymbol{x}_{i+1}), \ldots, p_n(\boldsymbol{x}_n)$ error. Since $d_i \wedge ((d_i \wedge f_i) \to e_{i+1}) = d_i \wedge (f_i \to e_{i+1}) = e_i$ it follows that $p_i(\boldsymbol{x}_i), \ldots, p_n(\boldsymbol{x}_n)$ will not error if its call is described by e_i. In particular, it follows that e_1 describes a safe calling mode for the body atoms of the clause $p(\boldsymbol{x})$:- $\mathsf{ask}(d), \mathsf{tell}(f), p_1(\boldsymbol{x}_1), \ldots, p_n(\boldsymbol{x}_n)$.

The next step is to calculate $g = d \wedge (f \to e_1)$. The abstraction f describes the grounding behaviour of the Herbrand constraint added to the store prior to executing the body atoms. Thus $(f \to e_1)$ describes the *weakest* mode that, in conjunction with f, ensures that e_1 holds, and hence the body atoms are called safely. Hence $d \wedge (f \to e_1)$ represents the weakest demand that both satisfies the body atoms and the assertion d. One subtlety which relates to the abstraction process is that d is required to be a lower-approximation of the assertion whereas f is required to be an upper-approximation of the constraint. Put another way, if the mode d describes the binding on the store, then the (concrete) assertion is satisfied, whereas if the (concrete) constraint is added to the store, then the store is described by the mode f.

Strengthening Lower Approximations The projection operator $\exists_x$ cannot be applied to eliminate variables in g that are not present in $p(\boldsymbol{x})$, since this could potentially weaken g and thereby compromise safety. Instead a dual projection operator $\forall_x$ is applied which is defined $\forall_x(f) = f'$ if $f' \in Pos$ otherwise $\forall_x(f) = false$ where $f' = f[x \mapsto false] \wedge f[x \mapsto true]$. Note that although $f[x \mapsto false] \vee f[x \mapsto true] \in Pos$ for all $f \in Pos$ it does not follow that $f[x \mapsto false] \wedge f[x \mapsto true] \in Pos$ for all $f \in Pos$. For example, $(x \leftarrow y)[x \mapsto false] \wedge (x \leftarrow y)[x \mapsto true] = \neg y$. Like $\exists_x(f)$, $\forall_x(f)$ eliminates a variable x from f. The fundamental difference is in the direction of approximation in that $\forall_x(f) \models f \models \exists_x(f)$. Thus if Y are the variables that are not present in $p(\boldsymbol{x})$, then $g' = \forall_Y(g)$ eliminates Y from g where $\forall_{\{y_1...y_n\}}(g) = \forall_{y_1}(\ldots \forall_{y_n}(g))$, whilst strengthening g. A safe calling mode for this particular clause is then given by g', since if g' holds then g holds also.

D_{k+1} will contain a call pattern $\langle p(\boldsymbol{x}), g'' \rangle$ and, assuming $g' \wedge g'' \neq g''$, this is updated with $\langle p(\boldsymbol{x}), g' \wedge g'' \rangle$. Thus the call patterns become progressively stronger on each iteration. Correctness is preserved because call patterns can be safely approximated from below. The space of call patterns forms a complete lattice which ensures that a gfp exists. In fact, because call patterns are approximated from below, the gfp is the most precise solution, and therefore the desired solution. (This contrasts to the norm in logic program analysis where approximation is from above and a lfp is computed). Moreover, since the space of call patterns is finite, termination is assured. In fact, the scheme will converge onto the gfp since (lower Kleene) iteration commences with the top element $D_0 = \{\langle p(\boldsymbol{x}), true \rangle \mid p \in \Pi\}$.

Greatest Fixpoint Calculation for Quicksort Under this procedure quicksort generates the following D_k sequence:

$$D_0 = \left\{ \begin{array}{c} \langle \mathsf{qs}(x_1, x_2, x_3), true \rangle \\ \langle \mathsf{pt}(x_1, x_2, x_3, x_4), true \rangle \\ \langle =<'(x_1, x_2), true \rangle \\ \langle >'(x_1, x_2), true \rangle \end{array} \right\} \quad D_1 = \left\{ \begin{array}{c} \langle \mathsf{qs}(x_1, x_2, x_3), true \rangle \\ \langle \mathsf{pt}(x_1, x_2, x_3, x_4), true \rangle \\ \langle =<'(x_1, x_2), x_1 \wedge x_2 \rangle \\ \langle >'(x_1, x_2), x_1 \wedge x_2 \rangle \end{array} \right\}$$

$$D_2 = \left\{ \begin{array}{c} \langle \mathsf{qs}(x_1, x_2, x_3), true \rangle \\ \langle \mathsf{pt}(x_1, x_2, x_3, x_4), x_2 \wedge (x_1 \vee (x_3 \wedge x_4)) \rangle \\ \langle =<'(x_1, x_2), x_1 \wedge x_2 \rangle \\ \langle >'(x_1, x_2), x_1 \wedge x_2 \rangle \end{array} \right\}$$

$$D_3 = \left\{ \begin{array}{c} \langle \mathsf{qs}(x_1, x_2, x_3), x_1 \rangle \\ \langle \mathsf{pt}(x_1, x_2, x_3, x_4), x_2 \wedge (x_1 \vee (x_3 \wedge x_4)) \rangle \\ \langle =<'(x_1, x_2), x_1 \wedge x_2 \rangle \\ \langle >'(x_1, x_2), x_1 \wedge x_2 \rangle \end{array} \right\}$$

These calculations are non-trivial so consider how D_2 is obtained from D_1 by applying the second (abstract) clause of pt as listed in Figure 2 – the clause with head pt(T1, M, T2, H). The following e_i and g formulae are generated from the demands d_i and the success patterns f_i:

$$e_3 = true$$

$$e_2 = d_2 \wedge (f_2 \rightarrow e_3)$$
$$= true \wedge ((\text{Xs} \wedge \text{L} \wedge \text{H}) \rightarrow true) = true$$

$$e_1 = d_1 \wedge (f_1 \rightarrow e_2)$$
$$= (\text{M} \wedge \text{X}) \wedge ((\text{M} \wedge \text{X}) \rightarrow true) = \text{M} \wedge \text{X}$$

$$g = d \wedge (f \rightarrow e_1)$$
$$= true \wedge (((\text{T1} \leftrightarrow \text{X} \wedge \text{Xs}) \wedge (\text{T2} \leftrightarrow \text{X} \wedge \text{L})) \rightarrow (\text{M} \wedge \text{X}))$$

To characterise those pt(T1, M, T2, H) calls which are safe, it is necessary to compute a function g' on the variables T1, M, T2, H which, if satisfied by the mode of a call, ensures that g is satisfied by the mode of the call. Put another way, it is necessary to eliminate the variables X, Xs and L from g (those variables which do not occur in the head pt(T1, M, T2, H)) to obtain a *Pos* function g' such that g holds whenever g' holds. This is accomplished by calculating $g' = \forall_\text{L} \forall_\text{Xs} \forall_\text{X}(g)$. First consider the computation of $\forall_\text{X}(g)$:

$$g[\text{X} \mapsto false] = ((\text{T1} \leftrightarrow false \wedge \text{Xs}) \wedge (\text{T2} \leftrightarrow false \wedge \text{L})) \rightarrow (\text{M} \wedge false)$$
$$= (\neg\text{T1} \wedge \neg\text{T2}) \rightarrow false$$
$$= \text{T1} \vee \text{T2}$$

$$g[\text{X} \mapsto true] = ((\text{T1} \leftrightarrow true \wedge \text{Xs}) \wedge (\text{T2} \leftrightarrow true \wedge \text{L})) \rightarrow (\text{M} \wedge true)$$
$$= ((\text{T1} \leftrightarrow \text{Xs}) \wedge (\text{T2} \leftrightarrow \text{L})) \rightarrow \text{M}$$

Since $g[\text{X} \mapsto false] \wedge g[\text{X} \mapsto true] \in Pos$ it follows that:

$$\forall_\text{X}(g) = (((\text{T1} \leftrightarrow \text{Xs}) \wedge (\text{T2} \leftrightarrow \text{L})) \rightarrow \text{M}) \wedge (\text{T1} \vee \text{T2})$$

(otherwise $\forall_\text{X}(g)$ would be set to *false*). Eliminating the other variables in a similar way we obtain:

$$\forall_\text{X}(g) = (((\text{T1} \leftrightarrow \text{Xs}) \wedge (\text{T2} \leftrightarrow \text{L})) \rightarrow \text{M}) \wedge (\text{T1} \vee \text{T2})$$
$$\forall_\text{Xs}\forall_\text{X}(g) = ((\text{T2} \leftrightarrow \text{L}) \rightarrow \text{M}) \wedge (\text{T1} \vee \text{T2})$$
$$g' = \forall_\text{L}\forall_\text{Xs}\forall_\text{X}(g) = \text{M} \wedge (\text{T1} \vee \text{T2})$$

Observe that if $\forall_\text{L}\forall_\text{Xs}\forall_\text{X}(g)$ holds then g holds. Thus if the mode of a call satisfies g' then the mode also satisfies g as required. This clause thus yields the call pattern $\langle \text{pt}(x_1, x_2, x_3, x_4), x_2 \wedge (x_1 \vee x_3) \rangle$. Similarly the first and third clauses contribute the patterns $\langle \text{pt}(x_1, x_2, x_3, x_4), true \rangle$ and $\langle \text{pt}(x_1, x_2, x_3, x_4), x_2 \wedge (x_1 \vee x_4) \rangle$. Observe also that

$$true \wedge (x_2 \wedge (x_1 \vee x_3)) \wedge (x_2 \wedge (x_1 \vee x_4)) = x_2 \wedge (x_1 \vee (x_3 \wedge x_4))$$

which gives the final call pattern formula for $\text{pt}(x_1, x_2, x_3, x_4)$ in D_2. The gfp is reached at D_3 since $D_4 = D_3$. The gfp often expresses elaborate calling modes, for example, it states that $pt(x_1, x_2, x_3, x_4)$ cannot generate an instantiation error (nor any predicate that it calls) if it is called with its second, third and fourth argument ground. This is a surprising result which suggests that the analysis can infer information that might be normally missed by a programmer.

2.4   Work Related to Mode Inference

Mode inference was partly motivated by the revival of interest in logic programming with assertions [4,56,64]. Interestingly, [56] observe that predicates are normally written with an expectation on the initial calling pattern, and hence provide an `entry` assertion to make the, moding say, of the top-level queries explicit. Mode inference gives a way of automatically synthesising `entry` assertions providing a provably correct way of ensuring that instantiation errors do not occur during program execution.

An analysis for type inference could be constructed by refining the analysis presented in this section by replacing the mode domain *Pos* with the domain of directional types [1,30,40]. This domain is condensing and therefore the domain comes equipped with the relative pseudo-complement operator that is necessary for backward reasoning. Interestingly, type inference can be performed even when the domain is not relatively pseudo-complemented [44]. This, however, relies on a radically different form of fixpoint calculation and therefore this approach to type inference is discussed separately in section 5.

3   Backwards Termination Inference

The aim of termination inference is to determine conditions under which calls to a predicate are guaranteed to terminate [24]. Termination inference is not a new idea in itself; it dates back to the pioneering work of Mesnard and his colleagues [34,50,52,53]. Recently it has been observed, however, that termination inference [24] can be performed by composing backwards analysis with a standard termination checker [10]. The elegance of this approach is that termination analysis can be reversed without dismantling an existing (forwards) termination analysis.

The key advantage of (backwards) termination inference over (forwards) termination checking is that termination inference can deduce, in a single application, a class of queries that lead to finite LD-derivations [24]. To illustrate this key idea, consider the program `split` listed in Figure 4. The `split` predicate arises in the classic mergesort algorithm where it is used to partition a list into sub-lists as preparation for an ordered merge [43]. For instance, the goal `split([a,b,c], L1, L2)` will terminate, binding L1 and L2 to `[a,c]` and `[b]` respectively. Correspondingly, a termination checker will ascertain that the call `split(L, L1, L2)` will terminate if L is bound to a list of fixed length [43]. However, a termination inference engine such as TerminWeb [24] or cTI [50] will deduce that `split(L, L1, L2)` terminates with either the first argument bound to a closed list or both the second and third arguments bound to closed lists. Of course, a termination checker could be reapplied to prove that

```
split([], [], []) :- true.
split([X | Xs], [X | L1], L2) :- split(Xs, L2, L1).
```

Fig. 4. split program expressed in Prolog

split(L, L1, L2) will terminate under the latter condition, but inference finds all the termination conditions in one application. Thus termination inference can discover termination conditions that are not observed by one, or possibly many, applications of a termination checker. Note that is not due to a failing of the checker; it is due to the programmer failing to realise that a condition warrants checking. (Actually, the conditions under which termination inference truly generalises termination checking are technical [24] and relate, among other things, to properties of the projection operators $\exists_x$ and $\forall_x$ [40].)

Termination inference can be realised in terms of the backwards analysis framework of [39] that was applied, in the previous section, to the problem of mode inference. In fact the only conceptual difference between mode inference and termination inference is in the way in which assertions are calculated. Whilst for mode analysis assertions are direct groundness abstractions of the builtins, for termination inference, assertions need to be calculated by an analysis of the loops within the program.

Termination analyses typically amount to showing that successive goals in an LD-derivation are decreasing with respect to some well-founded ordering. In the context of a termination checker founded on a binary clause semantics [20], this reduces to observing a size decrease between the arguments of the head and the body atom for each recursive binary clause [10]. From such a checker, a termination inference engine is obtained as follows:

- Firstly, the program is abstracted with respect to a chosen norm (or possibly a series of norms [25]). A norm maps each Herbrand term in the program to a linear expression that represents its size. Syntactic equations between Herbrand terms are replaced with linear inequations which express size relationships. The resulting program is abstract – it is a constraint program over the domain of linear constraints – but it is not binary; abstract clauses may contain more than one body atom.
- Secondly, an abstract version of the binary clause semantics is applied [10]. The (concrete) binary clause semantics of [20] provides a sound basis for termination analysis since the set of (concrete) binary clauses it defines precisely characterises the looping behaviour of the program. Specifically, a call to a given predicate will left-terminate if each corresponding recursive binary clause possesses a body atom that is strictly smaller than its head. Since this set of clauses is not finitely computable, an abstract version of binary clause semantics is used to compute a set of abstract binary clauses which, though finite, faithfully describes the set of concrete binary clauses. The linear in-

```
subset([], _) :-                    subset(0, Ys) :-
   true.                               0 ≤ Ys, true.
subset([X | Xs], Ys) :-             subset(1 + Xs, Ys) :-
   member(X, Ys), subset(Xs, Ys).      0 ≤ X, 0 ≤ Xs, 0 ≤ Ys,
                                        member(X, Ys), subset(Xs, Ys).
member(X, [X | Xs]) :-
   true.                            member(X, 1 + Xs) :-
member(X, [_ | Ys]) :-                 0 ≤ X, 0 ≤ Xs, true.
   member(X, Ys).                   member(X, 1 + Ys) :-
                                       0 ≤ X, 0 ≤ Ys, member(X, Ys).
```

Fig. 5. subset program expressed in Prolog, and its list-length abstraction

equalities in these abstract clauses capture size relationships between the arguments in the head and the body atom of the concrete clauses.

– Thirdly, combinations of ground arguments that are sufficient for termination are derived. The crucial point is that a decrease in size is only observable if sufficient arguments of a call are ground. These ground argument combinations are extracted from the linear inequalities in the abstract binary clauses, expressed as Boolean functions, and added to the original program in the form of assertions.

– Fourthly and finally, backwards mode analysis is performed on the program augmented with its assertions. The greatest fixpoint then yields groundness conditions which, if satisfied by an initial call, ensure that the call leads to a finite LD-derivation.

Note that backwards termination inference can be considered to be the composition of one black-box that infers binary clauses, with another which extracts assertions from the binary clauses with yet another performs mode inference. Because of this construction, readers who wish to skip the details on approximating loops can progress directly onto section 3.3.

3.1   Program Abstraction

Termination inference will be illustrated using the subset program listed in the first column of Figure 5. The predicate subset(L1, L2) holds iff each element of the list L1 occurs within the list L2. Observe that neither subset(L1, [a,b,c]) nor the call subset([a,b,c], L2) terminate when L1 and L2 are uninstantiated. However, both calls will terminate (albeit possibly in failure) when L1 and L2 are ground. The challenge is to automatically derive these grounding properties which are sufficient to guarantee termination.

Non-termination of logic programs is the result of infinite loops occurring during execution. Consequently recursive calls are the focus of termination analysis; a logic program will terminate if the arguments of successive calls to a predicate become progressively smaller with respect to a well-founded ordering. Thus, the notion of argument size (and more generally term size) is at the core of termination analyses. To measure term size, a norm is applied which maps a ground term to a natural number. To support program abstraction [28], the concept is normally lifted to terms that contain variables by defining a symbolic norm which maps a term to an expression over variables, non-negative integer constants and the functor $+$. For instance, the list-length norm is defined over the set of ground terms by:

$$|t|_{length} = \begin{cases} |t_2|_{length} + 1 \text{ if } t = [t_1|t_2] \\ 0 \qquad\qquad\qquad \text{otherwise} \end{cases}$$

whereas the symbolic list-length norm is given by:

$$|t|_{length} = \begin{cases} |t_2|_{length} + 1 \text{ if } t = [t_1|t_2] \\ t \qquad\qquad\qquad \text{if } t \text{ is a variable} \\ 0 \qquad\qquad\qquad \text{otherwise} \end{cases}$$

This symbolic norm describes the length of a list, using a variable to describe the variable length of an open list. For example $|[X \mid Xs]|_{length} = 1 + |Xs|_{length} = 1 + Xs$. Non-list terms are ascribed a length of zero. The second column of Figure 5 gives the list-length norm abstraction of subset and member in which terms are replaced by their sizes. The abstraction is obtained by replacing each term with its size. Since a norm can only map a variable to a non-negative value, extra inequalities are introduced to ensure that all (size) variables are non-negative. Observe that the resulting abstraction is a constraint program over the system of linear inequations.

3.2   Least Fixpoint Calculation over Binary Clauses

In [10] it is shown (using a semantics for call patterns similar to that of [20]) that a logic program is terminating iff its binary unfolding is. Informally, the binary unfolding of a program is the least set of binary clauses each with a head and body such that the head occurs as a head in the original program and, when the original program is called with the head as a goal, then the body occurs as a subsequent sub-goal in an LD-derivation. The binary unfolding is formally expressed in terms of the lfp of a T_P-style operator [10,20]. Moreover, an abstract binary unfolding can be obtained by applying an abstraction of the binary unfolding operator to the abstract program [10].

Calculation of this abstract lfp is complicated by the property that the domain of linear inequations does not satisfy the ascending chain condition [15]. This property compromises the termination of the abstract lfp calculation since it enables a set of abstract binary clauses to be repeatedly enlarged on successive iterates *ad infinitum*. Termination can be assured, however, by restricting the inequations that occur within abstract binary clauses to a finite sub-class, for example, the sub-class of monotonicity and equality constraints [5]. Alternatively widening can be applied to enforce convergence [3]. Using the latter technique the following set of abstract binary unfolding is obtained:

$$\left\{\begin{array}{l} \texttt{member}(x_1, x_2) \text{ :- } 0 \leq x_1 \wedge 1 \leq x_2, \texttt{true} \\ \texttt{member}(x_1, x_2) \text{ :- } 0 \leq x_1 \wedge 0 \leq y_2 \wedge 1 + y_2 \leq x_2 \wedge x_1 = y_1, \\ \qquad \texttt{member}(y_1, y_2) \\ \texttt{subset}(x_1, x_2) \text{ :- } 0 \leq x_1 \wedge 0 \leq x_2, \texttt{true} \\ \texttt{subset}(x_1, x_2) \text{ :- } y_2 \leq x_2 \wedge 1 \leq x_1 \wedge 0 \leq y_2 \wedge 0 \leq y_1, \\ \qquad \texttt{member}(y_1, y_2) \\ \texttt{subset}(x_1, x_2) \text{ :- } y_1 + 1 \leq x_1 \wedge y_2 = x_2 \wedge 1 \leq x_1 \wedge 1 \leq x_2, \\ \qquad \texttt{subset}(y_1, y_2) \end{array}\right\}$$

The set of abstract clauses contains at most $|\Pi|^2$ clauses where Π is the set of predicate symbols occurring in the program (which is assumed to include $\texttt{true}$). This follows because widening ensures that two abstract clauses cannot share the same predicate symbols in both the head and body. Note that if an abstract binary clause has $\texttt{true}$ as its body atom then the clause does not describe a loop and therefore has no bearing on the termination behaviour. Such clauses are given above simply for completeness.

3.3   Extracting the Assertions from the Binary Clauses

Those abstract binary clauses that involve recursive calls are as follows:

$$\texttt{member}(x_1, x_2) \text{ :-} \qquad\qquad \texttt{subset}(x_1, x_2) \text{ :-}$$
$$\quad 0 \leq x_1 \wedge 0 \leq y_2 \wedge \qquad\qquad y_1 + 1 \leq x_1 \wedge y_2 = x_2 \wedge$$
$$\quad 1 + y_2 \leq x_2 \wedge x_1 = y_1, \qquad\qquad 1 \leq x_1 \wedge 1 \leq x_2,$$
$$\quad \texttt{member}(y_1, y_2). \qquad\qquad\quad \texttt{subset}(y_1, y_2).$$

Consider the abstract clause for member. The inequality $1 + y_2 \leq x_2$ asserts that the recursive call is smaller than the previous call (as measured by the list-length norm). Therefore, assuming that the second argument of the original call to member is ground, each recursive call will operate on a strictly smaller list and thus terminate. Hence, although one abstract member clause approximates many concrete member clauses, the approximation is sufficiently precise to enable termination properties to be deduced. Likewise, the inequality $y_1 + 1 \leq x_1$ for subset ensures that termination follows if the first argument of the initial call to subset is ground.

Since termination is dependent on groundness, the inequalities in recursive abstract clauses induce groundness requirements that, if satisfied, assure termination. Since the number of ground argument combinations is exponential in the number of arguments, inferring the optimal set of ground argument combinations is potentially expensive (though experimentation suggests the contrary [51]). Therefore a subset of the argument combinations may only be considered [24]. Once extracted, the requirements are added to the original logic program in the form of assertions. Figure 6 lists the subset program complete with assertions that are sufficient for termination.

```
subset(A, B) :-               subset(A, B) :-
   tell(A = []),                 ask(A), tell(A),
   true.                         true.
subset(A, B) :-               subset(A, B) :-
   tell(A = [X | Xs]),           ask(A), tell(A ↔ (X ∧ Xs)),
   member(X, B),                 member(X, B),
   subset(Xs, B).                subset(Xs, B).

member(X, B) :-               member(A, B) :-
   tell(B = [X | Xs]),           ask(B), tell(B ↔ (X ∧ Xs)),
   true.                         true.
member(A, B) :-               member(A, B) :-
   tell(B = [Y | Ys]),           ask(B), tell(B ↔ (Y ∧ Ys)),
   member(A, Ys).                member(A, Ys).
```

Fig. 6. subset normalised and as a *Pos* abstraction with assertions

3.4 Backwards Mode Analysis

Backwards mode analysis can then be performed on the program with its assertions as specified in the previous section. Using the notation from that section,
backwards mode analysis yields the following sequence of iterates:

$$D_0 = \left\{ \begin{array}{l} \langle \texttt{member}(x_1, x_2), true \rangle \\ \langle \texttt{subset}(x_1, x_2), true \rangle \end{array} \right\} \qquad D_1 = \left\{ \begin{array}{l} \langle \texttt{member}(x_1, x_2), x_2 \rangle \\ \langle \texttt{subset}(x_1, x_2), x_1 \rangle \end{array} \right\}$$

$$D_2 = \left\{ \begin{array}{l} \langle \texttt{member}(x_1, x_2), x_2 \rangle \\ \langle \texttt{subset}(x_1, x_2), x_1 \wedge x_2 \rangle \end{array} \right\}$$

The fixpoint is reached and checked in the next iteration since $D_3 = D_2$. The
fixpoint specifies grounding conditions that are sufficient for termination. That
is, subset is guaranteed to left-terminate if both of its arguments are ground.
This is as expected, since the first argument of subset needs to be ground
in order that its own recursive call terminates. Moreover, the second argument
additionally needs to be ground in order that the call to member terminates. Both
the recursive call and the call to member are required to terminate to assure that
a call to the second clause of subset terminates.

3.5 Work Related to Termination Inference

Performing termination inference via backwards analysis is a comparatively
new idea [24] but termination inference was developed by Mesnard and others [34,50,51,52,53] long before this connection was made. Their system, the cTI
analyser, applied a μ-calculus solver to compute a greatest fixpoint. This seems
to suggest that greatest fixpoints are intrinsic to the problem itself. On the other

hand, the termination inference analyser reported in [24] (and described in this section) is composed from two components: a standard termination checker [10] and a backwards analysis. The resulting analyser is similar to cTI; the main difference is its design as two existing black-box components which, according to [24], simplifies the formal justification and implementation.

4   Backwards Suspension Inference

In mode inference [39] the assertions are synthesised from the builtins. In termination inference [24] the assertions are distilled from a separate analysis of the loops which occur within the program [10]. Both these analyses share the same backwards analysis component – a component which essentially propagates requirements right-to-left over sequences of goals against the control-flow. Interestingly, and perhaps surprisingly, backwards analysis can still be applied when the control is more loosely defined. In fact, backwards analysis is still applicable even when the control is specified by a delay mechanism which blocks the selection of a sub-goal until some condition is satisfied [7]. This, arguably, is one of the most flexible ways of specifying control within logic programming.

Delays have proved to be invaluable for handling negation [54], delaying non-linear constraints [32], enforcing termination [47], improving search and modelling concurrency [45]. However, reasoning about logic programs with delays is notoriously difficult and one reoccurring problem for the programmer is that of determining whether a given program and goal can reduce to a state which possesses a sub-goal that suspends indefinitely. A number of abstract interpretation schemes [8,11,17] have therefore been proposed for verifying that a program and goal cannot suspend in this fashion. These analyses are essentially forwards in that they simulate the operational semantics tracing the execution of the program in the direction of the control with collections of abstract states. This section reviews a suspension analysis that is performed backwards by propagating requirements against the control-flow. Specifically, rather than verifying that a particular goal will not lead to a suspension, the analysis infers a class of goals that will not lead to suspension. This approach has the computational advantage that the programmer need not rerun the analysis for different (abstract) queries. Moreover, like the previous analyses, this suspension analysis is formulated as two simple bottom-up fixpoint computations. The analysis strikes a good balance between tractability and precision. It avoids the complexity of goal interleaving by exploiting reordering properties of monotonic and positive Boolean functions.

Another noteworthy aspect of the analysis is that it verifies whether a logic program with delays can be scheduled with a *local* selection rule [63]. Under local selection, the selected atom is completely resolved, that is, those atoms it directly and indirectly introduces are also resolved, before any other atom is selected. Leftmost selection is one example of local selection. Knowledge about suspension within the context of local selection is useful within it own right [17,41]. In particular, [17] explains how various low-level optimisations, such as

```
inorder(nil, []) :- true.
inorder(tree(L, V, R), I) :-
    append(LI, [V|RI], I), inorder(L, LI), inorder(R, RI).

:- block append(-, ?, -).
append([], X, X) :- true.
append([X|Xs], Ys, [X|Zs]) :- append(Xs, Ys, Zs).
```

Fig. 7. inorder program in expressed in Prolog with block declarations

returning output values in registers, can be applied if goals can be scheduled left-to-right without suspension. Furthermore, any program that can be shown to be suspension-free under local selection is clearly suspension-free with a more general selection rule. Note, however, that the converse does not follow and the analysis cannot infer non-suspension if the program relies on coroutining techniques.

4.1 Worked Example on Suspension Inference

To illustrate the ideas behind suspension analysis, consider an analysis of the Prolog program listed in Figure 7. Declaratively, the program defines the relation that the second argument (a list) is an in-order traversal of the first argument (a tree). Operationally, the declaration :- block append(-, ?, -) delays (blocks) append goals until their arguments are sufficiently instantiated. The dashes in the first and third argument positions specify that a call to append is to be delayed until either its first or third argument are bound to non-variable terms. Thus append goals can be executed in one of two modes. The problem is to compute input modes which are sufficient to guarantee that any inorder query which satisfies the modes will not lead to a suspension under local selection. This problem can be solved with backwards analysis. Backwards analysis infers requirements on the input which ensure that certain properties hold at (later) program points [39]. Exactly like before, the analysis is tackled via an abstraction step followed by a least fixpoint (lfp) and then a greatest fixpoint (gfp) computation.

4.2 Program Abstraction

Abstraction reduces to two transformations: one from a Prolog with delay program to a concurrent constraint programming [60] (ccp) program and another from the ccp program to a *Pos* abstraction. The Prolog program is re-written to a ccp program to make blocking requirements explicit in the program as ask constraints. More exactly, a clause of a ccp program takes the form h :- ask(c'), tell(c''), g where h is an atom, g is a conjunction of body atoms and c' and c'' are the ask and tell constraints. The asks are guards that inspect the store and

```
inorder(T, I) :-                        inorder(T, I) :-
   ask(true),                              ask(true),
   tell(T = nil, I = []),                  tell(T ∧ I),
   true.                                   true.
inorder(T, I) :-                        inorder(T, I) :-
   ask(true),                              ask(true),
   tell(T = tree(L,V,R),A = [V|RI]),       tell(T ↔ (L ∧ V ∧ R),A ↔ (V ∧ RI)),
   append(LI, A, I),                       append(LI, A, I),
   inorder(L, LI),                         inorder(L, LI),
   inorder(R, RI).                         inorder(R, RI).


append(L, Ys, A) :-                     append(L, Ys, A) :-
   ask(nonvar(L) ∨ nonvar(A)),             ask(L ∨ A),
   tell(L = [], A = Ys),                   tell(L ∧ (A ↔ Ys)),
   true.                                   true.
append(L, Ys, A) :-                     append(L, Ys, A) :-
   ask(nonvar(L) ∨ nonvar(A)),             ask(L ∨ A),
   tell(L = [X|Xs], A = [X|Zs]),           tell(L ↔ (X ∧ Xs),A ↔ (X ∧ Zs)),
   append(Xs, Ys, Zs).                     append(Xs, Ys, Zs).
```

Fig. 8. inorder program expressed in ccp and as a *Pos* abstraction

specify synchronisation behaviour whereas the tells are writes that update the store. As before, empty conjunctions of atoms are denoted by true. Unlike before, ask does not denote an assertion but a synchronisation requirement. Moreover, a conjunction of goals g is not necessarily executed left-to-right: goals can only be reduced with a clause when the ask constraint within the clause is satisfied. A goal will suspend until this is the case, hence the execution order of the sub-goals within a goal does not necessarily concur with the textual (left-to-right) ordering of these sub-goals. In this particular example, the only ask constraint that appears in the program is $\mathtt{nonvar}(x)$ which formalises the requirement that x must be bound to a non-variable term.

The second transform abstracts the ask and tell constraints with Boolean functions which capture instantiation dependencies. The ask constraints are abstracted from below whereas the tell constraints are abstracted from above. More exactly, an ask abstraction is stronger than the ask constraint – whenever the abstraction holds then the ask constraint is satisfied; whereas the tell abstraction is weaker than the tell constraint – whenever the tell constraint holds then so does its abstraction. For example, the function L ∨ A describes states where either L or A is ground [2] which, in turn, ensure that the ask constraint nonvar(L) ∨ nonvar(A) holds. On the other hand, once the tell A = [V|RI] holds, then the grounding behaviour of the state (and all subsequent states) is described by A ↔ (V ∧ RI).

4.3   Least Fixpoint Calculation

The least fixpoint calculation approximates the success patterns of the ccp program (and thus the Prolog with delays program) by mimicking the T_P operator [28]. A success pattern is an atom with distinct variables for arguments paired with a *Pos* formula over those variables. This is the same notion of success pattern as used in mode inference and, just as in mode inference, a success pattern summarises the behaviour of an atom by describing the bindings it can make. The lfp of the *Pos* program can be computed in a finite number of iterates to give the following lfp:

$$F = \left\{ \begin{array}{l} \langle \texttt{inorder}(x_1, x_2), x_1 \leftrightarrow x_2 \rangle \\ \langle \texttt{append}(x_1, x_2, x_3), (x_1 \wedge x_2) \leftrightarrow x_3 \rangle \end{array} \right\}$$

4.4   Greatest Fixpoint Calculation

A gfp is computed to characterise the safe call patterns of the program. A call pattern has the same form as a success pattern. Iteration commences with

$$D_0 = \left\{ \begin{array}{l} \langle \texttt{inorder}(x_1, x_2), true \rangle \\ \langle \texttt{append}(x_1, x_2, x_3), true \rangle \end{array} \right\}$$

and incrementally strengthens the call pattern formulae until they are safe, that is, they describe queries which are guaranteed not to violate the ask constraints. The iterate D_{i+1} is computed by putting $D_{i+1} = D_i$ and then revising D_{i+1} by considering each $p(x)$:- $\mathsf{ask}(d), \mathsf{tell}(f), p_1(x_1), \ldots, p_n(x_n)$ in the abstract program and calculating a (monotonic) formula that describes input modes (if any) under which the atoms in the clause can be scheduled without suspension under local selection. A monotonic formula over set of variables X is any formula of the form $\vee_{i=1}^n (\wedge Y_i)$ where $Y_i \subseteq X$ [18]. Let d_i denote a monotonic formula that describes the call pattern requirement for $p_i(x_i)$ in D_i and let f_i denote the success pattern formula for $p_i(x_i)$ in the lfp (that is not necessarily monotonic). A new call pattern for $p(x)$ is computed using the following algorithm:

- Calculate $e = \wedge_{i=1}^n (d_i \rightarrow f_i)$ that describes the grounding behaviour of the compound goal $p_1(x_1), \ldots, p_n(x_n)$. The intuition is that $p_i(x_i)$ can be described by $d_i \rightarrow f_i$ since if the input requirements d_i hold then $p_i(x_i)$ can be executed without suspension, hence the output f_i must also hold.
- Compute $e' = \wedge_{i=1}^n d_i$ which describes a groundness property sufficient for scheduling all of the goals in the compound goal without suspension. Then $e \rightarrow e'$ describes a grounding property which, if satisfied, when the compound goal is called ensures the goal can be scheduled by local selection without suspension.
- Calculate $g = d \wedge (f \rightarrow (e \rightarrow e'))$ that describes a grounding property which is strong enough to ensure that both the ask is satisfied and the body atoms can be scheduled by local selection without suspension.

- Eliminate those variables not present in $p(\boldsymbol{x})$, Y say, by calculating $g' = \forall_Y(g)$ where $\forall_{\{y_1 \ldots y_n\}}(g) = \forall_{y_1}(\ldots \forall_{y_n}(g))$. Hence $\forall_x(f)$ entails f and g' entails g, so that a safe calling mode for this particular clause is then given by g'.
- Compute a monotonic function g'' that entails g'. Since g'' is stronger than g' it follows that g'' is sufficient for scheduling the compound goal by local selection without suspension. The function g' needs to be approximated by a monotonic function since the $e \rightarrow e'$ step relies on d_i being monotonic.
- Replace the pattern $\langle p(\boldsymbol{x}), g''' \rangle$ in D_{i+1} with $\langle p(\boldsymbol{x}), g'' \wedge g''' \rangle$.

This procedure generates the following D_i sequence:

$$D_1 = \left\{ \begin{array}{l} \langle \texttt{inorder}(x_1, x_2), true \rangle \\ \langle \texttt{append}(x_1, x_2, x_3), x_1 \vee x_3 \rangle \end{array} \right\}$$

$$D_2 = \left\{ \begin{array}{l} \langle \texttt{inorder}(x_1, x_2), x_1 \vee x_2 \rangle \\ \langle \texttt{append}(x_1, x_2, x_3), x_1 \vee x_3 \rangle \end{array} \right\}$$

The gfp is reached and checked in three iterations. The result asserts that a local selection rule exists for which inorder will not suspend if either its first or second arguments are ground. Indeed, observe that if the first argument is ground then body atoms of the second inorder clause can be scheduled as follows: inorder(L, LI), then inorder(R, RI), and then append(LI, A, I). Conversely, if the second argument is ground, then the reverse ordering is sufficient for non-suspension. These call patterns are intuitive and experimental evaluation [26] suggests that unexpected and counter-intuitive call patterns arise (almost exclusively) in buggy programs. This suggests that the analysis has a useful rôle in bug detection and program development.

4.5   Work Related to Suspension Inference

One of the most closely related works comes surprisingly from the compiling control literature and in particular the problem of *generating* a local selection rule under which a program universally terminates [34]. The technique of [34] builds on the termination inference method of [50] which infers initial modes for a query that, if satisfied, ensure that a logic program left-terminates. The chief advance in [34] over [50] is that it additionally infers how goals can be statically reordered so as to improve termination behaviour. This is performed by augmenting each clause with body atoms $a_1, \ldots, a_n$ with $n(n-1)$ Boolean variables $b_{i,j}$ with the interpretation that $b_{i,j} = 1$ if a_i precedes a_j in the reordered goal and $b_{i,j} = 0$ otherwise. The analysis of [50] is then adapted to include consistency constraints among the $b_{i,j}$, for instance, $b_{j,k} \wedge \neg b_{i,k} \rightarrow \neg b_{i,j}$. In addition, the $b_{i,j}$ are used to determine whether the post-conditions of a_i contribute to the pre-conditions of a_j. Although motivated differently and realised differently (in terms of the Boolean μ-calculus) this work also uses Boolean functions to finesse the problem of enumerating the goal reorderings.

A demand analysis for the ccp language Janus [61] is proposed in [16] which determines whether or not a predicate is uni-modal. A predicate is uni-modal iff the argument tuple for each clause shares the same minimal pattern of instantiation necessary for reduction. The demand analysis of a predicate simply traverses the head and guard of each clause to determine the extent to which arguments have to be instantiated. Body atoms need not be considered so the analysis does not involve a fixpoint computation. A related paper [17] presents a goal-dependent (forwards) analysis that detects those ccp predicates which can be scheduled left-to-right without deadlock. This work is unusual in that it attempts to detect suspension-freeness for goals under leftmost selection. Although this approach only considers one local selection rule, it is surprisingly effective because of the way data often flows left-to-right.

5   Backwards Type Inference

Backwards mode inference, termination inference and suspension inference analysis of the previous sections all apply the same operator to model reversed information flow – the relative pseudo-complement. The key idea that these analyses exploit is that if d_2 expresses a set of requirements that must hold after a constraint is added to the store, and d_1 models the constraint itself, then $d_1 \rightarrow d_2$ expresses the requirements that must hold on the store before the constraint. Comparatively few domains possess a relative pseudo-complement and, arguably, the most well-known type domain that comes equipped with a relative pseudo-complement operator is the domain of directional types [1,30]. This section demonstrates that backwards analysis is still applicable to problems in program development even when the domain is not relatively pseudo-complemented or when the relative pseudo-complement is not particularly tractable [40]. The section focuses on the problem of inferring type signatures for predicates that are sufficient to ensure that the execution of the program with a query satisfying the inferred type signatures will be free from type errors. This problem generalises backwards mode inference – types are richer than modes. It also generalises type checking in which the programmer declares type signatures for all predicates in the program and a type checker verifies that the program is well-typed with respect to these type signatures, that is, these type signatures are consistent with the operational semantics of the program.

The value of type inference is illustrated by returning to the quicksort program listed in Figure 1. A type checker would require the programmer to declare type signatures for qs and pt and then check if the program is well-typed with respect to these and the type signatures for builtin predicates $\leq$ and $>$ stipulated in the user manual. In contrast, type signature inference will infer that if qs is called with a list of numbers as the first argument then the execution of the program will not violate the type signatures of $\leq$ and $>$; the programmer need not declare types for qs nor pt. Backwards type analysis gives the programmer the flexibility not to declare and maintain type signatures for predicates that are subject to frequent modifications during program development. In the extreme situation, the programmer may choose to leave unspecified type signatures for all user-defined predicates and let the analyser to infer type signatures from builtin and library predicates. One application of the new analysis is automatic program documentation. Type signatures provide valuable information for both program development and maintenance [62]. Another application is in bug detection. The inferred type signature for a predicate can be compared with that intended by the programmer and any discrepancy indicates the possible existence of bugs.

5.1 Greatest Fixpoint Calculation

The analysis is performed by computing a greatest fixpoint. It starts by assuming that no call causes a type error and then checks this assumption by reasoning backwards over all clauses. If an assertion is violated, pre-conditions are strengthened, and the whole process is repeated. The basic datum of the analysis is a type constraint. A type constraint is a disjunction of conjunctive type constraints. A conjunctive type constraint, in turn, is a conjunction of atomic type constraints of the form $x{:}\tau$ where x is a variable and τ a type that denotes a set of terms closed under instantiation. Similarly to before, tell constraints distinguish syntactic equations from assertions which are themselves indicated by ask constraints. The assertions specify type constraints which must be respected by the execution of the program.

Each clause of the normalised program takes the form of $p(\boldsymbol{x})$:- $B_1, \ldots, B_k$ where each B_i is either:

- an assertion ask(ϕ) where ϕ is a type constraint or
- tell(E) where E is a syntactic equation (unification) or
- a call to an atom $q(\boldsymbol{y})$ where $\boldsymbol{y}$ is a vector of distinct variables.

Unlike previously, ask and tell constraints can occur multiply within the same clause. A conjunction of body atoms $B_1, \ldots, B_k$ is executed left-to-right.

As previously, backwards analysis reduces to computing a finite sequence of iterates D_i. Each D_i is a mapping from an atom $p(\boldsymbol{x})$ to a function that itself maps a type constraint ϕ_R to another ϕ_L such that the execution of $p(\boldsymbol{x})$ in a state satisfying ϕ_L succeeds (if it does) only in a state satisfying ϕ_R and respects type constraints given by the assertions. The pair $\langle p(\boldsymbol{x}), \phi_R \rangle$ is called a demand whereas ϕ_L is a pre-condition for $\langle p(\boldsymbol{x}), \phi_R \rangle$. D_{i+1} is computed from D_i by updating the pre-condition for each demand in D_i and adding new demands to D_{i+1} if necessary. For a demand $\langle p(\boldsymbol{x}), \phi_R \rangle$, a type constraint ϕ_L^C is computed from each clause $p(\boldsymbol{x})$:- $B_1, \ldots, B_k$ by computing a series $\psi_k, \ldots, \psi_0$ of type constraints. This starts by assigning $\psi_k = \phi_R$. Then every other ψ_{j-1} is computed from ψ_j as follows:

- If $B_j = \mathsf{ask}(\phi)$ then ψ_{j-1} is calculated by $\psi_{j-1} = \psi_j \wedge \phi$.
- If $B_j = \mathsf{tell}(E)$ then ψ_{j-1} is computed by performing backwards abstract unification. Backwards abstract unification ensures that the result of unifying E in the context of a store satisfying ψ_{j-1} is a store satisfying ψ_j. Since the domain is not condensing, backwards unification cannot coincide with

the relative pseudo-complement operator. The relative pseudo-complement operator is unique in that it delivers the weakest abstraction which when combined with one given abstraction, entails another given abstraction. This suggests there may exist a pre-condition which is strictly weaker than ψ_{j-1} or strictly incomparable with ψ_{j-1} which is also sufficient for ensuring that ψ_j holds after E. Put another way, backwards unification does not come with the precision guarantee that characterises the relative pseudo-complement.

- If $B_j = q(\boldsymbol{y})$ is a call to a user-defined predicate then ψ_{j-1} is computed as follows:
  - Let $\psi_j = \bigvee_{l=1}^m \mu_l$ where each μ_l is a conjunctive type constraint.
  - Apply existential quantification to project μ_l onto the variables $\boldsymbol{y}$ to obtain ν_l. Hence ν_l is weaker than μ_l, that is, ν_l holds if μ_l holds. Moreover, $\langle q(\boldsymbol{y}), \nu_l \rangle$ is a demand that constrains only variables in $\boldsymbol{y}$.
  - If $\langle q(\boldsymbol{y}), \nu_l \rangle$ (modulo renaming) is in D_i then $\omega_l = D_i(\langle q(\boldsymbol{y}), \nu_l \rangle)$; recall that D_i is interpreted as a mapping from demands to pre-conditions.
  - Otherwise, $\omega_l = true$ and $\langle q(\boldsymbol{y}), \nu_l \rangle \mapsto true$ is added into D_{i+1}, thereby introducing a new demand.
  - Put $\psi_{j-1} = \bigvee_{l=1}^m (\omega_l \wedge \upsilon_l)$ where each υ_l is obtained from μ_l by applying existential quantification to project out variables in $\boldsymbol{y}$.

  Then ψ_{j-1} is a pre-condition for $\langle q(\boldsymbol{y}), \psi_j \rangle$ provided that ω_l is a pre-condition for $\langle q(\boldsymbol{y}), \nu_l \rangle$ for each l.

Finally ϕ_L^C is computed from ψ_0 via universal quantification by projecting onto the variables within $p(\boldsymbol{x})$. As in the previous backwards analyses, this strengthens the pre-condition such that ψ_0 holds if ϕ_L^C holds.

5.2 Worked Example on Type Inference

To illustrate, consider the **insertionsort** program listed in the first column of Figure 9. The second column gives the program in a normalised form, decorated with **ask** and **tell** constraints. Note how the tests X > Y and X ≤ Y are both replaced with the tell constraint X:num ∧ Y:num where num denotes the set of numbers. Unlike the previous backwards analyses, the analysis is driven from an initial demand. The initial demand is the pair $\langle \text{sort}(\text{Xs}, \text{Ys}), true \rangle$ for which a pre-condition is required, hence D_0 is:

$$D_0 = \{\langle \text{sort}(\text{Xs}, \text{Ys}), true \rangle \mapsto true\}$$

The iterate D_1 is computed by successively updating D_0 by considering each clause in turn. To illustrate, consider the first clause for **sort** where $B_1 = \text{append}(\text{As}, \text{Cs}, \text{Xs})$, ..., $B_6 = \text{sort}(\text{Zs}, \text{Ys})$. This clause has 6 body atoms and analysis amounts to computing $\psi_5, \ldots, \psi_0$ where $\psi_6 = true$. The analysis proceeds as follows:

- Firstly, $\psi_5 = true$ is computed. Since $B_6 = \text{sort}(\text{Zs}, \text{Ys})$ is an atom, ψ_6 is projected onto the variables $\{\text{Zs}, \text{Ys}\}$, yielding $true$. Then D_1 is checked for

```
sort(Xs, Ys) :-                  sort(Xs, Ys) :-
   append(As, [X, Y|Bs], Xs),       append(As, Cs, Xs),
   X > Y,                            tell(Cs = [X, Y|Bs]),
   append(As, [Y, X|Bs], Zs),       ask(X:num ∧ Y:num),
   sort(Zs, Ys).                     tell(Ds = [Y, X|Bs]),
sort(Xs, Xs) :-                      append(As, Ds, Zs),
   order(Xs).                        sort(Zs, Ys).
                                  sort(Xs, Ys) :-
append([], Ys, Ys) :- true.          tell(Xs = Ys),
append([X|Xs], Ys, [X|Zs]) :-        order(Xs).
   append(Xs, Ys, Zs).

order([]) :- true.               append(Xs, Ys, Zs) :-
order([_]) :- true.                  tell(Xs = [], Ys = Zs).
order([X, Y|Xs]) :-              append(Xs, Ys, Zs) :-
   X ≤ Y,                            tell(Xs = [X|Xs1], Zs = [X|Zs1]),
   order([Y|Xs]).                    append(Xs1, Ys, Zs1).

                                 order(Xs) :-
                                     tell(Xs = []).
                                 order(Xs) :-
                                     tell(Xs = [_]).
                                 order(Xs) :-
                                     tell(Xs = [X|Xs1], Xs1 = [Y|Ys]),
                                     ask(X:num ∧ Y:num),
                                     order(Xs1).
```

Fig. 9. insertionsort expressed in Prolog and with type assertions

the demand $\langle B_6, true \rangle$. Because $\langle \text{sort}(\text{Zs}, \text{Ys}), true \rangle$ is a variant of $\langle \text{sort}(\text{Xs}, \text{Ys}), true \rangle$, no new demand is added to D_1 and thus $\psi_5 = D_1(\langle \text{sort}(\text{Zs}, \text{Ys}), true \rangle) = true$.

- Secondly, $\psi_4 = true$ is computed. As previously $B_5 = \text{append}(\text{As}, \text{Ds}, \text{Zs})$ is an atom. Thus $true$ is projected onto $\{\text{As}, \text{Ds}, \text{Zs}\}$, obtaining $true$. Unlike before, D_1 does not contain the demand $\langle B_5, true \rangle$ and therefore D_1 is updated to

$$D_1 = \left\{ \begin{array}{l} \langle \text{append}(\text{As}, \text{Ds}, \text{Zs}), true \rangle \mapsto true, \\ \langle \text{sort}(\text{Xs}, \text{Ys}), true \rangle \mapsto true \end{array} \right\}$$

and $\psi_4 = D_1(\langle \text{append}(\text{As}, \text{Ds}, \text{Zs}), true \rangle) = true$.

- Thirdly, $\psi_3 = true$ is computed. Because $B_4 = \text{tell}(\text{Ds} = [\text{Y}, \text{X}|\text{Bs}])$, backwards abstract unification is applied. Since $\psi_4 = true$, this requirement is trivially satisfied, hence $\psi_3 = true$.
- Fourthly, $\psi_2 = \text{X:num} \wedge \text{Y:num}$ is computed. Since $B_3 = \text{ask}(\text{X:num} \wedge \text{Y:num})$, $\psi_2 = \psi_3 \wedge \phi$ where $B_3 = \text{ask}(\phi)$.

- Fifthly, $\psi_1 = $ (X:num $\wedge$ Y:num) $\vee$ Cs:list(num) is computed where list is the standard polymorphic list constructor associated with the typing rules list$(\beta) ::= []$ and list$(\beta) ::= [\beta|\text{list}(\beta)]$. Abstract backwards unification is applied since $B_2 = \text{tell}(\text{Cs} = [\text{X}, \text{Y}|\text{Bs}])$. The conjunct (X:num $\wedge$ Y:num) derives from the fact that a type constraint that holds before unification also holds after unification. The conjunct Cs:list(num) derives from the fact that both Cs and [X, Y|Bs] are of the same type after unification and Cs:list(num) implies [X, Y|Bs]:list(num), hence (X:num $\wedge$ Y:num). More generally, backwards abstract unification takes as inputs an equational constraint E and a type constraint ψ and produces as output a type constraint ϕ which describes θ whenever ψ describes $mgu(\theta(E)) \circ \theta$.
- Sixthly, $\psi_0 = true$ is computed. Since $B_1 = \text{append}(\text{As}, \text{Cs}, \text{Xs})$ is an atom, (X:num $\wedge$ Y:num) is projected onto {As, Cs, Xs} yielding $true$. A variant of $\langle \text{append}(\text{As}, \text{Cs}, \text{Xs}), true \rangle$ is contained within D_1. However, projecting {As, Cs, Xs} out of (X:num $\wedge$ Y:num) yields (X:num $\wedge$ Y:num). Thus, one pre-condition for $\langle \text{append}(\text{As}, \text{Cs}, \text{Xs}), (\text{X:num} \wedge \text{Y:num}) \rangle$ is $(true \wedge (\text{X:num} \wedge \text{Y:num})) = (\text{X:num} \wedge \text{Y:num})$. Another is obtained by projecting Cs:list(num) onto {As, Cs, Xs} to obtain Cs:list(num), hence D_1 is updated with the new demand:

$$D_1 = \left\{ \begin{array}{c} \langle \text{append}(\text{As}, \text{Ds}, \text{Zs}), true \rangle \mapsto true, \\ \langle \text{append}(\text{As}, \text{Cs}, \text{Xs}), \text{Cs:list(num)} \rangle \mapsto true, \\ \langle \text{sort}(\text{Xs}, \text{Ys}), true \rangle \mapsto true \end{array} \right\}$$

Because $D_1(\langle \text{append}(\text{As}, \text{Cs}, \text{Xs}), \text{Cs:list(num)} \rangle) = true$, the other pre-condition for $\langle \text{append}(\text{As}, \text{Cs}, \text{Xs}), \text{Cs:list(num)} \rangle$ is $true$. Therefore $\psi_0 = $ (X:num $\wedge$ Y:num) $\vee\ true = true$.

Processing the second clause of sort gives the same pre-condition $true$ and introduces one more demand $\langle \text{order}(\text{Xs}), true \rangle$. Therefore

$$D_1 = \left\{ \begin{array}{c} \langle \text{append}(\text{As}, \text{Ds}, \text{Zs}), true \rangle \mapsto true, \\ \langle \text{append}(\text{As}, \text{Cs}, \text{Xs}), \text{Cs:list(num)} \rangle \mapsto true, \\ \langle \text{order}(\text{Xs}), true \rangle \mapsto true, \\ \langle \text{sort}(\text{Xs}, \text{Ys}), true \rangle \mapsto true \end{array} \right\}$$

Omitting details of the remaining computation, the gfp is reached at D_5 with

$$D_5 = \left\{ \begin{array}{c} \langle \text{append}(\text{Xs}, \text{Ys}, \text{Zs}), true \rangle \mapsto true, \\ \langle \text{append}(\text{Xs}, \text{Ys}, \text{Zs}), \text{Zs:list(num)} \rangle \mapsto \text{Zs:list(num)}, \\ \langle \text{append}(\text{Xs}, \text{Ys}, \text{Zs}), \text{Ys:list(num)} \rangle \mapsto \\ \text{Ys:list(num)} \vee \text{Zs:list(num)}, \\ \langle \text{order}(\text{Xs}), true \rangle \mapsto \text{Xs:list(num)}, \\ \langle \text{sort}(\text{Xs}, \text{Ys}), true \rangle \mapsto \text{Xs:list(num)} \end{array} \right\}$$

The gfp asserts that sort cannot generate a type error (nor any predicate it subsequently calls) if it is called with a list of numbers as its first argument. It also states that order will not generate a type error if it called with a list of numbers. Interestingly, it also asserts that calling **append** with its third argument instantiated to a list of numbers ensures that its second argument is instantiated to a list of numbers.

5.3   Work Related to Type Inference

Type analysis can be performed either with or without type definitions provided by the programmer. The former are easy for the programmer to understand whereas the latter are useful in compiler optimisation but can be more difficult for the programmer to interpret. If type definitions are not given by the programmer, then the analysis has to infer both the type definitions and the type descriptions for the program components. Traditionally unary regular logic programs [66] and type graphs [13] have been applied to this class of problem, though modern set-based techniques founded on non-deterministic finite tree automata offer a number of advantages [23].

Alternatively, if type definitions are supplied by the programmer, then the analysis need only infer type descriptions from the type constructors for the program components. In this class of problem of particular note is the work on formulating type dependency domains with ACI-unification [9] since the resulting domains condense. Directional type analysis [1,59] is likewise performed with type definitions provided by the programmer. A directional type $p(x) : \sigma \rightarrow \tau$ indicates that if $p(x)$ is called with x being of type σ then x is of type τ upon the success of $p(x)$. Aiken and Lakshman [1] provide a procedure for checking if a program is well-typed with respect to a given set of monomorphic directional types, whereas Rychlikowski and Truderung [59] provide type checking and inference algorithms for polymorphic types.

All the above type analyses propagate type information in the direction of program execution and compute upper approximations to the set of reachable program stores. In contrast, the backwards type analysis reviewed in this section propagates type information in the reverse direction of program execution and computes lower approximations to the set of program stores from which the execution will not violate any type assertions.

6   Directions for Research on Backwards Analysis

6.1   Backwards Analysis and Module Interaction

When reasoning about module interaction it can be advantageous to reverse the traditional deductive approach to abstract interpretation that is based on the abstract unfolding of abstract goals. In particular, [27] shows how abduction and abstraction can be combined to compute those properties that one module must satisfy to ensure that its composition with another fulfils certain requirements. Abductive analysis can, for example, determine how an optimisation in one module depends on a predicate defined in another module. Abductive analysis is related to backwards analysis since abduction is the inverse of deduction in much the same way that relative pseudo-complement is the reverse of conjunction. This suggests that the relationship between backwards analysis and abductive analysis warrants further investigation.

6.2   Backwards Analysis and Unfolding

Automatic program specialisation is a reoccurring theme in logic program development and one important aspect of this is the control of polyvariance [58]. Too much polyvariance (too many versions of a predicate) can lead to code bloat whereas too little polyvariance (too few versions of a predicate) can impede program specialisation and thereby efficiency. Surprisingly few works have addressed the problem of relating polyvariance to the ensuing optimisations [58], but recent work [49] has suggested that backwards analysis can be applied to control polyvariance by inferring specialisation conditions. Backwards analysis then becomes a pre-processing step that precedes the goal-dependent analysis and determines the degree of unfolding. Specifically, if the specialisation conditions are satisfied by an (abstract) call in a goal-dependent analysis then the call will possibly lead to valuable optimisations, and therefore it should not be merged with calls that lead to a lower level of optimisation. The backwards analysis in effect provides a convenient separation of concerns in that it enables version generation decisions to be made prior to applying top-down analysis. This work generalises and refines earlier work on compile-time garbage collection [48] that presents a kind of *ad hoc* backwards analysis for deriving reuse conditions for Mercury [62]. These works, and in particular [49], show how backwards analysis can provide a useful separation of concerns: the backwards analysis infers specialisation conditions which are later used in version control. This is reminiscent of the separation of control from unfolding that arises in off-line binding-time analysis [6]. In fact one promising direction for research would be to investigate how termination inference can be adapted to infer conditions under which loops can be partially unfolded.

6.3   Backwards Analysis and Hoare Logic

Pedreschi and Ruggieri [55] develop a calculus of weakest pre-conditions and weakest liberal pre-conditions, the latter of which is essentially a reformulation of Hoare's logic. Weakest liberal pre-conditions are characterised as the greatest fixpoint of a co-continuous operator on the space of interpretations. The work is motivated by, among other things, the desire to infer the absence of ill-typed arithmetic. Interestingly, it has been recently shown [40] that backwards analysis not only infers sufficient pre-conditions but the weakest pre-conditions. On the practical side, it means that backwards analysis need not be applied if forwards analysis cannot verify that a given query satisfies the assertions. Conversely, if an initial query is not inferred by backwards analysis, then it follows that forwards analysis cannot infer that the query satisfies the assertions. More generally, the expressive power of any backwards analysis needs to be compared against that of the forwards analysis that it attempts to reverse.

6.4   Backwards Analysis and Domain Refinement

Recent work in domain refinement [29] has shown that the problem of minimally enriching an abstract domain to make it condense reduces to the problem of making the domain complete with respect to unification. Specifically, the work shows that unification coincides with multiplicative conjunction in a quantale of (idempotent) substitutions and that elements in a complete refined (condensing) abstract domain can be expressed in terms of linear logic. The significance of this work for backwards analysis, is that it provides a pathway for synthesising condensing domains that are not necessarily downward-closed. This suggests that the framework of [39] needs to be revised to accommodate these domains.

6.5   Backwards Analysis and Transformation

Very recently Gallagher [22] has proposed program transformation as a tactic for realising backwards analysis in terms of forwards analysis. Assertions are realised with a meta-predicate $d(G, P)$ which expresses the relationship between an initial goal G and a property P to be checked at some program point. The meta-predicate $d(G,P)$ holds if there is a derivation starting from G leading to the program point. The transformed program defining the predicate d can be seen as a realisation of the resultants semantics [21]. Backwards analysis is performed by examining the meaning of d, which can be approximated using a standard forwards analysis, to deduce goals G that imply that the property P holds. This work is both promising and intriguing because it finesses the requirement of calculating a greatest fixpoint. One interesting line of enquiry would be to compare the expressive power of transformation – the pre-conditions its infers – against those deduced via a bespoke backwards analysis framework [39,44].

7   Concluding Discussion

This paper has shown how four classic program analysis and program development problems can be reversed. Reversal is a laudable goal in program analysis because it transforms a goal-dependent, checking problem into a goal-independent, inference problem; the latter being more general than the former. Arguably the greatest strength of backwards analysis is its ease of automation: backwards analyses can be surprisingly simple to implement and efficient to apply, and goal-independence means that it can be applied without any programmer interaction. Programmers merely have to interpret the inferred results and inspect the program if the results do not match their expectations. Thus, although backwards analysis is not yet a mainstream technology in the analysis of logic programs, its benefits need to be carefully weighed when a particular program development problem is being considered.

Backwards analysis is a modern approach to the analysis of logic programs in the sense that it relies on ideas that have been developed comparatively recently within the context of domain refinement. Backwards analysis thus illustrates the value of foundational work in logic program development. It also demonstrates the benefits of developing programs within the context of logic programming: the elegance of the underlying semantics manifests itself in the simplicity of the analyses. In fact it is fair to say that if we have seen slightly further in program development, it is only because we stand on the shoulders of those who have developed the underpinning semantics and abstract interpretation techniques.

Acknowledgements Our work on backwards analysis has greatly benefited from discussions with Maurice Bruynooghe, Mike Codish, John Gallagher, Samir Genaim, Roberto Giacobazzi, Bart Massey, Fred Mesnard, Germán Puebla, Francesca Scozzari to name but a few. We also thank the anonymous referees for their valuable comments. This work was supported, in part, by the Nuffield Foundation grant NAL/00478/G and the National Science Foundation grants CCR-0131862 and INT-0327760.

References

1. A. Aiken and T. K. Lakshman. Directional Type Checking of Logic Programs. In B. Le Charlier, editor, *Static Analysis Symposium*, volume 864 of *Lecture Notes in Computer Science*, pages 43–60. Springer-Verlag, 1994.
2. T. Armstrong, K. Marriott, P. Schachte, and H. Søndergaard. Two Classes of Boolean Functions for Dependency Analysis. *Science of Computer Programming*, 31(1):3–45, 1998.
3. F. Benoy and A. King. Inferring Argument Size Relationships with CLP($\mathcal{R}$). In J. Gallagher, editor, *Logic Program Synthesis and Transformation (Selected Papers)*, volume 1207 of *Lecture Notes in Computer Science*, pages 204–224. Springer-Verlag, 1996.
4. J. Boye, W. Drabent, and J. Małuszyński. Declarative Diagnosis of Constraint Programs: an Assertion-based Approach. In *Proceedings of the Third International Workshop on Automated Debugging*, pages 123–141. University of Linköping Press, 1997.
5. A. Brodsky and Y. Sagiv. Inference of Monotonicity Constraints in Datalog Programs. In *Symposium on Principles of Database Systems*, pages 190–199. ACM Press, 1989.
6. M. Bruynooghe, M. Leuschel, and K. Sagonas. A Polyvariant Binding-Time Analysis for Off-line Partial Deduction. In C. Hankin, editor, *European Symposium on Programming*, volume 1381 of *Lecture Notes in Computer Science*, pages 27–41. Springer-Verlag, 1998.
7. M. Carlsson. Freeze, Indexing, and Other Implementation Issues in the WAM. In J.-L. Lassez, editor, *International Conference on Logic Programming*, pages 40–58. MIT Press, 1987.
8. M. Codish, M. Falaschi, and K. Marriott. Suspension Analyses for Concurrent Logic Programs. *Transactions on Programming Languages and Systems*, 16(3):649–686, 1994.
9. M. Codish and V. Lagoon. Type Dependencies for Logic Programs using ACI-unification. *Theoretical Computer Science*, 238:131–159, 2000.
10. M. Codish and C. Taboch. A Semantic Basis for the Termination Analysis of Logic Programs. *The Journal of Logic Programming*, 41(1):103–123, 1999.

11. C. Codognet, P. Codognet, and M. Corsini. Abstract Interpretation for Concurrent Logic Languages. In S. K. Debray and M. V. Hermenegildo, editors, *North American Conference on Logic Programming*, pages 215–232. MIT Press, 1990.

12. M. Comini, R. Gori, G. Levi, and P. Volpe. Abstract Interpretation based Verification of Logic Programs. *Electronic Notes of Theoretical Computer Science*, 30(1), 1999.

13. A. Cortesi, B. Le Charlier, and P. Van Hentenryck. Type Analysis of Prolog using Type Graphs. *The Journal of Logic Programming*, 22(3):179–208, 1995.

14. P. Cousot and R. Cousot. Inductive Principles for Proving Invariance Properties of Programs. In *Tools and Notions for Program Construction*, pages 75–119. Cambridge University Press, 1982.

15. P. Cousot and N. Halbwachs. Automatic Discovery of Linear Restraints Among Variables of a Program. In *Symposium on Principles of Programming Languages*, pages 84–97. ACM Press, 1978.

16. S. K. Debray. QD-Janus: a Sequential Implementation of Janus in Prolog. *Software Practice and Experience*, 23(12):1337–1360, 1993.

17. S. K. Debray, D. Gudeman, and P. Bigot. Detection and Optimization of Suspension-free Logic Programs. *The Journal of Logic Programming*, 29(1–3):171–194, 1992.

18. P. Dyber. Inverse Image Analysis Generalises Strictness Analysis. *Information and Computation*, 90(2):194–216, 1991.

19. M. Falaschi, P. Hicks, and W. Winsborough. Demand Transformation Analysis for Concurrent Constraint Programs. *The Journal of Logic Programming*, 41(3):185–215, 2000.

20. M. Gabbrielli and R. Giacobazzi. Goal Independency and Call Patterns in the Analysis of Logic Programs. In *ACM Symposium on Applied Computing*, pages 394–399. ACM Press, 1994.

21. M. Gabbrielli, G. Levi, and M. C. Meo. Resultants Semantics for Prolog. *Journal of Logic and Computation*, 6(4):491–521, 1996.

22. J. P. Gallagher. A Program Transformation for Backwards Analysis of Logic Programs. In M. Bruynooghe, editor, *Pre-proceedings of the International Symposium on Logic-based Program Synthesis and Transformation*, volume CW 365 of *Katholieke Universiteit Leuven, Technical Report*, pages 113–122, 2003.

23. J. P. Gallagher and G. Puebla. Abstract Interpretation over Non-deterministic Finite Tree Automata for Set-based Analysis of Logic Programs. In S. Krishnamurthi and C. R. Ramakrishnan, editors, *Practical Aspects of Declarative Languages*, volume 2257 of *Lecture Notes in Computer Science*, pages 243–261. Springer-Verlag, 2002.

24. S. Genaim and M. Codish. Inferring Termination Conditions for Logic Programs using Backwards Analysis. In R. Nieuwenhuis and A. Voronkov, editors, *International Conference on Logic for Programming, Artificial Intelligence and Reasoning*, volume 2250 of *Lecture Notes in Artificial Intelligence*, pages 681–690. Springer-Verlag, 2001. Technical report version available at http://www.cs.bgu.ac.il/~mcodish/Papers/Pages/lpar01.html.

25. S. Genaim, M. Codish, J. P. Gallagher, and V. Lagoon. Combining Norms to Prove Termination. In A. Cortesi, editor, *Verification, Model Checking and Abstract Interpretation*, volume 2294 of *Lecture Notes in Computer Science*, pages 126–138. Springer-Verlag, 2002.

26. S. Genaim and A. King. Goal-Independent Suspension Analysis for Logic Programs with Dynamic Scheduling. In P. Degano, editor, *European Symposium on Programming*, volume 2618 of *Lecture Notes in Computer Science*, pages 84–98. Springer-Verlag, 2003.

27. R. Giacobazzi. Abductive Analysis of Modular Logic Programs. *Journal of Logic and Computation*, 8(4):457–484, 1998.

28. R. Giacobazzi, S. K. Debray, and G. Levi. Generalized Semantics and Abstract Interpretation for Constraint Logic Programs. *The Journal of Logic Programming*, 25(3):191–248, 1995.

29. R. Giacobazzi, F. Ranzato, and F. Scozzari. Making Abstract Domains Condensing. *ACM Transactions on Computational Logic*, To appear.

30. R. Giacobazzi and F. Scozzari. A Logical Model for Relational Abstract Domains. *ACM Transactions on Programming Languages and Systems*, 20(5):1067–1109, 1998.

31. C. Hall and D. Wise. Generating Function Versions with Rational Strictness Patterns. *Science of Computer Programming*, 12:39–74, 1989.

32. M. Hanus. Compile-time Analysis of Nonlinear Constraints in CLP($\mathcal{R}$). *New Generation Computing*, 13(2):155–186, 1995.

33. A. Heaton, M. Abo-Zaed, M. Codish, and A. King. A Simple Polynomial Groundness Analysis for Logic Programs. *The Journal of Logic Programming*, 45(1–3):143–156, 2000.

34. S. Hoarau and F. Mesnard. Inferring and Compiling Termination for Constraint Logic Programs. In P. Flener, editor, *Logic-based Program Synthesis and Transformation (Selected Papers)*, volume 1559 of *Lecture Notes in Computer Science*, pages 240–254. Springer-Verlag, 1998.

35. C. A. R. Hoare, I. J. Hayes, J. He, C. Morgan, A. W. Roscoe, J. W. Sanders, I. H. Sorensen, J. M. Spivey, and B. Sufrin. Laws of Programming. *Communications of the ACM*, 30(8):672–686, 1987.

36. J. M. Howe and A. King. Abstracting Numeric Constraints with Boolean Functions. *Information Processing Letters*, 75(1–2):17–23, 2000.

37. J. M. Howe and A. King. Positive Boolean Functions as Multiheaded Clauses. In P. Codognet, editor, *International Conference on Logic Programming*, volume 2237 of *Lecture Notes in Computer Science*, pages 120–134. Springer-Verlag, 2001.

38. J. M. Howe and A. King. Efficient Groundness Analysis in Prolog. *Theory and Practice of Logic Programming*, 3(1):95–124, 2003.

39. A. King and L. Lu. A Backward Analysis for Constraint Logic Programs. *Theory and Practice of Logic Programming*, 2:517–547, 2002.

40. A. King and L. Lu. Forward versus Backward Verification of Logic Programs. In C. Palamidessi, editor, *International Conference on Logic Programming*, volume 2916 of *Lecture Notes in Computer Science*, pages 315–330. Springer-Verlag, 2003.

41. A. King and P. Soper. Schedule Analysis of Concurrent Logic Programs. In K. R. Apt, editor, *Joint International Conference and Symposium on Logic Programming*, pages 478–492. MIT Press, 1992.

42. B. Le Charlier, C. Leclére, S. Rossi, and A. Cortesi. Automatic Verification of Prolog Programs. *The Journal of Logic Programming*, 39(1–3):3–42, 1999.

43. N. Lindenstrauss, Y. Sagiv, and A. Serebrenik. Unfolding the Mystery of Mergesort. In N. E. Fuchs, editor, *Logic Program Synthesis and Transformation (Selected Papers)*, volume 1463 of *Lecture Notes in Computer Science*, pages 206–225. Springer-Verlag, 1997.

44. L. Lu and A. King. Backward Type Inference Generalises Type Checking. In M. V. Hermenegildo and G. Puebla, editors, *Static Analysis Symposium*, volume 2477 of *Lecture Notes in Computer Science*, pages 85–101. Springer-Verlag, 2002.
45. K. Marriott, M. García de la Banda, and M. V. Hermenegildo. Analyzing Logic Programs with Dynamic Scheduling. In *Principles of Programming Languages*, pages 240–254. ACM Press, 1994.
46. K. Marriott and H. Søndergaard. Precise and Efficient Groundness Analysis for Logic Programs. *ACM Letters on Programming Languages and Systems*, 2(4):181–196, 1993.
47. J. C. Martin and A. King. Generating Efficient, Terminating Logic Programs. In *Theory and Practice of Software Development*, volume 1214 of *Lecture Notes in Computer Science*, pages 273–284. Springer-Verlag, 1997.
48. N. Mazur, G. Janssens, and M. Bruynooghe. A Module Based Analysis for Memory Reuse in Mercury. In *Computational Logic*, volume 1861 of *Lecture Notes in Artificial Intelligence*, pages 1255–1269, 2000.
49. N. Mazur, G. Janssens, and V. Van Hoof. Collecting Potential Optimizations. In M. Leuschel, editor, *Logic-based Program Synthesis and Transformation*, volume 2664 of *Lecture Notes in Computer Science*, pages 109–110, 2002.
50. F. Mesnard. Inferring Left-terminating Classes of Queries for Constraint Logic Programs. In *Joint International Conference and Symposium on Logic Programming*, pages 7–21. MIT Press, 1996.
51. F. Mesnard and U. Neumerkel. Applying Static Analysis Techniques for Inferring Termination Conditions of Logic Programs. In *Static Analysis Symposium*, volume 2126 of *Lecture Notes in Computer Science*, pages 93–110. Springer-Verlag, 2001.
52. F. Mesnard, É. Payet, and U. Neumerkel. Detecting Optimal Termination Conditions of Logic Programs. In M. V. Hermenegildo and G. Puebla, editors, *Static Analysis Symposium*, volume 2477 of *Lecture Notes in Computer Science*, pages 509–526. Springer-Verlag, 2002.
53. F. Mesnard and S. Ruggieri. On Proving Left Termination of Constraint Logic Programs. *ACM Transactions on Computational Logic*, 4(2):207–259, 2003.
54. L. Naish. Negation and Quantifiers in NU-Prolog. In E. Y. Shapiro, editor, *International Conference on Logic Programming*, volume 225 of *Lecture Notes in Computer Science*, pages 624–634. Springer-Verlag, 1986.
55. D. Pedreschi and S. Ruggieri. Weakest Preconditions for Pure Prolog Programs. *Information Processing Letters*, 67(3):145–150, 1998.
56. G. Puebla, F. Bueno, and M. V. Hermenegildo. An Assertion Language for Constraint Logic Programs. In *Analysis and Visualization Tools for Constraint Programming*, volume 1870 of *Lecture Notes in Computer Science*, pages 23–61. Springer-Verlag, 2000.
57. G. Puebla, F. Bueno, and M. V. Hermenegildo. A Generic Preprocessor for Program Validation and Debugging. In *Analysis and Visualization Tools for Constraint Programming*, volume 1870 of *Lecture Notes in Computer Science*, pages 63–107. Springer-Verlag, 2000.
58. G. Puebla and M. V. Hermenegildo. Abstract Multiple Specialization and its Application to Program Parallelization. *The Journal of Logic Programming*, 41(2&3):279–316, 1999.
59. P. Rychlikowski and T. Truderung. Polymorphic Directional Types for Logic Programming. In *International Conference on Principles and Practice of Declarative Programming*, pages 61–72. ACM Press, 2001.
60. V. A. Saraswat. *Concurrent Constraint Programming*. MIT Press, 1993.

61. V. A. Saraswat, K. Kahn, and J. Levy. Janus: a Step Towards Distributed Constraint Programming. In *North American Conference on Logic Programming*, pages 431–446. MIT Press, 1990.
62. Z. Somogyi, F. Henderson, and T. Conway. The Execution Algorithm of Mercury, an Efficient Purely Declarative Logic Programming Language. *The Journal of Logic Programming*, 29(1–3):17–64, 1996.
63. L. Vielle. Recursive Query Processing: The Power of Logic. *Theoretical Computer Science*, 69(1):1–53, 1989.
64. P. Volpe. A First-Order Language for Expressing Aliasing and Type Properties of Logic Programs. *Science of Computer Programming*, 39(1):125–148, 2001.
65. P. Wadler and R. J. M. Hughes. Projections for Strictness Analysis. In *Functional Programming and Computer Architecture*, volume 274 of *Lecture Notes in Computer Science*, pages 385–407. Springer-Verlag, 1987.
66. E. Yardeni and E. Y. Shapiro. A Type System for Logic Programs. *The Journal of Logic Programming*, 10(2):125–153, 1991.

Binding-Time Analysis for Mercury

Wim Vanhoof[1]*, Maurice Bruynooghe[2], and Michael Leuschel[3]

[1] University of Namur
wva@info.fundp.ac.be
[2] Katholieke Universiteit Leuven
Maurice.Bruynooghe@cs.kuleuven.ac.be
[3] University of Southampton
mal@ecs.soton.ac.uk

Abstract. In this work, we develop a binding-time analysis for the logic programming language Mercury. We introduce a precise domain of binding-times, based on the type information available in Mercury programs, that allows the analyser to reason with partially static data structures. The analysis is polyvariant, and deals with the module structure and higher-order capabilities of Mercury programs.

1 Introduction

Program specialisation is a technique that transforms a program into another program, by precomputing some of its operations. Assume we have a program P of which the input can be divided in two parts, say s and d. If one of the input parts, say s, is known at some point in the computation, we can *specialise* P with respect to the available input s. This specialisation process comprises performing those computations of P that depend only on s, and recording their *results* in a new program, together with the *code* for those computations that could not be performed (because they rely on the input part d – unknown at this point in the computation). The result of the specialisation is a new program, P_s that computes, when provided with the remaining input part d, the *same* result as P does when provided with the complete input $s + d$. Comprising a mixture of program evaluation and code generation, the program specialisation process is also often referred to by the names *partial evaluation, mixed computation* or *staged computation.*

Staging the computations of a program can be useful (usually in terms of efficiency) when different parts of a program's input become known at different times during the computation. The best benefit can be obtained when a single program must be run a number of times while a part of its input remains constant over the different runs. In this case, the program can first be specialised with respect to the constant part of the input, while afterwards the resulting program can be run a number of times, once for each of the remaining (different) input

---

* Sponsored by FWO Vlaanderen and Katholieke Universiteit Leuven at the time of this research.

M. Bruynooghe and K.-K. Lau (Eds.): Program Development in CL, LNCS 3049, pp. 189–232, 2004.

parts. In such a staged approach, the computations that depend only on the constant input part are performed only once – during specialisation. In the non-staged approach, *all* computations – including those depending on the constant part – are performed in every run of the program.

When using program specialisation to stage the computations of a program, the basic problem is deciding what computations can be safely performed during the specialisation process. The driving force behind this decision is twofold. Firstly, the specialisation process itself must terminate; that is, the specialiser must not to get into a loop when evaluating a sequence of computations from the program that is to be specialised. Secondly, the obtained degree of specialisation should be "as good as possible", meaning that a fair amount of computations that *can* be performed during specialisation *are* effectively performed during specialisation.

The key factor determining whether a computation can be performed during specialisation is the fact whether enough input values are available to compute a result. If that is the case, the specialiser can perform the computation; if not, it should generate code to perform this computation at a later stage. Binding-time analysis is a static analysis that, given the program and a description about the available partial input with respect to which the program will be specialised, computes for every statement in the program what input values will be known when that statement is reached during specialisation. In addition, the analysis computes — according to some control strategy — whether or not the statement should be evaluated during specialisation.

Once the program P and its available partial input s has been analysed by binding-time analysis, specialisation of P with respect to s boils down to evaluating those statements in P that are annotated as such by the binding-time analysis. This specialisation technique is called *offline*, the reason being that most of the control decisions about what statements should be evaluated have been taken by the binding-time analysis. This contrasts with the so-called *online* specialisation technique in which the program to be specialised is not analysed by any binding-time analysis, but is directly evaluated with respect to its partial input under the supervision of a control system that decides – for every statement under consideration – on the fly whether or not it can safely be evaluated. Both approaches towards specialisation have their advantages and disadvantages. In this work, we concentrate on *offline* specialisation and construct a binding-time analysis for the logic programming language Mercury.

1.1   Binding-Time Analysis and Logic Programming

Using binding-time analysis to control the behaviour of the specialisation has been thoroughly investigated in a number of programming paradigms. Breaking work on offline program specialisation of imperative languages include C-mix by Andersen [1] and more recently Tempo [10,20] by Consel and his group. In the context of functional language specialisation, most work focusing on binding-time analysis and offline specialisation was originally motivated by the desire to achieve better self-application [13,24]. Whereas initial analysis dealt with first-order languages [24], more recently developed analyses deal with higher-order aspects [15,4], polymorphism [32,19] and partially static data structures [28].

In the field of logic programming, however, only little attention has been paid to offline program specialisation. Known exceptions are LOGIMIX [33] and LOGEN [25] that develop different approaches to offline program specialisation for Prolog. Both cited works, however, lack an automatic binding-time analysis and rely on the user to provide the specialiser with suitable annotations of the program. To the best of our knowledge, the only attempt to construct an automatic binding-time analysis for logic programming is [6] and our own work about which we report in [30]. The approach of [6] is particular, in the sense that it obtains the required annotations not by analysing the subject program directly but rather by analysing the behaviour of an *online* program specialiser on the subject program. Although conceptually interesting, the latter approach is overly conservative and restricts the number of computations that can be performed during specialisation. Indeed, [6] decides whether to unfold a call or not based on the original program, not taking current annotations into account. This means that a call can either be completely unfolded or not at all. The binding-time analysis first described in [50] and employed in [30] is also particular in the sense that it obtains its annotations by repeatedly applying an automatic termination analysis. If the termination analysis identifies a call as possibly non-terminating, that call is marked such that it will not be reduced by the specialiser. Then the termination analysis is rerun to prove termination of the program under the assumption that each call that is marked as non-reducible is not evaluated. The process is repeated until termination of the (annotated) program can be proven.

Both the approach of [6] and [30] have been designed towards dealing with untyped and unmoded logic programming languages. The fact that most logic programming languages are untyped makes it harder to represent the availability of *partial* input in a sufficiently precise way during the analysis. More importantly, the lack of control flow information in the program makes it very difficult to approximate the data flow in a sufficiently precise way and renders the derivation of a binding-time analysis by "classic" abstract interpretation techniques not straightforward, hence the approaches of [6] and [30]. In this work, we construct a completely automatic binding-time analysis for the recently introduced logic programming language Mercury. Being a strongly typed and moded language, Mercury lifts the obstacles encountered in more traditional logic programming languages and allows to construct a "traditional" binding-time analysis along the lines of [15,23] based on data flow analysis. However, the more involved data- and control flow features – inherent to a logic programming language – render the derivation of an automatic binding-time analysis a daunting and not straightforward task.

1.2 Mercury

The design of Mercury was started in October 1993 by researchers at the University of Melbourne. While logic programming languages had been around for quite some time, no one seemed to fully realise the theoretical advantages such a language would have over more traditional, imperative languages. These advantages are widely known, and are summarised for example in [42]: a higher level of expressivity (enabling the programmer to concentrate on *what* has to be done rather than on *how* to do it), the availability of a useful formal semantics (required for the – relatively – straightforward design of analysis and transformation tools), a semantics that is independent of any order of evaluation (useful for parallelising the code), and a potential for declarative debugging [31]. While a language like Prolog does offer some of these advantages, others are destroyed by the impure features of the language.

The main objective of the Mercury designers was to create a logic programming language that would be *pure* and useful for the implementation of a large number of *real-world* applications. To achieve this goal, the main design objectives of Mercury can be summarised as follows [42]: *Support for the creation of reliable programs.* This involves a language that allows the compiler to detect some classes of bugs. *Support for programming in teams.* Large software systems are usually build by a number of programmers. The language must provide good support for creating a single application from multiple parts that are build (sometimes in isolation) by different programmers. These two objectives form a major departure from Prolog which, at the time, had basically no support for programming in the large, and which does not allow a lot of type-, mode- and determinism errors to be caught at compile-time. Another important objective was *support for the creation of efficient programs.* The compiler had to produce code whose performance is competitive with that produced by compilers of other languages. To meet these design objectives, Mercury was fitted with a strong system of type-, mode- and determinism declarations. Besides providing the programmer with some valuable documentation, these declarations enable the compiler to check the internal consistency of the program and to spot a substantial number of bugs that would go unnoticed in declaration free code submitted to a Prolog compiler. Also, the availability of declarations allows to adapt the evaluation order of the body atoms in a predicate and provides as such the basis for an efficient execution mechanism of the language [11,41,43]. Mercury is equipped with a modern module system that enables to hide some data definitions and to encapsulate both data and code, and provides as such support for programming-in-the-large activities.

1.3   Structure of the Paper

The remainder of this paper is organised as follows. In the following section, we introduce a domain of binding-times that is based on the type information available in Mercury programs. Next, in Section 3, we introduce a 2-phase binding-time analysis for a first-order subset of Mercury. The first part of the analysis performs a symbolic data flow analysis that – being call-independent – can be performed for each module in isolation, bottom-up over the module hierarchy. The second phase of the analysis, which computes the actual annotations, is call-dependent by nature and relies on the result of the symbolic analysis for all modules involved. In Section 4, we lift the first-order restriction and enhance the analysis such that it computes and propagates closure information throughout the program that is being analysed. In Section 5, we work through an example and discuss to what extent our method is also applicable to typed Prolog programs. We conclude this paper in Section 6 with a discussion of our binding-time analysis and its relation with existing work in the literature.

2   A Domain of Binding-Times

Binding-time analysis can be seen as an application of abstract interpretation over a domain of *binding-times*. A binding-time abstracts a value by specifying at what time during a 2-stage computation[4] the value becomes known. In their most basic form, the binding-time of a value is either *static* or *dynamic*, denoting a value that is known early, during specialisation, or late, during evaluation of the residual program, respectively.

It is recognised [23] that for a logic programming language, approximating values by either *static* or *dynamic* is too coarse grained in general. Indeed, most logic programs use a lot of *structured* data, where data values are represented by structured terms. Consequently, the input to the specialiser usually consists of a partially instantiated term: a term that is less instantiated than it would be at run-time. Approximating a partially instantiated term by *dynamic* usually results in too much information loss, possibly resulting in missed specialisation opportunities. Therefore, we use the structural information from the type system of Mercury to represent more detailed binding-times, capable of distinguishing between the computation stages in which *parts* of a value (according to that value's type) become known.

In what follows, we formally define the notions of type, type definition, type trees and type graphs, which we wil use later on as the basis of our abstract domain. Our formalisation is mainly based on [47,48] and [46], but similar notions and definitions can be found in related work on program analysis involving types, like e.g. [39,22,45,38,37]. Mercury's type system is based on a polymorphic many-sorted logic, and corresponds to the Mycroft-O'Keefe type system [34]. Basically, the types are discriminated union types and support parametric polymorphism: a type definition can be parametrised with some type variables, as the following example in Mercury syntax shows.

Example 1. :- type list(T) ---> [] ; [T | list(T)].

The above defines a polymorphic type list(T): it defines values of this type to be terms that are either [] (the empty list) or of the form [A|B] where A is a value of type T and B is a value of type list(T).

Formally, if we denote with Σ_T the set of type constructors and with V_T the set of type variables of a language $\mathcal{L}$, the set of *types* associated to $\mathcal{L}$ is

---

[4] Generalisations exist in which computations are staged over more than 2 stages (see e.g. [14]). In this work, we focus on a traditional 2-stage process, dividing the computations in a program over *specialisation-time* versus *run-time*.

represented by $\mathcal{T}(\Sigma_T, V_T)$; that is the set of terms that can be constructed from Σ_T and V_T. A type containing variables is said to be *polymorphic*, otherwise it is a *monomorphic* type. A *type substitution* is a substitution from type variables to types. The application of a type substitution to a polymorphic type results in a new type, which is an *instance* of the original type.

As usual, the set of program values is denoted by $\mathcal{T}(\mathcal{V}, \Sigma)$; that is the set of terms that can be constructed from a set Σ of function symbols and a set $\mathcal{V}$ of program variables.

The relation between a type and the values (terms) that constitute the type is made explicit by a *type definition* that consists of a number of *type rules*, one for every type constructor. Example 1 shows the type rule associated to the `list/1` type constructor. Formally, a type rule is defined as follows:

Definition 1 (type rule). *The* type rule *associated to a type constructor $h/n \in \Sigma_T$ is a definition of the form*

$$h(\overline{T}) \rightarrow f_1(\overline{\tau}_1) \,;\, \ldots \,;\, f_k(\overline{\tau}_k).$$

where $\overline{T}$ is a sequence of n type variables from V_T and for $1 \leq i \leq k$, $f_i/m \in \Sigma$ with $\overline{\tau}_i$ a sequence of m types from $\mathcal{T}(\Sigma_T, V_T)$ and all of the type variables occurring in the right hand side occur in the left hand side as well. The function symbols $\{f_1, \ldots, f_k\}$ are said to be associated with the type constructor h. A finite set of type rules is called a type definition.

Given a type substitution, we define the notion of an instance of a type rule in a straightforward way. In theory, every type (constructor) can be defined by a type rule as above. In practice, however, it is useful to have some types builtin in the system. For Mercury, the types `int`, `float`, `char`, `string` are builtin types whose denotation is predefined and is the set of integers, floating point numbers, characters and strings respectively. A type is called *atomic* if it is defined by a set of zero-arity function symbols $\{f_1, \ldots, f_k\}$.

Mercury is a statically typed language, in which the (possibly polymorphic) type of every term occurring in the program text is known at compile-time. In what follows, we use the type definition to construct, for every type occurring in the program, a finite description of the *structure* that values belonging to the denotation of a particular type can take. The relevance of such a description is in the fact that it can be used to abstract the values belonging to the denotation of the type according to their structure. This allows the construction of a precise abstract domain for program analysis, in particular binding-time analysis.

To extract a structural description of a type from a type definition, we introduce the notion of a type-path being a sequence of functor/argument position pairs that is meant to denote a path through the type definition from a type to an occurrence of one of its subtypes. In fact, a type itself can be represented as a (possibly infinite) set of such paths, one for every path from the type that is being defined to some subtype occurring at a particular position within some term belonging to the denotation of that type. More formally, we denote the set of all such sequences over $\Sigma \times \mathbb{N}$ by *TPath*. The empty sequence is denoted by $\langle\rangle$, and given $\delta, \gamma \in TPath$, we denote with $\delta.\gamma$ the sequence obtained by concatenating γ to δ. A *type tree* for a particular type can then be defined as follows:

Definition 2 (type tree). *Given a type $\tau \in \mathcal{T}(\Sigma_T, V_T)$, the type tree of τ, denoted by $\mathcal{L}_\tau$, is a set of sequences from TPath and is recursively defined as:*

- $\langle\rangle \in \mathcal{L}_\tau$
- *if $\tau = h(\overline{T})\theta$ and $h(\overline{T}) \rightarrow f_1(\overline{\tau}_1); \ldots; f_k(\overline{\tau}_k)$ is a type rule then $\langle(f_i, j)\rangle.\delta \in \mathcal{L}_\tau$ where (i) $i \in \{1 \ldots k\}$, (ii) f_i has arity m in Σ, (iii) $j \in \{1 \ldots m\}$, (iv) τ_{i_j} denotes the j-th type in $\overline{\tau}_i$, and (v) $\delta \in \mathcal{L}_{(\tau_{i_j})\theta}$.*

Note that the type tree of an atomic type is $\{\langle\rangle\}$ as a term belonging to an atomic type does not have any subterms. Likewise, also the type tree of a type variable T is defined as $\mathcal{L}_T = \{\langle\rangle\}$.

Example 2. Reconsider the type $list(T)$ from Example 1. As $\mathcal{L}_T = \{\langle\rangle\}$, the type tree of $list(T)$ is the infinite set of type paths

$$\mathcal{L}_{list(T)} = \left\{ \begin{array}{l} \langle\rangle \\ \langle([|], 1)\rangle \\ \langle([|], 2)\rangle \\ \langle([|], 2), ([|], 1)\rangle \\ \langle([|], 2), ([|], 2)\rangle \\ \langle([|], 2), ([|], 2), ([|], 1)\rangle \\ \langle([|], 2), ([|], 2), ([|], 2)\rangle \\ \langle([|], 2), ([|], 2), ([|], 2), ([|], 1)\rangle \\ \ldots \end{array} \right\}$$

The general idea now is to define, for any type τ, a finite approximation of $\mathcal{L}_\tau$ that provides a good characterisation of the structure of terms of type τ. First we introduce the following notation that formally defines the (sub)type that is identified by a type-path within another type.

Definition 3 (type selected by type-path). *Let $\tau = h(\overline{T})\theta$ be a type and δ a path in $\mathcal{L}_\tau$. If $\delta = \langle\rangle$ then $\tau^\delta = \tau$. Otherwise, δ has the form $\langle(f, i)\rangle.\gamma$, the type rule for $h(\overline{T})$ has in the right-hand side an alternative of the form $f(\tau_{i_1}, \ldots, \tau_{i_{k_i}})$ and $\tau^\delta = \tau_{j_i}^\gamma$.*

Note that a type path $\delta \in \mathcal{L}_\tau$ can also be used to identify a particular subterm in a term $t : \tau$, if it exists. Indeed, if $\delta \in TPath$ is of the form $\delta = \langle(f, i)\rangle.\gamma$ and $t = f(t_1, \ldots, t_n)$ we define $t^\delta = t_i^\gamma$.

Example 3. If $\tau = list(T)$ we have for example that

$$\tau^{\langle\rangle} = list(T), \tau^{\langle([|], 1)\rangle} = T \text{ and } \tau^{\langle([|], 2)\rangle} = \tau^{\langle([|], 2), ([|], 2)\rangle} = list(T).$$

Similarily for a term $t = [1, 2]$ we have for example that

$$t^{\langle\rangle} = [1, 2], t^{\langle([|], 1)\rangle} = 1 \text{ and } t^{\langle([|], 2)([|], 1)\rangle} = 2.$$

In what follows, we will use the notion of a type-graph as a finite approximation of a possibly infinite type-tree. Therefore, we introduce the following equivalence relation on the paths in a type tree $\mathcal{L}_\tau$. We define $\equiv$ (in $\mathcal{L}_\tau$) as the least transitive relation such that for any $\delta, \alpha \in \mathcal{L}_\tau$: if $\delta = \alpha.\gamma$ and $\tau^\delta = \tau^\alpha$ then $\alpha \equiv \delta$. Informally, two type paths in a type tree are equivalent if either one of the paths is an extension of the other while both identify the same type, or the paths share a common initial subpath of the same type as both paths in $\mathcal{L}_\tau$. In what follows, we restrict our attention to (possibly polymorphic) types that are not defined in terms of a strict instance of itself. That is, we assume for any type τ and $\delta \in \mathcal{L}_\tau$ that there doesn't exist a type substitution θ such that $\tau^\delta = \tau\theta$. This is a natural condition and is related to the polymorphism discipline of definitional genericity [27]. For any such type τ, the equivalence relation $\equiv$ partitions the (possibly infinite set) $\mathcal{L}_\tau$ into a finite number of equivalence classes. For any $\delta \in \mathcal{L}_\tau$, the equivalence class of δ is defined as

$$[\delta] = \{\gamma \in \mathcal{L}_\tau \mid \delta \equiv \gamma\}.$$

The least element of an equivalence class $[\delta]$ exists and is defined as follows.

$$\overline{[\delta]} = \alpha \in [\delta] \text{ such that } \forall \beta \in [\delta] : \beta = \alpha.\gamma \text{ for some } \gamma \in \mathit{TPath}$$

Next, we define, for a type τ, its *type graph* as the finite set of minimal elements of the equivalence classes of $\mathcal{L}_\tau$:

Definition 4 (type-graph). *For a type* $\tau \in \mathcal{T}(\Sigma_T, V_T)$, *we denote* τ*'s type graph by* $\mathcal{L}_\tau^\equiv$ *which is defined as*

$$\mathcal{L}_\tau^\equiv = \{\overline{[\delta]} \mid \delta \in \mathcal{L}_\tau\}.$$

A type graph $\mathcal{L}_\tau^\equiv$ provides a finite approximation of the structure of terms of type τ: every path in $\mathcal{L}_\tau^\equiv$ abstracts a number of subterms of the term according to their type and position in the term. For the $list(T)$ type from above, $\mathcal{L}_{list(T)}^\equiv = \{\langle\rangle, \langle([|], 1)\rangle\}$. The path $\langle\rangle$ represents all subterms of type $list(T)$ in a term of type $list(T)$, whereas $\langle([|], 1)\rangle$ represents all subterms of type T occurring in the first argument position of a functor $[|]$. In other words, $\langle\rangle$ can be seen as identifying the skeleton of the list, whereas $\langle([|], 1)\rangle$ as identifying the elements of the list. Note that as our notions of type-tree and type-graph describe the possible *positions* of subterms in terms of a particular type, they do not contain the zero-arity functors that possibly belong to the definition of the type. As such, our notions differ from more classic definions of type-trees and type-graphs like e.g. [22] or [39]. Also note that due to the particular definition of $\equiv$, two subterms of a same type are not necessarily abstracted by the same node in $\mathcal{L}_\tau^\equiv$. This is the case when $\mathcal{L}_\tau$ contains two type paths identifying the same type without them being equivalent, as in the next example.

Example 4. Consider the type $pair(T)$ defined as

$$pair(T) \longrightarrow (T - T).$$

A term of the type $pair(T)$ is a term $(A - B)$ where A and B are terms of type T. For $\tau = pair(T)$,

$$typetree_\tau = \mathcal{L}_\tau^\equiv = \left\{ \begin{matrix} \langle\rangle \\ \langle(-), 1\rangle \\ \langle(-), 2\rangle \end{matrix} \right\}$$

Although $\langle(-), 1\rangle$ and $\langle(-), 2\rangle$ identify subterms of the same type T, they are not equivalent according to the definition of equivalence.

The ability to distinguish between two occurrences of the same type in $\mathcal{L}_\tau^\equiv$ allows a characterisation of terms of type τ with a finer granularity than with type based analyses [51,7,26]. This is illustrated with Example 4. A type based analysis places the two components of a pair in the same equivalence class as $\langle(-), 1\rangle$ and $\langle(-), 2\rangle$ select nodes of the same type. We do not and can calculate different binding times for them.

Now, one can obtain an abstract characterisation of terms of type τ, based on the structure of the term (or at least the type it belongs to), by associating an abstract value to each of the paths in $\mathcal{L}_\tau^\equiv$. For binding-time analysis, we are interested in the time a (part of a) value becomes known in the computation process. We use the abstract values $\mathcal{B} = \{static, dynamic\}$. $static$ denotes that the binding certainly occurs at specialisation time; $dynamic$ that it is not known when (and in case of logic programs "if") the binding occurs. A binding-time associates a value from $\mathcal{B}$ to each of the paths in a type graph.

Definition 5 (binding-time). *A* binding-time *for a type* $t \in \mathcal{T}(\Sigma_T, V_T)$ *is a function*

$$\beta : \mathcal{L}_t^\equiv \mapsto \mathcal{B}$$

such that $\forall \delta \in dom(\beta)$ *holds that* $\beta(\delta) = dynamic$ *implies that* $\beta(\delta') = dynamic$ *for all* $\delta' \in dom(\beta)$ *with* $\delta' = \delta.\gamma$ *for some* $\gamma \in TPath$. *The set of all binding-times (independent of the type) is denoted by* $\mathcal{BT}$.

The relation between terms and the binding-times that approximate them is given by the following abstraction function.

Definition 6 (binding-time abstraction). *The* binding-time abstraction *is a function* $\alpha : \mathcal{T}(\Sigma, V) \mapsto \mathcal{BT}$ *and is defined as follows:*

$$\alpha(t : \tau) = \left\{ (\delta, v) \left| \begin{matrix} \delta \in \mathcal{L}_\tau^\equiv \text{ and } v = dynamic \text{ if } \exists\theta \text{ and a subterm } t^{\delta'} \text{ in } t\theta \\ \text{such that } t^{\delta'} \text{ is a variable and } \delta \equiv \delta' \\ v = static \text{ otherwise} \end{matrix} \right. \right\}$$

If a term $t : \tau$ contains a subterm $t^{\delta'}$ that is a variable, then the binding-time abstraction associates the value $dynamic$ to the path in $\mathcal{L}_\tau^\equiv$ that identifies this subterm and to all its extensions in $\mathcal{L}_\tau^\equiv$.

Example 5. Given the following terms of type $list(T)$ as defined in Example 1, their binding-time abstraction is:

$$
\begin{aligned}
\alpha([]) &= \{(\langle\rangle, static), (\langle\langle([], 1\rangle\rangle, static)\} \\
\alpha([X_1, X_2]) &= \{(\langle\rangle, static), (\langle\langle([], 1\rangle\rangle, dynamic)\} \\
\alpha(X) &= \{(\langle\rangle, dynamic), (\langle\langle([], 1\rangle\rangle, dynamic)\} \\
\alpha([X|Y]) &= \{(\langle\rangle, dynamic), (\langle\langle([], 1\rangle\rangle, dynamic)\}
\end{aligned}
$$

Since the term $[]$ does not contain any variable, it is abstracted by a binding-time specifying that the list's skeleton as well as its elements are *static*. A term $[X_1, X_2]$ is approximated by a binding-time specifying that the list's skeleton is *static*, but its elements are *dynamic*. A variable is abstracted by a binding-time specifying that the list's skeleton as well as its elements are *dynamic*. Also a term $[X|Y]$ is approximated by a binding-time stating that its list skeleton as well as its elements are dynamic due to the presence of the variable subterm $Y : list(T)$.

The following example shows why, if the value *dynamic* is associated to a path δ in a binding-time for a type τ, *dynamic* is also associated to all extensions of δ in $\mathcal{L}_\tau^{\equiv}$.

Example 6. Consider a type definition for a tree of integers:

```
inttree ---> nil ; t(int, inttree, inttree).
```

The type graph of $\tau = inttree$, $\mathcal{L}_\tau^{\equiv}$ contains only two paths: $\langle\rangle$ denoting the tree's skeleton, and $\langle t, 1\rangle$ denoting the integer elements in the tree. We have

$$
\alpha(t(0, X, t(1, nil, nil))) = \{(\langle\rangle, dynamic), (\langle t, 1\rangle, dynamic)\}.
$$

Although all subterms of type *int* in the term $t(0, X, t(1, nil, nil))$ are non-variable terms, we cannot abstract them to *static*. Indeed, the variable X in the term, being of type *inttree*, possibly represents some unknown integer elements.

To make our approximations suitable for a binding-time analysis, we define a partial order relation on $\mathcal{BT}$:

Definition 7 (covers). *Let β and $\beta' \in \mathcal{BT}$ such that $dom(\beta) \subseteq dom(\beta')$ or $dom(\beta') \subseteq dom(\beta)$. We say that β covers β', denoted by $\beta \succeq \beta'$ if and only if $\beta'(\delta) = dynamic \to \beta(\delta) = dynamic$ holds for all $\delta \in dom(\beta) \cap dom(\beta')$.*

If a binding-time β covers another binding-time β', then β is "at least as dynamic" as β'. Note that the relationship between $dom(\beta)$ and $dom(\beta')$ implies that the *covers* relation is only defined between two binding-times that are derived from types τ and τ' such that either τ is an instance of τ' or τ' is an instance of τ.

Example 7. Recall the binding-times obtained by abstracting the terms in Example 5. We have that

$$
\alpha(X) \succeq \alpha([X_1, X_2]) \succeq \alpha([])
$$

In what follows, we extend the notion of the $\succeq$ relation to include the elements $\{\top, \bot\}$ such that $\top \succeq \beta$ and $\beta \succeq \bot$ for all $\beta \in \mathcal{BT}$. If we denote with $\mathcal{BT}^+$ the set $\mathcal{BT}^+ = \mathcal{BT} \cup \{\top, \bot\}$, $(\mathcal{BT}^+, \succeq)$ forms a complete lattice. Wherever appropriate, we use $\bot$ and $\top$ to denote, for a particular type, a binding-time in which all paths are mapped to *static*, respectively a binding-time in which all paths are mapped to *dynamic*. Occasionally we will also call such binding-times completely static and completely dynamic, respectively.

We conclude this section by introducing some more notation. First, if β denotes a binding-time for a type τ and $\delta \in dom(\beta)$, then β^δ denotes the binding-time for a type τ^δ that is obtained as follows:

$$\beta^\delta = \left\{ \, (\gamma, \beta([\overline{\delta.\gamma}])) \big| \gamma \in \mathcal{L}_{\tau^\delta}^{\equiv} \, \right\} .$$

In other words, if $\beta = \alpha(t)$ then $\beta^\delta = \alpha(t^\delta)$. Finally, let $\tau, \tau_1, \ldots, \tau_n$ be types and $f \in \Sigma$ such that $f(t_1 : \tau_1, \ldots, t_n : \tau_n)$ is a term in the denotation of τ. If $\beta_1, \ldots, \beta_n$ are binding-times for the types $\tau_1, \ldots, \tau_n$, we denote with $f(\beta_1, \ldots, \beta_n)$ the *least dynamic* binding-time for type τ such that $\beta^{[\langle (f,i) \rangle]} \succeq \beta_i$ for all i.

3 A Modular Binding-Time Analysis for Mercury

In what follows, we develop a polyvariant binding-time analysis. The final output of the analysis is an annotated program in which each of the original procedures may occur in several annotated versions, depending on the binding-times of the (input) arguments with respect to which the procedure was called. Each such version contains the binding-times of the local variables and output arguments as well as instructions stating for each subgoal of the procedure's body whether or not it should be evaluated during specialisation. Correctness of the analysis ensures that if a particular call $p(t_1, \ldots, t_n)$ occurs during specialisation, the analysis has created a version of the called procedure that is annotated with respect to the particular call's binding-time abstraction $p(\alpha(t_1), \ldots, \alpha(t_n))$. Before we define the actual analysis, we introduce Mercury's module system and define some necessary machinery to base the analysis upon.

3.1 Mercury's Module System

A Mercury program is defined as a set of Mercury modules. The basic module system of Mercury is simple. A module consists of an *interface* part and an *implementation* part. The interface part contains those type definitions and procedure declarations that the module provides (or *exports*) towards other modules. In other words, the types and procedures declared in the interface part of a module are visible and can be used (or *imported*) by other modules. Apart from the implementation of the procedures that are declared in the module's interface, its implementation part possibly contains additional type definitions and the declaration and implementation of additional procedures. These types and procedures are only visible in the implementation part of this module, and can not be used by other modules.

Note that the way in which the modules import each other impose a hierarchy on the modules that constitute a program.[5] Following the terminology of [36], we use the notation $imports(M, M')$ to indicate that the module M imports the interface of M' and $imported(M)$ to denote the set of modules that are imported by M, that is: $imported(M) = \{M' \mid imports(M, M')\}$. Figure 1 shows an example of a module hierarchy in Mercury in which we graphically represent a module by a box, and denote $imports(M, M')$ by an arrow from M towards M'. In the example, we have that $imported(M_1) = \{M_2, M_3, M_5\}$. Note that in

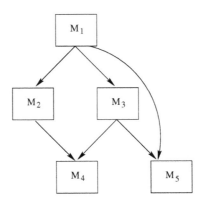

Fig. 1. A sample module hierarchy.

Mercury, the *imports* relation is not transitive; when a module M imports the interface of a module M', it becomes dependent on the interfaces imported by M' (and those imported therein) but it does not import these itself. The module system described above is to some extent a simplification of Mercury's real module system, in which modules can be constructed from submodules. While submodules do provide extra means to the programmer to control encapsulation and visibility of declarations, they do not pose additional conceptual difficulties and we do not consider them in the remainder of this work.

In this work, we aim at developing a binding-time analysis that is as modular as possible. Ultimately, a modular analysis deals with each module of a program in isolation. We will discuss throughout the text to what extent our binding-time analysis is modular in this respect.

3.2   Mercury Programs for Analysis

Mercury is an expressive language, in which programs can be composed of predicates and functions, one can use DCG notation, etc. However, if we consider

---

[5] While in Mercury modules may depend on each other in a circular way, we restrict our attention to programs in which no circular dependencies exist between the modules. We discuss how one could deal with circular dependencies in Section 6.

only programs that are type correct and well-moded – which is natural, since the compiler should reject programs that are not [43] – such a program can be translated into *superhomogeneous form* [43]. Translation to superhomogeneous form involves a number of analysis and transformation steps. These include translating an *n*-ary function definition into an $n + 1$ ary predicate definition [44], making the implicit arguments in DCG-predicate definitions and calls explicit, and copying and renaming predicate definitions and calls such that every remaining predicate definition has a single mode declaration associated with it [43] that specifies for each argument whether it is an input or output argument. As such, every predicate definition is transformed to a set of so-called *procedure* definitions, with one procedure for every mode in which the original predicate is used.

For our analysis purposes, we assume that a Mercury program is given in superhomogeneous form. This does not involve any loss of generality, as the transformation from a plain Mercury program into superhomogeneous form is completely defined and automated [43]. Formally, the syntax of Mercury programs in superhomogeneous form can be defined as follows. We use the symbol Π to refer to the set of *procedure* symbols underlying the language associated to the program. As such, we consider two procedures that are derived from the same predicate as having different procedure symbols.

Definition 8 (superhomogeneous form).

$Proc ::= p(\overline{X}) : -G.$
$Goal := Atom \mid not(G) \mid (G_1 , G_2) \mid (G_1 ; G_2) \mid if\,G_1\,then\,G_2\,else\,G_3$
$Atom ::= X := Y \mid X == Y \mid X \Rightarrow f(\overline{Y}) \mid X \Leftarrow f(\overline{Y}) \mid p(\overline{X})$

where $p/n \in \Pi$, X and Y are distinct variables and $\overline{X}$ is a sequence of n distinct variables of $\mathcal{V}$, $f/m \in \Sigma$, $\overline{Y}$ a sequence of m distinct variables of $\mathcal{V}$, and $G, G_1, G_2, G_3 \in Goal$.

The definition of a procedure p in superhomogeneous form consists of a single clause. The sequence of arguments in the head of the clause, denoted by $\mathcal{A}rgs(p)$, are distinct variables, explicit unifications are created for these variables in the body goal – denoted by $\mathcal{B}ody(p)$ – and complex unifications are broken down in several simpler ones. The arguments of a procedure p are divided in a set of input arguments, denoted by $in(p)$ and a set of output arguments denoted by $out(p)$. A goal is either an atom or a number of goals connected by *conjunction, disjunction, if then else* or *not*. An atom is either a unification or a procedure call. Note that, as an effect of mode analysis [43], unifications are categorised as follows:

– An *assignment* of the form $X := Y$. For such a unification, Y is input, whereas X is output.
– A *test* of the form $X == Y$. Both X and Y are input to the unification and of atomic type.
– A *deconstruction* of the form $X \Rightarrow f(\overline{Y})$. In this case, X is input to the unification whereas $\overline{Y}$ is a sequence of output variables.

– A *construction* of the form $X \Leftarrow f(\overline{Y})$. In this case X is output from the unification whereas $\overline{Y}$ is a sequence of input variables.

During the translation into superhomogeneous form, unifications between values of a complex data type may be transformed into a call to a newly generated procedure that (possibly recursively) performs the unification. For any goal G, we denote with $\text{in}(G)$ and $\text{out}(G)$ the set of its input, respectively output variables[6]

Example 8. Consider the classical definition of the append/3 predicate, both in normal syntax and in superhomogeneous form for the mode append(in,in,out) as depicted in Fig. 2.

append/3	append/3 in superhomogeneous form
append([],Y,Y).	append(X,Y,Z):-
append([E|Es],Y,[E|R]):-	(X⇒[], Z:=Y ;
append(Xs,Y,R).	X⇒[E|Es], append(Es, Y, R), Z⇐[E|R]).

Fig. 2. The append/3 predicate and append(in,in,out) in superhomogeneous form.

According to Definition 8, conjunctions and disjunctions are considered binary constructs. This differs from their representation inside the Melbourne compiler [40], where conjunctions and disjunctions are represented in flattened form. Our syntactic definition however facilitates the conceptual handling of these constructs during analysis.

For analysis purposes, we assume that every subgoal of a procedure body is identified by a unique program point, the set of all such program points is denoted by $\mathcal{Pp}$. If we are dealing with a particular procedure, we denote with η_0 the program point associated with the procedure's head atom, and with η_b the program point associated to its body goal. The set of program points identifying the subgoals of a goal G is denoted by $\mathcal{Pps}(G)$, this set includes the program point identifying G itself. If the particular program point identifying a goal G in a procedure's body is important, we subscribe the goal with its program point, as in G_η or explicitly state that $\mathcal{Pp}(G) = \eta$. An important use of program points is to identify those atoms in the body of a procedure in which a particular variable becomes initialised or, said otherwise, those atoms of which the variable is an output variable. This information is computed by mode analysis, and we assume the availability of a function

$$\text{init} : \mathcal{V} \mapsto \wp(\mathcal{Pp})$$

---

[6] Although Mercury has some support for more involved modes – other than input versus output – that are necessary to support *partially instantiated data structures* at run-time, release 0.9 of the Mercury implementation [40] does not fully support these.

with the intended meaning that, for a variable V used in some procedure, if $\text{init}(V) = \{\eta_1, \ldots, \eta_n\}$, the variable V is an output variable of the atoms identified by $\eta_1, \ldots, \eta_n$. Note that the function init is implicitly associated with a particular procedure, which we do not mention explicitly. When we use the function init, it will be clear from the context to what particular procedure it is associated.

Example 9. Let us recall the definition of $\texttt{append/3}$ in superhomogeneous form for the mode $\texttt{append(in,in,out)}$, with the atoms and structured goals occurring in the procedure's definition explicitly identified by subscripting them with their respective program point as in Figure 3. We denote the program points

$$\texttt{append(X,Y,Z)}_0 :-$$
$$((\texttt{X} \Rightarrow \texttt{[]}_1, \ \texttt{Z:=Y}_2)_{c_1} \ ;$$
$$(\texttt{X} \Rightarrow \texttt{[E|Es]}_3, \ (\texttt{append(Es, Y, R)}_4, \ \texttt{Z} \Leftarrow \texttt{[E|R]}_5)_{c_2})_{c_3})_{d_1} .$$

Fig. 3. $\texttt{append/3}$ with explicit program points.

associated to a structured goal by subscripting the goal with the characters 'c' for conjunction and 'd' for disjunction, accompanied by a natural number. From mode analysis, it follows that

$$\text{init}(X) = \{0\} \ \text{init}(E) = \{3\} \ \text{init}(R) = \{4\}$$
$$\text{init}(Y) = \{0\} \ \text{init}(Es) = \{3\} \ \text{init}(Z) = \{2,5\}$$

Or, put otherwise, X and Y (being input arguments) are initialised in the procedure's head, E and Es are initialised in the deconstruction identified by program point 3, R is initialised in the recursive call whereas Z is initialised either by the assignment $Z := Y$ (program point 2) or by the construction $Z \Leftarrow [E|R]$ (program point 5).

3.3 A Modular Analysis

In order to make the binding-time analysis as modular as possible, we devise an analysis that works in two phases. In a first phase, we represent binding-times and the relations that exist between them according the data flow in the program in a symbolic way. Doing so enables us to perform a large part of the data-flow analysis independent of a particular call pattern. It is only in the second phase that call patterns in the form of the binding-times of a procedure's input arguments are used — in combination with the symbolic information derived from the first phase— for computing the annotations and the actual binding-times of the procedure's other variables. The first phase of the analysis hence is *call independent* whereas the second phase is *call dependent*. Obviously, the call independent phase of the analysis does not need to be repeated in case a procedure is called with a different binding-time characterisation of its arguments and consequently, the result of a module's call independent analysis can be used regardless of the context the module is used in, and must not be repeated when the module is used in different programs. Since the domain of binding-times is condensing [21], the call-independent analysis preserves the precision that would be obtained by a call-dependent analysis.

To symbolically represent the binding-time of a variable at a particular program point, we introduce the concept of a *binding-time variable*, the set of which is denoted by $\mathcal{V}_{BT}$. We will denote elements of this set as variables subscribed by a program point. If V is a variable occurring in a goal G, and η is a program point identifying an atom in G, then the binding-time variable $V_\eta \in \mathcal{V}_{BT}$ symbolically represents the binding-time of V at program point η. Given a type path $\delta \in TPath$, we use the notation V_η^δ to denote the subvalue identified by δ in the binding-time of V at program point η[7].

Example 10. Given the definition of `append/3` from Example 9, the binding-time variables X_0, Z_2, Z_5 and Z_0 denote, respectively the binding-time of X at the program point 0 and the binding-times of Z at the program points $2, 5$ and 0.

Apart from the binding-time variables that correspond with program variables, we introduce a number of extra binding-time variables that we use to symbolically represent some control information that will be collected (and needed) during the binding-time analysis. For each program point η, we introduce two such variables, $\mathcal{R}_\eta$ and $\mathcal{C}_\eta$, that range over the set of binding-times $\{\bot, \top\}$. Their intended meaning is as follows:

- $\mathcal{R}_\eta = \bot$: Either the goal identified by η reduces to *true* or *fail* during specialisation, or its residual code is guaranteed not to fail at run-time.
- $\mathcal{R}_\eta = \top$: No claims are made about the outcome of the reduction at specialisation time.
- $\mathcal{C}_\eta = \top$: The goal identified by η is under dynamic control in the procedure's body. We say that an atom is under dynamic control if the fact whether it will be evaluated depends on the success or failure of another goal, say $G_{\eta'}$ while success or failure of that goal is undecided at specialisation-time (that is $\mathcal{R}_{\eta'} = \top$).
- $\mathcal{C}_\eta = \bot$: The goal identified by η is not under dynamic control in the procedure's body.

Note that these binding-time variables – which we will refer to as *control variables* – are boolean in the sense that they will only assume a value that is either $\bot$ or $\top$. During the binding-time analysis, these control variables collect the necessary information to implement the control strategy of the specialiser. Our analysis models a rather conservative specialisation strategy, in the sense that during specialisation, no atoms are reduced that are under dynamic control.

---

[7] Hence $V_\eta^\blacksquare$ and V_η denote the same binding-time value and we will use the latter in examples.

The idea behind this strategy is that in this way only atoms are reduced that would also be evaluated if the program is executed with a complete input that extends the static input for which the program is specialised.

Indeed, their being evaluated depends only on goals that are – during specialisation– sufficiently reduced in order to decide success or failure. Hence, no atoms are "speculatively" reduced, guaranteeing termination of the reduction process (constituting local termination) under the assumption that the equivalent single stage computation terminates.

Example 11. Consider the following code fragment

```
if X ⇒ [] then p(X) else q(X)
```

Both atoms $p(X)$ and $q(X)$ are under dynamic control if X's binding-time does not allow the specialiser to decide whether or not the test $X \Rightarrow []$ will succeed during specialisation. Indeed, the specialiser has no means of knowing which of the branches will be taken during the second stage of the computation.[8]

In general, the binding-time of a program variable can depend on the binding-times of other program variables (according to the data flow) and on the value of the appropriate control variables (according to the control strategy). The values of the control variables that are associated to a goal in turn depend on the binding-times of that goal's input variables. Symbolically, we can represent these dependencies by a number of constraints between the involved binding-time variables. In general:

Definition 9 (binding-time constraint). *A binding-time constraint is a constraint of the following form:*

$$V_\eta^\delta \succeq X_{\eta'}^\gamma, \ V_\eta^\delta \succeq \top$$

$$V_\eta^\delta \succeq^* X_{\eta'}^\gamma, \ V_\eta^\delta \succeq^* \top$$

where $V_\eta, X_{\eta'} \in \mathcal{V}_{\mathcal{BT}}$ and $\delta, \gamma \in TPath$. The set of all binding-time constraints is denoted by $\mathcal{BTC}$.

A constraint of the form $V_\eta^\delta \succeq X_{\eta'}^\gamma$ denotes that the binding-time represented by V_η^δ must be at least as dynamic as (or *cover*) the binding-time represented by $X_{\eta'}^\gamma$. Note that such a constraint requires the types of V and X, denoted by τ_V and τ_X to be such that τ_V^δ and τ_X^γ are instances of one another, in order

---

[8] Note that it can happen that the analysis cannot predict the outcome of the test while execution of the program with full input always selects the same branch, e.g. $q(X)$. Although the call to $p(X)$ is residualised, the code of the procedure $p/1$ is specialised. All reductions performed while specialising $p/1$ are then in fact speculative (and the specialisation could in extreme cases be non-terminating while execution of the program to be specialised with full input is always terminating).

for their binding-times to be comparable. The intended meaning of a constraint of the form $V_\eta^\delta \succeq^* X_{\eta'}^\gamma$ is that the binding-time represented by V_η^δ is at least as dynamic as the binding-time value associated to the path identified by γ in the binding-time represented by $X_{\eta'}^\gamma$. Note that such a constraint does not require τ_V^γ and τ_X^γ to be of comparable types; it simply expresses that if the node identified by γ in the binding-time represented by $X_{\eta'}$ is *dynamic*, so must be the node identified by δ in V_η and by definition of a binding-time, so must be all its descendant nodes. Remark that we also allow constraints in which the right-hand side is the constant $\top$. Although we occasionally also consider constraints of which the right-hand side is the constant $\bot$, we do not explicitly mention these in the definition, as these constraints are superfluous: for any $X_\eta \in \mathcal{V}_{BT}$ and $\delta \in TPath$, it holds by definition that $X_\eta^\delta \succeq \bot$.

Example 12. Reconsider the definition of **append/3** in Fig. 3. Some examples of binding-time constraints between binding-time variables from **append/3** and their intended meaning are:

$Z_2 \succeq Y_0$	The binding-time associated to Z at program point 2 is at least as dynamic as the binding-time associated to Y at program point 0.
$E_3 \succeq X_0^{\langle[|],1\rangle}$	The binding-time associated to E at program point 3 is at least as dynamic as the subvalue denoted by $\langle[|],1\rangle$ of the binding-time associated to X at program point 0.
$Z_5^{\langle[|],1\rangle} \succeq E_3$	The subvalue denoted by $\langle[|],1\rangle$ in the binding-time of Z at program point 5 is at least as dynamic as the binding-time associated to E at program point 3.
$\mathcal{R}_3 \succeq^* X_0$	If X_0 represents a binding-time in which the root node $\langle\rangle$ is bound to *dynamic* then one cannot assume that the atom at program point 3 reduces to *true*, *fail* or code that is guaranteed to succeed.
$\mathcal{C}_4 \succeq \mathcal{R}_3$	The atom at program point 4 must be under dynamic control if the specialisation of the atom at program point 3 possibly results in residual code that might fail at run-time.

A set of binding-time constraints is called a binding-time constraint system (or simply a constraint system). Given a constraint system $\mathcal{C}$, we define vars($\mathcal{C}$) as the set of all binding-time variables X_η that occur in some constraint $C \in \mathcal{C}$. The link between a binding-time constraint system and the actual binding-times it represents is formalised as a (minimal) solution to the constraint system.

Definition 10 (solution). *A solution to a binding-time constraint system $\mathcal{C}$ is a substitution $\sigma : \mathcal{V}_{BT} \mapsto \mathcal{BT}$ mapping binding-time variables to binding-times with dom(σ) = vars($\mathcal{C}$) such that*

- *for every constraint $V_\eta^\delta \succeq \top \in \mathcal{C}$ and $V_\eta^\delta \succeq^* \top \in \mathcal{C}$ it holds that $\sigma(V_\eta)^\delta \succeq \top$*
- *for every constraint $V_\eta^\delta \succeq X_{\eta'}^\gamma \in \mathcal{C}$ it holds that $\sigma(V_\eta)^\delta \succeq \sigma(X_{\eta'})^\gamma$*
- *for every constraint $V_\eta^\delta \succeq^* X_{\eta'}^\gamma \in \mathcal{C}$ it holds that $\sigma(X_{\eta'})(\gamma) = dynamic \Rightarrow \sigma(V_\eta)^\delta \succeq \top$*

Given two solutions σ and σ' to $\mathcal{C}$, we define that $\sigma \sqsupseteq \sigma'$ if for all $V_\eta \in dom(\sigma')$ it holds that $V_\eta \in dom(\sigma)$ and $\sigma(V_\eta) \succeq \sigma'(V_\eta)$. A solution σ is a least solution for $\mathcal{C}$ if for every solution σ' for $\mathcal{C}$ it holds that $\sigma' \sqsupseteq \sigma$.

Remember, a solution must also satisfy the condition of Definition 5, i.e. if $\sigma(X_{\eta'})^\gamma = dynamic$ then also $\sigma(X_{\eta'})^{\gamma \cdot \alpha} = dynamic$ for any extension α. We will sometimes use a constraint of the form $V_\eta^\delta \succeq X_{\eta'}^{\gamma'} \sqcup Y_{\eta''}^{\gamma''}$ (analogously for $\succeq^*$) as shorthand notation for the set of constraints $\{V_\eta^\delta \succeq X_{\eta'}^{\gamma'}, V_\eta^\delta \succeq Y_{\eta''}^{\gamma''}\}$. Indeed, from Definition 10 it can be seen that in any solution σ satisfying the latter two constraints, it holds that $\sigma(V_\eta)^\delta \succeq \sigma(X_{\eta'}^{\gamma'}) \sqcup \sigma(Y_{\eta''}^{\gamma''})$, where $\sqcup$ denotes the least upper bound on $(\mathcal{BT}^+, \succeq)$.

Example 13. Consider the following binding-time constraint system and its least solution. For sake of simplicity, we assume that all binding-time variables are boolean and range over the set $\{dynamic, static\}$.

Binding-time constraint system	Least solution
$X_{\eta_1} \succeq \top$	
$R_{\eta_3} \succeq X_{\eta_2}$	$\left\{ \begin{array}{ll} (X_{\eta_1}, dynamic) & (X_{\eta_2}, static) \\ (R_{\eta_3}, static) & (Y_{\eta_4}, dynamic) \end{array} \right\}$
$Y_{\eta_4} \succeq X_{\eta_1}$	
$Y_{\eta_4} \succeq R_{\eta_3}$	

In what follows, we formulate our analysis as a call-independent abstract semantics. We define the abstract "meaning" of a goal, be it an atom or a structured goal, as a set of binding-time constraints (description domain $\wp(\mathcal{BTC})$) that reflect the data flow between the input- and output arguments of the goal. An essential operator for the symbolic data flow analysis is a projection operator that basically rewrites a set of constraints such that every constraint expresses (or constrains) the binding-time of a local variable within a procedure in function of the binding-time(s) of that procedure's input arguments. Such a constraint is said to be in normal form:

Definition 11 (normal form). *A binding-time constraint is in* normal form *with respect to a procedure $p \in Proc$ if it is either of the form*

- $V_\eta^\delta \succeq \top$
- $V_\eta^\delta \succeq X_{\eta_0}^\gamma$ *with $X \in in(p)$ and η_0 the program point associated to p's head atom.*

and analogously for constraints of this form using $\succeq^*$.

Example 14. Reconsider the binding-time constraints from Example 12. The constraints

$$Z_2 \succeq Y_0 \qquad E_3 \succeq X_0^{\langle[|],1\rangle} \qquad \mathcal{R}_3 \succeq^* X_0$$

are in normal form with respect to append/3, whereas the constraints

$$Z_5^{\langle[|],1\rangle} \succeq E_3 \qquad C_4 \succeq \mathcal{R}_3$$

are not.

Projection of a constraint involves unfolding the (subvalue of the) binding-time variable in its right-hand side with respect to a single constraint on (a subvalue of) this variable. If we consider two subvalues of a binding-time variable, say X_η^δ and X_η^γ, one of them is a subvalue of the other if either δ is an extension of γ or vice versa. This is captured by the following definition:

Definition 12 (extension). *We define* $ext : TPath \times TPath \mapsto TPath \times TPath$ *as follows:*

$$ext(\gamma, \delta) = \begin{cases} (\langle\rangle, \alpha) & \text{if } \gamma = \delta.\alpha \\ (\alpha, \langle\rangle) & \text{if } \gamma.\alpha = \delta \\ \text{undefined otherwise} \end{cases}$$

Note that if $\text{ext}(\gamma, \delta) = (\alpha, \alpha')$ then $\gamma.\alpha = \delta.\alpha'$. Unfolding a constraint $X_\eta^\gamma \succeq Y_{\eta'}^\delta$ with respect to another constraint result in a new constraint on (a subvalue of) X_η^γ, with as right hand side the appropriate subvalue of the right hand side of the constraint that was used for unfolding. To denote a subvalue of a constraint's right hand side ϕ (which is either a binding-time variable or one of the constants $\top$ or $\bot$), we use the notation $\phi^{\cdot\overline{\alpha}}$. If ϕ denotes a variable X_η^γ, then $\phi^{\cdot\overline{\alpha}}$ equals $X_\eta^{\overline{[\gamma.\alpha]}}$. Otherwise, if ϕ denotes one of the constants $\bot$ or $\top$, $\phi^{\cdot\overline{\alpha}}$ simply equals ϕ. Note the use of the least element of the equivalence class, $\overline{[\gamma.\eta]}$, to denote an element of the appropriate type graph $\mathcal{L}_\top^\equiv$ (rather than the type tree $\mathcal{L}_\top$). The projection operation is defined in Definition 13 and basically consists of a fixed point iteration over an unfolding operator followed by a selection operation that retrieves the constraints of interest from the fixed point. Recall that η_0 identifies the head atom of the procedure of interest.

Definition 13 (projection). *The* projection *of a set* $S \subseteq \wp(\mathcal{BTC})$ *on a set of binding-time variables* $V \subseteq \mathcal{V}_{\mathcal{BT}}$ *is denoted by* $proj_V S$ *and defined as*

$$proj_V(S) = \{X \succeq^{(*)} \phi \in lfp(unf_S) \mid X \in V\}$$

where unf_S *is defined in Figure 4.*

The symbolic analysis is defined in Definition 14. The result of analysing a program is a mapping (from the semantic domain Den) that maps a procedure symbol p to a set of binding-time constraints on the variables that occur in the definition of the procedure p. The constraints are in normal form. Polyvariance is immediate, since all constraints are expressed in terms of the procedure's input arguments, which are represented symbolically and hence can be instantiated by any call pattern. The analysis is defined by a number of semantic functions defining the abstract semantics of a program $\mathbf{P} : Prog \mapsto Den$ in terms of the semantics of the individual procedures, goals and atoms.

Definition 14 (call independent abstract semantics). *The* call indepen-dent abstract semantics *for description domain* $\wp(\mathcal{BTC})$ *has semantic domain*

$$Den : \Pi \mapsto \wp(\mathcal{BTC})$$

$$\mathrm{unf}_S : \wp(\mathcal{BTC}) \mapsto \wp(\mathcal{BTC})$$

$$\mathrm{unf}_S(I) = \left\{ C \,\middle|\, \begin{array}{l} C \in S \cup S_1 \cup S_2 \cup S_3 \text{ and the form of } C \text{ is} \\ \text{either} X_\eta {\succeq}^{(*)} Y_{\eta_0} \text{ or } X_\eta {\succeq}^{(*)} \top \end{array} \right\}$$

where

$$S_1 = \{X_\eta^{\overline{[\gamma \cdot \alpha]}} \succeq \phi^{\overline{\cdot \alpha'}} \mid X_\eta^\gamma \succeq Y_{\eta'}^\delta \in S, Y_{\eta'}^{\delta'} \succeq \phi \in I, \text{ and } \mathrm{ext}(\delta, \delta') = (\alpha, \alpha')\}$$

$$S_2 = \{X_\eta^\gamma {\succeq}^* \phi \mid X_\eta^\gamma \succeq Y_{\eta'} \in S \text{ and } Y_{\eta'} {\succeq}^* \phi \in I\}$$

$$S_3 = \{X_\eta {\succeq}^* \phi^{\overline{\cdot \alpha}} \mid X_\eta {\succeq}^* Y_{\eta'}^\delta \in S, Y_{\eta'}^{\delta'} \succeq \phi \in I \text{ and } \mathrm{ext}(\delta, \delta') = (\langle\rangle, \alpha)\}$$

Fig. 4. The projection proj_V

and semantic functions

$$\mathbf{P} : Prog \mapsto Den$$

$$\mathbf{C} : Proc \mapsto Den \mapsto Den$$

$$\mathbf{G} : Goal \mapsto Den \mapsto \wp(\mathcal{BTC})$$

$$\mathbf{A} : Atom \mapsto Den \mapsto \wp(\mathcal{BTC})$$

and is defined in Figures 5 and 6.

The result of analysing a program is a denotation, $\mathbf{P}[\![P]\!]$, in the domain Den, which is a mapping from a predicate symbol to a set of binding-time constraints. This mapping is defined as the least fixed point of applying the analysis function $\mathbf{C}$ to each individual procedure. The analysis function $\mathbf{C}$ constructs a partial denotation for a particular procedure, given a (possibly incomplete) denotation that represents the result of analysis of the whole program so far. The analysis functions $\mathbf{G}$ and $\mathbf{A}$ map respectively a structured goal and an atomic goal to a set of binding-time constraints, given a denotation – again representing the result of analysing the whole program so far. In general, the result of analysing a complex goal is the union of the constraints obtained by analysing each subgoal in isolation, together with a number of additional constraints on the control variables associated with the goal and its subgoals. These constraints are simple, as they merely reflect the propagation of the control variable's value, either from the goal to its subgoals (in case of the control variable C) or from the goal's subgoals to the goal itself (in case of $\mathcal{R}$). The binding-time variables denoting dynamic control denote that a goal is under dynamic control *with respect to the procedure's body*. The negated goal (G) in a negation is under dynamic control only if the negation $(\neg G)$ itself is. Observe that if A reduces to true or is guaranteed to succeed, then $\mathrm{not}(A)$ fails. And if A fails then $\mathrm{not}(A)$ succeeds. So we can say that the negation reduces to true, fail, or residual code which is guaranteed to succeed if the negated goal does. The propagation in the other

$$\mathbf{P}[\![P]\!] = \mathrm{lfp}\Big(\bigcup_{p \in Proc(P)} \mathbf{C}[\![p]\!]\Big)$$

$$\mathbf{C}[\![p(\overline{X}) \leftarrow G_\eta]\!]d = \{(p, \mathbf{G}[\![G_\eta]\!]d)\}$$

$$
\begin{aligned}
\mathbf{G}[\![(G'_{\eta'}, G''_{\eta''})_\eta]\!]d &= \mathbf{G}[\![G'_{\eta'}]\!]d \cup \mathbf{G}[\![G''_{\eta''}]\!]d \cup CC_{\mathrm{conj}}(\eta, \eta', \eta'') \\
\mathbf{G}[\![not_\eta(G_{\eta'})]\!]d &= \mathbf{G}[\![G_{\eta'}]\!]d \cup CC_{\mathrm{not}}(\eta, \eta') \\
\mathbf{G}[\![if_\eta\ G'_{\eta'}\ then\ G''_{\eta''}\ else\ G'''_{\eta'''}]\!] &= \mathbf{G}[\![G'_{\eta'}]\!]d \cup \mathbf{G}[\![G''_{\eta''}]\!]d \cup \mathbf{G}[\![G'''_{\eta'''}]\!]d \\
&\quad \cup CC_{\mathrm{if}}(\eta, \eta', \eta'', \eta''') \\
\mathbf{G}[\![(G'_{\eta'}; G''_{\eta''})_\eta]\!]d &= \mathbf{G}[\![G'_{\eta'}]\!]d \cup \mathbf{G}[\![G''_{\eta''}]\!]d \cup CC_{\mathrm{disj}}(\eta, \eta', \eta'') \\
\mathbf{G}[\![A_\eta]\!]d &= \mathbf{A}[\![A_\eta]\!]d \\
&\quad \cup \{X_\eta \succeq X_{\eta'} \mid X \in \mathtt{in}(A), \eta' \in \mathtt{reach}(X, \eta)\}
\end{aligned}
$$

$$
\begin{aligned}
\mathbf{A}[\![X ==_\eta Y]\!]d &= \{\mathcal{R}_\eta \succeq^* X_\eta \sqcup Y_\eta\} \\
\mathbf{A}[\![X :=_\eta Y]\!]d &= \{X_\eta \succeq Y_\eta \sqcup \mathcal{C}_\eta, \mathcal{R}_\eta \succeq \bot\} \\
\mathbf{A}[\![X \Rightarrow_\eta f(\overline{Y})]\!]d &= \bigcup_{Y_i \in \overline{Y}}\{Y_{i_\eta} \succeq X_\eta^{\overline{[\langle f, i\rangle]}} \sqcup \mathcal{C}_\eta\} \cup \{\mathcal{R}_\eta \succeq^* X_\eta\} \\
\mathbf{A}[\![X \Leftarrow_\eta f(\overline{Y})]\!]d &= \bigcup_{Y_i \in \overline{Y}}\{X_\eta^{\overline{[\langle f, i\rangle]}} \succeq Y_{i_\eta} \sqcup \mathcal{C}_\eta\} \cup \{\mathcal{R}_\eta \succeq \bot\} \\
\mathbf{A}[\![p(X_1, \dots, X_n)_\eta]\!]d &= \rho(\mathrm{proj}_{Args(p), \mathcal{R}_{\eta_b}}d\,p) \sqcup \{X_{i_\eta} \succeq \mathcal{C}_\eta \mid X_i \in \mathtt{out}(p)\}
\end{aligned}
$$

where $Args(p)$ denotes the sequence of formal arguments in the definition of p/n, η_b is associated to the body goal in the definition of p/n and ρ is a renaming mapping the sequence of formal arguments $Args(p)$ to the sequence of actual arguments $\langle X_1, \dots, X_n\rangle$ and $\mathcal{R}_{\eta_b}$ to $\mathcal{R}_\eta$.

Fig. 5. The call independent abstract semantics

$$CC_{\mathrm{conj}}(\eta, \eta', \eta'') = \left\{\begin{array}{c} \mathcal{C}_{\eta'} \succeq \mathcal{C}_\eta\ \ \mathcal{C}_{\eta''} \succeq \mathcal{C}_\eta\ \ \mathcal{C}_{\eta''} \succeq \mathcal{R}_{\eta'} \\ \\ \mathcal{R}_\eta \succeq \mathcal{R}_{\eta'}\ \ \mathcal{R}_\eta \succeq \mathcal{R}_{\eta''} \end{array}\right\}$$

$$CC_{\mathrm{disj}}(\eta, \eta', \eta'') = \left\{\begin{array}{c} \mathcal{C}_{\eta'} \succeq \mathcal{C}_\eta\ \ \mathcal{C}_{\eta''} \succeq \mathcal{C}_\eta \\ \\ \mathcal{R}_\eta \succeq \mathcal{R}_{\eta'}\ \ \mathcal{R}_\eta \succeq \mathcal{R}_{\eta''} \end{array}\right\}$$

$$CC_{\mathrm{not}}(\eta, \eta') = \left\{\mathcal{C}_{\eta'} \succeq \mathcal{C}_\eta\ \ \mathcal{R}_\eta \succeq \mathcal{R}_{\eta'}\right\}$$

$$CC_{\mathrm{if}}(\eta, \eta', \eta'', \eta''') = \left\{\begin{array}{c} \mathcal{C}_{\eta'} \succeq \mathcal{C}_\eta\ \ \mathcal{C}_{\eta''} \succeq \mathcal{C}_\eta\ \ \mathcal{C}_{\eta'''} \succeq \mathcal{C}_\eta \\ \\ \mathcal{C}_{\eta''} \succeq \mathcal{R}_{\eta'}\ \ \mathcal{C}_{\eta'''} \succeq \mathcal{R}_{\eta'} \\ \\ \mathcal{R}_\eta \succeq \mathcal{R}_{\eta'}\ \ \mathcal{R}_\eta \succeq \mathcal{R}_{\eta''}\ \ \mathcal{R}_\eta \succeq \mathcal{R}_{\eta'''} \end{array}\right\}$$

Fig. 6. The call independent abstract semantics (ctd.)

constructs is similar: the subgoals of an if-then-else are under dynamic control if the if-then-else is under dynamic control. Moreover, both the then and else goals are under dynamic control if the test goal possibly reduces to residual code which could fail at run time. If each of the if-then-else's subgoals reduces to true, fail or code that is guaranteed to succeed, so does the if-then-else. The subgoals of a conjunction are under dynamic control if the conjunction itself is. Moreover, the second conjunct is under dynamic control if the first conjunct possibly reduces to residual code that could fail. If both conjuncts reduce to true, fail or code that is guaranteed to succeed, so does the conjunction. To conclude, if a disjunction is under dynamic control, so are both disjuncts. If both disjuncts reduce to true, fail or code that is guaranteed to succeed, so does the disjunction.

Example 15. Reconsider the definition of `append/3` in Figure 3. The body goal contains the following structured subgoals: a conjunction identified by program point c_1 with the atomic conjuncts identified by program points 1 and 2, a second conjunction identified by c_2 with the atomic conjuncts identified by program points 4 and 5, a third conjunction identified by c_3 with the conjuncts identified by program points 3 and c_2 and a disjunction identified by program point d_1 with the disjuncts identified by c_1 and c_3. The binding-time constraints that are associated to each of these structured goals are as follows:

$$
\begin{array}{c|ll}
(c_1) & \mathcal{C}_1 \succeq \mathcal{C}_{c_1} & \mathcal{R}_{c_1} \succeq \mathcal{R}_1 \\
& \mathcal{C}_2 \succeq \mathcal{C}_{c_1} & \mathcal{R}_{c_1} \succeq \mathcal{R}_2 \\
& \mathcal{C}_2 \succeq \mathcal{R}_1 & \\
\hline
(c_2) & \mathcal{C}_4 \succeq \mathcal{C}_{c_2} & \mathcal{R}_{c_2} \succeq \mathcal{R}_4 \\
& \mathcal{C}_5 \succeq \mathcal{C}_{c_2} & \mathcal{R}_{c_2} \succeq \mathcal{R}_5 \\
& \mathcal{C}_5 \succeq \mathcal{R}_4 & \\
\hline
(c_3) & \mathcal{C}_3 \succeq \mathcal{C}_{c_3} & \mathcal{R}_{c_3} \succeq \mathcal{R}_3 \\
& \mathcal{C}_{c_2} \succeq \mathcal{C}_{c_3} & \mathcal{R}_{c_3} \succeq \mathcal{R}_{c_2} \\
& \mathcal{C}_{c_2} \succeq \mathcal{R}_3 & \\
\hline
(d_1) & \mathcal{C}_{c_1} \succeq \mathcal{C}_{d_1} & \mathcal{R}_{d_1} \succeq \mathcal{R}_{c_1} \\
& \mathcal{C}_{c_3} \succeq \mathcal{C}_{d_1} & \mathcal{R}_{d_1} \succeq \mathcal{R}_{c_3} \\
\end{array}
$$

The binding-time constraints that are associated to an atomic goal are somewhat more involved. Apart from binding-time constraints on the atom's output variables, analysing an atom A_η also possibly results in a binding-time constraint on the control variable $\mathcal{R}_\eta$, indicating under what conditions the atom can be reduced to true, fail, or code that is guaranteed to succeed. Moreover, when creating the binding-time constraints on the atom's output variables, the control variable $\mathcal{C}_\eta$ must be taken into account, in order to guarantee that the particular binding-time is made $\top$ in case the atom is under dynamic control.

Note that in the definition of **A** the binding-time variables that refer to the *input* variables of an atom at program point η are indexed by the program point η. Consequently, a number of additional constraints must be created for each atom, relating the binding-time of such an input argument at program point η with its binding-time at the program point(s) where the binding-time was created, being output of some other atom.

A test does not have any output variables, so it only creates constraints on control variables. The atom reduces to true, fail or code that is guaranteed to succeed when both input variables are bound to an outermost functor. An assignment $X := Y$ introduces the constraints specifying that the binding-time of X at program point η must be at least as dynamic as the binding-time of Y at program point η. Recall that the latter's value is constrained to be at least as dynamic as the least upper bound of the binding-times of Y at the reachable program points where Y is assigned a value. Moreover, if the assignment is under dynamic control, X_η must be assigned the value $\top$. This is guaranteed by adding $\sqcup\, \mathcal{C}_\eta$ to the right-hand side of the constraint on X_η. Even if an assignment is not reduced, it can never fail at run time. Hence the (superfluous) constraint $\mathcal{R}_\eta \succeq \bot$. A deconstruction introduces some binding-time constraints indicating that the binding-time of the newly introduced variables must be at least as dynamic as the corresponding subvalue in the binding-time of the variable that is deconstructed. Also in this case, the least upper bound with $\mathcal{C}_\eta$ guarantees that, if the deconstruction is under dynamic control, the newly introduced binding-time variables will be forced to have the value $\top$. If the deconstructed variable is bound to at least an outermost functor, the deconstruction reduces to true or fail at specialisation time. Otherwise, a residualised deconstruction can either succeed or fail at run time which is reflected by the fact that in that case $\mathcal{R}_\eta$ will have the value $\top$. When handling a construction on the other hand, the binding-time of the constructed variable is constrained by the binding-times of the variables used in the construction. Again, if the construction is under dynamic control, the constructed binding-time is guaranteed to be $\top$ by the use of the least upper bound with $\mathcal{C}_\eta$. Even when residualised, a construction can never fail, so again the (superfluous) constraint $\mathcal{R}_\eta \succeq \bot$ is introduced.

Example 16. Reconsider the definition of append/3 in Figure 3. The constraints that are associated to the unifications in append/3's body goal are as follows. The numbers in the left hand side column denote the particular unification's program point.

(1)	$\mathcal{R}_1 \succeq^* X_0$	
(2)	$\mathcal{R}_2 \succeq \bot$	$Z_2 \succeq Y_0$
(3)	$\mathcal{R}_3 \succeq^* X_0$	$E_3 \succeq X_0^{\langle[|],1\rangle}$ $Es_3 \succeq X_0^{\langle\rangle}$
(5)	$\mathcal{R}_5 \succeq \bot$	$Z_5^{\langle[|],1\rangle} \succeq E_3$ $Z_5^{\langle\rangle} \succeq R_4$

Finally, handling a procedure $p(X_1, \ldots, X_n)$ call involves retrieving the constraints for the called procedure p from the denotation and projecting these onto the set of variables $\mathcal{A}rgs(p) \cup \{\mathcal{R}_{\eta_b}\}$. This projection operation makes sure that the constraints on these variables are in normal form, i.e. that they are expressed in terms of $in(p)$. The resulting set of constraints is then renamed to the context of the call. The formal arguments of p, $\mathcal{A}rgs(p)$ are renamed to their corresponding actual argument in $\langle X_1, \ldots, X_n \rangle$. The constraints on $\mathcal{R}_{\eta_b}$ are renamed to constraint on $\mathcal{R}_\eta$, expressing that the call reduces to true, fail or

code that is guaranteed to succeed if the body of the called procedure reduces
to true, fail or code that is guaranteed to succeed.

Example 17. Let P denote the program consisting only of the definition of
append/3 depicted in Figure 3 and let (1) and (2) denote, respectively, the
sets of constraints depicted in Examples 15 and 16. The fixed point computation
for $\mathbf{P}[\![P]\!]$ starts with an empty denotation and hence, in the first round of the
computation, the recursive call does not introduce any constraints; the result
of $\mathbf{C}[\![\text{append/3}]\!]\{\}$ is a denotation that maps append/3 to the constraint set
$(1) \cup (2)$. It is only in the second round, when the constraints are projected and
renamed, that the recursive call adds the constraints

$$R_4 \succeq Y_0 \qquad R_4^{\langle([\,]),1\rangle} \succeq Es_3^{\langle([\,]),1\rangle} \qquad \mathcal{R}_4 \succeq^* Es_0$$

One can verify that in a next round no new constraints are introduced by the
recursive call, and hence $\mathbf{P}[\![P]\!]$ results in a denotation that associates append/3
to the union of the constraints derived above with the sets (1) and (2).

3.4   From Constraints to Annotations

Once we have computed $\mathbf{P}[\![P]\!]$, it suffices to have a set of binding-times for the
input variables of a procedure p in order to compute the binding-times of the
remaining variables in the definition of p, as well as the annotations that are
associated with a particular atom in the definition of p. Let us first introduce
the semantic domain *Call*, that we use to represent a call in the domain of
binding-times:

$$Call = \{p(\beta_1, \ldots, \beta_n) \mid p/n \in \Pi \text{ and } \forall i : \beta_i \in \mathcal{BT}^+\}$$

To ease notation, we assume that such a call contains a binding-time for each
argument (input as well as output). However, since these calls are used to represent the binding-times of the *input* arguments of the call only, we asume the
binding-times of the output arguments to be $\perp$. We will denote elements of *Call*
by a single greek letter π if the particular procedure/argument combination is
irrelevant. We can now define the annotation of a procedure with respect to a
particular call as follows:

Definition 15 (procedure annotation). *Given a denotation $d \in Den$ for
a program P and a call $p(\beta_1, \ldots, \beta_n) \in Call$, the procedure annotation (of a
procedure $p \in Proc(P)$) induced by a call $p(\beta_1, \ldots, \beta_n)$ is defined as the least
solution σ of $(d\,p)$ in which $\sigma(X_i) = \beta_i$ for every $X_i \in \text{in}(p)$.*

Being a solution of the set of binding-time constraints associated to a procedure p, a procedure annotation not only provides binding-times for all program
variables in p, but also maps every binding-time variable of the form C_η to either
$\perp$ or $\top$, denoting respectively that the goal at program point η in the procedure's body should be evaluated during specialisation, or be residualised. Being a

least solution, a procedure annotation contains the least dynamic binding-times while still satisfying the congruence relation. As such, a procedure annotation of a procedure p with respect to a call π represents control information for a specialiser as to how to treat each subgoal of the body of p, when a call to p is approximated by π.

A polyvariant analysis for a program P and an initial call $p(\beta_1, \ldots, \beta_n)$ can then be performed by first computing the procedure annotation σ of p induced by $p(\beta_1, \ldots, \beta_n)$ and consecutively computing, for every call $q(X_1, \ldots, X_m)$ that occurs at some program point η in the definition of p, the procedure annotation of q induced by $q(\sigma(X_{1_\eta}), \ldots, \sigma(X_{m_\eta}))$. This process is repeated recursively until no more abstract calls are encountered for which no procedure annotation has been constructed yet. In other words, a polyvariant annotation process for a program P with initial call π boils down to computing the abstract callset of (P, π): The set of abstractions of all calls that can possibly be encountered during evaluation of P with respect to a call that is abstracted by π. Formally, we define also this annotation process by a number of semantic functions that define the meaning of a program P with respect to an initial call π as a set of calls in the domain of binding-times.

Definition 16 (annotation semantics). *The* first-order *annotation semantics has semantic domain $Den_c : \wp(Call)$ and semantic functions*

$$\mathbf{P_c} : Prog \mapsto Call \mapsto Den_c$$

$$\mathbf{C_c} : Proc \mapsto Call \mapsto Den_c \mapsto Den_c$$

$$\mathbf{G_c} : Goal \mapsto Call \mapsto Den_c$$

defined in Figure 7.

$$\mathbf{P_c}[P]\pi = \mathrm{lfp}\left(\bigcup_{p \in Proc(P)} \mathbf{C_c}[p]\pi \right)$$

$$\mathbf{C_c}[p(X_1, \ldots, X_n) \leftarrow B]\pi S = \bigcup_{p(\beta_1, \ldots, \beta_n) \in S \cup \{\pi\}} \mathbf{G_c}[B]p(\beta_1, \ldots, \beta_n)$$

$$
\begin{aligned}
\mathbf{G_c}[not(G)]\pi &= \mathbf{G_c}[G]\pi \\
\mathbf{G_c}[G_1, G_2]\pi &= \mathbf{G_c}[G_1]\pi \cup \mathbf{G_c}[G_2]\pi \\
\mathbf{G_c}[G_1; G_2]\pi &= \mathbf{G_c}[G_1]\pi \cup \mathbf{G_c}[G_2]\pi \\
\mathbf{G_c}[if\, G_1\, then\, G_2\, else\, G_3]\pi &= \mathbf{G_c}[G_1]\pi \cup \mathbf{G_c}[G_2]\pi \cup \mathbf{G_c}[G_3]\pi \\
\mathbf{G_c}[q(Y_1, \ldots, Y_n)]\pi &= \{q(\sigma_\pi(Y_1), \ldots, \sigma_\pi(Y_n))\}
\end{aligned}
$$

and $\mathbf{G_c}[A]\pi = \emptyset$ for any other atomic goal A and where σ_π denotes the procedure annotation induced by $\pi \in Call$.

Fig. 7. The annotation semantics

The definition of the semantic functions $\mathbf{P_c}$, $\mathbf{C_c}$ and $\mathbf{G_c}$ is straightforward. The semantic domain $Den_c = \wp(Call)$ represents the set of all abstract callsets. The semantics of a program P with respect to an initial call π is defined as the least fixed point of repeatedly computing the semantics of each procedure (by $\mathbf{C_c}$) in P within the context of this initial call and a (possibly incomplete) denotation containing the result of analysis so far. The analysis function $\mathbf{C_c}$ constructs a partial denotation for a particular procedure as the union of the denotations obtained by analysing the procedure's body goal with respect to every call to the procedure encountered so far. The semantics of an individual goal G in the body of a procedure p is defined with respect to a call π to p. The definition of $\mathbf{G_c}$ is straightforward, as it only collects the abstract calls encountered in the annotation of p induced by π. Note that the analysis is guaranteed to create a finite number of procedure annotations since every procedure has a finite number of arguments, every such argument can only be approximated by a finite number of binding-times, and hence only a finite number of call patterns can be constructed for a particular procedure.

3.5   On the Modularity of the Approach

In summary, the binding-time analysis we have developed so far is to be performed in two phases. The first phase of the process performs the data flow analysis in a symbolic way. A procedure is analysed independent of a particular call pattern, and the analysis handles procedure calls by projecting and renaming the constraints that are associated to the called procedure. For a program that is divided into several modules, this means that the constraint generating phase of the analysis can be performed one module at a time, bottom-up in the module hierarchy if we consider hierarchies without circularities. Reconsider the module hierarchy from Fig. 1. The result of bottom-up analysis of this hierarchy is depicted in Fig. 8. First, the modules at the bottom level, M_4 and M_5 are analysed. Since these modules do not import any other modules, they can be treated as regular programs, and we can simply compute $\mathbf{P}[\![M_4]\!]$ and $\mathbf{P}[\![M_5]\!]$. The rounded boxes in the figure denote the result of computing $\mathbf{P}[\![M]\!]$ for a particular module M. The shaded part of the box represent this denotation, restricted to the procedures from the module's interface. Subsequently, the modules M_2 and M_3 can be analysed, since their analysis only requires the constraints from the interface procedures of M_4, respectively M_4 and M_5. Computation of $\mathbf{P}[\![M_2]\!]$ and $\mathbf{P}[\![M_3]\!]$ can proceed as before, with the exception that the fixed point computation should not be started from the empty denotation, but rather from $\mathbf{P}[\![M_4]\!]$ and $\mathbf{P}[\![M_4]\!] \cup \mathbf{P}[\![M_5]\!]$ respectively. Finally, once the results of analysing M_2, M_3 and M_5 are available, the module M_1 can be analysed. Note that in this process, each module is analysed only once. If a module, like M_5 in the example, is imported in more than one module, analysing the latter modules only requires the *result* of analysing the former.

The second phase of the analysis, computing the procedure annotations, is naturally a call-dependent process. Consequently, annotating a multi-module program for an initial call to a procedure p in the top-level module requires the

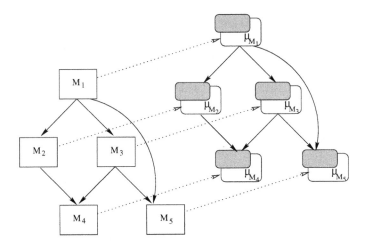

Fig. 8. Bottom-up analysis of the module hierarchy.

constraints for all the procedures (spread out over all modules) that are in the call graph for p. One could argue that this corresponds to analysing a multi-module program as if it was a single-module monolithic program. However, it should be noted that computing a procedure annotation induced by a particular call is a rather cheap process. Since the involved constraints are in normal form, it merely consists of performing a substitution on the right-hand side of the constraints and computing their least upper bounds. The hard part of the analysis – tracing the data flow between the input- and output arguments of a procedure – which possibly involves procedure calls over module boundaries, is done at the symbolic level, in a modular fashion.

4   Higher-Order Binding-Time Analysis

Mercury is a higher-order language in which *closures* can be created, passed as arguments of predicate calls, and in turn be called themselves. To describe the higher-order features of the language, it suffices to extend the definition of superhomogeneous form (see Definition 8) with two new kinds of atoms:

- A *higher-order unification* which is of the form $X \Leftarrow p(V_1, \ldots, V_k)$ where $X, V_1, \ldots, V_k \in \mathcal{V}$ and $p/n \in \Pi$ with $k \leq n$.
- A *higher-order call* which is of the form $X(V_{k+1}, \ldots, V_n)$ where X and $V_{k+1}, \ldots, V_n \in \mathcal{V}$ with $0 \leq k \leq n$.

A higher-order unification $X \Leftarrow p(V_1, \ldots, V_k)$ constructs a closure from an n-arity procedure p by *currying* the first k arguments (with $k \leq n$). The result of the construction is assigned to the variable X and denotes a procedure of arity $n - k$. Such a closure can be called by a higher-order call of the form $X(V_{k+1}, \ldots, V_n)$ where $V_{k+1}, \ldots, V_n$ are the $n - k$ remaining arguments. The effect of evaluating the conjunction $X \Leftarrow p(V_1, \ldots, V_k), X(V_{k+1}, \ldots, V_n)$ equals the effect of evaluating $p(V_1, \ldots, V_n)$.[9]

In order to represent higher-order *types* it suffices to add a special type constructor, *pred*, to Σ_T. This constructor is special in the sense that it can be used with any arity and it has no type rule associated with it. Consequently, a higher-order type corresponds with a leaf node in a type tree. In what follows we represent higher-order types as $pred(t_1, \ldots, t_k)$ with $t_1, \ldots, t_k$ first-order types. We furthermore assume that higher-order types are not used in the definition of other types; that is, values of higher-order type are only constructed, called, or passed around as arguments of a procedure call.[10]

The basic problem when analysing a procedure involving higher-order calls, is that the control flow in the procedure is determined by the values of the higher-order variables. To retrieve a set of suitable binding-time constraints between the in- and output arguments of a higher-order call $X(Y_{k+1}, \ldots, Y_n)$, it is necessary to know to some extent to what closures X can be bound to during specialisation. Consequently, to achieve an acceptable level of precision, the symbolic data flow analysis needs to be enhanced by some form of *closure analysis* [23,35] which basically computes for every higher-order call an approximation of the closures that may be bound to the higher-order variable involved. In what follows, we first define a suitable representation for such closure information; next we reformulate the first phase of our binding-time analysis in such a way that it integrates the derivation of closure information with the derivation of binding-time constraint systems. Doing so basically transforms the process of building constraint systems into a call dependent process, since closures can be passed around by procedure calls and hence the analysis needs to take the closure information from a particular call pattern into account. We conclude this section with a discussion on the modularity of the higher-order approach.

4.1   Representing Closures

In order to use closures during binding-time analysis, where concrete values of the closure's curried arguments are approximated by binding-times, we introduce the notion of a *binding-time closure* as follows.

Definition 17 (binding-time closure). *A* binding-time closure *is a term of the form* $p(\beta_1, \ldots, \beta_k)$ *where* $p/n \in \Pi$, $k \leq n$ *and* $\beta_1, \ldots, \beta_k \in \mathcal{BT}^+$. *The set of all such binding-time closures is denoted by* $\mathcal{C}los$.

---

[9] When writing Mercury code, the programmer can also use lambda expressions to construct closures. These can, however, be converted into a regular procedure definition which is then again used to construct the closure as above. The Melbourne Mercury compiler does this conversion as part of the translation into superhomogeneous form. Note that closures cannot be constructed from other closures: once a closure is created, one can only call it or pass it as an argument to another procedure.

[10] In fact, this is also a limitation of release 0.9 of the Mercury implementation [40].

If $p/n \in \Pi$, $p(\beta_1, \ldots, \beta_k)$ approximates a set of procedures of arity $n - k$, each being an instance of p in which the first k arguments are fixed and whose values are approximated by the binding-times $\beta_1, \ldots, \beta_k$.

Example 18. Given the traditional `append/3` procedure and β_l being a binding-time approximating terms of type `list(T)` that are instantiated at least up to a list skeleton, $append$, $append(\beta_l)$ and $append(\bot, \beta_l)$ are examples of binding-time closures of arity 3, 2 and 1 respectively.

In order to obtain a precise binding-time analysis, we approximate the value of a higher-order variable with a *set* of binding-time closures. A singleton set $\{c\}$ describes that the higher-order variable under consideration is, during specialisation, definitely bound to a closure that is approximated by c. In general, a set $\{c_1, \ldots, c_n\}$ describes that the higher-order variable under consideration is bound during specialisation to a closure that is approximated either by c_1, $c_2, \ldots$, or c_n. To make this representation explicit, we alter the definition of the domain $\mathcal{B}$. Instead of containing only the values *static* and *dynamic*, we now include a value $static(S)$ with S being a set of binding-time closures. Note that, if we define $dynamic > static$ as before and $static(S_1) > static(S_2)$ if and only if $S_1 \supseteq S_2$, $\mathcal{B}$ is still partially ordered. Since the binding-times now include higher-order binding-times, we alter the definition of the partial order relation on $\mathcal{BT}$:

Definition 18 (covers). *Let* $\beta, \beta' \in \mathcal{BT}$ *such that* $dom(\beta) \subseteq dom(\beta')$ *or* $dom(\beta') \subseteq dom(\beta)$. *We say that* β *covers* β', *denoted by* $\beta \succeq \beta'$ *if and only if it holds for all* $\delta \in dom(\beta) \cap dom(\beta')$ *that:*

- $\beta'(\delta) = dynamic$ *implies* $\beta(\delta) = dynamic$, *and*
- $\beta'(\delta) = static(S')$ *implies* $\beta(\delta) = static(S)$ *and* $S \supseteq S'$.

Note that, with this new definition, the covers relation remains only defined between two binding-times that are derived from types that are instances of each other. In case of higher-order binding-times this means that both sets of binding-time closures contain closures of identical arity and argument types. Like before, we denote with $\mathcal{BT}^+$ the set $\mathcal{BT} \cup \{\top, \bot\}$, and $(\mathcal{BT}^+, \succeq)$ forms a complete lattice.

4.2   Higher-Order Binding-Time Analysis

We now reformulate the analysis from Section 3 such that it takes the higher-order constructs of Mercury into account. As a first observation, note that the binding-time constraints that are associated to first-order unifications and structured goals (see Figures 5 and 6) remain unchanged in the context of a higher-order analysis. To deal with higher-order constructions, we add an extra form of binding-time constraint to $\mathcal{BTC}$; namely a constraint of the form $X_\eta \succeq p(X_1, \ldots, X_k)$. The intended meaning is that the (higher-order) binding-time associated to X at program point η should at least contain a closure constructed from p and the binding-times of its arguments at program point η.

Formally, we extend the definition of a solution (Definition 10) such that for every constraint of the form $X_\eta \succeq p(X_{1_\eta}, \ldots, X_{k_\eta})$ it holds that

$$\sigma(X_\eta) \succeq static(\{p(\beta_1, \ldots, \beta_k)\}) \text{ where } \beta_i \succeq \sigma(X_{i_\eta}) \text{ for } 1 \leq i \leq k.$$

The main difference with the symbolic data flow analysis of Section 3 in a higher-order setting is that a set of constraints can no longer be associated to a procedure symbol (as in the semantic domain Den) because a typical higher order predicate is passed a procedure as one of its input arguments (e.g., a call to map has as one of its inputs the predicate to be applied on the elements of the list it has to process) and the resulting set of binding time constraints depends on the input predicate. Instead, in the higher-order analysis, we associate a set of binding-time constraints with a particular abstract call. Therefore, we define the analysis as an abstract semantics as before, but over the new semantic domain

$$Den_{cc} : Call \mapsto \wp(\mathcal{BTC}).$$

The notion of a procedure annotation of a procedure p induced by a call $p(\beta_1, \ldots, \beta_n)$ is straightforwardly adapted for use with a denotation in Den_{cc} rather than in Den. Moreover, given two such mappings $f, g \in Den_{cc}$, we define $f \cup g$ as a mapping in Den_{cc} with $dom(f \cup g) = dom(f) \cup dom(g)$ and

$$\forall x \in dom(f \cup g) : (f \cup g)(x) = \begin{cases} f(x) \cup g(x) & \text{if } x \in dom(f) \cap dom(g) \\ f(x) & \text{if } x \in dom(f) \text{ and } x \notin dom(g) \\ g(x) & \text{if } x \in dom(g) \text{ and } x \notin dom(f) \end{cases}$$

The resulting analysis is a call-dependent analysis that is basically a combination of the call-independent and call-dependent analyses of Section 3.

Definition 19 (higher-order semantics).
The higher-order semantics *has semantic domain*

$$Den_{cc} : Call \mapsto \wp(\mathcal{BTC})$$

and semantic functions

$$\mathbf{P_{cc}} : Prog \mapsto Call \mapsto Den_{cc}$$

$$\mathbf{C_{cc}} : Proc \mapsto Call \mapsto Den_{cc} \mapsto Den_{cc}$$

$$\mathbf{G_{cc}} : Goal \mapsto Call \mapsto Den_{cc} \mapsto Den_{cc}$$

$$\mathbf{A_{cc}} : Atom \mapsto Call \mapsto Den_{cc} \mapsto Den_{cc}$$

defined in Figure 9.

Again, the meaning of a program is defined as a fixed point computation over the meaning of the individual procedures in the program given a binding-time abstraction of the call with respect to which the program must be specialised. Each procedure is analysed (by $\mathbf{C_{cc}}$) within the context of this initial call and a

$$\mathbf{P_{cc}}[P]\pi = \text{lfp}\left(\bigcup_{p \in Proc(P)} \mathbf{C_{cc}}[p]\pi\right)$$

$$\mathbf{C_{cc}}[p(X_1,\ldots,X_n) \leftarrow B]\pi d = \bigcup_{p(\beta_1,\ldots,\beta_n) \in dom(d) \cup \{\pi\}} \mathbf{G_{cc}}[B]p(\beta_1,\ldots,\beta_n)d$$

$\mathbf{G_{cc}}[(G'_{\eta'}, G''_{\eta''})_\eta]\pi d =$
$\qquad \mathbf{G_{cc}}[G'_{\eta'}]\pi d \cup \mathbf{G_{cc}}[G''_{\eta''}]\pi d \cup \{(\pi, CC_{\text{conj}}(\eta, \eta', \eta''))\}$
$\mathbf{G_{cc}}[not_\eta(G_{\eta'})]\pi d =$
$\qquad \mathbf{G_{cc}}[G_{\eta'}]\pi d \cup \{(\pi, CC_{\text{not}}(\eta, \eta'))\}$
$\mathbf{G_{cc}}[if_\eta\ G'_{\eta'}\ then\ G''_{\eta''}\ else\ vG'''_{\eta'''}]\pi d =$
$\qquad \mathbf{G_{cc}}[G'_{\eta'}]\pi d \cup \mathbf{G_{cc}}[G''_{\eta''}]\pi d \cup \mathbf{G_{cc}}[G'''_{\eta'''}]\pi d \cup \{(\pi, CC_{\text{if}}(\eta, \eta', \eta'', \eta'''))\}$
$\mathbf{G_{cc}}[(G'_{\eta'}; G''_{\eta''})_\eta]\pi d =$
$\qquad \mathbf{G_{cc}}[G'_{\eta'}]\pi d \cup \mathbf{G_{cc}}[G''_{\eta''}]\pi d \cup \{(\pi, CC_{\text{disj}}(\eta, \eta', \eta''))\}$
$\mathbf{G_{cc}}[A_\eta]\pi d =$
$\qquad \mathbf{A_{cc}}[A_\eta]\pi d \cup \{(\pi, S)\}$
$\qquad \text{where } S = \{X_\eta \succeq X_{\eta'} \mid X \in \text{in}(A), \eta' \in \mathbf{reach}(X, \eta)\})\}$

$\mathbf{A_{cc}}[U]\pi d = \{(\pi, \mathbf{A}[U]d)\}$ for a first-order unification U
$\mathbf{A_{cc}}[X \Leftarrow p(X_1,\ldots,X_k)_\eta]\pi d = \{(\pi, \{X_\eta \succeq p(X_1,\ldots,X_n), \mathcal{R}_\eta \succeq \bot\})\}$
$\mathbf{A_{cc}}[q(Y_1,\ldots,Y_n)_\eta]\pi d = S_1 \cup S_2$ where
$\qquad S_1 = \{(q(\beta_1,\ldots,\beta_n), \{\})\}$
$\qquad S_2 = \{(\pi, \rho(\text{proj}_{Args(q),\mathcal{R}_{\eta_b}}(d\ q(\beta_1,\ldots,\beta_n))) \sqcup \{Y_{i_\eta} \succeq C_\eta \mid Y_i \in \text{out}(q)\})\}$
$\qquad \text{with } \beta_i = \sigma_\pi(Y_{i_\eta})$
$\mathbf{A_{cc}}[X(Y_{k+1},\ldots,Y_n)_\eta]\pi d = S_1 \cup S_2$ where
$\qquad S_1 = \text{if } \sigma_\pi(X_\eta) = \top$
$\qquad\qquad \text{then } \{(q(\top,\ldots,\top), \{\}) \mid q/m \in Proc(P) \text{ and } m \geq n - k\}$
$\qquad\qquad \text{else } \{(q(\beta_1,\ldots,\beta_n), \{\}) \mid q(\beta_1,\ldots,\beta_k) \in S\}$
$\qquad\qquad \text{where } \sigma_\pi(X_\eta) = static(S) \text{ and } \beta_i = \sigma_\pi(Y_i) \text{ for } k+1 \leq i \leq n$
$\qquad S_2 = \{(\pi, \bigcup_{q(\beta_1,\ldots,\beta_n) \in dom(S_1)} \rho(\text{proj}_V(d(q\beta_1,\ldots,\beta_n))) \sqcup$
$\qquad\qquad \{Y_{i_\eta} \succeq C_\eta \mid Y_i \in \text{out}(q)\})\}$ where $V = Args(q) \cup \{\mathcal{R}_{\eta_b}\}$

Fig. 9. The higher-order semantics

denotation (in Den_{cc}) representing the (possibly incomplete) results of analysis so far. The definition of $\mathbf{G_{cc}}$, defining the abstract meaning of a goal, is basically identical to the definition of $\mathbf{G}$ from Section 3, apart from the facts that (1) it threads a denotation as well as the abstract call to the procedure that is currently being analysed and (2) it associates this abstract call to the constraints for a particular goal. The same observations hold for the definition of $\mathbf{A_{cc}}$. The constraints derived for a first-order unification are identical to those derived by $\mathbf{A}$. A higher-order construction results in a constraint stating that the binding-time of the higher-order variable must contain at least the abstract closure created at this program point. Note that we propagate the binding even when the construction is under dynamic control, as this binding allows to substantially simplify the analysis of higher-order calls. Being a construction, reduction can never result in code that might fail during exeuction, hence the (superfluous) constraint on $\mathcal{R}_\eta$.

Handling procedure calls is somewhat more involved than in the first-order case. Retrieving the constraints associated to a first-order call from the denotation now requires to compute the binding-times of the arguments in of the call. As before, σ_π represents the procedure annotation induced by the call π. The binding-time variables in the resulting (projected) constraints are again renamed to the actual arguments of the call $X_1, \ldots, X_n$ and the control variable $\mathcal{R}_{\eta_b}$ is renamed to $\mathcal{R}_\eta$, as before. As for the other goals, the resulting constraints are associated to the abstract call π for which the surrounding procedure is being analysed. The resulting mapping, in Figure 9 denoted by S_2, is updated with the mapping $\{(q(\beta_1, \ldots, \beta_n), \{\})\}$ in order to make sure that the call $q(\beta_1, \ldots, \beta_n)$ is in the domain of the newly constructed denotation, and hence will be analysed during a next round of the analysis. Note that the use of $\cup$ guarantees that if the call was already in the domain of the donation, the set of constraints associated to it remains unchanged. A higher-order call is basically handled as a set of first-order calls. First, the binding-time of the higher-order variable is retrieved from the procedure annotation σ_π for the currently analysed procedure/call combination. If this binding-time equals $static(S)$, each closure $q(\beta_1, \ldots, \beta_k) \in S$ is transformed to a first-order call by adding $\sigma_\pi(X_{k+1}), \ldots, \sigma_\pi(X_n)$ to its arguments. From then on, the call is handled as a first-order call. The constraints associated to this call are retrieved from the denotation and added to the denotation under construction, and the call itself is added to the domain of the denotation under construction.

4.3   On the Modularity of the Approach

In a higher-order setting, the constraint generation phase of our binding-time analysis is a call dependent process. Indeed, the data flow dependencies in a procedure are determined by the closures contained in the procedure's call pattern. This suggests that the advantage of modularity, associated to the constraint based technique in a first-order setting, might no longer hold in a higher-order setting. However, to some extent the analysis can still be performed in a bottom-up, modular way. For a module M that exports the predicates $p_1, \ldots, p_n$ we initiate the analysis with:

$$\bigcup_{p \in \{p_1, \ldots, p_n\}} \mathbf{P_{cc}}[\![P]\!]p(\top, \ldots, \top).$$

At first sight, it might seem strange to perform a call-dependent analysis with respect to an inital call in which all arguments are approximated by $\top$. However, recall that only the higher-order parts of the call patterns influence the resulting constraint systems. Hence, for those procedures that have no higher-order arguments, the constraint system derived by the call dependent analysis for a call $p(\top, \ldots, \top)$ equals the one derived by the call independent analysis of Section 3, and it can readily be used by other modules importing these procedures. Note that the call dependent nature of the process ensures that closure information that is constructed in a module M, is propagated inside M itself. It is only if closure information is "lost" over a module boundary that the resulting analysis is less precise than a full call dependent analysis over the complete multi-module program. This is the case when, in some module, closure information is available in some arguments of a call to an imported procedure p whereas, being imported, the constraints that are used for p are those obtained by analysing $p(\top, \ldots, \top)$.

5   Example

In this section, we present an example, and use it to discuss to what extent the proposed analysis is also applicable in the context of Prolog.

5.1   A Simple Interpreter

Consider the simple interpreter for arithmetic expressions depicted in Figure 10, adapted from a Prolog version discussed and specialized in a companion chapter [29]. The program consists of a number of type definitions and two predicates.

```
:- type env --> nil ; cons(elem, env).
:- type elem --> pair(ident,int).

:- type exp --> cst(int) ; var(ident) ; +(exp,exp).

:- pred lookup(ident, env, int).
:- mode lookup(in,in,out) is multi.

lookup(V,E,Val):- E⇒₁ cons(A,As), A⇒₂ pair(I,VI), (
     V==₃ I, Val:=₄ VI
     ;
     lookup(V,As,T)₅, Val:=₆ T).

:- pred int(exp,env,int).
:- mode int(in,in,out) is multi.

int(E,Env,R):-(
     E⇒₁ cst(C), R:=₂ C
     ;
     E⇒₃ var(V), lookup(V,Env,Val)₄, R:=₅ Val
     ;
     E⇒₆ +(A,B), int(A,Env,R1)₇, int(B,Env,R2)₈, plus(R1,R2,R)₉).
```

Fig. 10. A simple interpreter

The type `env` defines an environment as a list of elements, each element being a pair (type `elem`) consisting of an identifier (type `ident`) and an integer (type `int`). We assume that the types `ident` and `int` are atomic and builtin. The type `exp` defines an expression as either a constant integer, a variable denoted by an identifier, or the sum of two expressions.

The predicate `lookup/3` takes an identifier and an environment as input, searches the value associated to the identifier in the environment and returns this value or fails. Note that the predicate is defined as being non-deterministic in order to mimick a purely declarative implementation in Prolog. The interpreter itself is represented by the predicate `int` which takes an expression and an environment as input and returns the value of the expression or fails. Both predicates are given in superhomogeneous form.

After call-independent analysis, the binding-time constraints associated with the `lookup/3` predicate are as follows.

$$A \succeq E^{\langle (cons,1) \rangle}$$
$$As \succeq E$$
$$I \succeq E^{\langle (cons,1),(pair,1) \rangle}$$
$$I \succeq^* E$$
$$VI \succeq E^{\langle (cons,1),(pair,2) \rangle}$$
$$VI \succeq^* E$$
$$Val_4 \succeq E^{\langle (cons,1),(pair,2) \rangle}$$
$$Val_4 \succeq^* E \sqcup E^{\langle (cons,1) \rangle} \sqcup E^{\langle (cons,1),(pair,1) \rangle} \sqcup V$$
$$T \succeq E^{\langle (cons,1),(pair,2) \rangle}$$
$$T \succeq^* E \sqcup E^{\langle (cons,1) \rangle} \sqcup E^{\langle (cons,1),(pair,1) \rangle} \sqcup V$$
$$Val_6 \succeq E^{\langle (cons,1),(pair,2) \rangle}$$
$$Val_6 \succeq^* E \sqcup E^{\langle (cons,1) \rangle} \sqcup E^{\langle (cons,1),(pair,1) \rangle} \sqcup V$$

All constraints are in normalised form. Where relevant, a binding-time variable is indexed by a subscript indicating the program point at which the constraint holds. Recall that the $\succeq$-constraints express the regular data flow, whereas the $\succeq^*$-constraints reflect the specialisation-strategy: a constraint $X \succeq^* Y^\delta$ denotes that the binding-time of X cannot be static if the node δ in the binding-time of Y is marked *dynamic*. Such a constraint is due to the presence, earlier in the predicate, of a deconstruction (or test) on Y^δ that may be residualised and subsequently fail at run-time. The interpretation of these constraints is as follows. The data-flow (or $\succeq$) constraints are obtained in a straightforward way, by projecting the constraints obtained from the unifications. The strategy (or $\succeq^*$) constraints are somewhat more involved. The constraints $I \succeq^* E$ and $VI \succeq^* E$ denote that I and VI must be $\top$ in case E is not bound to an outermost functor. Indeed, if E is not bound to an outermost functor, the deconstruction at program point 1 cannot be reduced at specialisation-time and the atom at program point 2 (in which I and VI are assigned their value) is under dynamic control and hence cannot be reduced at specialisation time. Subsequently, the construction at program point 4 is under dynamic control if one of the preceeding atoms cannot be reduced or results in code that may fail at runtime, which is the case if either the environment E, the elements of the environment ($E^{\langle(cons,1)\rangle}$), the identifiers within each such element ($E^{\langle(cons,1),(pair,1)\rangle}$ or the variable V is not bound to an outermost function. Similar considerations explain the $\succeq^*$ constraints on T and Val at program point 6 in the other branch of the disjunction. The constraints on T are equal to the least upper bound of those (in the least fixed point) on Val_4 and Val_6. Recall that the constraints on T, which originate from the recursive call, are obtained from $T \succeq Val_4 \sqcup Val_6$.

The binding-time constraints derived for the int/3 predicate are as follows.

$C \succeq E^{\langle(cst,1)\rangle}$

$R_2 \succeq E^{\langle(cst,1)\rangle}$

$R_2 \succeq^* E$

$V \succeq E^{\langle(var,1)\rangle}$

$Val \succeq Env^{\langle(cons,1),(pair,2)\rangle}$

$Val \succeq^* Env \sqcup Env^{\langle(cons,1)\rangle} \sqcup Env^{\langle(cons,1),(pair,1)\rangle} \sqcup E^{\langle(var,1)\rangle}$

$R_5 \succeq Env^{\langle(cons,1),(pair,2)\rangle}$

$R_5 \succeq^* E \sqcup Env \sqcup Env^{\langle(cons,1)\rangle} \sqcup Env^{\langle(cons,1),(pair,1)\rangle} \sqcup E^{\langle(var,1)\rangle}$

$A \succeq E^{\langle(+,1)\rangle}$

$B \succeq E^{\langle(+,2)\rangle}$

$R1 \succeq E^{\langle(+,1),(cst,1)\rangle} \sqcup Env^{\langle(cons,1),(pair,2)\rangle}$

$R1 \succeq^* E \sqcup E^{\langle(+,1)\rangle} \sqcup E^{\langle(+,2)\rangle} \sqcup E^{\langle(+,1),(var,1)\rangle} \sqcup E^{\langle(+,2),(var,1)\rangle} \sqcup$
$\qquad Env \sqcup Env^{\langle(cons,1)\rangle} \sqcup Env^{\langle(cons,1),(pair,1)\rangle}$

$R2 \succeq E^{\langle(+,2),(cst,1)\rangle} \sqcup Env^{\langle(cons,1),(pair,2)\rangle}$

$R2 \succeq^* E \sqcup E^{\langle(+,1)\rangle} \sqcup E^{\langle(+,2)\rangle} \sqcup E^{\langle(+,1),(var,1)\rangle} \sqcup E^{\langle(+,2),(var,1)\rangle} \sqcup$
$\qquad Env \sqcup Env^{\langle(cons,1)\rangle} \sqcup Env^{\langle(cons,1),(pair,1)\rangle}$

$R_9 \succeq E^{\langle(+,1),(cst,1)\rangle} \sqcup E^{\langle(+,2),(cst,1)\rangle} \sqcup Env^{\langle(cons,1),(pair,2)\rangle}$

$R_9 \succeq^* E \sqcup E^{\langle(+,1)\rangle} \sqcup E^{\langle(+,2)\rangle} \sqcup E^{\langle(+,1),(var,1)\rangle} \sqcup E^{\langle(+,2),(var,1)\rangle} \sqcup$
$\qquad Env \sqcup Env^{\langle(cons,1)\rangle} \sqcup Env^{\langle(cons,1),(pair,1)\rangle}$

These constraints are obtained in a similar way as those for the lookup predicate.
Assume we want to specialise this program for the query

```
int(+(cst(2),+(var(x),cst(3))), [pair(y,Yval),(x,Xval)],Res)   (1)
```

i.e., the expression to compute is fully instantiated and the domain of the environment mapping is fully defined but the concrete values associated to the identifiers are as yet unknown. These degrees of instantiation are expressed by the binding-times β_{exp} defined for the type exp and β_{env} defined for the type env.

$$\beta_{exp} = \left\{ \begin{array}{ll} (\langle\rangle, static), & (\langle(cst,1)\rangle, static), \;\; (\langle(var,1)\rangle, static) \\ (\langle(+,1)\rangle, static), & (\langle(+,2)\rangle, static) \end{array} \right\}$$

$$\beta_{env} = \left\{ \begin{array}{l} (\langle\rangle, static) \\ (\langle(cons,1),(pair,1)\rangle, static) \\ (\langle(cons,1),(pair,2)\rangle, dynamic) \end{array} \right\}$$

Note that the abstract call int ($\beta_{exp}, \beta_{env}, \_$) will give rise to an abstract call lookup($static, \beta_{env}, \_$). In the least solution of the constraints for lookup with respect to this call, we obtain that the output argument $Val = Val_4 \sqcup Val_6 = dynamic$. However, the input to each test or deconstruction in lookup is at least bound to an outermost functor and hence is a candidate for reduction. In addition, if we look at the strategy constraints

$$C_2 \succeq^* E$$
$$C_3 \succeq^* E \sqcup E^{\langle(cons,1)\rangle}$$
$$C_4 \succeq^* E \sqcup E^{\langle(cons,1)\rangle} \sqcup V \sqcup E^{\langle(cons,1),(pair,1)\rangle}$$
$$C_5 \succeq^* E \sqcup E^{\langle(cons,1)\rangle}$$
$$C_6 \succeq^* E \sqcup E^{\langle(cons,1)\rangle} \sqcup V \sqcup E^{\langle(cons,1),(pair,1)\rangle}$$

we derive that none of the atoms is under dynamic control and consequently, each atom can be annotated as reducible.

Consequently, for the int predicate we obtain $R = dynamic$ but similarily to the case of the lookup predicate, none of the atoms is under dynamic control and the input to each unification is bound to at least an outermost constructor. Hence all unifications can be reduced. Only the predicate plus, which we assume builtin, has both input arguments *dynamic* and need to be residualised. The result of specialisation using the obtained annotations is the residual program
int(Xval,Yval,Res):- plus(Xval,3,T), plus(2,T,Res).

5.2   The Prolog Case

The basic characteristic of Mercury that make this work feasible is the presence of type- and mode information. Hence, one may ask to what extent the technique can be carried over to the analysis of (pure) Prolog programs. Let us assume that the same type information as above is available. Given that the normal use of the int/3 predicate is with mode (i,i,o), a mode analysis is able to show that lookup/3 is also called with mode (i,i,o) and that both predicates return a ground answer. Taking care that variables in output positions of predicates are first occurrences (hence free variables) one can obtain a normalisation that is almost a replica of the Mercury code.

```
lookup(V,E,Val):-E=cons(A,As), A=pair(I,VI), V=I, Val=VI.
lookup(V,E,Val):-E=cons(A,As), A=pair(I,VI), lookup(V,As,T),
                 Val=T.
```

```
int(E,Env,R):-E = cts(C), R=C.
int(E,Env,R):-E = var(V), lookup(E,Env,Val), R=Val .
int(E,Env,R):-E = +(A,B), int(A,Env,R1), int(B,Env,R2),
              is+(R1,R2,R).
```

Using the mode information about the variables participating in unifications, one could classify them into tests, assignments, constructions and deconstructions as in the Mercury code. There is one difference. In the case of Mercury, assignments and constructions are guaranteed to succeed. In the case of our mode analysis, a variable not having mode input can still be partially intantiated, hence the unfication could fail at run-time. This will not happen in the example at hand. Indeed a simple local analysis shows that the variables being assigned are effectively free. E.g. in Val=VI, Val is the first occurrence of the output variable. Whether a unification η can fail has to be properly encoded in the special binding-time analysis variable $\mathcal{R}_\eta$. Apart from this, given the type information and the specification of the query to be specialised, the binding time analysis as done for Mercury can be performed, leading to the same annotations and hence, a specialiser as LOGEN [30] could derive the same specialised code.

Finally, it is feasible to handle more complex modes than simply input and output. In [7], a more refined mode analysis, called rigidity analysis is developed. Given a term t of type τ, it considers all subtypes τ' of τ. The term is τ'-rigid if it cannot have a well-typed instance that has a variable as a subterm of type τ'. Such a type based rigidity analysis can provide more detailed mode information that has the potential to contribute to a better binding-time analysis. For example, such an analysis could show that a term of type elem (cnfr. the simple interpreter) that is not ground, is ident-rigid.

To conclude the discussion of this example, we note that — within the context of Prolog – the results obtained by the binding-time analysis could be directly fed to the LOGEN offline partial deduction system [25,30]. This system uses the notion of a *binding-type* to characterise specialisation-time values. Basic binding-types are *static* — characterising a value as ground — and *dynamic* – characterising a value as possibly non-ground – but more involved binding-types can be declared by the user using binding-type rules, much in the same way as types are declared by type rules.

In the interpreter example, the binding-times β_{exp} and β_{env} could be translated to the following binding-type definitions:

```
:- type exp ---> cst(static) ; var(static) ; +(static,static).

:- type elem --> pair(static,dynamic).

:- type env ---> nil ; cons(elem,env).
```

Input to the LOGEN system would then consist of the program in which every call is annotated as reducible (by means of the unfold annotation [25,30]) together with the binding-type classification of the query int(exp,env,dynamic). In the companion chapter [29] we present in more detail how this example program can be specialized using the LOGEN system and the so-derived annotations. Further work is needed to investigate whether our binding-time analysis can be adapted for the Prolog setting with LOGEN's binding-types.

6   Discussion

Constraint based (binding-time) analysis has been considered before. In [17], Henglein develops such a constraint-based (higher-order) binding-time analysis for λ-calculus by viewing the problem as a type inference problem for annotated λ-terms in a two-level λ-calculus. A set of constraints capturing local binding-time requirements is created and transformed into a normal form. A solver is used to find a consistent minimal binding-time classification. The analysis is re-developed, concentrating on the aspect of polyvariance, for a PCF-like language in [19]. Henglein's analysis is scaled up by Bondorf and Jørgensen in [5], where they construct three (monovariant) analyses to be used in the partial evaluator Similix [4]. An important conceptual advantage, mentioned among others in [5], of doing binding-time analysis by constraint normalisation is the fact that the constraint based approach is viewed as a more *elegant* description of the analysis, compared with a direct abstract interpretation approach in which the source code is abstractly interpreted over the domain of binding-times. Indeed, in the constraint-based approach, problem and solution are separated: the constraint system expresses the binding-time *requirements* on the involved variables, whereas actual binding-times are contained in a *solution* to the constraint system. A practical consequence of this separation is that the data flow analysis, being performed at the symbolic level, needs to be performed only once for each predicate (in a first-order setting) rather than performing a separate analysis for every (abstract) call to the predicate. This result extends – at least to some extent – to a higher-order setting in the sense that the data flow analysis needs to be performed only once for each combination of a predicate with the closure information from its arguments.

In this work, we have shown that a constraint-based approach is also feasible for the logic programming language Mercury. The available type information allows to construct a precise domain of binding-times, whereas the available mode information allows to express the data flow constraints in a sufficiently precise way. Apart from being modular, the resulting analysis is polyvariant, and able to deal with partially instantiated data structures. A prototype implementation of the analysis was made and in [49] we describe some experiments that show the practical feasibility of the analysis. An interesting topic for further research is to couple the binding-time analysis with an offline specialiser and to perform experiments to determine the obtainable speedups.

Strongly related to our domain of binding-times is the domain proposed and used by Launchbury [28] who defines a system of types and derives a finite domain of *projections* over each type. Such a projection maps a value to a part of the value that is definitely static, as such "blanking" out the dynamic part. In recent work [3,2], a binding-time analysis is presented for the lambda calculus that allows an expression to be both static and dynamic at the same time; the general idea is to be able to access statically the (static) components of a residualised data structure. The exact relation and/or integration with a fine-grained domain of binding-times as employed by our technique is an interesting topic for further research.

Upgrading binding-time analysis to deal with Mercury's higher-order constructs requires closure information. In the literature, also closure analysis has been formulated by means of abstract interpretation [4,9] as well as by constraint solving [16,35,18]. Bondorf and Jørgensen [5] develop a constraint-based flow analysis that traces higher-order flow as well as flow of constructed (first-order) values. In this work, we have combined closure analysis with binding-time analysis and used constraints to express the first-order as well as the higher-order data flow. We have enhanced the domain of binding-times to include a set of closures that represents the binding-time of a higher-order value, and formulated the constraint-generation phase as a call dependent process in which however only the higher-order parts of the call pattern determine the result of the analysis. During constraint generation, the constraints involving higher-order values are evaluated, and the resulting closure information is used to decide what constraints to incorporate, possibly propagating closure information down into the called procedures.

We have discussed in detail how the analysis can be applied to multi-module programs according to a one module at a time scenario in Sections 3.5 and 4.3. If we do not wish to propagate closure information over module boundaries, the constraint generation phase can be performed one module at a time, bottom-up in the module hierarchy. Remaining issues are precisely such inter-module closure propagation and the handling of circularities in the module hierarchy. Recent work [8] presents a framework for the (call-dependent) analysis of multi-module programs that solves both problems. The key invariant in the approach of [8] is that at each stage of the process, the analysis results are correct, but reanalysis may – when more information is available – produce more accurate results. The analysis performs some extra bookkeeping such that, when a module is analysed, it records both the call patterns occurring in the calls to the imported procedures, and the analysis results of the module's exported procedures. When the recorded information contains new calls (or calls with a more accurate call pattern) to the imported modules, the analysis may decide to re-analyse the relevant imported modules with respect to the more accurate call patterns. Likewise, the recording of more accurate analysis results for a module's exported procedures can trigger the reanalysis of those modules that would possibly profit from these more accurate results. Note that our binding-time analysis neatly fits such an approach: initially, a module's exported procedures are analysed with respect to $\top$ (no closure information is available). The resulting binding-time constraint systems are correct, but could possibly be rendered more precise, when the procedures are (re)analysed with respect to a more accurate call pattern (one that *does* contain some closure information). To the best of our knowledge, the binding-time analysis of modular programs has been considered only occasionally before. Henglein and Mossin [19] note that a symbolic representation of binding-times allows a modular approach. Based on such a symbolic analysis, [12] present a method to specialise a multi-module program – written in a simple yet higher-order functional language – by constructing, for each of the modules, a generating extension, while using only the result of a call-independent binding-time analysis. The analysis assumes that annotations indicating whether a function must be unfolded are given by hand and is restricted to module hierarchies without circular dependencies.

To summarise, we can state that few binding-time analyses have been developed that are polyvariant, deal with partially instantiated data, modules *and* higher-order constructs for a realistic language. Our binding-time analysis achieves this for the Mercury language by combining a number of known techniques: partially instantiated structures are dealt with by incorporating a structured and precise domain of binding-times, polyvariance and modularity are achieved by computing the binding-times symbolically and higher-order information is incorporated by propagating closure information during the symbolic phase of the analysis. Two important limitations of our technique are in the modularity of the approach, in particular the lack of propagation of closure information over module boundaries and the handling of circularities in the module dependency graph. Fortunately, both issues can be addressed by imposing a system like [8] on top of our technique.

Acknowledgments

We would like to thank the anonymous referees for providing valuable feedback. We are also grateful to Kim Henriksen for his comments.

References

1. L.O. Andersen. Binding-time analysis and the taming of C pointers. In *PEPM93*, pages 47–58. ACM, 1993.
2. K. Asai. Binding-time analysis for both static and dynamic expressions. *New Generation Computing*, 20(1):27–52, 2001.
3. Kenichi Asai. Binding-time analysis for both static and dynamic expressions. In *Static Analysis Symposium*, pages 117–133, 1999.
4. A. Bondorf. Automatic autoprojection of higher order recursive equations. *Science of Computer Programming*, 17:3–34, 1991.
5. A. Bondorf and J. Jørgensen. Efficient analyses for realistic off-line partial evaluation. *Journal of Functional Programming*, 3(3):315–346, 1993.
6. Maurice Bruynooghe, Michael Leuschel, and Kostis Sagonas. A polyvariant binding-time analysis for off-line partial deduction. In C. Hankin, editor, *Programming Languages and Systems, Proc. of ESOP'98, part of ETAPS'98*, pages 27–41, Lisbon, Portugal, 1998. Springer-Verlag. LNCS 1381.
7. Maurice Bruynooghe, Wim Vanhoof, and Michael Codish. Pos(T) : Analyzing dependencies in typed logic programs. In *Perspectives of System Informatics, 4th International Andrei Ershov Memorial Conference, PSI 2001, Revised Papers*, volume 2244 of *LNCS*, pages 406–420. Springer-Verlag, 2001.
8. F. Bueno, M. de la Banda, M. Hermenegildo, K. Marriott, G. Puebla, and P. Stuckey. A model for inter-module analysis and optimizing compilation. In K.K. Lau, editor, *Preproceedings of LOPSTR 2000*, pages 64–71, 2000.

9. C. Consel. Binding time analysis for higher order untyped functional languages. In *1990 ACM Conference on Lisp and Functional Programming, Nice, France*, pages 264–272. ACM, 1990.

10. C. Consel et al. A uniform approach for compile-time and run-time specialization. In O. Danvy, R. Glück, and P. Thiemann, editors, *Partial Evaluation*, volume 1110 of *Lecture Notes in Computer Science*, pages 54–72. Springer-Verlag, 1996.

11. Thomas Conway, Fergus Henderson, and Zoltan Somogyi. Code generation for Mercury. In John Lloyd, editor, *Proceedings of the International Symposium on Logic Programming*, pages 242–256, Cambridge, 1995. MIT Press.

12. D. Dussart, R. Heldal, and J. Hughes. Module-sensitive program specialisation. In *SIGPLAN '97 Conference on Programming Language Design and Implementation, June 1997, Las Vegas*, pages 206–214. ACM, 1997.

13. Y. Futamura. Partial evaluation of a computation process — an approach to a compiler-compiler. *Systems, Computers, Controls*, 2(5):45–50, 1971.

14. R. Glück and J. Jørgensen. An automatic program generator for multi-level specialization. *Lisp and Symbolic Computation*, 10:113–158, 1997.

15. C.K. Gomard and N.D. Jones. A partial evaluator for the untyped lambda-calculus. *Journal of Functional Programming*, 1(1):21–69, 1991.

16. N. Heintze. Set-based analysis of ML programs. In *ACM Conference on Lisp and Functional Programming*, pages 306–317, 1994.

17. F. Henglein. Efficient type inference for higher-order binding-time analysis. In J. Hughes, editor, *Functional Programming Languages and Computer Architecture, Cambridge, Massachusetts, August 1991 (Lecture Notes in Computer Science, vol. 523)*, pages 448–472. ACM, Springer-Verlag, 1991.

18. F Henglein. Simple closure analysis. Technical Report D-193, DIKU Semantics Report, 1992.

19. F. Henglein and C. Mossin. Polymorphic binding-time analysis. In D. Sannella, editor, *Programming Languages and Systems — ESOP'94. 5th European Symposium on Programming, Edinburgh, U.K., April 1994 (Lecture Notes in Computer Science, vol. 788)*, pages 287–301. Springer-Verlag, 1994.

20. L. Hornof and J. Noyé. Accurate binding-time analysis for imperative languages: Flow, context, and return sensitivity. In *PEPM97*, pages 63–73. ACM, 1997.

21. Dean Jacobs and Anno Langen. Static analysis of logic programs for independent AND-parallelism. *Journal of Logic Programming*, 13(2 &3):291–314, May/July 1992.

22. G. Janssens and M. Bruynooghe. Deriving descriptions of possible values of program variables by means of abstract interpretation. *Journal of Logic Programming*, 13(2&3):205–258, 1992.

23. N. D. Jones, C. K. Gomard, and P. Sestoft. *Partial Evaluation and Automatic Program Generation*. Prentice Hall, 1993.

24. N.D. Jones, P. Sestoft, and H. Søndergaard. An experiment in partial evaluation: The generation of a compiler generator. In J.-P. Jouannaud, editor, *Rewriting Techniques and Applications, Dijon, France. (Lecture Notes in Computer Science, vol. 202)*, pages 124–140. Springer-Verlag, 1985.

25. J. Jørgensen and M. Leuschel. Efficiently generating efficient generating extensions in Prolog. In O. Danvy, R. Glück, and P. Thiemann, editors, *Proceedings Dagstuhl Seminar on Partial Evaluation*, pages 238–262, Schloss Dagstuhl, Germany, 1996. Springer-Verlag, LNCS 1110.

26. Vitaly Lagoon, Fred Mesnard, and Peter Stuckey. Termination analysis with types is more accurate. In *Logic Programming, 19th International Conference, ICLP 2003,*, volume 2916 of *LNCS*, pages 254–268. Springer-Verlag, 2003.

27. T. K. Lakshman and Uday S. Reddy. Typed Prolog: A semantic reconstruction of the Mycroft-O'Keefe type system. In Kazunori Saraswat, Vijay; Ueda, editor, *Proceedings of the 1991 International Symposium on Logic Programming (ISLP'91)*, pages 202–220, San Diego, CA, 1991. MIT Press.

28. J. Launchbury. Dependent sums express separation of binding times. In K. Davis and J. Hughes, editors, *Functional Programming, Glasgow, Scotland, 1989*, pages 238–253. Springer-Verlag, 1990.

29. Michael Leuschel, Stephen J. Craig, Maurice Bruynooghe, and Wim Vanhoof. Specializing interpreters using offline partial deduction. In K.K. Lau and M. Bruynooghe, editors, *Program Development in Computational Logic*. Springer-Verlag, 2004.

30. Michael Leuschel, J. Jørgensen, Wim Vanhoof, and Maurice Bruynooghe. Offline specialisation in Prolog using a hand-written compiler generator. *Theory and Practice of Logic Programming*, 4(1):139–191, 2002.

31. J. W. Lloyd. Declarative error diagnosis. *New Generation Computing*, 5:133–154, 1987.

32. T Mogensen. Binding Time Analysis for Polymorphically Typed Higher Order Languages. In J. Diaz and F. Orejas, editors, *TAPSOFT'89, Barcelona, Spain*, volume 352 of *LNCS*, pages 298–312. Springer-Verlag, 1989.

33. T. Mogensen and A. Bondorf. Logimix: A self-applicable partial evaluator for Prolog. In K.-K. Lau and T. Clement, editors, *Proceedings LOPSTR'92*, pages 214–227. Springer-Verlag, Workshops in Computing Series, 1993.

34. A. Mycroft and R. A. O'Keefe. A polymorphic type system for Prolog. *Artificial Intelligence*, 23(3):295–307, 1984.

35. Jens Palsberg. Closure analysis in constraint form. *ACM Transactions on Programming Languages and Systems*, 17(1):47–62, 1995.

36. G. Puebla and M. Hermenegildo. Some issues in analysis and specialization of modular Ciao-Prolog programs. In M. Leuschel, editor, *Proceedings of the Workshop on Optimization and Implementation of Declarative Languages*, Las Cruces, 1999. In Electronic Notes in Theoretical Computer Science, Volume 30 Issue No.2, Elsevier Science.

37. Jan-Georg Smaus. Analysis of polymorphically typed logic programs using ACI-unification. In Robert Nieuwenhuis and Andrei Voronkov, editors, *8th International Conference on Logic for Programming, Artificial Intelligence and Reasoning*, volume 2250 of *Lecture Notes in Artificial Intelligence*, pages 280–295. Springer-Verlag, 2001.

38. Jan-Georg Smaus, Patricia M. Hill, and Andy King. Mode Analysis Domains for Typed Logic Programs. In *Logic Program Synthesis and Transformation*, pages 82–101, 1999.

39. Z. Somogyi. A system of precise modes for logic programs. In *International Conference on Logic Programming*, pages 769–787, 1987.

40. Zoltan Somogyi et al. The Melbourne Mercury compiler, release 0.9.

41. Zoltan Somogyi, Fergus Henderson, and Thomas Conway. The implementation of Mercury, an efficient purely declarative logic programming language. In *Proceedings of the ILPS'94 Postconference Workshop on Implementation Techniques for Logic Programming Languages*, 1994.

42. Zoltan Somogyi, Fergus Henderson, and Thomas Conway. Logic programming for the real world. In *Proceedings of the ILPS'95 Postconference Workshop on Visions for the Future of Logic Programming*, 1995.

43. Zoltan Somogyi, Fergus Henderson, and Thomas Conway. The execution algorithm of Mercury, an efficient purely declarative logic programming language. *Journal of Logic Programming*, 29(1–3):17–64, 1996.

44. Zoltan Somogyi, Fergus Henderson, Thomas Conway, Andres Bromage, Tyson Dowd, David Jeffery, Peter Ross, Peter Schachte, and Simon Taylor. Status of the Mercury system. In *Proceedings of the JICSLP'96 Workshop on Parallelism and Implementation Technology for (Constraint) Logic Programming Languages*, 1996.

45. P. Van Hentenryck, A. Cortesi, and B. Le Charlier. Type analysis of Prolog using type graphs. *Journal of Logic Programming*, 22(3):179–209, 1995.

46. W. Vanhoof. Binding-time analysis by constraint solving: a modular and higher-order approach for Mercury. In M. Parigot and A. Voronkov, editors, *Logic for Programming and Automated Reasoning, 7th Intl. Conference, LPAR2000*, volume 1955 of *Lecture Notes in Artificial Intelligence*, pages 399 – 416, Reunion Island, France, 2000.

47. W. Vanhoof and M. Bruynooghe. Binding-time analysis for Mercury. In D. De Schreye, editor, *16th International Conference on Logic Programming*, pages 500 – 514. MIT Press, 1999.

48. W. Vanhoof and M. Bruynooghe. Binding-time analysis for Mercury. In *Pre-proceedings of LOPSTR'99*, Venice, Italy, 1999. Technical Report, University of Venice.

49. Wim Vanhoof. *Techniques for on- and off-line specialisation of logic programs*. Phd, Department of Computer Science, K.U.Leuven, Leuven, Belgium, jun 2001. Pages: xiv+323+xxxiii.

50. Wim Vanhoof and Maurice Bruynooghe. Binding-time annotations without binding-time analysis. In *Logic for Programming, Artificial Intelligence, and Reasoning, 8th International Conference, Proceedings*, volume 2250 of *Lecture Notes in Artificial Intelligence*, pages 707–722. Springer-Verlag, 2001.

51. Wim Vanhoof and Maurice Bruynooghe. When size does matter - Termination analysis for typed logic programs. In *Logic-based Program Synthesis and Transformation, 11th International Workshop, LOPSTR 2001, Selected Papers*, volume 2372 of *Lecture Notes in Computer Science*, pages 129–147. Springer-Verlag, 2002.

A Generic Framework for Context-Sensitive Analysis of Modular Programs

Germán Puebla[1], Jesús Correas[1], Manuel V. Hermenegildo[1,2],
Francisco Bueno[1], María García de la Banda[3], Kim Marriott[3], and
Peter J. Stuckey[4]

[1] Department of Computer Science
Technical University of Madrid (UPM)
{german,jcorreas,herme,bueno}@fi.upm.es
[2] Depts. of Computer Science and Electrical and Computer Engineering
University of New Mexico (UNM)
[3] School of Computer Science and Software Engineering
Monash University
{mbanda,marriott}@mail.csse.monash.edu.au
[4] Department of Computer Science and Software Engineering
University of Melbourne
pjs@cs.mu.oz.au

Abstract. Context-sensitive analysis provides information which is potentially more accurate than that provided by context-free analysis. Such information can then be applied in order to validate/debug the program and/or to specialize the program obtaining important improvements. Unfortunately, context-sensitive analysis of modular programs poses important theoretical and practical problems. One solution, used in several proposals, is to resort to context-free analysis. Other proposals do address context-sensitive analysis, but are only applicable when the description domain used satisfies rather restrictive properties. In this paper, we argue that a general framework for context-sensitive analysis of modular programs, i.e., one that allows using all the domains which have proved useful in practice in the non-modular setting, is indeed feasible and very useful. Driven by our experience in the design and implementation of analysis and specialization techniques in the context of CiaoPP, the Ciao system preprocessor, in this paper we discuss a number of design goals for context-sensitive analysis of modular programs as well as the problems which arise in trying to meet these goals. We also provide a high-level description of a framework for analysis of modular programs which does substantially meet these objectives. This framework is generic in that it can be instantiated in different ways in order to adapt to different contexts. Finally, the behavior of the different instantiations w.r.t. the design goals that motivate our work is also discussed.

1 Introduction

Analysis of logic programs has received considerable theoretical and practical attention. A number of successful compile-time techniques have been proposed

M. Bruynooghe and K.-K. Lau (Eds.): Program Development in CL, LNCS 3049, pp. 233–260, 2004.
© Springer-Verlag Berlin Heidelberg 2004

and implemented which allow obtaining useful information on the program and using such information to debug, validate, and specialize the program, obtaining important improvements in correctness and efficiency. Unfortunately, most of the existing techniques are still only used in prototypes and, though numerous experiments demonstrate their effectiveness, they have not made their way into existing real-life systems. Perhaps one of the reasons for this is that most of these techniques were originally designed to be applied to a complete, monolithic program, while programs in practice invariably have a more complex structure combining a number of user modules with system libraries. Clearly, organizing program code in this modular way has many practical advantages for both program development and maintenance. On the other hand, performing global techniques such as program analysis on modular programs differs from doing so in a monolithic setting in several interesting ways and poses non-trivial problems which must be solved.

In this work we concentrate on *strict* module systems in which procedures external to a module are *visible* to it only if they are part of its *interface*. The interface of a module usually contains the names of the *exported* procedures and the names of the procedures *imported* from other modules. The module can only import procedures which are among the ones exported by the other modules. Procedures which are not exported are not visible outside the module.

Driven by our experience in the design and implementation of context-sensitive analysis and specialization techniques in the CiaoPP system [20,9], in this paper we present a high level description of a framework for analysis of modular programs. This framework is generic in that it can be instantiated in different ways in order to adapt to different contexts. The correctness, accuracy, and efficiency of the different instantiations is discussed and compared.

The analysis of modular programs has been addressed in a number of previous works. However, most of them have focused on specific analyses with particular properties and using more or less ad-hoc techniques. In [6] a framework is proposed for performing compositional analysis of logic programs in a modular fashion, using the concept of an *open program*, introduced in [2]. An open program is a program in which part of the code is not available to the analyzer. Nevertheless, this interesting framework is valid only for a particular set of abstract domains of analysis—those which are *compositional*.

Another interesting framework for compositional analysis for logic programs is presented in [23], in this case, for *binding-time analysis*. Although the most natural way to describe abstract interpretation-based binding-time analyses is arguably to use a top-down, goal-dependent framework, in this work a goal-independent analysis framework is used in order to simplify the handling of the issues stemming from modularity. The choice is based on the fact that context-sensitivity brings important problems to a top-down analysis framework. Both this paper and [6] stress compositionality as a very attractive property, since it greatly facilitates modular analysis. However, there are many useful abstract domains which do not meet this property, and thus these approaches are not of general applicability.

In [15] a control-flow analysis-based technique is proposed for call graph construction in the context of object oriented languages. Although there has been other work in this area, the novelty of this approach w.r.t. previous proposals is that it is context-sensitive. Also, [1] shows a way to perform modular class analysis by translating the object oriented program into *open* DATALOG programs, in the sense of [2]. These two contributions are tailored to specific analysis domains with particular properties, so an important part of their work is not generally applicable nor reusable in a general framework.

In [21] a two-phase analysis is proposed for incomplete imperative programs, starting with a fast, imprecise global analysis and then continuing with a (possibly context sensitive) analysis for each module in the program. This approach is not abstract interpretation-based. It is interesting to see that it appears to follow from the theory of abstract interpretation that if in such a two-pass approach the first pass "overshoots" the fixed-point, the maximum precision may not be recovered in the second pass.

In [22] a method for performing separate control-flow analysis by means of abstract interpretation is proposed. This paper does not deal with the intermodular approach studied in the present work, although it does have points in common with our module-aware analysis framework (Section 5). However, in this work the initial information needed by the abstract interpretation-based analyzer is provided by other analysis techniques (types and effects techniques), instead of taking advantage of the actual results from the analysis of the rest of the modules in the program.

A preliminary study of the extension of analysis and specialization to the case of modular programs was presented in [19]. A full practical proposal for modular program analysis was presented in [4], which also presented some preliminary data from its implementation in the context of the Ciao system. Also, an implementation of [4] in the context of the HAL system [8] has been reported in [14].

The rest of the paper proceeds as follows: Section 2 presents a review of program analysis based on abstract interpretation and of the non-modular framework that we use as a starting point. Section 3 then presents some additional notation related to modular programs and a first, simple approach to extending the framework to handling such modular programs: the "flattening" approach. This approach is used as baseline for comparison throughout the rest of the paper. Section 4 then identifies a number of characteristics that are desirable of a modular analysis system and which the simple approach does not meet in general. Achieving (at least a subset of) these characteristics justifies the more involved approach presented in the rest of the paper. To this end, Section 5 first discusses the modifications made to the analysis framework for non-modular programs in order to be able to handle one module at a time. Section 6 then presents the actual full framework for analysis of modular programs. The framework proposed is parametric on the *scheduling policies*. The following sections discuss two scheduling policies which are fundamentally different: *manual scheduling* (Section 7), which corresponds to a scenario where one or more users decide when and what modules to analyze individually (but in a context-sensitive way), such as in distributed program development, and *automatic scheduling* (Section 8), where a full scheduling policy automatically determines in which order the modules will be analyzed and continues until the process is completed (a fixed-point is reached). Section 9 addresses some practical implementation issues, including persistence and handling of libraries. Finally, Section 10 compares the behavior of the different instantiations of the generic framework proposed together with that of the flattening approach w.r.t. the desirable design features discussed in Section 4, and presents some conclusions.

2   A Non-modular Context-Sensitive Analysis Framework

The aim of context-sensitive program analysis is, for a particular description domain, to take a program and a set of initial call patterns and to annotate the program with information about the current environment at each program point whenever that point is reached when executing calls described by the initial call patterns.

2.1   Program Analysis by Abstract Interpretation

Abstract interpretation [7] is a technique for static program analysis in which execution of the program is simulated on a description (or abstract) domain (D_α) which is simpler than the actual (or concrete) domain (D). Values in the description domain and sets of values in the actual domain are related via a pair of monotonic mappings $\langle \alpha, \gamma \rangle$: *abstraction* $\alpha : 2^D \rightarrow D_\alpha$ and *concretization* $\gamma : D_\alpha \rightarrow 2^D$ which form a Galois connection, i.e.

$$\forall x \in 2^D : \gamma(\alpha(x)) \supseteq x \quad \text{and} \quad \forall \lambda \in D_\alpha : \alpha(\gamma(\lambda)) = \lambda.$$

The set of all possible descriptions represents a description domain D_α which is usually a complete lattice or cpo for which all ascending chains are finite. Note that in general $\sqsubseteq$ is induced by $\subseteq$ and α (in such a way that $\forall \lambda, \lambda' \in D_\alpha : \lambda \sqsubseteq \lambda' \Leftrightarrow \gamma(\lambda) \subseteq \gamma(\lambda'))$. Similarly, the operations of *least upper bound* ($\sqcup$) and *greatest lower bound* ($\sqcap$) mimic those of 2^D in some precise sense. A description $\lambda \in D_\alpha$ *approximates* a set of concrete values $x \in 2^D$ if $\alpha(x) \sqsubseteq \lambda$. Correctness of abstract interpretation guarantees that the descriptions computed approximate all of the actual values which occur during execution of the program.

Different description domains may be used which capture different properties with different accuracy and cost. Also, for a given description domain, program, and set of initial call patterns there may be many different analysis graphs. However, for a given set of initial call patterns, a program and abstract operations on the descriptions, there is a unique *least analysis graph* which gives the most precise information possible.

2.2   The Generic Non-modular Analysis Framework

We will now briefly describe the main ingredients of a generic context-sensitive analysis framework which computes the least analysis graph. This framework generalizes the particular analysis algorithms used in systems such as PLAI [12,13], GAIA [5], and the CLP($\mathcal{R}$) analyzer [11], and we believe captures the essence of most context-sensitive, non-modular analysis systems. More details on this generic framework can be found in [10,17].

We first introduce some notation. CD and AD stand for descriptions in the abstract domain. The expression $P : CD$ denotes a *call pattern*. This consists of a predicate call together with a call description for that predicate call. Similarly, $P : AD$ denotes an answer pattern, though it will be referred to as AD when it is associated to a call pattern $P : CD$ for the same predicate call.

The least analysis graph for the program is implicitly represented in the algorithm by means of two data structures, the *answer table* and the *dependency table*. Given the information in these data structures it is straightforward to construct the graph and the associated program point annotations. The answer table contains entries of the form $P : CD \mapsto AD$. It is interpreted as: the answer pattern for calls of the form CD to P is AD. A dependency is of the form $P : CD_0 \Rightarrow B_{key} : CD_1$. This is interpreted as follows: if the procedure P is called with description CD_0 then this causes the procedure B to be called with description CD_1. The subindex key can be used in order to uniquely identify the program point within P where B is called with calling pattern CD_1. Dependency arcs represent the arcs in the program analysis graph from procedure calls to the corresponding call pattern.

Intuitively, different analysis algorithms correspond to different graph traversal strategies which place entries in the answer table and dependency table as new nodes and arcs in the program analysis graph are encountered. To capture the different graph traversal strategies used in different fixed-point algorithms, we use a priority queue. The queue contains the events to process. Different priority strategies correspond to different analysis algorithms. Thus, the third, and final, structure used in our generic framework is a *tasks queue*.

When an event being added to the tasks queue is already in the queue, a single event with the maximum of the priorities is kept in the queue. Also, only one arc of the form $P : CD \Rightarrow B_{key} : CD'$ for each tuple (P, CD, B_{key}) exists in the dependency table: the last one added. The same holds for entries $P : CD \mapsto AD$ for each tuple (P, CD) in the answer table.

Figure 1 shows the architecture of the framework. The *Code* corresponds to the (source) code of the program to be analyzed. By *Entries* we denote the initial starting points for analysis. The box *Description Domain Operations* represents the definition of operations which are domain dependent. The circle represents the *Analysis Engine*, which has the three data-structures mentioned above, i.e., the answer table, the dependency table, and the tasks queue. Initially, for each analysis these three structures are empty and the analysis engine takes care of processing the events on the priority queue by repeatedly removing the highest priority event and calling the appropriate event-handling function. This in

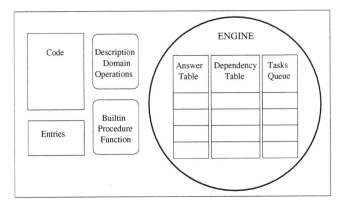

Fig. 1. Non-Modular Analysis Framework

turn consults and modifies the contents of the answer and dependency tables. When the tasks queue becomes empty then the analysis engine has reached a fixed-point. This implies that the least analysis graph has been found. We will use $Analysis_{D_\alpha}(Q, E) = (AT, DT)$ to denote that the analysis of program Q for initial descriptions E in domain D_α produces the answer table AT with dependency table DT.

2.3   Predefined Procedures

In order to simplify their presentation, formalizations of program analysis often do not consider *predefined* procedures. However, in practice, program analysis implementations allow the use of predefined (language built-in and/or library) procedures[5] in the programs to be analyzed. These *external* procedures whose code is not available in the program being analyzed are often handled in an *ad-hoc* way. Thus, in fairness, non-modular program analyses are more accurately represented by adding to the framework a *builtin procedure function* which essentially hardwires the answer table for these external procedures. This function is represented in Figure 1 by the box *builtin procedure function*. We will use $\mathcal{CP}$ and $\mathcal{AP}$ to denote, respectively, the set of all call patterns and the set of all answer patterns. The builtin procedure function can be formalized as a function $BF : \mathcal{CP} \rightarrow \mathcal{AP}$. For all call pattern $P : CD$ where P is a builtin procedure $BF(P : CD)$ returns a description AD which is assumed to be correct in the sense that it is a safe approximation, i.e. an over-approximation of the actual answer pattern for $P : CD$.

It is important to note that the data structures which are outside the analysis engine, *code, entries, description domain operations,* and *builtin procedure function* are read-only. However, though the code and entries are supposed to

---

[5] In our modular design, a library can be treated simply as (yet another) module in the program. However, special practical considerations for them will be discussed in Section 9.3.

change for the analysis of each particular program, the *builtin procedure function* can be considered to be fixed, for each description domain D_α, in that it does not vary from the analysis of one program to another. Indeed, it can be considered to be part of the analyzer. Thus, the builtin procedure function is not explicitly represented as an input to the analysis algorithm.

3   The Flattening Approach to Modular Processing

We start by introducing some notation. We will use m and m' to denote *modules*. Given a module m, by $imports(m)$ we denote the set of modules which m imports. Figure 2 presents a modular program. Modules are represented as boxes and there is an arrow from m to m' iff m imports m'. In our example, $imports(a) = \{b, c\}$. By $depends(m)$ we refer to the set generated by the transitive closure of *imports*, i.e. $depends(m)$ is the least set such that $imports(m) \subseteq depends(m)$ and $m' \in depends(m)$ implies that $imports(m') \subseteq depends(m)$. In our example, $depends(a) = \{b, c, d, e, f\}$. Note that there may be circular dependencies among modules. In our example, $e \in depends(d)$ and $d \in depends(e)$. A module m is a *leaf* if $depends(m) = \emptyset$. In our example, the only leaf module is f. By $callers(m)$ we denote the set of modules which import m. In the example, $callers(e) = \{b, c, d\}$. Also, we define $related(m) = callers(m) \cup imports(m)$. In our example, $related(b) = \{a, d, e\}$.

The *program unit* of a given module m is the finite set of modules containing m and the modules on which m depends: $program\_unit(m) = \{m\} \cup depends(m)$. m is called the *top-level* module of its program unit. In our example, $program\_unit(a) = \{a, b, c, d, e, f\}$ and $program\_unit(c) = \{c, d, e, f\}$. A program unit U is self-contained in the sense that $\forall m \in U : m' \in imported(m) \rightarrow m' \in U$.

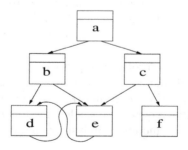

Fig. 2. An Example of Module Dependencies

Several *compilation tasks* such as program analysis and specialization are traditionally considered *global*, as opposed to *local*. Usually, local tasks process one procedure at a time and all the information required for performing the task can be obtained by inspecting that procedure. In contrast, in global tasks the results of processing a part of the program (say, a procedure) may be needed in order to process other parts of the program. Thus, global processing often requires iterating on the whole program until a fixed-point is reached.

In a modular setting, it may well be the case that part of the information needed to perform the task on (a procedure in) module m has to be computed in modules other than m. We will refer to the information originated in modules different from m as *inter-modular* information in contrast to the information originated in m itself, which we will call *intra-modular*.

Example 1. In context-sensitive program analysis there is an information flow of both call and success patterns to and from procedures in different modules. Thus, program analysis requires inter-modular information. For example, the module c receives call patterns from module a since $callers(c) = \{a\}$, and it has to propagate the corresponding success patterns to a. In turn, c provides $\{e, f\} = imports(c)$ with call patterns and receives success patterns from them.

3.1   Flattening a Program Unit Vs. Modular Processing

Applying a framework for non-modular programs to a module m has the difficulty that m may not be self-contained. However, there should be no problem in applying the framework if m is a leaf module. Furthermore, given a global process such as program analysis, at least in principle, it is not obvious that it makes much sense to apply the process to a module m alone. In principle, it makes more sense to apply it to program units since they are conceptually self-contained. Thus, given a module m one natural approach seems to be to apply the tool (simultaneously) to all the modules in $U = program\_unit(m)$.

Given a program unit U it is always possible to build a single module m_{flat} which is equivalent to U and which is a leaf. The process of constructing such a module m_{flat} usually only amounts to renaming apart identifiers in the different modules in U so as to avoid name clashes. We will use $flatten(U) = m_{flat}$ to denote that the module m_{flat} is the result of renaming apart the code in each module in U and concatenating its code into a monolithic module m_{flat}. This points to a simple solution to the problem of processing modular programs (at least for the case in which all the code is available): to transform $program\_unit(m)$ into the equivalent monolithic program m_{flat}. It is then straightforward to apply any tool for non-modular programs to the leaf module m_{flat}. Figure 3 represents the case in which the non-modular analysis framework is used on the flattened program.

Given the existence of an implementation for non-modular analysis, this approach is often simple to apply. Also, this flattening approach has theoretical interest. It can be used, for example, in order to compare the efficiency of different approaches to modular handling of programs w.r.t. the flattening approach. However, as a practical way in which to actually perform analysis of program units this approach has important drawbacks. This issue will be discussed in more detail in Section 10.

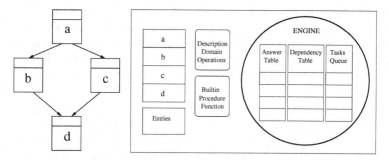

Fig. 3. Using non-modular analysis on a flattened program

4   Design Goals for Analysis of Modular Programs

Before presenting our proposals for analysis of modular programs, we will discuss the main features which should be taken into account when designing and/or implementing a tool for context-sensitive analysis of modular programs. As often happens in practice, some of the features presented are conflicting with others and this might make it impossible to find a framework which behaves optimally w.r.t. all of them.

Module-Awareness We consider a framework *module-aware* when it has been designed with modules in mind. Thus, it is applicable to a module m by using the code of m and some "interface" information for the modules in *imports*(m). Such interface information will in general consist of a summary of previous analysis results for such modules, if such results are available, or a safe approximation if they are not.

Though transforming a non-modular framework into a module-aware one may seem trivial, it requires identifying precisely which is the required information on the result of applying the tool in each of the modules in *imports*(m) which should be stored in order to apply the tool to m. This corresponds in general to the inter-modular information. It is also desirable that the amount of such information be minimal.

Example 2. The framework for non-modular analysis in Section 2 is indeed non-modular since it requires the code of all procedures (except possibly for some predefined ones) to be available to the analyzer. It will produce wrong results when applied to non-leaf modules since a missing procedure can only be deemed as an error, unless the framework is aware that such a procedure can be imported.

Correctness The results of applying the tool to a module m should produce results which are *correct*. The notion of correctness itself can in general be lifted from the non-modular case to the modular case without great difficulties. A more complex issue is how to extend a framework to the modular case in such a way that correctness is preserved.

Accuracy Similarly, the analysis results for a module m should be as accurate as possible. The notion of accuracy can be defined by comparing the analysis results with those which would be obtained using the flattening approach presented in Section 3.1 above, since the latter always computes the most accurate information possible, which corresponds to the least analysis graph.

Termination A framework for analysis of modular programs should guarantee termination (at least) in all cases in which the flattening approach terminates (which, typically, is for every program). Such termination is guaranteed by choosing description domains with some specific characteristics such as having finite height, finite ascending chains, etc., and/or incorporating a *widening operator*.

Efficiency in Time The time required to apply the tool should be reasonable. We will understand "reasonable" as not over an acceptable threshold on the time taken using the flattening approach.

Efficiency in Memory In general, one of the main expected advantages of the modular approach is that the total amount of memory required to handle each module separately should be smaller than that needed in the flattening approach.

No Need for Analyzing All Call Patterns Under certain circumstances, applying a tool on a module m may require processing only a subset of the call patterns rather than all call patterns for m. In order to achieve this, the model must keep track of fine-grained dependencies. This will allow marking exactly those call patterns which need processing. Other call patterns not marked do not need to be processed.

Support for the Co-Existence of Multiple Program Units/Applications In a modular setting it is often the case that a particular module is used in several applications. Support for software reuse is thus a desirable feature. However, this poses additional and interesting challenges to the tools, some of which will be discussed in Section 9.

Support for Source Changes What happens if the source of a module changes during processing? Some tools will not allow this at all and if it happens all the processing has to start again from scratch. This has the disadvantage that the tool is then not incremental since a (possibly minor) change in a module invalidates the information for all the program unit. Other tools may delete the information which may depend on the changed code, but still keep the information which does not depend on it.

Persistence This feature indicates that the inter-modular information can be stored in a persistent medium, such as a file stored on disk or a database, and allow later recovery of such information.

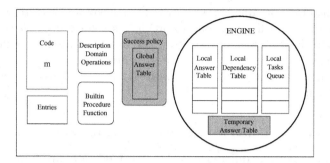

Fig. 4. Module-aware analysis framework

5   Analysis of Modular Programs: the Local Level

As a first step towards introducing our analysis framework for modular programs, which will be presented in Section 6 below, in this section we discuss the main ingredients which have to be added to an analysis framework for non-modular programs in order to be able to handle one module at a time.

Analyzing a module separately presents the difficulty that, from the point of view of analysis, the code to be analyzed is *incomplete* in the sense that the code for procedures imported from other modules is not available to analysis. More precisely, during analysis of a module m there may be calls $P : CD$ such that the procedure P is not defined in m but instead it is imported from another module $m' \in imports(m)$. We refer to determining the value of AD to be used for $P : CD \mapsto AD$ as the *imported success problem*. In addition, in order to obtain analysis information for m' which is as accurate as possible we need to somehow propagate the call $P : CD$ to m' so that the next time m' is analyzed such a call pattern is taken into account. We refer to this as the *imported calls problem*. Note that in this case analysis has to be module-aware in order to determine whether a given procedure is either local or imported (or predefined).

Figure 4 shows the architecture of an analysis framework which is module-aware. This framework is an extension of the non-modular framework in Figure 1. One minor change is that the read/write data structures internal to the analysis engine have been renamed with the prefix "local". So now we have the *local answer table*, the *local dependency table*, and the *local task queue*. Also, the box which represents the code now contains m indicating that it contains the single module m.

The shaded boxes in Figure 4 indicate the main differences w.r.t. the non-modular framework. One is that in the module-aware framework there is an additional read-only[6] data structure, the *global answer table*, or *GAT* for short. Its contents are identical in format to those in the answer table of the non-modular framework. There are however some differences: (1) the *GAT* contains analysis

---

[6] In fact, this data structure is read/write at the global level discussed in Section 6 below, but it is read-only as regards our engine for analysis of one module.

results which were obtained previously to the current analysis step. (2) The GAT contains entries which correspond to predicates defined in $imports(m)$, whereas all entries in the local answer table (or LAT for short) are for predicates defined in m itself. (3) Only information of exported predicates is available in GAT. The LAT contains information for all predicates in m regardless of whether they are exported or not.

5.1   Solving the Imported Success Problem

The second important difference is that the module-aware framework requires the use of a *success policy*, or SP for short, which is represented in Figure 4 with a shaded box surrounding the GAT. The SP can be seen as an intermediator between the GAT and the analysis engine. The behavior of the analysis engine for predicates defined in m remains exactly as before. SP is needed because though the information in the GAT will be used in order to obtain answer patterns for imported predicates, given a call pattern $P : CD$ it will often be the case that an entry of exactly the form $P : CD \mapsto AD$ does not exist in GAT. In such case, the information already present in GAT may be of value in order to obtain a (temporary) answer pattern AD. Note that the GAT together with SP will allow solving the "imported success problem".

In contrast, in many formalizations of non-modular analysis there is no explicit success policy. This is because if the call pattern $P : CD$ has not been analyzed yet, the analysis algorithm forces its computation. Thus, the results of analysis do not depend on any particular success policy: when analysis reaches a fixed-point there is always an entry of the form $P : CD \mapsto AD$ for any call pattern $P : CD$ which appears in the analysis graph. Unfortunately, in a modular setting it is not directly possible to force the analysis of predicates defined in other modules. Those modules may have already been analyzed or they may be analyzed in the future. We will simply do what we can given the information available in GAT.

We will use $\mathcal{GAT}$ to denote the set of all global answer tables. The success policy can be formalized as a function $SP : \mathcal{CP} \times \mathcal{GAT} \to \mathcal{AP}$. Several success policies can be defined which provide over- or under-approximations of the exact answer pattern $AD^=$ with different degree of accuracy. Note that this exact value $AD^=$ is the one which the flattening approach would compute. In this work we consider two kinds of success policies, those which are guaranteed to always provide over-approximations, i.e. $AD^= \sqsubseteq SP(P : CD, AT)$, and those which provide under-approximations, i.e., $SP(P : CD, AT) \sqsubseteq AD^=$. We will use the superscript $^+$ (resp $^-$) to indicate that a success policy over-approximates (resp. under-approximates). As will be discussed later in the paper, both over- and under-approximations are useful in different contexts and for different purposes. Since it is always required to know whether a success policy over- or under-approximates we will mark all success policies in either way.

Example 3. A very precise over-approximating success policy is the function SP_{All}^+ defined below, already proposed in [19]:

$$SP_{All}^+(P : CD, GAT) = topmost(CD) \sqcap_{AD' \in app} AD' \text{ where}$$
$$app = \{AD' \mid (P : CD' \mapsto AD') \in GAT \text{ and } CD \sqsubseteq CD'\}$$

The function *topmost* obtains the topmost answer pattern for a call pattern. The notion of *topmost description* was already introduced in [3]. Informally, a topmost description keeps those properties which are *downwards closed* whereas it loses those ones which are not. Note that taking $\top$ as answer pattern is a correct over-approximation, but often less accurate than using topmost substitutions. For example, if a variable is known to be ground in the call pattern, it will continue being ground in the answer pattern and taking $\top$ as the answer pattern would lose this information. However, the fact that a variable is free on call does not guarantee that it will keep on being free on success.

We refer to this success policy as SP_{All}^+ because it uses *all* entries in GAT which are *applicable* to the call pattern in the sense that the call pattern already computed is more general than the call being analyzed.

Example 4. The counter-part of SP_{All}^+ is the function SP_{All}^- which is defined as:

$$SP_{All}^-(P : CD, GAT) = \sqcup_{AD' \in app} AD' \text{ where}$$
$$app = \{AD' \mid (P : CD' \mapsto AD') \in GAT \text{ and } CD' \sqsubseteq CD\}$$

Note the change in the direction of the applicability relation (the call pattern in the GAT has to be more particular than the one being analyzed) and the use of the lub operator instead of the glb. Also, note that taking, for example, $\bot$ as an under-approximation is correct but SP_{All}^- is more precise.

5.2   Solving the Imported Calls Problem

The third important difference w.r.t. the non-modular framework is the use of the *temporary answer table* (or *TAT* for short) and which is represented as a shaded box within the analysis engine of Figure 4. This answer table will be used to store call patterns for imported predicates which are not yet present in GAT and whose answer pattern has been obtained (approximated) using the success policy on the entries currently stored in GAT. The TAT is used as a cache for imported call patterns and their corresponding answer patterns, thus avoiding having to repeatedly apply the success policy on the GAT for equivalent call patterns, which is an expensive operation. Also, after analysis of the current module is finished, the existence of the TAT simplifies the way in which the global data structures need to be updated. This will be discussed in more detail in Section 6 below.

We use $MAnalysis_{D_\alpha}(m, E_m, SP, GAT) = (LAT_m, LDT_m, TAT_M)$ to denote that the module-aware analysis framework returns (LAT_m, LDT_m, TAT_M) when applied to module m for initial call patterns E_m with SP and GAT.

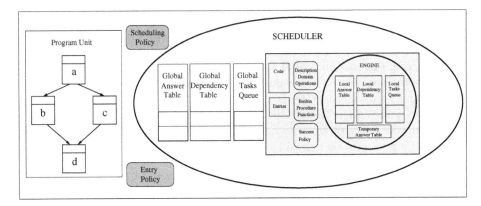

Fig. 5. A two-level framework for analysis of modular programs

6   Analysis of Modular Programs: the Global Level

After discussing the *local-level* issues which appear when analyzing a module, in this section we present a complete framework for the analysis of modular programs. Since analysis is a global task, an analysis framework should not only deal with local-level information, but also with global-level information. A graphical representation of our framework is depicted in Figure 5. The main idea is that we have to add a higher-level component to the framework which takes care of the *inter-modular* information, as opposed to the *intra-modular* information which is handled by the local-level subsystem described in the previous section.

As a result, analysis of modular programs is best seen as a two-level process. Note that the inner, lightly shaded, rectangle corresponds exactly to Figure 4 as it is a module-aware analysis system. It is interesting to see how the data structures in the global and local levels are indeed very similar. The similarities and differences between the GAT and LAT have been discussed already in Section 5 above. Regarding the global and local dependency tables (GDT and LDT respectively), they are used in order to be able to propagate as precisely as possible which parts of the analysis graph have to be recomputed. The GDT is used in order to add events to the global task queue (GTQ) whereas the LDT is used to add events (*arcs*) to be (re-)analyzed to the local task queue (LTQ). We can define the events to be processed at the global level using different levels of granularity. As usual, the finer-grained these events are, the more detailed and thus more effective the handling of the events can be. One obvious possibility is to use modules as events. This means that all call patterns which correspond to a module are handled simultaneously whenever the module is selected at the global level. A more refined possibility is to keep events at the call pattern level. This, together with sufficiently detailed information in the GDT will allow incrementality at the call pattern level rather than module level.

6.1   Parameters of the Framework

The framework has three parameters. The *program unit* corresponds to the program unit to be analyzed. Note that the code may not be physically stored in the tool's memory since it is already on external storage. However, the framework may maintain some information on the program unit, such as dependencies among modules, *strongly connected components*, and any other information which may be useful in order to guide analysis. In the figure the *program unit* is represented, as an example, containing a program unit composed of four modules. The second parameter is the *entry policy*, which determines the way in which the GTQ and GAT should be initialized whenever analysis of a program unit is started. Depending on how the success policy is defined, entries for all procedures exported in each of the modules in the program unit may be required in GAT and GTQ or not.

Finally, the *scheduling policy* determines the order in which the entries in the GTQ should be processed. The efficiency with which the fixed-point is reached can differ very much from some scheduling policies to others. Since the framework presented in Figure 5 has just one analysis engine, processing a call pattern in a different module from that currently loaded has a relevant cost associated to it, since this often requires context switching from the current module to a new module. Thus, it is often a good idea to process all or many of the call patterns in GTQ which correspond to the module which is being analyzed in order to minimize the number of times the analysis tool has to switch from one module to another. In the rest of the paper we consider that events in GTQ are answer patterns which would benefit from (re-)analysis. The role of the scheduling policy is to select a set of patterns from GTQ which must necessarily belong to the same module m to be analyzed. Note that a scheduling policy based on modules can always be obtained by simply processing at each analysis step all events in GTQ which correspond to m.

6.2   How the Global Level Works

As already mentioned, analysis of a modular program starts by initializing the global data structures as indicated by the entry policy. At each step, the scheduling policy is used to determine the set E_m of entries for module m which are to be processed. They are removed from GTQ and copied into the data structure *Entries*. The code of the module m is also copied to *code*. Then, $MAnalysis(m, E_m, SP) = (LAT_m, LDT_m, TAT_m)$ is computed. Then, the global data structures are updated, as detailed in Section 6.3 below. As a result of this, new events may be added to GTQ. Analysis terminates when there are no more events to process in GTQ or when the scheduling strategy does not select any further events.

Each entry in GTQ is of one of the following three types: *over-approximation*, *under-approximation*, or *invalid*, according to the reason why they should be re-analyzed. An entry $P : CP \mapsto AP$ which is an over-approximation is marked $P : CP \mapsto^+ AP$. This indicates that the answer pattern AP is possibly an over-approximation since it depends on a call pattern whose answer pattern has been determined to be an over-approximation. In other words, the accuracy of $P : CP \mapsto AP$ may be improved by re-analysis. Similarly, under-approximations are marked $P : CP \mapsto^- AP$ and they indicate that AP is probably an under-approximation since it depends on a call pattern whose success pattern has increased. As a result, the call pattern should be re-analyzed to guarantee correctness. Finally invalid entries are marked $P : CP \mapsto^\perp AP$. They indicate that the relation between the current answer pattern AP and one resulting from re-computing it for $P : CP$ is unpredictable. This often indicates that the source code of the module has changed in a way that the analysis results for some of the exported procedures are just incompatible with previous ones. Handling this kind of events is discussed in more detail in Section 6.4 below.

6.3   Updating the Global State

In Section 5 it has been presented how the local level subsystem, given a module m, can compute the corresponding LAT_m, LDT_m, and TAT_m. However, once analysis of module m is done, the analysis results of module m have to be used in order to update the global state prior to starting analysis of any other module.

We now briefly discuss how this updating is done. For each initial call pattern $P : CP$ in $Entries$ we compare the previous answer pattern AP with the newly computed one AP'. If $AP = AP'$ then this call pattern has not been affected by the latest analysis. However, it is also possible that the answer pattern "evolves" in different analysis iterations. If we use SP^+, the natural thing is that the new answer pattern is more specific than the previous one, i.e., $AP' \sqsubseteq AP$. In such case those call patterns which depend on $P : CP$ can also improve their success pattern. We use the GDT to locate all such patterns and we add them to the GTQ with the $^+$ mark. Conversely, if we use SP^-, the natural thing is that $AP \sqsubseteq AP'$. We then add events marked $^-$.

In a typical situation, and if modules do not change, all events in GTQ will be approximations of the same sign. This depends on the success policy used. If the success policy is of kind SP^+ (resp. SP^-) then the events which will be added to GTQ will also be over-approximations (resp. under-approximations). In turn, when they are processed they will introduce other over-approximations (resp. under-approximations).

The TAT_m is also used to update the global state. All entries in TAT_m are added to GAT and GTQ marked with the same sign as the success policy used. Last, we also have to update the GDT. For this, we first erase all entries for any of the call patterns which we have just analyzed, and which are thus stored in $entries_m$. Then we add an entry of the form $P : CP \rightarrow H : CP'$ for each imported procedure H which is reachable with call pattern CP' from an initial call pattern $P : CP$. Note that this can easily be determined using LDT.

6.4   Recovering from an Invalid State

If code of a module m has changed since it was last analyzed, it can be the case that the global information available is invalid. This happens when in the results of re-analysis of m any of the exported predicates has an answer pattern which is incompatible with the previous results. In this case, all information dependent on the new answer patterns might have become invalid, as discussed in Section 6.2. The question is how to minimize the impact of such a situation.

The simplest solution is to (transitively) erase any information of other modules which depends on the invalidated one. This solution may not be very efficient, as it ignores all results of previous analyses of other modules even if the changes performed in the module are minor, or only affect directly related modules. Another alternative is to launch an automatic recovery process as soon as invalid analysis results are detected (see [4]). This process has to reanalyze the modules directly affected by the invalidated answer pattern(s). If the new answer patterns coincide with the old ones then the changes do not affect this module and the process terminates. Otherwise, it continues transitively with the directly related modules.

7   Using a Manual Scheduling Policy

Consider, for example, the relevant case of independent development of different parts of the program, which can then even be performed in parallel by different teams. In this setting, it makes sense that the analyzer performs its job on the current module without analyzing other modules in the program unit, i.e., it allows separate analysis. This will typically allow early detection of compile-time errors in the current module without having to wait for the code of the dependent modules to be fully developed. Moreover, in this setting, it is the user (or users) who decide when and what to analyze. Thus, we refer to this as the *manual* setting. Furthermore, we assume that in this setting analysis for a module m has to do its best with only the code for m plus the results of previous analyses (if any) of the modules in *depends*(m). These assumptions have important implications. The setting allows the users of different modules to decide when they should be processed. And thus, any module could be (re-)analyzed at any point. As a result, strong requirements must hold for the whole approach to be correct. In return, the results obtained may not be optimal (in terms of error detection, degree of optimization, etc., depending on the particular tools) w.r.t. those achievable using automatic scheduling.

So the question is, is there any combination of the three parameters of the global analysis framework which allows handling the manual setting? The answer to this question is yes. Our earlier paper [4] essentially describes such an instantiation of the analysis framework. In the terminology of the current paper, the model in [4] corresponds to waiting until the user requests that a module m in the program unit U be analyzed. The success policy is over-approximating. This guarantees that in the absence of invalidated entries in the GTQ all events will be marked $^+$. This means that the analysis information available is correct, though perhaps not as accurate as possible. Since the scheduling is manual, no other analyses should be triggered until the user requires so. Finally, the entry policy is simply to include in GTQ an event such as $P : \top \mapsto^+ \top$ per predicate exported by any of the modules in U to be analyzed (it is called *all* entry policy). The initial events are required to be so general to keep the overall correctness of the analysis while allowing the users to choose the order of the modules to be analyzed.[7] The model in [4] has the very important feature of being guaranteed to always provide correct results without the need of reaching a global fixed-point.

8   Using an Automatic Scheduling Policy

In spite of the evident interest of the manual setting, there are situations in which the user is interested in obtaining the most accurate analysis results possible. For this, it may be required to analyze the modules in the program unit several times in order to converge to a distributed global fixed-point. We will refer to this as the *automatic* setting, in which the user decides when to start global analysis of a program unit. From then on it is the global analysis framework by means of its *scheduling policy* who decides when and what to analyze. Note that the manual and automatic settings roughly correspond to scenario 1 and scenario 2 of [19] respectively. Since we admit circular dependencies among modules, the strategy has to be able to deal with such circularities correctly and efficiently without entering infinite loops. The question now is what are the values for the different parameters to our generic framework which should be used in order to obtain satisfactory results? One major difference of the automatic setting w.r.t. the manual setting is that in addition to over-approximations, now also under-approximations can be used. This is because though under-approximations do not guarantee correctness in general, when an inter-modular fixed-point is reached, analysis results are guaranteed to be correct. Below we consider the use of SP^+ and SP^- separately.

8.1   Using Over-Approximating Success Policies

If a success policy SP^+ is used, we are in a situation similar to the one in Section 7 in that independently of how many times each module has been analyzed, if there have not been any code changes, the analysis results are guaranteed to be correct. The main difference is that now the system keeps on automatically requesting further analysis steps until a fixed-point is reached.

Regarding the entry policy, an important observation is that in the automatic mode, much as in the case of intra-modular analysis, inter-modular analysis will eventually compute all call patterns which are needed in order to obtain information which is correct w.r.t. calls, i.e., the set of computed call patterns covers all possible calls which may occur at run-time for the class of initial calls considered, i.e., those for the top-level of the program unit U. This will allow us to use a different entry policy from that used in the manual mode: rather than

---

[7] In the case of the Ciao system it is possible to use *entry* declarations (see for example [16]) in order to improve the set of initial call patterns for analysis.

introducing events of the form $P : \top \mapsto^+ \top$ in the GTQ for exported predicates in all modules in U, it suffices to introduce them for predicates exported by the top-level of U (this entry policy is named *top-level* entry policy). This has several important advantages: (1) It avoids analyzing all predicates for the most general call pattern, since this may end up introducing plenty of call patterns which are not used in our particular program unit U. (2) It will help to have a more guided scheduling policy since there are no requests for processing a module until it is certain that a call pattern should be analyzed. (3) If multiple specialization is being performed based on the set of call patterns for each procedure (possibly proceeded by a minimization step for eliminating useless versions [18]), the fact that a call pattern with the most general call pattern exists implies that a non-optimized version of the predicate must always exist. Another way out of this problem is to eliminate useless call patterns once an inter-modular fixed-point has been reached.

Since reaching a global fixed-point can be a costly task, one interesting possibility can be the introduction of a time-out. The user can ask the system to request (re-)analysis as needed towards improving the analysis information. However, if after performing n analysis steps the time-out is reached before analysis $n + 1$ is finished, the global state corresponding to state n is guaranteed to be correct. In this case, the entry policy used has to be to introduce most general call patterns for all exported predicates, either before starting analysis or when a time-out is reached.

8.2   Using Under-Approximating Success Policies

Another alternative is to use SP^-. As a result, the analysis results are not guaranteed to be correct until an inter-modular fixed-point is reached. Thus, it may take a large amount of time to perform this global analysis. On the other hand, once a fixed-point is reached, the accuracy which will be obtained is optimal, since it corresponds to the least analysis graph, which is exactly the same which the flattening approach would have obtained.

Regarding the entry policy, the same discussion as above applies. The only difference being that the GTQ should be initialized with events of the form $P : \top \mapsto^- \bot$ since now the framework computes under-approximations. Clearly, $\bot$ is an under-approximation of any description.

Another important thing to note is that, since the final results of automatic analysis are optimal, they do not depend on the use of a particular success policy SP_1^- or another SP_2^-. Of course, the efficiency using SP_1^- can be very different from that obtained using SP_2^-.

8.3   Hybrid Policy

In practice we may wish to use a manual scheduling policy with an over-approximating success policy during program development, and then use an automatic scheduling policy with an under-approximating success policy just before program release, so as to ensure that the analysis is as precise as possible, thus allowing as much optimization as possible in the final version.

Fortunately, in such a situation we can often reuse much of the analysis information obtained using the over-approximating success policy. The reason is that if the analysis with the over-approximating success policy has reached a fixed-point, the answers obtained for module m are as accurate as those obtained with an under-approximating success policy as long as there are no cyclic dependencies between the modules in $depends(m)$. Thus in the common case that no modules are mutually dependent we can simply use the answer tables from the manual scheduling policy and use an automatic scheduling policy with an over-approximating success policy to obtain the fixed-point. Even in the case that some modules are mutually dependent we can use this technique to compute the answers for the modules which do not contain cyclic dependencies or do not depend on modules that contain them (e.g., leaf-modules).

8.4   Computation of an Intermodular Fixed-Point

Determining the optimal order in which the different modules in the program unit should be analyzed in order to get to a fixed-point as efficiently as possible is not trivial and it is the topic of ongoing work.

Finding good scheduling strategies for intra-modular analysis is a topic which has received considerable attention and highly optimized algorithms exist which converge to a fixed-point quickly. Unfortunately, it is not possible to directly translate the same heuristics used in the intra-modular case to the inter-modular case. In the inter-modular case we have to take into account the time required to change from analysis of one module to another since this typically means reading a new module from disk. Thus, requests to process call patterns have to be grouped by modules in order to reduce the number of times we change context.

Taking the heuristics in [17,10] as a starting point we are investigating and experimenting with different scheduling policies which take into account different aspects of the structure of the program unit such as dependencies, strongly connected components, etc. with promising results. It also remains to be explored which of the approaches to success policy results in more efficiently reaching a global fixed-point and whether the heuristics to be applied in either case coincide or are mostly different.

9   Some Practical Implementation Issues

In this section we discuss several issues not addressed in the previous sections and which are very important in order to have practical implementations of context-sensitive analysis systems. These issues are related to the persistence of global information and the analysis of libraries.

9.1   Making Global Information Persistent

The two-level framework presented in Section 6 needs to keep information both at the local and global level. One relevant question, due to its practical implications, is where this global information actually resides. One possibility is to have the global analysis tool running continuously as a kind of "compilation server" which stores the global state in its program memory. In a *manual* setting, this global tool would wait for the user(s) to place requests to analyze modules. When a request is received, the corresponding module is analyzed for the appropriate call patterns and using the global information available at the time in the memory of the global analyzer. After analysis terminates, the global information is updated and remembered by the process for subsequent requests. If we are in an *automatic* setting, the global tool itself requests the analysis of different modules until a global fixed-point (or a time-out) is reached.

This approach outlined above is not fully persistent in the sense that if the computer crashes all information about the global state is lost and analysis would have to start from scratch again. In order to implement the more general kind of persistence discussed in Section 4, a way to save and restore the global state of analysis is needed. This requires storing the value of the three global-level data-structures: GAT, GDT, and GTQ. A level of granularity which seems appropriate in this context is clearly the module level. I.e., the global state of analysis is saved and restored between two consecutive steps of (module) analysis, but not during the analysis of a given module, which, from the point of view of the two-level framework, is an atomic operation.

The ability to save and restore the global state of analysis has several advantages:

1. The global tool does not need to be running continuously: it can save its state, stop, restart when needed, and restore the global state. This is specially interesting when using a manual scheduling policy, since two consecutive analysis requests can be separated by large intervals.
2. Even if the automatic scheduling policy is used, any information about the global state which is still valid can be directly used. This means that analysis can be *incremental* in the sense that (global level) analysis information which is known to be valid is reused.

9.2   Splitting Global Information

Consider the analysis of module b in the program unit $U = \{a, b, c, d, e, f, g, h\}$ depicted in Figure 6. In principle, the global state includes information regarding exported predicates in any of the modules in U. As a result, if we can save the global state to disk and restore it, this would involve storing and retrieving information about all modules in U. However, analysis of b only requires retrieving the information for modules in *related(m)*. The small boxes which appear on the side of every module represent the portion of the global structures related to each module. To analyze the module b, the information of the global tables that we need is that of modules a, d and e, as indicated by the dashed curved line.

This is straightforward to do in practice by splitting the information in the global data structures into several parts, each one associated to a module. This allows easily identifying the pieces of global information which are needed in order to process a given module.

This optimization of the handling of global information has several advantages:

1. The time required to save and restore the information to disk is reduced since the total amount of information transferred is smaller.
2. The use of the data structures during analysis can be more efficient since search space is reduced.
3. The total amount of memory required in order to analyze a module can be significantly reduced: only the local data structures plus a possibly very reduced part of the global data structures are actually required to analyze the module.

One question which we have intentionally left open is where the persistent information should reside. In fact, all the discussion above is independent on how and where the global state is stored, as long as it is persistent. One possibility is to use a database which stores the global state and information is grouped by modules in order to minimize the amount of information which has to be retrieved or updated for each analysis. Another, very common, possibility is to store the global information associated to each module to disk, in the same way as temporary information (such as relocatable code) is stored in many traditional compilers. In fact, the actual implementation of modular analysis in both CiaoPP and HAL [14] systems is based on this idea: a module m has a m.reg file associated to it which contains the part of the global data structures which are associated to m.

9.3   Handling Libraries and Predefined Modules

Many compilers and program development systems include a large number of predefined modules and libraries which can be readily reused by programmers –an obviously interesting feature since it greatly reduces the time required to develop applications. From the point of view of analysis, these predefined modules and libraries differ from user programs in a number of ways:

1. They are designed with reusability in mind and thus they can be used by a comparatively large number of user programs.
2. Sometimes the source code for libraries and predefined modules may not be available. One common reason for this is that they are implemented in a lower-level language.
3. The total amount of code available as libraries can be extremely large. Thus, reanalyzing the libraries over and over again for slightly different call patterns can be costly.

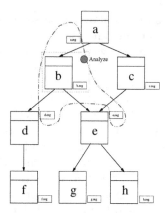

Fig. 6. Using Distributed Scheduling and Local Data Structures

Given these characteristics, it makes sense to develop a specialized treatment for libraries. We propose the following scheme. For each library module, the analysis results for a sufficient set of call patterns should be precomputed. This set should cover all possible correct call patterns for the library. In addition, the answer pattern for those call patterns have to be an over-approximation of the actual answers, independently of whether a SP^+ or SP^- success policy is used for the programs which use such library. In addition, in order to provide more accurate information, more particular call patterns which are expected to occur often in programs which use that library module can also be included. This information is added to the GAT of the program units which use the library. Thus, the success policy will be able to use this information directly for obtaining answer patterns. The reason for requiring pre-computed answer patterns for library modules to be over-approximations is that, much in the same way as for predefined procedures, even if an automatic scheduling policy is used, library modules are (in principle) not analyzed for calling patterns other than those which are pre-computed. Note that this is conceptually equivalent to considering the interface information of library modules *read-only*, since any program using them can read this information, but no additional call patterns will be analyzed. As a result, the global level framework will ignore new call patterns to library procedures that might be generated during the analysis of user programs. More precisely, entries of the form $P : CP \mapsto AP$ in TAT such that P is a library predicate do not need to be added to the GTQ since they will not be analyzed. In addition, no entries of the form $P : CP \rightarrow H : CP'$ need be added to GDT if H is a library predicate, since the answer pattern for library predicates is never modified and thus those dependencies are useless.

Deciding which is the best set of call patterns for which a library module should be analyzed is a non-trivial problem. One possibility can be to extract call patterns from correct programs which use the library and study which are the call patterns most often used. Another possibility is to have the library developer decide which are the call patterns of interest.

In spite of the considerations above, it is sometimes the case that we are interested in treating a library module using the general scheme, i.e., effectively considering the library information writable and allowing the analysis of new call patterns and the storage of the corresponding results. This can be interesting if the source code of a library is available and the set of initial call patterns for which it has been analyzed is not very representative. Note that hopefully this will happen often only when the library is relatively new. Once the code of the library stabilizes and a good set of initial patterns is obtained, it will generally be considered read-only. Allowing reanalysis of a library can also be useful when we are interested in using the analysis results from such call patterns to optimize the code of the library for the particular cases that correspond to those calls. For this case it may be interesting to store the corresponding information locally to the calling module, as opposed to inserting it into the library directories.

In summary, the implementation of the framework needs to treat libraries in a special way and also allow applying the general scheme for some designated library modules.

10   Discussion and Conclusions

Table 1 summarizes some characteristics of the different instantiations of the generic framework presented in the paper, in terms of the design features discussed in Section 4. The corresponding entries for the flattening approach of Section 3 –our baseline as usual– are also provided for comparison, listed in the column labeled Flattening. The Manual column lists the characteristics of the manual scheduling policy described in Section 7. The last two columns correspond to the two instantiations of the automatic scheduling policy, which were presented in Sections 8.1 and 8.2 respectively. Automatic$^+$ (resp. Automatic$^-$) indicate that an over-approximating (resp. under-approximating) success policy is used.

The first three rows, i.e., Scheduling policy, Success policy, and Entry policy correspond to the values of these parameters in each instantiation.

All instances of the framework for modular analysis are *module-aware*, in contrast to Flattening, which is not. Both instances described of the modular framework proposed are incremental, in the sense that only a subset (instead of every module) in the program unit needs to be re-analyzed, and they also both achieve the goal of *not needing to reanalyze all call patterns* every time a module is considered for analysis.

Regarding correctness, both the Flattening and Automatic$^-$ approaches have in common that correctness is only guaranteed when analysis comes to an end. This is because the approximations used are under-approximations and thus the results are only guaranteed to be correct when a (global) fixed-point is reached. However, in the Manual and Automatic$^+$ approaches the information in the global state is correct after any number of local analysis steps.

On the other hand, both the Flattening and Automatic$^-$ approaches are guaranteed to obtain the most accurate information possible, i.e., the least analysis graph, when a fixed-point is reached. In contrast, the Manual approach cannot guarantee optimal accuracy for two reasons. The first one is that there is no guarantee that modules will be processed the number of times that is necessary for an inter-modular fixed-point to be reached. Second, even if such a fixed-point is reached, it may not be the least fixed-point. This is because this approach uses over-approximations of the analysis results which are improved ("narrowed") in the different analysis iterations until a fixed-point is reached. On the other hand, if there are no circular dependencies among predicates in different modules, then the fixed-point obtained will be the least one, i.e., the most accurate.

Regarding efficiency in time we will consider two cases. The first one is when we have to perform analysis of the program unit from scratch. In this case, Flattening can be highly optimized in order to converge quickly to a fixed-point. In contrast, in this situation the instances of the modular framework have the disadvantage that loading and unloading modules during analysis introduces a significant overhead. As a result, in order to maintain the number of context changes low, call patterns may be solicited from imported modules which use temporary information and which are not needed in the final analysis graph. These call patterns which end up being useless are known as *spurious* versions. This problem also occurs in Flattening, though to a much lesser degree if good algorithms are used. Therefore, the modular approaches may end up performing work which is speculative, and thus the total amount of work performed in the automatic approaches to modular analysis is in principle an upper bound of that needed in Flattening.

On the other hand, consider the second case in which a relatively large amount of intra-modular analysis has already taken place for the modules to be analyzed in our programming unit and that the global information is persistent. In this case, the automatic approaches can update their global data structures using the precomputed information, rather than starting from scratch as is done in Flattening. In such a case the automatic approaches may perform much less work than Flattening. It is to be expected that once module m becomes stable, i.e., it is fully developed, it will quickly be analyzed for a relatively large set of calling patterns. In such a case it is likely that it will be possible to analyze any other module m' which uses m by simply reusing the existing analysis results for m. This is specially true in the case of *library modules*, as discussed in Section 9.3.

Regarding the efficiency in terms of memory, it is to be expected that the instances of the modular framework will outperform the non-modular, flattening approach. This was in fact already observed in the case of [4]. Indeed, one important practical difficulty that appears during the (monolithic) analysis of large programs is that the amount of information which is kept in memory is very large and the storage needed can become too large to fit in memory. The modular framework proposed needs less memory because: a) at each point in time, only one module requires to be loaded in the code area, and b) the local answer table only needs to hold entries for the module being analyzed, and not for other modules. Also, in general, the total amount of memory required to

Table 1. Comparison of Approaches to Modular Analysis

	Flattening	Manual	Automatic$^+$	Automatic$^-$
Scheduling policy	automatic	manual	automatic	automatic
Success policy	SP^-	SP^+	SP^+	SP^-
Entry policy	top-level	all	top-level	top-level
Module-aware	no	yes	yes	yes
No Rean. of all CPs	no	n/a	yes	yes
Correct	at fixed-point	yes	yes	at fixed-point
Accurate	yes	no	no circularities	yes
Efficient in time	yes	n/a	no	no
Efficient in memory	no	yes	yes	yes
Termination	finite asc. chains	finite asc. chains	finite chains	finite asc. chains

store the global data structures is not very high when compared to the memory required locally for the different modules. In addition, not all the global data structures are required when analyzing a module m, but only that associated with the modules in *related*(m).

Finally, regarding termination, except for Flattening, in which only one level of termination is required, the three other cases require two levels of termination: at the intra-modular and at the inter-modular level. In Flattening, since analysis results increase monotonically until a fixed-point is reached, termination is often guaranteed by considering description domains which do not contain infinite ascending chains: no matter what the current description is, top ($\top$), which is trivially guaranteed to be a fixed-point, is only a finite number of steps away. Exactly the same condition is required for guaranteeing termination of Automatic$^-$. The manual approach only requires guaranteeing intra-modular termination since the number of call patterns analyzed is finite. However, in the case Automatic$^+$, finite ascending chains are required for ensuring local termination *and* finite descending chains are required for ensuring global termination. As a result, termination requires domains with finite chains, or appropriate widening operators.

In summary, the proposed two-level generic framework for analysis and its instantiations meet a good subset of our stated objectives. We hope the discussion and the concrete proposal presented in this paper will provide a better understanding of the handling of context-sensitive program analysis on modular programs and contribute to the widespread use of such context-sensitive analysis techniques for modular programs in practical systems. An implementation of the framework, as a generalization of the pre-existing CiaoPP modular analysis components, is currently being completed. In this context, we are experimenting with different scheduling policies for the global level, for concrete, practical analysis situations.

Acknowledgments

This work was funded in part by projects ASAP (EU IST FET Programme Project Number IST-2001-38059) and CUBICO (MCYT TIC 2002-0055) and

ARC IREX Grant X00106666. Part of this work was performed during a research stay of Germán Puebla and Jesús Correas at UNM supported by grants from the Secretaría de Estado de Educación y Universidades and by the Madrid Regional Government (CAM), respectively. Manuel Hermenegildo is also supported by the Prince of Asturias Chair in Information Science and Technology at UNM.

References

1. F. Besson and T. Jensen. Modular class analysis with datalog. In *10th International Symposium on Static Analysis, SAS 2003*, number 2694 in LNCS. Springer, 2003.

2. A. Bossi, M. Gabbrieli, G. Levi, and M.C. Meo. A compositional semantics for logic programs. *Theoretical Computer Science*, 122(1,2):3–47, 1994.

3. F. Bueno, D. Cabeza, M. Hermenegildo, and G. Puebla. Global Analysis of Standard Prolog Programs. In *European Symposium on Programming*, number 1058 in LNCS, pages 108–124, Sweden, April 1996. Springer-Verlag.

4. F. Bueno, M. García de la Banda, M. Hermenegildo, K. Marriott, G. Puebla, and P. Stuckey. A Model for Inter-module Analysis and Optimizing Compilation. In *Logic-based Program Synthesis and Transformation*, number 2042 in LNCS, pages 86–102. Springer-Verlag, March 2001.

5. B. Le Charlier and P. Van Hentenryck. Experimental Evaluation of a Generic Abstract Interpretation Algorithm for Prolog. *ACM Transactions on Programming Languages and Systems*, 16(1):35–101, 1994.

6. M. Codish, S.K. Debray, and R. Giacobazzi. Compositional analysis of modular logic programs. In *Proc. POPL'93*, 1993.

7. P. Cousot and R. Cousot. Abstract Interpretation: a Unified Lattice Model for Static Analysis of Programs by Construction or Approximation of Fixpoints. In *Fourth ACM Symposium on Principles of Programming Languages*, pages 238–252, 1977.

8. María J. García de la Banda, Bart Demoen, Kim Marriott, and Peter J. Stuckey. To the Gates of HAL: A HAL Tutorial. In *International Symposium on Functional and Logic Programming*, pages 47–66, 2002.

9. M. Hermenegildo, G. Puebla, F. Bueno, and P. López-García. Program Development Using Abstract Interpretation (and The Ciao System Preprocessor). In *10th International Static Analysis Symposium (SAS'03)*, number 2694 in LNCS, pages 127–152. Springer-Verlag, June 2003.

10. M. Hermenegildo, G. Puebla, K. Marriott, and P. Stuckey. Incremental Analysis of Constraint Logic Programs. *ACM Transactions on Programming Languages and Systems*, 22(2):187–223, March 2000.

11. A. Kelly, A. Macdonald, K. Marriott, H. Søndergaard, and P.J. Stuckey. Optimizing compilation for CLP($\mathcal{R}$). *ACM Transactions on Programming Languages and Systems*, 20(6):1223–1250, 1998.

12. K. Muthukumar and M. Hermenegildo. Deriving A Fixpoint Computation Algorithm for Top-down Abstract Interpretation of Logic Programs. Technical Report ACT-DC-153-90, Microelectronics and Computer Technology Corporation (MCC), Austin, TX 78759, April 1990.

13. K. Muthukumar and M. Hermenegildo. Compile-time Derivation of Variable Dependency Using Abstract Interpretation. *Journal of Logic Programming*, 13(2/3):315–347, July 1992.

14. Nicholas Nethercote. The Analysis System of HAL. Master's thesis, Monash University, 2002.

15. Christian W. Probst. Modular Control Flow Analysis for Libraries. In *Static Analysis Symposium, SAS'02*, volume 2477 of *LNCS*, pages 165–179. Springer-Verlag, 2002.

16. G. Puebla, F. Bueno, and M. Hermenegildo. An Assertion Language for Constraint Logic Programs. In P. Deransart, M. Hermenegildo, and J. Maluszynski, editors, *Analysis and Visualization Tools for Constraint Programming*, number 1870 in LNCS, pages 23–61. Springer-Verlag, September 2000.

17. G. Puebla and M. Hermenegildo. Optimized Algorithms for the Incremental Analysis of Logic Programs. In *International Static Analysis Symposium*, number 1145 in LNCS, pages 270–284. Springer-Verlag, September 1996.

18. G. Puebla and M. Hermenegildo. Abstract Multiple Specialization and its Application to Program Parallelization. *J. of Logic Programming. Special Issue on Synthesis, Transformation and Analysis of Logic Programs*, 41(2&3):279–316, November 1999.

19. G. Puebla and M. Hermenegildo. Some Issues in Analysis and Specialization of Modular Ciao-Prolog Programs. In *Special Issue on Optimization and Implementation of Declarative Programming Languages*, volume 30 of *Electronic Notes in Theoretical Computer Science*. Elsevier - North Holland, March 2000.

20. G. Puebla and M. Hermenegildo. Abstract Specialization and its Applications. In *ACM Partial Evaluation and Semantics based Program Manipulation (PEPM'03)*, pages 29–43. ACM Press, June 2003. Invited talk.

21. A. Rountev, B.G. Ryder, and W. Landi. Data-flow analysis of program fragments. In *ESEC/FSE'99*, volume 1687 of *LNCS*, pages 235–252. Springer-Verlag, 1999.

22. Y. M. Tang and P. Jouvelot. Separate abstract interpretation for control-flow analysis. In *Theoretical Aspects of Computer Software (TACS '94)*, number 789 in LNCS. Springer, 1994.

23. W. Vanhoof and M. Bruynooghe. Towards modular binding-time analysis for first-order mercury. In *Special Issue on Optimization and Implementation of Declarative Programming Languages*, volume 30 of *Electronic Notes in Theoretical Computer Science*. Elsevier - North Holland, March 2000.

Unfold/Fold Transformations for Automated Verification of Parameterized Concurrent Systems

Abhik Roychoudhury[1] and C.R. Ramakrishnan[2]

[1] School of Computing, National University of Singapore, Singapore
`abhik@comp.nus.edu.sg`
[2] Dept. of Computer Science, SUNY Stony Brook, Stony Brook, NY 11794, USA
`cram@cs.sunysb.edu`

Abstract. Formal verification of reactive concurrent systems is important since many hardware and software components of our computing environment can be modeled as reactive concurrent systems. Algorithmic techniques for verifying concurrent systems such as model checking can be applied to finite state systems only. This chapter investigates the verification of a common class of infinite state systems, namely parameterized systems. Such systems are parameterized by the number of component processes, for example an n-process token ring for any n. Verifying the entire infinite family represented by a parameterized system lies beyond the reach of traditional model checking. On the other hand, deductive techniques to verify infinite state systems often require substantial user guidance.

The goal of this work is to integrate algorithmic and deductive techniques for automating proofs of temporal properties of parameterized concurrent systems. Here, the parameterized system to be verified and the temporal property are encoded together as a logic program. The problem of verifying the temporal property is then reduced to the problem of determining equivalence of predicates in this logic program. These predicate equivalences are established by transforming the program such that the semantic equivalence of the predicates can be inferred from the structure of their clauses in the transformed program.

For transforming the predicates, we use the well-established unfold/fold transformations of logic programs. Unfolding represents a step of resolution and can be used to evaluate the base case and the finite part of the induction step in an induction proof. Folding and other transformations represent deductive reasoning and can be used to recognize the induction hypothesis. Together these transformations are used to construct induction proofs of temporal properties. Strategies are developed to help guide the application of the transformation rules. The transformation rules and strategies have been implemented to yield an automatic and programmable first order theorem prover for parameterized systems. Case studies include multi-processor cache coherence protocols and the Java Meta-Locking protocol from Sun Microsystems. The program transformation based prover has been used to automatically prove various safety properties of these protocols.

M. Bruynooghe and K.-K. Lau (Eds.): Program Development in CL, LNCS 3049, pp. 261–290, 2004.

1   Introduction

Many hardware and software components of our everyday computing environment can be modeled as a *reactive concurrent system*. These include hardware controllers, operating systems, network protocols, and distributed applications *e.g.* air traffic control systems. Intuitively, a reactive concurrent system is a collection of nonterminating processes which run concurrently, and communicate with each other as well as an external environment to perform a common task. Proving correctness of such a system involves showing that it displays some desired behavior. Formally proving correctness of such systems has been a topic of intense research for the past two decades, leading to the birth of successful techniques like *model checking* [8].

Formal verification of reactive systems involves: *(i)* constructing the "specification" *i.e.* the description of the desired behavior(s) of the program, *(ii)* constructing the "implementation" *i.e.* the formal description of the reactive system being verified, and *(iii)* formally proving that the implementation satisfies the specification. Given appropriate formalisms for expressing the specification and implementation, we then need a proof system for establishing that a given implementation satisfies a given specification. Given a proof system and a proof obligation (*i.e.* a given implementation and specification), one needs to construct a proof tree by repeated application of the rules to the proof obligation. In general, this proof tree construction is undecidable [31].

However, for *finite state* concurrent systems, this can be achieved algorithmically by searching *the* finite model of the implementation, *i.e.* by searching the states of the finite state transition system representing the behaviors of the concurrent system. This is the basic idea behind model checking. Model checking [8] is an *automated* formal verification technique for proving properties of finite state concurrent programs. Here the specification is typically provided as a temporal logic formula. The implementation is often expressed using a process calculus, which is translated to a finite state transition system. Verifying the truth of the temporal formula is accomplished by traversing the states of this transition system based on the structure of the temporal formula. If the formula is true, then the search succeeds; otherwise the search fails and yields a counterexample.

The Problem Addressed The applicability of model checking is inherently restricted to finite state systems. Many of the verification tasks one would like to conduct however deal with infinite state systems. In particular, we often need to verify "parameterized" systems such as an n-bit adder or an n-process token ring for any n. Intuitively, a parameterized system is an infinite family of finite state systems parameterized by a recursively defined type *e.g.* the set of natural numbers $\mathbb{N}$. Thus an n-bit adder is a parameterized system, the parameter in question being $n \in \mathbb{N}$, the width of the adder circuit. Verification of distributed algorithms can be naturally cast as verifying parameterized systems, the parameter being the number of processes. For example, consider a distributed algorithm where n users share a resource and follow some protocol to ensure mutually exclusive access. Using model checking, we can verify mutual exclusion only for finite instances of the algorithm, *i.e.* for $n = 2$, $n = 3, \ldots$, but not for every n. The verification of parameterized systems lies beyond the reach of traditional model checkers: the representations and the model-checking algorithms that manipulate these representations are designed to work on finite state systems and it is not at all trivial to adapt them for parameterized system verification.

In general, automated verification of parameterized systems has been shown to be undecidable [3]. Thus, verification of parameterized systems is often accomplished via *theorem proving*, i.e. mechanically checking the steps of a human proof using a deductive system. Even with substantial help from the deductive system in dispensing routine parts of the proof, such theorem proving efforts require considerable user guidance. Alternatively, one can identify subclasses of parameterized systems for which verification is decidable [21, 33]. Using this approach meaningful subclasses have been identified, such as token rings of similar processes [14] and classes of parameterized synchronous systems [17].

The Approach Taken A parameterized system represents an infinite family parameterized by a recursively defined type. Therefore, it is natural to attempt proving properties of parameterized systems by inducting over this type. In this work, we aim to automate the construction of such induction proofs by restricting the deductive machinery for constructing proofs. We construct an automatic and programmable first order logic prover with limited deductive capability.

The research reported in this chapter is part of recent efforts to exploit logic programming technology for developing new tools and techniques to specify and verify concurrent systems. For example, constraint logic programming has been used for the analysis and verification of hybrid systems [49] and more recently for model checking of finite-state [34] / infinite-state systems [13]. In [40], a memoized logic programming engine is used to develop XMC, an efficient and flexible model checker whose performance is comparable to that of highly optimized model checkers such as Spin [22]. Recently, [12] used constraint logic programming to construct proofs of safety properties of parameterized cache coherence protocols. Essentially, these techniques aim to use (constraint) logic program evaluation to efficiently construct verification proofs involving state space search (accomplished via resolution) and (possibly) constraint solving. These techniques do not construct induction proofs and are not applicable to parameterized networks of different topologies; thus, the technique of [12] cannot be used to prove properties of parameterized tree networks. On the other hand, we construct an automatic and programmable first order logic prover with limited deductive capability. This prover is geared to construct nested induction proofs which typically proceed by inducting on the structure of the parameterized network. The core technology of our prover is provided by logic program transformations. We discuss related proof techniques based on program transformations in Section 9.

Our work provides a methodology for constructing induction proofs by suitably extending the resolution based evaluation mechanism of logic programs [42, 44]. In this approach, the parameterized system and the property to be verified is expressed as a logic program. The verification problem is reduced to the problem of determining the equivalence of predicates in this program. The predicate equivalences are then established by transforming the predicates such that their semantic equivalence can be inferred from the syntax of their transformed definitions. The proof of semantic equivalence of two transformed predicates p, p' then proceeds automatically by a routine induction on the size of the proofs of ground instances of $p(\overline{X})$ and $p'(\overline{X})$.

For transforming the predicates, we use the well-established *unfold/fold* transformations of logic programs [46] which have been previously used for program optimization [11, 38] and automated deduction [23, 25, 36]. The major transformations in such a transformation framework are unfolding, folding and goal replacement. One of these transformations (unfolding) represents an application of resolution. In particular, an application of the unfold transformation represents a single resolution step. Therefore, one can achieve on-the-fly explicit state *algorithmic* model checking by repeated unfolding of the verification proof obligation. In constructing induction proofs, unfold transformations are used to evaluate away the base case and the finite portions of the proof in the induction step of the induction argument. Folding and goal replacement, on the other hand, represent a form of *deductive* reasoning. They are used to simplify the given program so that applications of the induction hypothesis in the induction proof can be recognized. The reader should note that the folding transformation is more powerful that the memoing involved in traditional tabled resolution [7, 40, 48]. Folding remembers (disjunctions of) conjunctions of atoms and can be used to remember/recognize the induction hypothesis in an induction proof.

Contributions The contributions of this work can be summarized as follows.

- First, it shows how logic program evaluation based techniques for verifying finite state systems can be flexibly extended to yield a program transformation framework for constructing inductive proofs of temporal properties of parameterized systems. Since one of our transformations corresponds to a model checking step and the others correspond to deductive reasoning, model checking emerges as a special case when the deductive steps are applied lazily.[3]
- The program transformation framework presented here allows for tight integration of algorithmic and deductive verification steps in a proof. Note that application of unfolding and folding steps can be arbitrarily interleaved in the verification proof of a parameterized system. This constitutes a tighter integration of model checking computation with deductive reasoning as compared to the integration of model checking as a decision procedure in a theorem prover.
- Finally, we present terminating strategies for controlling the application of the transformation rules, thereby leading to the implementation of a programmable and fully automatic prover (which is incomplete). These strate-

---

[3] However, unlike model checking, our augmented proof technique does not generate counter-example evidence. We discuss this issue further in Section 9.

gies are used to construct safety proofs of parameterized systems of various "structures" including uni and bi-directional chains, rings and trees of processes. The prover has been used to construct automated proofs of safety properties of cache coherence protocols. It has also been used to automatically verify mutual exclusion in the Java Meta-Locking Algorithm (a recently developed algorithm to ensure secure access of Java objects by multiple Java threads) from Sun Microsystems [1].

Organization The rest of this chapter is organized as follows. In Section 2 we discuss how we encode the problem of verifying temporal properties of parameterized systems as a logic program. Section 3 presents an overview of our proof technique, while Section 4 presents the proof rules on which our technique is based. Section 5 discusses the automation of each application of a proof rule while Section 6 presents a framework to guide application of proof rules when several of them are applicable. Section 7 presents an example proof using our technique. Section 8 summarizes some applications of our proof technique along with experimental results. Finally, section 9 provides concluding remarks and comparisons to related work.

2   Encoding the Verification Problem

In this section, we discuss how to encode the problem of verifying parameterized concurrent systems as a logic program. Intuitively, a parameterized concurrent system can be viewed as a network of an unbounded number of finite state processes which communicate in a specific pattern. These finite state processes constituting the network have a finite number of process types, and their communication pattern is called the *network topology*. For example, an n bit shift register (for any n) is a parameterized system. It represents an unbounded number of finite state processes communicating along a chain. These finite state processes are "similar", each of them representing a single bit. To model a parameterized system as a logic program, the local states of the constituent finite state processes are represented by terms of finite size. The global state of the parameterized system is represented by a term of unbounded size consisting of these finite terms as sub-terms. The initial states and the transition relation of the parameterized system are then encoded as logic program predicates with such unbounded terms as arguments.

2.1   System Specification

In our encoding, the global states of the parameterized system to be verified are represented by unbounded terms. This is because (i) a global state is a composition of local states of the constituent processes and (ii) a parameterized system typically contains unbounded number of processes (recall that a parameterized system is an infinite family of finite state systems). The initial states and the transition relation of the parameterized system are specified as two logic program predicates gen/1 and trans/2 over these terms. Thus, for any ground term $\bar{t}$, gen($\bar{t}$) is true iff $\bar{t}$ is an initial state of one member of the parameterized family being verified. Similarly for any two ground terms $\bar{t}$, $\bar{t}'$ we require that trans($\bar{t}$,$\bar{t}'$) is true iff $\bar{t} \to \bar{t}'$ is a transition in one of the members of the parameterized family. The recursive structure of gen and trans depends on the topology of the parameterized network being verified.

```
gen([1]).
gen([0|X]) :- gen(X).
trans([0,1|T], [1,0|T]).
trans([H|T], [H|T1]) :- trans(T,T1).
```

System description

```
thm(X) :- gen(X), live(X).
live(X) :- X = [1|_].
live(X) :- trans(X,Y), live(Y).
```

Property description

Fig. 1. Example: Liveness in an unbounded length shift register

For example, in an n bit shift register (for any n), the local states of the bit process are represented by the terms 0 and 1 (corresponding to the situations where the value stored in the bit is 0 and 1 respectively). A global state of the register is then represented by an unbounded list where each element of the list is 0 or 1. Now, let us consider an n bit shift register where initially the rightmost bit of the chain contains 1 and all other bits contain 0. The system evolves by passing the 1 leftward. A logic program describing the system is given in Figure 1. The predicate gen generates the initial states of an n-process chain for all n. As mentioned above, a global state of the register is represented as an ordered list (a list in Prolog-like notation is of the form [Head|Tail]) of zeros and ones. The set of bindings of variable S upon evaluation of the query gen(S) is { [1], [0,1], [0,0,1], ... }. The predicate trans in the program encodes a single transition of the global automaton. The first clause in the definition of trans captures the transfer of the 1 from right to left; the second clause recursively searches the state representation until the first clause can be applied. (i.e., when the 1 is not already in the left-most bit).

2.2   Temporal Property and Proof Obligations

So far, we have illustrated how the parameterized system to be verified can be encoded as a logic program. The temporal property to be verified can also be encoded as a logic program predicate over global states of the system. In this chapter, we only consider those properties φ such that φ *(or its negation) can be encoded as a definite logic program*. This includes weak liveness properties such as EFp and invariant properties such as AGp where p is an atomic proposition about system states and A, E, F, G are operators of the branching time temporal logic CTL [16]. These temporal properties have a single fixed point operator.

For our shift register example, we consider the CTL property EF $[1|\_]$, that is, eventually the 1 reaches the left most bit. This is encoded by the predicate live in Figure 1. The first clause of live succeeds for global states where the 1 is already in the left-most bit (a good state). The second (recursive) clause of live checks if a good state is reachable after a (finite) sequence of transitions. Every member of the parameterized family satisfies the liveness property if and only if $\forall$ X gen(X) $\Rightarrow$ live(X). Moreover, this is the case if

$$\forall X \; \text{thm}(X) \Leftrightarrow \text{gen}(X)$$

i.e. if thm and gen are semantically equivalent. Thus, we have encoded the verification problem as a logic programs and reduced the proof obligation to establishing equivalence of program predicates.

3 Overview of Our Proof Technique

We now illustrate how we can construct induction based proofs arising in parameterized system verification via logic program transformations. Essentially, this is accomplished using the following steps:

1. Encode the temporal property to be verified as well as the parameterized system as a logic program P_0.
2. Convert the verification proof obligation to predicate equivalence proof obligations of the form $P_0 \vdash \text{p} \equiv \text{q}$ (p, q are predicates)
3. Construct a transformation sequence $P_0, P_1, \ldots, P_k$ s.t.
   (a) Semantics of P_0 = Semantics of P_k
   (b) from the syntax of P_k we infer $P_k \vdash \text{p} \equiv \text{q}$

The construction of a transformation sequence proceeds by repeated application of transformation rules. If several rules are applicable, strategies are used for rule selection. Inferring $P_k \vdash \text{p} \equiv \text{q}$ from syntax is achieved by a sufficient condition called *Syntactic Equivalence* which is formally defined in Section 5.1 (see Definition 4). Also, note that we are dealing with definite logic programs, and the semantics that we consider for a definite logic program is its least Herbrand model [10].

In the shift register example, we have encoded the problem of verifying liveness in an n bit shift register as the logic program P_0 in Figure 1. We have reduced the verification proof obligation to establishing the equivalence of thm and gen predicates in program P_0. We then apply program transformations to program P_0 to obtain a program P_k where thm and gen are defined as follows:

In this example, the transformed definitions of thm and gen are identical modulo predicate (and variable) renaming. In general, we have a sufficient condition called *syntactic equivalence* s.t. if two predicates p and q are syntactically equivalent in program P_k then p and q are semantically equivalent in P_k. Furthermore, we ensure that checking syntactic equivalence of two predicates in a

```
gen([1]).                    thm([1]).
gen([0|X]) :- gen(X).        thm([0|X]) :- thm(X).
```

Fig. 2. Fragment of Transformed Program for Shift Register Example

given program is decidable. In the shift register example, the transformed definitions of gen and thm given in Figure 2 are syntactically equivalent. The formal definition of syntactic equivalence is presented in Section 5.1. The definitions of gen and thm given above both represent the infinite set $\{[0^n, 1] \mid n \in \mathbb{N}\}$. For each element X in this set, we can therefore construct a *ground proof* of thm(X) and gen(X). Formally, we define a ground proof as:

Definition 1 (Ground Proof) *Let T be a tree, each of whose nodes is labeled with a ground atom. Then T is a ground proof in a definite program P, if every node A in T satisfies the condition : $A :- A_1, ..., A_n$ is a ground instance of a clause in P, where $A_1, ..., A_n$ $(n \geq 0)$ are the children of A in T.*

For example, a ground proof tree[4] of gen([0,0,1]) and thm([0,0,1]) (using the above clauses of thm and gen) are shown below.

Inferring the equivalence of thm and gen from the transformed definitions in Figure 2 involves an *induction* on the size of the proof trees of gen(X) and thm(X) for any ground term X. In general, to prove the equivalence of two predicates p, p' of same arity we first transform their definitions to syntactically equivalent forms. Then, the proof of semantic equivalence of two syntactically equivalent predicates p, p' proceeds (by definition of syntactic equivalence) as follows:

- show that for every ground proof of $p(\overline{X})\theta$ (where $\overline{X}$ are variables and θ is any ground substitution of $\overline{X}$) there exists a ground proof of $p'(\overline{X})\theta$. This follows by induction on the size of ground proofs of $p(\overline{X})\theta$.
- show that for every ground proof of $p'(\overline{X})\theta$ (where $\overline{X}$ are variables and θ is any ground substitution of $\overline{X}$) there exists a ground proof of $p(\overline{X})\theta$. This follows by induction on the size of ground proofs of $p'(\overline{X})\theta$.

Thus, transforming gen and thm to obtain the definitions of Figure 2 and then inferring the equivalence from these transformed definitions amounts to an induction proof of the liveness property. Note that even though we are actually

---

[4] In this particular example, these are the only ground proofs of gen([0,0,1]) and thm([0,0,1]).

inducting on the size of ground proofs, here this is same as inducting on the process structure of the parameterized system: the length of the shift register.

We now formally describe our proof technique. Since we always prove equivalence of logic program predicates, we start by constructing a proof system for predicate equivalence proof obligations. Formally, the *predicate equivalence problem* is: given a definite logic program P and a pair of predicates p and p' of the same arity, determine if $P \models p \equiv p'$ *i.e.* whether p and p' are semantically equivalent in P. In other words, we need to determine whether for all ground substitutions θ, $p(\overline{X})\theta \in M(P) \Leftrightarrow p'(\overline{X})\theta \in M(P)$. Here $M(P)$ denotes the least Herbrand model [30] of program P. *Henceforth, whenever we refer to the "semantics" of a definite logic program P, we mean its least Herbrand model $M(P)$.*

4   A Proof System for Predicate Equivalences

We develop a tableau-based proof system for establishing predicate equivalence. The proof system presented here can be straightforwardly extended to prove goal equivalences[5] instead of predicate equivalences. Our process is analogous to SLD resolution. Recall that given a goal $\mathcal{G}$ and a definite logic program P, SLD resolution is used to prove whether instances of $\mathcal{G}$ are in $M(P)$. This proof is constructed recursively by deriving new goals via resolution. The truth of $\mathcal{G}$ is then shown by establishing the truth of these new goals. In contrast, each node in our proof tree denotes a pair of predicates (p, p'). To establish their equivalence we must establish that the predicates in the pair represented by each child node are equivalent. Note that the predicates in the child node are to be obtained from the syntax of the current definitions of p, p'. We now define:

Definition 2 (e-atom) *Let $\Gamma = P_0, P_1, \ldots, P_i$ be a sequence of programs. An e-atom is of the form $\Gamma \vdash p \equiv p'$ where p and p' are predicates of same arity appearing in each of the programs in Γ. It represents the proof obligation*

$$\forall 0 \leq j \leq i \; P_j \models p \equiv p'$$

Thus, an e-atom $\Gamma \vdash p \equiv p'$ represents the proof obligation that p, p' are semantically equivalent in each of the programs in Γ. We generalize the problem of establishing a single e-atom to that of establishing a sequence of e-atoms. We define an *e-goal* as a (possibly empty) sequence of e-atoms. We will often denote an e-goal by $\mathcal{E}$, possibly with primes and subscripts. Recall that SLD resolution proves a goal by unfolding an atom in the goal. Similarly, we proceed to prove an e-goal by transforming the relevant clauses of an e-atom (*i.e.* the clauses of the predicates appearing in the e-atom) in the e-goal.

The three rules used to construct an equivalence tableau are shown in Table 1. In the description of the proof rules Γ denotes a sequence of programs $P_0, \ldots, P_i$. Given a definite logic program P_0, and a pair of predicates of same arity p, p', we construct a tableau for the proof obligation $P_0 \vdash p \equiv p'$ by repeatedly applying the inference rules in Table 1.

---

[5] Recall that in a definite logic program, a goal is a conjunction of atoms.

Name	Top-down Inference (one step)	Side Condition
(Ax)	$\dfrac{\mathcal{E}, \quad \Gamma \vdash p \equiv p', \quad \mathcal{E}'}{\mathcal{E}, \quad \mathcal{E}'}$	$p \overset{P_i}{\cong} p'$
(Tx)	$\dfrac{\mathcal{E}, \quad \Gamma \vdash p \equiv p', \quad \mathcal{E}'}{\mathcal{E}, \quad \Gamma, P_{i+1} \vdash p \equiv p', \quad \mathcal{E}'}$	$M(P_{i+1}) = M(P_i)$
(Gen)	$\dfrac{\mathcal{E}, \quad \Gamma \vdash p \equiv p', \quad \mathcal{E}'}{\mathcal{E}, \quad \Gamma, P_{i+1} \vdash p \equiv p', \quad P_0 \vdash q \equiv q', \quad \mathcal{E}'}$	$P_0 \models q \equiv q'$ $\Rightarrow M(P_{i+1}) = M(P_i)$

Table 1. Proof System for Showing Predicate Equivalences

The *axiom elimination rule* (**Ax**) is applicable whenever the equivalence of the predicates p and p' can be established by some automatic mechanism, denoted in the rule by $p \overset{P_i}{\cong} p'$. Thus, $\overset{P_i}{\cong}$ is a decision procedure which infers the equivalence of p, p' in program P_i. Axiom elimination will typically be an application of what we call **syntactic equivalence**, a decidable equivalence of predicates based on the syntactic form of the clauses defining them.

The *program transformation rule* (**Tx**) attempts to simplify the program in order to expose the equivalence of predicates (which can then be inferred via an application of **Ax**). The program P_{i+1} is constructed from Γ using a *semantics preserving* program transformation. We use this rule whenever we apply an unfolding, folding, or any other (semantics-preserving) transformation that does not add any equivalence proof obligations. We give a brief presentation of these transformation rules in the next section.

The *equivalence generation rule* (**Gen**) proves an e-atom $\Gamma \vdash p \equiv p'$ by performing replacements in the clauses of p, p'. In particular, occurrence of some predicate q in the clauses of p, p' is replaced by occurrence of another predicate q'. The guarantee is that if the predicates q, q' are semantically equivalent then the program thus obtained is semantics preserving. This appears as the side condition of the **Gen** rule. The notation $P_0 \models q \equiv q'$ is a shorthand for the following: for all ground substitution θ, $q(\overline{X})\theta) \in M(P_0) \Leftrightarrow q'(\overline{X})\theta) \in M(P_0)$ where $M(P_0)$ is the least Herbrand model of P_0. Note the proof of semantic equivalence of p and p' is being constructed by using the semantic equivalence of q and q'. This allows us to simulate nested induction proofs. Typically, an application of the **Gen** rule corresponds to applying the goal replacement transformation.[6]

The notion of a tableau for a predicate equivalence proof obligation in a definite logic program P_0 is then defined in the usual way.

---

[6] The **Gen** rule does not require $\{p, p'\} \cap \{q, q'\} = $. When we synthesize an algorithmic framework for applying the proof rules we will keep track of the past history of equivalence proof obligations.

Definition 3 (Equivalence Tableau) *An equivalence tableau of an e-goal $\mathcal{E}_0$ is a finite sequence of e-goals $\mathcal{E}_0, \mathcal{E}_1, \ldots, \mathcal{E}_n$ where $\mathcal{E}_{i+1}$ is obtained from $\mathcal{E}_i$ by applying one of the rules described in Table 1 and $\mathcal{E}_n$ is empty.*

Now, let P_0 be a definite logic programs and p, p' be predicates of same arity appearing in P_0. Then we use our proof system to construct an equivalence tableau of $\mathcal{E}_0 = (P_0 \vdash p \equiv p')$.

Theorem 1 (Soundness of Proof System) *Let $\mathcal{E}_0, \mathcal{E}_1, \ldots, \mathcal{E}_n$ be a successful tableau with $\mathcal{E}_0 = (P_0 \vdash p \equiv p')$ for some definite logic program P_0. Then $P_0 \models p \equiv p'$ i.e. predicates p and p' are semantically equivalent in the least Herbrand model of P_0.*

Proof: We prove a stronger result. For any successful tableau of an e-goal $\mathcal{E}_0$ if $\Gamma \vdash p \equiv p'$ is an e-atom in $\mathcal{E}_0$ where $\Gamma = P_0, \ldots, P_i$ then $P_i \models p \equiv p'$.

The proof for this result is established by induction on the length of the tableau. For the base case, we have a tableau of length 1, which is formed by an application of the **Ax** rule. For such a tableau the result holds trivially since **Ax** is applied only when the semantic equivalence of p, p' can be automatically inferred in P_i. For the induction step, we consider a tableau $\mathcal{E}_0, \mathcal{E}_1, \ldots, \mathcal{E}_{k+1}$ of length $k + 1$. For all e-atoms of $\mathcal{E}_0$ which are not modified in the step $\mathcal{E}_0 \to \mathcal{E}_1$, the result follows by induction hypothesis. Let $P_0, \ldots, P_i \vdash p \equiv p'$ be the e-atom in $\mathcal{E}_0$ that is modified.

- **Ax**: If the rule applied to $\mathcal{E}_0$ is **Ax**, then from the side condition of **Ax** we have $P_i \models p \equiv p'$.
- **Tx** : If the rule applied to $\mathcal{E}_0$ is **Tx**, then $P_0, \ldots, P_i, P_{i+1} \vdash p \equiv p'$ is an e-atom in $\mathcal{E}_1$. Since $\mathcal{E}_1, \ldots, \mathcal{E}_{k+1}$ is a successful tableau of $\mathcal{E}_1$, therefore by induction hypothesis $P_{i+1} \models p \equiv p'$. By the side condition of **Tx**, we have $M(P_i) = M(P_{i+1})$ and therefore $P_i \models p \equiv p'$.
- **Gen** : If the rule applied to $\mathcal{E}_0$ is **Gen**, then $P_0, \ldots, P_i, P_{i+1} \vdash p \equiv p'$ and $P_0 \vdash q \equiv q'$ are e-atoms in $\mathcal{E}_1$. Again $\mathcal{E}_1, \ldots, \mathcal{E}_{k+1}$ is a successful tableau of $\mathcal{E}_1$. By induction hypothesis, we have $P_{i+1} \models p \equiv p'$ and $P_0 \models q \equiv q'$. From the side condition of **Gen** we have $M(P_i) = M(P_{i+1})$ and therefore $P_i \models p \equiv p'$.

If $\mathcal{E}_0, \ldots, \mathcal{E}_n$ is a successful tableau of $\mathcal{E}_0 = P_0 \vdash p \equiv p'$ then $P_0 \models p \equiv p'$.   □

The tableau can be readily extended to use some transformations that may not preserve least models, but only ensure that the least models, with respect to the predicates in the original program, are same. A transformation that adds new predicates to a program has this property, and is often useful in predicate equivalence proofs. From the soundness of the proof system, we can also infer the following property for any equivalence tableau: for any e-atom $\Gamma \vdash \ldots$ appearing in an equivalence tableau, all programs in Γ are semantically equivalent. The proof appears in [41].

Lemma 2 *Let $\mathcal{E}_0, \mathcal{E}_1, \ldots, \mathcal{E}_n$ be an equivalence tableau of $\mathcal{E}_0 = P_0 \vdash p \equiv p'$. For every e-atom $(\Gamma \vdash \ldots)$ in the tableau, if $\Gamma = P_0, \ldots, P_i$ then we have $M(P_0) = \ldots = M(P_i)$.*

Note that the proof system given in Table 1 is not complete. There can be no such complete proof system as attested to by the following theorem.

Theorem 3 (Incompleteness)   *Determining equivalence of predicates described by logic programs is not recursively enumerable.*

The theorem is easily proved using a reduction described in [3]. For a Turing machine M, we construct a program having two predicates, one that describes the natural numbers and the other that identifies an n such that M does not halt within n moves. These predicates are equivalent if and only if M does not halt. The non-halting problem is not recursively enumerable and so the predicate equivalence problem cannot be recursively enumerable.

5   Automated Instances of Proof Rules

In this section, we discuss the automation of each application of an **Ax**, **Tx** or **Gen** rule. The application of the **Tx** and **Gen** rules is achieved by unfolding, folding and goal replacement transformations (which we also discuss).

5.1   Automating the Ax Rule

The *axiom elimination rule* (**Ax**) infers the equivalence of two predicates p, p' in a semantics preserving program transformation sequence $\Gamma = P_0, \ldots, P_i$. In the light of Theorem 3, any such rule will be incomplete. Therefore, we will construct an effectively checkable sufficient condition for predicate equivalence. We call this sufficient condition as syntactic equivalence. Given a program transformation sequence $\Gamma = P_0, \ldots, P_i$ and two predicates p, p', we apply **Ax** if p, p' are syntactically equivalent in program P_i.

As an illustration, consider the program P (with clauses annotated with integer clause measures) in Figure 3. We can infer that $P \models r \equiv s$ since r and s have identical definitions. Using the equivalence of r and s we can infer that $P \models p \equiv q$, since the definitions of p and q are, in a sense, isomorphic.

```
p(X) :- r(X).          q(X) :- s(X).
p(X) :- e(X,Y), p(Y).  q(X) :- e(X,Y), q(Y).
r(X) :- b(X).          s(X) :- b(X).
```

Fig. 3. Program with syntactically equivalent predicates.

We formalize this notion of equivalence in the following definition. The following definition partitions the predicate symbols of a program into equivalence classes. Each predicate is assumed to be assigned a *label*, the partition number of the equivalence class to which it belongs. The labels of all predicates belonging to the same equivalence class is thus the same, and each equivalence class has a unique label.

Definition 4 (Syntactic Equivalence) *A syntactic equivalence relation $\overset{P}{\sim}$, is an equivalence relation on the set of predicates of a program P such that for all predicates p, q in P, if $p \overset{P}{\sim} q$ then the following conditions hold:*

1. *p and q have same arity, and*
2. *Let the clauses defining p and q be $\{C_1, \ldots, C_m\}$ and $\{D_1, \ldots, D_n\}$ respectively. Let $\{C'_1, \ldots, C'_m\}$ and $\{D'_1, \ldots, D'_n\}$ be such that C'_l (D'_l) is obtained by replacing every predicate symbol r in C_l (D_l) by s, where s is the label of the equivalence class of r (w.r.t. $\overset{P}{\sim}$). Then there exist two functions $f : \{1, \ldots, m\} \rightarrow \{1, \ldots, n\}$ and $g : \{1, \ldots, n\} \rightarrow \{1, \ldots, m\}$ such that*
   (i) $\forall 1 \leq i \leq m$ C'_i is an instance of $D'_{f(i)}$
   (ii) $\forall 1 \leq j \leq n$ D'_j is an instance of $C'_{g(j)}$.

Note that there is a largest syntactic equivalence relation. It can be computed by starting with all predicates in the same class, and repeatedly splitting the classes that violate properties (1) and (2) until a fixed point is reached. The existence of the mapping f ensures that for any ground substitution θ we have $p(\overline{X})\theta \in M(P) \Rightarrow q(\overline{X})\theta \in M(P)$ whereas the mapping g ensures $q(\overline{X})\theta \in M(P) \Rightarrow p(\overline{X})\theta \in M(P)$. The proof of the lemma proceeds by induction on size of ground proofs (see [41] for details).

Lemma 4 (Syntactic Equivalence $\Rightarrow$ Semantic Equivalence) *Let $\overset{P}{\sim}$ be the syntactic equivalence relation of the predicates of a program P. For all predicates p, q, if $p \overset{P}{\sim} q$, then $P \models p \equiv q$.*

5.2   Automating Tx: Transformations as Proof Rules

The transformation rule **Tx** corresponds to applying a program transformation which does not add any new equivalence proof obligations. Typically an application of this step is either unfolding or folding, or other standard transformations like generalization and equality introduction, deletion of subsumed clauses and deletion of failed clauses [35]. A single application of all these transformations can be automated.

We transform a logic program to another logic program by applying transformations that include unfolding and folding. A simple illustration of these transformations appears in Figure 4. Program P_1 is obtained from P_0 by unfolding the occurrence of q(X) in the definition of p. P_2 is obtained by folding q(X) in the second clause of p in P_1 using the definition of p in P_0 (an earlier program). Intuitively, unfolding is a step of clause resolution whereas folding replaces an instance of a clause body (in some earlier program in the transformation sequence) with its head.

$$
\begin{array}{l}
\texttt{p(X)} \texttt{ :- } \boxed{\texttt{q(X)}}. \\
\texttt{q(0)}. \\
\texttt{q(s(X))} \texttt{ :- q(X)}.
\end{array}
\quad \xrightarrow{Unf.} \quad
\begin{array}{l}
\texttt{p(0)}. \\
\texttt{p(s(X))} \texttt{ :- } \boxed{\texttt{q(X)}}. \\
\texttt{q(0)}. \\
\texttt{q(s(X))} \texttt{ :- q(X)}.
\end{array}
\quad \xrightarrow{Fold} \quad
\begin{array}{l}
\texttt{p(0)}. \\
\texttt{p(s(X))} \texttt{ :- p(X)}. \\
\texttt{q(0)}. \\
\texttt{q(s(X))} \texttt{ :- q(X)}.
\end{array}
$$

$$\qquad \text{Program } P_0 \qquad\qquad\qquad \text{Program } P_1 \qquad\qquad\qquad \text{Program } P_2$$

Fig. 4. Illustration of unfold/fold transformations

In the following, we present a (simplified) version of the unfolding and folding transformation rules. Note that each application of these rules is automated. We say that $P_0, P_1, \ldots, P_n$ is an *unfold/fold transformation sequence* if the program P_{i+1} is obtained from P_i $(i \geq 0)$ by an application of unfolding or a folding. We always assume that the clauses of each program in such a transformation sequence are "standardized apart". In other words, the variables of the clauses of P_i are suitably renamed such that no two clauses have any variables in common.

Transformation 1 Unfolding *Let C be a clause in P_i and A an atom in the body of C. Let $C_1, \ldots, C_m$ be the clauses in P_i whose heads are unifiable with A with most general unifier $\sigma_1, \ldots, \sigma_m$. Let C'_j be the clause that is obtained by replacing $A\sigma_j$ by the body of $C_j\sigma_j$ in $C\sigma_j$ $(1 \leq j \leq m)$. Assign $(P_i - \{C\}) \cup \{C'_1, \ldots, C'_m\}$ to P_{i+1}.* ☐

Transformation 2 Folding *Let $\{C_1, \ldots, C_m\} \subseteq P_i$ where C_l denotes the clause*

$$A :- A_{l,1}, \ldots, A_{l,n_l}, A'_1, \ldots, A'_n$$

and $\{D_1, \ldots, D_m\} \subseteq P_j$ $(j \leq i)$ where D_l is $B_l :- B_{l,1}, \ldots, B_{l,n_l}$. Further, let:

1. $\forall 1 \leq l \leq m \; \exists \sigma_l \; \forall 1 \leq k \leq n_l \; A_{l,k} = B_{l,k}\sigma_l$
2. $B_1\sigma_1 = B_2\sigma_2 = \cdots = B_m\sigma_m = B$
3. $D_1, \ldots, D_m$ *are the only clauses in P_j whose heads are unifiable with B.*
4. $\forall 1 \leq l \leq m$, σ_l *substitutes the internal variables[7] of D_l to distinct variables which do not appear in $\{A, B, A'_1, \ldots A'_n\}$.*

Then $P_{i+1} := (P_i - \{C_1, \ldots, C_m\}) \cup \{C'\}$ where $C' \equiv A :- B, A'_1, \ldots, A'_n$. ☐

$D_1, \ldots, D_m$ are the *folder* clauses, $C_1, \ldots, C_m$ are the *folded* clauses, and B is the *folder* atom.

Semantics preservation While unfolding is semantics preserving, folding may introduce circularity and change the program semantics. Recall that we are dealing with definite logic programs and we consider the least Herbrand model semantics. For example consider the program P_1 in Figure 5; P_1 is obtained from P_0 by unfolding the occurrence of q(X) in the body of p's second clause. We

---

[7] Variables appearing in the body of a clause, but not its head

perform folding where the second clause of p in P_1 serves as the folded clause and the second clause of q in P_0 serves as the folder clause. We get the program P_2 of Figure 5. Now, let us fold again. We use the second clause of q in P_2 as the folded clause and the second clause of p in P_1 as the folder clause. This produces the program P_3 of Figure 5. The program transformation sequence $P_0 \rightarrow P_1 \rightarrow P_2 \rightarrow P_3$ is not semantics preserving since the least Herbrand model of P_3 differs from that of P_0.

`p(X):-q(X).`
`q(a).`
`q(f(X)):-q(X).`
	`p(a).`
	`p(f(X)):-q(X).`
	`q(a).`
	`q(f(X)):-q(X).`
		`p(a).`
		`p(f(X)):-q(f(X)).`
		`q(a).`
		`q(f(X)):-q(X).`
			`p(a).`
			`p(f(X)):-q(f(X)).`
			`q(a).`
			`q(f(X)):-p(f(X)).`

Program P_0	Program P_1	Program P_2	Program P_3

Fig. 5. An example of incorrect unfold/fold transformation sequence

Due to this problem of semantics preservation, existing unfold/fold transformation systems have restricted the folding rule. Thus, in a program transformation sequence $P_0, P_1, \ldots, P_i$, folding of clause(s) in P_i is restricted [20, 26, 46, 47]. The restrictions are of two kinds: (a) based on the unfold/fold steps used to derive the transformation sequence $P_0, \ldots, P_i$, and (b) based on the syntax of the folder clauses used. In [43] we have shown that restrictions on the syntax of folder clauses is unnecessary for semantics preservation. As a consequence of this result, in a folding step we can use multiple clauses as folder; furthermore some of these clauses may be recursive.

The additional power of our transformation rules is useful in our transformation based proofs of temporal properties. Note that temporal properties contain fixed point operators. These properties are typically encoded as a logic program predicate with multiple recursive clauses *e.g.* a least fixed point property containing disjunctions is encoded using multiple recursive clauses. A simple reachability property EFp (which specifies that a state in which proposition p holds is reachable) [9] will be encoded as a logic program as follows:

```
ef(X) :- p(X).
ef(X) :- trans(X,Y), ef(Y).
```

where the predicate **trans** captures the transition relation of the system being verified, and p(X) is true if the proposition p holds in state X. This encoding contains two clauses, one of which is recursive.

5.3   Automating the Gen Rule

The **Gen** rule attempts to prove the e-atom $\Gamma \vdash p \equiv p'$ by proving the e-atoms $\Gamma, P_{i+1} \vdash p \equiv p'$ and $P_0 \vdash q \equiv q'$ where $\Gamma = P_0, \ldots, P_i$ is a program transformation sequence. It generates a new lemma $P_0 \vdash q \equiv q'$ whose proof is used to ensure that $M(P_i) = M(P_{i+1})$. An application of **Gen** corresponds to an application of the Goal Replacement transformation (given in the following). Here, we replace an occurrence of q with q' in a clause of p or p' as shown below.

$$\cdots \atop C : p(\bar{\ }) :- \mathcal{G}, q(\bar{s}), \mathcal{G'}. \qquad \cdots \atop C' : p(\bar{\ }) :- \mathcal{G}, q'(\bar{s}), \mathcal{G'}. \atop \cdots$$

Program P_i Program P_{i+1}

This requires us to show $P_0 \models q \equiv q'$ and therefore we obtain a new proof obligation $P_0 \vdash q \equiv q'$. We prove $P_0 \vdash q \equiv q'$ by constructing a different transformation sequence $P_0, P'_1, \ldots, P'_k$ s.t. $q \overset{P'_k}{\sim} q'$ i.e. q, q' are syntactically equivalent in P'_k. Note that since we are replacing q with q' in program P_i, the goal replacement rule requires $P_i \models q \equiv q'$. However for any e-atom $\Gamma \vdash \ldots$ appearing in a successful tableau, $M(P_0) = \ldots = M(P_i)$ where $\Gamma = P_0, \ldots, P_i$ (refer Lemma 2). Thus, $P_0 \models q \equiv q'$ implies $P_i \models q \equiv q'$.

A (simplified) definition of the Goal Replacement Transformation is given below. Again, to ensure semantics preservation, the transformation rule needs to impose *additional restrictions* on the transformation sequence $P_0, P_1, \ldots, P_i$. We omit these restrictions here (refer [43] for details). For a conjunction of atoms $A_1, \ldots, A_n$, we use the notation $vars(A_1, \ldots, A_n)$ to denote the set of variables in $A_1, \ldots, A_n$.

Transformation 3 Goal Replacement Let C be a clause $A :- A_1, \ldots, A_k, G$ in P_i, and G' be an atom such that $vars(G) = vars(G') \subseteq vars(A, A_1, \ldots, A_k)$. Suppose for all ground instantiation θ of G, G' we have $G\theta \in M(P_i) \Leftrightarrow G'\theta \in M(P_i)$. Then $P_{i+1} := (P_i - \{C\}) \cup \{C'\}$ where $C' \equiv A :- A_1, \ldots, A_k, G'$. $\qquad\square$

6 An Algorithmic Framework for Proof Strategies

We describe an algorithmic framework for creating strategies to automate the construction of the equivalence tableau of an e-atom. The objective is to: (a) find equivalence proofs that arise in verification with little or no user intervention, and (b) apply deduction rules lazily, i.e. for finite state systems a proof using the strategy is equivalent to algorithmic verification.

Our framework specifies the order in which the different program transformations (corresponding to each tableau rule) will be applied. If multiple transformations of the same kind (e.g., two folding steps) are possible at any point in the proof, the framework itself does not specify which transformations to apply. That is done by a separate selection function (analogous to literal selection in SLD resolution). *Thus we only present a framework for constructing strategies, rather than concrete strategies. Concrete strategies can be constructed by instantiating this framework.*

The tableau rules and associated transformations are applied in the following order. As would be expected, the axiom elimination rule (**Ax**) is used whenever

```
p1(a).                              p1(a).
p1(f(X)):- p1(X),s1(X).            p1(f(X)):- p1(X), s1(X).
p1(f(X)):- p1(X),t1(X), q1(X) .    p1(f(X)):- p1(X), t1(X), q2(X) .
r1(X):- s1(X).                      r1(X):- s1(X).
r1(X):- t1(X),q2(X).               r1(X):- t1(X),q2(X).
           P₀                                  Pᵢ
```

```
                p1(a).
                p1(f(X)):- p1(X),r1(X).
                r1(X):- s1(X).
                r1(X):- t1(X),q2(X).
                       Pᵢ₊₁
```

Fig. 6. Goal replacements to facilitate other transformations.

it is applicable. When the choice is between the **Tx** and **Gen** rules, we choose the former since the default transformation employed by **Tx** is unfolding, *i.e.* resolution. This will ensure that our strategies will perform on-the-fly model checking, a' la XMC [40] for finite-state systems. To create finite unfolding sequences we impose a finiteness condition *FIN* on transformation sequences. We do not give an exact definition of *FIN* but only a sufficient condition such that the resultant unfolding sequences terminate.

Definition 5 (Finiteness condition) *Given an a-priori fixed constant $k \in \mathbb{N}$, an unfolding program transformation sequence $\Gamma = P_0, \ldots, P_i, \ldots$ satisfies the finiteness condition $FIN(\Gamma, k)$ if for the clause C and atom A selected for unfolding at every P_i: (1) A is distinct modulo variable renaming from any atom B which was selected in unfolding some clause $D \in P_j (j < i)$ where C is obtained by repeated unfolding of D (2) the term depth of each argument of A is $\leq k$.*

Typically, we will assume a suitable choice of k and write the finiteness condition simply as $FIN(\Gamma)$. Condition 1 prohibits infinite unfolding sequences of the form: unfolding p(X) using the clause p(X) :- p(X) *i.e.* unfolding sequences where the same atom is infinitely unfolded. Condition 2 prohibits infinite unfolding sequences of the form: unfolding p(X) using the clause p(X) :- p(s(X)) *i.e.* where a different atom is unfolded every time, but there are infinitely many atoms to unfold.

We note that various online techniques for ensuring termination of unfolding sequences have been studied in the context of partial deduction [28, 32]. These techniques proceed by establishing a well-founded / well-quasi order among the atoms unfolded. This order may be fixed before hand, or refined online as the unfolding proceeds. Such techniques could be adapted for controlling unfolding in our predicate equivalence prover.

If *FIN* prohibits any further unfolding we either apply the folding transformation associated with **Tx** or use the **Gen** rule. Care must be taken, however, when **Gen** is chosen. Recall from the definition of **Gen** (refer Table 1) that

$\Gamma, P_{i+1} \vdash p \equiv p'$ implies $\Gamma \vdash p \equiv p'$ only if we can prove a new equivalence $P_0 \vdash q \equiv q'$. In other words, $P_{i+1} \models p \equiv p'$ implies $P_i \models p \equiv p'$ only if $P_0 \models q \equiv q'$. Since **Gen** itself does not specify the goals q and q' in the new equivalence, its application is highly nondeterministic. We limit the nondeterminism by using **Gen** only to enable **Ax** or **Tx** rules. For instance, consider the transformation sequence in Figure 6 (the intermediate programs $P_1, \ldots, P_{i-1}$ in the program transformation sequence $P_0, P_1, \ldots, P_{i-1}, P_i$ are not shown). Applying goal replacement in P_0 under the assumption that $P_0 \models \mathtt{q1} \equiv \mathtt{q2}$ enables the subsequent folding which transforms P_i into P_{i+1}.

Thus, when no further unfoldings are possible, we apply any possible folding. If no foldings are enabled, we check if there are new goal equivalences that will enable a folding step. We call this a *conditional folding* step. For instance, in program P_0 of Figure 6, equivalence of $\mathtt{q1(X)}$ and $\mathtt{q2(X)}$ enables folding. Note that the test for syntactic equivalence is only done on predicates, whereas a goal is a conjunction of atoms. However, we can reduce a goal equivalence check to a predicate equivalence check by introducing new predicate names for the goals. A keen point needs to be noted here. When we introduce new predicate names to a program, clearly the least Herbrand model cannot be preserved. As is common in program transformation literature [46, 20], we rectify this apparent anomaly by assuming that all new predicate names introduced are present in the initial program P_0 of a program transformation sequence.

Finally, we look for new goal equivalences, which, if valid, can lead to syntactic equivalence. This is called a *conditional equivalence* step. For instance, suppose in program P_{i+1} (in Figure 6), there are two additional predicates $\mathtt{p2}$ and $\mathtt{r2}$ and further assume that $\mathtt{p2}$ is defined using clauses

```
p2(a).
p2(f(Y)):- p2(Y), r2(Y).
```

Now if $\mathtt{r2}$ and $\mathtt{r1}$ are semantically equivalent, we can perform this goal replacement to obtain a program P_{i+2} where $\mathtt{p1}$ and $\mathtt{p2}$ are defined as follows. Thus, in P_{i+2} we can conclude that $\mathtt{p1} \overset{P_{i+2}}{\sim} \mathtt{p2}$.

```
p1(a).                          p2(a).
p1(f(X)):- p1(X), r1(X).        p2(f(Y)):- p2(Y), r1(Y).
```

The above intuitions are formalized in algorithmic framework *Prove* (see Figure 7). Given a program transformation sequence Γ, and a pair of predicates p, p', *Prove* attempts to prove that $\Gamma \vdash p \equiv p'$. *Prove* searches nondeterministically for a proof: if multiple cases of the nondeterministic choice are enabled, then they will be tried in the order specified in *Prove*. If none of the cases apply, then evaluation fails, and backtracks to the most recent unexplored case. There may also be nondeterminism within a case; for instance, many fold transformations may be applicable at the same time. We again select nondeterministically from this set of applicable transformations. By providing selection functions to pick from these applicable transformations, one can implement a variety of concrete strategies. Note that *Prove* uses two different markings in the process of constructing a proof for $\Gamma \vdash p \equiv p'$. The marking *proved* remembers predicate equivalences which have been already proved. This marking allows us to cache subproofs in a proof. The marking *proof_attempt* keeps track of predicate pairs whose equivalence has not yet been established, but is being attempted by *Prove* via transformations. This marking is essential for ensuring termination of *Prove*. The proof of $P_0 \vdash p \equiv p'$ may (via a conditional equivalence step) generate the (sub)-equivalence $P_0 \vdash p \equiv p'$. *Prove* deems this proof path as failed and explores other proof paths.

Our algorithmic framework *Prove* uses the following functions. Functions $unfold(P)$, $fold(P)$ apply unfolding and folding transformations respectively to program P and return a new program. Whenever conditional folding is possible, the function $new\_goal\_equiv\_for\_fold(P)$ finds a pair of goals whose replacement is necessary to do a fold transformation. Similarly, when conditional equivalence is possible, $new\_goal\_equiv\_for\_equiv(p, p', P)$ finds a pair of goals $\mathcal{G}, \mathcal{G}'$ s.t. syntactic equivalence of p and p' can be established after replacing $\mathcal{G}$ with $\mathcal{G}'$ in P.

Finally, *replace_and_prove* constructs nested proofs for sub-equivalences created by applying the **Gen** rule. Thus, $replace\_and\_prove(p, p', \mathcal{G}, \mathcal{G}', \Gamma)$ performs the following sequence of steps (where $\Gamma = P_0, \ldots, P_i$):

1. first introduces new predicate definitions q and q' for goals $\mathcal{G}$ and $\mathcal{G}'$ respectively (if such definitions do not already exist),
2. proves the equivalence $P_0 \vdash q \equiv q'$ by invoking *Prove*,
3. replaces goal $\mathcal{G}$ by goal $\mathcal{G}'$ in clauses of p or p' in program P_i to obtain program P_{i+1}, and
4. finally invokes *Prove* to dispense the obligation $\Gamma, P_{i+1} \vdash p \equiv p'$. This completes the proof of $\Gamma \vdash p \equiv p'$.

Termination of *Prove* It can be verified that only finite unfolding sequences satisfy *FIN*. This is because in any unfolding sequence of clauses $C_1, \ldots, C_n$ where C_{i+1} is obtained from C_i via unfolding, condition 1 of Definition 5 ensures that the selected atom each C_i is distinct, and condition 2 ensures that there are only finitely many atoms which can ever be selected for unfolding.

Therefore, the length of each predicate equivalence proof itself is finite (assuming folding always reduces program size which can be ensured). However, a proof for $p \equiv p'$ may require $q \equiv q'$ as a lemma, whose proof in turn may require $r \equiv r'$ as a lemma, and so on. Since the number of distinct equivalences are quadratic in the number of predicate symbols in the program, the number of subproofs is finite if the number of new predicates names introduced is finite. Thus, we have :

Lemma 5 *Prove (refer Figure 7) terminates provided the number of definitions introduced (i.e. new predicate symbols added) is finite.*

Efficiency of unfolding/folding The algorithmic framework *Prove* does not clarify how we implement $unfold(P)$ and $fold(P)$, *i.e.* the heuristics for choosing unfolding/folding steps. These heursitics are extremely important for the purposes of efficient proof construction via program transformation. Full details of these heuristics appear in [41, 44].

algorithm $Prove(p, p'$: predicates, Γ:prog. seq.)
begin
  if $proof\_attempt(p, p')$ is marked **then return** false
  mark $proof\_attempt(p, p')$
  let $\Gamma = P_0, \ldots, P_i$
  (* **Ax** rule *)
  if $(p \overset{P_i}{\sim} p' \vee proved(p, p'))$ **then**
    return true
  else nondeterministic choice
    (* **Tx** rule *)
    case $FIN(\langle \Gamma, unfold(P_i)\rangle)$: (* Unfolding *)
      return $Prove(p, p', \langle \Gamma, unfold(P_i)\rangle)$
    case Folding is possible in P_i:
      return $Prove(p, p', \langle \Gamma, fold(P_i)\rangle)$
    (* **Gen** rule *)
    case Conditional folding is possible in P_i:
      let $(\mathcal{G}, \mathcal{G}') = new\_goal\_equiv\_for\_fold(P_i)$
      return $replace\_and\_prove(p, p', \mathcal{G}, \mathcal{G}', \Gamma)$
    case Conditional equivalence is possible in P_i:
      let $(\mathcal{G}, \mathcal{G}') = new\_goal\_equiv\_for\_equiv(p, p', P_i)$
      return $replace\_and\_prove(p, p', \mathcal{G}, \mathcal{G}', \Gamma)$
  end choices
  mark $proved(p, p')$
  unmark $proof\_attempt(p, p')$
end

Fig. 7. Algorithmic framework for equivalence tableau construction.

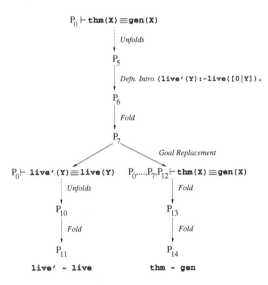

Fig. 8. Liveness Proof of n-bit shift register

Proving Predicate Implications Note that the proof system given in Table 1, the algorithmic framework *Prove* and the strategies to guide the transformations in *Prove* are aimed at proving equivalence of program predicates. Our proof technique can be readily extended to prove predicate implications *i.e.* proof obligations of the form

$$\forall \text{ ground substitutions } \theta \;\; p(\overline{X})\theta \in M(P_0) \Rightarrow p'(\overline{X})\theta \in M(P_0)$$

This extension involves (1) relaxing the definition of syntactic equivalence (Definition 4) to test for implications only, and (2) generating conditions of the form $q \Rightarrow q'$ by applying conditional folding and conditional equivalence.

7   An Example Proof

Recall the logic program of Figure 1 (page 266) which formulates a liveness property about token-passing chains, namely, that the token eventually reaches the left-most process in any arbitrarily long chain. We obtain P_0, the starting point of our transformation sequence from the encoding of the verification problem in Figure 1. To establish the liveness property, we prove that $P_0 \vdash \text{thm(X)} \equiv \text{gen(X)}$, by invoking $Prove(\text{thm}, \text{gen}, \langle P_0 \rangle)$. The proof is illustrated in Figure 8.

Proof of $P_0 \vdash \text{thm} \equiv \text{gen}$: Since thm $\overset{P_0}{\not\equiv}$ gen, we must transform the predicates. By repeatedly unfolding the definition of thm in P_0, we obtain program P_5 where thm is defined as:

```
thm([1]).
thm([0|X]) :- gen(X), X = [1|_].
thm([0|X]) :- gen(X), trans(X,Y), live([0|Y]).
```

Further unfolding in P_5 is not possible since it involves unfolding an atom which is already unfolded in the sequence $P_0, \ldots, P_5$, thereby risking non-termination. In addition no folding transformation is applicable at this stage. However, if $\forall Y \text{ live([0|Y])} \Leftrightarrow \text{live(Y)}$ we can fold the last two clauses of thm. Thus, *conditional folding* is true at P_5, and hence *replace_and_prove* is invoked with $\mathcal{G} = \text{live([0|Y])}$ and $\mathcal{G}' = \text{live(Y)}$. Since live([0|Y]) is not an open atom, a new name:

```
live'(Y) :- live([0|Y]).
```

is added to P_5 to yield P_6. This simply converts the goal equivalence problem of showing $\forall Y \text{ live([0|Y])} \Leftrightarrow \text{live(Y)}$ to a predicate equivalence problem. We fold the third clause of thm above using the newly introduced clause as folder, obtaining P_7:

```
thm([1]).
thm([0|X]) :- gen(X), X = [1|_].
thm([0|X]) :- gen(X), trans(X,Y), live'(Y).
```

We then proceed to show $P_0 \vdash \text{live'} \equiv \text{live}$. This subproof is shown in the left branch of the tree in Figure 8). Then we replace live'(X) with live(X) in the definition of thm in P_7 (right branch in Figure 8).

Proof of $P_0 \vdash$ live' $\equiv$ live: $Prove(\text{live'}, \text{live}, \langle P_0 \rangle)$ performs a series of unfoldings, yielding programs P_8, P_9 and P_{10}. Any further unfolding involves unfolding an atom already unfolded in the sequence P_0, P_8, P_9, P_{10} and risks non-termination. In P_{10}, live' is defined by the following clauses:

```
live'([1|Z]).
live'(X) :- trans(X,Z), live([0|Z]).
```

Folding is applicable is P_{10}, in the second clause of live', yielding P_{11} with

```
live'([1|Z]).
live'(X) :- trans(X,Z), live'(Z).
```

Now, live' $\overset{P_{11}}{\sim}$ live and hence $Prove(\text{live'}, \text{live}, \langle P_0 \rangle)$ terminates. We assume that all occurrences of the equality predicate in the clause bodies are removed (via unification) prior to any syntactic equivalence check.

Resuming Proof of $P_0 \vdash$ thm $\equiv$ gen: Now *replace_and_prove* replaces live'(X) with live(X) in the definition of thm in P_7, yielding P_{12} with:

```
thm([1]).
thm([0|X]) :- gen(X), X = [1|_].
thm([0|X]) :- gen(X), trans(X,Y), live(Y).
```

We can now fold the last two clauses of thm using the definition of live in P_0. Note that the folding uses a recursive definition of a predicate with multiple clauses. The program-transformation system developed by us in [43] was the first to permit such folding. Thus we obtain P_{13}:

```
thm([1]).
thm([0|X]) :- gen(X), live(X).
```

This completes the conditional folding step (which had invoked *replace_and_prove* and thereby constructed live' $\equiv$ live as a subproof). We can fold again using the definition of thm in P_0, giving P_{14} where thm is defined as:

```
thm([1]).
thm([0|X]) :- thm(X).
```

We now have thm $\overset{P_{14}}{\sim}$ gen, thereby completing the equivalence proof.

It is interesting to observe in Figure 8 that the unfolding steps that transform P_0 to P_5 and P_7 to P_{10} are interleaved with folding steps. In other words, algorithmic and deductive verification steps are interleaved in the proof of the equivalence $P_0 \vdash$ thm $\equiv$ gen.

8 Experiments

So far, we have presented a tableau based proof system for proving equivalence of predicates in a logic program. Furthermore, we presented an algorithmic framework *Prove* for guiding the application of the rules in the proof system. However, this algorithmic framework *Prove* is nondeterministic since at each step several transformations may be applicable. Hence it is necessary to develop appropriate selection functions to distill concrete strategies from the algorithmic framework. Indeed we have implemented such strategies in a predicate equivalence prover for verifying parameterized protocols of different *network topologies* (the communication pattern between the different constituent processes of a parameterized network is called its network topology). Given a parameterized system and a liveness/invariant property to be proved, our prover extracts the predicate equivalences that need to be established. It tries to use the network topology of the parameterized system being verified to construct concrete proof strategies. These strategies then guide the proof search which proceeds without any user intervention. The proof search is terminating, sound but incomplete (*i.e.* the prover may fail to establish a correct property). *A full-fledged discussion of the concrete proof strategies (obtained by instantiating the algorithmic framework Prove of the last section) appears in [41, 44].*

In this section, we present the experimental results obtained using our predicate equivalence prover. The prover is built on top of the XSB tabled logic programming system [50] which supports top-down memoized evaluation of logic programs. We report results on parameterized cache coherence protocols, including (a) single bus broadcast protocols *e.g.* Mesi, (b) single bus protocols with global conditions *e.g.* Illinois and (b) multiple bus hierarchical protocols. We also report experimental results for the Java Meta-locking algorithm [1], a distributed algorithm to ensure secure access of shared objects by various Java threads. The benchmarks cover various network topologies including star, tree and complete graph networks.

Results In Table 2, *Meta-lock* denotes the Java meta-locking algorithm from Sun Microsystems. The Java Meta-Locking Algorithm is a distributed algorithm recently proposed by Sun Microsystems to ensure mutually exclusive access of shared Java objects by Java threads. A proof of correctness of the algorithm involves proving mutual exclusion in the access of a Java object by arbitrary number of Java threads. Previously, model checking has been used to verify mutual exclusion for different instances of the protocol, obtained by fixing the number of threads [5]. We have used our program transformation based prover to automatically construct a proof of mutual exclusion for the entire infinite family. The sources of infiniteness in the Meta-locking algorithm include (a) unbounded number of Java threads, and (b) data variables of infinite domain in the shared Java object.

Mesi and *Berkeley RISC* are single bus broadcast protocols [4, 15, 18]. *Illinois* is a single bus cache coherence protocol with global conditions which cannot be modeled as a broadcast protocol [12]. *Tree-cache* is a binary tree network which simulates the interactions between the cache agents in a hierarchical cache coherence protocol [41].

Table 2 presents experimental results obtained using our prover: a summary of the invariants proved along with the time taken, the number of unfolding steps and the number of deductive steps (*i.e.* folding, conditional equivalence

Protocol	Invariant	Time(sec) in [12]	Our time(secs)	# Unf	#Ded
Meta-Lock	#owner + #handout < 2	-	129.8	1981	311
Mesi	#m + #e < 2	1	3.2	325	69
	#m + #e = 0 ∨ #s = 0	0.5	2.9	308	63
Illinois	#dirty < 2	5.3	35.7	2501	137
Berkeley	#dirty < 2	0.6	6.8	503	146
	#ex + #sh < 2	-	Fails	-	-
Tree-cache	#bus_with_data < 2	-	9.9	178	18

Table 2. Summary of protocol verification results

etc.) performed in constructing the proof. The total time involves time taken by (a) unfolding steps (b) deductive steps, and (c) the time to invoke nested proof obligations. All experiments reported here were conducted on a Sun Ultra-Enterprise workstation with two 336 MHz CPUs and 2 GB of RAM. In the table, we have used the following notational shorthand: $\#s$ denotes the number of processes in local state s. In column 3 of the table, we have shown the timings for the same proofs using the constraint logic program evaluation based checker of [12]. The work of [12] was aimed at verifying parameterized cache coherence protocols. Note that the timings of [12] were obtained using a Pentium 133 with Linux 2.0.32.

Comparison with CLP-based Verifier [12] The running times of our prover are slower than the times for verifying single bus cache coherence protocols reported in [12]. In fact, there is up to an order of magnitude difference between the time taken by our prover and the time taken by the CLP-based verifier. One source of the relative inefficiency of our prover arises from the way the proof steps are applied. The prototype implementation of our prover implements both the unfolding and folding steps via meta-programming. While meta-programming appears inevitable to perform the folding steps, the unfolding steps can be performed directly at the level of the underlying evaluation engine. Such an implementation would improve running times, can be directly compared to the CLP-based verifier, and can be used to evaluate whether the overheads due to folding steps in our prover exceed the overheads due to constraint solving in the CLP-based verifier. Also, the abstraction technique of [12] is not suitable for parameterized tree networks such as *Tree-cache*, which can be verified by our inductive proof technique.

Comparison across Benchmarks Note that the number of deductive steps in a proof is consistently small compared to the number of unfolding steps. This is owing to our proof search strategy which repeatedly applies unfolding steps until none are applicable. Furthermore, note that the tree network example consumes larger running time with fewer unfolding and deductive steps as compared to other cache coherence protocols like the Mesi protocol. Due to its network topology, the state representation in the tree network has a different term structure than the other protocols (where the global states are typically represented as lists). This partially accounts for the increase in the running time. In addition, certain deductive steps (such as conditional equivalence) employ more expensive search heuristics for the tree topology. Finally, the Java meta-locking algorithm represents global states as lists, but involves nested induction over both control and the data of the protocol thereby increasing the number of predicate equivalence proof obligations. Extra proof obligations are incurred due to nested induction on the infinite data domain thereby increasing the time to construct the proof.

9 Discussion

In this chapter, we have presented a technique for proving predicate equivalences in a definite logic program. This is used for verifying infinite-state concurrent systems, in particular the class of parameterized concurrent systems. We have described how the parameterized system verification problem can be reduced to proving equivalence of logic program predicates. First we review related work on using logic program transformations to construct proofs.

9.1 Related Work

Unfold/fold transformations of logic programs have been widely used for program specialization and optimization. Relatively little work has been done on using these transformations for constructing *proofs*. Unfold/fold transformations can be used to construct induction proofs of program properties. In such proofs, unfolding accomplishes the base case and the finite part of the induction step, and folding roughly corresponds to application of induction hypothesis. This observation has been exploited in [23, 25, 27, 36, 37] to construct inductive proofs of program properties.

Hsiang and Srivas in [23] extended Prolog's evaluation with "limited forward chaining" to perform inductive theorem proving. This limited forward chaining step is in fact a very restricted form of folding: only the theorem statement (which is restricted to be conjunctive) can be used as a folder clause. The works of [25, 27] is closer to ours. They proved certain first order theorems about the Least Herbrand Model of a definite logic program via induction. In particular, they observed that the least fixed point semantics of logic programs could be exploited to employ fixed point induction. Our usage of the transformations is similar. Given a program P we intend to prove $p \equiv q$ in the Least Herbrand Model of P. To do this proof by induction, we transform p and q to obtain a program P'. If the transformed definitions of p and q in P' are "syntactically equivalent" (Definition 4) then our proof is finished. Note that *the syntactic equivalence check is in fact an application of fixed point induction*. It allows us to show $p \equiv q$ in $M(P')$ (the least Herbrand model of P'). Furthermore, since $M(P') = M(P)$ this amounts to showing $p \equiv q$ in program P. Thus, in our work predicates are transformed to facilitate the construction of induction schemes (for proving predicate equivalence). [25] also exploits transformations for similar purposes. However, their method performs *conjunctive* folding using only a single non-recursive clause. Apart from the restriction in their folding rule, they also do not employ goal replacement in their induction proofs.

The idea of using logic program transformations for proving goal equivalences was explored by Pettorossi and Proietti in [36, 37]. These works employ more restricted unfold/fold transformation rules *e.g.* folding using non-recursive clauses. In [19], a proof technique based on transformation of constraint logic programs was proposed. It is used to verify safety properties of systems with arbitrary number of (potentially infinite state) process. Unlike our work, the proof technique of [19] is not based on mathematical induction. Instead it produces uniform proofs by abstracting away the number of processes. The work of [12] proves safety properties of parameterized systems via evaluation of constraint logic programs (the evaluation includes acceleration techniques to ensure termination). Partial deduction and abstract interpretation of logic programs is used in [29] for proving safety properties of infinite state systems; these techniques can be applied to parameterized families as well.

The reader might notice similarities between a proof system based on unfold/fold transformations and a proof system based on tabled resolution [7, 48]. Tabled resolution combines resolution proofs with memoing of calls and answers. Since folding corresponds to remembering the original definition of predicates, there is some correspondence between folding and memoing. However, folding can remember conjunctions and/or disjunctions of atoms as the definition of a predicate. This is not possible in tabled resolution. Furthermore, in tabled resolution when a tabled call C is encountered, the answers produced so far for C are used to produce new answers for C. In folding, when the clause bodies in old definition of a predicate is encountered, it is replaced by the clause head.

We note that there is a lot of research work on using logic program transformations for optimization and/or partial evaluation [35]. Furthermore, the area of automated inductive theorem proving has substantial literature of its own [6]. These works are not discussed here. Instead, we have concentrated only on techniques which extend logic program evaluation for proving program properties.

9.2 Summary

In a broader perspective, our proof technique is geared to automate nested induction proofs, where each induction proceeds without hypothesis strengthening. Furthermore, the induction schema as well as the requisite lemmas should be implicitly encoded in the logic program itself. We have employed our lightweight inductive proof technique for verifying a specific class of infinite state concurrent systems: *parameterized systems*. Such systems occur widely in computing since many distributed algorithms in telecommunication and information processing applications constitute a parameterized concurrent system. We have used our proof technique to verify parameterized networks of various interconnection patterns: chain, ring, tree, star and complete graph networks. A prover based on our technique has been used to verify design invariants of real-life distributed algorithms such as the recently developed Java meta-locking algorithm from Sun Microsystems [1].

Our program transformation based proof technique unifies algorithmic and deductive verification steps (*i.e.* model checking and theorem proving steps) in a framework. Essentially the proof technique amounts to integrating limited deductive steps by enhancing the search based evaluation of a model checker. This is different from the traditional way of integrating model checking and theorem proving where a model checker is incorporated as a decision procedure into a theorem prover [39].

The reader should however note that unlike model checking, our inductive proof technique currently *does not generate counter-example evidence*. Due to the undecidability of parameterized system verification, the problem of counter-example generation is more involved. This is because a proof attempt may fail due to either the temporal property being false or the inability of the proof system to construct a proof. The problem of navigating and explaining proof attempts has been studied for interactive theorem provers [24]. For our transformation based automated prover, we can a-posteriori provide explanation of success/failure of a proof attempt. In particular, we can provide to the user the tree of predicate equivalence proof obligations constructed. Once a node in this tree is selected (by the user), we can provide snapshots of the transformation sequence constructed which led to the success/failure of the proof attempt of that predicate equivalence. Developing tools and techniques for explaining transformation based proof runs is an attractive topic of future work.

In conclusion, we would like highlight some interesting aspects of our proposed integration (of algorithmic and deductive verification). First, the proof technique thus obtained allows arbitrary interleaving of algorithmic and deductive steps in a proof. In contrast, by incorporating model checking as a decision procedure into a theorem prover, the model checker is always invoked as a subroutine. Secondly, the integration is not only *tight* but also *extensible* for verification of different flavors of concurrent systems. Our transformation based proof technique is a flexible extension of model checking via logic program evaluation (since one of our transformations correspond to logic program evaluation). By extending the underlying programming language to constraint logic programs one can verify families of timed systems with similar proof techniques. Finally, note that the proof technique supports zero overhead theorem proving [45]. Concurrent systems which can be verified without deductive reasoning (such as finite state and data independent systems) are verified via model checking since the deductive transformations are applied lazily.

Acknowledgments The work reported in this chapter was conducted as part of the first author's Ph.D. thesis at SUNY Stony Brook [41]. Many discussions with K. Narayan Kumar, I.V. Ramakrishnan and Scott A. Smolka shaped the work.

This work was partially supported by NSF grants CCR-9711386, CCR-9876242, CDA-9805735 and EIA-9705998.

References

[1] O. Agesen, D. Detlefs, A. Garthwaite, R. Knippel, Y. S. Ramakrishna, and D. White. An efficient meta-lock for implementing ubiquitous synchronization. In *ACM SIGPLAN International Conference on Object-Oriented Programming Systems, Languages and Applications (OOPSLA)*, 1999.

[2] R. Alur and T. A. Henzinger, editors. *Computer Aided Verification (CAV '96)*, volume 1102 of *Lecture Notes in Computer Science*, New Brunswick, New Jersey, July 1996. Springer-Verlag.

[3] K. Apt and D. Kozen. Limits for automatic verification of finite-state systems. *Information Processing Letters*, 15:307–309, 1986.

[4] J. Archibald and J.-L. Baer. Cache coherence protocols: Evaluation using a multi-processor simulation model. *ACM Transactions on Computer Systems*, 4(4):273–298, 1986.

[5] S. Basu, S.A. Smolka, and O.R. Ward. Model checking the Java meta-locking algorithm. In *IEEE International Conference on the Engineering of Computer Based Systems*. IEEE Press, April 2000.

[6] A. Bundy. *The Automation of Proof by Mathematical Induction*, volume 1 of *Handbook of Automated Reasoning*, pages 845–911. Elsevier and MIT Press, 2001.

[7] W. Chen and D.S. Warren. Tabled evaluation with delaying for general logic programs. *Journal of the ACM*, 43(1):20–74, 1996.

[8] E.M. Clarke, E.A. Emerson, and A.P. Sistla. Automatic verification of finite-state concurrent systems using temporal logic specifications. *ACM Transactions on Programming Languages and Systems (TOPLAS)*, 8(2), 1986.

[9] E.M. Clarke, O. Grumberg, and D. Peled. *Model Checking*. MIT Press, 1999.

[10] S.K. Das. *Deductive Databases and Logic Programming*. Addison-Wesley, 1992.

[11] D. De Schreye, R. Glück, J. Jørgensen, M. Leuschel, B. Martens, and M. H. Sørensen. Conjunctive partial deduction: Foundations, control, algorithms, and experiments. *Journal of Logic Programming*, 41(2–3):231–277, 1999.

[12] G. Delzanno. Automatic verification of parameterized cache coherence protocols. In *International Conference on Computer Aided Verification (CAV), LNCS 1855*, 2000.

[13] G. Delzanno and A. Podelski. Model checking in CLP. In *International Conference on Tools and Algorithms for Construction and Analysis of Systems (TACAS)*, volume LNCS 1579, pages 74–88. Springer-Verlag, 1999.

[14] E. Emerson and K.S. Namjoshi. Reasoning about rings. In *ACM SIGPLAN International Conference on Principles of Programming Languages (POPL)*, pages 85–94, 1995.

[15] E. Emerson and K.S. Namjoshi. On model checking for non-deterministic infinite state systems. In *IEEE Annual Symposium on Logic in Computer Science (LICS)*, pages 70–80, 1998.

[16] E.A. Emerson. *Temporal and Modal Logic*, volume B of *Handbook of Theoretical Computer Science*, pages 995–1072. Elsevier/North-Holland, 1990.

[17] E.A. Emerson and K.S. Namjoshi. Automated verification of parameterized synchronous systems. In Alur and Henzinger [2].

[18] J. Esparza, A. Finkel, and R. Mayr. On the verification of broadcast protocols. In *IEEE Annual Symposium on Logic in Computer Science (LICS)*, pages 352–359, 1999.

[19] F. Fioravanti, A. Pettorossi, and M. Proietti. Verifying CTL properties of infinite state systems by specializing constraint logic programs. In *Logic-Based Program Synthesis and Transformation (LOPSTR '01)*, LNCS 2372, 2002.

[20] M. Gergatsoulis and M. Katzouraki. Unfold/fold transformations for definite clause programs. In *International Symposium on Programming Language Implementation and Logic Programming (PLILP)*, LNCS 844, pages 340–354, 1994.

[21] S. German and A. Sistla. Reasoning about systems with many processes. *Journal of the ACM*, 39:675–735, 1992.

[22] G. J. Holzmann. The model checker SPIN. *IEEE Transactions on Software Engineering*, 23(5):279–295, May 1997.

[23] J. Hsiang and M. Srivas. Automatic inductive theorem proving using Prolog. *Theoretical Computer Science*, 54:3–28, 1987.

[24] INRIA Rocquencourt, URL : http://pauillac.inria.fr/coq/doc/main.html, Paris, France. *The Coq Proof Assistant : Reference Manual*, 1999.

[25] T. Kanamori and H. Fujita. Formulation of Induction Formulas in Verification of Prolog Programs. In *International Conference on Automated Deduction (CADE)*, pages 281–299, 1986.

[26] T. Kanamori and H. Fujita. Unfold/fold transformation of logic programs with counters. In *USA-Japan Seminar on Logics of Programs*, 1987.

[27] T. Kanamori and H. Seki. Verification of prolog programs using an extension of execution. In *International Conference on Logic Programming (ICLP)*, 1986.

[28] M. Leuschel and M. Bruynooghe. Logic program specialisation through partial deduction: Control issues. *Theory and Practice of Logic Programming*, 2(4&5):461–515, 2002.

[29] M. Leuschel and T. Massart. Infinite state model checking by abstract interpretation and program specialisation. In Annalisa Bossi, editor, *Logic-Based Program Synthesis and Transformation (LOPSTR '99)*, LNCS 1817, pages 63–82, Venice, Italy, 2000.

[30] J.W. Lloyd. *Foundations of Logic Programming, Second Edition.* Springer-Verlag, 1993.

[31] Z. Manna and A. Pnueli. *The Temporal Logic of Reactive and Concurrent Systems.* Springer Verlag, 1991.

[32] B. Martens, D. De Schreye, and T. Horváth. Sound and complete partial deduction with unfolding based on well-founded measures. *Theoretical Computer Science*, 122:97–117, 1994.

[33] K.S. Namjoshi. *Ameliorating the State Explosion Problem.* PhD thesis, University of Texas at Austin, 1998.

[34] U. Nilsson and J. Lubcke. Constraint logic programming for local and symbolic model checking. In *Computational Logic, LNCS 1861*, 2000.

[35] A. Pettorossi and M. Proietti. *Transformation of logic programs*, volume 5 of *Handbook of Logic in Artificial Intelligence*, pages 697–787. Oxford University Press, 1998.

[36] A. Pettorossi and M. Proietti. Synthesis and transformation of logic programs using unfold/fold proofs. *Journal of Logic Programming*, 41(2–3):197–230, 1999.

[37] A. Pettorossi and M. Proietti. Perfect model checking via unfold/fold transformations. In *Computational Logic, LNCS 1861*, 2000.

[38] A. Pettorossi, M. Proietti, and S. Renault. Reducing nondeterminism while specializing logic programs. In *ACM SIGPLAN International Conference on Principles of Programming Languages (POPL)*, pages 414–427, 1997.

[39] S. Rajan, N. Shankar, and M. K. Srivas. An integration of model checking with automated proof checking. In *International Conference on Computer Aided Verification (CAV), LNCS 939*, 1995.

[40] Y. S. Ramakrishna, C. R. Ramakrishnan, I. V. Ramakrishnan, S. A. Smolka, T. L. Swift, and D. S. Warren. Efficient model checking using tabled resolution. In O. Grumberg, editor, *Computer Aided Verification (CAV '97)*, volume 1254 of *Lecture Notes in Computer Science*, Haifa, Israel, June 1997. Springer-Verlag.

[41] A. Roychoudhury. *Program Transformations for Verifying Parameterized Systems*. PhD thesis, State University of New York at Stony Brook, Available from http://www.comp.nus.edu.sg/~abhik/papers.html, 2000.

[42] A. Roychoudhury, K. Narayan Kumar, C. R. Ramakrishnan, I. V. Ramakrishnan, and S. A. Smolka. Verification of parameterized systems using logic program transformations. In *International Conference on Tools and Algorithms for Construction and Analysis of Systems (TACAS)*, volume LNCS 1785, pages 172–187. Springer-Verlag, 2000.

[43] A. Roychoudhury, K. Narayan Kumar, C.R. Ramakrishnan, and I.V. Ramakrishnan. An unfold/fold transformation framework for definite logic programs. *ACM Transactions on Programming Languages and Systems (TOPLAS)*, To appear. Preliminary version appeared in International Conference on Principles and Practice of Declarative Programming (PPDP) 1999, LNCS 1702.

[44] A. Roychoudhury and I.V. Ramakrishnan. Inductively verifying invariant properties of parameterized systems. *Automated Software Engineering Journal*, 2004. Preliminary version appeared in International Conference on Computer Aided Verification (CAV) 2001, LNCS 2102.

[45] Carl Seger. Combining functional programming and hardware verification. In *ACM SIGPLAN International Conference on International Conference on Functional Programming, Invited Talk*, 2000.

[46] H. Tamaki and T. Sato. Unfold/fold transformations of logic programs. In *Proceedings of International Conference on Logic Programming*, pages 127–138, 1984.

[47] H. Tamaki and T. Sato. A generalized correctness proof of the unfold/ fold logic program transformation. Technical report, Ibaraki University, Japan, 1986.

[48] H. Tamaki and T. Sato. OLDT resolution with tabulation. In *Third International Conference on Logic Programming*, pages 84–98, 1986.

[49] L. Urbina. Analysis of hybrid systems in CLP(R). In *Constraint Programming (CP'96)*, volume LNCS 1102. Springer-Verlag, 1996.

[50] XSB. The XSB logic programming system v2.2, 2000. Available for downloading from http://xsb.sourceforge.net/.

Transformation Rules
for Locally Stratified Constraint Logic Programs

Fabio Fioravanti[1], Alberto Pettorossi[2], and Maurizio Proietti[3]

[1] Dipartimento di Informatica, Universit dell'Aquila, L'Aquila, Italy
`fioravan@univaq.it`
[2] DISP, University of Tor Vergata, Roma, Italy
`adp@iasi.rm.cnr.it`
[3] IASI-CNR, Roma, Italy
`proietti@iasi.rm.cnr.it`

Abstract. We propose a set of transformation rules for constraint logic programs with negation. We assume that every program is locally stratified and, thus, it has a unique perfect model. We give sufficient conditions which ensure that the proposed set of transformation rules preserves the perfect model of the programs. Our rules extend in some respects the rules for logic programs and constraint logic programs already considered in the literature and, in particular, they include a rule for unfolding a clause with respect to a negative literal.

1 Introduction

Program transformation is a very powerful methodology for developing correct and efficient programs from formal specifications. This methodology is particularly convenient in the case of declarative programming languages, where programs are formulas and program transformations can be viewed as replacements of formulas by new, equivalent formulas.

The main advantage of using the program transformation methodology for program development is that it allows us to address the correctness and the efficiency issues at separate stages. Often little effort is required for encoding formal specifications (written by using equational or logical formalisms) as declarative programs (written as functional or logic programs). These programs are correct by construction, but they are often computationally inefficient. Here is where program transformation comes into play: from a correct (and possibly inefficient) initial program version we can derive a correct and efficient program version by means of a sequence of program transformations that preserve correctness. We say that a program transformation preserves correctness, or it is *correct*, if the semantics of the initial program is equal to the semantics of the derived program.

A very popular approach followed when applying the program transformation methodology, is the one based on *transformation rules* and *strategies* [9]: the rules are elementary transformations that preserve the program semantics and the strategies are (possibly nondeterministic) procedures that guide the application of transformation rules with the objective of deriving efficient programs. Thus, a

M. Bruynooghe and K.-K. Lau (Eds.): Program Development in CL, LNCS 3049, pp. 291–339, 2004.

program transformation is realized by a sequence $P_0, \ldots, P_n$ of programs, called a *transformation sequence*, where, for $i = 0, \ldots, n-1$, P_{k+1} is derived from P_k by applying a transformation rule according to a given transformation strategy. A transformation sequence is said to be *correct* if the programs $P_0, \ldots, P_n$ have the same semantics.

Various sets of program transformation rules have been proposed in the literature for several declarative programming languages, such as, functional [9,39], logic [44], constraint [7,11,27], and functional-logic languages [1]. In this paper we consider a constraint logic programming language with negation [19,28] and we study the correctness of a set of transformation rules that extends the sets which were already considered for constraint logic programming languages. We will not deal here with transformation strategies, but we will show through some examples (see Section 5) that the transformation rules can be applied in a rather systematic (yet not fully automatic) way.

We assume that constraint logic programs are *locally stratified* [4,35]. This assumption simplifies our treatment because the semantics of a locally stratified program is determined by its unique *perfect model* which is equal to its unique *stable model*, which is also its unique, total *well-founded model* [4,35]. (The definitions of locally stratified programs, perfect models, and other notions used in this paper are recalled in Section 2.)

The set of transformation rules we consider in this paper includes the *unfolding* and *folding* rules (see, for instance, [7,11,16,17,23,27,29,31,37,38,40,42,43,44]). In order to understand how these rules work, let us first consider propositional programs. The *definition* of an atom a in a program is the set of clauses that have a as head. The atom a is also called the *definiendum*. The disjunction of the bodies of the clauses that constitute the definition of a, is called the *definiens*. Basically, the application of the unfolding rule consists in replacing an atom occurring in the body of a clause by its definiens and then applying, if necessary, some suitable boolean laws to obtain clauses. For instance, given the following programs P_1 and P_2:

$$P_1: \; p \leftarrow q \wedge r \qquad\qquad P_2: \; p \leftarrow \neg a \wedge r$$
$$q \leftarrow \neg a \qquad\qquad\qquad\qquad p \leftarrow b \wedge r$$
$$q \leftarrow b \qquad\qquad\qquad\qquad\quad q \leftarrow \neg a$$
$$\qquad\qquad\qquad\qquad\qquad\qquad q \leftarrow b$$

we have that by unfolding the first clause of program P_1 we get program P_2.

Folding is the inverse of unfolding and consists in replacing an occurrence of a definiens by the corresponding occurrence of the definiendum (before this replacement we may apply suitable boolean laws). For instance, by folding the first two clauses of P_2 using the definition of q, we get program P_1. An important feature of the folding rule is that the definition used for folding may occur in a previous program in the transformation sequence. The formal definitions of the unfolding and folding transformation rules for constraint logic programs will be given in Section 3. The usefulness of the program transformation approach based on the unfolding and folding rules, is now very well recognized in the scientific community as indicated by a large number of papers (see [29] for a survey).

A relevant property we will prove in this paper is that the unfolding of a clause w.r.t. an atom occurring in a negative literal, also called *negative unfolding*, preserves the perfect model of a locally stratified program. This property is interesting, because negative unfolding is useful for program transformation, but it may *not* preserve the perfect models (nor the stable models, nor the well-founded model) if the programs are not locally stratified. For instance, let us consider the following programs P_1 and P_2:

$$P_1: \begin{array}{l} p \leftarrow \neg q \\ q \leftarrow \neg p \end{array} \qquad\qquad P_2: \begin{array}{l} p \leftarrow p \\ q \leftarrow \neg p \end{array}$$

Program P_2 can be obtained by unfolding the first clause of P_1 (i.e., by first replacing q by the body $\neg p$ of the clause defining q, and then replacing $\neg\neg p$ by p). Program P_1 has two perfect models: $\{p\}$ and $\{q\}$, while program P_2 has the unique perfect model $\{q\}$.

In this paper we consider the following transformation rules (see Section 3): definition introduction and definition elimination (for introducing and eliminating definitions of predicates), positive and negative unfolding, positive and negative folding (that is, unfolding and folding w.r.t. a positive and a negative occurrence of an atom, respectively), and also rules for applying boolean laws and rules for manipulating constraints.

Similarly to other sets of transformation rules presented in the literature (see, for instance, [1,7,9,11,27,39,44]), a transformation sequence constructed by arbitrary applications of the transformation rules presented in this paper, may be incorrect. As customary, we will ensure the correctness of transformation sequences only if they satisfy suitable properties: we will call them *admissible* sequences (see Section 4). Although our transformation rules are extensions or adaptations of transformation rules already considered for stratified logic programs or logic programs, in general, for our correctness proof we cannot rely on already known results. Indeed, the definition of an admissible transformation sequence depends on the interaction among the rules and, in particular, correctness may not be preserved if we modify even one rule only.

To see that known results do not extend in a straightforward way when adding negative unfolding to a set of transformation rules, let us consider the transformation sequences constructed by first (1) unfolding all clauses of a definition δ and then (2) folding some of the resulting clauses by using the definition δ itself. If at Step (1) we use positive unfolding only, then the perfect model semantics is preserved [37,42], while this semantics may not be preserved if we use negative unfolding, as indicated by the following example.

Example 1. Let us consider the transformation sequence P_0, P_1, P_2, where:

$$P_0: \begin{array}{l} p(X) \leftarrow \neg q(X) \\ q(X) \leftarrow X \geq 0 \\ q(X) \leftarrow q(X) \end{array} \quad P_1: \begin{array}{l} p(X) \leftarrow X < 0 \wedge \neg q(X) \\ q(X) \leftarrow X \geq 0 \\ q(X) \leftarrow q(X) \end{array} \quad P_2: \begin{array}{l} p(X) \leftarrow X < 0 \wedge p(X) \\ q(X) \leftarrow X \geq 0 \\ q(X) \leftarrow q(X) \end{array}$$

Program P_1 is derived by unfolding the first clause of P_0 w.r.t. the negative literal $\neg q(X)$ (that is, by replacing the definiendum $q(X)$ by its definiens $X \geq 0 \vee q(X)$, and then applying De Morgan's law). Program P_2 is derived by folding the first clause of P_1 using the definition $p(X) \leftarrow \neg q(X)$ in P_0. We have that, for any $a < 0$, the atom $p(a)$ belongs to the perfect model of P_0, while $p(a)$ does not belong to the perfect model of P_2.

The main result of this paper (see Theorem 3 in Section 4) shows the correctness of a transformation sequence constructed by first (1) unfolding all clauses of a (non-recursive) definition δ w.r.t. a *positive* literal, then (2) unfolding zero or more clauses w.r.t. a *negative* literal, and finally (3) folding some of the resulting clauses by using the definition δ. The correctness of such transformation sequences cannot be established by the correctness results presented in [37,42].

The paper is structured as follows. In Section 2 we present the basic definitions of locally stratified constraint logic programs and perfect models. In Section 3 we present our set of transformation rules and in Section 4 we give sufficient conditions on transformation sequences that ensure the preservation of perfect models. In Section 5 we present some examples of program derivation using our transformation rules. In all these examples the negative unfolding rule plays a crucial role. Finally, in Section 6 we discuss related work and future research.

2   Preliminaries

In this section we recall the syntax and semantics of constraint logic programs with negation. In particular, we will give the definitions of locally stratified programs and perfect models. For notions not defined here the reader may refer to [2,4,19,20,26].

2.1   Syntax of Constraint Logic Programs

We consider a first order language $\mathcal{L}$ generated by an infinite set *Vars* of *variables*, a set *Funct* of *function symbols* with arity, and a set *Pred* of *predicate symbols* (or *predicates*, for short) with arity. We assume that *Pred* is the union of two disjoint sets: (i) the set $Pred_c$ of *constraint* predicate symbols, including the *equality* symbol $=$, and (ii) the set $Pred_u$ of *user defined* predicate symbols.

A *term* of $\mathcal{L}$ is either a variable or an expression of the form $f(t_1, \ldots, t_n)$, where f is an n-ary function symbol and $t_1, \ldots, t_n$ are terms. An *atomic formula* is an expression of the form $p(t_1, \ldots, t_n)$ where p is an n-ary predicate symbol and $t_1, \ldots, t_n$ are terms. A *formula* of $\mathcal{L}$ is either an atomic formula or a formula constructed from atomic formulas by means of connectives ($\neg, \wedge, \vee, \rightarrow, \leftarrow, \leftrightarrow$) and quantifiers ($\exists, \forall$).

Let e be a term, or a formula, or a set of terms or formulas. The set of variables occurring in e is denoted by $vars(e)$. Given a formula φ, the set of the *free variables* occurring in φ is denoted by $FV(\varphi)$. A term or a formula is *ground* iff it does not contain variables. Given a set $X = \{X_1, \ldots, X_n\}$ of n variables, by $\forall X \, \varphi$ we denote the formula $\forall X_1 \ldots \forall X_n \, \varphi$. By $\forall(\varphi)$ we denote the *universal closure* of φ, that is, the formula $\forall X \, \varphi$, where $FV(\varphi) = X$. Analogous notations will be adopted for the existential quantifier $\exists$.

A *primitive constraint* is an atomic formula $p(t_1, \ldots, t_n)$ where p is a predicate symbol in $Pred_c$. The set C of *constraints* is the smallest set of formulas of $\mathcal{L}$ that contains all primitive constraints and is closed w.r.t. negation, conjunction, and existential quantification. This closure assumption simplifies our treatment, but as we will indicate at the end of this section, we can do without it.

An *atom* is an atomic formula $p(t_1, \ldots, t_n)$ where p is an element of $Pred_u$ and $t_1, \ldots, t_n$ are terms. A *literal* is either an atom A, also called *positive literal*, or a negated atom $\neg A$, also called *negative literal*. Given any literal L, by $\overline{L}$ we denote: (i) $\neg A$, if L is the atom A, and (ii) A, if L is the negated atom $\neg A$. A *goal* is a (possibly empty) conjunction of literals (here we depart from the terminology used in [2,26], where a goal is defined as the negation of a conjunction of literals). A *constrained literal* is the conjunction of a constraint and a literal. A *constrained goal* is the conjunction of a constraint and a goal.

A *clause* γ is a formula of the form $H \leftarrow c \wedge G$, where: (i) H is an atom, called the *head* of γ and denoted $hd(\gamma)$, and (ii) $c \wedge G$ is a constrained goal, called the *body* of γ and denoted $bd(\gamma)$. A conjunction of constraints and/or literals may be empty (in which case it is equivalent to *true*). A clause of the form $H \leftarrow c$, where c is a constraint and the goal part of the body is the empty conjunction of literals, is called a *constrained fact*. A clause of the form $H \leftarrow$, whose body is the empty conjunction, is called a *fact*.

A *constraint logic program* (or *program*, for short) is a finite set of clauses. A *definite clause* is a clause whose body has no occurrences of negative literals. A *definite program* is a finite set of definite clauses.

Given two atoms $p(t_1, \ldots, t_n)$ and $p(u_1, \ldots, u_n)$, we denote by $p(t_1, \ldots, t_n) = p(u_1, \ldots, u_n)$ the constraint: $t_1 = u_1 \wedge \ldots \wedge t_n = u_n$. For the notion of *substitution* and for the application of a substitution to a term we refer to [2,26]. Given a formula φ and a substitution $\{X_1/t_1, \ldots, X_n/t_n\}$ we denote by $\varphi\{X_1/t_1, \ldots, X_n/t_n\}$ the result of simultaneously replacing in φ all free occurrences of $X_1, \ldots, X_n$ by $t_1, \ldots, t_n$.

We say that a predicate p *immediately depends on* a predicate q in a program P iff there exists in P a clause of the form $p(\ldots) \leftarrow B$ and q occurs in B. We say that p *depends on* q in P iff there exists a sequence $p_1, \ldots, p_n$, with $n > 1$, of predicates such that: (i) $p_1 = p$, (ii) $p_n = q$, and (iii) for $i = 1, \ldots, n-1$, p_i immediately depends on p_{i+1}. Given a user defined predicate p and a program P, the *definition of p in P*, denoted $Def(p, P)$, is the set of clauses γ in P such that p is the predicate symbol of $hd(\gamma)$.

A *variable renaming* is a bijective mapping from *Vars* to *Vars*. The application of a variable renaming ρ to a formula φ returns the formula $\rho(\varphi)$, which is said to be a *variant* of φ, obtained by replacing each (bound or free) variable occurrence X in φ by the variable $\rho(X)$. A variant of a set $\{\varphi_1, \ldots, \varphi_n\}$ of formulas is the set $\{\rho(\varphi_1), \ldots, \rho(\varphi_n)\}$, also denoted $\rho(\{\varphi_1, \ldots, \varphi_n\})$. During program transformation we will feel free to silently apply variable renamings to clauses and to sets of clauses because, as the reader may verify, they preserve program semantics (see Section 2.2). Moreover, we will feel free to change the names of the bound variables occurring in constraints, as usually done in predicate calculus.

2.2   Semantics of Constraint Logic Programs

In this section we present the definition of the semantics of constraint logic programs with negation. This definition extends similar definitions given in the literature for definite constraint logic programs [19] and logic programs with negation [4,35].

We proceed as follows: (i) we define an *interpretation for the constraints*, following the approach used in first order logic (see, for instance, [2]), (ii) we introduce the notion of $\mathcal{D}$-*model*, that is, a model for constraint logic programs which is parametric w.r.t. the interpretation $\mathcal{D}$ for the constraints, (iii) we introduce the notion of *locally stratified program*, and finally, (iv) we define the *perfect $\mathcal{D}$-model* (also called *perfect model*, for short) of locally stratified programs.

An *interpretation $\mathcal{D}$ for the constraints* consists of: (1) a non-empty set D, called *carrier*, (2) an assignment of a function $f_{\mathcal{D}}: D^n \rightarrow D$ to each n-ary function symbol f in *Funct*, and (3) an assignment of a relation $p_{\mathcal{D}}$ over D^n to each n-ary predicate symbol in $Pred_c$. In particular, $\mathcal{D}$ assigns the set $\{\langle d, d \rangle \,|\, d \in D\}$ to the equality symbol $=$.

We assume that D is a set of ground terms. This is not restrictive because we may add suitable 0-ary function symbols to $\mathcal{L}$.

Given a formula φ whose predicate symbols belong to $Pred_c$, we consider the satisfaction relation $\mathcal{D} \models \varphi$, which is defined as usual in first order predicate calculus (see, for instance, [2]). A constraint c is said to be *satisfiable* iff its existential closure is satisfiable, that is, $\mathcal{D} \models \exists(c)$. If $\mathcal{D} \not\models \exists(c)$, then c is said to be *unsatisfiable* in $\mathcal{D}$.

Given an interpretation $\mathcal{D}$ for the constraints, a $\mathcal{D}$-*interpretation* I assigns a relation over D^n to each n-ary user defined predicate symbol in $Pred_u$, that is, I can be identified with a subset of the set $\mathcal{B}_{\mathcal{D}}$ of ground atoms defined as follows:

$$\mathcal{B}_{\mathcal{D}} = \{p(d_1, \ldots, d_n) \,|\, p \text{ is a predicate symbol in } Pred_u \text{ and } (d_1, \ldots, d_n) \in D^n\}.$$

A *valuation* is a function $v: Vars \rightarrow D$. We extend the domain of a valuation v to terms, constraints, literals, and clauses as we now indicate. Given a term t, we inductively define the term $v(t)$ as follows: (i) if t is a variable X then $v(t) = v(X)$, and (ii) if t is $f(t_1, \ldots, t_n)$ then $v(t) = f_{\mathcal{D}}(v(t_1), \ldots, v(t_n))$. Given a constraint c, $v(c)$ is the constraint obtained by replacing every free variable $X \in FV(c)$ by the ground term $v(X)$. Notice that $v(c)$ is a closed formula which may be not ground. Given a literal L, (i) if L is the atom $p(t_1, \ldots, t_n)$, then $v(L)$ is the ground atom $p(v(t_1), \ldots, v(t_n))$, and (ii) if L is the negated atom $\neg A$, then $v(L)$ is the ground, negated atom $\neg v(A)$. Given a clause $\gamma: H \leftarrow c \wedge L_1 \wedge \ldots \wedge L_m$, $v(\gamma)$ is the clause $v(H) \leftarrow v(c) \wedge v(L_1) \wedge \ldots \wedge v(L_m)$.

Let I be a $\mathcal{D}$-interpretation and v a valuation. Given a literal L, we say that $v(L)$ *is true in* I iff either (i) L is an atom and $v(L) \in I$, or (ii) L is a negated atom $\neg A$ and $v(A) \notin I$. We say that the literal $v(L)$ *is false in* I iff it is not true in I. Given a clause $\gamma: H \leftarrow c \wedge L_1 \wedge \ldots \wedge L_m$, $v(\gamma)$ *is true in* I iff either (i) $v(H)$ is true in I, or (ii) $\mathcal{D} \not\models v(c)$, or (iii) there exists $i \in \{1, \ldots, m\}$ such that $v(L_i)$ is false in I.

A $\mathcal{D}$-interpretation I is a $\mathcal{D}$-*model* of a program P iff for every clause γ in P and for every valuation v, we have that $v(\gamma)$ is true in I. It can be shown that every definite constraint logic program P has a *least* $\mathcal{D}$-model w.r.t. set inclusion (see, for instance [20]).

Unfortunately, constraint logic programs which are not definite may fail to have a least $\mathcal{D}$-model. For example, the program consisting of the clause $p \leftarrow \neg q$ has the two minimal (not least) models $\{p\}$ and $\{q\}$. This fact has motivated the introduction of the set of *locally stratified* programs [4,35]. For every locally stratified program one can associate a unique (minimal, but not least, w.r.t. set inclusion) model, called *perfect model*, as follows.

A *local stratification* is a function $\sigma: \mathcal{B}_{\mathcal{D}} \to W$, where W is the set of countable ordinals. If $A \in \mathcal{B}_{\mathcal{D}}$ and $\sigma(A)$ is the ordinal α, we say that the *stratum* of A is α. Given a clause γ in a program P, a valuation v, and a local stratification σ, we say that a clause $v(\gamma)$ of the form: $H \leftarrow c \wedge L_1 \wedge \ldots \wedge L_m$ is *locally stratified* w.r.t. σ iff *either* $\mathcal{D} \models \neg c$ *or*, for $i = 1, \ldots, m$, if L_i is an atom A then $\sigma(H) \geq \sigma(A)$ else if L_i is a negated atom $\neg A$ then $\sigma(H) > \sigma(A)$. Given a local stratification σ, we say that program P is *locally stratified w.r.t.* σ, or σ is a *local stratification for P*, iff for every clause γ in P and for every valuation v, the clause $v(\gamma)$ is locally stratified w.r.t. σ. A program P is *locally stratified* iff there exists a local stratification σ such that P is *locally stratified w.r.t.* σ. For instance, let us consider the following program *Even*:

$$even(0) \leftarrow$$
$$even(X) \leftarrow X = Y+1 \wedge \neg even(Y)$$

where the interpretation for the constraints is as follows: (1) the carrier is the set of the natural numbers, and (2) the addition function is assigned to the function symbol $+$. The program *Even* is locally stratified w.r.t. the stratification function σ such that for every natural number n, $\sigma(even(n)) = n$.

The perfect model of a program P which is locally stratified w.r.t. a stratification function σ is the least $\mathcal{D}$-model of P w.r.t. a suitable ordering based on σ, as specified by the following definition. This ordering is, in general, different from set inclusion.

Definition 1. (*Perfect Model*) [35]. *Let P be a locally stratified program, let σ be any local stratification for P, and let I, J be $\mathcal{D}$-interpretations. We say that I is* preferable *to J, and we write $I \prec J$ iff for every $A_1 \in I - J$ there exists $A_2 \in J - I$ such that $\sigma(A_1) > \sigma(A_2)$. A $\mathcal{D}$-model M of P is called a* perfect $\mathcal{D}$-model (*or a* perfect model, *for short*) *iff for every $\mathcal{D}$-model N of P different from M, we have that $M \prec N$.*

It can be shown that the perfect model of a locally stratified program always exists and does not depend on the choice of the local stratification function σ, as stated by the following theorem.

Theorem 1. [35] *Every locally stratified program P has a unique perfect model $M(P)$.*

By Theorem 1, $M(P)$ is the least $\mathcal{D}$-model of P w.r.t. the $\prec$ ordering. For instance, the perfect model of the program consisting of the clause $p \leftarrow \neg q$ is $\{p\}$ because $\sigma(p) > \sigma(q)$ and, thus, the $\mathcal{D}$-model $\{p\}$ is preferable to the $\mathcal{D}$-model $\{q\}$ (i.e., $\{p\} \prec \{q\}$). Similarly, it can be verified that the perfect model of the program $Even$ is $M(Even) = \{even(n) \,|\, n$ is an even non-negative integer$\}$. In Section 4 we will provide a method for constructing the perfect model of a locally stratified program based on the notion of *proof tree*.

Let us conclude this section by showing that the assumption that the set $\mathcal{C}$ of constraints is closed w.r.t. negation, conjunction, and existential quantification is not really needed. Indeed, given a locally stratified clause $H \leftarrow c \wedge G$, where the constraint c is written by using negation, or conjunction, or existential quantification, we can replace $H \leftarrow c \wedge G$ by an equivalent set of locally stratified clauses. For instance, if c is $\exists X\, d$ then we can replace $H \leftarrow c \wedge G$ by the two clauses:

$$H \leftarrow newp(Y_1, \ldots, Y_n) \wedge G$$
$$newp(Y_1, \ldots, Y_n) \leftarrow d$$

where $newp$ is a new, user defined predicate and $\{Y_1, \ldots, Y_n\} = FV(\exists X\, d)$. Analogous replacements can be applied in the case where a constraint is written by using negation or conjunction.

3   The Transformation Rules

In this section we present a set of rules for transforming locally stratified constraint logic programs. We postpone to Section 6 the detailed comparison of our set of transformation rules with other sets of rules which were proposed in the literature for transforming logic programs and constraint logic programs. The application of our transformation rules is illustrated by simple examples. More complex examples will be given in Section 5.

The transformation rules are used to construct a *transformation sequence*, that is, a sequence $P_0, \ldots, P_n$ of programs. We assume that P_0 is locally stratified w.r.t. a fixed local stratification function $\sigma \colon \mathcal{B}_{\mathcal{D}} \to W$, and we will say that $P_0, \ldots, P_n$ is constructed *using* σ. We also assume that we are given a set $Pred_{int} \subseteq Pred_u$ of predicates of interest.

A transformation sequence $P_0, \ldots, P_n$ is constructed as follows. Suppose that we have constructed a transformation sequence $P_0, \ldots, P_k$, for $0 \leq k \leq n-1$, the next program P_{k+1} in the transformation sequence is derived from program P_k by the application of a transformation rule among R1–R10 defined below.

Our first rule is the *definition introduction* rule, which is applied for introducing a new predicate definition. Notice that by this rule we can introduce a new predicate defined by m (≥ 1) non-recursive clauses.

R1. Definition Introduction. Let us consider m (≥ 1) clauses of the form:

$$\delta_1 : newp(X_1, \ldots, X_h) \leftarrow c_1 \wedge G_1$$
$$\cdots$$
$$\delta_m : newp(X_1, \ldots, X_h) \leftarrow c_m \wedge G_m$$

where:

(i) *newp* is a predicate symbol not occurring in $\{P_0, \ldots, P_k\}$,

(ii) $X_1, \ldots, X_h$ are distinct variables occurring in $FV(\{c_1 \wedge G_1, \ldots, c_m \wedge G_m\})$,

(iii) every predicate symbol occurring in $\{G_1, \ldots, G_m\}$ also occurs in P_0, and

(iv) for every ground substitution ϑ with domain $\{X_1, \ldots, X_h\}$,

$\sigma(newp(X_1, \ldots, X_h)\vartheta)$ is the least ordinal α such that, for every valuation v and for every $i = 1, \ldots, m$,

either (iv.1) $\mathcal{D} \models \neg v(c_i\vartheta)$ *or* (iv.2) for every literal L occurring in $v(G_i\vartheta)$, if L is an atom A then $\alpha \geq \sigma(A)$ else if L is a negated atom $\neg A$ then $\alpha > \sigma(A)$.

By *definition introduction* (or *definition*, for short) from program P_k we derive the program $P_{k+1} = P_k \cup \{\delta_1, \ldots, \delta_m\}$. For $k \geq 0$, $Defs_k$ denotes the set of clauses introduced by the definition rule during the transformation sequence $P_0, \ldots, P_k$. In particular, $Defs_0 = \emptyset$.

Condition (iv), which is needed to ensure that σ is a local stratification for each program in the transformation sequence $P_0, \ldots, P_{k+1}$ (see Proposition 1), is not actually restrictive, because *newp* is a predicate symbol *not* occurring in P_0 and, thus, we can always choose the local stratification σ for P_0 so that Condition (iv) holds. As a consequence of Condition (iv), $\sigma(newp(X_1, \ldots, X_h)\vartheta)$ is the least upper bound of $S_p \cup S_n$ w.r.t. $<$ where:

$$S_p = \{\sigma(A) \quad | 1 \leq i \leq m, v \text{ is a valuation}, A \text{ occurs in } v(G_i\vartheta),$$
$$\mathcal{D} \models v(c_i\vartheta)\}, \text{ and}$$
$$S_n = \{\sigma(A)+1 \mid 1 \leq i \leq m, v \text{ is a valuation}, \neg A \text{ occurs in } v(G_i\vartheta),$$
$$\mathcal{D} \models v(c_i\vartheta)\}.$$

In particular, if for $i = 1, \ldots, m$, $\mathcal{D} \models \neg \exists (c_i\vartheta)$, then $S_p \cup S_n = \emptyset$ and we have that $\sigma(newp(X_1, \ldots, X_h)\vartheta) = 0$.

The *definition elimination* rule is the inverse of the definition introduction rule. It can be used to discard from a given program the definitions of predicates which are not of interest.

R2. Definition Elimination. Let p be a predicate such that no predicate of the set $Pred_{int}$ of the predicates of interest depends on p in P_k. By *eliminating* the definition of p, from program P_k we derive the new program $P_{k+1} = P_k - Def(p, P_k)$.

The *unfolding* rule consists in: (i) replacing an atom $p(t_1, \ldots, t_m)$ occurring in the body of a clause, by a suitable instance of the disjunction of the bodies of the clauses which are the definition of p, and (ii) applying suitable boolean laws for deriving clauses. The suitable instance of Step (i) is computed by adding a constraint of the form $p(t_1, \ldots, t_m) = K$ for each head K of a clause in $Def(p, P_k)$. There are two unfolding rules: (1) the positive unfolding rule, and (2) the negative unfolding rule, corresponding to the case where $p(t_1, \ldots, t_m)$ occurs positively and negatively, respectively, in the body of the clause to be unfolded. In order to perform Step (ii), in the case of positive unfolding we apply the distributivity law, and in the case of negative unfolding we apply De Morgan's, distributivity, and double negation elimination laws.

R3. Positive Unfolding. Let $\gamma : H \leftarrow c \wedge G_L \wedge A \wedge G_R$ be a clause in program P_k and let P'_k be a variant of P_k without common variables with γ. Let

$$\gamma_1 : K_1 \leftarrow c_1 \wedge B_1$$
$$\dots$$
$$\gamma_m : K_m \leftarrow c_m \wedge B_m$$

where $m \geq 0$ and $B_1, \dots, B_m$ are conjunction of literals, be all clauses of program P'_k such that, for $i = 1, \dots, m$, $\mathcal{D} \models \exists (c \wedge A = K_i \wedge c_i)$.
By *unfolding clause γ w.r.t. the atom A* we derive the clauses

$$\eta_1 : H \leftarrow c \wedge A = K_1 \wedge c_1 \wedge G_L \wedge B_1 \wedge G_R$$
$$\dots$$
$$\eta_m : H \leftarrow c \wedge A = K_m \wedge c_m \wedge G_L \wedge B_m \wedge G_R$$

and from program P_k we derive the program $P_{k+1} = (P_k - \{\gamma\}) \cup \{\eta_1, \dots, \eta_m\}$.

Notice that if $m = 0$ then, by positive unfolding, clause γ is deleted from P_k.

Example 2. Let P_k be the following program:

1. $p(X) \leftarrow X \geq 1 \wedge q(X)$
2. $q(Y) \leftarrow Y = 0$
3. $q(Y) \leftarrow Y = Z + 1 \wedge q(Z)$

where we assume that the interpretation for the constraints is given by the structure $\mathcal{R}$ of the real numbers. Let us unfold clause 1 w.r.t. the atom $q(X)$. The constraint $X \geq 1 \wedge X = Y \wedge Y = 0$ constructed from the constraints of clauses 1 and 2 is unsatisfiable, that is, $\mathcal{R} \models \neg \exists X \exists Y (X \geq 1 \wedge X = Y \wedge Y = 0)$, while the constraint $X \geq 1 \wedge X = Y \wedge Y = Z + 1$ constructed from the constraints of clauses 1 and 3, is satisfiable. Thus, we derive the following program P_{k+1}:

1u. $p(X) \leftarrow X \geq 1 \wedge X = Y \wedge Y = Z + 1 \wedge q(Z)$
2. $q(Y) \leftarrow Y = 0$
3. $q(Y) \leftarrow Y = Z + 1 \wedge q(Z)$

R4. Negative Unfolding. Let $\gamma : H \leftarrow c \wedge G_L \wedge \neg A \wedge G_R$ be a clause in program P_k and let P'_k be a variant of P_k without common variables with γ. Let

$$\gamma_1 : K_1 \leftarrow c_1 \wedge B_1$$
$$\dots$$
$$\gamma_m : K_m \leftarrow c_m \wedge B_m$$

where $m \geq 0$ and $B_1, \dots, B_m$ are conjunction of literals, be all clauses of program P'_k such that, for $i = 1, \dots, m$, $\mathcal{D} \models \exists (c \wedge A = K_i \wedge c_i)$. Suppose that, for $i = 1, \dots, m$, there exist an idempotent substitution $\vartheta_i = \{X_{i1}/t_{i1}, \dots, X_{in}/t_{in}\}$ and a constraint d_i such that the following conditions hold:

(i) $\mathcal{D} \models \forall (c \rightarrow ((A = K_i \wedge c_i) \leftrightarrow (X_{i1} = t_{i1} \wedge \dots \wedge X_{in} = t_{in} \wedge d_i)))$,

(ii) $\{X_{i1}, \dots, X_{in}\} \subseteq V_i$, where $V_i = FV(\gamma_i)$, and

(iii) $FV(d_i \wedge B_i \vartheta_i) \subseteq FV(c \wedge A)$.

Then, from the formula

$$\psi_0 : c \wedge G_L \wedge \neg (\exists V_1 (A = K_1 \wedge c_1 \wedge B_1) \vee \dots \vee \exists V_m (A = K_m \wedge c_m \wedge B_m)) \wedge G_R$$

we get an equivalent disjunction of constrained goals by performing the following steps. In these steps we silently apply the associativity of $\wedge$ and $\vee$.

Step 1. (*Eliminate* $\exists$) Since Conditions (i), (ii), and (iii) hold, we derive from ψ_0 the following equivalent formula:

$$\psi_1 : \quad c \wedge G_L \wedge \neg((d_1 \wedge B_1 \vartheta_1) \vee \ldots \vee (d_m \wedge B_m \vartheta_m)) \wedge G_R$$

Step 2. (*Push* $\neg$ *inside*) We apply to ψ_1 as long as possible the following rewritings of formulas, where d is a constraint, At is an atom, G, G_1, G_2 are goals, and D is a disjunction of constrained literals:

$$\neg((d \wedge G) \vee D) \quad \longrightarrow \quad \neg(d \wedge G) \wedge \neg D$$
$$\neg(d \wedge G) \quad \longrightarrow \quad \neg d \vee (d \wedge \neg G)$$
$$\neg(G_1 \wedge G_2) \quad \longrightarrow \quad \neg G_1 \vee \neg G_2$$
$$\neg\neg At \quad \longrightarrow \quad At$$

Thus, from ψ_1 we derive the following equivalent formula:

$$\psi_2 : \quad c \wedge G_L \wedge (\neg d_1 \vee (d_1 \wedge (\overline{L_{11}\vartheta_1} \vee \ldots \vee \overline{L_{1p}\vartheta_1})))$$
$$\wedge \ \ldots$$
$$\wedge (\neg d_m \vee (d_m \wedge (\overline{L_{m1}\vartheta_m} \vee \ldots \vee \overline{L_{mq}\vartheta_m})))$$
$$\wedge G_R$$

where $L_{11} \wedge \ldots \wedge L_{1p}$ is B_1, ..., and $L_{m1} \wedge \ldots \wedge L_{mq}$ is B_m.

Step 3. (*Push* $\vee$ *outside*) We apply to ψ_2 as long as possible the following rewriting of formulas, where φ_1, φ_2, and φ_3 are formulas:

$$\varphi_1 \wedge (\varphi_2 \vee \varphi_3) \quad \longrightarrow \quad (\varphi_1 \wedge \varphi_2) \vee (\varphi_1 \wedge \varphi_3)$$

and then we move constraints to the left of literals by applying the commutativity of $\wedge$. Thus, from ψ_2 we get an equivalent formula of the form:

$$\psi_3 : \quad (c \wedge e_1 \wedge G_L \wedge Q_1 \wedge G_R) \vee \ldots \vee (c \wedge e_r \wedge G_L \wedge Q_r \wedge G_R)$$

where $e_1, \ldots, e_r$ are constraints and $Q_1, \ldots, Q_r$ are goals.

Step 4. (*Remove unsatisfiable disjuncts*) We remove from ψ_3 every disjunct ($c \wedge e_j \wedge G_L \wedge Q_j \wedge G_R$), with $1 \leq j \leq r$, such that $\mathcal{D} \models \neg\exists(c \wedge e_j)$, thereby deriving an equivalent disjunction of constrained goals of the form:

$$\psi_4 : \quad (c \wedge e_1 \wedge G_L \wedge Q_1 \wedge G_R) \vee \ldots \vee (c \wedge e_s \wedge G_L \wedge Q_s \wedge G_R)$$

By *unfolding clause* γ *w.r.t. the negative literal* $\neg A$ we derive the clauses

$$\eta_1 : \quad H \leftarrow c \wedge e_1 \wedge G_L \wedge Q_1 \wedge G_R$$
$$\ldots$$
$$\eta_s : \quad H \leftarrow c \wedge e_s \wedge G_L \wedge Q_s \wedge G_R$$

and from program P_k we derive the program $P_{k+1} = (P_k - \{\gamma\}) \cup \{\eta_1, \ldots, \eta_s\}$.

Notice that: (i) if $m = 0$, that is, if we unfold clause γ w.r.t. a negative literal $\neg A$ such that the constraint $c \wedge A = K_i \wedge c_i$ is satisfiable for no clause $K_i \leftarrow c_i \wedge B_i$ in P'_k, then we get the new program P_{k+1} by deleting $\neg A$ from the body of clause γ, and (ii) if we unfold clause γ w.r.t. a negative literal $\neg A$ such that for some clause $K_i \leftarrow c_i \wedge B_i$ in P'_k, $\mathcal{D} \models \forall(c \rightarrow \exists V_i (A = K_i \wedge c_i))$ and B_i is the empty conjunction, then we derive the new program P_{k+1} by deleting clause γ from P_k.

An application of the negative unfolding rule is illustrated by the following example.

Example 3. Suppose that the following clause belongs to program P_k:

$\gamma : h(X) \leftarrow X \geq 0 \wedge \neg p(X)$

and let

$p(Y) \leftarrow Y = Z + 1 \wedge Z \geq 0 \wedge q(Z)$
$p(Y) \leftarrow Y = Z - 1 \wedge Z \geq 1 \wedge q(Z) \wedge \neg r(Z)$

be the definition of p in P_k. Suppose also that the constraints are interpreted in the structure $\mathcal{R}$ of the real numbers. Now let us unfold clause γ w.r.t. $\neg p(X)$. We start off from the formula:

$\psi_0 : \ X \geq 0 \wedge \neg (\ \exists Y \exists Z \ (X = Y \wedge Y = Z + 1 \wedge Z \geq 0 \wedge q(Z)) \vee$
$\exists Y \exists Z \ (X = Y \wedge Y = Z - 1 \wedge Z \geq 1 \wedge q(Z) \wedge \neg r(Z)))$

Then we perform the four steps indicated in rule R4 as follows.

Step 1. Since we have that:

$\mathcal{R} \models \forall X \forall Y \forall Z \ (X \geq 0 \rightarrow (\ (X = Y \wedge Y = Z + 1 \wedge Z \geq 0) \leftrightarrow$
$(Y = X \wedge Z = X - 1 \wedge X \geq 1)))$

and

$\mathcal{R} \models \forall X \forall Y \forall Z \ (X \geq 0 \rightarrow (\ (X = Y \wedge Y = Z - 1 \wedge Z \geq 1) \leftrightarrow$
$(Y = X \wedge Z = X + 1)))$

we derive the formula:

$\psi_1 : \ X \geq 0 \wedge \neg((X \geq 1 \wedge q(X - 1)) \vee (q(X + 1) \wedge \neg r(X + 1)))$

Steps 2 and 3. By applying the rewritings indicated in rule R4 we derive the following formula:

$\psi_3 : \ (X \geq 0 \wedge \neg X \geq 1 \wedge \neg q(X + 1)) \vee$
$(X \geq 0 \wedge \neg X \geq 1 \wedge r(X + 1)) \vee$
$(X \geq 0 \wedge X \geq 1 \wedge \neg q(X - 1) \wedge \neg q(X + 1)) \vee$
$(X \geq 0 \wedge X \geq 1 \wedge \neg q(X - 1) \wedge r(X + 1))$

Step 4. Since all constraints in the formula derived at the end of Steps 2 and 3 are satisfiable, no disjunct is removed.

Thus, by unfolding $h(X) \leftarrow X \geq 0 \wedge \neg p(X)$ w.r.t. $\neg p(X)$ we derive the following clauses:

$h(X) \leftarrow X \geq 0 \wedge \neg X \geq 1 \wedge \neg q(X + 1)$
$h(X) \leftarrow X \geq 0 \wedge \neg X \geq 1 \wedge r(X + 1)$
$h(X) \leftarrow X \geq 0 \wedge X \geq 1 \wedge \neg q(X - 1) \wedge \neg q(X + 1)$
$h(X) \leftarrow X \geq 0 \wedge X \geq 1 \wedge \neg q(X - 1) \wedge r(X + 1)$

The validity of Conditions (i), (ii), and (iii) in the negative folding rule allows us to eliminate the existential quantifiers as indicated at Step 1. If these conditions do not hold and nonetheless we eliminate the existential quantifiers, then negative unfolding may be incorrect, as illustrated by the following example.

Example 4. Let us consider the following programs P_0 and P_1, where P_1 is obtained by negative unfolding from P_0, but Conditions (i)–(iii) do not hold:

$P_0: \ p \leftarrow \neg q$ $\qquad\qquad\qquad$ $P_1: \ p \leftarrow \neg r(X)$
$\quad\ \ q \leftarrow r(X)$ $\qquad\qquad\qquad\qquad$ $q \leftarrow r(X)$
$\quad\ \ r(X) \leftarrow X = 0$ $\qquad\qquad\qquad\ \ \ r(X) \leftarrow X = 0$

We have that: $p \notin M(P_0)$ while $p \in M(P_1)$. (We assume that the carrier of the interpretation for the constraints contains at least one element different from 0.)

The reason why the negative unfolding step of Example 4 is incorrect is that the clause $q \leftarrow r(X)$ is, as usual, implicitly universally quantified at the front, and $\forall X\,(q \leftarrow r(X))$ is logically equivalent to $q \leftarrow \exists X\, r(X)$. Now, a correct negative unfolding rule should replace the clause $p \leftarrow \neg q$ in program P_0 by $p \leftarrow \neg \exists X\, r(X)$, while in program P_1 we have derived the clause $p \leftarrow \neg r(X)$ which, by making the quantification explicit at the front of the body, can be written as $p \leftarrow \exists X\, \neg r(X)$.

The *folding* rule consists in replacing instances of the bodies of the clauses that are the definition of a predicate by the corresponding head. As for unfolding, we have a positive folding and a negative folding rule, depending on whether folding is applied to positive or negative occurrences of (conjunctions of) literals. Notice that by the positive folding rule we may replace $m\,(\geq 1)$ clauses by one clause only.

R5. Positive Folding. Let $\gamma_1, \ldots, \gamma_m$, with $m \geq 1$, be clauses in P_k and let $Defs'_k$ be a variant of $Defs_k$ without common variables with $\gamma_1, \ldots, \gamma_m$. Let the definition of a predicate in $Defs'_k$ consist of the clauses

$$\delta_1 : K \leftarrow d_1 \wedge B_1$$
$$\ldots$$
$$\delta_m : K \leftarrow d_m \wedge B_m$$

where, for $i = 1, \ldots, m$, B_i is a non-empty conjunction of literals. Suppose that there exists a substitution ϑ such that, for $i = 1, \ldots, m$, clause γ_i is of the form $H \leftarrow c \wedge d_i \vartheta \wedge G_L \wedge B_i \vartheta \wedge G_R$ and, for every variable X in the set $FV(d_i \wedge B_i) - FV(K)$, the following conditions hold: (i) $X\vartheta$ is a variable not occurring in $\{H, c, G_L, G_R\}$, and (ii) $X\vartheta$ does not occur in the term $Y\vartheta$, for any variable Y occurring in $d_i \wedge B_i$ and different from X.
By *folding clauses* $\gamma_1, \ldots, \gamma_m$ *using clauses* $\delta_1, \ldots, \delta_m$ we derive the clause η: $H \leftarrow c \wedge G_L \wedge K\vartheta \wedge G_R$ and from program P_k we derive the program $P_{k+1} = (P_k - \{\gamma_1, \ldots, \gamma_m\}) \cup \{\eta\}$.

The following example illustrates an application of rule R5.

Example 5. Suppose that the following clauses belong to P_k:

$\gamma_1: \ h(X) \leftarrow X \geq 1 \wedge Y = X - 1 \wedge p(Y, 1)$
$\gamma_2: \ h(X) \leftarrow X \geq 1 \wedge Y = X + 1 \wedge \neg q(Y)$

and suppose that the following clauses constitute the definition of a predicate *new* in $Defs_k$:

$\delta_1: \ new(Z, C) \leftarrow V = Z - C \wedge p(V, C)$
$\delta_2: \ new(Z, C) \leftarrow V = Z + C \wedge \neg q(V)$

For $\vartheta = \{V/Y, Z/X, C/1\}$, we have that $\gamma_1 = h(X) \leftarrow X \geq 1 \wedge (V = Z - C \wedge p(V, C))\vartheta$ and $\gamma_2 = h(X) \leftarrow X \geq 1 \wedge (V = Z + C \wedge \neg q(V))\vartheta$, and the substitution

ϑ satisfies Conditions (i) and (ii) of the positive folding rule. By folding clauses γ_1 and γ_2 using clauses δ_1 and δ_2 we derive:

η: $h(X) \leftarrow X \geq 1 \wedge new(Z, 1)$

R6. Negative Folding. Let γ be a clause in P_k and let $Defs'_k$ be a variant of $Defs_k$ without common variables with γ. Suppose that there exists a predicate in $Defs'_k$ whose definition consists of a single clause $\delta : K \leftarrow d \wedge A$, where A is an atom. Suppose also that there exists a substitution ϑ such that clause γ is of the form: $H \leftarrow c \wedge d\vartheta \wedge G_L \wedge \neg A\vartheta \wedge G_R$ and $FV(K) = FV(d \wedge A)$.

By *folding clause γ using clause δ* we derive the clause η: $H \leftarrow c \wedge d\vartheta \wedge G_L \wedge \neg K\vartheta \wedge G_R$ and from program P_k we derive the program $P_{k+1} = (P_k - \{\gamma\}) \cup \{\eta\}$.

The following is an example of application of the negative folding rule.

Example 6. Let the following clause belong to P_k:

γ: $h(X) \leftarrow X \geq 0 \wedge q(X) \wedge \neg r(X, 0)$

and let *new* be a predicate whose definition in $Defs_k$ consists of the clause:

δ: $new(X, C) \leftarrow X \geq C \wedge r(X, C)$

By folding γ using δ we derive:

η: $h(X) \leftarrow X \geq 0 \wedge q(X) \wedge \neg new(X, 0)$

The positive and negative folding rule are not fully symmetric for the following three reasons.

(1) By positive folding we can fold several clauses at a time by using *several* clauses whose body may contain several literals, while by negative folding we can fold a *single* clause at a time by using a single clause whose body contains precisely one atom. This is motivated by the fact that a conjunction of more than one literal cannot occur inside negation in the body of a clause.

(2) By positive folding, for $i = 1, \ldots, m$, the constraint $d\vartheta_i$ occurring in the body of clause γ_i is removed, while by negative folding the constraint $d\vartheta$ occurring in the body of clause γ is not removed. Indeed, the removal of the constraint $d\vartheta$ would be incorrect. For instance, let us consider the program P_k of Example 6 above and let us assume that γ is the only clause defining the predicate h. Let us also assume that the predicates q and r are defined by the following two clauses: $q(X) \leftarrow X < 0$ and $r(X, 0) \leftarrow X < 0$. We have that $h(-1) \notin M(P_k)$. Suppose that we apply the negative folding rule to clause γ and we remove the constraint $X \geq 0$, thereby deriving the clause $h(X) \leftarrow q(X) \wedge \neg new(X, 0)$, instead of clause η. Then we obtain a program whose perfect model has the atom $h(-1)$.

(3) The conditions on the variables occurring in the clauses used for folding are less restrictive in the case of positive folding (see Conditions (i) and (ii) of R5) than in the case of negative folding (see the condition $FV(K) = FV(d \wedge A)$). Notice that a negative folding rule where the condition $FV(K) = FV(d \wedge A)$ is replaced by Conditions (i) and (ii) of R5 would be incorrect, in general. To see this, let us consider the following example which may be viewed as the inverse derivation of Example 4.

Example 7. Let us consider the following programs P_0, P_1, and P_2, where P_1 is obtained from P_0 by definition introduction, and P_2 is obtained from P_1 by incorrectly folding $p \leftarrow \neg r(X)$ using $q \leftarrow r(Y)$. Notice that $FV(q) \neq FV(r(X))$ but Conditions (i) and (ii) are satisfied by the substitution $\{Y/X\}$.

$$
\begin{array}{lll}
P_0\colon\ p \leftarrow \neg r(X) & P_1\colon\ p \leftarrow \neg r(X) & P_2\colon\ p \leftarrow \neg q \\
\quad\ r(X) \leftarrow X = 0 & \quad\ r(X) \leftarrow X = 0 & \quad\ r(X) \leftarrow X = 0 \\
 & \quad\ q \leftarrow r(Y) & \quad\ q \leftarrow r(Y)
\end{array}
$$

We have that: $p \in M(P_0)$ while $p \notin M(P_2)$. (We assume that the carrier of the interpretation for the constraints contains at least one element different from 0.)

If we consider the folding and unfolding rules outside the context of a transformation sequence, either rule can be viewed as the inverse of the other. However, given a transformation sequence $P_0, \ldots, P_n$, it may be the case that from a program P_k in that sequence we derive program P_{k+1} by folding, and from program P_{k+1} we *cannot* derive by unfolding a program P_{k+2} which is equal to P_k. This is due to the fact that in the transformation sequence $P_0, \ldots, P_k, P_{k+1}$, in order to fold some clauses in program P_k, we may use clauses in $Defs_k$ which are neither in P_k nor in P_{k+1}, while for unfolding program P_{k+1} we can only use clauses which belong to P_{k+1}. Thus, according to the terminology introduced in [29], we say that folding is, in general, not *reversible*. This fact is shown by the following example.

Example 8. Let us consider the transformation sequence:

$$
\begin{array}{llll}
P_0\colon\ p \leftarrow q & P_1\colon\ p \leftarrow q & P_2\colon\ p \leftarrow q & P_3\colon\ p \leftarrow r \\
\quad\ q \leftarrow & \quad\ q \leftarrow & \quad\ q \leftarrow & \quad\ q \leftarrow \\
 & \quad\ r \leftarrow q & \quad\ r \leftarrow & \quad\ r \leftarrow
\end{array}
$$

where P_1 is derived from P_0 by introducing the definition $r \leftarrow q$, P_2 is derived from P_1 by unfolding the clause $r \leftarrow q$, and P_3 is derived from P_2 by folding the clause $p \leftarrow q$ using the definition $r \leftarrow q$. We have that from program P_3 we cannot derive a program equal to P_2 by applying the positive unfolding rule.

Similarly, the unfolding rules are not reversible in general. In fact, if we derive a program P_{k+1} by unfolding a clause in a program P_k and we have that $Defs_k = \emptyset$, then we cannot apply the folding rule and derive a program P_{k+2} which is equal to P_k, simply because no clause in $Defs_k$ is available for folding.

The following *replacement* rule can be applied to replace a set of clauses with a new set of clauses by using laws based on equivalences between formulas. In particular, we consider: (i) boolean laws, (ii) equivalences that can be proved in the chosen interpretation $\mathcal{D}$ for the constraints, and (iii) properties of the equality predicate.

R7. Replacement Based on Laws. Let us consider the following rewritings $\Gamma_1 \Rightarrow \Gamma_2$ between sets of clauses (we use $\Gamma_1 \Leftrightarrow \Gamma_2$ as a shorthand for the two rewritings $\Gamma_1 \Rightarrow \Gamma_2$ and $\Gamma_2 \Rightarrow \Gamma_1$). Each rewriting is called a *law*.

Boolean Laws

(1) $\{H \leftarrow c \wedge A \wedge \neg A \wedge G\}$ $\qquad\qquad \Leftrightarrow \emptyset$

(2) $\{H \leftarrow c \wedge H \wedge G\}$ $\qquad\qquad\quad \Leftrightarrow \emptyset$

(3) $\{H \leftarrow c \wedge G_1 \wedge A_1 \wedge A_2 \wedge G_2\} \Leftrightarrow \{H \leftarrow c \wedge G_1 \wedge A_2 \wedge A_1 \wedge G_2\}$

(4) $\{H \leftarrow c \wedge A \wedge A \wedge G\}$ $\qquad\quad \Rightarrow \{H \leftarrow c \wedge A \wedge G\}$

(5) $\begin{aligned}\{&H \leftarrow c \wedge G_1, \\ &H \leftarrow c \wedge d \wedge G_1 \wedge G_2\}\end{aligned}$ $\quad \Leftrightarrow \{H \leftarrow c \wedge G_1\}$

(6) $\begin{aligned}\{&H \leftarrow c \wedge A \wedge G, \\ &H \leftarrow c \wedge \neg A \wedge G\}\end{aligned}$ $\qquad \Rightarrow \{H \leftarrow c \wedge G\}$

Laws of Constraints

(7) $\{H \leftarrow c \wedge G\} \Leftrightarrow \emptyset$

$\qquad\qquad$ if the constraint c is unsatisfiable, that is, $\mathcal{D} \models \neg \exists (c)$

(8) $\{H \leftarrow c_1 \wedge G\} \Leftrightarrow \{H \leftarrow c_2 \wedge G\}$

$\qquad\qquad$ if $\mathcal{D} \models \forall (\exists Y \, c_1 \leftrightarrow \exists Z \, c_2)$, where:

$\qquad\qquad\qquad$ (i) $Y = FV(c_1) - FV(\{H, G\})$, and

$\qquad\qquad\qquad$ (ii) $Z = FV(c_2) - FV(\{H, G\})$

(9) $\{H \leftarrow c \wedge G\} \Leftrightarrow \{H \leftarrow c_1 \wedge G, \; H \leftarrow c_2 \wedge G\}$

$\qquad\qquad$ if $\mathcal{D} \models \forall (c \leftrightarrow (c_1 \vee c_2))$

Laws of Equality

(10) $\{(H \leftarrow c \wedge G)\{X/t\}\} \Leftrightarrow \{H \leftarrow X = t \wedge c \wedge G\}$

$\qquad\qquad$ if the variable X does not occur in the term t

$\qquad\qquad$ and t is free for X in c.

Let Γ_1 and Γ_2 be sets of clauses such that: (i) $\Gamma_1 \Rightarrow \Gamma_2$, and (ii) Γ_2 is locally stratified w.r.t. the fixed local stratification function σ. By *replacement* from Γ_1 we derive Γ_2 and from program P_k we derive the program $P_{k+1} = (P_k - \Gamma_1) \cup \Gamma_2$.

Condition (ii) on Γ_2 is needed because a replacement based on laws (1), (2), (5), and (7), used from right to left, may not preserve local stratification. For instance, the first law may be used to introduce a clause of the form $p \leftarrow p \wedge \neg p$, which is not locally stratified. We will see at the end of Section 4 that if we add the reverse versions of the boolean laws (4) or (6), then the correctness result stated in Theorem 3 does not hold.

The following definition is needed for stating rule R8 below. The set of *useless predicates* in a program P is the maximal set U of predicate symbols occurring in P such that a predicate p is in U iff every clause γ in $Def(p, P)$ is of the form $H \leftarrow c \wedge G_1 \wedge q(\ldots) \wedge G_2$ for some q in U. For example, in the following program:

$$p(X) \leftarrow q(X) \wedge \neg r(X)$$
$$q(X) \leftarrow p(X)$$
$$r(X) \leftarrow X > 0$$

p and q are useless predicates, while r is not useless.

R8. Deletion of Useless Predicates. If p is a useless predicate in P_k, then from program P_k we derive the program $P_{k+1} = P_k - Def(p, P_k)$.

Neither of the rules R2 and R8 subsumes the other. Indeed, on one hand the definition of a predicate p on which no predicate of interest depends, can be deleted by rule R2 even if p is not useless. On the other hand, the definition of a useless predicate p can be deleted by rule R8 even if a predicate of interest depends on p.

The *constraint addition* rule R9 which we present below, can be applied to add to the body of a clause a constraint which is implied by that body. Conversely, the *constraint deletion* rule R10, also presented below, can be applied to delete from the body of a clause a constraint which is implied by the rest of the body. Notice that these implications should hold in the perfect model of program P_k, while the applicability conditions of rule R7 (see, in particular, the replacements based on laws 7–9) are independent of P_k. Thus, for checking the applicability conditions of rules R9 and R10 we may need a program analysis based, for instance, on abstract interpretation [10].

R9. Constraint Addition. Let $\gamma_1 : H \leftarrow c \wedge G$ be a clause in P_k and let d be a constraint such that $M(P_k) \models \forall((c \wedge G) \rightarrow \exists X\, d)$, where $X = FV(d) - FV(\gamma_1)$. By *constraint addition* from clause γ_1 we derive the clause $\gamma_2 : H \leftarrow c \wedge d \wedge G$ and from program P_k we derive the program $P_{k+1} = (P_k - \{\gamma_1\}) \cup \{\gamma_2\}$.

The following example shows an application of the constraint addition rule that cannot be realized by applying laws of constraints according to rule R7.

Example 9. Let us consider the following program P_k:

1. $nat(0) \leftarrow$
2. $nat(N) \leftarrow N = M + 1 \wedge nat(M)$

Since $M(P_k) \models \forall M\, (nat(M) \rightarrow M \geq 0)$, we can add the constraint $M \geq 0$ to the body of clause 2. This constraint addition improves the termination of the program when using a top-down strategy.

R10. Constraint Deletion. Let $\gamma_1 : H \leftarrow c \wedge d \wedge G$ be a clause in P_k and let d be a constraint such that $M(P_k) \models \forall((c \wedge G) \rightarrow \exists X\, d)$, where $X = FV(d) - FV(H \leftarrow c \wedge G)$. Suppose that the clause $\gamma_2 : H \leftarrow c \wedge G$ is locally stratified w.r.t. the fixed σ. By *constraint deletion* from clause γ_1 we derive clause γ_2 and from program P_k we derive the program $P_{k+1} = (P_k - \{\gamma_1\}) \cup \{\gamma_2\}$.

We assume that γ_2 is locally stratified w.r.t. σ because otherwise, the constraint deletion rule may not preserve local stratification. For instance, let us consider the following program P:

$p(X) \leftarrow$
$p(X) \leftarrow X \neq X \wedge \neg p(X)$

P is locally stratified because for all elements d in the carrier of the interpretation $\mathcal{D}$ for the constraints, we have that $\mathcal{D} \models d = d$. We also have that $M(P) \models \forall X\, (\neg p(X) \rightarrow X \neq X)$. However, if we delete the constraint $X \neq X$ from the second clause of P we derive the clause $p(X) \leftarrow \neg p(X)$ which is not locally stratified w.r.t. any local stratification function.

4   Preservation of Perfect Models

In this section we present some sufficient conditions which ensure that a transformation sequence constructed by applying the transformation rules listed in Section 3, preserves the perfect model semantics.

We will prove our correctness theorem for *admissible* transformation sequences, that is, transformation sequences constructed by applying the rules according to suitable restrictions. The reader who is familiar with the program transformation methodology, will realize that most transformation strategies can, indeed, be realized by means of admissible transformation sequences. In particular, all examples of Section 5 are worked out by using this kind of transformation sequences.

We proceed as follows. (i) First we show that the transformation rules preserve local stratification. (ii) Then we introduce the notion of an *admissible* transformation sequence. (iii) Next we introduce the notion of a *proof tree* for a ground atom A and a program P and we show that $A \in M(P)$ iff there exists a proof tree for A and P. Thus, the notion of proof tree provides the operational counterpart of the perfect model semantics. (iv) Then, we prove that given any admissible transformation sequence $P_0, \ldots, P_n$, any set $Pred_{int}$ of predicates of interest, and any ground atom A whose predicate is in $Pred_{int}$, we have that for $k = 0, \ldots, n$, there exists a proof tree for A and P_k iff there exists a proof tree for A and $P_0 \cup Defs_n$. (v) Finally, by using the property of proof trees considered at Point (iii), we conclude that an admissible transformation sequence preserves the perfect model semantics (see Theorem 3).

Let us start off by showing that the transformation rules preserve the local stratification function σ which was fixed for the initial program P_0 at the beginning of the construction of the transformation sequence.

Proposition 1. [Preservation of Local Stratification]. *Let P_0 be a locally stratified program, let $\sigma : \mathcal{B}_\mathcal{D} \to W$ be a local stratification function for P_0, and let $P_0, \ldots, P_n$ be a transformation sequence using σ. Then the programs $P_0, \ldots, P_n$, and $P_0 \cup Defs_n$ are locally stratified w.r.t. σ.*

The proof of Proposition 1 is given in Appendix A.

An admissible transformation sequence is a transformation sequence that satisfies two conditions: (1) every clause used for positive folding is unfolded w.r.t. a positive literal, and (2) the definition elimination rule cannot be applied before any other transformation rule. An admissible transformation sequence is formally defined as follows.

Definition 2. [Admissible Transformation Sequence] *A transformation sequence $P_0, \ldots, P_n$ is said to be* admissible *iff the following two conditions hold:*
(1) for $k = 0, \ldots, n-1$, if P_{k+1} is derived from P_k by applying the positive folding rule to clauses $\gamma_1, \ldots, \gamma_m$ using clauses $\delta_1, \ldots, \delta_m$, then for $i = 1, \ldots, m$ there exists j, with $0 < j < n$, such that $\delta_i \in P_j$ and program P_{j+1} is derived from P_j by positive unfolding of clause δ_i, and

(2) *if for some $m < n$, P_{m+1} is derived from P_m by the definition elimination rule then for all $k = m, \ldots, n-1$, P_{k+1} is derived from P_k by applying the definition elimination rule.*

When proving our correctness theorem (see Theorem 3 below), we will find it convenient to consider transformation sequences which are admissible and satisfy some extra suitable properties. This motivates the following notion of *ordered* transformation sequences.

Definition 3. [Ordered Transformation Sequence] *A transformation sequence $P_0, \ldots, P_n$ is said to be* ordered *iff it is of the form:*

$$P_0, \ldots, P_i, \ldots, P_j, \ldots, P_m, \ldots, P_n$$

where:
(1) *the sequence $P_0, \ldots, P_i$, with $i \geq 0$, is constructed by applying i times the definition introduction rule, that is, $P_i = P_0 \cup Defs_i$;*
(2) *the sequence $P_i, \ldots, P_j$ is constructed by unfolding w.r.t. a positive literal each clause in $Defs_i$ which is used for applications of the folding rule in $P_j, \ldots, P_m$;*
(3) *the sequence $P_j, \ldots, P_m$, with $j \leq m$, is constructed by applying any rule, except the definition introduction and definition elimination rules; and*
(4) *the sequence $P_m, \ldots, P_n$, with $m \leq n$, is constructed by applying the definition elimination rule.*

Notice that in an ordered transformation sequence we have that $Defs_i = Defs_n$. Every ordered transformation sequence is admissible, because of Points (2) and (4) of Definition 3. Conversely, by the following Proposition 2, in our correctness proofs we will assume, without loss of generality, that any admissible transformation sequence is ordered.

Proposition 2. *For every admissible transformation sequence $P_0, \ldots, P_n$, there exists an ordered transformation sequence $Q_0, \ldots, Q_r$ (with r possibly different from n), such that: (i) $P_0 = Q_0$, (ii) $P_n = Q_r$, and (iii) the set of definitions introduced during $P_0, \ldots, P_n$ is equal to the set of definitions introduced during $Q_0, \ldots, Q_r$.*

The easy proof of Proposition 2 is omitted for reasons of space. It is based on the fact that the applications of some transformation rules can be suitably rearranged without changing the initial and final programs in a transformation sequence.

Now we present the operational counterpart of the perfect model semantics, that is, the notion of a proof tree. A proof tree for a ground atom A and a locally stratified program P is constructed by transfinite induction as indicated in the following definition.

Definition 4. [Proof Tree] *Let A be a ground atom, P be a locally stratified program, and σ be any local stratification for P. Let $PT_{<A}$ be the set of proof trees for ground atoms B and P with $\sigma(B) < \sigma(A)$. A proof tree for A and P is a finite tree T of goals such that: (i) the root of T is A, (ii) a node N of T has* *children $L_1, \ldots, L_r$ iff N is a ground atom B and there exists a clause $\gamma \in P$ and a valuation v such that $v(\gamma)$ is $B \leftarrow c \wedge L_1 \wedge \ldots \wedge L_r$ and $\mathcal{D} \models c$, and (iii) every leaf of T is either the empty conjunction true or a negated ground atom $\neg B$ such that there is no proof tree for B and P in $PT_{<A}$.*

The following theorem establishes that the operational semantics based on proof trees is equivalent to the perfect model semantics.

Theorem 2. [Proof Trees and Perfect Models] *Let P be a locally stratified program. For all ground atoms A, there exists a proof tree for A and P iff $A \in M(P)$.*

Our proofs of correctness use induction w.r.t. suitable *well-founded measures* over proof trees, ground atoms, and ground goals (see, in particular, the proofs of Propositions 3 and 5 in Appendices B and C). We now introduce these measures.

Let T be a proof tree for a ground atom A and a locally stratified program P. By $size(T)$ we denote the number of atoms occurring at non-leaf nodes of T. For any ground atom A, locally stratified program P, and local stratification σ for P, we define the following measure:

$$\mu(A, P) = min_{lex}\{\langle \sigma(A), size(T)\rangle \mid T \text{ is a proof tree for } A \text{ and } P\}$$

where min_{lex} denotes the minimum w.r.t. the lexicographic ordering $<_{lex}$ over $W \times N$, where W is the set of countable ordinals and N is the set of natural numbers. $\mu(A, P)$ is undefined if there is no proof tree for A and P. The measure μ is extended from ground atoms to ground literals as follows. Given a ground literal L, we define:

$\mu(L, P) = $ if L is an atom A then $\mu(A, P)$
            else if L is a negated atom $\neg A$ then $\langle \sigma(A), 0\rangle$

Now we extend μ to ground goals. First, we introduce the binary, associative operation $\oplus : (W \times N)^2 \rightarrow (W \times N)$ defined as follows:

$$\langle \alpha_1, m_1\rangle \oplus \langle \alpha_2, m_2\rangle = \langle max(\alpha_1, \alpha_2), m_1 + m_2\rangle$$

Then, given a ground goal $L_1 \wedge \ldots \wedge L_n$, we define:

$$\mu(L_1 \wedge \ldots \wedge L_n, P) = \mu(L_1, P) \oplus \ldots \oplus \mu(L_n, P)$$

The measure μ is well-founded in the sense that there is no infinite sequence of ground goals $G_1, G_2, \ldots$ such that $\mu(G_1, P) > \mu(G_2, P) > \ldots$

In order to show that an ordered transformation sequence $P_0, \ldots, P_i, \ldots, P_j, \ldots, P_m, \ldots, P_n$ (where the meaning of the subscripts is the one of Definition 3) preserves the perfect model semantics, we will use Theorem 2 and we will show that, for $k = 0, \ldots, n$, given any ground atom A whose predicate belongs to the set $Pred_{int}$ of predicates of interest, there exists a proof tree for A and P_k iff there exists a proof tree for A and $P_0 \cup Defs_n$. Since $P_i = P_0 \cup Defs_n$, it is sufficient to show the following properties, for any ground atom A:

(P1) there exists a proof tree for A and P_i iff there exists a proof tree for A and P_j,

(P2) there exists a proof tree for A and P_j iff there exists a proof tree for A and P_m, and

(P3) if the predicate of A is in $Pred_{int}$, then there exists a proof tree for A and P_m iff there exists a proof tree for A and P_n.

Property P1 is proved by the following proposition.

Proposition 3. *Let P_0 be a locally stratified program and let $P_0, \ldots, P_i, \ldots,$ $P_j, \ldots, P_m, \ldots, P_n$ be an ordered transformation sequence. Then there exists a proof tree for a ground atom A and P_i iff there exists a proof tree for A and P_j.*

The proof of Proposition 3 is given in Appendix B. It is a proof by induction on $\sigma(A)$ and on the size of the proof tree for A.

   In order to prove the only-if part of Property P2, we will show a stronger invariant property based on the following consistency notion.

Definition 5. *[P_j-consistency] Let $P_0, \ldots, P_i, \ldots, P_j, \ldots, P_m, \ldots, P_n$ be an ordered transformation sequence, P_k be a program in this sequence, and A be a ground atom. We say that a proof tree T for A and P_k is P_j-consistent iff for every ground atom B and ground literals $L_1, \ldots, L_r$, if B is the father of $L_1, \ldots, L_r$ in T, then $\mu(B, P_j) > \mu(L_1 \wedge \ldots \wedge L_r, P_j)$.*

The invariant property is as follows: for every program P_k in the sequence $P_j, \ldots, P_m$, if there exists a P_j-consistent proof tree for A and P_j, then there exists a P_j-consistent proof tree for A and P_k.

   It is important that P_j-consistency refers to the program P_j obtained by applying the positive unfolding rule to each clause that belongs to $Defs_i$ and is used in $P_j, \ldots, P_m$ for a folding step. Indeed, if the positive unfolding rule is not applied to a clause in $Defs_i$, and this clause is then used (possibly, together with other clauses) in a folding step, then the preservation of P_j-consistent proof trees may not be ensured and the transformation sequence may not be correct. This is shown by Example 1 of the Introduction where we assume that the first clause $p(X) \leftarrow \neg q(X)$ of P_0 has been added by the definition introduction rule in a previous step.

   We have the following.

Proposition 4. *If there exists a proof tree for a ground atom A and program P_j then there exists a P_j-consistent proof tree for A and P_j.*

Proof. Let T be a proof tree for A and P_j such that $\langle \sigma(A), size(T) \rangle$ is minimal w.r.t. $<_{lex}$. Then T is P_j-consistent.   □

Notice that in the proof of Proposition 4 we state the existence of a P_j-consistent proof tree for a ground atom A and program P_j without providing an effective method for constructing this proof tree. In fact, it should be noticed that no effective method can be given for constructing the minimal proof tree for a given atom and program, because the existence of such a proof tree is not decidable and not even semi-decidable.

   By Proposition 4, in order to prove Property P2 it is enough to show the following Proposition 5.

Proposition 5. *Let P_0 be a locally stratified program and let $P_0, \ldots, P_i, \ldots,$ $P_j, \ldots, P_m, \ldots, P_n$ be an ordered transformation sequence. Then, for every ground atom A we have that:*

(Soundness) if there exists a proof tree for A and P_m, then there exists a proof tree for A and P_j, and

(Completeness) if there exists a P_j-consistent proof tree for A and P_j, then there exists a P_j-consistent proof tree for A and P_m.

The proof of Proposition 5 is given in Appendix C.

In order to prove Property P3, it is enough to prove the following Proposition 6, which is a straightforward consequence of the fact that the existence of a proof tree for a ground atom with predicate p is determined only by the existence of proof trees for atoms with predicates on which p depends.

Proposition 6. *Let P be a locally stratified program and let $Pred_{int}$ be a set of predicates of interest. Suppose that program Q is derived from program P by eliminating the definition of a predicate q such that no predicate in $Pred_{int}$ depends on q. Then, for every ground atom A whose predicate is in $Pred_{int}$, there exists a proof tree for A and P iff there exists a proof tree for A and Q.*

Now, as a consequence of Propositions 1–6, and Theorem 2, we get the following theorem which ensures that an admissible transformation sequence preserves the perfect model semantics.

Theorem 3. *[Correctness of Admissible Transformation Sequences] Let P_0 be a locally stratified program and let $P_0, \ldots, P_n$ be an admissible transformation sequence. Let $Pred_{int}$ be the set of predicates of interest. Then $P_0 \cup Defs_n$ and P_n are locally stratified and for every ground atom A whose predicate belongs to $Pred_{int}$, $A \in M(P_0 \cup Defs_n)$ iff $A \in M(P_n)$.*

This theorem does not hold if we add to the boolean laws listed in rule R7 of Section 3 the inverse of law (4), as shown by the following example.

Example 10. Let us consider the following transformation sequence:
$$P_0: \; p \leftarrow q \wedge q \qquad P_1: p \leftarrow q \qquad P_2: \; p \leftarrow q \wedge q \qquad P_3: \; p \leftarrow p$$
$$q \leftarrow \qquad\qquad\quad q \leftarrow \qquad\qquad\quad q \leftarrow \qquad\qquad\quad q \leftarrow$$
We assume that the clause for p in P_0 is added to P_0 by the definition introduction rule, so that it can be used for folding. Program P_1 is derived from P_0 by unfolding, program P_2 is derived from P_1 by replacement based on the reverse of law (4), and finally, program P_3 is derived by folding the first clause of P_2 using the first clause of P_0. We have that $p \in M(P_0)$, while $p \notin M(P_3)$.

Analogously, the reader may verify that Theorem 3 does not hold if we add to the boolean laws of rule R7 the inverse of law (6).

5   Examples of Use of the Transformation Rules

In this section we show some program derivations realized by applying the transformation rules of Section 3. These program derivations are examples of the following three techniques: (1) the *determinization* technique, which is used for deriving a deterministic program from a nondeterministic one [14,33], (2) the *program synthesis* technique, which is used for deriving a program from a first order logic specification (see, for instance, [18,41] and [6] in this book for a recent survey), and (3) the *program specialization* technique, which is used for deriving a specialized program from a given program and a given portion of its input data (see, for instance, [21] and [24] for a recent survey).

Although we will *not* provide in this paper any automatic transformation strategy, the reader may realize that in the examples we will present, there is a systematic way of performing the program derivations. In particular, we perform all derivations according to the repeated application of the following sequence of steps: (i) first, we consider some predicate definitions in the initial program or we introduce some new predicate definitions, (ii) then we unfold these definitions by applying the positive and, possibly, the negative unfolding rules, (iii) then we manipulate the derived clauses by applying the rules of replacement, constraint addition, and constraint deletion, and (iv) finally, we apply the folding rules. The final programs are derived by applying the definition elimination rule, and keeping only those clauses that are needed for computing the predicates of interest.

5.1   Determinization: Comparing Even and Odd Occurrences of a List

Let us consider the problem of checking whether or not, for any given list L of numbers, the following property $r(L)$ holds: every number occurring in L in an even position is greater or equal than every number occurring in L in an odd position. The locally stratified program *EvenOdd* shown below, solves the given problem by introducing a new predicate $p(L)$ which holds iff there is a pair $\langle X, Y \rangle$ of numbers such that X occurs in the the list L in an even position, Y occurs in L in an odd position, and $X < Y$. Thus, for any list L, the property $r(L)$ holds iff $p(L)$ does not hold.

EvenOdd:

1. $r(L) \leftarrow list(L) \wedge \neg p(L)$
2. $p(L) \leftarrow I \geq 1 \wedge J \geq 1 \wedge X < Y \wedge$
   $occurs(X, I, L) \wedge even(I) \wedge occurs(Y, J, L) \wedge \neg even(J)$
3. $even(X) \leftarrow X = 0$
4. $even(X+1) \leftarrow X \geq 0 \wedge \neg even(X)$
5. $occurs(X, I, [H|T]) \leftarrow I = 1 \wedge X = H$
6. $occurs(X, I+1, [H|T]) \leftarrow I \geq 1 \wedge occurs(X, I, T)$
7. $list([]) \leftarrow$
8. $list([H|T]) \leftarrow list(T)$

In this program $occurs(X, I, L)$ holds iff X is the I-th element (with $I \geq 1$) of the list L starting from the left. When executed by using SLDNF resolution, this *EvenOdd* program may generate, in a nondeterministic way, all possible pairs $\langle X, Y \rangle$, occurring in even and odd positions, respectively. This program has an $O(n^2)$ time complexity in the worst case, where n is the length of the input list.

We want to derive a more efficient *definite* program that can be executed in a *deterministic* way, in the sense that for every constrained goal $c \wedge A \wedge G$ derived from a given ground query by LD-resolution [3] there exists at most one clause $H \leftarrow d \wedge K$ such that $c \wedge A = H \wedge d$ is satisfiable.

To give a sufficient condition for determinism we need the following notion. We say that a variable X is a *local variable* of a clause γ iff $X \in FV(bd(\gamma)) - FV(hd(\gamma))$. The determinism of a program P can be ensured by the following syntactic conditions: (i) no clause in P has local variables and (ii) any two clauses $H_1 \leftarrow c_1 \wedge G_1$ and $H_2 \leftarrow c_2 \wedge G_2$ in P are *mutually exclusive*, that is, the constraint $H_1 = H_2 \wedge c_1 \wedge c_2$ is unsatisfiable.

Our derivation consists of two transformation sequences. The first sequence starts from the program made out of clauses 2–8 and derives a deterministic, definite program Q for predicate p. The second sequence starts from $Q \cup \{1\}$ and derives a deterministic, definite program *EvenOdd*$_{det}$ for predicate r.

Let us show the construction of the first transformation sequence. Since clause 2 has local variables, we want to transform it into a set of clauses that have no local variables and are mutually exclusive, and thus, they will constitute a deterministic, definite program. We start off by applying the positive unfolding rule to clause 2, followed by applications of the replacement rule based on laws of constraints and equality. We derive:

9. $p([A|L]) \leftarrow J \geq 1 \wedge Y < A \wedge occurs(Y, J, L) \wedge even(J+1)$
10. $p([A|L]) \leftarrow I \geq 1 \wedge J \geq 1 \wedge X < Y \wedge occurs(X, I, L) \wedge$
$ even(I+1) \wedge occurs(Y, J, L) \wedge \neg even(J+1)$

Now, by applications of the positive unfolding rule, negative unfolding, and replacement rules, we derive the following clauses for p:

11. $p([A, B|L]) \leftarrow B < A$
12. $p([A, B|L]) \leftarrow B \geq A \wedge I \geq 1 \wedge X < A \wedge occurs(X, I, L) \wedge even(I)$
13. $p([A, B|L]) \leftarrow B \geq A \wedge I \geq 1 \wedge B < X \wedge occurs(X, I, L) \wedge \neg even(I)$
14. $p([A, B|L]) \leftarrow B \geq A \wedge I \geq 1 \wedge J \geq 1 \wedge X < Y \wedge occurs(X, I, L) \wedge even(I) \wedge$
$ occurs(Y, J, L) \wedge \neg even(J)$

Notice that the three clauses 12, 13, and 14, are not mutually exclusive. In order to derive a deterministic program for p, we introduce the following new definition:

15. $new1(A, B, L) \leftarrow I \geq 1 \wedge X < A \wedge occurs(X, I, L) \wedge even(I)$
16. $new1(A, B, L) \leftarrow I \geq 1 \wedge B < X \wedge occurs(X, I, L) \wedge \neg even(I)$
17. $new1(A, B, L) \leftarrow I \geq 1 \wedge J \geq 1 \wedge X < Y \wedge occurs(X, I, L) \wedge even(I) \wedge$
$ occurs(Y, J, L) \wedge \neg even(J)$

and we fold clauses 12, 13, and 14 by using the definition of $new1$, that is, clauses 15, 16, and 17. We derive:

18. $p([A, B|L]) \leftarrow B \geq A \wedge new1(A, B, L)$

Clauses 11 and 18 have no local variables and are mutually exclusive. We are left with the problem of deriving a deterministic program for the newly introduced predicate $new1$.

By applying the positive unfolding, negative unfolding, and replacement rules, from clauses 15, 16, and 17, we get:

19. $new1(A, B, [C|L]) \leftarrow B < C$
20. $new1(A, B, [C|L]) \leftarrow I \geq 1 \wedge B < X \wedge occurs(X, I, L) \wedge even(I)$
21. $new1(A, B, [C|L]) \leftarrow I \geq 1 \wedge X < A \wedge occurs(X, I, L) \wedge \neg even(I)$
22. $new1(A, B, [C|L]) \leftarrow I \geq 1 \wedge X < C \wedge occurs(X, I, L) \wedge \neg even(I)$
23. $new1(A, B, [C|L]) \leftarrow I \geq 1 \wedge J \geq 1 \wedge X < Y \wedge occurs(X, I, L) \wedge$
    $\neg even(I) \wedge occurs(Y, J, L) \wedge even(J)$

In order to derive mutually exclusive clauses without local variables we first apply the replacement rule and derive sets of clauses corresponding to mutually exclusive cases, and then we fold each of these sets of clauses. We use the replacement rule based on law (5) and law (9) which is justified by the equivalence: $\forall X \forall Y (true \leftrightarrow X \geq Y \vee X < Y)$. We get:

24. $new1(A, B, [C|L]) \leftarrow B < C$
25. $new1(A, B, [C|L]) \leftarrow B \geq C \wedge A \geq C \wedge I \geq 1 \wedge B < X \wedge$
    $occurs(X, I, L) \wedge even(I)$
26. $new1(A, B, [C|L]) \leftarrow B \geq C \wedge A \geq C \wedge I \geq 1 \wedge X < A \wedge$
    $occurs(X, I, L) \wedge \neg even(I)$
27. $new1(A, B, [C|L]) \leftarrow B \geq C \wedge A \geq C \wedge I \geq 1 \wedge J \geq 1 \wedge X < Y \wedge$
    $occurs(X, I, L) \wedge \neg even(I) \wedge$
    $occurs(Y, J, L) \wedge even(J)$
28. $new1(A, B, [C|L]) \leftarrow B \geq C \wedge A < C \wedge I \geq 1 \wedge B < X \wedge$
    $occurs(X, I, L) \wedge even(I)$
29. $new1(A, B, [C|L]) \leftarrow B \geq C \wedge A < C \wedge I \geq 1 \wedge X < C \wedge$
    $occurs(X, I, L) \wedge \neg even(I)$
30. $new1(A, B, [C|L]) \leftarrow B \geq C \wedge A < C \wedge I \geq 1 \wedge J \geq 1 \wedge X < Y \wedge$
    $occurs(X, I, L) \wedge \neg even(I) \wedge$
    $occurs(Y, J, L) \wedge even(J)$

The three sets of clauses: {24}, {25, 26, 27}, and {28, 29, 30} correspond to the mutually exclusive cases: $(B < C)$, $(B \geq C \wedge A \geq C)$, and $(B \geq C \wedge A < C)$, respectively. Now, in order to fold each set {25, 26, 27} and {28, 29, 30} and derive mutually exclusive clauses without local variables, we introduce the following new definition:

31. $new2(A, B, L) \leftarrow I \geq 1 \wedge B < X \wedge occurs(X, I, L) \wedge even(I)$
32. $new2(A, B, L) \leftarrow I \geq 1 \wedge X < A \wedge occurs(X, I, L) \wedge \neg even(I)$
33. $new2(A, B, L) \leftarrow I \geq 1 \wedge J \geq 1 \wedge X < Y \wedge occurs(X, I, L) \wedge \neg even(I) \wedge$
    $occurs(Y, J, L) \wedge even(J)$

By folding clauses 25, 26, 27 and 28, 29, 30 using clauses 31, 32, and 33, for predicate $new1$ we get the following mutually exclusive clauses without local variables:

34. $new1(A, B, [C|L]) \leftarrow B < C$
35. $new1(A, B, [C|L]) \leftarrow B \geq C \land A \geq C \land new2(A, B, L)$
36. $new1(A, B, [C|L]) \leftarrow B \geq C \land A < C \land new2(C, B, L)$

Unfortunately, the clauses for the new predicate $new2$ have local variables and are not mutually exclusive. Thus, we continue our derivation and, by applying the positive unfolding, negative unfolding, replacement, and folding rules, from clauses 31, 32, and 33 we derive the following clauses (this derivation is similar to the derivation that lead from $\{15, 16, 17\}$ to $\{34, 35, 36\}$ and we omit it):

37. $new2(A, B, [C|L]) \leftarrow C < A$
38. $new2(A, B, [C|L]) \leftarrow C \geq A \land B \geq C \land new1(A, C, L)$
39. $new2(A, B, [C|L]) \leftarrow C \geq A \land B < C \land new1(A, B, L)$

The set of clauses derived so far starting from the initial clause 2, that is, $\{11, 18, 34, 35, 36, 37, 38, 39\}$ constitutes a deterministic program for p, call it Q.

Now we construct the second transformation sequence starting from $Q \cup \{1\}$ for deriving a deterministic, *definite* program for r. We start off by considering clause 1 which defines r and, by positive unfolding, negative unfolding, and replacement we derive:

40. $r([]) \leftarrow$
41. $r([A]) \leftarrow$
42. $r([A, B|L]) \leftarrow list(L) \land B \geq A \land \neg new1(A, B, L)$

By introducing the following definition:

43. $new3(A, B, L) \leftarrow list(L) \land B \geq A \land \neg new1(A, B, L)$

and then folding clause 42 using clause 43, we derive the following definite clauses:

44. $r([]) \leftarrow$
45. $r([A]) \leftarrow$
46. $r([A, B|L]) \leftarrow B \geq A \land new3(A, B, L)$

Now, we want to transform clause 43 into a set of definite clauses. By positive unfolding, negative unfolding, and replacement, from clause 43 we derive:

47. $new3(A, B, []) \leftarrow B \geq A$
48. $new3(A, B, [C|L]) \leftarrow B \geq C \land A < C \land list(L) \land B \geq C \land \neg new2(C, B, L)$
49. $new3(A, B, [C|L]) \leftarrow B \geq C \land A \geq C \land list(L) \land B \geq A \land \neg new2(A, B, L)$

In order to transform clauses 48 and 49 into definite clauses, we introduce the following definition:

50. $new4(A, B, L) \leftarrow list(L) \land B \geq A \land \neg new2(A, B, L)$

and we fold clauses 48 and 49 using clause 50. We get:

51. $new3(A, B, []) \leftarrow B \geq A$
52. $new3(A, B, [C|L]) \leftarrow B \geq C \land A < C \land new4(C, B, L)$
53. $new3(A, B, [C|L]) \leftarrow B \geq C \land A \geq C \land new4(A, B, L)$

Now we are left with the task of transforming clause 50 into a set of definite clauses. By applying the positive unfolding, negative unfolding, replacement, and folding rules, we derive:

54. $new4(A, B, [\,]) \leftarrow B \geq A$
55. $new4(A, B, [C|L]) \leftarrow B < C \wedge C \geq A \wedge new3(A, B, L)$
56. $new4(A, B, [C|L]) \leftarrow B \geq C \wedge C \geq A \wedge new3(A, C, L)$

Finally, by eliminating the definitions of the predicates on which r does not depend, we get, as desired, the following final program which is a deterministic, definite program.

$EvenOdd_{det}$:

44. $r([\,]) \leftarrow$
45. $r([A]) \leftarrow$
46. $r([A, B|L]) \leftarrow B \geq A \wedge new3(A, B, L)$
51. $new3(A, B, [\,]) \leftarrow B \geq A$
52. $new3(A, B, [C|L]) \leftarrow B \geq C \wedge A < C \wedge new4(C, B, L)$
53. $new3(A, B, [C|L]) \leftarrow B \geq C \wedge A \geq C \wedge new4(A, B, L)$
54. $new4(A, B, [\,]) \leftarrow B \geq A$
55. $new4(A, B, [C|L]) \leftarrow B < C \wedge C \geq A \wedge new3(A, B, L)$
56. $new4(A, B, [C|L]) \leftarrow B \geq C \wedge C \geq A \wedge new3(A, C, L)$

Given a list of numbers L of length n, the $EvenOdd_{det}$ program checks that $r(L)$ holds by performing at most $2n$ comparisons between numbers occurring in L. Program $EvenOdd_{det}$ works by traversing the input list L only once (without backtracking) and storing, for every initial portion L_1 of the input list L, the maximum number A occurring in an odd position of L_1 and the minimum number B occurring in an even position of L_1 (see the first two arguments of the predicates $new3$ and $new4$). When looking at the first element C of the portion of the input list still to be visited (i.e., the third argument of $new3$ or $new4$), the following two cases are possible: either (Case 1) the element C occurs in an odd position of the input list L, i.e., a call of the form $new3(A, B, [C|L_2])$ is executed, or (Case 2) the element C occurs in an even position of the input list L, i.e., a call of the form $new4(A, B, [C|L_2])$ is executed. In Case (1) program $EvenOdd_{det}$ checks that $B \geq C$ holds and then updates the value of the maximum number occurring in an odd position with the maximum between A and C. In Case (2) program $EvenOdd_{det}$ checks that $C \geq A$ holds and then updates the value of the minimum number occurring in an even position with the minimum between B and C.

5.2 Program Synthesis: The N-queens Problem

The N-queens problem has been often considered in the literature for presenting various programming techniques, such as recursion and backtracking. We consider it here as an example of the program synthesis technique, as it has been done in [41]. Our derivation is different from the one presented in [41], because the derivation in [41] makes use of the unfold/fold transformation rules for definite programs together with an *ad hoc* transformation rule (called *negation technique*) for transforming general programs (with negation) into definite programs. In contrast, we use unfold/fold transformation rules for general programs, and in particular, our negative unfolding rule of Section 3.

The N-queens problem can be informally specified as follows. We are required to place $N(\geq 0)$ queens on an $N \times N$ chess board, so that no two queens attack each other, that is, they do not lie on the same row, column, or diagonal. A board configuration with this property is said to be *safe*. By using the fact that no two queens should lie on the same row, we represent an $N \times N$ chess board as a list L of N positive integers: the k-th element on L represents the column of the queen on row k.

In order to give a formal specification of the N-queens problem we follow the approach presented in [32], which is based on first order logic. We introduce the following constraint logic program:

$P:$ $nat(0) \leftarrow$
$nat(N) \leftarrow N = M+1 \wedge M \geq 0 \wedge nat(M)$
$nat\_list([\,]) \leftarrow$
$nat\_list([H|T]) \leftarrow nat(H) \wedge nat\_list(T)$
$length([\,], 0) \leftarrow$
$length([H|T], N) \leftarrow N = M+1 \wedge M \geq 0 \wedge length(T, M)$
$member(X, [H|T]) \leftarrow X = H$
$member(X, [H|T]) \leftarrow member(X, T)$
$in\_range(X, M, N) \leftarrow X = N \wedge M \leq N$
$in\_range(X, M, N) \leftarrow N = K+1 \wedge M \leq K \wedge in\_range(X, M, K)$
$occurs(X, I, [H|T]) \leftarrow I = 1 \wedge X = H$
$occurs(X, I+1, [H|T]) \leftarrow I \geq 1 \wedge occurs(X, I, T)$

and the following first order formula:

$\varphi(N, L):$ $nat(N) \wedge nat\_list(L) \wedge$ (1)
$length(L, N) \wedge \forall X\, (member(X, L) \rightarrow in\_range(X, 1, N)) \wedge$ (2)
$\forall A, B, M, N\, ((1 \leq M \wedge M \leq N \wedge occurs(A, M, L) \wedge occurs(B, N, L))$ (3)
$\rightarrow (A \neq B \wedge A - B \neq N - M \wedge B - A \neq N - M))$ (4)

In the above program and formula $in\_range(X, M, N)$ holds iff $X \in \{M, M+1, \ldots, N\}$ and $N \geq 0$. The other predicates have been defined in previous programs or do not require explanation. Now we define the relation $queens(N, L)$ where N is a nonnegative integer and L is a list of positive integers, as follows:

$queens(N, L)$ iff $M(P) \models \varphi(N, L)$

Line (2) of the formula $\varphi(N, L)$ above specifies a chess board as a list of N integers each of which is in the range $[1, \ldots, N]$. If $N = 0$ the list is empty. Lines (3) and (4) of $\varphi(N, L)$ specify the safety property of board configurations. Now, we would like to derive a constraint logic program R which computes the relation $queens(N, L)$, that is, R should define a predicate $queens(N, L)$ such that:

(π) $M(R) \models queens(N, L)$ iff $M(P) \models \varphi(N, L)$

Following the approach presented in [32], we start from the formula (called a *statement*) $queens(N, L) \leftarrow \varphi(N, L)$ and, by applying a variant of the *Lloyd-Topor transformation* [26], we derive the following stratified logic program:

F : 1. $queens(N, L) \leftarrow nat(N) \wedge nat\_list(L) \wedge length(L, N) \wedge$
$\qquad\qquad \neg aux1(L, N) \wedge \neg aux2(L)$

   2. $aux1(L, N) \leftarrow member(X, L) \wedge \neg in\_range(X, 1, N)$

   3. $aux2(L) \leftarrow 1 \leq K \wedge K \leq M \wedge$
$\qquad\qquad \neg(A \neq B \wedge A - B \neq M - K \wedge B - A \neq M - K) \wedge$
$\qquad\qquad occurs(A, K, L) \wedge occurs(B, M, L)$

This variant of the Lloyd-Topor transformation is a fully automatic transformation, but it cannot be performed by using our transformation rules, because it operates on first order formulas. It can be shown that this variant of the Lloyd-Topor transformation preserves the perfect model semantics and, thus, we have that: $M(P \cup F) \models queens(N, L)$ iff $M(P) \models \varphi(N, L)$.

The derived program $P \cup F$ is not very satisfactory from a computational point of view because, when using SLDNF resolution with the left-to-right selection rule, it may not terminate for calls of the form $queens(n, L)$ where n is a nonnegative integer and L is a variable. Thus, the process of program synthesis proceeds by applying the transformation rules listed in Section 3, thereby transforming program $P \cup F$ into a program R such that: (i) Property (π) holds, (ii) R is a definite program, and (iii) R terminates for all calls of the form $queens(n, L)$, where n is any nonnegative integer and L is a variable. Actually, the derivation of the final program R is performed by constructing two transformation sequences: (i) a first one, which starts from the initial program P, introduces clauses 2 and 3 by definition introduction, and ends with a program Q, and (ii) a second one, which starts from program Q, introduces clause 1 by definition introduction, and ends with program R.

We will illustrate the application of the transformation rules for deriving program R without discussing in detail how this derivation can be performed in an automatic way using a particular strategy. As already mentioned, the design of suitable transformation strategies for the automation of program derivations for constraint logic programs, is beyond the scope of the present paper.

The program transformation process starts off from program $P \cup \{2, 3\}$ by transforming clauses 2 and 3 into a set of clauses without local variables, so that they can be subsequently used for unfolding clause 1 w.r.t. $\neg aux1(L, N)$ and $\neg aux2(L)$ (see the negative unfolding rule R4).

By positive unfolding, replacement, and positive folding, from clause 2 we derive:

   4. $aux1([H|T], N) \leftarrow \neg in\_range(X, 1, N)$

   5. $aux1([H|T], N) \leftarrow aux1(T, N)$

Similarly, by positive unfolding, replacement, and positive folding, from clause 3 we derive:

   6. $aux2([A|T]) \leftarrow M \geq 1 \wedge \neg(A \neq B \wedge A - B \neq M \wedge B - A \neq M) \wedge$
$\qquad\qquad occurs(B, M, T)$

   7. $aux2([A|T]) \leftarrow aux2(T)$

In order to eliminate the local variables B and M occurring in clause 6, by the definition introduction rule we introduce the following new clause, whose body is a generalization of the body of clause 6:

8. $new1(A, T, K) \leftarrow M \geq 1 \wedge \neg(A \neq B \wedge A - B \neq M + K \wedge B - A \neq M + K) \wedge$
    $occurs(B, M, T)$

By replacement and positive folding, from clause 6 we derive:

6f. $aux2([A|T]) \leftarrow new1(A, T, 0)$

Now, by positive unfolding, replacement, and positive folding, from clause 8 we derive:

9. $new1(A, [B|T], K) \leftarrow \neg(A \neq B \wedge A - B \neq K + 1 \wedge B - A \neq K + 1)$
10. $new1(A, [B|T], K) \leftarrow new1(A, T, K + 1)$

The program, call it Q, derived so far is $P \cup \{4, 5, 6f, 7, 9, 10\}$, and clauses 4, 5, 6f, 7, 9, and 10 have no local variables.

Now we construct a new transformation sequence which takes Q as initial program. We start off by applying the definition introduction rule and adding clause 1 to program Q. Our objective is to transform clause 1 into a set of definite clauses. We first apply the definition rule and we introduce the following clause, whose body is a generalization of the body of clause 1:

11. $new2(N, L, K) \leftarrow nat(M) \wedge nat\_list(L) \wedge length(L, M) \wedge$
    $\neg aux1(L, N) \wedge \neg aux2(L) \wedge N = M + K$

By replacement and positive folding, from clause 11 we derive:

1f. $queens(N, L) \leftarrow new2(N, L, 0)$

By positive and negative unfolding, replacement, constraint addition, and positive folding, from clause 11 we derive:

12. $new2(N, [\,], K) \leftarrow N = K$
13. $new2(N, [H|T], K) \leftarrow N \geq K + 1 \wedge new2(N, T, K + 1) \wedge$
    $nat(H) \wedge nat\_list(T) \wedge in\_range(H, 1, N) \wedge$
    $\neg new1(H, T, 0)$

In order to derive a definite program we introduce a new predicate $new3$ defined by the following clause:

14. $new3(A, T, N, M) \leftarrow nat(A) \wedge nat\_list(T) \wedge in\_range(A, 1, N) \wedge$
    $\neg new1(A, T, M)$

We fold clause 13 using clause 14 and we derive the following definite clause:

13f. $new2(N, [H|T], K) \leftarrow N \geq K + 1 \wedge new2(N, T, K + 1) \wedge new3(H, T, N, 0)$

By positive and negative unfolding, replacement, and positive folding, from clause 14 we derive the following definite clauses:

15. $new3(A, [\,], N, M) \leftarrow in\_range(A, 1, N) \wedge nat(A)$
16. $new3(A, [B|T], N, M) \leftarrow A \neq B \wedge A - B \neq M + 1 \wedge B - A \neq M + 1 \wedge$
    $nat(B) \wedge new3(A, T, N, M + 1)$

Finally, by assuming that the set of predicates of interest is the singleton $\{queens\}$, by definition elimination we derive the following program:

R: 1f. $queens(N, L) \leftarrow new2(N, L, 0)$
  12. $new2(N, [\,], K) \leftarrow N = K$
  13f. $new2(N, [H|T], K) \leftarrow N \geq K+1 \land new2(N, T, K+1) \land new3(H, T, N, 0)$
  15. $new3(A, [\,], N, M) \leftarrow in\_range(A, 1, N) \land nat(A)$
  16. $new3(A, [B|T], N, M) \leftarrow A \neq B \land A - B \neq M+1 \land B - A \neq M+1 \land$
        $nat(B) \land new3(A, T, N, M+1)$

together with the clauses for the predicates in_range and nat.

Program R is a definite program and, by Theorem 3, we have that $M(R) \models queens(N, L)$ iff $M(P \cup F \cup Defs) \models queens(N, L)$, where $F \cup Defs$ is the set of all clauses introduced by the definition introduction rule during the transformation sequences from P to R. Since $queens$ does not depend on $Defs$ in $P \cup F \cup Defs$, we have that $M(R) \models queens(N, L)$ iff $M(P \cup F) \models queens(N, L)$ and, thus, Property (π) holds. Moreover, it can be shown that R terminates for all calls of the form $queens(n, L)$, where n is any nonnegative integer and L is a variable.

Notice that program R computes a solution of the N-queens problem in a clever way: each time a queen is placed on the board, program R checks that it does not attack any other queen already placed on the board.

5.3   Program Specialization: Derivation of Counter Machines from Constrained Regular Expressions

Given a set $\mathcal{N}$ of variables ranging over natural numbers, a set $\mathcal{C}$ of constraints over natural numbers, and a set K of identifiers, we define a *constrained regular expression* e over the alphabet $\{a, b\}$ as follows:

$$e ::= \ a \mid b \mid e_1 \cdot e_2 \mid e_1 + e_2 \mid e^\wedge N \mid not(e) \mid k$$

where $N \in \mathcal{N}$ and $k \in K$. An identifier $k \in K$ is defined by a *definition* of the form $k \equiv (c : e)$, where $c \in \mathcal{C}$ and e is a constrained regular expression. For instance, the set $\{a^m b^n \mid m = n \geq 0\}$ of strings in $\{a, b\}^*$ is denoted by the identifier k which is defined by the following definition:

$$k \equiv (M = N : (a^\wedge M \cdot b^\wedge N)).$$

Obviously, constrained regular expressions may denote languages which are *not* regular.

Given a string S and a constrained regular expression e, the following locally stratified program P checks whether or not S belongs to the language denoted by e. We assume that constraints are definable as conjunctions of equalities and disequalities over natural numbers.

P : $string([\,]) \leftarrow$
    $string([a|S]) \leftarrow string(S)$
    $string([b|S]) \leftarrow string(S)$
    $symbol(a) \leftarrow$
    $symbol(b) \leftarrow$
    $app([\,], L, L) \leftarrow$
    $app([A|X], Y, [A|Z]) \leftarrow app(X, Y, Z)$
    $in\_language([A], A) \leftarrow symbol(A)$

$$in\_language(S, (E1 \cdot E2)) \leftarrow app(S1, S2, S) \wedge$$
$$in\_language(S1, E1) \wedge in\_language(S2, E2)$$
$$in\_language(S, E1 + E2) \leftarrow in\_language(S, E1)$$
$$in\_language(S, E1 + E2) \leftarrow in\_language(S, E2)$$
$$in\_language(S, not(E)) \leftarrow \neg\, in\_language(S, E)$$
$$in\_language([\,], E^\wedge I) \leftarrow I = 0$$
$$in\_language(S, E^\wedge I) \leftarrow I = J + 1 \wedge J \geq 0 \wedge app(S1, S2, S) \wedge$$
$$in\_language(S1, E) \wedge in\_language(S2, E^\wedge J)$$
$$in\_language(S, K) \leftarrow (K \equiv (C : E)) \wedge solve(C) \wedge in\_language(S, E)$$
$$solve(X = Y) \leftarrow X = Y$$
$$solve(X \geq Y) \leftarrow X \geq Y$$
$$solve(C_1 \wedge C_2) \leftarrow solve(C_1) \wedge solve(C_2)$$

For example, in order to check whether a string S does *not* belong to the language denoted by k, where k is defined by the following definition: $k \equiv (M = N : (a^\wedge M \cdot b^\wedge N))$, we add to program P the clause:

$$(k \equiv (M = N : (a^\wedge M \cdot b^\wedge N))) \leftarrow$$

and we evaluate a query of the form:

$$string(S) \wedge in\_language(S, not(k))$$

Now, if we want to specialize program P w.r.t. this query, we introduce the new definition:

  1. $new1(S) \leftarrow string(S) \wedge in\_language(S, not(k))$

By unfolding clause 1 we get:

  2. $new1(S) \leftarrow string(S) \wedge \neg\, in\_language(S, k)$

We cannot perform the negative unfolding of clause 2 w.r.t. $\neg\, in\_language(S, k)$ because of the local variables in the clauses for $in\_language(S, k)$. In order to derive a predicate which is equivalent to $in\_language(S, k)$ and is defined by clauses without local variables, we introduce the following clause:

  3. $new2(S) \leftarrow in\_language(S, k)$

By unfolding clause 3 we get:

  4. $new2(S) \leftarrow M = N \wedge app(S1, S2, S) \wedge$
$$in\_language(S1, a^\wedge M) \wedge in\_language(S2, b^\wedge N)$$

We generalize clause 4 and we introduce the following clause 5:

  5. $new3(S, I) \leftarrow M = N + I \wedge app(S1, S2, S) \wedge$
$$in\_language(S1, a^\wedge M) \wedge in\_language(S2, b^\wedge N)$$

By unfolding clause 5, performing replacements based on laws of constraints, and folding, we get:

  6. $new3(S, N) \leftarrow in\_language(S, b^\wedge N)$
  7. $new3([a|S], N) \leftarrow new3(S, N + 1)$

In order to fold clause 6 we introduce the following definition:

  8. $new4(S, N) \leftarrow in\_language(S, b^\wedge N)$

By unfolding clause 8, performing some replacements based on laws of constraints, and folding, we get:

    9. $new4([\,],0) \leftarrow$
    10. $new4([b|S],N) \leftarrow N \geq 1 \wedge new4(S,N-1)$

By negative folding of clause 2 and positive folding of clauses 4 and 6 we get the following program:

    2f. $new1(S) \leftarrow string(S) \wedge \neg new2(S)$
    4f. $new2(S) \leftarrow new3(S,0)$
    6f. $new3(S,N) \leftarrow new4(S,N)$
    7. $new3([a|S],N) \leftarrow new3(S,N+1)$
    9. $new4([\,],0) \leftarrow$
    10. $new4([b|S],N) \leftarrow N \geq 1 \wedge new4(S,N-1)$

Now from clause 2f, by positive and negative unfoldings, replacements based on laws of constraints, and folding, we get:

    11. $new1([a|S]) \leftarrow string(S) \wedge \neg new3(S,1)$
    12. $new1([b|S]) \leftarrow string(S)$

In order to fold clause 11 we introduce the following definition:

    13. $new5(S,N) \leftarrow string(S) \wedge \neg new3(S,N)$

By positive and negative unfolding and folding we get:

    14. $new5([\,],N) \leftarrow$
    15. $new5([a|S],N) \leftarrow new5(S,N+1)$
    16. $new5([a|S],N) \leftarrow string(S) \wedge \neg N \geq 1$
    17. $new5([b|S],N) \leftarrow string(S) \wedge \neg new4(S,N-1)$

In order to fold clause 17 we introduce the following definition:

    18. $new6(S,N) \leftarrow string(S) \wedge \neg new4(S,N)$

Now, starting from clause 18, by positive and negative unfolding, replacements based on laws of constraints, folding, and elimination of the predicates on which $new1$ does not depend, we get the following final, specialized program:

P_{spec} : 11f. $new1([a|S]) \leftarrow new5(S,1)$
      12. $new1([b|S]) \leftarrow string(S)$
      14. $new5([\,],N) \leftarrow$
      15. $new5([a|S],N) \leftarrow new5(S,N+1)$
      16. $new5([b|S],0) \leftarrow string(S)$
    17f. $new5([b|S],N) \leftarrow new6(S,N-1)$
      19. $new6([\,],N) \leftarrow N \neq 0$
      20. $new6([a|S],N) \leftarrow string(S)$
      21. $new6([b|S],0) \leftarrow string(S)$
      22. $new6([b|S],N) \leftarrow new6(S,N-1)$

This specialized program corresponds to a one-counter machine (that is, a pushdown automaton where the stack alphabet contains one letter only [5]) and it takes $O(n)$ time to test that a string of length n does *not* belong to the language $\{a^m \cdot b^n \mid m = n \geq 0\}$.

6   Related Work and Conclusions

During the last two decades various sets of unfold/fold transformation rules have been proposed for different classes of logic programs. The authors who first introduced the unfold/fold rules for logic programs were Tamaki and Sato in their seminal paper [44]. That paper presents a set of rules for transforming definite logic programs and it also presents the proof that those rules are correct w.r.t. the least Herbrand model semantics. Most of the subsequent papers in the field have followed Tamaki and Sato's approach in that: (i) the various sets of rules which have been published can be seen as extensions or variants of Tamaki and Sato's rules, and (ii) the techniques used for proving the correctness of the rules are similar to those used by Tamaki and Sato (the reader may look at the references given later in this section, and also at [29] for a survey). In the present paper we ourselves have followed Tamaki and Sato's approach, but we have considered the more complex framework of locally stratified constraint logic programs with the perfect model semantics.

Among the rules we have presented, the following ones were initially introduced in [44] (in the case of definite logic programs): (R1) definition introduction, restricted to one clause only (that is, with $m=1$), (R3) positive unfolding, (R5) positive folding, restricted to one clause only (that is, with $m=1$). Our rules of replacement, deletion of useless predicates, constraint addition, and constraint deletion (that is, rules R7, R8, R9, and R10, respectively) are extensions to the case of constraint logic programs with negation of the *goal replacement* and *clause addition/deletion* rules presented in [44]. In comparing the rules in [44] and the corresponding rules we have proposed, let us highlight also the following important difference. The goal replacement and clause addition/deletion of [44] are very general, but their applicability conditions are based on properties of the least Herbrand model and properties of the proof trees (such as goal equivalence or clause implication) which, in general, are very difficult to prove. On the contrary, (i) the applicability conditions of our replacement rule require the verification of (usually decidable) properties of the constraints, (ii) the property of being a useless predicate is decidable, because it refers to predicate symbols only (and not to the value of their arguments), and (iii) the applicability conditions for constraint addition and constraint deletion can be verified in most cases by program analysis techniques based on abstract interpretation [10].

For the correctness theorem (see Theorem 3) relative to admissible transformation sequences we have followed Tamaki and Sato's approach, and as in [44], the correctness is ensured by assuming the validity of some suitable conditions on the construction of the transformation sequences.

Let us now relate our work here to that of other authors who have extended in several ways the work by Tamaki and Sato and, in particular, those who have extended it to the cases of: (i) general logic programs, and (ii) constraint logic programs.

Tamaki and Sato's unfolding and folding rules have been extended to general logic programs (without constraints) by Seki. He proved his extended rules correct w.r.t. various semantics, including the perfect model semantics [42,43].

Building upon previous work for definite logic programs reported in [17,22,38], paper [37] extended Seki's folding rule by allowing: (i) *multiple* folding, that is, one can fold m (≥ 1) clauses at a time using a definition consisting of m clauses, and (ii) *recursive* folding, that is, the definition used for folding can contain recursive clauses.

Multiple folding can be performed by applying our rule R5, but recursive folding *cannot*. Indeed, by rule R5 we can fold using a definition introduced by rule R1, and this rule does *not* allow the introduction of recursive clauses. Thus, in this respect the folding rule presented in this paper is less powerful than the folding rule considered in [37]. On the other hand, the set of rules presented here is more powerful than the one in [37] because it includes negative unfolding (R4) and negative folding (R6). These two rules are very useful in practice, and both are needed for the program derivation examples we have given in Section 5. They are also needed in the many examples of program verification presented in [13]. For reasons of simplicity, we have presented our non-recursive version of the positive folding rule because it has much simpler applicability conditions. In particular, the notion of admissible transformation sequence is much simpler for non-recursive folding. We leave for future research the problem of studying the correctness of a set of transformation rules which includes positive and negative unfolding, as well as recursive positive folding and recursive negative folding.

Negative unfolding and negative folding were also considered in our previous work [32]. The present paper extends the transformation rules presented in [32] by adapting them to a logic language with constraints. Moreover, in [32] we did not present the proof of correctness of the transformation rules and we only showed some applications of our transformation rules to theorem proving and program synthesis.

In [40] Sato proposed a set of transformation rules for *first order programs*, that is, for a logic language that extends general logic programs by allowing arbitrary first order formulas in the bodies of the clauses. However, the semantics considered in [40] is based on a three valued logic with the three truth values *true*, *false*, and *undefined* (corresponding to non terminating computations). Thus, the results presented in [40] cannot be directly compared with ours. In particular, for instance, the rule for eliminating useless predicates (R8) does not preserve the three valued semantics proposed in [40], because this rule may transform a program that does not terminate for a given query, into a program that terminates for that query. Moreover, the conditions for the applicability of the folding rule given in [40] are based on the chosen three valued logic and cannot be compared with those presented in this paper.

Various other sets of transformation rules for general logic programs (including several variants of the goal replacement rule) have been proved correct w.r.t. other semantics, such as, the operational semantics based on SLDNF resolution [16,42], Clark's completion [16], and Kunen's and Fitting's three valued extensions of Clark's completion [8]. We will not enter into a detailed comparison with these works here. It will suffice to say that these works are not directly comparable with ours because of the different set of rules (in particular, none of these works considers the negative unfolding rule) and the different semantics considered.

The unfold/fold transformation rules have also been extended to constraint logic programs in [7,11,12,27]. Papers [7,11] deal with definite programs, while [27] considers locally stratified programs and proves that, with suitable restrictions, the unfolding and folding rules preserve the perfect model semantics. Our correctness result presented here extends that in [27] because: (i) the rules of [27] include neither negative unfolding nor negative folding, and (ii) the folding rule of [27] is *reversible*, that is, it can only be applied for folding a set of clauses in a program P by using a set of clauses that occur in P. As already mentioned in Section 3, our folding rule is not reversible, because we may fold clauses in program P_k of a transformation sequence by using definitions occurring in $Defs_k$, but possibly not in P_k. Reversibility is a very strong limitation, because it does not allow the derivation of recursive clauses from non-recursive clauses. In particular, the derivations presented in our examples of Section 5 could not be performed by using the reversible folding rule of [27].

Finally, [12] proposes a set of transformation rules for locally stratified constraint logic programs tailored to a specific task, namely, program specialization and its application to the verification of infinite state reactive systems. Due to their specific application, the transformation rules of [12] are much more restricted than the ones presented here. In particular, by using the rules of [12]: (i) we can only introduce *constrained atomic definitions*, that is, definitions that consist of single clauses whose body is a constrained atom, (ii) we can unfold clauses w.r.t. a negated atom only if that atom succeeds or fails in one step, and (iii) we can apply the positive and negative folding rules by using constrained atomic definitions only.

We envisage several lines for further development of the work presented in this paper. As a first step forward, one could design strategies for automating the application of the transformation rules proposed here. In our examples of Section 5 we have demonstrated that some strategies already considered in the literature for the case of definite programs, can be extended to general constraint logic programs. This extension can be done, in particular, for the following strategies: (i) the elimination of local variables [34], (ii) the derivation of deterministic programs [33], and (iii) the rule-based program specialization [24].

It has been pointed out by recent studies that there is a strict relationship between program transformation and various other methodologies for program development and software verification (see, for instance, [13,15,25,30,31,36]). Thus, strategies for the automatic application of transformation rules can be exploited in the design of automatic techniques in these related fields and, in particular, in program synthesis and theorem proving. We believe that transformation methodologies for logic and constraint languages can form the basis of a very powerful framework for machine assisted software development.

Acknowledgements

We would like to thank Maurice Bruynooghe and Kung-Kiu Lau for inviting us to contribute to this volume. We would like also to acknowledge the very stimulating conversations we have had over the years with the members of the LOPSTR community since the beginning of the series of the LOPSTR workshops. Finally, we express our thanks to the anonymous referees for their helpful comments and suggestions.

7   Appendices

7.1   Appendix A

In this Appendix A we will use the fact that, given any two atoms A and B, and any valuation v, if $\sigma(v(A)) \geq \sigma(v(B))$ then for every substitution ϑ, $\sigma(v(A\vartheta)) \geq \sigma(v(B\vartheta))$. The same holds with $>$, instead of $\geq$.

Proof of Proposition 1. [Preservation of Local Stratification]. We will prove that, for $k = 0, \ldots, n$, P_k is locally stratified w.r.t. σ by induction on k.

Base case ($k = 0$). By hypothesis P_0 is locally stratified w.r.t. σ.

Induction step. We assume that P_k is locally stratified w.r.t. σ and we show that P_{k+1} is locally stratified w.r.t. σ. We proceed by cases depending on the transformation rule which is applied to derive P_{k+1} from P_k.

Case 1. Program P_{k+1} is derived by definition introduction (rule R1). We have that $P_{k+1} = P_k \cup \{\delta_1, \ldots, \delta_m\}$, where P_k is locally stratified w.r.t. σ by the inductive hypothesis and $\{\delta_1, \ldots, \delta_m\}$ is locally stratified w.r.t. σ by Condition (iv) of R1. Thus, P_{k+1} is locally stratified w.r.t. σ.

Case 2. Program P_{k+1} is derived by definition elimination (rule R2). Then P_{k+1} is locally stratified w.r.t. σ because $P_{k+1} \subseteq P_k$.

Case 3. Program P_{k+1} is derived by positive unfolding (rule R3). We have that $P_{k+1} = (P_k - \{\gamma\}) \cup \{\eta_1, \ldots, \eta_m\}$, where γ is a clause in P_k of the form $H \leftarrow c \wedge G_L \wedge A \wedge G_R$ and clauses $\eta_1, \ldots, \eta_m$ are derived by unfolding γ w.r.t. A. Since, by the induction hypothesis, $(P_k - \{\gamma\})$ is locally stratified w.r.t. σ, it remains to show that, for every valuation v, for $i = 1, \ldots, m$, clause $v(\eta_i)$ is locally stratified w.r.t. σ. Take any valuation v. For $i = 1, \ldots, m$, there exists a clause γ_i in a variant of P_k of the form $K_i \leftarrow c_i \wedge B_i$ such that η_i is of the form $H \leftarrow c \wedge A = K_i \wedge c_i \wedge G_L \wedge B_i \wedge G_R$. By the inductive hypothesis, $v(H \leftarrow c \wedge G_L \wedge A \wedge G_R)$ and $v(K_i \leftarrow c_i \wedge B_i)$ are locally stratified w.r.t. σ. We consider two cases: (a) $\mathcal{D} \models \neg v(c \wedge A = K_i \wedge c_i)$ and (b) $\mathcal{D} \models v(c \wedge A = K_i \wedge c_i)$. In Case (a), $v(\eta_i)$ is locally stratified w.r.t. σ by definition. In Case (b), we have that: (i) $\mathcal{D} \models v(c)$, (ii) $\mathcal{D} \models v(A) = v(K_i)$, and (iii) $\mathcal{D} \models v(c_i)$. Let us consider a literal $v(L)$ occurring in the body of $v(\eta_i)$. If $v(L)$ is an atom occurring positively in $v(G_L \wedge G_R)$ then $\sigma(v(H)) \geq \sigma(v(L))$ because $v(H \leftarrow c \wedge G_L \wedge A \wedge G_R)$ is locally stratified w.r.t. σ and $\mathcal{D} \models v(c)$. Similarly, if $v(L)$ is a negated atom occurring in $v(G_L \wedge G_R)$ then $\sigma(v(H)) > \sigma(\overline{v(L)})$. If $v(L)$ is an atom occurring positively in $v(B_i)$ then $\sigma(v(H)) \geq \sigma(v(L))$. Indeed:

$$\sigma(v(H)) \geq \sigma(v(A)) \quad \text{(because } v(H \leftarrow c \wedge G_L \wedge A \wedge G_R) \text{ is locally stratified}$$
$$\text{w.r.t. } \sigma \text{ and } \mathcal{D} \models v(c))$$
$$= \sigma(v(K_i)) \quad \text{(because } v(A) = v(K_i))$$
$$\geq \sigma(v(L)) \quad \text{(because } v(K_i \leftarrow c_i \wedge B_i) \text{ is locally stratified w.r.t. } \sigma$$
$$\text{and } \mathcal{D} \models v(c_i))$$

Similarly, if $v(L)$ is a negated atom occurring in $v(B)$ then $\sigma(v(H)) > \sigma(\overline{v(L)})$. Thus, the clause $v(\eta_i)$ is locally stratified w.r.t. σ.

Case 4. Program P_{k+1} is derived by negative unfolding (rule R4). As in Case 3, we have that $P_{k+1} = (P_k - \{\gamma\}) \cup \{\eta_1, \dots, \eta_s\}$, where γ is a clause in P_k of the form $H \leftarrow c \wedge G_L \wedge \neg A \wedge G_R$ and clauses $\eta_1, \dots, \eta_s$ are derived by negative unfolding γ w.r.t. $\neg A$. Since, by the induction hypothesis, $(P_k - \{\gamma\})$ is locally stratified w.r.t. σ, it remains to show that, for every valuation v, for $j = 1, \dots, s$, clause $v(\eta_j)$ is locally stratified w.r.t. σ. Take any valuation v. Let $K_1 \leftarrow c_1 \wedge B_1, \dots, K_m \leftarrow c_m \wedge B_m$ be the clauses in a variant of P_k such that, for $i = 1, \dots, m$, $\mathcal{D} \models \exists (c \wedge A = K_i \wedge c_i)$. Then, we have that, for $j = 1, \dots, s$, the clause $v(\eta_j)$ is of the form $v(H \leftarrow c \wedge e_j \wedge G_L \wedge Q_j \wedge G_R)$, where $v(Q_j)$ is a conjunction of literals. By the applicability conditions of the negative unfolding rule and by construction (see Steps 1–4 of R4), we have that there exist m substitutions $\vartheta_1, \dots, \vartheta_m$ such that the following two properties hold:

(P.1) for every literal $v(L)$ occurring in $v(Q_j)$ there exists a (positive or negative) literal $v(M)$ occurring in $v(B_i \vartheta_i)$ for some $i \in \{1, \dots, m\}$, such that $v(L)$ is $\overline{v(M)}$, and

(P.2) if $v(L)$ occurs in $v(Q_j)$ and $v(L)$ is $\overline{v(M)}$ with $v(M)$ occurring in $v(B_i \vartheta_i)$ for some $i \in \{1, \dots, m\}$, then $\mathcal{D} \models v((c \wedge e_j) \rightarrow (A = K_i \vartheta_i \wedge c_i \vartheta_i))$.

We will show that $v(\eta_j)$ is locally stratified w.r.t. σ. By the inductive hypothesis, we have that $v(H \leftarrow c \wedge G_L \wedge \neg A \wedge G_R)$ and $v(K_i \vartheta_i \leftarrow c_i \vartheta_i \wedge B_i \vartheta_i)$ are locally stratified w.r.t. σ.

We consider two cases: (a) $\mathcal{D} \models \neg v(c \wedge e_j)$ and (b) $\mathcal{D} \models v(c \wedge e_j)$. In Case (a), $v(\eta_j)$ is locally stratified w.r.t. σ by definition. In Case (b), take any literal $v(L)$ occurring in $v(Q_j)$. By Properties (P.1) and (P.2), $v(L)$ is $\overline{v(M)}$ for some $v(M)$ occurring in $v(B_i)$. We also have that: (i) $\mathcal{D} \models v(A) = v(K_i \vartheta_i)$ and (ii) $\mathcal{D} \models v(c_i \vartheta_i)$. Moreover $\mathcal{D} \models v(c)$, because we are in Case (b). Now, if $v(M)$ is a positive literal occurring in $v(B_i)$ we have:

$$\sigma(v(H)) > \sigma(v(A)) \quad \text{(because } v(H \leftarrow c \wedge G_L \wedge \neg A \wedge G_R) \text{ is locally stratified}$$
$$\text{w.r.t. } \sigma \text{ and } \mathcal{D} \models v(c))$$
$$= \sigma(v(K_i \vartheta_i)) \quad \text{(because } v(A) = v(K_i \vartheta_i))$$
$$(\dagger) \quad \geq \sigma(v(M)) \quad \text{(because } v(K_i \vartheta_i \leftarrow c_i \vartheta_i \wedge B_i \vartheta_i) \text{ is locally stratified}$$
$$\text{w.r.t. } \sigma \text{ and } \mathcal{D} \models v(c_i \vartheta_i)).$$

Thus, we get: $\sigma(v(H)) > \sigma(v(M))$, and we conclude that $v(\eta_j)$ is locally stratified w.r.t. σ. Similarly, if $v(M)$ is a negative literal occurring in $v(B_i \vartheta_i)$, we also get: $\sigma(v(H)) > \sigma(\overline{v(M)})$. (In particular, if $v(M)$ is a negative literal, at Point ($\dagger$) above, we have $\sigma(v(K_i \vartheta_i)) > \sigma(\overline{v(M)})$.) Thus, we also conclude that $v(\eta_j)$ is locally stratified w.r.t. σ.

Case 5. Program P_{k+1} is derived by positive folding (rule R5). For reasons of simplicity, we assume that we fold one clause only, that is, $m = 1$ in rule R5. The general case where $m \geq 1$ is analogous. We have that $P_{k+1} = (P_k - \{\gamma\}) \cup \{\eta\}$, where η is a clause of the form $H \leftarrow c \wedge G_L \wedge K\vartheta \wedge G_R$ derived by positive folding of clause γ of the form $H \leftarrow c \wedge d\vartheta \wedge G_L \wedge B\vartheta \wedge G_R$ using a clause δ of the form $K \leftarrow d \wedge B$ introduced by rule R1. We have to show that, for every valuation v, $v(H \leftarrow c \wedge G_L \wedge K\vartheta \wedge G_R)$ is locally stratified w.r.t. σ. By the inductive hypothesis, we have that: (i) for every valuation v, $v(\gamma)$ is locally stratified w.r.t. σ, and (ii) for every valuation v, $v(\delta)$ is locally stratified w.r.t. σ. Take any valuation v. There are two cases: (a) $\mathcal{D} \models \neg v(c)$ and (b) $\mathcal{D} \models v(c)$. In Case (a), $v(\eta)$ is locally stratified w.r.t. σ by definition. In Case (b), take any literal $v(L)$ occurring in $v(B\vartheta)$. Now, *either* (b1) $v(L)$ is a positive literal, *or* (b2) $v(L)$ is a negative literal. In Case (b1) there are two subcases: (b1.1) $\mathcal{D} \models \neg v(d\vartheta)$, and (b1.2) $\mathcal{D} \models v(d\vartheta)$. In Case (b1.1) by Condition (iv) of rule R1, $\sigma(v(K\vartheta)) = 0$ and thus, $\sigma(v(H)) \geq \sigma(v(K\vartheta))$. Hence, $v(\eta)$ is locally stratified w.r.t. σ. In Case (b1.2), we have that $\mathcal{D} \models v(c \wedge d\vartheta)$ and, by the inductive hypothesis, $\sigma(v(H)) \geq \sigma(v(L\vartheta))$. Thus, $\sigma(v(H)) \geq \sigma(v(K\vartheta))$, because by Condition (iv) of rule R1, $\sigma(v(K\vartheta))$ is the smallest ordinal α such that $\alpha \geq \sigma(v(L\vartheta))$. Thus, $v(\eta)$ is locally stratified w.r.t. σ.

Case (b2), when $v(L)$ is a negative literal occurring in $v(B\vartheta)$, has a proof similar to the one of Case (b1), except that $\sigma(v(H)) > \sigma(v(L\vartheta))$, instead of $\sigma(v(H)) \geq \sigma(v(L\vartheta))$.

Case 6. Program P_{k+1} is derived by negative folding (rule R6). We have that $P_{k+1} = (P_k - \{\gamma\}) \cup \{\eta\}$, where η is a clause of the form $H \leftarrow c \wedge d\vartheta \wedge G_L \wedge \neg K\vartheta \wedge G_R$ derived by negative folding of clause γ of the form $H \leftarrow c \wedge d\vartheta \wedge G_L \wedge \neg A\vartheta \wedge G_R$ using a clause δ of the form $K \leftarrow d \wedge A$ introduced by rule R1. We have to show that, for every valuation v, $v(\eta)$ is locally stratified w.r.t. σ. By the inductive hypothesis, we have that: (i) for every valuation v, $v(H \leftarrow c \wedge d\vartheta \wedge G_L \wedge \neg A\vartheta \wedge G_R)$ is locally stratified w.r.t. σ, and (ii) for every valuation v, $v(K \leftarrow d \wedge A)$ is locally stratified w.r.t. σ. Take any valuation v. There are two cases: (a) $\mathcal{D} \models \neg v(c \wedge d\vartheta)$, and (b) $\mathcal{D} \models v(c \wedge d\vartheta)$. In Case (a), $v(\eta)$ is locally stratified w.r.t. σ by definition. In Case (b), by the inductive hypothesis, we have only to show that $\sigma(v(H)) > \sigma(v(K\vartheta))$. Since $\mathcal{D} \models v(c \wedge d\vartheta)$, by the inductive hypothesis we have that $\sigma(v(H)) > \sigma(v(A\vartheta))$. By Condition (iv) of the rule R1, we have that $\sigma(v(H)) > \sigma(v(K\vartheta))$. Hence, $v(\eta)$ is locally stratified w.r.t. σ.

Case 7. Program P_{k+1} is derived by replacement (rule R7). We have that $P_{k+1} = (P_k - \Gamma_1) \cup \Gamma_2$, where $(P_k - \Gamma_1)$ is locally stratified w.r.t. σ by the inductive hypothesis and Γ_2 is locally stratified w.r.t. σ by the applicability conditions of rule R7. Thus, P_{k+1} is locally stratified w.r.t. σ.

Case 8. Program P_{k+1} is derived by deletion of useless clauses (rule R8). P_{k+1} is locally stratified w.r.t. σ by the inductive hypothesis because $P_{k+1} \subseteq P_k$.

Case 9. Program P_{k+1} is derived by constraint addition (rule R9). We have that $P_{k+1} = (P_k - \{\gamma_1\}) \cup \{\gamma_2\}$, where $\gamma_2 : H \leftarrow c \wedge d \wedge G$ is the clause in P_{k+1} derived by constraint addition from the clause $\gamma_1 : H \leftarrow c \wedge G$ in P_k. For every valuation v, $v(H \leftarrow c \wedge d \wedge G)$ is locally stratified w.r.t. σ because: (i) by the induction hypothesis $v(H \leftarrow c \wedge G)$ is locally stratified w.r.t. σ and (ii) if $\mathcal{D} \models v(c \wedge d)$ then $\mathcal{D} \models v(c)$. Since, by the inductive hypothesis, $(P_k - \{\gamma_1\})$ is locally stratified w.r.t. σ, also P_{k+1} is locally stratified w.r.t. σ.

Case 10. Program P_{k+1} is derived by constraint deletion (rule R10). We have that $P_{k+1} = (P_k - \{\gamma_1\}) \cup \{\gamma_2\}$, where $\gamma_2 \colon H \leftarrow c \wedge G$ is the clause in P_{k+1} derived by constraint deletion from clause $\gamma_1 \colon H \leftarrow c \wedge d \wedge G$ in P_k. By the applicability conditions of R10, γ is locally stratified w.r.t. σ. Since, by the inductive hypothesis, $(P_k - \{\gamma_1\})$ is locally stratified w.r.t. σ, also P_{k+1} is locally stratified w.r.t. σ.

Finally, $P_0 \cup Defs_n$ is locally stratified w.r.t. σ by the hypothesis that P_0 is locally stratified w.r.t. σ and by Condition (iv) of rule R1.   □

7.2 Appendix B

In the proofs of Appendices B and C we use the following notions. Given a clause $\gamma \colon H \leftarrow c \wedge L_1 \wedge \ldots \wedge L_m$ and a valuation v such that $\mathcal{D} \models v(c)$, we denote by γ_v the clause $v(H \leftarrow L_1 \wedge \ldots \wedge L_m)$. We define $ground(\gamma) = \{\gamma_v \mid v$ is a valuation and $\mathcal{D} \models v(c)\}$. Given a set Γ of clauses, we define $ground(\Gamma) = \bigcup_{\gamma \in \Gamma} ground(\gamma)$.

Proof of Proposition 3. Recall that $P_0, \ldots, P_i$ is constructed by $i \, (\geq 0)$ applications of the definition rule, that is, $P_i = P_0 \cup Defs_i$, and $P_i, \ldots, P_j$ is constructed by applying once the positive unfolding rule to each clause in $Defs_i$. Let σ be the fixed stratification function considered at the beginning of the construction of the transformation sequence. By Proposition 1, each program in the sequence $P_i, \ldots, P_j$ is locally stratified w.r.t. σ.

Let us consider a ground atom A. By complete induction on the ordinal $\sigma(A)$ we prove that, for $k = i, \ldots, j-1$, there exists a proof tree for A and P_k iff there exists a proof tree for A and P_{k+1}. The inductive hypothesis is:

(I1) for every ground atom A', if $\sigma(A') < \sigma(A)$ then there exists a proof tree for A' and P_k iff there exists a proof tree for A' and P_{k+1}.

(*If Part*) We consider a proof tree U for A and P_{k+1}, and we show that we can construct a proof tree T for A and P_k. We proceed by complete induction on $size(U)$. The inductive hypothesis is:

(I2) given any proof tree U_1 for a ground atom A_1 and P_{k+1}, if $size(U_1) < size(U)$ then there exists a proof tree T_1 for A_1 and P_k.

Let γ be a clause of P_{k+1} and let $\gamma_v \colon A \leftarrow L_1 \wedge \ldots \wedge L_r$ be the clause in $ground(\gamma)$ used at the root of U. Thus, $L_1, \ldots, L_r$ are the children of A in U. For $h = 1, \ldots, r$, if L_h is an atom then the subtree U_h of U rooted at L_h is a proof tree for L_h and P_{k+1}. Since $size(U_h) < size(U)$, by the inductive hypothesis (I2) there exists a proof tree T_h for L_h and P_k. For $h = 1, \ldots, r$, if L_h is a negated atom $\neg A_h$ then, by the definition of proof tree, there exists no proof tree for A_h and P_{k+1}. Since σ is a local stratification for P_{k+1}, we have that $\sigma(A_h) < \sigma(A)$ and, by the inductive hypothesis (I1) there exists no proof tree for A_h and P_k.

Now, we proceed by cases.

Case 1. $\gamma \in P_k$. We construct T as follows. The root of T is A. We use γ_v: $A \leftarrow L_1 \wedge \ldots \wedge L_r$ to construct the children of A. If $r = 0$ then *true* is the only child of A in T, and T is a proof tree for A and P_k. Otherwise $r \geq 1$ and, for $h = 1, \ldots, r$, if L_h is an atom A_h then T_h is the subtree of T at A_h, and if L_h is a negated atom then L_h is a leaf of T. By construction we have that T is a proof tree for A and P_k.

Case 2. $\gamma \notin P_k$ and $\gamma \in P_{k+1}$ because γ is derived by positive unfolding. Thus, there exist: a clause α in P_k of the form $H \leftarrow c \wedge G_L \wedge A_S \wedge G_R$ and a variant β of a clause in P_k of the form $K \leftarrow d \wedge B$ such that clause γ is of the form $H \leftarrow c \wedge A_S = K \wedge d \wedge G_L \wedge B \wedge G_R$. Thus, (i) $v(H) = A$, (ii) $\mathcal{D} \models v(c \wedge A_S = K \wedge d)$, and (iii) $v(G_L \wedge B \wedge G_R) = L_1, \ldots, L_r$. By (ii) we have that $\alpha_v \in ground(P_k)$ and $\beta_v \in ground(P_k)$. (Notice that, since β is a variant of a clause in P_k, then $\beta_v \in ground(P_k)$.)

We construct T as follows. The root of T is A. We use α_v to construct the children of A and then we use β_v to construct the children of A_S. The leaves of the tree constructed in this way are $L_1, \ldots, L_r$. If $r = 0$ then *true* is the only leaf of T, and T is a proof tree for A and P_k. Otherwise $r \geq 1$ and, for $h = 1, \ldots, r$, if L_h is an atom then T_h is the subtree of T rooted at L_h, and if L_h is a negated atom then L_h is a leaf of T. By construction we have that T is a proof tree for A and P_k.

(*Only-if Part*) We consider a proof tree T for a ground atom A and program P_k, for $k = i, \ldots j-1$, and we show that we can construct a proof tree U for A and P_{k+1}. We proceed by complete induction on $size(T)$. The inductive hypothesis is:

(I3) given any proof tree T_1 for a ground atom A_1 and P_k, if $size(T_1) < size(T)$ then there exists a proof tree U_1 for A_1 and P_{k+1}.

Let γ be a clause of P_k and let γ_v: $A \leftarrow L_1 \wedge \ldots \wedge L_r$ be the clause in $ground(\gamma)$ used at the root of T. Now we proceed by cases.

Case 1. $\gamma \in P_{k+1}$. We construct the proof tree U for A and P_{k+1} as follows. We use γ_v to construct the children $L_1, \ldots, L_r$ of the root A. If $r = 0$ then *true* is the only child of A in U, and U is a proof tree for A and P_{k+1}. Otherwise, $r \geq 1$ and, for $h = 1, \ldots, r$, if L_h is an atom, we consider the subtree T_h of T rooted at L_h. We have that T_h is a proof tree for L_h and P_k with $size(T_h) < size(T)$ and, therefore, by the inductive hypothesis (I3), there exists a proof tree U_h for L_h and P_{k+1}. For $h = 1, \ldots, r$, if L_h is a negated atom $\neg A_h$, then $\sigma(A) > \sigma(A_h)$ because σ is a stratification function for P_k. Thus, by the inductive hypothesis (I1) we have that there is no proof tree for A_h and P_{k+1}. The construction of U continues as follows. For $h = 1, \ldots, r$, if L_h is an atom then we use U_h as a subtree of U rooted at L_h and, if L_h is a negated atom, then L_h is a leaf of U. Thus, by construction we have that U is a proof tree for A and P_{k+1}.

Case 2. $\gamma \in P_k$ and $\gamma \notin P_{k+1}$ because γ has been unfolded w.r.t. an atom in its body. Let us assume that γ is of the form $H \leftarrow c \wedge G_L \wedge A_S \wedge G_R$ and γ has been unfolded w.r.t. A_S. We have that: (i) $v(H) = A$, (ii) $\mathcal{D} \models v(c)$, and (iii) the ground literals $L_1, \ldots, L_r$ such that $L_1 \wedge \ldots \wedge L_r = v(G_L \wedge A_S \wedge G_R)$ are the children of A in T. Let β: $K \leftarrow d \wedge B$ be the clause in P_k which has been used for constructing the children of $v(A_S)$ in T. Thus, there exists a valuation v' such that: (iv) $v(A_S) = v'(K)$, (v) $\mathcal{D} \models v'(d)$, and (vi) the literals in $v'(B)$ are the children of $v(A_S)$ in T. Without loss of generality we may assume that γ and β have no variables in common and $v = v'$. Thus, the ground literals $M_1, \ldots, M_s$ such that $M_1 \wedge \ldots \wedge M_s = v(G_L \wedge B \wedge G_R)$ are descendants of A in T. For $h = 1, \ldots, s$, if M_h is an atom, let us consider the subtree T_h of T rooted at M_h. We have that T_h is a proof tree for M_h and P_k with $size(T_h) < size(T)$ and, therefore, by the inductive hypothesis (I3), there exists a proof tree U_h for M_h and P_{k+1}. For $h = 1, \ldots, s$, if M_h is a negated atom $\neg A_h$ then M_h is a leaf of T and there exists no proof tree for A_h and P_k. Since σ is a stratification function for P_k, we have that $\sigma(A) > \sigma(A_h)$ and thus, by the inductive hypothesis (I1), there exists no proof tree for A_h and P_{k+1}.

Now let us consider the clause $\eta : H \leftarrow c \wedge A_S = K \wedge d \wedge G_L \wedge B \wedge G_R$. η is one of the clauses derived by unfolding γ because $\beta \in P_k$ and, by (ii), (iv), (v) and the assumption that $v = v'$, we have that $\mathcal{D} \models v(c \wedge A_S = K \wedge d)$ and hence $\mathcal{D} \models \exists (c \wedge A_S = K \wedge d)$. Thus, we construct a proof tree U for A and P_{k+1} as follows. Since $A = v(H)$ and $M_1 \wedge \ldots \wedge M_s = v(G_L \wedge B \wedge G_R)$, we can use η_v: $v(H \leftarrow G_L \wedge B \wedge G_R)$ to construct the children $M_1, \ldots, M_s$ of A in U. If $s = 0$ then $true$ is the only child of A in U, and U is a proof tree for A and P_{k+1}. Otherwise, $s \geq 1$ and, for $h = 1, \ldots, s$, if M_h is an atom then U_h is the proof tree rooted at M_h in U. If M_h is a negated atom then M_h is a leaf of U. The proof tree U is the proof tree for A and P_{k+1} to be constructed.   □

7.3   Appendix C

Proof of Proposition 5. Recall that the transformation sequence $P_0, \ldots, P_i,$ $\ldots, P_j, \ldots, P_m$ is constructed as follows (see Definition 3):
(1) the sequence $P_0, \ldots, P_i$, with $i \geq 0$, is constructed by applying i times the definition introduction rule, that is, $P_i = P_0 \cup Defs_i$;
(2) the sequence $P_i, \ldots, P_j$ is constructed by applying once the positive unfolding rule to each clause in $Defs_i$ which is used for applications of the folding rule in $P_j, \ldots, P_m$;
(3) the sequence $P_j, \ldots, P_m$, with $j \leq m$, is constructed by applying any rule, except the definition introduction and definition elimination rules.
Let σ be the fixed stratification function considered at the beginning of the construction of the transformation sequence. By Proposition 1, each program in the sequence $P_0 \cup Defs_i, \ldots, P_j, \ldots, P_m$ is locally stratified w.r.t. σ.

We will prove by induction on k that, for $k = j, \ldots, m$,
(*Soundness*) if there exists a proof tree for a ground atom A and P_k then there exists a proof tree for A and P_j, and
(*Completeness*) if there exists a P_j-consistent proof tree for a ground atom A and P_j then there exists a P_j-consistent proof tree for A and P_k.
The base case ($k = j$) is trivial.
For proving the induction step, consider any k in $\{j, \ldots, m-1\}$. We assume that the soundness and completeness properties hold for that k, and we prove that they hold for $k+1$. For the soundness property it is enough to prove that:

- if there exists a proof tree for a ground atom A and P_{k+1} then there exists a proof tree for A and P_k,

and for the completeness property it is enough to prove that:

- if there exists a P_j-consistent proof tree for a ground atom A and P_k then there exists a P_j-consistent proof tree for A and P_{k+1}.

We proceed by complete induction on the ordinal $\sigma(A)$ associated with the ground atom A. The inductive hypotheses are:

(IS) for every ground atom A' such that $\sigma(A') < \sigma(A)$, if there exists a proof tree for A' and P_{k+1} then there exists a proof tree for A' and P_k, and

(IC) for every ground atom A' such that $\sigma(A') < \sigma(A)$, if there exists a P_j-consistent proof tree for A' and P_k then there exists a P_j-consistent proof tree for A' and P_{k+1}.

By the inductive hypotheses on soundness and completeness for k, (IS), (IC), and Proposition 4, we have that:

(ISC) for every ground atom A' such that $\sigma(A') < \sigma(A)$, there exists a proof tree for A' and P_k iff there exists a proof tree for A' and P_{k+1}.

Now we give the proofs for the soundness and the completeness properties.

Proof of Soundness. Given a proof tree U for A and P_{k+1} we have to prove that there exists a proof tree T for A and P_k. The proof is by complete induction on $size(T)$. The inductive hypothesis is:

(Isize) Given any proof tree U' for a ground atom A' and P_{k+1}, if $size(U') < size(U)$ then there exists a proof tree T' for A' and P_k.

Let γ be a clause in P_{k+1} and v be a valuation. Let $\gamma_v \in ground(\gamma)$ be the ground clause of the form $A \leftarrow L_1 \wedge \ldots \wedge L_r$ used at the root of U. We proceed by considering the following cases: *either* (Case 1) γ belongs to P_k *or* (Case 2) γ does not belong to P_k and it has been derived from some clauses in P_k by applying a transformation rule among R3, R4, R5, R6, R7, R9, R10. (Recall that R1 and R2 are not applied in $P_j, \ldots, P_m$, and by R8 we delete clauses.)

The proof of Case 1 and the proofs of Case 2 for rules R3, R4, R9, and R10 are left to the reader. Now we present the proofs of Case 2 for rules R5, R6, and R7.

Case 2, rule R5. Clause γ is derived by positive folding. Let γ be derived by folding clauses $\gamma_1, \ldots, \gamma_m$ in P_k using clauses $\delta_1, \ldots, \delta_m$ where, for $i = 1, \ldots, m$, clause δ_i is of the form $K \leftarrow d_i \wedge B_i$ and clause γ_i is of the form $H \leftarrow c \wedge d_i\vartheta \wedge G_L \wedge B_i\vartheta \wedge G_R$, for a substitution ϑ satisfying Conditions (i) and (ii) given in (R5). Thus, γ is of the form: $H \leftarrow c \wedge G_L \wedge K\vartheta \wedge G_R$ and we have that: (a) $v(H) = A$, (b) $\mathcal{D} \models v(c)$, and (c) $v(G_L \wedge K\vartheta \wedge G_R) = L_1 \wedge \ldots \wedge L_r$. Since program P_{k+1} is locally stratified w.r.t. σ, by the inductive hypotheses (ISC) and (Isize) we have that: for $h = 1, \ldots, r$, if L_h is an atom then there exists a proof tree T_h for L_h and P_k, and if L_h is a negated atom $\neg A_h$ then there is no proof tree for A_h and P_k. The atom $v(K\vartheta)$ is one of the literals $L_1, \ldots, L_r$, say L_f, and thus, there exists a proof tree for $v(K\vartheta)$ and P_k. By the inductive hypothesis

(Soundness) for P_k and Proposition 3, there exists a proof tree for $v(K\vartheta)$ and P_i. Since $P_i = P_0 \cup Defs_n$ and $\delta_1, \ldots, \delta_m$ are all clauses in (a variant of) $P_0 \cup Defs_n$ which have the same predicate symbol as K, there exists $\delta_p \in \delta_1, \ldots, \delta_m$ such that δ_p is of the form $K \leftarrow d_p \wedge B_p$ and δ_p is used to construct the children of $v(K\vartheta)$ in the proof tree for $v(K\vartheta)$ and P_i. By Conditions (i) and (ii) on ϑ given in (R5), we have that: (d) $\mathcal{D} \models v(d_p\vartheta)$ and (e) $v(B_p\vartheta) = M_1 \wedge \ldots \wedge M_s$. By the definition of proof tree, for $h = 1, \ldots, s$, if M_h is an atom then there exists a proof tree for M_h and P_i, else if M_h is a negated atom $\neg E_h$ then there is no proof tree for E_h and P_i. By Propositions 3 and 4 and the inductive hypotheses (Soundness and Completeness) we have that, for $h = 1, \ldots, s$, if M_h is an atom then there exists a proof tree $\widehat{T_h}$ for M_h and P_k, else if M_h is a negated atom $\neg E_h$ then there is no proof tree for E_h and P_k.

Now we construct the proof tree T for A and P_k as follows. By (a), (b), and (d), we have that $v(H) = A$ and $\mathcal{D} \models v(c \wedge d_p\vartheta)$. Thus, we construct the children of A in T by using the clause $\gamma_p \colon H \leftarrow c \wedge d_p\vartheta \wedge G_L \wedge B_p\vartheta \wedge G_R$. Since $v(G_L \wedge B_p\vartheta \wedge G_R) = L_1 \wedge \ldots \wedge L_{f-1} \wedge M_1 \wedge \ldots \wedge M_s \wedge L_{f+1} \wedge \ldots \wedge L_r$, the children of A in T are: $L_1, \ldots, L_{f-1}, M_1, \ldots, M_s, L_{f+1}, \ldots, L_r$. By the applicability conditions of the positive folding rule, we have that $s > 0$ and A has a child different from the empty conjunction *true*. The children of A are constructed as follows. For $h = 1, \ldots, r$, if L_h is an atom then T_h is the subtree of T rooted in L_h, else if L_h is a negated atom then L_h is a leaf of T. For $h = 1, \ldots, s$, if M_h is an atom then $\widehat{T_h}$ is the subtree of T rooted in M_h, else if M_h is a negated atom then M_h is a leaf of T.

Case 2, rule R6. Clause γ is derived by negative folding. Let γ be derived by folding a clause α in P_k of the form $H \leftarrow c \wedge G_L \wedge \neg A_F\vartheta \wedge G_R$ by using a clause $\delta \in Defs_i$ of the form $K \leftarrow d \wedge A_F$. Thus, γ is of the form $H \leftarrow c \wedge G_L \wedge \neg K\vartheta \wedge G_R$.

Let γ_v be of the form $A \leftarrow L_1 \wedge \ldots \wedge L_{f-1} \wedge \neg v(K\vartheta) \wedge L_{f+1} \wedge \ldots \wedge L_r$, that is, $v(H) = A$ and $\mathcal{D} \models v(c)$. By the conditions on the applicability of rule R6, we also have that $\mathcal{D} \models v(d\vartheta)$. Since program P_{k+1} is locally stratified w.r.t. σ, we have that $\sigma(v(K\vartheta)) < \sigma(A)$. By the definition of proof tree, there is no proof tree for $v(K\vartheta)$ and P_{k+1}. Thus, by hypothesis (ISC) there exists no proof tree for $v(K\vartheta)$ and P_k. By the inductive hypothesis (Completeness) and Propositions 3 and 4, there exists no proof tree for $v(K\vartheta)$ and $P_0 \cup Defs_i$ and thus, since $K \leftarrow d \wedge A_F$ is the only clause defining the head predicate of K and $\mathcal{D} \models v(d\vartheta)$, there is no proof tree for $v(A_F\vartheta)$ and $P_0 \cup Defs_i$. By Proposition 3 and the inductive hypothesis (Soundness), there exists no proof tree for $v(A_F\vartheta)$ and P_k. Since $\mathcal{D} \models v(c)$ there exists a clause α_v in $ground(\alpha)$ of the form $A \leftarrow L_1 \wedge \ldots \wedge L_{f-1} \wedge \neg v(A_F\vartheta) \wedge L_{f+1} \wedge \ldots \wedge L_r$. We begin the construction of T by using α_v at the root. For all $h = 1, \ldots, f-1, f+1, \ldots, r$ such that L_h is an atom and U_h is the subtree of U rooted in L_h, we have that $size(U_h) < size(U)$. By hypothesis (Isize) there exists a proof tree T_h for L_h and P_k which we use as a subtree of T rooted in L_h. For all $h = 1, \ldots, f-1, f+1, \ldots, r$ such that L_h is a negated atom $\neg A_h$ we have that $\sigma(A_h) < \sigma(A)$, because program P_{k+1} is locally stratified w.r.t. σ. Moreover, there is no proof tree for A_h in P_{k+1}, because U is a proof tree. By hypothesis (ISC) we have that there is no proof tree for A_h in

P_k. Thus, for all $h = 1, \ldots, f-1, f+1, \ldots, r$ such that L_h is a negated atom we take L_h to be a leaf of T.

Case2, rule R7. Clause γ is derived by replacement. We only consider the case where P_{k+1} is derived from program P_k by applying the replacement rule based on law (8). The other cases are left to the reader. Suppose that a clause η: $H \leftarrow c_1 \wedge G$ in P_k is replaced by clause γ: $H \leftarrow c_2 \wedge G$ and $\mathcal{D} \models \forall (\exists Y \, c_1 \leftrightarrow \exists Z \, c_2)$, where: (i) $Y = FV(c_1) - FV(\{H, G\})$ and (ii) $Z = FV(c_2) - FV(\{H, G\})$. Thus, $ground(\gamma) = ground(\eta)$ and we can construct a proof tree for the ground atom A and P_k by using a clause in $ground(\eta)$, instead of a clause in $ground(\gamma)$.

Proof of Completeness. Given a P_j-consistent proof tree for A and P_k, we prove that there exists a P_j-consistent proof tree for A and P_{k+1}. The proof is by well-founded induction on $\mu(A, P_j)$. The inductive hypothesis is:

(Iμ) for every ground atom A' such that $\mu(A', P_j) < \mu(A, P_j)$, if there exists a P_j-consistent proof tree T' for A' and P_k then there exists a P_j-consistent proof tree U' for A' and P_{k+1}.

Let γ be a clause in P_k and v be a valuation such that $\gamma_v \in ground(\gamma)$ is the ground clause of the form $H \leftarrow L_1 \wedge \ldots \wedge L_r$ used at the root of T.

The proof proceeds by considering the following cases: *either* γ belongs to P_{k+1} *or* γ does not belong to P_{k+1} because it has been replaced (together with other clauses in P_k) with new clauses derived by an application of a transformation rule among R3, R4, R5, R6, R7, R8, R9, R10 (recall that R1 and R2 are not applied in $P_j, \ldots, P_m$). We present only the case where P_{k+1} is derived from P_k by positive folding (rule R5). The other cases are similar and are left to the reader.

Suppose that P_{k+1} is derived from P_k by folding clauses $\gamma_1, \ldots, \gamma_m$ in P_k using clauses $\delta_1, \ldots, \delta_m$ in (a variant of) $Defs_k$, and let γ be γ_p, with $1 \leq p \leq m$. Suppose also that, for $i = 1, \ldots, m$, clause δ_i is of the form $K \leftarrow d_i \wedge B_i$ and clause γ_i is of the form $H \leftarrow c \wedge d_i \vartheta \wedge G_L \wedge B_i \vartheta \wedge G_R$, for a substitution ϑ satisfying Conditions (i) and (ii) given in (R5). The clause η derived by folding $\gamma_1, \ldots, \gamma_m$ using $\delta_1, \ldots, \delta_m$ is of the form: $H \leftarrow c \wedge G_L \wedge K\vartheta \wedge G_R$. Since we use γ_v at the root of T, we have that: (a) $v(H) = A$, (b) $\mathcal{D} \models v(c \wedge d_p\vartheta)$, and (c) $v(G_L \wedge B_p\vartheta \wedge G_R) = L_1 \wedge \ldots \wedge L_r$, that is, for some $f1, f2, v(G_L) = L_1 \wedge \ldots \wedge L_{f1}, v(B_p\vartheta) = L_{f1+1} \wedge \ldots \wedge L_{f2}$, and $v(G_R) = L_{f2+1} \wedge \ldots \wedge L_r$. By Proposition 4 and the inductive hypotheses (Soundness and Completeness), for $h = f1+1, \ldots, f2$, if L_h is an atom then there exists a proof tree for L_h and P_j, and if L_h is a negated atom $\neg A_h$ then there is no a proof tree for A_h and P_j. By Proposition 3, by the fact that (by ii) $\mathcal{D} \models v(d_p\vartheta)$, and by the fact that $\delta_p \in P_i$ (recall that $Defs_k \subseteq P_i$), we have that there exists a proof tree for $v(K\vartheta)$ and P_j. Moreover, since $K \leftarrow d_p \wedge B_p$ has been unfolded w.r.t. a positive literal, we have that:

$$(\dagger) \quad \mu(v(B_p\vartheta), P_j) \geq \mu(v(K\vartheta), P_j)$$

By Proposition 4 and the inductive hypothesis (Completeness), there exists a proof tree for $v(K\vartheta)$ and P_k. Since T is P_j-consistent we have that, for $h = 1, \ldots, r, \mu(A, P_j) > \mu(L_h, P_j)$. Moreover, we have that:

$$\mu(A, P_j) > \mu(v(G_L \wedge B_p\vartheta \wedge G_R), P_j) \qquad \text{(because } T \text{ is } P_j\text{-consistent)}$$
$$= \mu(v(G_L), P_j) \oplus \mu(v(B_p\vartheta), P_j) \oplus \mu(v(G_R), P_j) \qquad \text{(by definition of } \mu)$$
$$\geq \mu(v(G_L), P_j) \oplus \mu(v(K\vartheta), P_j) \oplus \mu(v(G_R), P_j) \qquad \text{(by (†))}$$
$$\geq \mu(v(K\vartheta), P_j) \qquad \text{(by definition of } \mu)$$

By the inductive hypotheses (Iμ) and (IS), for $h = 1, \ldots, f1, f2+1, \ldots, r$, if L_h is an atom then there exists a P_j-consistent proof tree U_h for L_h and P_{k+1}, and if L_h is a negated atom $\neg A_h$ then there is no a proof tree for A_h and P_{k+1}. Moreover, by the inductive hypothesis (Iμ), there exists a P_j-consistent proof tree $\widehat{U}$ for $v(K\vartheta)$ and P_{k+1}.

Now we construct a P_j-consistent proof tree U for A and P_{k+1} as follows. By (a) and (b) we have that $v(H) = A$ and $\mathcal{D} \models v(c)$. Thus, we construct the children of A in U by using the clause η: $H \leftarrow c \wedge G_L \wedge K\vartheta \wedge G_R$. Since $v(G_L \wedge K\vartheta \wedge G_R) = L_1 \wedge \ldots \wedge L_{f1} \wedge v(K\vartheta) \wedge L_{f2+1} \wedge \ldots \wedge L_r$, the children of A in U are: $L_1, \ldots, L_{f1}, v(K\vartheta), L_{f2+1}, \ldots, L_r$. The construction of U continues as follows. For $h = 1, \ldots, f1, f2+1, \ldots, r$, if L_h is an atom then U_h is the P_j-consistent subtree of U rooted in L_h, else if L_h is a negated atom then L_h is a leaf of U. Finally, the subtree of U rooted in $v(K\vartheta)$ is the P_j-consistent proof tree $\widehat{U}$.

The proof tree U is indeed P_j-consistent because: (i) for $h = 1, \ldots, f1, f2+1, \ldots, r$, $\mu(A, P_j) > \mu(L_h, P_j)$, (ii) $\mu(A, P_j) \geq \mu(v(K\vartheta), P_j)$, and (iii) every subtree rooted in one of the literals $L_1, \ldots, L_{f1}, v(K\vartheta), L_{f2+1}, \ldots, L_r$ is P_j-consistent. $\qquad \square$

References

1. M. Alpuente, M. Falaschi, G. Moreno, and G. Vidal. A transformation system for lazy functional logic programs. In A. Middeldorp and T. Sato, editors, *Proceedings of the 4th Fuji International Symposium on Functional and Logic Programming, FLOPS'99*, Lecture Notes in Computer Science 631, pages 147–162. Springer-Verlag, 1999.
2. K. R. Apt. Introduction to logic programming. In J. van Leeuwen, editor, *Handbook of Theoretical Computer Science*, pages 493–576. Elsevier, 1990.
3. K. R. Apt. *From Logic Programming to Prolog*. Prentice Hall, London, UK, 1997.
4. K. R. Apt and R. N. Bol. Logic programming and negation: A survey. *Journal of Logic Programming*, 19, 20:9–71, 1994.
5. J.-M. Autebert, J. Berstel, and L. Boasson. Context-free languages and pushdown automata. In G. Rozenberg and A. Salomaa, editors, *Handbook of Formal Languages*, volume 1, pages 111–174. Springer, Berlin, 1997.
6. D. Basin, Y. Deville, P. Flener, A. Hamfelt, and J.F. Nilsson. Synthesis of programs in computational logic. In M. Bruynooghe and K.-K. Lau, editors, *Program Development in Computational Logic*. Springer, 2004. This volume.
7. N. Bensaou and I. Guessarian. Transforming constraint logic programs. *Theoretical Computer Science*, 206:81–125, 1998.
8. A. Bossi, N. Cocco, and S. Etalle. Transforming normal programs by replacement. In A. Pettorossi, editor, *Proceedings 3rd International Workshop on Meta-Programming in Logic, Meta '92, Uppsala, Sweden*, Lecture Notes in Computer Science 649, pages 265–279, Berlin, 1992. Springer-Verlag.

9. R. M. Burstall and J. Darlington. A transformation system for developing recursive programs. *Journal of the ACM*, 24(1):44–67, January 1977.
10. M. Garcia de la Banda, M. Hermenegildo, M. Bruynooghe, V. Dumortier, G. Janssens, and W. Simoens. Global analysis of constraint logic programs. *ACM Transactions on Programming Languages and Systems*, 18(5):564–614, 1996.
11. S. Etalle and M. Gabbrielli. Transformations of CLP modules. *Theoretical Computer Science*, 166:101–146, 1996.
12. F. Fioravanti. *Transformation of Constraint Logic Programs for Software Specialization and Verification*. PhD thesis, Università di Roma "La Sapienza", Italy, 2002.
13. F. Fioravanti, A. Pettorossi, and M. Proietti. Verifying CTL properties of infinite state systems by specializing constraint logic programs. In *Proceedings of the ACM Sigplan Workshop on Verification and Computational Logic VCL'01, Florence (Italy)*, Technical Report DSSE-TR-2001-3, pages 85–96. University of Southampton, UK, 2001.
14. F. Fioravanti, A. Pettorossi, and M. Proietti. Specialization with clause splitting for deriving deterministic constraint logic programs. In *Proceedings of the IEEE International Conference on Systems, Man and Cybernetics, Hammamet (Tunisia)*. IEEE Computer Society Press, 2002.
15. L. Fribourg and H. Olsén. Proving safety properties of infinite state systems by compilation into Presburger arithmetic. In *CONCUR '97*, Lecture Notes in Computer Science 1243, pages 96–107. Springer-Verlag, 1997.
16. P. A. Gardner and J. C. Shepherdson. Unfold/fold transformations of logic programs. In J.-L. Lassez and G. Plotkin, editors, *Computational Logic, Essays in Honor of Alan Robinson*, pages 565–583. MIT, 1991.
17. M. Gergatsoulis and M. Katzouraki. Unfold/fold transformations for definite clause programs. In M. Hermenegildo and J. Penjam, editors, *Proceedings Sixth International Symposium on Programming Language Implementation and Logic Programming (PLILP '94)*, Lecture Notes in Computer Science 844, pages 340–354. Springer-Verlag, 1994.
18. C. J. Hogger. Derivation of logic programs. *Journal of the ACM*, 28(2):372–392, 1981.
19. J. Jaffar and M. Maher. Constraint logic programming: A survey. *Journal of Logic Programming*, 19/20:503–581, 1994.
20. J. Jaffar, M. Maher, K. Marriott, and P. Stuckey. The semantics of constraint logic programming. *Journal of Logic Programming*, 37:1–46, 1998.
21. N. D. Jones, C. K. Gomard, and P. Sestoft. *Partial Evaluation and Automatic Program Generation*. Prentice Hall, 1993.
22. T. Kanamori and H. Fujita. Unfold/fold transformation of logic programs with counters. Technical Report 179, ICOT, Tokyo, Japan, 1986.
23. T. Kanamori and K. Horiuchi. Construction of logic programs based on generalized unfold/fold rules. In *Proceedings of the Fourth International Conference on Logic Programming*, pages 744–768. The MIT Press, 1987.
24. M. Leuschel and M. Bruynooghe. Logic program specialisation through partial deduction: Control issues. *Theory and Practice of Logic Programming*, 2(4&5):461–515, 2002.
25. M. Leuschel and T. Massart. Infinite state model checking by abstract interpretation and program specialization. In A. Bossi, editor, *Proceedings of LOPSTR '99, Venice, Italy*, Lecture Notes in Computer Science 1817, pages 63–82. Springer, 1999.

26. J. W. Lloyd. *Foundations of Logic Programming*. Springer-Verlag, Berlin, 1987. Second Edition.
27. M. J. Maher. A transformation system for deductive database modules with perfect model semantics. *Theoretical Computer Science*, 110:377–403, 1993.
28. K. Marriott and P. Stuckey. *Programming with Constraints: An Introduction*. The MIT Press, 1998.
29. A. Pettorossi and M. Proietti. Transformation of logic programs: Foundations and techniques. *Journal of Logic Programming*, 19,20:261–320, 1994.
30. A. Pettorossi and M. Proietti. Synthesis and transformation of logic programs using unfold/fold proofs. *Journal of Logic Programming*, 41(2&3):197–230, 1999.
31. A. Pettorossi and M. Proietti. Perfect model checking via unfold/fold transformations. In J. W. Lloyd, editor, *First International Conference on Computational Logic, CL'2000, London, UK, 24-28 July, 2000*, Lecture Notes in Artificial Intelligence 1861, pages 613–628. Springer, 2000.
32. A. Pettorossi and M. Proietti. Program Derivation = Rules + Strategies. In A. Kakas and F. Sadri, editors, *Computational Logic: Logic Programming and Beyond (Essays in honour of Bob Kowalski, Part I)*, Lecture Notes in Computer Science 2407, pages 273–309. Springer, 2002.
33. A. Pettorossi, M. Proietti, and S. Renault. Reducing nondeterminism while specializing logic programs. In *Proc. 24-th ACM Symposium on Principles of Programming Languages, Paris, France*, pages 414–427. ACM Press, 1997.
34. M. Proietti and A. Pettorossi. Unfolding-definition-folding, in this order, for avoiding unnecessary variables in logic programs. *Theoretical Computer Science*, 142(1):89–124, 1995.
35. T. C. Przymusinski. On the declarative semantics of stratified deductive databases and logic programs. In J. Minker, editor, *Foundations of Deductive Databases and Logic Programming*, pages 193–216. Morgan Kaufmann, 1987.
36. A. Roychoudhury, K. Narayan Kumar, C. R. Ramakrishnan, I. V. Ramakrishnan, and S. A. Smolka. Verification of parameterized systems using logic program transformations. In *Proceedings of the Sixth International Conference on Tools and Algorithms for the Construction and Analysis of Systems, TACAS 2000, Berlin, Germany*, Lecture Notes in Computer Science 1785, pages 172–187. Springer, 2000.
37. A. Roychoudhury, K. Narayan Kumar, C. R. Ramakrishnan, and I.V. Ramakrishnan. Beyond Tamaki-Sato style unfold/fold transformations for normal logic programs. *International Journal on Foundations of Computer Science*, 13(3):387–403, 2002.
38. A. Roychoudhury, K. Narayan Kumar, C.R. Ramakrishnan, and I.V. Ramakrishnan. A parameterized unfold/fold transformation framework for definite logic programs. In *Proceedings of Principles and Practice of Declarative Programming (PPDP)*, Lecture Notes in Computer Science 1702, pages 396–413. Springer-Verlag, 1999.
39. D. Sands. Total correctness by local improvement in the transformation of functional programs. *ACM Toplas*, 18(2):175–234, 1996.
40. T. Sato. An equivalence preserving first order unfold/fold transformation system. *Theoretical Computer Science*, 105:57–84, 1992.
41. T. Sato and H. Tamaki. Transformational logic program synthesis. In *Proceedings of the International Conference on Fifth Generation Computer Systems*, pages 195–201. ICOT, 1984.
42. H. Seki. Unfold/fold transformation of stratified programs. *Theoretical Computer Science*, 86:107–139, 1991.

43. H. Seki. Unfold/fold transformation of general logic programs for well-founded semantics. *Journal of Logic Programming*, 16(1&2):5–23, 1993.
44. H. Tamaki and T. Sato. Unfold/fold transformation of logic programs. In S.-Å. Tärnlund, editor, *Proceedings of the Second International Conference on Logic Programming*, pages 127–138, Uppsala, Sweden, 1984. Uppsala University.

Specialising Interpreters Using Offline Partial Deduction

Michael Leuschel[1], Stephen J. Craig[1],
Maurice Bruynooghe[2], and Wim Vanhoof[3]

[1] Department of Electronics and Computer Science
University of Southampton
mal@ecs.soton.ac.uk
[2] Department of Computer Science
Katholieke Universiteit Leuven
Maurice.Bruynooghe@cs.kuleuven.ac.be
[3] University of Namur
wva@info.fundp.ac.be

Abstract. We present the latest version of the LOGEN partial evaluation system for logic programs. In particular we present new binding-types, and show how they can be used to effectively specialise a wide variety of interpreters. We show how to achieve Jones-optimality in a systematic way for several interpreters. Finally, we present and specialise a non-trivial interpreter for a small functional programming language. Experimental results are also presented, highlighting that the LOGEN system can be a good basis for generating compilers for high-level languages.

1 Introduction

Partial evaluation [21] is a source-to-source program transformation technique which specialises programs by fixing part of the input of some source program P and then pre-computing those parts of P that only depend on the known part of the input. The so-obtained transformed programs are less general than the original but can be much more efficient. The part of the input that is fixed is referred to as the *static* input, while the remainder of the input is called the *dynamic* input.

Partial evaluation is especially useful when applied to interpreters. In that setting the static input is typically the object program being interpreted, while the actual call to the object program is dynamic. Partial evaluation can then produce a more efficient, specialised version of the interpreter, which is sometimes akin to a compiled version of the object program [10].

The ultimate goal in that setting is to achieve so-called *Jones optimality* [19,21,36], i.e., fully getting rid of a layer of interpretation (called the "optimality criterion" in [21]). More precisely, if we have a self-interpreter sint for a programming language L, i.e., an interpreter for L written in that same language L, and then specialise sint for a particular object program p we would like to obtain a specialised interpreter p' which is as least as efficient as p (see

M. Bruynooghe and K.-K. Lau (Eds.): Program Development in CL, LNCS 3049, pp. 340–375, 2004.

Figure 1). The reason one uses a self-interpreter, rather than an interpreter in general, is so as to be able to directly compare the running times of p and p' (as they are written in the same programming language L).

More formally, if D is the input domain of p and $t_p(i)$ is the running time of the program p on the input i, we want that $\forall d \in D : t_{p'}(d) \leq t_p(d)$.

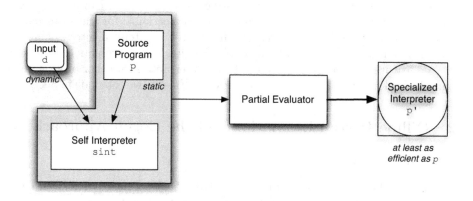

Fig. 1. Jones Optimality

In this paper we study systematically how to specialise a wide variety of interpreters written in Prolog using so-called offline partial evaluation. We will illustrate this using the partial evaluation system LOGEN. Starting from very simple interpreters we will progress towards more complicated interpreters. We will also show how we can actually achieve the goal of Jones optimality for a logic programming self-interpreter, as well as for a debugger derived from it; i.e., when specialising the debugger for an object program p with none of its predicates being spied on we will always get a specialised debugger equivalent to p. We believe this to be the first result of its kind in a logic programming setting. In fact, how to effectively specialise interpreters has been a matter of ongoing research for many years, and has been of big interest in the logic programming community, see e.g., [42,47,44,5,7,26,50,28] to mention just a few. However, despite these efforts, achieving Jones optimality in a systematic way has remained mainly a dream. To our knowledge, Jones optimiality has been achieved only for a simple Vanilla self-interpreter in [50], but the technique does not scale up to more involved interpreters. All of these works have mainly tried to tackle the problem using fully automatic online partial evaluation techniques, while in this paper we are using the offline approach. Basically, an *online* specialiser takes all of its control decisions during the specialisation process itself, while an *offline* specialiser is guided by a preliminary *binding-time analysis*, which in our case will be (partially) done by hand. The basic reason we opt for the offline approach is that it allows to steer the specialisation process far better than online techniques.

This steering is of particular importance in the current setting, since all of the previous research using automatic online techniques has shown that specialising interpreters (in general and especially Jones optimality) is hard to achieve.

The paper is structured as follows. In Section 2 we present the basics of offline partial evaluation and of the so-called cogen approach to specialisation employed by LOGEN. The LOGEN system itself is introduced in Section 2.3. In Section 3 we focus on offline techniques in logic programming as employed by LOGEN. We then show how a simple, non-recursive interpreter can be specialised in Section 4 before moving to a self-interpreter in Section 5, for which we achieve Jones-optimality. In Section 6 this self-interpreter is extended into a debugger, for which Jones-optimality is also achieved. Section 7 then presents more sophisticated features of LOGEN, required to tackle interpreters for other programming paradigms. Their use is illustrated in Section 8. Finally, we conclude in Section 9.

2   Offline Partial Evaluation and the Cogen Approach

2.1   Offline Specialisation

Inspired by the seminal work of Futamura [10], the functional partial evaluation community has put a lot of effort in developing self-applicable partial evaluators. The first successful self-application was reported in [22], and later refined in [23] (see also [21]). The main idea which made this self-application possible was to separate the specialisation process into two phases, as depicted in Figure 2:

- First a *binding-time analysis* (*BTA* for short) is performed which, given a program and an approximation of the input available for specialisation, approximates all values within the program and generates annotations that steer (or control) the specialisation process.
- A (simplified) *specialisation phase*, which is guided by the result of the *BTA*.

Such an approach is *offline* because most control decisions are taken beforehand. The interest for self-application lies with the fact that only the second, simplified phase has to be self-applied. We refer to [22,23,21] for further details. In the context of logic programming languages the offline approach was used to achieve self-application in [39,15] and more recently in [8].

2.2   The Cogen Approach

Given a self-applicable partial evaluator, one can construct a so-called *compiler generator* (a *cogen* for short) using Futamura's third projection (see e.g. [21]). A *cogen* is a program that given a binding-time annotated program produces a specialiser for that program. If the annotated program is an interpreter, this specialiser can be viewed as a compiler, hence the name "compiler generator."

Obtaining an efficient cogen by self-application is a quite difficult task. This has led several researchers to pursue the so-called *cogen approach* to program specialisation [17,18,4,1,14,48]. The idea behind this approach is to write the *cogen* directly by hand, rather than trying to obtain it by self-application. This

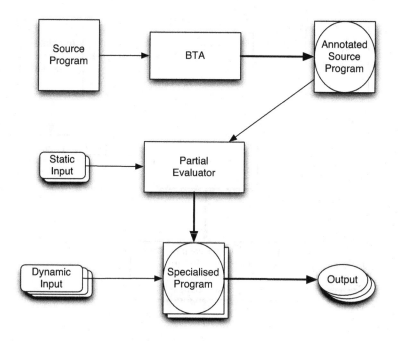

Fig. 2. Offline Partial Evaluation

turns out to be less difficult than one could imagine. Also, from a user's point of view, it is not important how a *cogen* was generated; what is important is that a *cogen* exists and that it is efficient and produces efficient, non-trivial specialised specialisers.

2.3   Overview of LOGEN

The application of the cogen approach in a logic programming setting has lead to the LOGEN system [24,31], which we describe in more detail in the next section.

Figure 3 highlights the way the LOGEN system works. Typically, a user would proceed as follows:

– First the source program is annotated using the BTA, which produces an annotated source program. This annotated source program can be further edited.[4] This also allows an expert to inspect and manually refine the annotations to get better specialisation.

---

[4] We have developed a special LOGEN Emacs mode as well as a Tcl/Tk editor for this task. The figure does not show that LOGEN now also contains a term expansion package (for SICStus and Ciao Prolog) that strips the annotations when loading the annotated source program, allowing the annotated source program to be run directly.

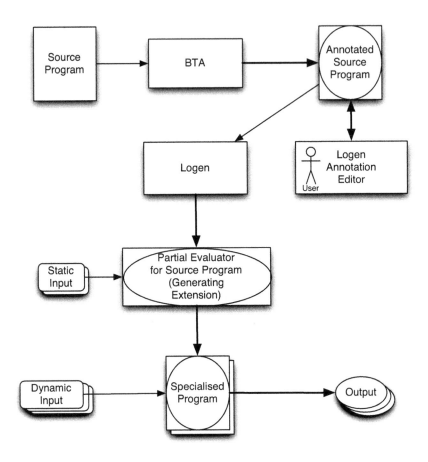

Fig. 3. Illustrating the LOGEN system and the *cogen* approach

- Second, LOGEN is run on the annotated source program and produces a specialiser for the source program, called a *generating extension*.
- This generating extension can now be used to specialise the source program for some static input. Note that the same generating extension can be run many times for different static inputs (i.e., there is no need to re-run LOGEN on the annotated source program unless the annotated source program itself changes).
- When the remainder of the input is known, the specialised program can now be run and will produce the same output as the original source program. Note again, that the same specialised program can be run for different dynamic inputs; one only has to re-generate the specialised program if the static input changes (or the original program itself changes).

3   Offline Partial Deduction of Logic Programs

We now describe the process of offline partial evaluation of logic programs and give a better understanding of how LOGEN specialises its source programs.

Throughout this paper, we suppose familiarity with basic notions in logic programming. We follow the notational conventions of [34]. In particular, in programs, we denote variables by strings starting with an upper-case symbol, while the notations for constants, functions and predicates begin with a lower-case character.

3.1   Partial Deduction

The term "partial deduction" has been introduced in [25] to replace the term partial evaluation in the context of pure logic programs (no side effects, no cuts). Though in some parts of the paper we briefly touch upon the consequences of impure language constructs, we adhere to this terminology because the word "deduction" places emphasis on the purely logical nature of most of the source programs. Before presenting partial deduction, we first present some aspects of the logic programming execution model.

Formally, executing a logic program P for an atom A consists of building a so-called *SLD-tree* for $P \cup \{\leftarrow A\}$ and then extracting the *computed answer substitutions* from every non-failing branch of that tree. Take for example the well-known append program:

```
append([],L,L).
append([H|X],Y,[H|Z]) :- append(X,Y,Z).
```

For example, the SLD-tree for append([a,b],[c],R) is presented on the left in Figure 4. The underlined atoms are called selected atoms. Here there is only one branch, and its computed answer is R = [a,b,c].

```
append([a,b],[c],R)

   append([b],[c],R2)

      append([],[c],R3)

□
```

Partial deduction builds upon this approach with two major differences:

- At some step in building the SLD-tree, it is possible *not* to select an atom, hence leaving a leaf with a non-empty goal. The motivation is that lack of the full input may cause the SLD-tree to have extra branches, in particular infinite ones. For example, in Figure 4 the rightmost tree is an incomplete SLD-tree for append(X,[c],R), whose full SLD-tree would be infinite. The partial evaluator should not only avoid constructing infinite branches, but also other branches causing inefficiencies in the specialised program. Building such a tree is called *unfolding*. An *unfolding rule* tells us which atom to select at which point. Incomplete branches do not produce computed answers, they produce conditional answers which can be expressed as program clauses by taking the resultants of the branches as defined below.
- Because of the atoms left in the leaves (in the bodies of the resultants), we may have to build a series of SLD-trees to ensure that every such atom is covered by some root of some tree. The fact that every leaf is an instance of a root is called *closedness* (sometimes also *coveredness*). In the example of Figure 4 the leaf atom append(X2,[c],R2) is already an instance of its root atom, hence closedness is already ensured and there is no need to build more trees.

Definition 1. *Let P be a program, $G =\leftarrow Q$ a goal, D a finite SLD-derivation of $P \cup \{G\}$ ending in $\leftarrow B$, and θ the composition of the mgus in the derivation steps. Then the formula $Q\theta \leftarrow B$ is called the* **resultant** *of D.*

E.g., the resultants of the derivations in the right tree of Figure 4 are:

```
append([],[c],[c]).
append([H|X2],[c],[H|R2]) :- append(X2,[c],R2).
```

Partial deduction starts from an initial set of atoms A provided by the user that is chosen in such a way that all runtime queries of interest are closed, i.e., are an instance of some atom in A. As we have seen, constructing a specialised program requires us to construct an SLD-tree for each atom in A. Moreover, one can easily imagine that ensuring closedness may require revision of the set A. Hence, when controlling partial deduction, it is natural to separate the control into two components (as already pointed out in [11,38]):

- The *local control* controls the construction of the finite SLD-tree for each atom in A and thus determines *what* the residual clauses for the atoms in A are.
- The *global control* controls the content of A, it decides *which* atoms are ultimately partially deduced (taking care that A remains closed for the initial atoms provided by the user).

More details on exactly how to control partial deduction in general can be found, e.g., in [29]. In offline partial deduction the local control is hardwired, in the form of annotations added to the source program (either by the BTA, the user, or both). The global control is also partially hard-wired, by specifying which arguments to which predicate are dynamic and which ones are static.

3.2   An Offline Partial Deduction Algorithm

As already outlined earlier, an offline specialiser works on an annotated version of the source program. In our approach, we use two kinds of annotations:

- *Filter declarations*, which declare which arguments to which predicates are static and which ones dynamic. This influences the global control only.
- *Clause annotations*, which indicate for every call in the body how that call should be treated during unfolding. This thus influences the local control only. For now, we assume that a call is either annotated by **memo** — indicating that it should not be unfolded – or by **unfold** — indicating that it should be unfolded. We introduce more annotations later on.

There is of course an interplay between these two kinds of annotations, and we return to this below.

First, let us consider as example an annotated version of the append program from above in which the filter declarations annotate the second argument as static while the others are dynamic and the clause annotations annotate the recursive call as **memo** to prevent its unfolding. Given such annotations and a specialisation query append(X,[c],Z), offline partial deduction would unfold exactly as depicted in the right tree of Figure 4 and produce the resultants above.

The following is a general algorithm for offline partial deduction given filter declarations and clause annotations.

Algorithm 3.1 (offline partial deduction)
Input: A program P and an atom A

> $M = \{A\}$
> **repeat**
>> select an unmarked atom A in M and mark it
>> unfold A using the clause annotations in the annotated source program
>> **if** a selected atom S is annotated as **memo then**
>>> generalise S into S' by replacing all arguments declared as dynamic
>>>> by the filter declarations with a fresh variable
>>> **if** no variant of S' is in M **then** add it to M **end**
>> **end**
>> pretty print the specialised clauses of A
> **until** all atoms in M are marked

In practice, renaming transformations [12] are also involved: Every atom in M is assigned a new predicate name, whose arity is the number of arguments declared as dynamic (static arguments do not need to be passed around; they have already been built into the specialised code). For example, the resultants of the derivations in the right tree of Figure 4 would get transformed into the following, where the second static argument has been removed:

```
append__0([],[c]).
append__0([H|X2],[H|R2]) :- append__0(X2,R2).
```

To give a more precise picture, we present a Prolog version of the above algorithm. The code is runnable (using an implementation of gensym, see [45], to generate new predicate names). We assume that the filter declarations and clause annotations of the source program are represented by the definition of a filter/2 and rule/2 predicate respectively. We discuss a more user-friendly representation of these annotations in LOGEN later in the chapter.

An atom A is specialised by calling memo(A,Res) in the code below. The memo/2 and memo_table/2 predicates return in their second argument the call to the new specialised predicate where the static arguments are removed and the dynamic ones generalised. This generalisation and filtering is performed by the generalise_and_filter/3 predicate that returns in its second argument the generalised original call (to be unfolded) with fresh variables and in its third argument the corresponding call to the specialised predicate. It uses the annotations as defined by the filter/2 predicate to perform its task. The call memo_table(X,ResX) within the definition of memo/2 simply binds ResX to the residual version of the call X. Note the difference between ResX, GenX and FX. Consider for example the filter declaration for app given below with X = app(S,[],S) as call. The generalised call to be unfolded, GenX becomes app(Y,[],Z); FX, the head of the specialised version becomes for example app__0(Y,Z) in which case the original call is to be replaced by ResX = app__0(S,S).

The predicate unfold/2 computes the bodies of the specialised predicates. A call annotated as **memo** is replaced by a call to the specialised version. It is created, if it does not exist, by the call to memo/2. A call annotated as **unfolded** is further unfolded. To be able to deal with built-ins, we also add two more annotations: a call annotated as **call** is completely evaluated; finally, a call annotated as **rescall** is added to the residual code without modification (for built-ins that cannot be evaluated). These two annotations can also be useful for user-predicates (a user predicate marked as **call** is completely unfolded without further examination of the annotations, while the **rescall** annotation can be useful for predicates defined elsewhere or whose code is not annotated). All clauses defining the new predicate are collected using findall/3 and pretty printed.

```
:- dynamic memo_table/2.
memo(X,ResX) :- (memo_table(X,ResX)
    -> true /* nothing to be done: already specialised */
    ; (generalise_and_filter(X,GenX,FX),
        assert(memo_table(GenX,FX)),
        findall((FX:-B),unfold(GenX,B),XClauses),
        pretty_print_clauses(XClauses),nl,
        memo_table(X,ResX) ) ).

unfold(X,Code) :- rule(X,B), body(B,Code).
body((A,B),(CA,CB)) :- body(A,CA), body(B,CB).
body(memo(X),ResX) :- memo(X,ResX).
body(unfold(X),ResCode) :- unfold(X,ResCode).
body(call(C),true) :- call(C).
body(rescall(C),C).
```

```
generalise_and_filter(Call,GCall,FCall) :- filter(Call,ArgTypes),
        Call =.. [P|Args],
        gen_filter(ArgTypes,Args,GenArgs,FiltArgs),
        GCall =.. [P|GenArgs],
        gensym(P,NewP), FCall =.. [NewP|FiltArgs].
gen_filter([],[],[],[]).
gen_filter([static|AT],[Arg|ArgT],[Arg|GT],FT) :-
        gen_filter(AT,ArgT,GT,FT).
gen_filter([dynamic|AT],[_|ArgT],[GenArg|GT],[GenArg|FT]) :-
        gen_filter(AT,ArgT,GT,FT).
```

Let us now examine the behaviour of this specialiser for our earlier append example. First, we have to produce an annotated version of the append program:

```
/* the annotated source program: */
/* filter indicates how to generalise and filter */
filter(app(_,_,_),[dynamic,static,dynamic]).

/* rule annotates the clauses and indicates how to unfold */
rule(app([],L,L),call(true)).
rule(app([H|X],Y,[H|Z]),memo(app(X,Y,Z))).
```

Calling the specialiser with memo(app(X,[c],Y)) produces the following specialised program as output:

```
app__1([],[c]):-true
app__1([_12855|_12856],[_12855|_12854]) :- app__1(_12856,_12854).
```

The full treatment in LOGEN is a lot more complicated as LOGEN supports a more user friendly syntax as well as various features to be introduced in the next sections.

3.3   Local and Global Termination

Without proper annotations of the source program, the above offline specialiser may fail to terminate. There are essentially two reasons for nontermination.

- **Local nontermination:** The unfolding predicate unfold/2 may fail to terminate or provide infinitely many answers.
- **Global nontermination:** Even if all calls to unfold/2 terminate, we may still run into problems because the partial evaluator may try to build infinitely many specialised versions of some predicate for infinitely many different static values.[5]

To overcome the first problem, we may have to annotate certain calls as **memo** rather than **unfold**. In the worst case, every call is annotated as **memo**

---

[5] One often tries to ensure that a static argument is of so-called *bounded static variation* [21], so that global termination is guaranteed.

which always ensures local termination (but means that little or no specialisation is performed).

To overcome global termination problems, we have to play with the filter declarations and declare more arguments as **dynamic** rather than **static**.

Another possible problem appears when built-ins lack enough input to behave as they do at run-time (either by triggering an error or by giving a different result). When this happens, we have to mark the offending call as **rescall** rather than **call**.

4   Propositional Logic Interpreter

We first introduce a simple propositional logic interpreter to demonstrate the basic annotations. The interpreter will accept *and*, *or*, *not*, *implies* and propositional variables. The *int(Prog, Env, Result)* predicate takes two input arguments, the propositional formula and the environment containing a truth function for the propositional variables and produces the result. The environment is a list of truth values; *var(i)* indexes the ith element in the environment.

```
not(true,false).
not(false,true).
and(true,true ,true).          or(true ,_ ,true).
and(false,_ ,false).           or(false,true,true).
and(true,false,false).         or(false,false,false).

int(true,_,true).
int(false,_,false).
int(implies(X,Y),Env, Z) :- int(or(not(X),Y),Env,Z).
int(and(X,Y),Env, Z)  :- int(X,Env,R1),int(Y,Env,R2),and(R1,R2,Z).
int(or(X,Y),Env, Z)  :- int(X,Env,R1),int(Y,Env,R2),or(R1,R2,Z).
int(not(X),Env, Z)  :- int(X,Env,R1),not(R1,Z).
int(var(X),Env, Z)  :- lookup(X,Env,Z).

lookup(0,[X|_],X).
lookup(N,[X|T],Y) :- N>0, N1 is N-1, lookup(N1,T,Y).
```

As was indicated in Figure 3, the source program that serves as input for LOGEN needs annotations. The **filter** declaration declares how the arguments of the residual predicates have to be treated. The annotation **static** announces that the value of argument will be known at specialisation time; the annotation **dynamic** that the value of the argument will not necessarily be known at specialisation time. Top level predicates that one intends to specialise must be declared in this way, as well as any subsidiary predicate which cannot be fully unfolded.

The syntax for LOGEN's filter declarations is more user-friendly than that used in the previous section. For example, for the propositional interpreter we could declare:

```
:- filter int(static, dynamic, dynamic).
:- filter lookup(dynamic, dynamic, dynamic).
```

In other words, we assume that the propositional formula (the first argument of int/3) is known at specialisation time (**static**) while the environment will only be known at runtime (**dynamic**).

Next we must annotate the clauses in the original program to control the specialisation. This has to be done either manually by the user (possibly with the help of some annotation aware editor) or by an automatic binding-time analysis. The following constructs can be used to annotate the calls in the clause bodies of the program:

- **unfold** for reducible predicates; they will be unravelled during specialisation,
- **memo** for non-reducible predicates; they will be added to the memoisation table and replaced with a generalised residual predicate,
- **call** for built-ins or user defined predicates that should be fully evaluated without further intervention of the specialiser.
- **rescall** for calls to be kept as such in the specialised code. In contrast to the **memo** annotation, no specialised predicate definition is produced for the call. This annotation is especially useful for built-ins, but can also be useful for user predicates (e.g., because the code is not available at specialisation time). The example below will highlight the difference with the **memo** annotation.

As the propositional formula is known at specialisation time (**static**) all calls to int/3 can be unfolded. As concerns the variable lookups in the environment, let us first be cautious and mark the call to lookup as a **rescall**:

$$\text{int(var(X),Env, Z)} \;\; :- \; \underbrace{\text{lookup(X, Env, Z)}}_{rescall}.$$

Let us specialise the interpreter for the logical formula:
$((var(0) \lor (var(1) \land \neg var(2))) \lor false) \land true$. The output from specialisation is a new version of the program representing the truth table for the formula; as the call to lookup was marked as **rescall**, several instantiated occurrences appear in each resultant.

```
int(and(or(or(var(0),and(not(var(1)),var(2))),false),true),Env,R)
     :- int__0(Env,R).
int__0(A,true) :-
     lookup(0,A,true),lookup(1,A,true),lookup(2,A,C).
int__0(A,false) :-
     lookup(0,A,false),lookup(1,A,true),lookup(2,A,C).
int__0(A,true) :-
     lookup(0,A,true),lookup(1,A,false),lookup(2,A,true).
int__0(A,true) :-
     lookup(0,A,false),lookup(1,A,false),lookup(2,A,true).
int__0(A,true) :-
     lookup(0,A,true),lookup(1,A,false),lookup(2,A,false).
```

```
int__0(A,false) :-
    lookup(0,A,false),lookup(1,A,false),lookup(2,A,false).
```

Observe that no specialised predicate has been produced for lookup/3, as we have used the **rescall** annotation. If we mark the call in int/3 to lookup/3 as **memo** rather than **rescall** and within the clauses of lookup/3 we mark the built-ins as **rescall** and the recursive call as **memo**, we obtain a specialised program containing lookup__1/3, a specialised version of lookup/3; however, the specialised version is but a renaming of the original as all its arguments where declared as dynamic:

```
int__0(A,true) :-
    lookup__1(0,A,true),lookup__1(1,A,true),lookup__1(2,A,B).
...
lookup__1(0,[B|C],B).
lookup__1(B,[C|D],E) :- B > 0, F is (B - 1), lookup__1(F,D,E).
```

One may notice that in all calls to lookup/3 the first argument is actually static. One may thus think of changing the filter declaration for lookup/3 into:

```
:- filter lookup(static, dynamic, dynamic).
```

Unfortunately, if we now run LOGEN we get a specialisation time error. Indeed, in the recursive call lookup(N1,T,Y) in second clause of lookup/3 the variable N1 will be unbound at specialisation time, and hence LOGEN will complain. The problem is that we have not evaluated the call N1 is N-1 which binds N1. Indeed, what we need to do is to annotate the clause as follows:

$$\texttt{lookup(N,[X|T],Y)} :- \underbrace{\texttt{N > 0}}_{call}, \underbrace{\texttt{N1 is N - 1}}_{call}, \underbrace{\texttt{lookup(N1,T,Y)}}_{memo}.$$

There is actually no need to **memo** the calls to lookup: given that we know the first argument we can annotate all calls to lookup/3 as **unfold** and LOGEN will produce the following program:

```
int__0([true,true,B|C],true).
int__0([false,true,B|C],false).
int__0([true,false,true|B],true).
int__0([false,false,true|B],true).
int__0([true,false,false|B],true).
int__0([false,false,false|B],false).
```

It is actually possible to obtain an even better specialisation than this, by providing more information about the structure of the environment. For that we need more sophisticated filter annotations, which we introduce later in Section 7. As a teaser, after declaring

```
:- filter int(static,list(dynamic), dynamic).
```

one can specialise the interpreter for the call:

```
int(and(or(or(var(0),and(not(var(1)),var(2))),false),true),[A,B,C],D)
```

obtaining the following more efficient specialised program:

```
int__0(true,true,B,true).
int__0(false,true,B,false).
int__0(true,false,true,true).
int__0(false,false,true,true).
int__0(true,false,false,true).
int__0(false,false,false,false).
```

Indeed, the environment list has vanished and need not to be manipulated.

5   Specialising the Vanilla Self-interpreter

5.1   Background

A classical benchmark for partial deduction has been the so-called *vanilla meta-interpreter* (see, e.g., [16,3]). This interpreter is a self-interpreter because it can handle the language in which it is written. The following is the vanilla meta-interpreter, along with an encoding of the double-append object program:

```
solve(empty).
solve(and(A,B)) :- solve(A), solve(B).
solve(X) :-  clause(X,Y), solve(Y).
clause(dapp(X,Y,Z,R),and(app(Y,Z,YZ),app(X,YZ,R))).
clause(app([],L,L),empty).
clause(app([H|X],Y,[H|Z]),app(X,Y,Z)).
```

The clause/2 facts describe the object program to be interpreted, while solve/1 is the meta-interpreter executing the object program. In practice, solve will often be instrumented so as to provide extra functionality for, e.g., debugging, analysis (e.g., using abstract unifications instead of concrete unification) or transformation. We will actually do so later in this section. However, even without these extensions the vanilla interpreter provides enough challenges for partial deduction. Indeed, we would like to specialise the interpreter so as to obtain a residual program at least as efficient as the object program being interpreted. For example, one would like to specialise our vanilla interpreter for the query solve(dapp(X,Y,Z,R)) and obtain a specialised interpreter which is at least as efficient as:

```
dapp(X,Y,Z,R) :- app(Y,Z,YZ),app(X,YZ,R).
app([],L,L).
app([H|X],Y,[H|Z]) :- app(X,Y,Z).
```

As we have seen in the introduction (cf. Figure 1), achieving such a feat for every object program and query is called "Jones-optimality" [19,36].

Online partial evaluators such as ECCE [32] or MIXTUS [43] come close to achieving Jones-optimality for many object programs. However, they will not do so for *all* object programs and we refer the reader to [37] (discussing the parsing problem) and the more recent [50] and [28] for more details. [50] presents a particular specialisation technique that can achieve Jones-optimality for the vanilla interpreter, but the technique is very specific to that interpreter and, as far as we understand, does not scale to extensions of it.

In the rest of this section we show how LOGEN *can* achieve Jones-optimality for the vanilla interpreter, and we show how we can then handle extensions of the basic interpreter.

5.2   The Nonvar Binding Time Annotation

First, we have to present a new feature of LOGEN which is useful when specialising interpreters. In addition to marking arguments to predicates as static or dynamic, LOGEN also supports the annotation **nonvar**. This means that the argument is not necessarily ground but has at least a top-level function symbol at specialisation time. When generalising the call, LOGEN keeps the top-level function symbol while replacing all its sub-arguments by fresh variables. Finally, these subarguments become arguments in the specialised version constructed by LOGEN.

A small example will help to illustrate this annotation:

```
:- filter p(nonvar).
p(f(X,X)) :- p(g(a)).
p(g(X)) :- p(h(X)).
p(h(a)).
p(h(X)) :- p(f(X,X)).
```

Marking every call as **memo** (hence no unfolding), we obtain the following specialised program for the call $p(f(Z,Z))$. The first comment line indicates the renamings that LOGEN has performed.

```
%%% p(f(A,B)) :- p__0(A,B).  p(g(A)):-p__1(A).  p(h(A)):-p__2(A).
p__0(A,A) :-  p__1(a).
p__1(A) :-    p__2(A).
p__2(a).
p__2(A) :-    p__0(A,A).
```

If we mark the last call as **memo** and all others as **unfold**, we obtain:

```
%%% p(f(A,B)) :- p__0(A,B).
p__0(A,A).
p__0(A,A) :- p__0(a,a).
```

5.3   Jones-Optimality for Vanilla

The vanilla interpreter as shown above, is actually a badly written program as it mixes the control structures **and** and **empty** with the actual calls to predicates of the object program. This means that the vanilla interpreter will not behave correctly if the object program contains predicates and/2 or empty/0. This fact also poses problems typing the program. Even more importantly for us, it also prevents one from annotating the program effectively for LOGEN. Indeed, statically there is no way to know whether any of the three recursive calls to solve/1 has a control structure or a user call as its argument. For LOGEN this means that we can only mark the call clause(X,Y) as **unfold**. Indeed, if we mark any of the solve/1 calls as **unfold** we may get into trouble, i.e., non-termination of the specialisation process. This also means that we cannot even mark the argument to solve/1 as **nonvar**, as it may actually become a variable. Indeed, take the call solve(and(p,q)): it will be generalised into solve(and(X,Y)) and after unfolding with the second clause we get the calls solve(X) and solve(Y). Hence we obtain very little specialisation and we will not achieve Jones-optimality.

Two ways to solve this problem are as follows:

- Assume that the control structures are used in a principled, predictable way that will allow us to produce a better annotation.
- Rewrite the interpreter so that it is clearly typed, allowing us to produce an effective annotation as well as solving the problem with the name clashes between object program and control structures.

We will pursue these solutions in the remainder of this section. A third possible solution is to use more precise annotations which we introduce later in Section 7. This will give some improvements, but not full Jones optimality, due to the bad way in which solve is written.

Structuring Conjunctions. The first solution is to enforce a standard way of writing down conjunctions within clause/2 facts by requesting that every conjuctions is either empty or is an and whose left part is an atom and the right hand a conjunction. For the example above, this means that we have to rewrite the clause/2 facts as follows:

```
clause(dapp(X,Y,Z,R),and(app(Y,Z,YZ),and(app(X,YZ,R),empty))).
clause(app([],L,L),empty).
clause(app([H|X],Y,[H|Z]),and(app(X,Y,Z),empty)).
```

This allows us to predict what to find within the arguments of a conjunction and thus we can now annotate the interpreter more effectively, without risking non-termination:

```
:- filter solve(nonvar).
solve(empty).
solve(and(A,B)) :- solve(A), solve(B).
                    ‾‾‾‾‾‾‾  ‾‾‾‾‾‾‾
                     memo      unfold
solve(X) :- clause(X,Y), solve(Y).
            ‾‾‾‾‾‾‾‾‾‾‾  ‾‾‾‾‾‾‾
             unfold       unfold
```

Given our assumption about the structure of conjunctions, the above annotation will still ensure termination of the generating extension:

- **Local termination**: The call to clause(X,Y) can be unfolded as before as clause/2 is defined by facts. The calls solve(B) and solve(Y) can be

unfolded as we know that B and Y are conjunctions. LOGEN will deconstruct
the and/2 and empty/0 function symbols. However, as solve(A) is marked
memo, the possibly recursive predicates of the object program are not unfolded.

– **Global termination**: At the point when we memo solve(A) the variable
A will be bound to a predicate call. As we have marked the argument to
solve/1 as **nonvar**, generalization will just keep the top-level predicate
symbol. As there are only finitely many predicate symbols, global termination is ensured.

Specialising for solve(dapp(X,Y,Z,R)) now gives a Jones-optimal output.

```
%%% solve(dapp(A,B,C,D)) :- solve__0(A,B,C,D).
%%% solve(app(A,B,C)) :- solve__1(A,B,C).
solve__0(B,C,D,E) :-  solve__1(C,D,F), solve__1(B,F,E).
solve__1([],B,B).
solve__1([B|C],D,[B|E]) :-  solve__1(C,D,E).
```

LOGEN will in general produce a specialised program which is slightly better
than the original program in the sense that it will generate code only for those
predicates that are reachable in the predicate dependency graph from the initial
call. E.g., for solve(app(X,Y,R)) only two clauses for app/3 will be produced,
not a clause for dapp/4.

It is relatively easy to see that Jones optimality will be achieved for any properly encoded object program and any call to the object program. Indeed, any
call of the form solve(p($t_1, \ldots, t_n$)) will be generalised into solve(p(_,...,_))
keeping information about the predicate being called; unfolding this will only
match the clauses of p as the call clause(X,Y) is marked **unfold** and all of the
parsing structure (and/2 and empty/0) will then be removed by further unfolding, leaving only predicate calls to be memoised. These are then generalised and
specialised in the same manner.

Rewriting Vanilla. The more principled solution is to rewrite the vanilla interpreter, so that the conjunction encoding and the object level atoms are clearly
separated. The attentive reader may have noticed that above we have actually
enforced that conjunctions are encoded as lists, with empty/0 playing the role of
nil/0 and and/2 playing the role of ./2. The following vanilla interpreter makes
this explicit and thus properly enforces this encoding. It is also more efficient,
as it no longer attempts to find definitions of empty and and within the clause
facts.

```
solve([]).
solve([H|T]) :- solve_atom(H), solve(T).
solve_atom(H) :- clause(H,Bdy), solve(Bdy).
```

```
clause(dapp(X,Y,Z,R), [app(Y,Z,YZ), app(X,YZ,R)]).
clause(app([],R,R), []).
clause(app([H|X],Y,[H|Z]), [app(X,Y,Z)]).
```

We can now annotate all calls to `solve` as **unfold**, knowing that this will only deconstruct the conjunction represented as a list. However, the call to `solve_atom` cannot be unfolded, as with recursive object programs we may perform infinite unfolding. LOGEN now produces the following specialised program for the query `solve_atom(dapp(X,Y,Z,R))`, having marked the argument to `solve_atom` calls as **nonvar**.[6]

```
solve_atom__0(B,C,D,E) :-
    solve_atom__1(C,D,F),solve_atom__1(B,F,E).
solve_atom__1([],B,B).
solve_atom__1([B|C],D,[B|E]) :- solve_atom__1(C,D,E).
```

We have again achieved Jones-Optimality, which holds for any object program and any object-level query.

An almost equivalent solution would be to improve the original vanilla interpreter so that atoms are tagged by a special function symbol, e.g., as follows:

```
solve(empty).
solve(and(A,B)) :- solve(A), solve(B).
solve(atom(X)) :-  solve_atom(X).
solve_atom(H) :- clause(H,Bdy), solve(Bdy).
clause(dapp(X,Y,Z,R),and(atom(app(Y,Z,YZ)),atom(app(X,YZ,R)))).
clause(app([],L,L),empty).
clause(app([H|X],Y,[H|Z]),atom(app(X,Y,Z))).
```

We have again clearly separated the control structures from the predicate calls and we can basically get the same result as above (by marking all calls to solve as **unfold** and the call to solve_atom as **memo**).

Reflections. So, what are the essential ingredients that allowed us to achieve Jones optimality where others have failed?

– First, the offline approach allows us to precisely steer the specialisation process in a predictable manner: we know exactly how the interpreter will be specialised independently of the complexity of the object program. A problem with online techniques is that they may work well for some object programs, but then be "fooled" by other (more or less contrived) object programs; see [50,28]. (On the other hand, online techniques are capable of removing several layers of self-interpretation in one go. An offline approach will typically only be able to remove one layer at a time.)

---

[6] The predicate `solve` does not have to be given a filter declaration as it is only unfolded and never residualised.

– Second, it was also important to have sufficiently refined annotations at our
disposal. Without the **nonvar** annotation we would not have been able to
specialise the original vanilla self-interpreter: we cannot mark the argument
to `solve` as static and marking it as dynamic means that no specialisation
will occur. Hence, considerable rewriting of the interpreter would have been
required if we just had **static** and **dynamic** at our disposal.[7]

– Third, it is important that the meta-interpreter is written in such a way
that the specialiser can distinguish between conjunctions and object level
calls and can treat them differently.

6   Jones-Optimality for a Debugger

Let us now try to extend the above interpreter, to do something more useful.
The code below implements a tracing version of `solve` which takes two extra
arguments: a counter for the current indentation level and a list of predicates to
trace.

```
dsolve([],_,_).
dsolve([H|T],Level,ToTrace) :-
      (debug(H,ToTrace)
       -> (indent(Level),print('Call: '),print(H),nl,
            dsolve_atom(H,s(Level),ToTrace),
            indent(Level),print('Exit: '),print(H),nl)
        ;  dsolve_atom(H,Level,ToTrace)
        ),
      dsolve(T,Level,ToTrace).

debug(Call,ToTrace) :- Call=..[P|Args],
      length(Args,Arity), member(P/Arity,ToTrace).

:- filter indent(dynamic).
indent(0).
indent(s(X)) :- print('>'),indent(X).

:- filter dsolve_atom(nonvar,dynamic,static).
dsolve_atom(H,Level,TT) :-
    clause(H,Bdy), dsolve(Bdy,Level,TT).
```

Basically, the annotation of `dsolve` and `dsolve_atom` calls are exactly as
before: calls to `dsolve` are marked as **unfold** while calls to `dsolve_atom` are
marked as **memo**. The if-then-else is marked **call**, i.e., it will be executed at
specialisation time. As far as the new predicates are concerned, all calls to `indent`
are marked **memo**, and all calls to `print` and `nl` are marked **rescall**. All other
user defined predicate are marked as **unfold** and built-ins as **call**. Note that the

---

[7] We leave this as an exercise for the reader. See also Section 7.1 later in the paper.

above interpreter uses non-declarative predicates, and hence one has to be careful about "left-propagation" of bindings [43]. In our case, one has to be careful not to left-propagate bindings onto the first `print(H)` call, as this could change the observable behaviour of the debugger. LOGEN provides special annotations (such as `hide_nf`, see [31]) to prevent these problems. However, in our case we do not need those annotations as the call `dsolve_atom(H,s(Level),ToTrace)` is marked **memo** and hence will not generate any bindings that could affect `print(H)`.

For `dsolve_atom(dapp([a,a,a],[b],[c],R),0,[])` we get the following almost optimal code:

```
dsolve_atom__0(B,C,D,E,F) :-
  dsolve_atom__1(C,D,G,F), dsolve_atom__1(B,G,E,F).
dsolve_atom__1([],B,B,C).
dsolve_atom__1([B|C],D,[B|E],F) :- dsolve_atom__1(C,D,E,F).
```

In fact, the extra last argument of both predicates can be easily removed by the FAR redundant argument filtering post-processing of [33] which produces a Jones-optimal result:

```
dsolve_atom__0(A,B,C,D) :-
  dsolve_atom__1(B,C,E),dsolve_atom__1(A,E,D).
dsolve_atom__1([],A,A).
dsolve_atom__1([A|B],C,[A|D]) :-  dsolve_atom__1(B,C,D).
```

Again, is is not too difficult to see that LOGEN together with the FAR post-processor [33] produces a Jones-optimal result for every object program P and call C, provided that none of the predicates reachable from C are traced.

For `dsolve_atom(dapp([a,a,a],[b],[c],R),0,[app/3])` we get the following very efficient tracing version of our object program, where the debugging statements have been weaved into the code. This specialised code now runs with minimal overhead, and there is no more runtime checking whether a call should be traced or not:

```
dsolve_atom__0(B,C,D,E,F) :-
  indent__1(F),print('Call: '),print(app(C,D,G)),nl,
  dsolve_atom__2(C,D,G,s(F)),
  indent__1(F),print('Exit: '),print(app(C,D,G)),nl,
  indent__1(F),print('Call: '),print(app(B,G,E)),nl,
  dsolve_atom__2(B,G,E,s(F)),
  indent__1(F),print('Exit: '),print(app(B,G,E)),nl.
indent__1(0).
indent__1(s(B)) :-  print('>'),indent__1(B).
dsolve_atom__2([],B,B,C).
dsolve_atom__2([B|C],D,[B|E],F) :-
  indent__1(F),print('Call: '),print(app(C,D,E)),nl,
  dsolve_atom__2(C,D,E,s(F)),
  indent__1(F),print('Exit: '),print(app(C,D,E)),nl.
```

Running the specialised program for dsolve_atom__0([a,b,c],[],[d],R,0),
corresponding to the call dsolve_atom(dapp([a,b,c],[],[d],R),0,[app/3])
to the original program, prints the following trace:

```
| ?- dsolve_atom__0([a,b,c],[],[d],R,0).
Call: app([],[d],_837)
Exit: app([],[d],[d])
Call: app([a,b,c],[d],_525)
>Call: app([b,c],[d],_1341)
>>Call: app([c],[d],_1601)
>>>Call: app([],[d],_1891)
>>>Exit: app([],[d],[d])
>>Exit: app([c],[d],[c,d])
>Exit: app([b,c],[d],[b,c,d])
Exit: app([a,b,c],[d],[a,b,c,d])
R = [a,b,c,d] ?
yes
```

Some Experimental Results. We now present some experimental results for
specialising the solve and dsolve interpeters. The results are summarised in
Table 1. The results were obtained on a Powerbook G4 running at 1 Ghz with
1Gb RAM and using SICStus Prolog 3.10.1.

The partition4 object program calls append to partition a list into 4 identical sublists, and has been run for a list of 1552 elements. The fibonacci
object program computes the Fibonacci numbers in the naive way using Peano
arithmetic. This program was benchmarked for computing the 24th Fibonacci
number. Exact queries can be found in the DPPD library [27]. The FAR filtering [33] has not been applied to the specialised programs. The time needed to
generate and run the generating extensions was negligible (more results, with
full times can be found later in the paper for more involved interpreters where
this time is more significant).

Table 1. Specialising solve and dsolve using LOGEN

object program	solve	specialised	speedup	dsolve	specialised	speedup
partition4	350 ms	200 ms	1.75	1590 ms	220 ms	7.23
fibonacci	890 ms	170 ms	5.24	4670 ms	180 ms	25.94

Adding More Functionality. It should be clear how one can extend the above
logic program interpreters. A good exercise is to add more logical connectives,
such as disjunction and implication, to the debugging interpreter dsolve and
then see whether one can obtain something similar to the Lloyd-Topor transformations [35] automatically by specialisation (with the added benefit that debugging can still be performed at the source level).

We will now show how one can handle interpreters for other programming paradigms. In such a setting variables and their values may have to be stored in some environment structure rather than relying on the Prolog variable model. This will raise a new challenge, which we tackle next.

7   More Sophisticated Annotations

So far we have come by with just three annotations for arguments in filter declarations: static, dynamic, and nonvar. The latter denotes a simple kind of so-called *partially static* data [21]. For more realistic programs, however, it is often essential to be able to deal with more sophisticated partially static data. For example, interpreters often have an environment, and at specialisation time we may know the actual variables store in the environment but not their value. Take the following simple interpreter for arithmetic expressions using addition, constants and variables whose value is stored in an environment:

```
int(cst(C),_E,C).
int(var(V),E,R) :- lookup(V,E,R).
int(+(A,B),E,R) :- int(A,E,Ra), int(B,E,Rb), R is Ra+Rb.

lookup(V,[(V,Val)|_T],Val).
lookup(V,[(_Var,_)|T],Res) :- lookup(V,T,Res).
```

A typical query to the above program would be

```
| ?- int(+(var(a),var(b)),[(a,1),(b,3),(c,5)],Res).
Res = 4 ?
yes
```

Now, if at specialisation time we know the variables of the environment list but not their value, this would be represented by an atom to specialise `int(+(var(a),var(b)),[(a,_),(b,_),(c,_)],R)`. We cannot declare the environment as static and the best we can do, given the binding types we have seen so far, is to declare the environment as nonvar:

```
:- filter int(static,nonvar,dynamic).
```

Unfortunately, this means that LOGEN will replace `[(a,_),(b,_),(c,_)]` by `[_|_]`, hence leading to suboptimal specialisation. For example, we cannot annotate `lookup` with **unfold** because the environment is an open ended list at specialisation time.

7.1   Binding-Time Improvements and Bifurcation

One way to overcome such limitations is often to rewrite the program to be specialised into a semantically equivalent program which specialises better, i.e., in which more arguments can be classified as static and/or more calls can be unfolded. This process is called *binding-time improvement*, see, e.g., Chapter 12 of [21].

One simple binding-time improvement for this particular problem is to define an auxiliary entry point as follows:

```
aux(Expr,A,B,C,Res) :- int(Expr,[(a,A),(b,B),(c,C)],Res).
```

Now, we can annotate the calls to int and lookup with **unfold** and the calls to is with **rescall** and use the following filter declaration:

```
:- filter aux(static,dynamic,dynamic,dynamic,dynamic).
```

However, this solution only works because we can completely unfold the predicates int and lookup. Hence, this solution is rather ad-hoc and works only in special circumstances. For example, if the object language supports recursive procedures, this will not work.

A more principled solution, is to apply a binding-time improvement sometimes called *bifurcation* [9,40]. This consists of splitting the environment into two parts (the static and the dynamic part) and then rewriting the interpreter accordingly. Here, a solution is to split the environment into two lists: a static one containing the variable names and a dynamic list containing the actual values. We would then rewrite our interpreter as follows:

```
:- filter int(static,static,dynamic,dynamic).
int(cst(C),_E,_E2,C).
int(var(V),E,E2,R) :- lookup(V,E,E2,R).
int(+(A,B),E,E2,R) :- int(A,E,E2,Ra), int(B,E,E2,Rb), R is Ra+Rb.

:- filter lookup(static,static,dynamic,dynamic).
lookup(V,[V|_],[Val|_],Val).
lookup(V,[_|T],[_|ValT],Res) :- lookup(V,T,ValT,Res).
```

One can annotate now all calls to int and lookup with **unfold**. It is even possible to annotate calls to int or to lookup(V,E,E2,R) as **memo** without loosing much specialisation as one part of the split environment is static and still available when specialising lookup.

There are however several problems with this approach:
- It can be very cumbersome and errorprone to rewrite the program.
- For every different annotation we may have to rewrite the program in a different way.
- If the dynamic and static data are not as neatly separated as above, it can be non-trivial to find a proper separation.
- The final result is not always "optimal". E.g., in the example above the information that the variable list and the value list must be of the same length is no longer explicit, resulting in a suboptimal residual program. For example, specialising for lookup(b,[a,b,c],[1,X,Y],Res) gives

```
%%% lookup(b,[a,b,c],[1,X,Y],Res) :- lookup__0([1,X,Y],Res).
%%% lookup(b,[a,b,c],A,B) :- lookup__0(A,B).
lookup__0([B,C|D],C).
```

This is less efficient than the result we will obtain later below, mainly because the value list has still to be deconstructed and examined at runtime (via the unification with [B,C|D]).

LOGEN provides a better way of solving this problem by allowing its users to define their own annotations using what we will call binding-types. For the interpreter above we would like to be able to define a custom annotation describing a list of pairs whose first element is static and the second dynamic. In the rest of this section we formalise and describe how this can be achieved.

7.2 Formal Definition of Binding-Types

In what follows, we present a polished version of the notion of a *binding-type* as introduced in [31] in order to characterise partially instantiated specialisation-time values in a more precise way. Like a traditional type in logic programming [2], a binding-type is conceptually defined as a set of terms closed under substitution and represented by a term constructed from *type variables* and *type constructors* in the same way that a data term is constructed from ordinary variables and function symbols. However, the underlying type system is different from the one of Mercury used in [49] for developing binding-types where the right hand side of a rule consists of a number of alternatives of the form $f(\tau_1, \ldots, \tau_k)$ with f a function symbol and the τ_i types. The LOGEN user has to cope with untyped Prolog programs and his interest is not in well-typing them but in concisely expressing the relevant binding-types. Hence LOGEN allows for union types and for function symbols anywhere in the names of types and in the right hand side of type rules. To distinguish between function symbols and type constructors, a wrapper type/1 is used for the latter. The wrapper is ommitted for the predefined binding-types *static/0, dynamic/0, nonvar/0,* and *list/1*. Formally, a type is inductively defined as follows:

Definition 2. *The set of types is the least set defined by the following rules:*
- *A type variable is a type.*
- static, dynamic, *and* nonvar *are types.*
- *If* t *is a type then* list(t) *is a type.*
- *If* c/n *is a type constructor different from* static, dynamic, nonvar *and* list/1 *and* $\tau_1, \ldots, \tau_n$ *are types then* type(c($\tau_1, \ldots, \tau_n$)) *is a type.*
- *If* f/n *is a function symbol and* $\tau_1, \ldots, \tau_n$ *are types then* f($\tau_1, \ldots, \tau_n$) *is a type.*

As user programs may use the predefined binding-types as function symbols, the need could arise to refer to these function symbols in a binding type. Therefore, LOGEN also provides a wrapper term/1. For example, term(static) is the type denoting the singleton set with the function symbol *static* and not the binding-type static. To keep the exposition simple, we have not included the term wrapper in the above definition of types and we will ommit it entirely in what follows.

The set of terms denoted by a type of the form $f(\tau_1,\ldots,\tau_n)$ are all the terms of the form $f(t_1,\ldots,tn)$ with for all i: $t_i \in \tau_i$. For types of the form $\texttt{type}(c(\tau_1,\ldots,\tau_n))$, the denotation has to be defined by a type rule.

Definition 3. *A* type rule *for a type constructor c of arity n is of the form:*

$$\texttt{:- type } c(V_1,\ldots,V_n) \texttt{ ---> } (\tau_1 \; ; \; \ldots \; ; \; \tau_k).$$

with $k \geq 1$, $n \geq 0$ and where $V_1,\ldots,V_n$ are distinct type variables, and $\tau_1,\ldots,\tau_k$ are distinct types. Any type variable occurring in the right hand side must occur also in the left hand side. A set of type rules is a type definition.

With $n = 0$, a type rule defines a monomorphic or ground type, with $n > 0$, the type is polymorhic and the type rule defines the denotation for every type instance of the polymorhic type. For example the type rule corresponding with the predefined type $\texttt{list(V)}$ is:

```
:- type list(V) ---> [ ] ; [V | list(V)].
```

Every type $\texttt{type}(c(\tau_1,\ldots,\tau_n))$ used in the annotations of LOGEN's input must be defined, i.e., there must be a type rule with left hand side $c(V_1,\ldots,V_n)$ and, for all types $\texttt{type}(\tau)$ occurring in the right hand side of the type rule, the type $\texttt{type}(\tau\{V_1/\tau_1,\ldots,V_n/\tau_n\})$ must be defined.

Now we can formally define the denotations of types:

Definition 4. $[[\tau]]$, *the set of terms denotated by a type τ is defined as follows:*
- $[[dynamic]] = \{t \mid t \text{ is a term}\}$.
- $[[static]] = \{t \mid t \text{ is a ground term}\}$.
- $[[nonvar]] = \{t \mid t \text{ is a non-variable term}\}$.
- $[[type(c(\tau_1,\ldots,\tau_n))]] = \{t \mid t \in [[\tau]] \text{ and there is a type rule of the form}$
  $\texttt{:- type } c(V_1,\ldots,V_n) \texttt{ ---> } (\ldots;\tau;\ldots) \text{ and } t \in [[\tau\{V_1/\tau_1,\ldots,V_n/\tau_n\}]]$.
- $[[f(\tau_1,\ldots,\tau_n)]] = \{f(t_1,\ldots,t_n) \mid t_i \in [[\tau_i]] \text{ for all } i\}$.
- $[[list(\tau)]] = \{[]\} \cup \{[t_1 \mid t_2] \mid t_1 \in [[\tau]] \text{ and } t_2 \in [[list(\tau)]]\}$

Note that our definitions guarantee that types are downwards-closed (i.e., $t \in [[\tau]]$ implies $t\theta \in [[\tau]]$).

A few examples are as follows: $[] \in [[static]]$, $[] \in [[[\,]]]$, $[] \in [[list(static)]]$, $[] \in [[list(dynamic)]]$; $s(0) \in [[static]]$ hence $[s(0)] \in [[list(static)]]$; $X \in [[dynamic]]$ and $Y \in [[dynamic]]$ hence $[X,Y] \in [[list(dynamic)]]$.

7.3   Using Binding-Types

The three basic binding types that are now used to control generalisation and filtering (the predicate $\texttt{generalise\_and\_filter}$) within the offline partial deduction algorithm of Section 3.2 are as follows:
- An argument marked as **dynamic** is replaced by a fresh variable and there will be a corresponding argument in the residual predicate.

- An argument marked as **static** is not generalised, and there will be no corresponding argument in the residual predicate.
- The top-level function symbol of an argument marked as **nonvar** will be kept, while all of its arguments are replaced by fresh variables. There will be one argument in the residual predicate for each argument of the top-level function symbol.
- An argument marked as $f(\tau_1, \ldots, \tau_n)$ is basically dealt with like the **nonvar** case, except that the top-level function symbol has to be f and every sub-argument of f will be recursively generalised and filtered according to the binding-types τ_i.
- For an argument marked as $type(c(\tau_1, \ldots, \tau_n))$ the type rule of c will be looked at and the argument will be treated according to the body of the rule. For disjunctions like $\tau_1 ; \tau_2$ the algorithm will first attempt to apply τ_1, and if that is not successful it will apply τ_2.

For example, given the declaration :- filter p(static,dynamic,nonvar). the call p(a,[b],f(c,d)) is generalised into p(a,_,f(_,_)) and the residual version of the call is of the form p__1([b],c,d). Given the declaration" :- filter p(static,dynamic,f(static,dynamic))." the call is generalised into p(a,_,f(c,_)) and the residual version is of the form p__2([b],d). Finally, using ":- filter p(static,list(dynamic),static)." as filter declaration, the same call is generalised into p(a,[_],f(c,d)) with the residual version being of the form p__3(b).

Let us now try to tackle the original arithmetic int/3 interpreter using the more refined binding-types. First, we define a new type, describing a list of pairs whose first element is static and whose second element is given by a parameter of the type constructor (so as to show how parameters can be used):

```
:- type bind_list(X) ---> list((static,X)).
```

For the interpreter we can now simply provide the following filter declarations:

```
:- filter int(static,type(bind_list(dynamic)),dynamic).
:- filter lookup(static,type(bind_list(dynamic)),dynamic).
```

Given these filter declarations, we can now annotate the clause bodies as follows:
```
int(cst(C),_E,C).
int(var(V),E,R)  :- lookup(V, E, R)).
```
$$\underbrace{\qquad}_{unfold}$$
```
int(+(A,B),E,R)  :- int(A, E, Ra)), int(B, E, Rb)), RisRa + Rb).
```
$$\underbrace{\qquad}_{unfold} \quad \underbrace{\qquad}_{unfold} \quad \underbrace{\qquad}_{rescall}$$
```
lookup(V,[(V,Val)|_T],Val).
lookup(V,[(_Var,_)|T],Res)  :- lookup(V, T, Res).
```
$$\underbrace{\qquad}_{unfold}$$

While these annotations and types were derived by hand, we believe that it is possible to derive them automatically. One approach is to adapt the polymorphic binding-time analysis for Mercury presented in a companion chapter [49] of this book. For more details see [49]. A fully automatic monomorphic binding-time analysis, refining earlier work in [6,31] is currently being implemented within the EU-funded project ASAP (see http://clip.dia.fi.upm.es/Projects/ASAP/).

Let us now use LOGEN to specialise the original int/3 interpreter for the query lookup(b,[(a,1),(b,X),(c,Y)],Res). This results in the following specialised code:

```
%%% lookup(b,[(a,A),(b,B),(c,C)],D) :- lookup__0(A,B,C,D).
lookup__0(B,C,D,C).
```

This code is much more efficient, as linear time lookup of variable bindings has been replaced by basically constant time lookup in the argument list.

Let us now specialise the interpreter for a full-fledged query:
int(+(cst(3),+(+(cst(2),cst(5)),+(var(y),+(var(x),var(y))))),
[(a,1),(b,2),(x,3),(y,4)],X). This produces the following satisfactory result, where the arithmetic expression has been fully compiled into Prolog code.

```
int__0(B,C,D,E,F) :-  G is (2 + 5), H is (D + E),
                      I is (E + H), J is (G + I), F is (3 + J).
```

One can see that the reduction G is (2+5) has not been performed by the specialiser. This shows an aspect where an online specialiser could have fared better, as it could have realised that, for this particular instruction, the right hand side of the is/2 was actually known (even though it is in general dynamic). Still, it is possible to instruct LOGEN to try to perform calls using the so-called **semicall** annotation [31]. Another alternative is to binding-time improve the program by inserting an explicit if-statement, changing the 3rd clause of the interpreter as follows:

$$\texttt{int(+(A,B),E,E2,R)} :- \underbrace{\texttt{int(A,E,E2,Ra)}}_{unfold}, \underbrace{\texttt{int(B,E,E2,Ra)}}_{unfold},$$

$$(\underbrace{\texttt{ground((Ra,Rb))}}_{call} \ \texttt{->} \ \underbrace{\texttt{R is Ra+Rb}}_{call} \ ; \ \underbrace{\texttt{R is Ra+Rb}}_{rescall}).$$

where the if-statement itself is marked **call** and executed at specialisation time. The resulting specialised interpreter is then:

```
int__0(B,C,D,E,F) :-  G is (D + E), H is (E + G),
                      I is (7 + H),  F is (3 + I).
```

7.4   Revisiting Vanilla Again

Finally, let us present a third solution for specialising the Vanilla self-interpreter from Section 5.3. Indeed, we can now use the following more precise binding types on the original interpreter, thus ensuring that relevant information will be kept by the generalisation:

```
:- type vexp ---> (empty ; and(type(vexp),type(vexp))
                          ; type(predcall)).
:- type predcall ---> (app(dynamic,dynamic,dynamic)
                      ;  dapp(dynamic,dynamic,dynamic,dynamic)).
:- filter solve(type(vexp)).
```

Given these filter declarations, we can mark the calls solve(A), solve(B) and clause(X,Y as **unfold**, and mark the call solve(Y) as **memo**. This will not give full Jones optimality, due to the bad way in which the original solve is written, but it will at least give much better specialisation than was possible using just **static**, **dynamic**, and **nonvar**.

8   Lambda Interpreter

Based on the insights of the previous section, we now tackle a more substantial example. We will present an interpreter for a small functional language. The interpreter still leaves much to be desired from a functional programming language perspective, but the main purpose is to show how to specialise a non-trivial interpreter for another programming paradigm. The interpreter will use an environment, very much like the one in the previous section, to store values for variables and function arguments. The full annotated source code is available with the LO-GEN distribution at http://www.ecs.soton.ac.uk/~mal/systems/logen.html.

To keep things simple, we will not use a parser but simply use Prolog's operator declarations to encode the functional programs. The following shows how to encode the Fibonacci function for our interpreter:

```
:- op(150,fx,$). /* to indicate variables */
:- op(150,fx,&). /* to indicate constants */
:- op(150,yfx,'==='). /* to define functions */
:- op(150,yfx,@). /* to do calls to defined functions */
:- op(250,yfx,'->'). /* for sequential composition */

fib ===  lambda(x,if($x = &0,  &1,
                     if($x = &1,  &1,
                        (fib @ ($x - &1) + fib @ ($x - &2)))))).
```

The source code of the interpreter is as shown below. As usual in functional programming, one distinguishes between constructors (encoded using constr/2) and functions (encoded using lambda/2). Functions can be defined statically using the === declarations which can then be extracted using the fun/1 expression. One can use @ as a shorthand to call such defined functions. One can introduce local variables using the let/3 expression. The predicate eval/3 computes the normal form of an expression. The rest of the code should be pretty much self-explanatory. To keep the code simpler, we have not handled renaming of the arguments of lambda expressions (it is not required for the examples we will deal with).

```
eval('&'(C),_Env,constr(C,[])).   /* 0-ary constructor */
eval(constr(C,Args),Env,constr(C,EArgs)) :- l_eval(Args,Env,EArgs).
eval('$'(VKey),Env,Val) :-  /* variable */ lookup(VKey,Env,Val).
eval('+'(X,Y),Env,constr(XY,[])) :- eval(X,Env,constr(VX,[])),
        eval(Y,Env,constr(VY,[])), XY is VX+VY.
eval('-'(X,Y),Env,constr(XY,[])) :- eval(X,Env,constr(VX,[])),
        eval(Y,Env,constr(VY,[])), XY is VX-VY.
eval('*'(X,Y),Env,constr(XY,[])) :- eval(X,Env,constr(VX,[])),
        eval(Y,Env,constr(VY,[])), XY is VX*VY.
eval(let(VKey,VExpr,InExpr),Env,Result) :- eval(VExpr,Env,VVal),
        store(Env,VKey,VVal,InEnv), eval(InExpr,InEnv,Result).
eval(if(Test,Then,Else),Env,Res) :- eval_if(Test,Then,Else,Env,Res).
eval(lambda(X,Expr),_Env,lambda(X,Expr)).
eval(apply(Arg,F),Env,Res) :- eval(F,Env,FVal),
        eval(Arg,Env,ArgVal), eval_apply(ArgVal,FVal,Env,Res).
eval(fun(F),_,FunDef) :- '==='(F,FunDef).
eval('@'(F,Args),E,R) :- eval(apply(Args,fun(F)),E,R).
eval(print(X),Env,FVal) :- eval(X,Env,FVal),print(FVal),nl.
eval('->'(X,Y),Env,Res) :-  /* seq. composition */
        eval(X,Env,_), eval(Y,Env,Res).

eval_apply(ArgVal,FVal,Env,Res) :- rename(FVal,Env,lambda(X,Expr)),
        store(Env,X,ArgVal,NewEnv), eval(Expr,NewEnv,Res).

rename(Expr,_Env,RenExpr) :- RenExpr=Expr.  /* sufficient for now */

l_eval([],_E,[]).
l_eval([H|T],E,[EH|ET]) :- eval(H,E,EH), l_eval(T,E,ET).

eval_if(Test,Then,_Else,Env,Res) :- test(Test,Env), !, eval(Then,Env,Res).
eval_if(_Test,_Then,Else,Env,Res)) :- eval(Else,Env,Res).

test('='(X,Y),Env) :- eval(X,Env,VX),eval(Y,Env,VX).

store([],Key,Value,[Key/Value]).
store([Key/_Value2|T],Key,Value,[Key/Value|T]).
store([Key2/Value2|T],Key,Value,[Key2/Value2|BT]) :-
        Key\==Key2,store(T,Key,Value,BT).

lookup(Key,[Key/Value|_T],Value).
lookup(Key,[Key2/_Value2|T],Value) :-
        Key\==Key2,lookup(Key,T,Value).
```

Handling the Cut. One may notice that the above program does use a cut in the code for eval_if. Previous version of LOGEN did not support the cut, but it turns out that specialising the cut is actually very easy to do: basically all one has to do is to simply mark the cuts using either the **call** or **rescall** annotations we have already encountered. It is up to the binding time analysis to ensure that this is sound, i.e., one has to ensure that:

- If a cut is marked **call**, then whenever it is reached and executed at specialisation time the calls to the left of the cut will never fail at runtime.
- If a cut is marked as **rescall** within a predicate p, then no calls to p are unfolded. One can relax this condition somewhat, e.g., one may to be able to unfold such a predicate p if all computations are deterministic (like in our functional interpreter) but one has to be very careful when doing that.

These conditions are sufficient to handle the cut in a sound, but still useful manner. Details about handling the cut in an online specialiser can be found in [41,43].

Annotations. To be able to specialise this interpreter we need the power of LOGEN's binding types. The structure of the environment is much like in the previous section, but here we have more information about the structure of values that the interpreter manipulates and stores. Basically, values are encoded using constr/2, whose first argument is the symbol of the constructor being encoded and the second argument is a list containing the encoding of the arguments. A lambda expression is also a valid value.

```
:- type value_expression =
      (constr(dynamic,list(type(value_expression))) ;
       lambda(static,static)).
:- type env = list( static / type(value_expression)).
```

We can now annotate the calls of our program. Basically, all built-ins have to be marked **rescall** but all user calls can be marked as **unfold** except for the call eval_apply(ArgVal,FVal,Env,Res). We thus supply the following filter declaration:

```
:- type result = ( type(value_expression) ; dynamic).
:- filter eval_apply(type(result),type(result),type(env),dynamic).
```

Note that we use a union type for result, because often (but not always) we will have partial information about the result types. Union types are thus a way to allow LOGEN to make some online decisions: during specialisation it will check whether the first and second argument of eval_apply match the value_expression type and it will treat the arguments as dynamic (the second alternative in the type result) when they do not.

Experiments When specialising this program for, e.g., calling the fib function we get something very similar to the (naive) fibonacci program one would have written in Prolog in the first place:

```
%% eval_apply(constr(A,[]),lambda(x,if($x= &0,&1,if($x= &1,&1,
%%    fib@($x- &1)+fib@($x- &2)))),[x/constr(B,[])],C) :-
%%    eval_apply__2(A,B,C).
eval_apply__2(0,B,constr(1,[])) :-  !.
```

```
eval_apply__2(1,B,constr(1,[])) :-  !.
eval_apply__2(B,C,constr(D,[])) :-
  E is (B - 1), eval_apply__2(E,B,constr(F,[])),
  G is (B - 2), eval_apply__2(G,B,constr(H,[])),  D is (F + H).
```

This specialised code runs about 14 times faster than the original, and even when including the specialisation time, i.e., the time to run LOGEN and the generating extension, the specialised program is still 7 times faster than running the original program. Full details of this experiment can be found in Table 2.

Furthermore, the experiments described below indicate that speedups are getting bigger for more complicated object programs with more functions and more arguments and variables. One reason being that more complicated object programs will have more variables, and hence looking up variable values in the list environment will get more and more expensive, whereas lookup in the specialised program will be basically a constant time operation (relevant variables are arguments of the specialised predicates). Indeed, the results of specialising the interpreter for the following slightly bigger functional program that has extra loop variables results in bigger speedups.

```
loop_fib === lambda(cur,let(cur1,$cur + &1, let(cur2, $cur1 + &1,
               let(cur3, $cur2 + &1,  if(($cur = &21),
                 (fib @ ($cur)),
                 (print(constr(fibonacci,[$cur,fib @ ($cur)]))
                  ->  (loop_fib @ ($cur1)))))))).
```

In the same table one can see figures for loop_fib2, loop_fib3, loop_fib4, loop_fib5, each with 3 more variables in the environment than its predecessor, but apart from that behaving identically to loop_fib. As can be seen, the specialised programs basically all run in the same time (60–70 ms), whereas the original interpreter runs considerably slower with more variables, increasing the speedup to 45 for loop_fib5.

Note that LOGEN has only to be run once for the eval interpreter; the same generating extension can then be used for specialising the interpreter with respect to any functional program. Similarly, the specialised code can then be used for any call to the given functional program.[8]

9   Discussion and Conclusion

Probably the most closely related work is [20] which treats untyped first-order functional languages, and gives a list of recommendations on how to write interpreters that specialise well. Even though [20] does of course not address the specific issues that arise when specialising logic programming interpreters, many

---

[8] In the speedup figures we suppose that the time needed for consulting is the same for the original and specialised program. In our experiments consulting the specialised program was actually slightly faster, but this may not always be the case.

Table 2. Specialising `eval` using LOGEN

function call	eval runtime	logen time	genex time	specialised runtime	speedup	speedup (incl. gx)	speedup (incl. gx,logen)
fib(24)	1050 ms	60 ms	15ms	75 ms	14.0	11.7	7
loop_fib(0)	1430 ms	60 ms	30ms	60 ms	23.8	15.9	9.5
loop_fib2(0)	1940 ms	60 ms	40ms	60 ms	32.3	19.4	12.1
loop_fib3(0)	2460 ms	60 ms	50ms	60 ms	41.0	22.4	14.5
loop_fib4(0)	2540 ms	60 ms	50ms	70 ms	36.3	21.2	14.1
loop_fib5(0)	3150 ms	60 ms	60ms	70 ms	45.0	24.2	16.6

points raised in [20] are also valid in the logic programming setting. For example, [20] suggests that you should "Write your interpreter compositionally" which is exactly what we have done for our lambda interpreter in Section 8 and which makes it much easier to ensure termination of the specialisation process. [20] also warns of "data structures that contain static data, but can grow unboundedly under dynamic control" (such as a stack). The environment in the lambda interpreter contained static data but its length was fixed and so caused no problem; however if we were to add an activation stack to our interpreter in Section 8 we would have to resort to the recipes suggested in [20].

We have already discussed related work in the logic programming community [42,47,44,5,7,26,50,28]. In the functional community there has been a lot of recent interest in Jones optimality; see [19,36,46,13]. For example, [13] shows theoretically the interest of having a Jones-optimal specialiser and the results should also be relevant for logic programming.

As far as future work is concerned, the most challenging topic is probably to provide a fully automatic binding-time analysis. As already mentioned, the binding-time analysis in [49] may prove to be a good starting point. Still, it is likely that at least some user intervention will be required in the foreseeable future to specialise more complicated interpreters.

Another avenue for further investigation is to move from interpreters to program transformers and analysers. A particular kind of program transformer is of course a partial evaluator, and one may wonder whether we can specialise, e.g., the code from Section 3. Actually, it turns out we can now do this and, surprisingly or not, the specialised specialisers we obtain in this way are quite similar to the one generated by LOGEN directly. This issue is investigated in [8], proving some first encouraging results.

In conclusion, we have shown how to use offline specialisation in general and LOGEN in particular to specialise logic programming interpreters. We have shown how to obtain Jones-optimality for simple self-interpreters, as well as for more involved interpreter such as a debugger. We have also shown how to specialise interpreters for other programming paradigms, using more sophisticated binding-types. We have also presented some experimental results, highlighting the speedups that can be obtained, and showing that the LOGEN system can be a useful basis for generating compilers for high-level languages. Indeed, we soon hope to be able to apply LOGEN to derive a compiler from the interpreter in [30], and then compiling high-level B specifications into Prolog code for fast animation and verification.

Acknowledgements

We would like to thank Mauricio Varea for helping us out with some of the figures and for valuable discussions. We are also very grateful to Armin Rigo for developing the initial Emacs mode. We also thank the ASAP project participants for their stimulating feedback and their help in adapting LOGEN for Ciao-Prolog. Finally, we thank the reviewers for their thoughtful comments.

References

1. L. O. Andersen. *Program Analysis and Specialization for the C Programming Language*. PhD thesis, DIKU, University of Copenhagen, May 1994. (DIKU report 94/19).
2. K. R. Apt and E. Marchiori. Reasoning about Prolog programs: from modes through types to assertions. *Formal Aspects of Computing*, 6(6A):743–765, 1994.
3. K. R. Apt and F. Turini. *Meta-logics and Logic Programming.* MIT Press, 1995.
4. L. Birkedal and M. Welinder. Hand-writing program generator generators. In M. Hermenegildo and J. Penjam, editors, *Programming Language Implementation and Logic Programming. Proceedings, Proceedings of PLILP'91*, LNCS 844, pages 198–214, Madrid, Spain, 1994. Springer-Verlag.
5. A. F. Bowers and C. A. Gurr. Towards fast and declarative meta-programming. In K. R. Apt and F. Turini, editors, *Meta-logics and Logic Programming*, pages 137–166. MIT Press, 1995.
6. M. Bruynooghe, M. Leuschel, and K. Sagonas. A polyvariant binding-time analysis for off-line partial deduction. In C. Hankin, editor, *Proceedings of the European Symposium on Programming (ESOP'98)*, LNCS 1381, pages 27–41. Springer-Verlag, April 1998.
7. Y. Cosmadopoulos, M. Sergot, and R. W. Southwick. Data-driven transformation of meta-interpreters: A sketch. In H. Boley and M. M. Richter, editors, *Proceedings of the International Workshop on Processing Declarative Knowledge (PDK'91)*, volume 567 of *LNAI*, pages 301–308, Kaiserslautern, FRG, July 1991. Springer Verlag.
8. S. Craig and M. Leuschel. Lix: An effective self-applicable partial evaluator for Prolog. In *Proceedings of FLOPS'04*, April 2004. To appear.
9. A. De Niel, E. Bevers, and K. De Vlaminck. Partial evaluation of polymorphically typed functional languages: The representation problem. In M. Billaud and et al., editors, *Analyse Statique en Programmation Équationelle, Fonctionelle, et Logique (Bigre, vol. 74)*, pages 90–97, October 1991.
10. Y. Futamura. Partial evaluation of a computation process — an approach to a compiler-compiler. *Systems, Computers, Controls*, 2(5):45–50, 1971.
11. J. Gallagher. Tutorial on specialisation of logic programs. In *Proceedings of PEPM'93, the ACM Sigplan Symposium on Partial Evaluation and Semantics-Based Program Manipulation*, pages 88–98. ACM Press, 1993.

12. J. Gallagher and M. Bruynooghe. Some low-level transformations for logic programs. In M. Bruynooghe, editor, *Proceedings of Meta90 Workshop on Meta Programming in Logic*, pages 229–244, Leuven, Belgium, 1990.
13. R. Glück. Jones optimality, binding-time improvements, and the strength of program specializers. In *Proceedings of the ASIAN symposium on Partial evaluation and semantics-based program manipulation*, pages 9–19. ACM Press, 2002.
14. R. Glück and J. Jørgensen. Efficient multi-level generating extensions for program specialization. In S. Swierstra and M. Hermenegildo, editors, *Programming Languages, Implementations, Logics and Programs (PLILP'95)*, LNCS 982, pages 259–278, Utrecht, The Netherlands, September 1995. Springer-Verlag.
15. C. A. Gurr. *A Self-Applicable Partial Evaluator for the Logic Programming Language Gödel.* PhD thesis, Department of Computer Science, University of Bristol, January 1994.
16. P. Hill and J. Gallagher. Meta-programming in logic programming. In D. M. Gabbay, C. J. Hogger, and J. A. Robinson, editors, *Handbook of Logic in Artificial Intelligence and Logic Programming*, volume 5, pages 421–497. Oxford Science Publications, Oxford University Press, 1998.
17. C. K. Holst. Syntactic currying: yet another approach to partial evaluation. Technical report, DIKU, Department of Computer Science, University of Copenhagen, 1989.
18. C. K. Holst and J. Launchbury. Handwriting cogen to avoid problems with static typing. In *Draft Proceedings, Fourth Annual Glasgow Workshop on Functional Programming, Skye, Scotland*, pages 210–218. Glasgow University, 1991.
19. N. D. Jones. Partial evaluation, self-application and types. In M. S. Paterson, editor, *Automata, Languages and Programming*, LNCS 443, pages 639–659. Springer-Verlag, 1990.
20. N. D. Jones. What not to do when writing an interpreter for specialisation. In O. Danvy, R. Glück, and P. Thiemann, editors, *Partial Evaluation, International Seminar*, LNCS 1110, pages 216–237, Schloß Dagstuhl, 1996. Springer-Verlag.
21. N. D. Jones, C. K. Gomard, and P. Sestoft. *Partial Evaluation and Automatic Program Generation.* Prentice Hall, 1993.
22. N. D. Jones, P. Sestoft, and H. Søndergaard. An experiment in partial evaluation: The generation of a compiler generator. In J.-P. Jouannaud, editor, *Rewriting Techniques and Applications*, LNCS 202, pages 124–140, Dijon, France, 1985. Springer-Verlag.
23. N. D. Jones, P. Sestoft, and H. Søndergaard. Mix: a self-applicable partial evaluator for experiments in compiler generation. *LISP and Symbolic Computation*, 2(1):9–50, 1989.
24. J. Jørgensen and M. Leuschel. Efficiently generating efficient generating extensions in Prolog. In O. Danvy, R. Glück, and P. Thiemann, editors, *Partial Evaluation, International Seminar*, LNCS 1110, pages 238–262, Schloß Dagstuhl, 1996. Springer-Verlag.
25. J. Komorowski. An introduction to partial deduction. In A. Pettorossi, editor, *Proceedings Meta'92*, LNCS 649, pages 49–69. Springer-Verlag, 1992.
26. A. Lakhotia and L. Sterling. How to control unfolding when specializing interpreters. *New Generation Computing*, 8:61–70, 1990.
27. M. Leuschel. The ECCE partial deduction system and the DPPD library of benchmarks. Obtainable via http://www.ecs.soton.ac.uk/~mal, 1996-2002.
28. M. Leuschel. Homeomorphic embedding for online termination of symbolic methods. In T. Æ. Mogensen, D. Schmidt, and I. H. Sudborough, editors, *The Essence*

of Computation - Essays dedicated to Neil Jones, LNCS 2?56, pages 379–403. Springer-Verlag, 2002.

29. M. Leuschel and M. Bruynooghe. Logic program specialisation through partial deduction: Control issues. *Theory and Practice of Logic Programming*, 2(4 & 5):461–515, July & September 2002.

30. M. Leuschel and M. Butler. ProB: A model checker for B. In K. Araki, S. Gnesi, and D. Mandrioli, editors, *FME 2003: Formal Methods*, LNCS 2805, pages 855–874. Springer-Verlag, 2003.

31. M. Leuschel, J. Jørgensen, W. Vanhoof, and M. Bruynooghe. Offline specialisation in Prolog using a hand-written compiler generator. *Theory and Practice of Logic Programming*, 4(1):139–191, 2004.

32. M. Leuschel, B. Martens, and D. De Schreye. Controlling generalisation and polyvariance in partial deduction of normal logic programs. *ACM Transactions on Programming Languages and Systems*, 20(1):208–258, January 1998.

33. M. Leuschel and M. H. Sørensen. Redundant argument filtering of logic programs. In J. Gallagher, editor, *Logic Program Synthesis and Transformation. Proceedings of LOPSTR'96*, LNCS 1207, pages 83–103, Stockholm, Sweden, August 1996. Springer-Verlag.

34. J. W. Lloyd. *Foundations of Logic Programming.* Springer-Verlag, 1987.

35. J. W. Lloyd and R. W. Topor. Making Prolog more expressive. *Journal of Logic Programming*, 1(3):225–240, 1984.

36. H. Makholm. On Jones-optimal specialization for strongly typed languages. In W. Taha, editor, *Semantics, Applications, and Implementation of Program Generation*, LNCS 1924, pages 129–148. Springer-Verlag, 2000.

37. B. Martens. *On the Semantics of Meta-Programming and the Control of Partial Deduction in Logic Programming.* PhD thesis, K.U. Leuven, February 1994.

38. B. Martens and J. Gallagher. Ensuring global termination of partial deduction while allowing flexible polyvariance. In L. Sterling, editor, *Proceedings ICLP'95*, pages 597–613, Kanagawa, Japan, June 1995. MIT Press.

39. T. Mogensen and A. Bondorf. Logimix: A self-applicable partial evaluator for Prolog. In K.-K. Lau and T. Clement, editors, Logic Program Synthesis and Transformation. *Proceedings of LOPSTR'92*, pages 214–227. Springer-Verlag, 1992.

40. T. Æ. Mogensen. Separating binding times in language specifications. In *Proceedings of FPCA'89*, pages 12–25. ACM press, 1989.

41. S. Prestwich. An unfold rule for full Prolog. In K.-K. Lau and T. Clement, editors, Logic Program Synthesis and Transformation. *Proceedings of LOPSTR'92*, Workshops in Computing, pages 199–213, University of Manchester, 1992. Springer-Verlag.

42. S. Safra and E. Shapiro. Meta interpreters for real. In H.-J. Kugler, editor, *Proceedings of IFIP'86*, pages 271–278, 1986.

43. D. Sahlin. Mixtus: An automatic partial evaluator for full Prolog. *New Generation Computing*, 12(1):7–51, 1993.

44. L. Sterling and R. D. Beer. Metainterpreters for expert system construction. *The Journal of Logic Programming*, 6(1 & 2):163–178, 1989.

45. L. Sterling and E. Shapiro. *The Art of Prolog.* MIT Press, 1986.

46. W. Taha, H. Makholm, and J. Hughes. Tag elimination and Jones-optimality. In O. Danvy and A. Filinski, editors, *Programs as Data Objects, Second Symposium, PADO 2001*, LNCS 2053, pages 257–275, Aarhus, Denmark, May 2001. Springer-Verlag.

47. A. Takeuchi and K. Furukawa. Partial evaluation of Prolog programs and its application to meta programming. In H.-J. Kugler, editor, *Information Processing 86*, pages 415–420, 1986.
48. P. Thiemann. Cogen in six lines. In *International Conference on Functional Programming*, pages 180–189. ACM Press, 1996.
49. W. Vanhoof, M. Bruynooghe, and M. Leuschel. Binding-time analysis for Mercury. In M. Bruynooghe and K.-K. Lau, editors, *Program Development in Computational Logic*, LNCS this Volume. Springer-Verlag, 2004.
50. W. Vanhoof and B. Martens. To parse or not to parse. In N. Fuchs, editor, *Logic Program Synthesis and Transformation. Proceedings of LOPSTR'97*, LNCS 1463, pages 322–342, Leuven, Belgium, July 1997.

Characterisations of Termination
in Logic Programming

Dino Pedreschi[1], Salvatore Ruggieri[1], and Jan-Georg Smaus[2]

[1] Dipartimento di Informatica, Università di Pisa
Via F. Buonarroti 2, 56125 Pisa, Italy
{pedre,ruggieri}@di.unipi.it
[2] Institut für Informatik, Universität Freiburg
Georges-Köhler-Allee 52, 79110 Freiburg im Breisgau, Germany
smaus@informatik.uni-freiburg.de

Abstract. The procedural interpretation of logic programs and queries is parametric to the selection rule, i.e. the rule that determines which atom is selected in each resolution step. Termination of logic programs and queries depends critically on the selection rule. In this survey, we present a unified view and comparison of seven notions of universal termination considered in the literature, and the corresponding classes of programs. For each class, we focus on a sufficient, and in most cases even necessary, declarative characterisation for determining that a program is in that class. By unifying different formalisms and making appropriate assumptions, we are able to establish a formal hierarchy between the different classes and their respective declarative characterisations.

1 Introduction

The paradigm of logic programming originates from the discovery that a fragment of first-order logic can be given an elegant computational interpretation. Kowalski [40] advocates the separation of the *logic* and *control* aspects of a logic program and has coined the famous formula

Algorithm = Logic + Control.

The programmer should be responsible for the logic part, and hence a logic program should be a (first-order logic) specification. The control should be taken care of by the logic programming system. One aspect of control in logic programs is the *selection rule*. This is a rule stating which atom in a query is selected in each derivation step. It is well-known that soundness and completeness of SLD-resolution is independent of the selection rule [2]. However, a stronger property is usually required for a selection rule to be useful in programming, namely termination.

Definition 1.1. A *terminating control* for a program P and a query Q is a selection rule s such that every SLD-derivation of P and Q via s is finite.

M. Bruynooghe and K.-K. Lau (Eds.): Program Development in CL, LNCS 3049, pp. 376–431, 2004.

In reality, logic programming is far from the ideal that the logic and control aspects are separated. Without the programmer being aware of the control and writing programs accordingly, logic programs would usually be hopelessly inefficient or even non-terminating.

The usual selection rule of early systems is the *LD* selection rule: in each derivation step, the leftmost atom in a query is selected for resolution. This selection rule is based on the assumption that programs are written in such a way that the data flow within a query or clause body is from left to right. Under this assumption, this selection rule is usually a terminating control. For most applications, this selection rule is appropriate in that it allows for an efficient implementation.

Second generation logic programming languages allow for *dynamic scheduling*, i.e. they have primitives for addressing logic and control separately. Program clauses have their usual logical reading. In addition, programs are augmented by *delay declarations* or *annotations* that specify restrictions on the admissible selection rules. These languages include NU-Prolog [74] and Gödel [38].

In this survey, we classify programs and queries according to the selection rules for which they terminate, hence investigating the influence of the selection rule on termination. Like most approaches to the termination problem, we are interested in *universal* termination of logic programs and queries, that is, showing that *all* derivations for a program and query (via a certain selection rule) are finite. This is in contrast to *existential* termination [10,23,48]. Also, we consider *definite* logic programs, as opposed to logic programs that also contain negated literals in clause bodies.

Figure 1 gives an overview of the classes we consider. Arrows drawn with solid lines stand for set inclusion ("→ corresponds to ⊆"). The numbers in the figure correspond to statements and examples related to the pair of classes in question.

A program P and query Q *strongly terminate* if they terminate for *all* selection rules. This class of programs has been studied mainly by Bezem [11]. Naturally, this class is the smallest we consider. A program P and query Q *left-terminate* if they terminate for the *LD* selection rule. The vast majority of the literature is concerned with this class; see [23] for an overview. A program P and query Q ∃-*terminate* if there *exists* a selection rule for which they terminate. This notion of termination has been introduced by Ruggieri [62,63]. Surprisingly, this is still not the largest class we consider. Namely, there is the class of programs for which there are only finitely many *successful* derivations (although there could also be infinite derivations). We say that these programs have *bounded nondeterminism*, a notion studied by Pedreschi & Ruggieri [58]. Such programs can be transformed into equivalent programs which strongly terminate, as indicated in the figure and stated in Theorem 10.11.

The three remaining classes shown in the figure are related to *dynamic scheduling*, i.e. selection rules where the selection of an atom depends on its degree of instantiation at runtime. To explain these classes and their relationship with left-terminating programs, we have to introduce the concept of *modes*.

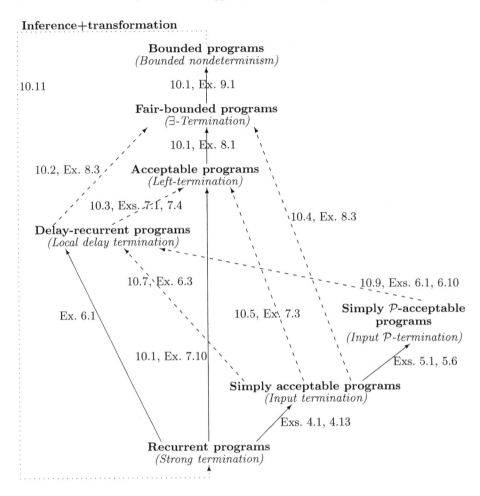

Fig. 1. An overview of the classes

A mode is a labelling of each argument position of a predicate as either input or output. It indicates the intended data flow in a query or clause body.

An *input-consuming* derivation is a derivation where an atom can be selected only when its input arguments are instantiated to a sufficient degree, so that unification with the head of the clause does not instantiate them further. A program and a query *input terminate* if all input-consuming derivations for this program and query are finite. This class of programs has been studied by Smaus [67] and Bossi *et al.* [15,16,17].

Input-consuming derivations can be restricted by imposing some additional instantiation property $\mathcal{P}$ that each selected atom must have. For example, $\mathcal{P}$ might be the set of all atoms that are bounded w.r.t. a given level mapping. A program and a query *input $\mathcal{P}$-terminate* if all input-consuming derivations for this program and query, restricted by $\mathcal{P}$, are finite. This class of programs has been studied by Smaus in very recent work [68].

A *local* selection rule is a selection rule specifying that an atom can only be selected if there is no other atom which was introduced (by resolution) more recently. Marchiori & Teusink [47] have studied termination for selection rules that are both local and *delay-safe*, i.e. they respect the *delay declarations*. We will call termination w.r.t. such selection rules *local delay* termination.

A priori, the LD selection rule, input-consuming selection rules (possibly restricted by a property $\mathcal{P}$) and local delay-safe selection rules are not formally comparable. Under reasonable assumptions however, one can say that assuming input-consuming selection rules is weaker than assuming local and delay-safe selection rules, which is again weaker than assuming the LD selection rule. While assuming input-consuming selection rules is trivially (though not necessarily strictly) weaker than assuming input-consuming selection rules with an additional property $\mathcal{P}$, there is little sense in making general comparisons between selection rules restricted by some $\mathcal{P}$ and the other classes — it depends on the $\mathcal{P}$. However, we can choose $\mathcal{P}$ so that it exactly captures delay-safe selection rules, and then it follows of course that assuming $\mathcal{P}$-selection rules is weaker than assuming local and delay-safe selection rules. All these inclusions that depend on additional assumptions are indicated in the figure by dashed lines. Again, the numbers in the figure correspond to statements and examples.

In this survey, we present declarative characterisations of the classes of programs and queries that terminate with respect to each of the mentioned notions of termination. The characterisations make use of level mappings and Herbrand models in order to provide proof obligations on program clauses and queries. All characterisations are sound. Except for the cases of local delay termination and input $\mathcal{P}$-termination, they are also complete (in the case of input termination, this holds only under certain restrictions).

This survey is organised as follows. The next section introduces some basic concepts and fixes the notation. Then we have seven sections corresponding to the seven classes in Fig. 1, defined by increasingly strong assumptions about the selection rule. In each section, we introduce a notion of termination and provide a declarative characterisation for the corresponding class of terminating programs and queries. In Sec. 10, we establish relations between the classes, formally showing the implications of Fig. 1. Section 11 discusses the related work, and Sec. 12 concludes.

2   Background and Notation

We use the notation of Apt [2], when not otherwise specified. In particular, throughout this article we consider a fixed language L in which programs and queries are written. All the results are *parametric* with respect to L, provided that L is rich enough to contain the symbols of the programs and queries under consideration.

We denote by U_L (resp., B_L) the Herbrand universe (resp., base) on L. We denote by $Term_L$ (resp., $Atom_L$) the set of terms (resp., atoms) on L. We use typewriter font for logical variables, e.g. X, Ys, upper case letters for arbitrary terms, e.g. Xs, and lower case letters for ground terms, e.g. t, x, xs. We denote by $inst_L(P)$ ($ground_L(P)$) the set of (ground) instances of all clauses in P that are in language L. The notation $ground_L(Q)$ for a query Q is defined analogously. The domain (resp., set of variables in the range) of a substitution θ is denoted as $Dom(\theta)$ (resp., $Ran(\theta)$).

The set $\{1, \ldots, n\}$ is denoted by $[1, n]$.

2.1   Modes

For a predicate p/n, a *mode* is an atom $p(m_1, \ldots, m_n)$, where $m_i \in \{I, O\}$ for $i \in [1, n]$. Positions with I are called *input positions*, and positions with O are called *output positions* of p. To simplify the notation, an atom written as $p(\mathbf{s}, \mathbf{t})$ means: $\mathbf{s}$ is the vector of terms filling in the input positions, and $\mathbf{t}$ is the vector of terms filling in the output positions. An atom $p(\mathbf{s}, \mathbf{t})$ is *input-linear* if $\mathbf{s}$ is linear, i.e. each variable occurs at most once in $\mathbf{s}$. The atom is *output-linear* if $\mathbf{t}$ is linear. A mode for a program consists of a mode for each of its predicates.

In the literature, several correctness criteria concerning the modes have been proposed, most importantly nicely-modedness and well-modedness [2]. In this article, we need *simply* moded programs [4] and *well moded* programs. The former are a special case of nicely moded programs. Note that the use of the letters $\mathbf{s}$ and $\mathbf{t}$ is reversed for clause heads. We believe that this notation naturally reflects the data flow within a clause.

Definition 2.1. A   clause $p(\mathbf{t}_0, \mathbf{s}_{n+1}) \leftarrow p_1(\mathbf{s}_1, \mathbf{t}_1), \ldots, p_n(\mathbf{s}_n, \mathbf{t}_n)$ is   *simply moded* if $\mathbf{t}_1, \ldots, \mathbf{t}_n$ is a linear vector of variables and for all $i \in [1, n]$

$$Var(\mathbf{t}_i) \cap Var(\mathbf{t}_0) = \emptyset \quad \text{and} \quad Var(\mathbf{t}_i) \cap \bigcup_{j=1}^{i} Var(\mathbf{s}_j) = \emptyset.$$

A query $\mathbf{B}$ is *simply moded* if the clause $\mathbf{p} \leftarrow \mathbf{B}$ is simply moded, where $\mathbf{p}/0$ is a fresh predicate symbol. A program is *simply moded* if all of its clauses are.

A query (clause, program) is *permutation simply moded* if it is simply moded modulo reordering of the atoms of the query (each clause body).

Thus, a clause is simply moded if the output positions of the body atoms are filled in by distinct variables, and every variable occurring in an output position of a body atom does not occur in an earlier input position. In particular, every unit clause is simply moded.

Definition 2.2. A query $Q = p_1(\mathbf{s}_1, \mathbf{t}_1), \ldots, p_n(\mathbf{s}_n, \mathbf{t}_n)$ is *well moded* if for all $i \in [1, n]$ and $K = 1$

$$Vars(\mathbf{s}_i) \subseteq \bigcup_{j=K}^{i-1} Vars(\mathbf{t}_j) \tag{1}$$

The clause $p(\mathbf{t}_0, \mathbf{s}_{n+1}) \leftarrow Q$ is *well moded* if (1) holds for all $i \in [1, n+1]$ and $K = 0$. A program is *well moded* if all of its clauses are.

A query (clause, program) is *permutation well moded* if it is well moded modulo reordering of the atoms of the query (each clause body).

Almost all programs we consider in this article are permutation well and simply moded with respect to the same set of modes. The program in Fig. 9 is an exception due to the fact that our notion of modes cannot capture that sub-arguments of a term can have different modes. We do not always give the modes explicitly, but they are usually easy to guess.

Conceptually, we assume that whenever modes are used in this article, the mode of a predicate is unique. To realise the use of one predicate in several modes, one can introduce multiple (renamed) versions of the predicate [4,5,32,55]. But it is also possible to realise multiple modes without any actual code duplication. Then, a mode should be associated with each *occurrence* of a predicate in a program [66,69].

2.2   Norms and Level Mappings

All the characterisations of terminating programs we propose make use of the notions of norm and level mapping [20]. Depending on the approach, such notions are defined on ground or arbitrary objects.

In the following definition, $Term_L/\!\sim$ denotes the set of equivalence classes of terms modulo variance. Similarly, we define $Atom_L/\!\sim$.

Definition 2.3. A *norm* is a function $|.| : U_L \to \mathbb{N}$. A *level mapping* is a function $|.| : B_L \to \mathbb{N}$. For a ground atom A, $|A|$ is called the *level* of A.

An atom A is *bounded* w.r.t. the level mapping $|.|$ if there exists $k \in \mathbb{N}$ such that for every $A' \in ground_L(A)$, we have $k > |A'|$.

A *generalised norm* is a function $|.| : Term_L/\!\sim \to \mathbb{N}$. A *generalised level mapping* is a function $|.| : Atom_L/\!\sim \to \mathbb{N}$. Abusing notation, we write $|T|$ ($|A|$) to denote the value of $|.|$ on the equivalence class of the term T (the atom A).

(Generalised) level mappings are used to measure the "size" of a query and show that this size decreases along a derivation, hence showing termination. They are usually defined based on (generalised) norms.

Of course, a generalised norm or level mapping can be interpreted as an ordinary norm or level mapping by restricting its domain to ground objects. Therefore, we now give some examples of *generalised* norms and level mappings.

One commonly used generalised norm is the term size norm, defined as

$$size(f(T_1, \ldots, T_n)) = 1 + size(T_1) + \ldots + size(T_n) \text{ if } n > 0$$
$$size(T) = 0 \qquad\qquad\qquad \text{if } T \text{ constant/variable.}$$

Intuitively, the size of a term T is the number of function symbols occurring in T, excluding constants. Another widely used norm is the list-length function, defined as

$$length([T \,|\, Ts]) = 1 + length(Ts)$$
$$length(T) = 0 \qquad\qquad \text{if } T \neq [\ldots | \ldots].$$

In particular, for a nil-terminated list $[T_1, \ldots, T_n]$, the list-length is n. We call a term of the form $[T_1, \ldots, T_n|\mathtt{Ts}]$, where $n \geq 0$, an *open list*. In particular, any variable is an open list.

We will see later that usually, level mappings measure the *input* arguments of a query, even though this is often just an intuitive understanding and not explicit. Moreover, the choice of a particular selection rule often reflects a particular mode of the program. In this sense, the choice of the level mapping must depend on the selection rule, via the modes. This will be seen in our examples.

However, apart form the dependency just mentioned, the choice of level mapping is an aspect of termination which is rather independent from the choice of the selection rule. In particular, one does not find any interesting relationship between the underlying *norms* and the selection rule. This is why the detailed study of various norms and level mappings is beyond the scope of this article, although it is an important aspect of automated proofs of termination [14,27].

We now define level mappings where the dependency on the modes is made explicit [32].

Definition 2.4. A *moded (generalised) level mapping* $|.|$ is a (generalised) level mapping such that for any (not necessarily) ground $\mathbf{s}$, $\mathbf{t}$ and $\mathbf{u}$, $|p(\mathbf{s}, \mathbf{t})| = |p(\mathbf{s}, \mathbf{u})|$.

The condition $|p(\mathbf{s}, \mathbf{t})| = |p(\mathbf{s}, \mathbf{u})|$ states that the *level* of an atom is independent from the terms in its output positions.

2.3   Selection Rules

Let *INIT* be the set of initial fragments of SLD-derivations in which the last query is non-empty. The standard definition of *selection rule* is as follows: a selection rule is a function that, when applied to an element in *INIT*, yields an occurrence of an atom in its last query [2]. In this article, we assume an extended definition: we also allow that a selection rule may select no atom (a situation called *deadlock*), and we allow that it not only returns the selected atom, but also specifies the set of program clauses that may be used to resolve the atom. Whenever we want to emphasise that a selection rule always selects exactly one atom together with the entire set of clauses for that atom's predicate, we speak of a *standard* selection rule. Note that for the extended definition, completeness of SLD-resolution is lost in general. Selection rules are denoted by s.

In practice, selection rules should always be *computable* functions, but we are not concerned with this issue here.

We now define the various notions of selection rules used in this article.

A $\mathcal{P}$-selection rule is a selection rule where each selected atom is in some set of atoms $\mathcal{P}$, closed under instantiation. Note that this notion is very abstract, but this does not mean that every selection rule can be defined as a $\mathcal{P}$-selection rule.

Definition 2.5. Input-consuming selection rules are defined w.r.t. a given mode. A selection rule s is *input-consuming* for a program P if either

- s selects an atom $p(\mathbf{s}, \mathbf{t})$ and a non-empty set of clauses of P such that $p(\mathbf{s}, \mathbf{t})$ and each head of a clause in the set are unifiable with an mgu σ, and $Dom(\sigma) \cap Vars(\mathbf{s}) = \emptyset$, or
- s selects an atom $p(\mathbf{s}, \mathbf{t})$ that unifies with no clause head from P, together with all clauses in P (this models *failure*), or
- if the previous cases are impossible, s selects no atom (i.e. we have *deadlock*).

A selection rule is *delay-safe w.r.t. a level mapping* $|.|$ if it specifies that an atom A can be selected only when A is bounded w.r.t. $|.|.$[3]

Consider a query, containing atoms A and B, in an initial fragment ξ of a derivation. Then A is *introduced more recently* than B if the derivation step introducing A comes after the step introducing B, in ξ. A *local selection rule* is a selection rule that specifies that an atom in a query can be selected only if there is no more recently introduced atom in the query.

The usual *LD* selection rule (also called *leftmost* selection rule) always selects the leftmost atom in the last query of an element in *INIT*. The *RD* selection rule (also called *rightmost*) always selects the rightmost atom.

A standard selection rule s is *fair* if for every SLD-derivation ξ via s either ξ is finite or for every atom A in ξ, (some further instantiated version of) A is eventually selected.

2.4   Universal Termination

In general terms, the problem of universal termination of a program P and a query Q w.r.t. a set of selection rules consists of showing that every rule in the set is a terminating control for P and Q.

Definition 2.6. A program P and a query Q *universally terminate* w.r.t. a set of selection rules $\mathcal{S}$ if every SLD-derivation of P and Q via any selection rule from $\mathcal{S}$ is finite.

Note that, since SLD-trees are finitely branching, by König's Lemma, "every SLD-derivation for P and Q via a selection rule s is finite" is equivalent to stating that the SLD-tree of P and Q via s is finite.

We say that a class of programs and queries is a *sound* characterisation of universal termination w.r.t. $\mathcal{S}$ if every program and query in the class universally terminate w.r.t. $\mathcal{S}$. Conversely, it is *complete* if every program and query that universally terminate w.r.t. $\mathcal{S}$ are in the class.

2.5   Models

Several of the criteria for termination we consider rely on information supplied by a model of the program under consideration. We provide the definition of Herbrand interpretations and models [2].

---

[3] The reader may be surprised that delay-safe selection rules make no reference to *delay declarations*. This is a terminological shortcut.

A *Herbrand interpretation* I is a set of ground atoms. A ground atom A is *true in* I, written $I \models A$, if $A \in I$. This notation is extended to ground queries in the obvious way. I is a Herbrand *model* of program P if for each $A \leftarrow B_1, \dots, B_n \in ground_L(P)$, we have that $I \models B_1, \dots, B_n$ implies $I \models A$.

When speaking of the *least* Herbrand model of P, we mean least w.r.t. set inclusion. In termination analysis, it is usually not necessary to consider the least Herbrand model, which may be difficult or impossible to determine. Instead, one uses models that capture some *argument size relationship* between the arguments of each predicate [23]. For example, a model for the usual `append` predicate is

$$\{\texttt{append}(xs, ys, zs) \mid length(zs) = length(xs) + length(ys)\}.$$

3   Strong Termination

3.1   Operational Definition

Early approaches to the termination problem treated universal termination w.r.t. *all* selection rules, called *strong* termination. Generally speaking, strongly terminating programs and queries are either very trivial or especially written for theoretical considerations.

Definition 3.1. A program P and query Q *strongly terminate* if they universally terminate w.r.t. the set of all selection rules.

3.2   Declarative Characterisation

In the following, we recall the approach of Bezem [11], who defined the class of recurrent programs and queries. Intuitively, a program is recurrent if for every ground instance of a clause, the level of the body atoms is smaller than the level of the head.

Definition 3.2. Let $|.|$ be a level mapping.
A program P is *recurrent by* $|.|$ if for every $A \leftarrow B_1, \dots, B_n \in ground_L(P)$:

$$\text{for } i \in [1, n] \quad |A| > |B_i|.$$

A query Q is *recurrent by* $|.|$ if there exists $k \in \mathbb{N}$ such that for every $A_1, \dots, A_n \in ground_L(Q)$:

$$\text{for } i \in [1, n] \quad k > |A_i|.$$

In the above definition, the proof obligations for a query Q are derived from those for the program $\{\mathsf{p} \leftarrow Q\}$, where $\mathsf{p}/0$ is a fresh predicate symbol. Intuitively, this is justified by the fact that the termination behaviour of the query Q and a program P is the same as for the query p and the program $P \cup \{\mathsf{p} \leftarrow Q\}$. So k plays the role of the level of the atom p. In the original work [11], the query was called *bounded*. Throughout the paper, we prefer to maintain a uniform naming convention both for programs and queries.

Termination properties of recurrent programs are summarised in the following theorem.

```
%  sat(Formula) ←
%     there is a true instance of Formula

sat(true).
sat(X ∧ Y) ←
    sat(X), sat(Y).
sat(not X) ← inval(X).
```

```
inval(false).
inval(X ∧ Y)  ←  inval(X).
inval(X ∧ Y)  ←  inval(Y).
inval(not X)  ←  sat(X).
```

Fig. 2. SAT

Theorem 3.3 ([11]). Let P be a program and Q a query.

If P and Q are both recurrent by some $|.|$, then they strongly terminate.

Conversely, if P and every *ground query* strongly terminate, then P is recurrent by some level mapping $|.|$. If in addition P and Q strongly terminate, then P and Q are both recurrent by some level mapping $|.|$.

Proof. The result is shown in [11] for standard selection rules. It easily extends to our generalisation of selection rules by noting that P and Q strongly terminate iff they universally terminate w.r.t. the set of standard selection rules. The only-if part is immediate. The if-part follows by noting that a derivation via an arbitrary selection rule is a (prefix of a) derivation via a *standard* selection rule.

3.3   Examples

Example 3.4. The program SAT in Fig. 2 decides propositional satisfiability. The program is readily checked to be recurrent by $|.|$, where we define

$$|\mathtt{sat}(t)| = |\mathtt{inval}(t)| = size(t).$$

Note that Def. 3.2 imposes no proof obligations for unit clauses. The query $\mathtt{sat}(X)$ is recurrent iff there exists a natural k such that for every ground instance x of X, we have that $size(x)$ is bounded by k. Obviously, this is the case iff X is already a ground term. For instance, the query $\mathtt{sat}(\mathtt{not}(\mathtt{true}) \wedge \mathtt{false})$ is recurrent, while the query $\mathtt{sat}(\mathtt{false} \wedge X)$ is not.

Note that the choice of an appropriate level mapping depends on the intended mode of the program and query. Even though this is usually not explicit, level mappings measure the size of the *input* arguments of an atom [32].

Example 3.5. Figure 3 shows the APPEND program. It is easy to check that APPEND is recurrent by the level mapping $|\mathtt{append}(xs, ys, zs)| = length(xs)$ and also by $|\mathtt{append}(xs, ys, zs)| = length(zs)$. A query $\mathtt{append}(Xs, Ys, Zs)$ is recurrent by the first level mapping iff Xs is anything other than an open list, and by the second iff Zs is anything other than an open list. The level mapping

$$|\mathtt{append}(xs, ys, zs)| = min\{length(xs), length(zs)\}$$

combines the advantages of both level mappings. APPEND is easily seen to be recurrent by it, and if Xs or Zs is anything other than an open list, then $\mathtt{append}(Xs, Ys, Zs)$ is recurrent by it.

```
%  reverse(Xs,Ys)  ←              %  append(Xs,Ys,Zs)  ←
%      Xs is the reverse of list Ys.      %      Zs is the result of concatenating
                                  %      lists Xs and Ys.
   reverse([X|Xs],Ys)  ←
      append(Zs,[X],Ys),             append([X|Xs],Ys,[X|Zs])  ←
      reverse(Xs,Zs).                   append(Xs,Ys,Zs).
   reverse([],[]).                   append([],Ys,Ys).
```

Fig. 3. APPEND and NAIVE_REVERSE

```
%  even(X)  ←                    %  lte(X,Y)  ←
%      X  is an even natural number.      %      X,Y are natural numbers
                                  %      s.t. X is smaller or equal than Y.
   even(s(s(X)))  ←  even(X).
   even(0).                          lte(s(X),s(Y))  ←  lte(X,Y).
                                     lte(0,Y).
```

Fig. 4. EVEN

3.4 On Completeness of the Characterisation

Note that completeness is not stated in full general terms, i.e. recurrence is not a complete proof method for strong termination. Informally speaking, incompleteness is due to the use of level mappings, which are functions that must specify a value for every ground atom. Therefore, if P strongly terminates for a certain ground query Q but not for all ground queries, we cannot conclude that P is recurrent. We provide a general completeness result in Sec. 7 for a class of programs containing recurrent programs.

4 Input Termination

In this section, we consider input-consuming selection rules [17].

We have said above that the class of strongly terminating programs and queries is very limited. Even if a program is recurrent, it may not strongly terminate for a query of interest since the query is not recurrent.

Example 4.1. The program EVEN in Fig. 4 is recurrent by defining

$$|\text{even}(x)| = size(x)$$
$$|\text{lte}(x,y)| = size(y).$$

Now consider the query $Q = \text{even}(X), \text{lte}(X, s^{100}(0))$, which is supposed to compute the even numbers not exceeding 100. By always selecting the leftmost atom, one can easily obtain an infinite derivation for EVEN and Q. As a consequence of Theorem 3.3, Q is not recurrent.

4.1   Operational Definition

Definition 4.2. A program P and query Q *input terminate* if they universally terminate w.r.t. the set consisting of the input-consuming selection rules.

The requirement of input-consuming derivations merely reflects the very meaning of *input*: an atom must only consume its own input, not produce it. In existing implementations, input-consuming derivations can be ensured using control constructs such as delay declarations [38,70,73,74].

In the above example, the obvious mode is $even(I)$, $lte(O, I)$. With this mode, we will show that EVEN and Q input terminate. If we assume a selection rule that is input-consuming while always selecting the leftmost atom if possible, then the above example is a contrived instance of the *generate-and-test* paradigm. This paradigm involves two procedures, one which generates a set of candidates, and another which tests whether these candidates are solutions to the problem. The test occurs to the left of the generator so that tests take place as soon as possible, i.e. as soon as sufficient input has been generated for the derivation to be input-consuming.

Proofs of input termination differ from proofs of strong termination in an important respect. For the latter, we require that the initial query is recurrent, and as a consequence we have that all queries in any derivation from it are recurrent (we say that recurrence is *persistent* under resolution). This means that, at the time an atom is selected, the depth of its SLD-tree is bounded. In contrast, input termination does not have such a strong requirement on each selected atom.

Example 4.3. Consider the EVEN program in Fig. 4 and the following input-consuming derivation, where we underline the selected atom in each step:

$$\text{even(X)}, \ \underline{\text{lte(X}, \text{s}^{100}(0))} \longrightarrow \text{even(s(X'))}, \ \underline{\text{lte(X', s}^{99}(0))} \longrightarrow$$
$$\underline{\text{even(s(s(X'')))}}, \ \text{lte(X'', s}^{98}(0)) \longrightarrow \text{even(X'')}, \ \underline{\text{lte(X'', s}^{98}(0))} \dots$$

At the time when even(s(s(X''))) is selected, the depth of its SLD-tree is not bounded. In fact, this depth depends on the eventual instantiation of X''.

The method for showing input termination inherently relies on a notion of *level* for atoms such as even(s(s(X''))), although this level is not bounded. This is the key to showing termination for derivations with coroutining (interleaving subderivations). In contrast, most approaches to termination assume that the level of the selected atom is bounded. We refer to Subsec. 11.7 and [66, Sec. 11.1].

4.2   Information on Data Flow: Simply-Local Substitutions and Models

Since the depth of the SLD-tree of the selected atom depends on further instantiation of the atom, it is important that programs are well-behaved w.r.t. the modes. This is illustrated in the following example.

Example 4.4. Consider the APPEND program (Fig. 3) in mode $append(I, I, O)$ and the query

$$append([1|As], [], Bs), \; append(Bs, [], As).$$

Then we have the following infinite input-consuming derivation:

$$
\begin{array}{l}
\underline{append([1|As], [], Bs)}, \; append(Bs, [], As) \longrightarrow \\
\underline{append(As, [], Bs')}, \; append([1|Bs'], [], As) \longrightarrow \\
append([1|As'], [], Bs'), \; \underline{append(Bs', [], As')} \longrightarrow \cdots
\end{array}
$$

This well-known termination problem of programs with coroutining has been identified as *circular modes* by Naish [55].

To avoid the above situation, we require programs and queries to be simply moded (see Subsec. 2.1).

We now define *simply-local* substitutions, which reflect the way simply moded clauses become instantiated in input-consuming derivations. Given a clause $c = p(\mathbf{t}_0, \mathbf{s}_{n+1}) \leftarrow p_1(\mathbf{s}_1, \mathbf{t}_1), \ldots, p_n(\mathbf{s}_n, \mathbf{t}_n)$ used in an input-consuming derivation, first $\mathbf{t}_0$ becomes instantiated, and the range of that substitution contains only variables from outside of c. Then, by resolving $p_1(\mathbf{s}_1, \mathbf{t}_1)$, the vector $\mathbf{t}_1$ becomes instantiated, and the range of that substitution contains variables from outside of c in addition to variables from $\mathbf{s}_1$. Continuing in the same way, finally, by resolving $p_n(\mathbf{s}_n, \mathbf{t}_n)$, the vector $\mathbf{t}_n$ becomes instantiated, and the range of that substitution contains variables from outside of c in addition to variables from $\mathbf{s}_1 \ldots \mathbf{s}_n$. A substitution is *simply-local* if it is composed from substitutions as sketched above. We now give the formal definition [17].

Definition 4.5. A substitution θ is *simply-local* w.r.t. the clause $c = p(\mathbf{t}_0, \mathbf{s}_{n+1}) \leftarrow p_1(\mathbf{s}_1, \mathbf{t}_1), \ldots, p_n(\mathbf{s}_n, \mathbf{t}_n)$ if there exist substitutions $\sigma_0, \sigma_1 \ldots, \sigma_n$ and disjoint sets $V_0, V_1, \ldots, V_n$ consisting of of fresh (w.r.t. c) variables such that $\theta = \sigma_0 \sigma_1 \cdots \sigma_n$ where for $i \in \{0, \ldots, n\}$,

- $Dom(\sigma_i) \subseteq Vars(\mathbf{t}_i)$,
- $Ran(\sigma_i) \subseteq Vars(\mathbf{s}_i \sigma_0 \sigma_1 \cdots \sigma_{i-1}) \cup V_i.$[4]

θ is *simply-local* w.r.t. a query $\mathbf{B}$ if θ is simply-local w.r.t. the clause $p \leftarrow \mathbf{B}$ where $p/0$ is a fresh predicate symbol.

Note that in the case of a simply-local substitution w.r.t. a query, σ_0 is the empty substitution, since $Dom(\sigma_0) \subseteq Var(\mathbf{p})$ where $\mathbf{p}$ is a fresh predicate symbol. Note also that if $A, B, \mathbf{C} \longrightarrow (\mathbf{A}, \mathbf{B}, \mathbf{C})\theta$ is an input-consuming derivation step using clause $c = H \leftarrow \mathbf{B}$, then $\theta_{|H}$ is simply-local w.r.t. the clause $H \leftarrow$ and $\theta_{|B}$ is simply-local w.r.t. the atom B [17].

Example 4.6. Consider the PERMUTE_BACK program in Fig. 5 (the name has been chosen to distinguish it from PERMUTE to be introduced later). Assume mode $permute(O, I), insert(O, O, I)$. We examine the recursive clause for insert.

---

[4] Note that $\mathbf{s}_0$ is undefined. By abuse of notation, $Vars(\mathbf{s}_0 \ldots) = \emptyset$.

```
%  permute(Xs,Ys)  ←              %  insert(Xs,X,Zs)  ←
%     Ys is a permutation of the list Xs. %    Zs is obtained by inserting X into Xs.

   permute([X|Xs],Ys)  ←            insert(Xs,X,[X|Xs]).
      insert(Zs,X,Ys),              insert([Y|Xs],X,[Y|Zs])  ←
      permute(Xs,Zs).                  insert(Xs,X,Zs).
   permute([],[]).
```

Fig. 5. PERMUTE_BACK

The substitution $\sigma = \{Y/V, Zs/[W], Xs/[], X/W\}$ is simply-local w.r.t. it: let $\sigma_0 = \{Y/V, Zs/[W]\}$, $\sigma_1 = \{X/W, Xs/[]\}$; then $Dom(\sigma_0) \subseteq \{Y, Zs\}$, $Ran(\sigma_0) \subseteq V_0$ where $V_0 = \{V, W\}$, $Dom(\sigma_1) \subseteq \{Xs, X\}$, and $Ran(\sigma_1) \subseteq Vars(Zs \, \sigma_0)$.

Based on simply-local substitutions, we now define a restricted notion of model.

Definition 4.7. Let $I \subseteq Atom_L$. We say that I is a *simply-local model* of $c = H \leftarrow B_1, \ldots, B_n$ if for every substitution θ simply-local w.r.t. c,

$$\text{if } B_1\theta, \ldots, B_n\theta \in I \text{ then } H\theta \in I. \tag{2}$$

I is a *simply-local model* of a program P if it is a simply-local model of each clause of it.

Note that a simply-local model is not necessarily a model in the classical sense, since I is not necessarily a set of ground atoms, and the substitution in (2) is required to be simply-local. For example, given the program $\{q(1), p(X) \leftarrow q(X)\}$ with mode $q(I)$, $p(O)$, a model must contain the atom $p(1)$, whereas a simply-local model does not necessarily contain $p(1)$, since $\{X/1\}$ is not simply-local w.r.t. $p(X) \leftarrow q(X)$. The next subsection will further clarify the role of simply-local models.

Let SM_P be the set of all simply moded atoms[5] in $Atom_L$. It has been shown that the least simply-local model of P containing SM_P exists and can be computed by a variant of the well-known T_P-operator [17]. We denote the least simply-local model of P containing SM_P by PM_P^{SL}, for *partial model*.

Example 4.8. Recall Ex. 4.6. SM_P consists of all atoms $insert(Us, U, Vs)$ where $Us, U \notin Vars(Vs)$. To construct PM_P^{SL}, we iterate T_P^{SL} starting from any atom in SM_P (the resulting atoms are written on the l.h.s. below) and the fact clause (r.h.s.). Each line below corresponds to one iteration of T_P^{SL}. We have $PM_P^{SL} =$

$$\{ insert(Us, U, Vs),$$
$$insert([Y_1|Us], U, [Y_1|Vs]), \qquad insert(Xs_1, X_1, [X_1|Xs_1]),$$
$$insert([Y_2, Y_1|Us], U, [Y_2, Y_1|Vs]), insert([Y_1|Xs_1], X_1, [Y_1, X_1|Xs_1]), \tag{3}$$
$$\cdots \qquad\qquad\qquad \cdots$$
$$| \, Vs, Xs_1, X_1, Y_1, Y_2, \ldots \text{arbitrary where } Us, U \notin Vars(Vs)\}.$$

---

[5] We sometimes say "atom" for "query containing only one atom".

Observe the variable occurrences of U, Us in the atoms on the l.h.s. In Ex. 5.5, we will see the importance of such variable occurrences.

4.3   Declarative Characterisation

Bossi *et al.* [17] define *simply-acceptability*, which is the notion of decrease used for proving input termination.

We write $p \simeq q$ if p and q are mutually recursive predicates [2]. Abusing notation, we also use $\simeq$ for *atoms*, where $p(\mathbf{s}, \mathbf{t}) \simeq q(\mathbf{u}, \mathbf{v})$ stands for $p \simeq q$.

Definition 4.9. Let P be a simply moded program, $|.|$ a moded generalised[6] level mapping and I a simply-local model of P containing SM_P. A clause $A \leftarrow B_1, \ldots, B_n$ is *simply acceptable by* $|.|$ *and* I if for every substitution θ simply-local w.r.t. it,

$$\text{for all } i \in [1, n], \quad (B_1, \ldots, B_{i-1})\theta \in I \text{ and } A \simeq B_i \quad \text{imply} \quad |A\theta| > |B_i\theta|.$$

The program P is *simply acceptable by* $|.|$ *and* I if each clause of P is simply acceptable by $|.|$ and I.

Admittedly, the proof obligations may be difficult to verify, especially in the cases where a small (precise) simply-local model is required. However, as our examples show, often it is not necessary at all to consider the model, as one can show the decrease for arbitrary instantiations of the clause.

Simply-acceptability, and $\mathcal{P}$-simply-acceptability to be introduced in the next section, are not based on ground instances of clauses, but rather on instances obtained by applying simply-local substitutions, which arise in input-consuming derivations of simply moded programs. This is in contrast to all other character-isations in this article, and explains why we use *generalised* level mappings and a special kind of models.

Also note that in contrast to recurrence and other decreasing notions to be defined later, simply-acceptability has no proof obligation on queries (apart from the requirement that queries must be simply moded). Intuitively, such a proof obligation is made redundant by the mode conditions (simply-acceptability and moded level mapping) and the fact that derivations must be input-consuming. We also refer to Subsec. 10.1.

Simply-acceptability characterises the class of input terminating programs.

Theorem 4.10 ([17]). Let P and Q be a simply moded program and query.
If P is simply acceptable by some $|.|$ and I, then P and Q input terminate.
Conversely, if P and every simply moded query input terminate, then P is simply acceptable by some moded generalised level mapping $|.|$ and PM_P^{SL}.

The formulation of the theorem differs slightly from the original for reasons of consistency, but one can easily see that the formulations are equivalent.

---

[6] In [17], the word "generalised" is dropped, but here we prefer to emphasise that non-ground atoms are included in the domain.

```
permute([X|Xs],Ys) ←              insert(Xs,X,[X|Xs]).
    permute(Xs,Zs),               insert([Y|Xs],X,[Y|Zs]) ←
    insert(Zs,X,Ys).                  insert(Xs,X,Zs).
permute([],[]).
```

Fig. 6. PERMUTE

Remark 4.11. The definition of input-consuming derivations is independent from the textual order of atoms in a query, and so the textual order is irrelevant for termination. Therefore, if we can prove input termination for a program and query, we have also proven termination for a program obtained by permuting the body atoms of each clause and the query in an arbitrary way.

It would have been possible to state this remark explicitly in the above theorem, but that would have complicated the definition of simply-local substitution and subsequent definitions. Generally, the question of when it is necessary to make the permutations of body atoms explicit is discussed in [66, Sec. 5.3].

4.4 Examples

Example 4.12. The program EVEN in Fig. 4 is simply acceptable with mode $even(I)$, $lte(O, I)$ by using the level mapping in Ex. 4.1, interpreted as moded *generalised* level mapping in the obvious way, and using any simply-local model. Moreover, the query $even(X)$, $lte(X, s^{100}(0))$ is permutation simply moded (see Remark 4.11). Hence EVEN and this query input terminate.

Example 4.13. The program PERMUTE is shown in Fig. 6. Assume the mode $permute(I, O)$, $insert(I, I, O)$. Note that compared to Fig. 5, two body atoms have been reordered to make the program simply moded in this mode. Note also that $permute \not\simeq insert$. The program is readily checked to be simply acceptable, using the moded generalised level mapping

$$|permute(Xs, Ys)| = |insert(Xs, Ys, Zs)| = size(Xs)$$

and any simply-local model. Thus the program and any simply moded query input terminate. It can also easily be shown that the program is not recurrent.

Example 4.14. Figure 7 shows program 15.3 from [72]: QUICKSORT using a form of difference lists (we permuted two body atoms for the sake of clarity). This program is simply moded with mode $quicksort(I, O)$, $quicksort\_dl(I, O, I)$, $partition(I, I, O, O)$, $=<(I, I)$, $>(I, I)$.

We use the following moded generalised level mapping (positions with _ are irrelevant)

$$|quicksort\_dl(Xs, \_, \_)| = length(Xs),$$
$$|partition(Xs, \_, \_, \_)| = length(Xs).$$

```
%     quicksort(Xs, Ys) ← Ys is an ordered permutation of Xs.

quicksort(Xs,Ys) ← quicksort_dl(Xs,Ys,[]).

quicksort_dl([X|Xs],Ys,Zs) ←
    partition(Xs,X,Littles,Bigs),
    quicksort_dl(Bigs,Ys1,Zs).
    quicksort_dl(Littles,Ys,[X|Ys1]),
quicksort_dl([],Xs,Xs).

partition([X|Xs],Y,[X|Ls],Bs) ← X =< Y, partition(Xs,Y,Ls,Bs).
partition([X|Xs],Y,Ls,[X|Bs]) ← X > Y, partition(Xs,Y,Ls,Bs).
partition([],Y,[],[]).
```

Fig. 7. QUICKSORT

The level mapping of all other atoms can be set to 0. Concerning the model, the simplest solution is to use the model that expresses the dependency between the list lengths of the arguments of `partition`, i.e. I should contain all atoms of the form $\text{partition}(S_1, X, S_2, S_3)$ where $|S_1| \geq |S_2|$ and $|S_1| \geq |S_3|$. Note that this includes all simply moded atoms using `partitition`, and that this model is a fortiori simply-local since (2) in Def. 4.7 is true even for arbitrary θ.

The program is then simply acceptable by $|.|$ and I and hence input terminates for every simply moded query.

In essence, looking at the clause before any instantiation, there is a decrease between the input of the clause head and the recursive body atoms ([X|Xs] is bigger than both `Bigs` and `Littles`). Moreover, by the model information about the atom `partition(Xs, X, Littles, Bigs)` we know that this decrease is preserved as the clause becomes instantiated.

5 Input $\mathcal{P}$-Termination

In this section, we consider input-consuming selection rules that are additionally parametrised by some instantiation property $\mathcal{P}$ that each selected atom must have. In particular, delay-safe derivations can be modelled this way. This section is based on very recent work [68].

We first give an example of a program that is not input terminating.

Example 5.1. Consider again the PERMUTE_BACK program in Fig. 5. So the mode is $\text{permute}(O, I), \text{insert}(O, O, I)$. It is immediate to check that the program is not input terminating: by repeatedly selecting the rightmost atom that may be selected, the query $\text{permute}(\text{Xs}, [1])$ generates an infinite input-consuming derivation.

One can understand this by explaining why the program cannot be simply acceptable. Recall Ex. 4.8. $PM^{SL}_{\text{PERMUTE\_BACK}}$ contains every atom of the form $\text{insert}(Us, U, Vs)$, i.e. every simply moded atom whose predicate is `insert`.

Therefore in particular $\text{insert}(\text{Us}, \text{U}, \text{Vs}) \in PM^{SL}_{\text{PERMUTE\_BACK}}$ (note that Vs is a variable). Consider the recursive clause for permute. The substitution $\theta = \{\text{Ys/Vs}, \text{Zs/Us}, \text{X/U}\}$ is simply-local w.r.t. the clause. Therefore, for the clause to be simply acceptable, there would have to be a moded generalised level mapping such that $|\text{permute}([\text{U}|\text{Xs}], \text{Vs})| > |\text{permute}(\text{Xs}, \text{Us})|$. This is a contradiction since a *moded* generalised level mapping is necessarily defined as a generalised norm of the second argument of permute, and Vs and Us are equivalent modulo variance.

However, all derivations for $\text{permute}(\text{Xs}, [1])$ are finite if we require input-consuming derivations where each atom must be bounded w.r.t. an appropriate level mapping.

The attentive reader may have noticed that PERMUTE_BACK falls out of the class of input terminating programs for a very simple reason: Due to the variable Ys in the input position of the clause head, it follows that an atom using permute can *always* be selected.

Now it is tempting to think that the program misses the property of input termination "just narrowly", and that there is a simple fix to obtain input termination: replace Ys by [Y|Ys] in the above clause. This is a fallacy. The resulting program is still not input terminating. This is related to *speculative output bindings* and has first been observed by Naish [55].

Programs that "just narrowly" miss the property of input termination may also be analysed using the methods of this section. We refer to [68].

5.1   Operational Definition

We now define termination for input-consuming P-derivations, i.e. derivations via an input-consuming P-selection rule.

Definition 5.2. A program P and query Q *input P-terminate* if they universally terminate w.r.t. the set consisting of the input-consuming P-selection rules.

Of course, input termination is just a special case of input P-termination for a trivial P containing all atoms. However, in contrast to the previous section, it is unknown if the characterisation given here is complete. This justifies having the previous section on its own. Also, the previous section surveys well-established work while the work reported here is very recent.

5.2   Declarative Characterisation

Definition 5.3. Let P be a simply moded program, $|.|$ a moded generalised level mapping and I a simply-local model of P containing SM_P. A clause $A \leftarrow B_1, \ldots, B_n$ is *simply P-acceptable by $|.|$ and I* if for every substitution σ simply-local w.r.t. it, for all $i \in [1, n]$,

$$B_1\sigma, \ldots, B_{i-1}\sigma \in I \text{ and } A \simeq B_i \text{ and } B_i\sigma \in \mathcal{P} \quad \text{imply} \quad |A\sigma| > |B_i\sigma|. \quad (4)$$

The program P is *simply P-acceptable by $|.|$ and I* if each clause of P is simply P-acceptable by $|.|$ and I.

The only difference to *simply acceptable* clauses is the condition $B_i\sigma \in \mathcal{P}$. Simply-local models capture all input-consuming derivations of a simply moded query, including the ones where we impose an additional condition $\mathcal{P}$. Hence this small modification gives us a sufficient criterion for input $\mathcal{P}$-termination.

Theorem 5.4 ([68]). *Let P and Q be a simply moded program and query. If P is simply $\mathcal{P}$-acceptable by some $|.|$ and I, then P and Q input $\mathcal{P}$-terminate.*

5.3   Examples

We give two examples where $\mathcal{P}$ is used exactly to model *delay-safe* selection rules. These programs need delay-safe selection rules to overcome the problem of speculative output bindings [55].

Example 5.5. Consider PERMUTE_BACK (Fig. 5) assuming mode permute(O, I), insert(O, O, I). Recall Ex. 4.8. We define the level mapping as

$$|\texttt{permute}(Xs,\, Ys)| = length(Ys)$$
$$|\texttt{insert}(Zs,\, X,\, Ys)| = length(Ys).$$

Now for all atoms insert(Zs, X, Ys) $\in PM_P^{SL}$, we have $|Ys| \geq |Zs|$; for the ones on the r.h.s. in (3) even $|Ys| > |Zs|$. Let $\mathcal{P}$ be the set of bounded atoms w.r.t. $|.|$.

Now let us look at the recursive clause for permute. We verify that the second body atom fulfills the requirement of Def. 5.3, where I is PM_P^{SL}. So we have to consider all simply-local substitutions σ such that insert(Zs, X, Ys)$\sigma \in PM_P^{SL}$. For the atoms on the l.h.s. in (3), this means that

$$\sigma \supseteq \{\texttt{Ys}/[Y_n, \ldots, Y_1 | Vs], \texttt{Zs}/[Y_n, \ldots, Y_1 | Us], \texttt{X}/\texttt{U}\} \qquad (n \geq 0).$$

Clearly, permute(Xs, Zs)$\sigma \notin \mathcal{P}$, and hence no proof obligation arises. For the atoms on the r.h.s. in (3), this means that

$$\sigma \supseteq \{\texttt{Ys}/[Y_n, \ldots, Y_1, X_1 | Xs_1], \texttt{Zs}/[Y_n, \ldots, Y_1 | Xs_1], \texttt{X}/X_1\} \qquad (n \geq 0).$$

But then $|\texttt{permute}([X|Xs], Ys)\sigma| > |\texttt{permute}(Xs, Zs)\sigma|$.

The other clauses are trivial to check, and so PERMUTE_BACK is simply $\mathcal{P}$-acceptable.

Example 5.6. The program NAIVE_REVERSE (Fig. 3) in mode reverse(O, I), append(O, O, I) is not input terminating, but it is input $\mathcal{P}$-terminating for $\mathcal{P}$ chosen in perfect analogy to Ex. 5.5.

In our opinion, the difference between delay-safe selection rules and (just) input-consuming selection rules is a fundamental one. Looking at the literature, the termination problem for the latter has been considered a much harder problem than for the former [45,47,49,55]. We also refer to Subsec. 11.7.

```
r(X)  ← p(X,Y), r(Y).              p(X,s(X)) ← fail.
r(0).                              p(s(X),X).
```

Fig. 8. A program for which locality is crucial

5.4   On Completeness of the Characterisation

Our investigations so far suggest that the criterion of simply $\mathcal{P}$-acceptability is *not* a necessary criterion, but that modifications are needed. More specifically, it seems that the condition (4) in Def. 5.3 must be "weakened" to something like

$$B_1\sigma, \ldots, B_{i-1}\sigma \in I \text{ and } A \simeq B_i \text{ and } B_i\sigma \in \mathcal{P} \text{ and } A\sigma \in \mathcal{P} \text{ imply } |A\sigma| > |B_i\sigma|,$$

but it is not clear if this is *strictly* weaker. Therefore, we cannot provide a counterexample showing that $\mathcal{P}$-acceptability is not a necessary criterion.

So while the completeness issue is still work in progress, we hope that a modified criterion will eventually be found. It should then probably be take over the name *simply $\mathcal{P}$-acceptability*, replacing our current definition.

Another interesting topic for future work would consist of investigating the automatic inference of properties $\mathcal{P}$ for which termination of a given program can be established.

6   Local Delay Termination

In this section, we consider selection rules that are both local and delay-safe. We first give an example of a program that is not input $\mathcal{P}$-terminating, for a $\mathcal{P}$ that ensures delay-safe selection rules. We shall see that the program terminates for all selection rules that are local in addition to being delay-safe (see Ex. 6.9).

Example 6.1. Let P be the program in Fig. 8 in mode $r(I), p(I, O)$. Setting $\mathcal{P} = \{p(x, Y) \mid x \text{ ground}, Y \text{ arbitrary}\} \cup \{r(x) \mid x \text{ ground}\}$, we have the following infinite input-consuming $\mathcal{P}$-derivation:

$$\underline{r(0)} \longrightarrow p(0, Y_1), \underline{r(Y_1)} \longrightarrow \text{fail}, \underline{r(s(0))} \longrightarrow$$
$$\text{fail}, \underline{p(s(0), Y_1)}, \underline{r(Y_1)} \longrightarrow \text{fail}, \text{fail}, \underline{r(s(s(0)))} \longrightarrow \ldots$$

We give an intuitive explanation why P cannot be $\mathcal{P}$-simply acceptable. Since fail is a simply moded atom, it turns out that for any X, we have $p(X, s(X)) \in PM_P^{SL}$. So for the recursive clause to be $\mathcal{P}$-simply acceptable, we would need $|X| > |s(X)|$ for all X, which is impossible since there are no infinite descending chains in $\mathbb{N}$.

This example also demonstrates that the class of local delay terminating programs strictly includes the class of strongly terminating programs.

The example is artificial. We will come back to this point in the conclusion. In any case, the assumption of local selection rules is crucial for the method for showing termination of this section.

6.1   Operational Definition

Marchiori and Teusink [47] have considered local selection rules controlled by delay declarations. They define a *safe delay declaration* so that an atom can be selected only when it is bounded w.r.t. a level mapping. In order to avoid even having to define delay declarations, we took a shortcut by assuming *delay-safe* selection rules. This seems legitimate given that Marchiori and Teusink do not give the exact syntax of delay declarations either.

Definition 6.2. A program P and query Q *local delay terminate* (w.r.t. $|.|$) if they universally terminate w.r.t. the set of selection rules that are both local and delay-safe (w.r.t. $|.|$).

Unlike in the previous two sections, modes are not used explicitly in the definition of delay-safe selection rules. Therefore it is possible to contrive an example of a program and a query that input terminate (and hence a fortiori input $\mathcal{P}$-terminate) but do not local delay terminate. The example is obtained by deliberately choosing a level mapping that does not reflect the mode of the query at hand.

Example 6.3. The APPEND program and the query

$$\mathtt{append([],[],X), \; append(X,[],Y)}$$

input terminate for the mode $\mathtt{append}(I, I, O)$. However, they do not local delay terminate w.r.t. a level mapping $|.|$ such that $|A| = 0$ for every A (e.g. consider the RD selection rule).

However, in Subsec. 10.2 we will see that under natural assumptions (in particular, the level mapping must be moded) delay-safe selection rules are also input-consuming. Then, input termination implies local delay termination. As is witnessed by Ex. 6.1, a program which local delay terminates but does not even input $\mathcal{P}$-terminate, this implication is strict.

6.2   Information on Data Flow: Covers

Delay-safe selection rules ensure that selected atoms are bounded. To ensure that the level mapping *decreases* during a derivation, we exploit additional information provided by a model of the program. Given an atom B in a query, we are interested in other atoms that share variables with B, so that instantiating these variables makes B bounded. A set of such atoms is called a *direct cover*. The only way of making B bounded is by resolving away one of its direct covers. The formal definition is as follows.

Definition 6.4. Let $|.|$ be a level mapping, $A \leftarrow Q$ a clause containing a body atom B, and $\tilde{C}$ a subset[7] of Q such that $B \notin \tilde{C}$. We say that $\tilde{C}$ is a *direct cover for B (w.r.t. $A \leftarrow Q$ and $|.|$)* if there exists a substitution θ such that $B\theta$ is bounded w.r.t. $|.|$ and $Dom(\theta) \subseteq Vars(A, \tilde{C})$.

A direct cover is *minimal* if no proper subset is a direct cover.

---

[7] By abuse of terminology, here we identify a query with the set of atoms it contains.

Note that the above concept is similar to well-modedness, assuming a moded level mapping. In this case, for each atom, the atoms to the left of it are a direct cover. This generalises in the obvious way to *permutation* well moded queries.

Considering an atom B, we have said that the only way of making B bounded is by resolving away one of B's direct covers. However, for an atom in a direct cover, say atom A, to be selected, A must be bounded, and the only way of making A bounded is by resolving away one of A's direct covers. Iterating this reasoning gives rise to a kind of closure of the notion of direct cover. In the following definition, *Pow* stands for the powerset.

Definition 6.5. Let $|.|$ be a level mapping and $A \leftarrow Q$ a clause. Consider the least set $\mathcal{C}$, subset of $Pow(Q \times Pow(Q))$, such that

1. $\langle B, \emptyset \rangle \in \mathcal{C}$ whenever $\emptyset$ is a minimal direct cover for B in $A \leftarrow Q$;
2. $\langle B, \tilde{C} \rangle \in \mathcal{C}$ whenever $B \notin \tilde{C}$, and $\tilde{C} = \{C_1, \ldots, C_k\} \cup \tilde{D}_1 \cup \ldots \tilde{D}_k$, where $\{C_1, \ldots, C_k\}$ is a minimal direct cover of B in $A \leftarrow Q$, and for $i \in [1, k]$, $\langle C_i, \tilde{D}_i \rangle \in \mathcal{C}$.

The set $Covers(A \leftarrow Q) \subseteq Q \times Pow(Q)$ is defined as the set obtained by deleting from $\mathcal{C}$ each element of the form $\langle B, \tilde{C} \rangle$ if there exists another element of $\mathcal{C}$ of the form $\langle B, \tilde{C}' \rangle$ such that $\tilde{C}' \subset \tilde{C}$.

We say that $\tilde{C}$ is a *cover for B (w.r.t. $A \leftarrow Q$ and $|.|$)* if $\langle B, \tilde{C} \rangle$ is an element of $Covers(A \leftarrow Q)$.

6.3   Declarative Characterisation

The following concept is used to show that programs terminate for local and delay-safe selection rules. We present a definition slightly different from the original one [47], albeit equivalent.

Definition 6.6. Let $|.|$ be a level mapping and I a Herbrand interpretation. A program P is *delay-recurrent by $|.|$ and I* if I is a model of P, and for every clause $c = A \leftarrow B_1, \ldots, B_n$ of P, for every $i \in [1, n]$, for every cover $\tilde{C}$ for B_i, for every substitution θ such that $c\theta$ is ground,

$$\text{if } I \models \tilde{C}\theta \text{ then } |A\theta| > |B_i\theta|.$$

We believe that this notion should have better been called *delay-acceptable*, since the convention is to call decreasing notions that involve models *(. . .)-acceptable*, and the ones that do not involve models *(. . .)-recurrent*.

Just as simply-acceptability, delay-recurrence imposes no proof obligation on queries. Such a proof obligation is made redundant by the fact that selected atoms must be bounded. Note that if no most recently introduced atom in a query is bounded, we obtain termination by deadlock.

In order for delay-recurrence to ensure termination, it is crucial that when an atom is selected, its cover is resolved away *completely* (this allows to use the premise $I \models \tilde{C}\theta$ in Def. 6.6). This is the reason why the selection rule is assumed to be local. We can now state the result of this section.

Theorem 6.7 ([47]). Let P be a program. If P is delay-recurrent by some $|.|$ and I, then for every query Q, P and Q local delay terminate.

Remark 6.8. Remark 4.11 applies to local delay termination as well.

6.4   Examples

Example 6.9. Consider again the program in Fig. 8, with the level mapping and model

$$|\mathtt{p}(x, y)| = size(x)$$
$$|\mathtt{r}(x)| = size(x) + 1$$
$$I = \{\mathtt{p}(\mathtt{s}(z), z) \mid z \text{ arbitrary}\} \cup \{\mathtt{r}(\mathtt{s}^n(0)) \mid n \geq 0\}.$$

The program is delay-recurrent by $|.|$ and I. We check the recursive clause for r. Consider an arbitrary ground instance

$$\mathtt{r}(x) \leftarrow \mathtt{p}(x, y), \ \mathtt{r}(y). \tag{5}$$

First, we observe that I is a model of this instance. In fact, if its body is true in I, then $x = \mathtt{s}^{n+1}(0)$ and $y = \mathtt{s}^n(0)$ for some $n \geq 0$, and so $\mathtt{r}(x)$ is true in I.

Consider the first body atom. It has an empty cover. Since $size(x) + 1 > size(x)$, we have a decrease as required.

Consider now the second body atom. There is only one cover $\mathtt{p}(\mathtt{X}, \mathtt{Y})$, so we must show that

$$x = \mathtt{s}^{n+1}(0) \text{ and } y = \mathtt{s}^n(0) \quad \text{imply} \quad size(x) + 1 > size(y) + 1,$$

which is evident. Hence we have shown that the clause is delay-recurrent.

Note that for the $\mathcal{P}$ given in Ex. 6.1, any input-consuming $\mathcal{P}$-derivation is delay-safe. So it is the locality property that makes the difference to that example.

We now give another example, which seems even more contrived than Ex. 6.1, but turns out to be interesting because of the similarity to Ex. 7.1.

Example 6.10. Consider

```
p(X)  ← q(Y), p(Y).
q(0)  ← fail.
```

with $|\mathtt{p}(0)| = 0$.

For the sake of comparison, assume the mode $\mathtt{p}(I), \mathtt{q}(O)$ and let $\mathcal{P} = \{\mathtt{p}(0)\} \cup \{\mathtt{q}(X) \mid X \text{ arbitrary}\}$.

Then the program local delay terminates but does not input $\mathcal{P}$-terminate for the query $\mathtt{p}(0)$. We will discuss this example further in the conclusion.

In an article that was the predecessor of this one [60], we gave PERMUTE_BACK (Fig. 5) as an example of a delay-recurrent program, but since then, it has been shown that this program does not require locality for termination (Ex. 5.5).

6.5   On Completeness of the Characterisation

Note that delay-recurrence is a sufficient but not necessary condition for local delay termination. The limitation lies in the notion of cover: to make an atom bounded, one has to resolve one of its covers; but conversely, resolving a cover will not necessarily make the atom bounded.

Example 6.11. Consider the following simple program

```
z ← p(X), q(X), r(X).
p(0).
q(s(X)) ← q(X).
r(X).
```

The program and any query z local delay terminate w.r.t. the level mapping:

$$|z| = |p(t)| = |r(t)| = 0$$
$$|q(t)| = size(t).$$

In fact, the only source of non-termination for a query might be an atom q(X). However, for any such atom selected by a delay-safe selection rule, X is a ground term. Hence the recursive clause in the program cannot generate an infinite derivation. On the other hand, it is not the case that the program is delay-recurrent. Consider the first clause. Since r(X) is a cover for q(X) and since every model of the program contains $r(t)$ for every t, we would have to show for some $|.|'$ that for every t:

$$|z|' > |q(t)|'.$$

This is impossible, since delay-recurrence on the third clause implies $|q(s^k(0))|' \geq k$ for any natural k.

7   Left-Termination

In this section, we consider the LD selection rule. We first give an example of a program that is not local delay terminating.

Example 7.1. Consider the program

```
p ← q, p.
```

with query p, where $|p| = 1$ and $|q| = 0$. It terminates for the LD selection rule but does not local delay terminate.

The example is artificial, and hence not a convincing motivation for studying the LD selection rule. We discuss this further in the conclusion, but in any case, there are several reasons for studying the LD selection rule in its own right. First, the conditions for termination are easier to formulate than for local delay termination. Secondly, the vast majority of works consider this rule, being the standard selection rule of Prolog. Finally, for the class of programs and queries that terminate w.r.t. the LD selection rule we are able to provide a sound and complete characterisation.

7.1   Operational Definition

Definition 7.2. A program P and query Q *left-terminate* if they universally terminate w.r.t. the set consisting of only the LD selection rule.

Formally comparing this class to the three previous ones is difficult. In particular, left-termination is not necessarily stronger than input or local delay termination, e.g. when applied to programs written with the RD selection rule in mind.

Example 7.3. Consider the program PERMUTE_BACK in Fig. 5, but this time in mode permute(I, O), insert(I, I, O). This program input terminates but does not left-terminate (see Ex. 4.13 and note Remark 4.11).

Example 7.4. Consider the program in Fig. 8, where we permute two body atoms in the first clause to obtain

$$r(X) \leftarrow r(Y), \ p(X,Y).$$

By Remark 6.8 and Ex. 6.9, the program and every query local delay terminate w.r.t. the level mapping given there. Moreover, no derivation deadlocks. However, the program and the query $r(0)$ do not left-terminate.

Also, local delay termination may not imply left-termination because of the deadlock problem. We will comment on this in the conclusion.

7.2   Extended Level Mappings

Left-termination was addressed by Apt & Pedreschi [7], who introduced the class of acceptable logic programs. However, their characterisation encountered a completeness problem similar to the one highlighted for Theorem 3.3.

Example 7.5. Figure 9 shows TRANSP, a program that terminates on a strict subset of ground queries only. In the intended meaning of the program, trans(x, y, e) succeeds iff $x \leadsto_e y$, i.e. if arc(x, y) is in the transitive closure of a direct acyclic graph (DAG) e, which is represented as a list of arcs. It is readily checked that if e is a graph that contains a cycle, infinite derivations may occur.

In the approach of [7], TRANSP cannot be reasoned about, since the same incompleteness problem as for recurrent programs occurs, namely that they characterise a class of programs that (left-)terminate for every ground query.

The cause of the restricted form of completeness of Theorem 3.3 lies in the use of level mappings, which must specify a natural number for every ground atom — hence termination is forced for every ground query. A more subtle problem with using level mappings is that one must specify values also for *uninteresting atoms*, such as trans(x, y, e) when e is not a DAG. The solution to both problems is to consider *extended* level mappings [61,62].

```
%  trans(x,y,e)  ← x ↝ₑ y for a DAG e

   trans(X,Y,E)  ←                          member(X,[X|Xs]).
      member(arc(X,Y),E).
                                            member(X,[Y|Xs])  ←
   trans(X,Y,E)  ←                             member(X,Xs).
      member(arc(X,Z),E), trans(Z,Y,E).
```

Fig. 9. TRANSP

Definition 7.6. An *extended level mapping* is a function $|.| : B_L \to \mathbb{N}^\infty$ of ground atoms to $\mathbb{N}^\infty$, where $\mathbb{N}^\infty = \mathbb{N} \cup \{\infty\}$.

In particular, we define $n \rhd m$ for $n, m \in \mathbb{N}^\infty$ iff $n = \infty$ or $n > m$. We write $n \unrhd m$ iff $n \rhd m$ or $n = m$.

We have $\infty \rhd m$ for every $m \in \mathbb{N}^\infty$. In particular $\infty \rhd \infty$. For (only) this reason, $\rhd$ is not well-founded. However, this makes sense since the inclusion of ∞ in the codomain is intended to model non-termination and uninteresting instances of program clauses.

7.3   Declarative Characterisation

With the above notation we are now ready to introduce (a modified definition of) acceptable programs and queries. A program P is acceptable if for every ground instance of a clause from P, the level of the head is greater than the level of each atom in the body such that the body atoms to its left are true in a Herbrand model of the program.

The modification w.r.t. [7] lies in the fact that the definition of an acceptable clause may involve clause *instances* where both the head and a body atom have level ∞. Intuitively, a non-terminating derivation would start in a query of level ∞ and always use clause instances where head and recursive body atoms have level ∞, while an acceptable (and terminating) query must have a level in $\mathbb{N}$.

Definition 7.7. Let $|.|$ be an extended level mapping, and I a Herbrand interpretation. A program P is *acceptable by* $|.|$ *and I* if I is a model of P, and for every $A \leftarrow B_1, \dots, B_n \in ground_L(P)$,

$$\text{for all } i \in [1,n], \quad I \models B_1, \dots, B_{i-1} \quad \text{implies} \quad |A| \rhd |B_i|.$$

A query Q is *acceptable by* $|.|$ *and I* if there exists $k \in \mathbb{N}$ such that for every $A_1, \dots, A_n \in ground_L(Q)$,

$$\text{for all } i \in [1,n], \quad I \models A_1, \dots, A_{i-1} \quad \text{implies} \quad k \rhd |A_i|.$$

Let us compare this definition to the definition of delay-recurrence (Def. 6.6). In the case of local and delay-safe selection rules, an atom cannot be selected before one of its covers is completely resolved. In the case of the LD selection rule, an atom cannot be selected before the atoms to its left are completely resolved. Because of the correctness of LD resolution [2], this explains why, in both cases, a decrease is only required if the instance of the cover, resp. the instance of the atoms to the left, are in some model of the program. We also refer to Subsec. 10.1.

Acceptable programs and queries precisely characterise left-termination.

Theorem 7.8 ([7,61]). Let P be a program and Q a query.

If P and Q are both acceptable by some $|.|$ and I, then P and Q left-terminate.

Conversely, if P and Q left-terminate, then there exist an extended level mapping $|.|$ and a Herbrand interpretation I such that P and Q are both acceptable by $|.|$ and I.

7.4   Examples

Example 7.9. The program in Ex. 7.1 is trivially acceptable. Let $|\mathsf{p}| = 1$ and $|\mathsf{q}| = 0$ and $I = \emptyset$. Then $|\mathsf{p}| \rhd |\mathsf{q}|$, and since I is a model of the program, $I \models \mathsf{q}$ implies $|\mathsf{p}| \rhd |\mathsf{p}|$.

We now give an example that highlights the use of extended level mappings in termination proofs. Note that we do not intend this example to be contrasted with the three preceding termination classes.

Example 7.10. We will show that TRANSP is acceptable. We have pointed out that in the intended use of the program, e is supposed to be a DAG. We define:

$$|\mathsf{trans}(x,y,e)| = \begin{cases} length(e) + 1 + Card\{v \mid x \leadsto_e v\} & \text{if } e \text{ is a DAG} \\ \infty & \text{otherwise} \end{cases}$$

$$|\mathsf{member}(x,e)| = length(e)$$

$$\begin{aligned} I = \{&\mathsf{trans}(x,y,e) \mid x,y,e \in U_L\} \cup \\ &\{\mathsf{member}(x,e) \mid x \text{ is in the list } e\}. \end{aligned}$$

where $Card$ is the set cardinality operator. It is easy to check that TRANSP is acceptable by $|.|$ and I. In particular, consider a ground instance of the second clause:

$$\mathsf{trans}(x,y,e) \leftarrow \mathsf{member}(\mathsf{arc}(x,z),e),\ \mathsf{trans}(z,y,e).$$

It is immediate to see that I is a model of it. In addition, we have the proof obligations:

(i) $\qquad\qquad\qquad\qquad |\mathsf{trans}(x,y,e)| \rhd |\mathsf{member}(\mathsf{arc}(x,z),e)|$

(ii) $\mathsf{arc}(x,z)$ is in e implies $|\mathsf{trans}(x,y,e)| \rhd |\mathsf{trans}(z,y,e)|$.

The first one is easy to show since $|\mathsf{trans}(x,y,e)| \rhd length(e)$. Considering the second one, we distinguish two cases. If e is not a DAG, the conclusion is immediate. Otherwise, $\mathsf{arc}(x,z)$ in e implies that $Card\{v \mid x \leadsto_e v\} > Card\{v \mid z \leadsto_e v\}$, and so:

$$\begin{aligned} |\mathsf{trans}(x,y,e)| &= length(e) + 1 + Card\{v \mid x \leadsto_e v\} \\ &\rhd length(e) + 1 + Card\{v \mid z \leadsto_e v\} = |\mathsf{trans}(z,y,e)|. \end{aligned}$$

(s)	`system(N) ←` `    prod(Bs), cons(Bs,N).`	*(c)*	`cons([D|Bs],s(N)) ←` `    cons(Bs,N), wait(D).`
(p1)	`prod([s(0)|Bs])) ←` `    prod(Bs).`		`cons([], 0).`

(p2)	`prod([s(s(0))|Bs])) ←`
	`    prod(Bs).`
	`prod([]).`
		(w)	`wait(s(D)) ←`
			`    wait(D).`
			`wait(0).`

Fig. 10. PRODCONS

Finally, observe that for a DAG e, the queries $\mathtt{trans}(x, \mathtt{Y}, e)$ and $\mathtt{trans}(\mathtt{X}, \mathtt{Y}, e)$ are acceptable by $|.|$ and I. The first one is intended to compute all nodes y such that $x \leadsto_e y$, while the second one computes the binary relation $\leadsto_e$. Therefore, the TRANSP program and those queries left-terminate.

Note that this is of course also an example of a program and a query which left-terminate but do not strongly terminate (e.g. consider the RD selection rule).

8   ∃-Termination

So far we have considered five classes of terminating programs, making increasingly strong assumptions about the selection rule, or in other words, considering in each section a smaller set of selection rules. In the previous section we have arrived at a singleton set containing the LD selection rule. Therefore we can clearly not strengthen our assumptions, in the same sense as before, any further.

We will now consider an assumption about the selection rule which is the dual to assuming *all* selection rules (Sec. 3). We introduce ∃-*termination* of logic programs [63], claiming that it is an essential concept for separating the *logic* and *control* aspects of a program.

Before, however, we motivate the limitations of left-termination.

Example 8.1. The program PRODCONS in Fig. 10 abstracts a (concurrent) system composed of a producer and a consumer. For notational convenience, we identify the term $\mathbf{s}^n(0)$ with the natural number n. Intuitively, prod is the producer of a non-deterministic sequence of 1's and 2's, and cons the consumer of the sequence. The shared variable Bs in clause *(s)* acts as an unbounded buffer. The overall system is started by the query $\mathtt{system}(n)$. Note that the program is well moded with the obvious mode $\mathtt{prod}(O), \mathtt{cons}(I, I), \mathtt{wait}(I)$, but assuming LD (and hence, input-consuming) derivations does not ensure termination. The crux is that prod can produce a message sequence of arbitrary length. Now cons can only consume a message sequence of length n, but for this to ensure termination, atoms using cons must be eventually selected. We will see that a selection rule exists for which this program and the query $\mathtt{system}(n)$ terminate.

8.1   Operational Definition

Definition 8.2. A program P and a query Q $\exists$-*terminate* if there exists a non-empty set S of standard selection rules such that P and Q universally terminate w.r.t. S.

If P and Q do not $\exists$-terminate, then no standard selection rule can be terminating. For extensions of the standard definition of selection rule, such as input-consuming and delay-safe rules, this is not always true.

Example 8.3. The simple program

```
p(s(X)) ← p(X).
p(X).
```

with mode $p(I)$ and query $p(X)$ input terminates by deadlock, but does not $\exists$-terminate. The same program and query local delay terminate (w.r.t. $|p(t)| = size(t)$).

We will come back to the issue of deadlock in Subsec. 10.2.

We observe that $\exists$-termination coincides with universal termination w.r.t. the set of fair selection rules. Therefore, any fair selection rule is a terminating control for any program and query for which a terminating control exists.

Theorem 8.4 ([62,63]). A program P and a query Q $\exists$-terminate iff they universally terminate w.r.t. the set of fair selection rules.

Concerning Ex. 8.1, it can be said that viewed as a concurrent system, the program inherently relies on fairness for termination.

8.2   Declarative Characterisation

Ruggieri [62,63] offers a characterisation of $\exists$-termination using the notion of *fair-bounded* programs and queries. Just as Def. 7.7, it is based on *extended* level mappings.

Definition 8.5. Let $|.|$ be an extended level mapping, and I a Herbrand interpretation. A program P is *fair-bounded by* $|.|$ *and* I if I is a model of P such that for every $A \leftarrow B_1, \dots, B_n \in ground_L(P)$:

(a) $I \models B_1, \dots, B_n$ implies that for every $i \in [1, n]$, $|A| \rhd |B_i|$, and
(b) $I \not\models B_1, \dots, B_n$ implies that for some $i \in [1, n]$ with $I \not\models B_i \wedge |A| \rhd |B_i|$.

A query Q is *fair-bounded by* $|.|$ *and* I if there exists $k \in \mathbb{N}$ such that for every $A_1, \dots, A_n \in ground_L(Q)$:

(a) $I \models A_1, \dots, A_n$ implies that for every $i \in [1, n]$, $k \rhd |A_i|$, and
(b) $I \not\models A_1, \dots, A_n$ implies that for some $i \in [1, n]$ with $I \not\models A_i \wedge k \rhd |A_i|$.

Note that the hypotheses of conditions *(a)* and *(b)* are *mutually exclusive*.

Let us discuss in more detail the meaning of proof obligations *(a)* and *(b)* in Def. 8.5. Consider a ground instance $A \leftarrow B_1, \dots, B_n$ of a clause.

If the body $B_1, \dots, B_n$ is true in the model I, then there might exist a SLD-refutation for it. Condition *(a)* is then intended to bound the length of the refutation.

If the body is not true in the model I, then it cannot have a refutation. In this case, termination actually means that there is an atom in the body that has a finitely failed SLD-tree. Condition *(b)* is then intended to bound the depth of the finitely failed SLD-tree. As a consequence of this, the complement of I is necessarily included in the finite failure set of the program.

Compared to acceptability, the model and the extended level mapping in the proof of fair-boundedness have to be chosen more carefully, due to more binding proof obligations. As we will see in Subsec. 10.2, however, the simpler proof obligations of recurrence and acceptability are sufficient conditions for proving fair-boundedness. Note also that, as in the case of acceptable programs, the inclusion of ∞ in the codomain of extended level mapping allows for excluding *unintended atoms* and *non-terminating atoms* from the termination analysis. In fact, if $|A| = \infty$ then *(a, b)* in Def. 8.5 are trivially satisfied.

Fair-bounded programs and queries precisely characterise $\exists$-termination, i.e. the class of logic programs and queries for which a terminating control exists.

Theorem 8.6 ([62,63]). Let P be a program and Q a query.

If P and Q are both fair-bounded by some $|.|$ and I, then P and Q $\exists$-terminate.

Conversely, if P and Q $\exists$-terminate, then there exist an extended level mapping $|.|$ and a Herbrand interpretation I such that P and Q are both fair-bounded by $|.|$ and I.

8.3 Example

Example 8.7. The PRODCONS program is fair-bounded. First, we introduce the *list-max* norm:

$$lmax(f(x_1, \dots, x_n)) = 0 \qquad\qquad \text{if } f \neq [.|.]$$
$$lmax([x|xs]) = max\{lmax(xs), size(x)\} \quad \text{otherwise.}$$

Note that for a ground list xs, $lmax(xs)$ equals the maximum size of an element in xs. Then we define:

$$|\texttt{system}(n)| = size(n) + 3$$
$$|\texttt{prod}(bs)| = length(bs)$$
$$|\texttt{cons}(bs, n)| = \begin{cases} size(n) + lmax(bs) & \text{if } I \models \texttt{cons}(bs, n) \\ size(n) & \text{if } I \not\models \texttt{cons}(bs, n) \end{cases}$$
$$|\texttt{wait}(t)| = size(t)$$

$$I = \{\texttt{system}(n) \mid n \in U_L\} \cup \{\texttt{prod}(bs) \mid lmax(bs) \leq 2\} \cup$$
$$\{\texttt{cons}(bs, n) \mid length(bs) = size(n)\} \cup \{\texttt{wait}(x) \mid x \in U_L\}.$$

Let us show the proof obligations of Def. 8.5. Those for unit clauses are trivial. Consider now the recursive clauses *(w)*, *(c)*, *(p1)*, *(p2)*, and *(s)*.

(w). I is obviously a model of *(w)*. In addition, $|\mathtt{wait}(\mathtt{s}(d))| = size(d) + 1 \vartriangleright size(d) = |\mathtt{wait}(d)|$. This implies *(a, b)*.

(c). Consider a ground instance $\mathtt{cons}([d|bs], \mathtt{s}(n)) \leftarrow \mathtt{cons}(bs, n), \mathtt{wait}(d)$ of *(c)*. If $I \models \mathtt{cons}(bs, n), \mathtt{wait}(d)$, then $length(bs) = size(n)$, and so

$$length([d|bs]) = length(bs) + 1 = size(n) + 1 = size(\mathtt{s}(n)),$$

i.e. $I \models \mathtt{cons}([d|bs], \mathtt{s}(n))$. Therefore, I is a model of *(c)*. Let us show proof obligations *(a, b)* of Def. 8.5.

(a) Suppose that $I \models \mathtt{cons}(bs, n), \mathtt{wait}(d)$. We have already shown that $I \models \mathtt{cons}([d|bs], \mathtt{s}(n))$. We calculate:

$$
\begin{aligned}
|\mathtt{cons}([d|bs], \mathtt{s}(n))| &= size(n) + 1 + max\{lmax(bs), size(d)\} \\
&\vartriangleright size(n) + lmax(bs) = |\mathtt{cons}(bs, n)| \\
|\mathtt{cons}([d|bs], \mathtt{s}(n))| &= size(n) + 1 + max\{lmax(bs), size(d)\} \\
&\vartriangleright size(d) = |\mathtt{wait}(d)|.
\end{aligned}
$$

These two inequalities show that *(a)* holds.

(b) If $I \not\models \mathtt{cons}(bs, n), \mathtt{wait}(d)$, then necessarily $I \not\models \mathtt{cons}(bs, n)$. Therefore

$$
\begin{aligned}
|\mathtt{cons}([d|bs], \mathtt{s}(n))| &\trianglerighteq size(n) + 1 \\
&\vartriangleright size(n) = |\mathtt{cons}(bs, n)|,
\end{aligned}
$$

and so we have *(b)*. Recall that *(b)* states that the depth of the finitely failed SLD-tree must be bounded. In fact, it is the decrease of the "counter", the second argument of $\mathtt{cons}$, which in this case bounds the depth of the SLD-tree.

(p1,p2). I is obviously a model of *(p1)*. Moreover we have

$$|\mathtt{prod}([\mathtt{s}(0)|bs])| = length(bs) + 1 \vartriangleright length(bs) = |\mathtt{prod}(bs)|,$$

which implies *(a)* and *(b)*. The reasoning for *(p2)* is analogous.

(s). Consider a ground instance $\mathtt{system}(n) \leftarrow \mathtt{prod}(bs), \mathtt{cons}(bs, n)$ of *(s)*. Obviously I is a model of *(s)*. Let us show *(a,b)*.

(a) Suppose that $I \models \mathtt{prod}(bs), \mathtt{cons}(bs, n)$. This implies $lmax(bs) \leq 2$ and $length(bs) = size(n)$. These imply:

$$
\begin{aligned}
|\mathtt{system}(n)| &= size(n) + 3 \vartriangleright length(bs) = |\mathtt{prod}(bs)| \\
|\mathtt{system}(n)| &= size(n) + 3 \vartriangleright size(n) + lmax(bs) = |\mathtt{cons}(bs, n)|.
\end{aligned}
$$

```
%   even(X)  ←                              %   odd(X)  ←
%       X is an even natural number.        %       X is an odd natural number.

    even(s(X))  ←  odd(X).                      odd(s(X))  ←  even(X).
    even(0).
```

Fig. 11. ODDEVEN

(b) Suppose that $I \not\models \text{prod}(bs),\ \text{cons}(bs, n)$. Intuitively, this means that the query $\text{prod}(bs),\ \text{cons}(bs, n)$ has no refutation. We distinguish two cases. If $I \not\models \text{cons}(bs, n)$ ($\text{cons}(bs, n)$ has no refutation) then:

$$|\text{system}(n)| \ = \ size(n) + 3 \ \triangleright \ size(n) \ = \ |\text{cons}(bs, n)|.$$

If $I \models \text{cons}(bs, n)$ and $I \not\models \text{prod}(bs)$ ($\text{prod}(bs)$ has no refutation) then $length(bs) = size(n)$, which implies:

$$|\text{system}(n)| = size(n) + 3 \triangleright length(bs) = |\text{prod}(bs)|.$$

To conclude the example, note that for every $n \in \mathbb{N}$ the query $\text{system}(n)$ is fair-bounded by $|.|$ and I, and so every fair SLD-derivation of PRODCONS and $\text{system}(n)$ is finite.

9   Bounded Nondeterminism

In the previous section, we have made the strongest possible assumption about the selection rule, in that we considered programs and queries for which there *exists* a terminating control. In general, a terminating control may not exist. Even in this case however, all is not lost. If we can establish that a program and query have only finitely many successful derivations, then we can transform the program so that it terminates.

Example 9.1. The program ODDEVEN in Fig. 11 defines the **even** and **odd** predicates, with the usual intuitive meaning. The query **even(X), odd(X)** is intended to check whether there is a number that is both even and odd. It is readily checked that ODDEVEN and the query do not ∃-terminate. However, ODDEVEN and the query have only finitely many, namely zero, successful derivations.

9.1   Operational Definition

Pedreschi & Ruggieri [58] propose the notion of *bounded nondeterminism* to model programs and queries with finitely many refutations.

Definition 9.2. A program P and query Q have *bounded nondeterminism* if for every standard selection rule s there are finitely many SLD-refutations of P and Q via s.

By the Switching Lemma [2], each refutation via some standard selection rule is isomorphic to some refutation via any other standard selection rule. Therefore, bounded nondeterminism could have been defined by requiring finitely many SLD-refutations of P and Q via *some* standard selection rule. Also, note that, while bounded nondeterminism implies that there are finitely many refutations also for non-standard selection rules, the converse implication does not hold, in general (see Ex. 8.3).

Bounded nondeterminism, although not being a notion of termination in the strict sense, is closely related to termination. In fact, if P and Q ∃-terminate, then P and Q have bounded nondeterminism. Conversely, if P and Q have bounded nondeterminism then there exists an upper bound for the length of the SLD-refutations of P and Q. If the upper bound is known, then we can syntactically transform P and Q into an equivalent program and query that strongly terminate, i.e. any selection rule will be a terminating control for them. Note that this transformation is even interesting for programs and queries that ∃-terminate, since few existing systems adopt fair selection rules. In addition, even if we adopt a selection rule that ensures termination, we may apply the transformation to prune the SLD-tree from unsuccessful branches.

9.2 Declarative Characterisation

In the following, we present a declarative characterisation of programs and queries that have bounded nondeterminism, by introducing the class of *bounded* programs and queries. Just as Defs. 7.7 and 8.5, it is based on *extended* level mappings.

Definition 9.3. Let $|.|$ be an extended level mapping, and I a Herbrand interpretation. A program P is *bounded by $|.|$ and I* if I is a model of P such that for every $A \leftarrow B_1, \ldots, B_n \in ground_L(P)$:

$$I \models B_1, \ldots, B_n \text{ implies that for every } i \in [1, n], |A| \rhd |B_i|.$$

A query Q is *bounded by $|.|$ and I* if there exists $k \in \mathbb{N}$ such that for every $A_1, \ldots, A_n \in ground_L(Q)$:

$$I \models A_1, \ldots, A_n \text{ implies that for every } i \in [1, n], \ k \rhd |A_i|.$$

It is straightforward to check that the definition of bounded programs is a simplification of Def. 8.5 of fair-bounded programs, where proof obligation *(b)* is discarded. Intuitively, the definition of boundedness only requires the decreasing of the extended level mapping when the body atoms are true in some model of the program, i.e. they might have a refutation.

Bounded programs and queries precisely characterise the notion of bounded nondeterminism.

Theorem 9.4 ([58,62]). Let P be a program and Q a query.

If P and Q are both bounded by some $|.|$ and I, then P and Q have bounded nondeterminism.

Conversely, if P and Q have bounded nondeterminism, then there exist an extended level mapping $|.|$ and a Herbrand interpretation I such that P and Q are both bounded by $|.|$ and I.

9.3   Examples

Example 9.5. Consider again the ODDEVEN program. It is readily checked that it is bounded by defining:

$$|\texttt{even}(x)| = |\texttt{odd}(x)| = size(x)$$
$$I = \{\texttt{even}(\texttt{s}^{2 \cdot i}(0)),\ \texttt{odd}(\texttt{s}^{2 \cdot i+1}(0)) \mid i \geq 0\}.$$

The query `even(X), odd(X)` is bounded by $|.|$ and I. In fact, since no instance of it is true in I, Def. 9.3 imposes no requirement. Therefore, ODDEVEN and the query above have bounded nondeterminism.

Generally, for a query that has no instance in a model of the program (it is *unsolvable*), the k in Def. 9.3 can be chosen as 0. An automatic method to check whether a query (at a node of a SLD-tree) is unsolvable has been proposed by [19]. Of course, the example is somewhat a limit case, since one does not even need to run a query if it has been shown to be unsolvable. However, we have already mentioned that the benefits of characterising bounded nondeterminism also apply to programs and queries belonging to the previously introduced classes. In addition, it is still possible to devise an example program and a *satisfiable* query that do not ∃-terminate but have bounded nondeterminism.

Example 9.6. We define the predicate `all` such that the query `all`$(n_0, n_1, \texttt{Xs})$ collects in `Xs` the answers of a query `q`(m, A) for values m ranging from n_0 to n_1.

```
all(N,N,[A]) ← q(N,A).
all(N,N1,[A|As]) ← q(N,A), all(s(N),N1,As).
q(Y,Y). %just as an example
```

The program and the query `all(0, s(s(0)), As)` do not ∃-terminate, but they have only one computed answer, namely `As` $= [0, \texttt{s}(0), \texttt{s}(\texttt{s}(0))]$. The program and the query are bounded (and thus have bounded nondeterminism) by defining:

$$|\texttt{all}(n, m, x)| = max\{size(m) - size(n), 0\} + 1$$
$$|\texttt{q}(x, y)| = 0$$

$$I = \{\texttt{all}(n, m, x) \mid size(n) \leq size(m)\} \cup \{\texttt{q}(x, y) \mid x, y,\ \text{arbitrary}\}.$$

10   Relations between Classes

We have defined seven classes of programs and queries, which provide declarative characterisations of operational notions of universal termination and bounded nondeterminism. In this section we summarise the relationships between these classes.

Table 1. Comparison of characterisations

	only ground?	only recursive?	uses model?	query oblig.?	∞ in codomain?	neg. model info.?
boundedness	yes	no	yes	yes	yes	no
fair-boundedness	yes	no	yes	yes	yes	yes
acceptability	yes	no	yes	yes	yes	no
delay-recurrence	yes	no	yes	no	no	no
$\mathcal{P}$-simply-acceptability	no	yes	yes	no	no	no
recurrence	yes	no	no	yes	no	n.a.

10.1   Comparison of Characterisations

We now try to provide an intuitive understanding of the technical differences between the characterisations of termination we have proposed. These are summarised in Table 1. Note that simply-acceptability is a special case of $\mathcal{P}$-simply-acceptability that does not need to be distinguished in this context.

The first difference concerns the question of whether a decrease is defined for all ground instances of a clause, or rather for instances specified in some other way. All characterisations except $\mathcal{P}$-simply-acceptability require a decrease for all ground instances of a clause. One cannot attribute this difference to the termination classes themselves: the first criterion for input-termination by Smaus [67] also required a decrease for the ground instances of a clause, just as there are characterisations of left-termination [14,25] based on generalised level mappings and hence non-ground instances of clauses. However, one can say that our characterisation of input $\mathcal{P}$-termination inherently relies on measuring the level of non-ground atoms, which may change via further instantiation. Nevertheless, this instantiation is not arbitrary: it is controlled by the fact that derivations are input-consuming and the programs are simply moded. This is reflected in the condition that a decrease holds for all simply-local instantiations of a clause.

The second difference concerns the question of whether a decrease is required for recursive body atoms only, or whether recursion plays no role. $\mathcal{P}$-Simply-acceptability is the only characterisation that requires a decrease for recursive body atoms only. We attribute this difference essentially to the explicit use of modes. Broadly speaking, modes restrict the data flow of a program in a way that allows for termination proofs that are inherently *modular*. Therefore one does not explicitly require a decrease for non-recursive calls, but rather one requires that for the predicate of the non-recursive call, termination has already been shown (independently). To support this explanation, we refer to [32], where left-termination for *well moded* programs is shown, using *well-acceptability*. Well-acceptability requires a decrease only for recursive body atoms.

The third difference concerns the question of whether the method relies on (some kind of) models or not. It is not surprising that a method for showing strong termination cannot rely on models: one cannot make any assumptions about certain atoms being resolved before an atom is selected. However, the first methods for showing termination of input-consuming derivations were also not based on models [16,67], and it was remarked that the principle underlying the use of models in proofs of left-termination cannot be easily transferred to input termination. By restricting to simply moded programs and defining a special notion of model, this was nevertheless achieved. For a clause $H \leftarrow A_1, \ldots, A_n$, assuming that A_i is the selected atom, we exploited that provided that programs and queries are simply moded, we know that even though $A_1, \ldots, A_{i-1}$ may not be resolved completely, $A_1, \ldots, A_{i-1}\theta$ will be in any "partial model" of the program.

The fourth difference concerns the question of whether proof obligations are imposed on queries. Delay-recurrence and $\mathcal{P}$-simply-acceptability are the characterisations that impose no proof obligations for queries (except that in the latter case, the query must be simply moded). The reason is that the restrictions on the selectability of an atom, which depends on the degree of instantiation, take the role of such a proof obligation.

The fifth difference concerns the question of whether ∞ is in the codomain of level mappings. This is the case for acceptability, fair-boundedness and boundedness. In all three cases, this allows for excluding *unintended atoms* and *nonterminating atoms* from the termination analysis, which is crucial for achieving full completeness of the characterisation. For an atom A with $|A| = \infty$ the proof obligations are trivially satisfied. However, we do not see any reason why some of the other characterisations could not also be generalised by allowing ∞ in the codomain of level mappings.

A final difference concerns the way information on data flow (modes, models, covers) is used in the declarative characterisations. For recurrence this is not applicable. Apart from that, in all except fair-boundedness, such information is used only in a "positive" way, i.e. "if ... *is* in the model then ...". In fair-boundedness, it is also used in a "negative" way, namely "if ... *is not* in the model then ...". Intuitively, in all characterisation, except fair-boundedness, the relevant part of the information concerns a characterisation of atoms that are logical consequences of the program. In fair-boundedness, it is also relevant the characterisation of atoms that are not logical consequences, since for those atoms we must ensure finite failure.

10.2   From Strong Termination to Bounded Nondeterminism

In this subsection, we show inclusions between the introduced classes, i.e. we justify each arrow in Fig. 1. Note that in that figure, we have not only given the numbers of the statements, but also the numbers of two kinds of examples: examples that demonstrate that an inclusion is strict, and "counterexamples" that demonstrate that an inclusion does not hold without making additional assumptions.

We first leave aside the classes involving dynamic scheduling, i.e. input ($\mathcal{P}$-)termination and local delay termination, since for these classes, the comparison is much less clearcut.

Looking at the four remaining classes from an operational point of view, we note that strong termination of a program and a query implies left-termination, which in turn implies $\exists$-termination, which in turn implies bounded nondeterminism. Examples 7.10, 8.1 and 9.1 show that these implications are strict.

Since the declarative characterisations of those notions are sound and complete, the same strict inclusions hold among recurrence, acceptability, fair-boundedness and boundedness. This allows for reusing or simplifying termination proofs.

Theorem 10.1. Let P be a program and Q a query, $|.|$ an extended level mapping and I a Herbrand model of P. Each of the following statements strictly implies the statements below it:

- P and Q are recurrent by $|.|$,
- P and Q are acceptable by $|.|$ and I,
- P and Q are fair-bounded by $|.|$ and I,
- P and Q are bounded by $|.|$ and I.

Consider now local delay termination. Obviously, it is implied by strong termination, and this implication is strict (Ex. 6.1). However, we have observed with the programs and queries of Exs. 7.4 and 8.3 that local delay termination does not imply left-termination or $\exists$-termination, in general. These results can be obtained under reasonable assumptions, which, in particular, rule out deadlock.

The following proposition relates local delay termination with $\exists$-termination.

Proposition 10.2. Let P and Q be a permutation well moded program and query, and $|.|$ a moded level mapping.

If P and Q local delay terminate (w.r.t. $|.|$) then they $\exists$-terminate.

If P is delay-recurrent by $|.|$ and some Herbrand interpretation then P and Q are fair-bounded by some extended level mapping and Herbrand interpretation.

Proof. Since P and Q are permutation well moded, every query Q' in a derivation of P and Q is permutation well moded [66], and so by Def. 2.2, Q' contains an atom that is ground in its input positions and hence bounded w.r.t. $|.|$. Consider the selection rule that always selects this atom together with all program clauses. This selection rule is local and delay-safe, and it is a standard selection rule (since there is always a selected atom). Therefore, local delay termination implies $\exists$-termination.

Concerning the second claim, since fair-boundedness is a complete characterisation of $\exists$-termination, we have the conclusion.

The next proposition relates local delay termination with left-termination. In this case, programs must be well moded, not just *permutation* well moded. The proof is similar to the previous one but simpler.

Proposition 10.3. Let P and Q be a well moded program and query, and $|.|$ a moded level mapping.

If P and Q local delay terminate (w.r.t. $|.|$) then they left-terminate.

If P is delay-recurrent by $|.|$ and some Herbrand interpretation then P and Q are acceptable by some extended level mapping and Herbrand interpretation.

Marchiori & Teusink [47] propose a program transformation such that the original program is delay-recurrent iff the transformed program is acceptable. This transformation allows us to use automated proof methods originally designed for acceptability for the purpose of showing delay-recurrence.

Consider now input termination. As before, it is implied by strong termination, and this implication is strict (Exs. 4.1 and 4.13). However, as observed in Exs. 6.3, 7.3 and 8.3, input termination does not imply local delay termination, left-termination, or ∃-termination, in general. Again, these results can be obtained under reasonable assumptions.

The following proposition relates input termination to ∃-termination.

Proposition 10.4. Let P and Q be a permutation well moded program and query. If P and Q input terminate then they ∃-terminate.

Let P and Q be a permutation well and simply moded program and query. If P is simply acceptable by some $|.|$ and I then P and Q are fair-bounded by some extended level mapping and Herbrand interpretation.

Proof. The selection rule s constructed as in the proof of Prop. 10.2 is an input-consuming selection rule, and also a standard selection rule. Therefore, input termination implies universal termination w.r.t. $\{s\}$ and hence ∃-termination.

Concerning the second claim, by Theorem 4.10, P and Q input terminate. As shown above, this implies that they ∃-terminate. Since fair-boundedness is a complete characterisation of ∃-termination, we have the conclusion.

The next proposition gives a direct comparison between input and left-termination. The proof is similar to the previous one.

Proposition 10.5. Let P and Q be a well moded program and query. If P and Q input terminate then they left-terminate.

Let P and Q be a well and simply moded program and query. If P is simply acceptable by some $|.|$ and I then P and Q are acceptable by some extended level mapping and Herbrand interpretation.

To relate input termination to local delay termination, we introduce a notion that relates delay-safe derivations with input-consuming derivations, based on an a similar concept from [5].

Definition 10.6. Let P be a program and $|.|$ a moded generalised level mapping.

We say that $|.|$ *implies matching* (w.r.t. $|.|$) if for every atom $A = p(\mathbf{s}, \mathbf{t})$ bounded w.r.t. $|.|$ and for every $B = p(\mathbf{v}, \mathbf{u})$ head of a renaming of a clause from P which is variable-disjoint with A, if A and B unify, then $\mathbf{s}$ is an instance of $\mathbf{v}$.

Note that, in particular, $|.|$ implies matching if every atom bounded by $|.|$ is ground in its input positions.

Proposition 10.7. Let P and Q be a permutation simply moded program and query, and $|.|$ a moded generalised level mapping that implies matching.

If P and Q input terminate then they local delay terminate (w.r.t. $|.|$).

Proof. The conclusion follows by showing that any derivation of P and any permutation simply moded query Q' via a local delay-safe selection rule (w.r.t. $|.|$) is also a derivation via an input-consuming selection rule. So, let s be a local delay-safe selection rule and Q' a permutation simply moded query such that s selects atom $A = p(\mathbf{s}, \mathbf{t})$. Then by Def. 10.6, for each $B = p(\mathbf{v}, \mathbf{u})$, head of a renaming of a clause from P, if A and B unify, then $\mathbf{s}$ is an instance of $\mathbf{v}$, i.e. $\mathbf{s} = \mathbf{v}\theta$ for some substitution θ such that $dom(\theta) \subseteq Vars(\mathbf{v})$. By [5, (Apt & Luitjes, 1995, Corollary 31)], this implies that the resolvent of Q' and any clause in P is again permutation simply moded. Moreover, by applying the unification algorithm [2], it is readily checked that, if A and B unify, then $\sigma = \theta \cup \{\mathbf{t}/\mathbf{u}\theta\}$ is an mgu. Permutation simply-modedness implies that $\mathbf{s}$ and $\mathbf{t}$ are variable-disjoint. Moreover, $\mathbf{s}$ and $\mathbf{v}$ are variable-disjoint. This implies that $Dom(\sigma) \cap Vars(\mathbf{s}) = \emptyset$, and so the derivation step is input-consuming.

By repeatedly applying this argument to all queries in the SLD-derivation of P and Q via s, it follows that the derivation is via some input-consuming selection rule.

Definition 10.6 seems to express the natural condition for level mappings that ensure input-consuming derivations. Note that the proposition is not straightforward to generalise to, say, nicely moded programs, since in this case one cannot in general construct an mgu by matching as in the above proof.

It remains an open question if simply-acceptability implies delay-recurrence under some general hypotheses. The problem with showing such a result lies in the fact that delay-recurrence is a sufficient but not necessary condition for local delay termination.

Example 10.8. Consider again the program and the level mapping $|.|$ of Ex. 6.11. We have already observed that the program and any query local delay terminate.

In addition, given the mode $\{\mathbf{p}(O), \mathbf{q}(I), \mathbf{r}(I)\}$, it is readily checked that the program is simply moded, and that the level mapping is moded and implies matching. Also, note that the program is simply acceptable by $|.|$ and any simply-local model.

However, this is not sufficient to show that the program is delay-recurrent, as proved in Ex. 6.11. Intuitively, the problem with showing delay-recurrence lies in the fact that the notion of cover does not appropriately describe the data flow in this program given by the modes.

Finally, we consider input $\mathcal{P}$-termination. Obviously, if a program and query input terminate, then they input $\mathcal{P}$-terminate. Whether or not this inclusion is strict depends on whether $\mathcal{P}$ is a trivial property or not. Examples 5.1 and 5.6 demonstrate situations where it is strict.

There is little sense in making general comparisons between $\mathcal{P}$-selection rules and the other classes — everything depends on $\mathcal{P}$. However, the following generalisation of Prop. 10.7 is particularly interesting.

Proposition 10.9. Let P and Q be a permutation simply moded program and query, and $|.|$ a moded generalised level mapping that implies matching. Let $\mathcal{P}$ be the set of atoms atoms that are bounded w.r.t. $|.|$.

If P and Q input $\mathcal{P}$-terminate then they local delay terminate (w.r.t. $|.|$).

Proof. By the same proof as the one of Prop. 10.7, any derivation of P and any permutation simply moded query Q' via a local delay-safe selection rule (w.r.t. $|.|$) is also a derivation via an input-consuming selection rule. Moreover, by the definition of $\mathcal{P}$, such a derivation is also a $\mathcal{P}$-derivation.

10.3   From Bounded Nondeterminism to Strong Termination

Consider now a program P and a query Q which either do not universally terminate for a set of selection rules in question, or simply for which we (or our compiler) fail to *prove* termination. We have already mentioned that, if P and Q have bounded nondeterminism then there exists an upper bound for the length of the SLD-refutations of P and Q. If the upper bound is known, then we can syntactically transform P and Q into an equivalent program and query that strongly terminate. As shown by Pedreschi & Ruggieri [58], such an upper bound is related to the natural number k of Def. 9.3 of bounded queries. As in our notation for moded atoms, we use boldface letters to denote vectors of (possibly non-ground) terms.

Definition 10.10. Let P be a program and Q a query both bounded by $|.|$ and I, and let $k \in \mathbb{N}$. We define $Ter(P)$ as the program such that:

- for every clause $p_0(\mathbf{t}_0) \leftarrow p_1(\mathbf{t}_1), \ldots, p_n(\mathbf{t}_n)$ in P, with $n > 0$, the clause

$$p_0(\mathbf{t}_0, \mathbf{s}(\mathrm{D})) \leftarrow p_1(\mathbf{t}_1, \mathrm{D}), \ldots, p_n(\mathbf{t}_n, \mathrm{D})$$

is in $Ter(P)$, where D is a fresh variable,
- and, for every clause $p_0(\mathbf{t}_0)$ in P, the clause

$$p_0(\mathbf{t}_0, \_) \leftarrow$$

is in $Ter(P)$.

Also, for the query $Q = p_1(\mathbf{t}_1), \ldots, p_n(\mathbf{t}_n)$, we define $Ter(Q, k)$ as the query

$$p_1(\mathbf{t}_1, \mathbf{s}^k(0)), \ldots, p_n(\mathbf{t}_n, \mathbf{s}^k(0))$$

The transformed program relates to the original one as shown in the following theorem.

Theorem 10.11 ([58,62]). Let P be a program and Q a query both bounded by $|.|$ and I, and let k be a given natural number satisfying Def. 9.3.

Then, for every $n \in \mathbb{N}$, $Ter(P)$ and $Ter(Q, n)$ strongly terminate.

Moreover, there is a bijection between SLD-refutations of P and Q via a selection rule s and SLD-refutations of $Ter(P)$ and $Ter(Q, k-1)$ via s.

The intuitive reading of this result is that the transformed program and query maintain the *success semantics* of the original program and query. Note that no assumption is made on the selection rule s, i.e. any selection rule is a terminating control for the transformed program and query.

Example 10.12. Reconsider the program ODDEVEN and $Q = $ even(X), odd(X) of Ex. 9.1. The transformed program Ter(ODDEVEN) is:

```
even(s(X),s(D))  ←  odd(X,D).
even(0,_).

odd(s(X),s(D))  ←  even(X,D).
```

and the transformed query $Ter(Q, k-1)$ for $k = 3$ is

$$\text{even}(X, s^2(0)), \text{odd}(X, s^2(0)).$$

By Theorem 10.11, the transformed program and query terminate for *any* selection rule, and the semantics w.r.t. the original program is preserved modulo the extra argument added to each predicate.

The transformations $Ter(P)$ and $Ter(Q, k)$ are of purely theoretical interest. In practice, one would implement these counters directly into the compiler/interpreter. Also, the compiler/interpreter should include a module that infers an upper bound k automatically. Approaches to the automatic inference of level mappings and models are briefly recalled in the next section. Pedreschi & Ruggieri [58] give an example showing how the approach of Decorte *et al.* [29] could be rephrased to infer boundedness.

11   Related Work

Termination in logic programming (and its extensions) has been the subject of intense research over the last fifteen years. The survey of De Schreye & Decorte [23], dated 1994, distinguishes three types of approaches: the ones that express necessary and sufficient conditions for termination, the ones that provide decidable *sufficient* conditions, and the ones that prove decidability or undecidability for subclasses of programs and queries. Under this classification, this survey paper has been mainly concerned with the first type. While we do not even try to survey the large amount of literature on automatic or semi-automatic approaches [14,21,29,23,44,52,53,71], it must be observed that existing tools typically implement conditions for checking proof obligations of the characterisations we surveyed. As an example, a challenging topic of the research in automatic termination inference consists in finding standard forms of level mappings and models, so that the solution of the resulting proof obligations can be reduced to known problems for which efficient algorithms exist. Note that on a theoretical level the problem of deciding whether a program belongs to one of the classes studied in this article is undecidable. This was formally shown by Bezem [11] for recurrence, and by Ruggieri [62] for acceptability, fair-boundedness and boundedness. Therefore, the conditions implemented by automatic tools are, inevitably, *sufficient* conditions.

In the following, we recall other characterisations of the various notions of termination and relate them to those presented in this survey.

11.1   Acceptability: the Modularity Issue

A termination characterisation is modular if the proof obligations for the program $P = P_1 \cup \ldots \cup P_n$ can be obtained from separate proof obligations of programs $P_1, \ldots, P_n$. The modularity property is essential both in paper & pencil proofs and in automatic tools, since it allows for reasoning on termination of a large program by breaking it down to several small modules.

Since non-termination can only arise from recursion, the decomposition P_1, $\ldots, P_n$ should partition P in such a way that all clauses defining two mutually recursive predicates appear in a same module P_i. Therefore, a termination characterisation is modular if the proof obligations for a clause defining a predicate p depend only on predicates mutually recursive with p.

Apt & Pedreschi [8] refined acceptability to provide a partially modular method. The resulting notion, called *semi-acceptability*, requires that: for every $A \leftarrow B_1, \ldots, B_n \in ground_L(P)$,

$$\text{for all } i \in [1, n] : \ I \models B_1, \ldots, B_{i-1} \ \text{implies} \ \begin{cases} |A| > |B_i| \text{ if } \ rel(A) \simeq rel(B) \\ |A| \geq |B_i| \text{ otherwise.} \end{cases}$$

Compared to acceptability, a strict decrease is now required for mutually recursive predicates only. Even if this simplifies proofs, it is a restricted notion of modularity, since changes in the level mapping of atoms defined in one module may make the proof obligations in higher modules invalid.

Etalle *et al.* [32] proposed a refinement of acceptability (*well-acceptability*) for well moded programs and queries. The requirement of well-modedness simplifies proofs of acceptability. On the one hand, the decrease of the level mapping is now required only for mutually recursive calls, i.e. for every $A \leftarrow B_1, \ldots, B_n \in ground_L(P)$,

$$\text{for all } i \in [1, n], \ I \models B_1, \ldots, B_{i-1} \ \text{and} \ rel(A) \simeq rel(B) \ \text{imply} \ |A| > |B_i|.$$

On the other hand, level mappings are assumed to be moded, and this leads to no proof obligation on *queries* (or better, queries are bounded as an immediate consequence). Also, it is interesting to observe that the definition of well-acceptability is then very close to simply-acceptability (Def. 4.9). Actually, well-modedness of a program and a query implies that atoms selected by the LD selection rule are ground in their input positions, hence a derivation via the LD selection rule is input-consuming.

De Schreye & Serebrenik [24] generalised well-acceptability to *order-accepta-bility*, by having any well-founded ordering, not necessarily $\mathbb{N}$, as codomain of level mappings. This allows us to show the same termination results and to simplify termination proofs when complex level mappings may be needed.

11.2   Non-ground Characterisations of Left-Termination

Alternative characterisations of left-termination consider proof obligations on generalised level mappings and thus on possibly non-ground instances of clauses and queries. Let us recall the well-known approach of Decorte *et al.* [25,29].

First, they use a non-ground notion of model.

Definition 11.1. A *generalised model*[8] of a program P is a set $I \subseteq Atom_L$ such that for every $A \leftarrow B_1 , \dots , B_n \in inst_L(P)$,

$$B_1 , \dots , B_n \in I \text{ implies } A \in I.$$

Second, they require (generalised) level mappings to be invariant under instantiation for atoms that may appear in a derivation starting from a set of intended queries. This is the counterpart of acceptability of a(n atomic) query.

Definition 11.2. For a program P and a set of queries $\mathcal{Q}$, let $Call(P, \mathcal{Q})$ be the set of atoms selected along a SLD-derivation of P and any $Q \in \mathcal{Q}$ via the LD selection rule.

A generalised level mapping $|.|$ is *rigid* if for every $A \in Call(P, \mathcal{Q})$ and every substitution θ, we have $|A| = |A\theta|$.

Usually, abstract interpretation techniques allow us to compute a superset of $Call(P, \mathcal{Q})$ given P and $\mathcal{Q}$, while for a broad class of norms, rigidity can be verified syntactically [14].

The proof method, called *rigid acceptability w.r.t. a set* $\mathcal{Q}$, requires that for a rigid level mapping $|.|$ and a generalised model I: for every $A \leftarrow B_1 , \dots , B_n \in inst_L(P)$,

for all $i \in [1, n]$, $I \models B_1 , \dots , B_{i-1}$ and $rel(A) \simeq rel(B)$ imply $|A| > |B_i|$.

If those proof obligations are satisfied, then P and every $A \in \mathcal{Q}$ left-terminate.

This characterisation is fully modular, i.e. it does not require P to be well-moded as in the case of well-acceptability. However, the characterisation is not complete. The main problem is due to the notion of rigidity.

Example 11.1. The query p(X) and the simple program P below left-terminate.

    p(a) ←p(b).
    p(b).

---

[8] A generalised model coincides with a set of *valid interargument relations* in the terminology of [25,29].

Consider now $\mathcal{Q} = \{\text{p(X)}\}$. We have $Call(P, \mathcal{Q}) = \{\text{p(X)},\text{p(a)},\text{p(b)}\}$. However, for any generalised level mapping $|.|$, proof obligations require $|\text{p(a)}| > |\text{p(b)}|$, which implies that $|.|$ cannot be rigid on $Call(P, \mathcal{Q})$.

The source of the problem lies in the requirement $|A| = |A\theta|$ of Def. 11.2. By assuming $|A| \geq |A\theta|$, the example program and query above can be reasoned about.

De Schreye and Serebrenik [24] have adapted this approach, i.e. the use of call sets, to *general orderings*, as opposed to level mappings. However, the aspect of incompleteness is pretty much the same as in the approach of Decorte *et al.* (see [24, Example 6]).

A general solution is provided by Bossi *et al.* [14] consisting of: (1) generalised level mappings with an arbitrary well-founded ordering as the codomain that *do not increase w.r.t. substitutions*; (2) a specification $(Pre, Post)$, with Pre, $Post \subseteq Atom_L$, which is intended to characterise call patterns (Pre) and correct instances ($Post$) of atomic queries. Call patterns provide information on the structure of selected atoms, while correct instances provide information on data flow. However, the proof obligations are not well suited for *paper & pencil* proofs, since they require to reason on the strongly connected components of a graph abstracting the flow of control of the program under consideration.

11.3   Left-Termination with Respect to a Set of Queries

Acceptability w.r.t. a set allows us to reason on a program and a *set* of queries, while acceptability seems to concentrate on a program and a *single* query at once. The benefit of acceptability w.r.t. a set consists of having just one single proof of termination for a set of queries rather than a set of proofs, one for each query in the set.

However, we observe that in our examples on acceptability, proofs can easily be generalised to a set of queries. If this was not the case, the practical use of termination analysis would be very limited. For instance, given a level mapping such that $|\text{p}(t)| = length(t)$, it is immediate to conclude that all queries $\text{p}(T)$, where T is a list, are acceptable.

Conversely, is it the case that if P and all queries in a set $\mathcal{Q}$ left-terminate then P and every $Q \in \mathcal{Q}$ are acceptable by a same $|.|$ and I?

The answer is affirmative. In fact, from the proof of the Completeness Theorem 7.8 [62, Theorem 2.3.20], if P and Q left-terminate then they are acceptable by a level mapping $|.|_P$ and a Herbrand model I_P that *only* depend on P. This implies that every $Q \in \mathcal{Q}$ is acceptable by $|.|_P$ and I_P. In conclusion, acceptability by $|.|_P$ and I_P precisely characterises the maximal set $\mathcal{Q}$ such that P and Q left-terminate for each $Q \in \mathcal{Q}$.

11.4   Permutation Terminating Programs

A permutation of a program P (resp., query Q) is any program (query) obtained by reordering clause body atoms in P (atoms in Q). We say that P and Q

permutation terminate if for some permutation P' of P and Q' of Q, P' and Q' left-terminate. Observe that permutation termination is strictly weaker than left-termination, and strictly stronger than $\exists$-termination (e.g. program PRODCONS in Fig. 10 and system(n), with $n \in \mathbb{N}$, $\exists$-terminate but do not permutation terminate).

We have not included permutation termination in our formal hierarchy since it is trivial from a theoretical point of view to relate it to left-termination: simply analyse all possible permutations of the program and query for left-termination. Permutation termination is mainly an issue for automatic tools, since one would like to compute this permutation efficiently.

Deransart & Małuszyński [30] presented the proof obligations of their method by considering a generic permutation of body atoms. However, the choice of the permutation is left to the user.

The inference of an appropriate permutation has been proposed by Speirs *et al.* [71] and by Hoarau & Mesnard [39]. In [71], mode and type information provided by the programmer are used to reorder the body atoms. The resulting static termination algorithm is part of the Mercury system [70]. In contrast, the approach of [39] aims at *inferring* an as large as possible set of queries for which a program permutation terminate without involving the programmer in additional specifications.

11.5   Transformational Approaches

It is possible to investigate termination of logic programs by transforming them to some other formal system. If the transformation preserves termination, one can resort to the compendium of techniques of those formal systems for the purpose of proving termination of the original logic program.

Baudinet [10] considered transforming logic programs into functional programs. Termination of the transformed programs can then be studied by structural induction. Her approach covers general logic programs, existential termination and the effects of the Prolog cut. Also, there is a considerable body of literature on transforming logic programs to term rewriting systems (TRSs), where a large set of well-founded orderings is available for reasoning about termination . It is very common in these transformational approaches to use modes. The intuitive idea is usually that the input of an atom has to rewrite into the output of that atom. Most of those works assume the LD selection rule [9,35,41,56]. One notable exception is due to Krishna Rao *et al.* [43], where termination is considered w.r.t. selection rules that respect a producer-consumer relation among variables in clauses. Such a producer-consumer relation is formalised with an extension of the notion of well-modedness.

While the transformation must be sound (if the transformed program terminates then the original one terminates as well), the converse (if the original program terminates then the transformed one terminates as well) is not well studied. One remarkable exception is the approach by Aguzzi & Modigliani [1], whose transformation is complete, albeit only for the limited class of *input driven* logic programs [4]. So for this limited class, a program terminates if and only if the corresponding TRS terminates.

11.6   Integer and Floating-Point Computations

For efficiency reasons, integers and integer predicates are implemented in Prolog (and other logic programming languages) by means of special terms and predicates, built-in's of the system. As an example, 3 < (2+2) is an atom containing the less-than predicate < and the ground arithmetic expression terms 3 and (2+2). As one could expect, the resolution of the atom above leads to success.

Integer arithmetic does not require special treatment when termination does not depend on integer computation, such as in the definition of the partition predicate in Ex. 7. In contrast, in presence of integer computations, the definition of the level mapping might take into account integer arguments of atoms. The approach of Dershowitz et al. [31] deduces automatically from a given program a finite abstract domain for representing ranges of integer expressions involved in program clauses. The abstract domain serves as a basis for checking the decreasing of level mappings over recursive calls.

Serebrenik [64] shows that the definition of a level mapping when integer arguments are critical for termination may be not as simple as expected, e.g. it may be non-linear. He proposed and implemented a sufficient condition for partitioning integers into intervals (called *adornments*) such that a linear level mapping can be defined on each of them. Even further, Serebrenik & De Schreye [65] extended the approach to reason on floating-point computations, i.e. in presence of rounding errors.

Also, Apt et al. [6] proposed a variant of acceptability for reasoning on built-in predicates, including arithmetic ones, var() and ground(). Their key concept is a specialised semantics (called Θ-semantics) and a notion of model w.r.t. such semantics to be used instead of Herbrand models in the definition of acceptability.

11.7   Dynamic Scheduling

The term *dynamic scheduling* refers to selection rules where the selection of an atom depends on its degree of instantiation at runtime. Dynamic scheduling can be implemented using delay declarations as provided by Gödel [38] or SICStus [73], or using *guards* (see Subsec. 11.12).

We believe that *modes* are important for understanding dynamic scheduling, even though some authors have not used them explicitly [45,47,49,55]. Modes are the basis for defining input-consuming derivations, which are a formalism for describing dynamic scheduling while abstracting from the technical details of delay declarations. We also believe that within dynamic scheduling, there is an important qualitative distinction between what we call (here) *weak* and *strong* selection rules. *Weak* selection rules are achieved by delay declarations that test for arguments being at least non-variable, and ideally correspond to input-consuming selection rules. *Strong* selection rules ensure that the depth of the SLD-tree of an atom is bounded at the time of selection, and more or less correspond to delay-safe selection rules.

Naish [55] considers delay declarations that would fall under weak selection rules. Naish has given two intuitive causes for loops: *circular modes* and *speculative output bindings*. The first cause (see Ex. 4.4) can be eliminated by requiring programs to be *permutation nicely moded*[9]. Speculative output bindings are indeed a good explanation for the fact that `permute(O, I)` (see Ex. 5.1) does not input terminate. Naish then makes the additional assumption that the selection rule always selects the leftmost selectable atom, and proposes to put recursive calls last in clause bodies. Effectively, this guarantees that the recursive calls are *ground* in their input positions, which would fall under strong selection rules.

Lüttringhaus-Kappel [45] proposed a method for generating delay declarations automatically. The method finds *acceptable* delay declarations, ensuring that the most general selectable atoms have finite SLD-trees. What is required however are *safe* delay declarations, ensuring that *instances* of most general selectable atoms have finite SLD-trees. A *safe* program is a program for which every acceptable delay declaration is safe. Lüttringhaus-Kappel states that all programs he has considered are safe, but gives no hint as to how this might be shown in general. This work is hence not about *proving* termination. Sometimes the generated delay declarations would fall under weak selection rules, but in some cases, the delay declarations require an argument of an atom to be a list before that atom can be selected, which would fall under strong selection rules.

Apt & Luitjes [5] made a first attempt to show termination for dynamic scheduling. They considered deterministic programs, i.e. programs where for each selectable atom (according to the delay declarations) there is at most one clause head unifiable with it. For such programs, the existence of one successful derivation implies that *all* derivations are finite. Such a class of programs, however, is of limited interest. Apt & Luitjes also give conditions for the termination of `APPEND`, but these are ad-hoc and do not address the general problem.

The work by Marchiori & Teusink [47], which we surveyed in Sec. 6, not only assumes strong selection rules, but in addition selection rules must be *local*. A limitation of their method lies in the fact that the notion of cover is just an approximation of the data flow in a program (see Ex. 6.11). No implementation of local selection rules is mentioned by the authors. We refer to the conclusion for further discussion.

Martin & King [49] ensure termination by imposing a depth bound on the SLD-tree. This is realised by a program transformation introducing additional argument positions for each predicate, which are counters for the depth of the computation. Of course, this falls under strong selection rules.

Naish's proposal [55] has been formalised and refined by Smaus et al. [69]. The authors consider atoms that may loop when called with insufficient input. It is proposed to place such atoms sufficiently late; all producers of input for such atoms must occur textually earlier. Effectively, this is a hybrid selection rule where strong assumptions are made only for certain atoms.

---

[9] A generalisation of "permutation *simply* moded".

Concerning input termination, the first sound but incomplete characterisation assumed well and nicely moded programs [67]. It was then found that the condition of well-modedness could easily be lifted [16]. By restricting to *simply moded* programs, it was possible to give a characterisation that is also complete [17], which is the work we survey in Sec. 4. It has been shown that under natural conditions, input-consuming derivations can be implemented using delay declarations [15,17,66].

The recent work of [68] considers input-consuming selection rules with additional assumptions. In one dimension, a selection rule can be parametrised by a property $\mathcal{P}$ that the selected atoms must have. This can be used to formalise delay-safe selection rules as we did in Sec. 5. However, the notion of $\mathcal{P}$-derivation abstracts from the distinction between weak and strong selection rules, since $\mathcal{P}$ could be any instantiation property. In another dimension, a selection rule can be local or not (necessarily) local. These dimensions can freely be combined.

11.8   ∃-Termination

Concerning termination w.r.t. fair selection rules, i.e. ∃-termination, we are aware only of the works of Gori [36] and McPhee [50]. Gori proposed an automatic system based on abstract interpretation analysis that infers ∃-termination. McPhee proposed the notion of *prioritised fair selection rules*, where atoms that are known to terminate are selected first, with the aim of improving efficiency of fair selection rules. He adopts the automatic test of Lindenstrauss & Sagiv [44] to infer (left-)termination, but, in principle, the idea applies to any automatic termination inference system.

11.9   Bounded Nondeterminism

Sufficient (semi-)automatic methods to approximate the number of computed instances by means of lower and upper bounds have been studied in the context of cost analysis of logic programs [26] and of cardinality analysis of Prolog programs [18]. As an example, cost analysis is exploited in the Ciao-Prolog system [37]. Of course, if ∞ is a lower bound to the number of computed instances of P and Q then they do not have bounded nondeterminism. Dually, if $n \in N$ is an upper bound then P and Q have bounded nondeterminism. In this case, however, we are still left with the problem of determining a depth of the SLD-tree that includes all the refutations.

The idea of cutting unsuccessful SLD-derivations is common to the research area of *loop checking* (see e.g. [12]). While a run-time analysis is potentially able to cut more unsuccessful branches, the evaluation of a pruning condition at run-time, such as for loop checks, involves a considerably higher computational overhead than statically checking the boundedness proof obligations.

11.10   General Programs

General programs admit negative literals in clause bodies and in queries. In presence of negation, there are several execution models proposed in the literature.

The most widely known is *SLDNF-resolution*, where negation is interpreted by the *negation-as-failure* rule. A declarative characterisation of strong termination for general logic programs and queries was proposed by Apt & Bezem [3]. They assume *safe* (not to be confused with *delay-safe* [47]) selection rules, meaning that negative literals can be selected only if they are ground. Apt & Pedreschi [7] have generalised acceptability to reason on programs with negation under SLDNF resolution. The characterisation is sound. Also, it is complete for safe selection rules.

When turning on other execution models, the class of (left-)terminating programs and queries may differ. A declarative characterisation of left-termination was provided by Marchiori [46] in the context of *constructive negation* by extending acceptability. Also, an elaborated notion extension of recurrence has been proposed in the context of *SLDNFA-resolution* by Verbaeten [76], and in the context of the EK-proof procedure by Mancarella *et al.* [57].

Finally, the modularity issue for general programs is discussed by Bossi *et al.* [13].

11.11   Extensions of LP: Constraint Logic Programs

The first work on characterisations of (left-)termination in *constraint* logic programming (CLP) is due to Colussi *et al.* [22], who proposed a necessary and sufficient condition inspired by the method of Floyd for termination of flowchart programs [33]. Their method consists of assigning a data flow graph to a program, where each node is labelled with the set of constraint stores of calls that may reach the associated program point. The decreasing of a function on every cycle of the data flow graph is then a necessary and sufficient condition for left-termination. A drawback of the method is that the set of constraints associated to nodes must be specified (the approach is not automated), which means reasoning operationally (as opposed to declaratively in terms of level mappings) on the program.

Ruggieri [61] proposed an extension of acceptability that is sound and complete for *ideal* CLP languages. A CLP language is ideal if its constraint solver, the procedure used to test consistency of constraints, returns *true* on a consistent constraint and *false* on an inconsistent one. In contrast, a non-ideal constraint solver may return *unknown* if it is unable to determine (in)consistency. An example of non-ideal CLP language is the CLP($\mathcal{R}$) system, for which Ruggieri proposes proof obligations (based on a notion of modes) in addition to acceptability in order to obtain a sound characterisation of left-termination.

Mesnard [51] provided sufficient termination conditions based on approximation techniques and Boolean μ-calculus, with the aim of *inferring* a class of left-terminating CLP queries. Recently, the approaches of Mesnard and Ruggieri have been merged into a unified framework [54], for which an implementation is described in [52].

Finally, Frühwirth [34] adapted the notion of recurrent logic programs to show termination of *constraint handling rules*, a language closely related to concurrent constraint programming and especially designed for writing constraint solvers.

11.12   Extensions of LP: Programs with Guards

The definition of input-consuming derivations has a certain resemblance with derivations in the parallel logic language of *(Flat) Guarded Horn Clauses* [75]. In (F)GHC, an atom and clause may be resolved only if the atom is an instance of the clause head, and a test (*guard*) on clause selectability is satisfied. Termination of GHC programs was studied by Krishna Rao *et al.* [42] by transforming them into TRSs.

Pedreschi & Ruggieri [59] characterised a class of programs (with guards and delay declarations) and queries that have no failed derivation. For those programs, termination for one selection rule implies termination (with success) for all selection rules. This situation has been previously described as saying that a program does not make speculative bindings [69]. The approach by Pedreschi & Ruggieri is an improvement w.r.t. the latter one, since what might be called "shallow" failure does not count as failure. For example, the program QUICKSORT is considered failure-free in the approach of [59].

11.13   Extensions of LP: Tabled Programs

Tabled logic programming is particularly interesting since tabling improves the termination behaviour of a logic program, compared to ordinary execution.

A declarative characterisation of tabled left-termination has been given by Decorte *et al.* [28]. The method can show termination in interesting cases where ordinary execution does not terminate. The approach has been extended and automated by Verbaeten *et al.* [77], where a mix of tabled and ordinary SLD-resolution is also studied. The characterisation provided is in general sound, and complete under some conditions on tabled predicates.

12   Conclusion

In this article, we have surveyed seven different classes of terminating logic programs and queries. For each of them, we have provided a sound declarative characterisation of termination, which, in five cases, was also complete. We have offered a unified view of those classes allowing for non-trivial formal comparisons. In particular, we have shown strict inclusions among the classes, establishing the hierarchy shown in Fig. 1. We conclude by discussing two questions: Why, in some cases, did we need additional assumptions to obtain a unified view? How significant are the classes of the hierarchy?

To make the first question more specific: why do the inclusions between termination for dynamic selection rules on the one hand and left-termination and ∃-termination on the other hand not simply hold without additional assumptions? We have two kinds of counterexamples.

We have counterexamples where the textual order of atoms in the clause bodies of a program makes the program unsuitable for the LD selection rule (Exs. 7.3 and 7.4). It is not pathological for a program to be written for, say, the

RD selection rule, but we should not be surprised about pathological (i.e. non-termination) behaviour when we run the program using the LD selection rule.

Moreover, we have counterexamples where a program input terminates, or local delay terminates, thanks to deadlock (Ex. 8.3). Is a program that relies on deadlock for termination pathological? Generally, deadlock is considered an undesirable situation, but it is still preferable to non-termination. Also, it should be noted that deadlock cannot necessarily be blamed on the program. The APPEND program and the query append($[1|Xs]$, Ys, Zs) do not ∃-terminate, but they input terminate (for the mode input(I, I, O)), and in this sense, one could argue that selection rules allowing for deadlock are a *stronger* assumption for termination than any standard selection rule. This is in contrast to Props. 10.2, 10.3, 10.4 and 10.5 (where the hypotheses imply absence of deadlock).

Concerning the second question, there is of course a general answer: this is a survey article, and so we surveyed those works that are commonly recognised as most relevant in the field of termination for various selection rules, even if sometimes the significance of a result is diminished by a later result. However, we also have a few more specific answers.

The interest in strong termination, ∃-termination and bounded nondeterminism is evident because they are cornerstones of the whole spectrum of classes. The interest in left-termination is motivated by the fact that the standard selection rule of Prolog is assumed. With the three classes related to dynamic scheduling, we have captured the important distinction between *weak* selection rules, *strong* selection rules, and *strong* and *local* selection rules, as explained in Subsec. 11.7.

The question can also be phrased differently: for each inclusion between classes, how significant is it that the inclusion is strict? If $A \subset B$ but $B \setminus A$ contains only some very obscure and contrived programs, then is it worthwhile to study B in detail?

The strict inclusion between input termination and input $\mathcal{P}$-termination, for an appropriate $\mathcal{P}$, is witnessed by Exs. 5.1 and 5.6. These programs are not contrived, in fact they are famous in this context [55], but they are small programs, and it remains to be seen if other examples can be found.

In our opinion, the strict inclusion between local delay termination and left-termination demonstrated by Ex. 7.1 is insignificant. The example is artificial. Most of the time, the LD selection rule turns out to be simple implementation of a local delay-safe selection rule — no more and no less.

Example 6.10 is very similar to Ex. 7.1 and suggests that the strict inclusion between input $\mathcal{P}$-termination and local delay termination is also insignificant, or put differently, that the difference made by assuming local selection rules is insignificant. Actually, we are not aware of a realistic program where locality matters for termination. However, Ex. 6.1 exhibits a certain pattern that suggests that there could be a realistic example: consider the clause $r(X) \leftarrow p(X, Y), r(Y)$. There are two derivations for $p(X, Y)$, one that generates a Y bigger (say, by the term size norm) than X but is bound to fail, and one that generates a Y smaller than X and succeeds. Locality is crucial so that this failure occurs before the recursive call r(Y).

Marchiori & Teusink justify the restriction of local derivations saying that "the termination behaviour of 'delay until nonvar'[10] is poorly understood", and that "the class of local selection rules [...] supports simple tools for proving termination" [47]. In the meantime, as discussed in Sections 4 and 5, both termination for input-consuming derivations and termination for delay-safe (but not necessarily local) derivations are well understood.

Can we conclude from the above that the strict inclusion between input $\mathcal{P}$-termination and left-termination is insignificant, and so all the research effort currently devoted to left-termination should be redirected towards input $\mathcal{P}$-termination? Not quite. Left-termination is the most important notion of termination in practice and has been studied under every conceivable aspect. One cannot expect that all this work will readily translate to input $\mathcal{P}$-termination.

References

1. G. Aguzzi and U. Modigliani. Proving termination of logic program by transforming them into equivalent term rewriting systems. In R. K. Shyamasundar, editor, *Proc. of the 13th Conference on Foundations of Software Technology and Theoretical Computer Science*, volume 761 of *LNCS*, pages 114–124. Springer-Verlag, 1993.

2. K. R. Apt. *From Logic Programming to Prolog*. Prentice Hall, 1997.

3. K. R. Apt and M. Bezem. Acyclic programs. *New Generation Computing*, 29(3):335–363, 1991.

4. K. R. Apt and S. Etalle. On the unification free Prolog programs. In A. Borzyszkowski and S. Sokolowski, editors, *Proc. of the 18th International Symposium on Mathematical Foundations of Computer Science*, volume 711 of *LNCS*, pages 1–19. Springer-Verlag, 1993.

5. K. R. Apt and I. Luitjes. Verification of logic programs with delay declarations. In V. S. Alagar and M. Nivat, editors, *Proc. of the 4th International Conference on Algebraic Methodology and Software Technology*, volume 936 of *LNCS*, pages 66–90. Springer-Verlag, 1995.

6. K. R. Apt, E. Marchiori, and C. Palamidessi. A declarative approach for first-order built-in's of Prolog. *Applicable Algebra in Engineering, Communication and Computation*, 5(3/4):159–191, 1994.

7. K. R. Apt and D. Pedreschi. Reasoning about termination of pure Prolog programs. *Information and Computation*, 106(1):109–157, 1993.

8. K. R. Apt and D. Pedreschi. Modular termination proofs for logic and pure Prolog programs. In G. Levi, editor, *Advances in Logic Programming Theory*, pages 183–229. Oxford University Press, 1994.

9. T. Arts. *Automatically proving termination and innermost normalisation of term rewriting systems*. PhD thesis, Universiteit Utrecht, 1997.

10. M. Baudinet. Proving termination properties of Prolog programs: a semantic approach. *Journal of Logic Programming*, 14:1–29, 1992.

---

[10] This amounts to input-consuming derivations.

11. M. A. Bezem. Strong termination of logic programs. *Journal of Logic Programming*, 15(1 & 2):79–98, 1993.

12. R. N. Bol, K. R. Apt, and J. W. Klop. An analysis of loop checking mechanism for logic programs. *Theoretical Computer Science*, 86(1):35–79, 1991.

13. A. Bossi, N. Cocco, S. Etalle, and S. Rossi. On modular termination proofs of general logic programs. *Theory and Practice of Logic Programming*, 2(3):263–291, 2002.

14. A. Bossi, N. Cocco, and M. Fabris. Norms on terms and their use in proving universal termination of a logic program. *Theoretical Computer Science*, 124(2):297–328, 1994.

15. A. Bossi, S. Etalle, and S. Rossi. Semantics of input-consuming logic programs. In J. W. Lloyd et al., editor, *Proc. of the 1st International Conference on Computational Logic*, volume 1861 of *LNCS*, pages 194–208. Springer-Verlag, 2000.

16. A. Bossi, S. Etalle, and S. Rossi. Properties of input-consuming derivations. *Theory and Practice of Logic Programming*, 2(2):125–154, 2002.

17. A. Bossi, S. Etalle, S. Rossi, and J.-G. Smaus. Semantics and termination of simply moded logic programs with dynamic scheduling. *Transactions on Computational Logic*, 2004. To appear in summer 2004.

18. C. Braem, B. Le Charlier, S. Modart, and P. Van Hentenryck. Cardinality analysis of Prolog. In M. Bruynooghe, editor, *Proc. of the International Logic Programming Symposium*, pages 457—471. MIT Press, 1994.

19. M. Bruynooghe, H. Vandecasteele, D. A. de Waal, and M. Denecker. Detecting unsolvable queries for definite logic programs. In C. Palamidessi et al., editor, *Proc. of PLILP/ALP '98*, volume 1490 of *LNCS*, pages 118–133. Springer-Verlag, 1998.

20. L. Cavedon. Continuity, consistency, and completeness properties for logic programs. In G. Levi and M. Martelli, editors, *Proceedings of the 6th International Conference on Logic Programming*, pages 571–584. The MIT Press, 1989.

21. M. Codish and C. Taboch. A semantic basis for the termination analysis of logic programs. *Journal of Logic Programming*, 41(1):103–123, 1999.

22. L. Colussi, E. Marchiori, and M. Marchiori. On termination of constraint logic programs. In M. Bruynooghe and J. Penjam, editors, *Proc. of the 1st International Conference of Principles and Practice of Constraint Programming*, volume 976 of *LNCS*, pages 431–448. Springer-Verlag, 1995.

23. D. De Schreye and S. Decorte. Termination of logic programs: the never-ending story. *Journal of Logic Programming*, 19-20:199–260, 1994.

24. D. De Schreye and A. Serebrenik. Acceptability with general orderings. In F. Sadri and A. Kakas, editors, *Computational Logic: Logic Programming and Beyond, Part I*, volume 2407 of *LNCS*, pages 187–210. Springer-Verlag, 2002.

25. D. De Schreye, K. Verschaetse, and M. Bruynooghe. A framework for analyzing the termination of definite logic programs with respect to call patterns. In *Proc. of the International Conference on Fifth Generation Computer Systems*, pages 481–488. Institute for New Generation Computer Technology, 1992.

26. S. K. Debray and N. W. Lin. Cost analysis of logic programs. *ACM Transactions on Programming Languages and Systems*, 15(5):826–875, 1993.

27. S. Decorte, D. De Schreye, and M. Fabris. Automatic inference of norms: A missing link in automatic termination analysis. In D. Miller, editor, *Proc. of the International Logic Programming Symposium*, pages 420–436. The MIT Press, 1993.

28. S. Decorte, D. De Schreye, M. Leuschel, B. Martens, and K. Sagonas. Termination analysis for tabled logic programming. In N. E. Fuchs, editor, *Proc. of the*

7th International Workshop on Logic Programming Synthesis and Transformation, volume 1463 of *LNCS*, pages 111–127. Springer-Verlag, 1998.

29. S. Decorte, D. De Schreye, and H. Vandecasteele. Constraint-based termination analysis of logic programs. *ACM Transactions on Programming Languages and Systems*, 21(6):1137–1195, 1999.

30. P. Deransart and J. Małuszyński. *A Grammatical View of Logic Programming*. The MIT Press, 1993.

31. N. Dershowitz, N. Lindenstrauss, Y. Sagiv, and A. Serebrenik. A general framework for automatic termination analysis of logic programs. *Applicable Algebra in Engineering, Communication and Computing*, 2001(1/2):117–156, 2001.

32. S. Etalle, A. Bossi, and N. Cocco. Termination of well-moded programs. *Journal of Logic Programming*, 38(2):243–257, 1999.

33. R. W. Floyd. Assigning meaning to programs. In J. T. Schwartz, editor, *Proc. Symposium in Applied Mathematics, vol. 19 of Mathematical Aspects in Computer Science*, pages 19–32. AMS, 1967.

34. T. Frühwirth. Proving termination of constraint solver programs. In K. R. Apt et al., editor, *New Trends in Constraints*, volume 1865 of *LNAI*, 2000.

35. H. Ganzinger and U. Waldmann. Termination proofs of well-moded logic programs via conditional rewrite systems. In M. Rusinowitch and J. L. Rémy, editors, *Proc. of the 3rd International Workshop on Conditional Term Rewriting Systems*, volume 656 of *LNCS*, pages 430–437. Springer-Verlag, 1992.

36. R. Gori. An abstract interpretation approach to termination of logic programs. In M. Parigot and A. Voronkov, editors, *Proc. of the 7th International Conference on Logic for Programming and Automated Reasoning*, volume 1955 of *LNCS*, pages 362–380. Springer-Verlag, 2000.

37. M. V. Hermenegildo, F. Bueno, G. Puebla, and P. López. Program analysis, debugging, and optimization using the Ciao system preprocessor. In D. De Schreye, editor, *Proc. of the International Conference on Logic Programming*, pages 52–66. MIT Press, 1999.

38. P. M. Hill and J. W. Lloyd. *The Gödel Programming Language*. The MIT Press, 1994.

39. S. Hoarau and F. Mesnard. Inferring and compiling termination for constraint logic programs. In P. Flener, editor, *Proc. of the 8th International Workshop on Logic Programming Synthesis and Transformation*, volume 1559 of *LNCS*, pages 240–254. Springer-Verlag, 1998.

40. R. A. Kowalski. Algorithm = Logic + Control. *Communications of the ACM*, 22(7):424–436, 1979.

41. M .R. K. Krishna Rao, D. Kapur, and R. K. Shyamasundar. A transformational methodology for proving termination of logic programs. In E. Börger, G. Jäger, H. Kleine Büning, and M. M. Richter, editors, *Proc. of the 5th Workshop on Computer Science Logic*, volume 626 of *LNCS*, pages 213–226. Springer-Verlag, 1992.

42. M. R. K. Krishna Rao, D. Kapur, and R. K. Shyamasundar. Proving termination of GHC programs. *New Generation Computing*, 15(3):293–338, 1997.

43. M. R. K. Krishna Rao, D. Kapur, and R. K. Shyamasundar. Transformational methodology for proving termination of logic programs. *Journal of Logic Programming*, 34(1):1–41, 1998.

44. N. Lindenstrauss and Y. Sagiv. Automatic termination analysis of logic programs. In L. Naish, editor, *Proc. of the 14th International Conference on Logic Programming*, pages 63–77. The MIT Press, 1997.

45. S. Lüttringhaus-Kappel. Control generation for logic programs. In D. S. Warren, editor, *Proceedings of the 10th International Conference on Logic Programming*, pages 478–495. MIT Press, 1993.

46. E. Marchiori. On termination of general logic programs w.r.t. constructive negation. *Journal of Logic Programming*, 26(1):69–89, 1996.

47. E. Marchiori and F. Teusink. On termination of logic programs with delay declarations. *Journal of Logic Programming*, 39(1-3):95–124, 1999.

48. M. Marchiori. Proving existential termination of normal logic programs. In M. Wirsing and M. Nivat, editors, *Proc. of the 5th International Conference on Algebraic Methodology and Software Technology*, volume 1101 of *LNCS*, pages 375–390. Springer-Verlag, 1996.

49. J. Martin and A. King. Generating efficient, terminating logic programs. In M. Bidoit and M. Dauchet, editors, *Proc. of the 7th International Conference on Theory and Practice of Software Development*, volume 1214 of *LNCS*, pages 273–284. Springer-Verlag, 1997.

50. R. McPhee. *Compositional Logic Programming*. PhD thesis, Oxford University Computing Laboratory, 2000.

51. F. Mesnard. Inferring left-terminating classes of queries for constraint logic programs. In M. Maher, editor, *Proc. of the Joint International Conference and Symposium on Logic Programming*, pages 7–21. The MIT Press, 1996.

52. F. Mesnard and U. Neumerkel. Applying static analysis techniques for inferring termination conditions of logic programs. In P. Cousot, editor, *Proc. of the 8th Static Analysis Symposium*, volume 2126 of *LNCS*, pages 93–110. Springer-Verlag, 2001.

53. F. Mesnard, É. Payet, and U. Neumerkel. Detecting optimal termination conditions of logic programs. In M. V. Hermenegildo and G. Puebla, editors, *Proc. of the 9th Static Analysis Symposium*, volume 2477 of *LNCS*, pages 509–526. Springer-Verlag, 2002.

54. F. Mesnard and S. Ruggieri. On proving left-termination of constraint logic programs. *ACM Transactions on Computational Logic*, 4(2):207–259, 2003.

55. L. Naish. Coroutining and the construction of terminating logic programs. Technical Report 92/5, Department of Computer Science, University of Melbourne, 1992.

56. E. Ohlebusch, C. Claves, and C. Marché. TALP: A tool for the termination analysis of logic programs. In Leo Bachmair, editor, *Proc. of the 11th International Conference on Rewriting Techniques and Applications*, volume 1833 of *Lecture Notes in Computer Science*, pages 270–273. Springer-Verlag, 2000.

57. D. Pedreschi P. Mancarella and S. Ruggieri. Negation as failure through abduction: Reasoning about termination. In F. Sadri and A. Kakas, editors, *Computational Logic: Logic Programming and Beyond, Part I*, volume 2407 of *LNCS*, pages 240–272. Springer-Verlag, 2002.

58. D. Pedreschi and S. Ruggieri. Bounded nondeterminism of logic programs. In D. De Schreye, editor, *Proc. of the International Conference on Logic Programming*, pages 350–364. The MIT Press, 1999. Extended version to appear in *Annals of Mathematics and Artificial Intelligence*.

59. D. Pedreschi and S. Ruggieri. On logic programs that always succeed. *Science of Computer Programming*, 48(2-3):163–196, 2003. Extended version of the paper "On logic programs that do not fail", Proc. of ICLP 1999 Workshop on Verification of Logic Programs, ENTCS 30(1) 1999.

60. D. Pedreschi, S. Ruggieri, and J.-G. Smaus. Classes of terminating logic programs. *Theory and Practice of Logic Programming*, 2(3):369–418, 2002.

61. S. Ruggieri. Termination of constraint logic programs. In P. Degano, R. Gorrieri, and A. Marchetti-Spaccamela, editors, *Proc. of the 24th International Colloquium on Automata, Languages and Programming (ICALP '97)*, volume 1256 of *LNCS*, pages 838–848. Springer-Verlag, 1997.

62. S. Ruggieri. *Verification and Validation of Logic Programs*. PhD thesis, Dipartimento di Informatica, Università di Pisa, 1999.

63. S. Ruggieri. ∃-universal termination of logic programs. *Theoretical Computer Science*, 254(1-2):273–296, 2001.

64. A. Serebrenik. *Termination Analysis of Logic Programs*. PhD thesis, Katholieke Universiteit, Leuven, 2003.

65. A. Serebrenik and D. De Schreye. On termination of logic programs with floating point computations. In M. V. Hermenegildo and G. Puebla, editors, *Proc. of the 9th Static Analysis Symposium*, volume 2477 of *LNCS*, pages 151–164. Springer-Verlag, 2002.

66. J.-G. Smaus. *Modes and Types in Logic Programming*. PhD thesis, University of Kent at Canterbury, 1999.

67. J.-G. Smaus. Proving termination of input-consuming logic programs. In D. De Schreye, editor, *Proc. of the International Conference on Logic Programming*, pages 335–349. MIT Press, 1999.

68. J.-G. Smaus. Termination of logic programs for various dynamic selection rules. Technical Report 191, Insitut für Informatik, Universität Freiburg, 2003.

69. J.-G. Smaus, P. M. Hill, and A. M. King. Verifying termination and error-freedom of logic programs with block declarations. *Theory and Practice of Logic Programming*, 1(4):447–486, 2001.

70. Z. Somogyi, F. Henderson, and T. Conway. The execution algorithm of Mercury, an efficient purely declarative logic programming language. *Journal of Logic Programming*, 29(1–3):17–64, 1996.

71. C. Speirs, Z. Somogyi, and H. Søndergaard. Termination analysis for Mercury. In P. Van Hentenryck, editor, *Proc. of the 4th International Static Analysis Symposium*, volume 1302 of *LNCS*, pages 160–171. Springer-Verlag, 1997.

72. L. Sterling and E. Shapiro. *The Art of Prolog*. The MIT Press, 1986.

73. Swedish Institute of Computer Science. *SICStus Prolog User's Manual*, 2003. http://www.sics.se/isl/sicstuswww/site/documentation.html.

74. J. Thom and J. Zobel. NU-Prolog reference manual, version 1.3. Technical report, Department of Computer Science, University of Melbourne, Australia, 1988.

75. K. Ueda. Guarded Horn Clauses, a parallel logic programming language with the concept of a guard. In M. Nivat and K. Fuchi, editors, *Programming of Future Generation Computers*, pages 441–456. North Holland, Amsterdam, 1988.

76. S. Verbaeten. Termination analysis for abductive general logic programs. In D. De Schreye, editor, *Proc. of the International Conference on Logic Programming*, pages 365–379. The MIT Press, 1999.

77. S. Verbaeten, K. Sagonas, and D. De Schreye. Termination proofs for logic programs with tabling. *ACM Transactions on Computational Logic*, 2(1):57–92, 2001.

On the Inference of
Natural Level Mappings

Jonathan C. Martin and Andy King

University of Kent, Canterbury, CT2 7NF, UK
`a.m.king@ukc.ac.uk`

Abstract. Reasoning about termination is a key issue in logic program development. One classic technique for proving termination is to construct a well-founded order on goals that decreases between successive goals in a derivation. In practise, this is achieved with the aid of a level mapping that maps atoms to natural numbers. This paper examines why it can be difficult to base termination proofs on natural level mappings that directly relate to the recursive structure of the program. The notions of bounded-recurrency and bounded-acceptability are introduced to alleviate these problems. These concepts are equivalent to the classic notions of recurrency and acceptability respectively, yet provide practical criteria for constructing termination proofs in terms of natural level mappings for definite logic programs. Moreover, the construction is entirely modular in that termination conditions are derived in a bottom-up fashion by considering, in turn, each the strongly connected components of the program.

1 Introduction

The classes of recurrent and acceptable programs are, arguably, two of the most influential classes of logic program that occur in the termination literature. Acceptable programs are precisely those which, for ground input, terminate under the left-to-right selection rule of Prolog [2]. Programs which, for ground input, terminate under *any* selection rule are classified as being recurrent [5].

Whilst the notions of recurrency and acceptability provide a sound theoretical basis for studying termination, they do not provide much insight into the practicalities of deriving the level mappings which are needed to prove that a logic program is terminating or left-terminating. Instead, intuition has served as the guide in the development of automatic techniques. In particular, there has been a desire to derive natural level mappings based on the recursive structure of the program at hand. For example, given the program

$$\mathsf{p}([\mathsf{H}|\mathsf{T}]) \leftarrow \mathsf{p}(\mathsf{T}).$$

it is natural to define a level mapping $|.|$ to prove termination by $|\mathsf{p}(x)| = |x|_{\text{length}}$ where $|.|_{\text{length}}$ is the list-length norm because the predicate is inductively defined over the length of its argument which is a list. Other definitions, such as

M. Bruynooghe and K.-K. Lau (Eds.): Program Development in CL, LNCS 3049, pp. 432–452, 2004.
© Springer-Verlag Berlin Heidelberg 2004

$|\mathsf{p}(x)| = |x|_{\text{length}} + 1$ and $|\mathsf{p}(x)| = 2|x|_{\text{length}}$ do not possess the same natural correspondence with the termination behaviour of the program.

This paper examines the reasons why termination proofs based on recurrency and acceptability are often difficult to obtain. The observations are not new in themselves [3,6,12,18] and, by way of a solution, Apt and Pedreschi [3] define alternative characterisations of terminating and left-terminating programs which they call semi-recurrency and semi-acceptability respectively. This paper argues that these concepts do not, in fact, form an ideal basis for automatic termination analyses (though this approach has been followed by others [25,28]); some difficulties complicate the construction of the level mapping that arises in the termination proof. To alleviate these problems, this paper introduces notions of bounded-recurrency and bounded-acceptability for definite logic programs and shows that these concepts are equivalent to recurrency and acceptability respectively. These new characterisations of the two classes provide practical criteria for constructing termination proofs in terms of natural level mappings. The construction is entirely modular: termination conditions are derived in a bottom-up fashion by considering, in turn, each the strongly connected components of the predicate dependency graph. A bottom-up approach is more in tune with program specialisation, and partial deduction in particular [10,24], since the overall computation is unlikely to be terminating but some sub-computations probably will be. More exactly, it is more useful to derive sufficient termination conditions for individual predicates rather than proving that a given top-level goal will terminate. The notion of bounded-acceptability lends itself naturally to this process. Moreover, there has been much recent interest in the inference of level mappings [9,15,19,20,23,27] in order to fully automate termination analysis. Thus the desire for natural level mappings is much more than an aesthetic predilection.

The paper is structured as follows. Section 2 introduces the concepts necessary for discussing termination, and in particular reviews the notions of recurrency and acceptability. Section 3 argues that level mappings have traditionally been overloaded in that they address two different termination issues. Sections 4 and 5 reviews the concepts of semi-recurrency and semi-acceptability, arguing that these notions also lead to artificial level mappings. Sections 6 and 7 explain how the concepts of bounded-recurrency and bounded-acceptability permit simpler, more natural level mappings to be used within termination proofs. Section 8 presents the concluding discussion, reflecting on other approaches to modularity [6,18].

2   Preliminaries: the Nuts and Bolts of Termination

2.1   Level Mappings, Norms, and Boundedness

The fundamental idea underlying all termination proofs is to define an order on the goals that can occur within a derivation. Given a program P and goal G_0, the finiteness of derivation $G_0, G_1, G_2, \ldots$ is in principle straightforward to demonstrate: it is sufficient to construct a well-founded order $<$ such that $G_{i+1} < G_i$ for all $i \geq 0$. The problem is to find such an order. To simplify the problem, it is convenient to define the order on abstractions of goals rather than on the goals themselves. Thus the order $<$ is defined such that $G' < G$ holds iff $\mathcal{A}(G') < \mathcal{A}(G)$ holds where $\mathcal{A}$ is an abstraction function. For example, $\mathcal{A}$ might be defined to map each goal G to a multiset of natural numbers, where each atom in G maps to a single number in the multiset. The idea of abstracting goals by mapping atoms to natural numbers leads to the concept of a level mapping.

Definition 1 (level mapping [11]). Let P be a program. A level mapping for P is a function $|.| : B_P \mapsto \mathbb{N}$ from the Herbrand base of P to the set of natural numbers $\mathbb{N}$. For an atom $A \in B_P$, $|A|$ denotes the level of A. □

Example 1. Let P be the program

p(a, X) ← p(b, X).
p(b, a).
p(b, b).

The function $|.| : \{p(a, a), p(a, b), p(b, a), p(b, b)\} \mapsto \mathbb{N}$ defined by $|p(a, a)| = 34$, $|p(a, b)| = 12$, $|p(b, a)| = 0$ and $|p(b, b)| = 27$ is a level mapping for P. □

Since a level mapping is defined over the Herbrand base it is not defined for non-ground atoms. (The reader is referred to Lloyd [21] for the standard definitions of the Herbrand base, Herbrand interpretations, Herbrand models, *etc.*) The lifting of the mapping to non-ground atoms was proposed in [4].

Definition 2 (bounded atom [4]). An atom A is bounded wrt a level mapping $|.|$ if $|.|$ is bounded on the set $[A]$ of variable free instances of A. If A is bounded then $||[A]||$ denotes the maximum that $|.|$ takes on $[A]$. □

The importance of the notion of boundedness cannot be over stressed. Since goals which are ground cannot be used to compute values, they are the exception rather than the norm in logic programming. Thus practical termination proofs must be able to deal with non-ground goals and boundedness provides the basis for this.

Example 2. Let P be the program and $|.|$ the level mapping of example 1. The atom $p(a, X)$ is bounded since $|.|$ is bounded on the set $[p(a, X)] = \{p(a, a), p(a, b)\}$. Moreover, $||[p(a, X)]|| = \max(\{|p(a, a)|, |p(a, b)|\})$ and in particular $||[p(a, X)]|| = \max(\{34, 12\}) = 34$. □

Level mappings are usually defined in terms of norms. Basically, a norm is a mapping from terms to natural numbers which provides some measure of the size of a term.

Example 3. The list-length norm $|.|_{\text{length}} : U_P \mapsto \mathbb{N}$ from the Herbrand universe to the natural numbers can be defined by

$$|t|_{\text{length}} = \begin{cases} 1 + |t_2|_{\text{length}} & \text{if } t = [t_1|t_2] \\ 0 & \text{otherwise} \end{cases}$$

Then, for example, $||[X, Y, Z]||_{\text{length}} = 3$. □

Example 4. The term-size norm $|.|_{\text{size}} : U_P \mapsto \mathbb{N}$ is defined by

$$|f(t_1, \ldots, t_n)|_{\text{size}} = n + \sum_{i=1}^{n} |t_i|_{\text{size}}$$

Thus, for example, $|f(a, g(b))|_{\text{size}} = 2 + 1 = 3.$ □

The next two lemmas follow easily from definition 2.

Lemma 1. Let $|.|$ be a level mapping and A a bounded atom. Then for every substitution θ, the atom $A\theta$ is also bounded and moreover $|[A]| \geq |[A\theta]|$. □

Proof. Recall that $[A] = \{A\phi \mid \phi \text{ is a grounding substitution for } A\}$. Then $[A] \supseteq [A\theta]$, so $|[A]| \geq |[A\theta]|$. □

Lemma 2. Let H be a bounded atom, B an atom and $|.|$ a level mapping. If for every grounding substitution θ for H and B, $|H\theta| > |B\theta|$, then B is also bounded and moreover $|[H]| > |[B]|$. □

Proof. Recall that $[B] = \{B\theta \mid \theta \text{ is a grounding substitution for } B\}$. But $|H\theta| > |B\theta|$ for every grounding substitution θ for H and B, so $|.|$ is bounded on $[B]$. Let θ be any grounding substitution for H and B such that $|B\theta| = |[B]|$. Then, by lemma 1, $|[H]| \geq |[H\theta]| = |H\theta| > |B\theta| = |[B]|$. □

2.2 Recurrency

In [4,5], level mappings are used to define a class of terminating programs.

Definition 3 (recurrency [4,5]). Let P be a definite logic program and $|.|$ a level mapping for P. A clause $H \leftarrow B_1, \ldots, B_n$ is recurrent (wrt $|.|$) iff for every grounding substitution θ and for all $i \in [1, n]$ it follows that $|H\theta| > |B_i\theta|$. P is recurrent (wrt $|.|$) iff every clause in P is recurrent (wrt $|.|$). □

Henceforth all logic programs are assumed to be definite, that is, each clause contains precisely one atom in its consequent (its head).

Example 5. Consider the append program below

app_1 append([], X, X).
app_2 append([U|X], Y, [U|Z]) ← append(X, Y, Z).

The clause app_2 is recurrent wrt to the level mapping $|\text{append}(t_1, t_2, t_3)|_1 = |t_1|_{\text{length}}$ since for every grounding substitution θ for app_2,

$$\begin{aligned}
|\text{append}([U|X], Y, [U|Z])\theta|_1 &= |[U|X]\theta|_{\text{length}} \\
&= 1 + |X\theta|_{\text{length}} \\
&> |X\theta|_{\text{length}} \\
&= |\text{append}(X, Y, Z)\theta|_1
\end{aligned}$$

Similarly, it can be shown that the program is recurrent wrt $|.|_i$ for all $i \in [2, 4]$ where $|.|_2$, $|.|_3$ and $|.|_4$ are defined by

$$|append(t_1, t_2, t_3)|_2 = 3|t_1|_{length} + 1$$
$$|append(t_1, t_2, t_3)|_3 = |t_3|_{length}$$
$$|append(t_1, t_2, t_3)|_4 = \min(|t_1|_{length}, |t_3|_{length})$$

Moreover, the clause app_1 is trivially recurrent wrt to any level mapping.   □

Bezem formalised the concept of termination relating it to recurrency.

Definition 4 (termination [4]). Let P be a logic program and G a goal. Then G is terminating wrt P iff every SLD-derivation for $P \cup \{G\}$ is finite. P is terminating iff every variable-free goal is terminating wrt P.   □

Theorem 1 (recurrency [4]). Every recurrent program is terminating.

The same result was also obtained independently by Cavedon [11] in the more general context of recurrent programs with negation (called locally ω-hierarchical programs in [11] and later renamed acyclic programs in [1]). The proof in [4] relies on the following definition.

Definition 5 (bounded goal [4]). A goal $G =\leftarrow A_1, \ldots, A_n$ is bounded wrt a level mapping $|.|$ iff every A_i is bounded wrt $|.|$. If G is bounded then $|[G]|$ denotes the finite multiset of natural numbers $\{|[A_1]|, \ldots, |[A_n]|\}$.   □

The proof of theorem 1 applies the abstraction function $\mathcal{A} = |[.]|$ and as a result a well-founded order $<$ is defined over the set of bounded goals by taking $G' < G$ iff $|[G']| <_{mul} |[G]|$ where $<_{mul}$ is the multiset ordering over the natural numbers. Recall that this ordering is defined by $s_1 <_{mul} s_2$ iff there exists $n_1, \ldots, n_m \in s_1$ and $n \in s_2$ such that $s_1 = (s_2/\{n\}) \cup \{n_1, \ldots, n_m\}$ and $n_i < n$ for all $i \in [1, m]$ [26]. The proof is completed by showing for every SLD-resolvent G' of a bounded goal G, that G' is bounded and $G' < G$. In fact, this proof suggests a stronger corollary (bounded goals are not necessarily variable-free, that is, ground).

Corollary 1 (recurrency [4]). Let P be a logic program, G a goal and $|.|$ a level mapping. If P is recurrent wrt $|.|$ and G is bounded wrt $|.|$ then G is terminating wrt P.

Example 6. Reconsider append and the level mappings of example 5. Then

$\leftarrow$ append([U, V, W], Y, Z) is bounded wrt $|.|_1, |.|_2$ and $|.|_4$,
$\leftarrow$ append(X, Y, [U, V, W]) is bounded wrt $|.|_3$ and $|.|_4$

Hence these goals are terminating wrt append. Also, for a goal G observe that G is bounded wrt $|.|_1$ iff G is bounded wrt $|.|_2$. Moreover, G is bounded wrt $|.|_4$ if (*not iff*) G is bounded wrt $|.|_1$ or G is bounded wrt $|.|_3$. Thus by proving recurrency of append wrt $|.|_4$ a larger class of goals can be proven terminating than by proving recurrency wrt $|.|_1$, $|.|_2$ or $|.|_3$. This illustrates that the choice of the level mapping effects the set of goals which can be shown to be terminating.   □

As a final remark, Bezem also proved the converse of theorem 1.

Theorem 2 (recurrency [4]). A logic program is recurrent iff it is terminating.

2.3   Acceptability

The notion of recurrency is a theoretical one and is not of much use in proving termination of Prolog programs. Many Prolog programs only terminate under a left-to-right selection rule. This observation led Apt and Pedreschi [3] to refine the notion of termination as follows.

Definition 6 (left-termination [3]). Let P be a logic program and G a goal. Then G is left-terminating wrt P iff every LD-derivation for $P \cup \{G\}$ is finite. P is left-terminating iff every variable-free goal is left-terminating wrt P.   □

Example 7. Consider the permute program below

$perm_1$ permute([], []).
$perm_2$ permute([H|T], [A|P]) ← delete(A, [H|T], L), permute(L, P).

del_1 delete(X, [X|Y], Y).
del_2 delete(X, [Y|Z], [Y|W]) ← delete(X, Z, W).

The goal ← permute([1], [1]) is terminating wrt permute and as a consequence is left-terminating also. The goal ← permute([1, 2], [1, 2]) is left-terminating but *not* terminating, since there exists a computation rule which results in the following infinite derivation

  ← permute([1, 2], [1, 2]),
  ← delete(1, [1, 2], L), permute(L, [2]),
  ← delete(1, [1, 2], L), delete(2, L, L′), permute(L′, []),
  ← delete(1, [1, 2], L), delete(2, Z, W), permute(L′, []),
  ← delete(1, [1, 2], L), delete(2, Z′, W′), permute(L′, []),
  ← . . .

By theorem 2, it follows that the program is not recurrent. However, the program can be proven to be left-terminating.   □

The class of recurrent programs was extended in [3] to the class of acceptable programs in order to provide a theoretical basis for proving termination of left-terminating programs.

Definition 7 (acceptability [3]). Let $|.|$ be a level mapping and I an interpretation for a logic program P. A clause $c : H \leftarrow B_1, \ldots, B_n$ is acceptable wrt $|.|$ and I iff

1. I is a model for c and
2. for all $i \in [1, n]$ and for every grounding substitution θ for c such that $I \models \{B_1, \ldots, B_{i-1}\}\theta$ it follows that $|H\theta| > |B_i\theta|$.

P is acceptable (wrt $|.|$ and I) iff every clause in P is acceptable (wrt $|.|$ and I). □

Analogous results to those for recurrent programs (theorem 1, corollary 1 and theorem 2) have been proven for acceptable programs. The abstraction function used, however, is rather more complicated than that which is applied in the proof of recurrency. First, observe that if a goal $G =\leftarrow A_1, \ldots, A_n$ terminates under a left-to-right computation rule, then each atom A_i is not necessarily bounded, but should be once the atoms to its left have been resolved. This idea forms the basis of the following definitions.

Definition 8 (maximum function). The maximum function $\max : \wp(\mathbb{N}) \mapsto \mathbb{N} \cup \{\infty\}$ is defined as

$$\max\ S = \begin{cases} 0 & \text{if } S = \emptyset \\ n & \text{else if } S \text{ is finite and } n \text{ is the maximum of } S \\ \infty & \text{otherwise} \end{cases}$$

Then $\max\ S \neq \infty$ iff the set S is finite. □

Definition 9 (left-bounded goal [3]). Let $|.|$ be a level mapping, I an interpretation and $G =\leftarrow A_1, \ldots, A_n$ a goal. Then G is left-bounded wrt $|.|$ and I iff the set

$$|[G]_I^i| = \left\{ |A_i\theta| \ \middle| \ \begin{matrix} \theta \text{ is a grounding substitution for } G \\ I \models \{A_1, \ldots, A_{i-1}\}\theta \end{matrix} \right\}$$

is finite for each $i \in [1, n]$. If G is left-bounded wrt $|.|$ and I then $|[G]_I|$ denotes the finite multiset $\{\!| \max |[G]_I^1|, \ldots, \max |[G]_I^n| |\!\}$. □

Note that the term left-bounded is introduced here to avoid confusion with definition 5.

Using the abstraction function $\mathcal{A} = |[.]_I|$ allows one to prove that for a goal G which is left-bounded wrt $|.|$, any SLD-resolvent G' of G is left-bounded and furthermore $|[G']_I| <_{mul} |[G]_I|$. The result is the analogue of corollary 1.

Corollary 2 (acceptability [3]). Let P be a logic program, G a goal, $|.|$ a level mapping and I an interpretation for P. If P is acceptable wrt $|.|$ and I and G is left-bounded wrt $|.|$ and I then G is left-terminating wrt P. □

Sufficient and necessary conditions for left-termination are characterised by the following theorem.

Theorem 3 (acceptability). A logic program is acceptable iff it is left-terminating.

Example 8. Considering the **permute** program again, let $|.|$ be the level mapping defined by

$$|\text{permute}(t_1, t_2)| = |t_1|_{\text{length}} + 1$$
$$|\text{delete}(t_1, t_2, t_3)| = |t_2|_{\text{length}}$$

and I be the interpretation

$$\{\text{delete}(t_1, t_2, t_3) \mid |t_2|_{\text{length}} = |t_3|_{\text{length}} + 1\} \cup$$
$$\{\text{permute}(t_1, t_2) \mid |t_1|_{\text{length}} = |t_2|_{\text{length}}\}$$

Now I is a model for the program and, in particular, for the clause $perm_2$, and for every grounding substitution θ for $perm_2$,

$$|\text{permute}([H|T], [A|P])\theta| = |[H|T]\theta|_{\text{length}} + 1$$
$$> |[H|T]\theta|_{\text{length}}$$
$$= |\text{delete}(A, [H|T], L)\theta|$$

and for every grounding substitution θ for $perm_2$ with $I \models \text{delete}(a, [H|T], L)\theta$,

$$|\text{permute}([H|T], [A|P])\theta| = |[H|T]\theta|_{\text{length}} + 1$$
$$= (|L\theta|_{\text{length}} + 1) + 1$$
$$> |L\theta|_{\text{length}} + 1$$
$$= |\text{permute}(L, P)\theta|$$

Hence $perm_2$ is acceptable wrt $|.|$ and I. The clauses $perm_1$ and del_1 are trivially acceptable wrt $|.|$ and I since I is a model for them, while the clause del_2 can easily be shown to be acceptable wrt $|.|$ and I in the same way as for $perm_2$. This proves the program **permute** is left-terminating.   □

3   The Recurrent Problem

The main problem with recurrency, as noted by [3] and [12], is that it does not intuitively relate to recursion, the principal cause of non-termination in a logic program. Definition 3 requires that, for every ground instance of a clause, the level of its head atom is greater than the level of every body atom irrespective of the recursive relation between the two. There is a temptation to address this issue by using a modified definition of recurrency which only requires a decrease for mutually recursive body atoms. The following example, from [12], shows that this revision, by itself, is too weak to prove termination.

Example 9. Using the weaker form of recurrency suggested above, the following program would be classed as recurrent.

```
p([H|T]) ← append(X, Y, Y), p(T).
```

```
append([U|X], Y, [U|Z]) ← append(X, Y, Z).
append([], X, X).
```

Using the left-to-right computation rule and the top-down search rule, however, the goal $\leftarrow$ p([1,2]) admits an infinite computation. Of course, the clause defining the predicate p should not be classified as recurrent. The reason is that, while append is truly recurrent, only bounded goals are guaranteed to terminate and the predicate p contains an unbounded call to append. $\square$

This example shows that the level mapping decrease between the head and the non-recursive atoms of a clause implied by definition 3, is required to ensure that all subcomputations are initiated from a bounded goal. Enforcing boundedness in this way, however, complicates the derivation of level mappings. The following example, illustrating this, also comes from [12].

Example 10. Consider the following program

p_1 p([]).
p_2 p([H|T]) $\leftarrow$ q([H|T]), p(T).

q_1 q([]).
q_2 q([H|T]) $\leftarrow$ q(T).

It is clear that this program is terminating for any goal $\leftarrow$ p(x) where x is a rigid list, that is, $|x|_{\text{length}} = |x\theta|_{\text{length}}$ for every grounding substitution θ. To construct an automatic proof of termination one would like to use the level mapping $|.|$ defined by

$$|p(x)| = |x|_{\text{length}} |q(x)| = |x|_{\text{length}}$$

The problem is that the clause p_2 is not recurrent wrt this level mapping since it is not the case that $|p([H|T])\theta| > |q([H|T])\theta|$ for all grounding substitutions θ. For the inequality to hold, an unnatural offset must be included in the level mapping definition by taking for example $|p(x)| = |x|_{\text{length}} + 1$. $\square$

These examples show that the strict decrease in level between the head and body atoms of a recurrent clause is required for two distinct purposes:

1. To ensure that the levels of mutually recursive calls are strictly decreasing.
2. To ensure that subcomputations are initiated from a bounded goal.

4   Semi-recurrency

Apt and Pedreschi observed that, for termination, while it is necessary for the level mapping to decrease between the head of a clause and each mutually recursive body atom, a strict decrease is not required for the non-recursive body atoms. To distinguish between recursive and non-recursive body atoms the notion of predicate dependency is introduced.

Definition 10 (predicate dependency). Let $p, q \in \Pi$ where Π is the set of predicate symbols in a logic program P. Then p directly depends on q iff

$$p(t_1, \ldots, t_{n_p}) \leftarrow B_1, \ldots, B_n \in P$$

and $B_i = q(s_1, \ldots, s_{n_q})$ for some $i \in [1, n]$. The depends on relation, denoted $\sqsupseteq$, is defined as the reflexive, transitive closure of the directly depends on relation. If $p \sqsupseteq q$ and $q \sqsupseteq p$ then p and q are mutually dependent and this is denoted by $p \simeq q$. Furthermore, let $p \sqsupset q$ iff $p \sqsupseteq q$ and $p \not\simeq q$ and finally let $p \sqsubset q$ iff $q \sqsupset p$. □

Apt and Pedreschi then introduced the notion of semi-recurrency to exploit the observation that a strict decrease in level in only required for the mutually recursive body atoms. In what follows $rel(A)$ denotes the predicate symbol of the atom A.

Definition 11 (semi-recurrency [3]). Let P be a logic program and $|.|$ a level mapping for P. A clause $H \leftarrow B_1, \ldots, B_n$ is semi-recurrent (wrt $|.|$) iff for every grounding substitution θ and for all $i \in [1, n]$ it follows that

1. $|H\theta| > |B_i\theta|$ if $rel(H) \simeq rel(B_i)$,
2. $|H\theta| + 1 > |B_i\theta|$ if $rel(H) \not\simeq rel(B_i)$.

P is semi-recurrent (wrt $|.|$) if every clause in P is semi-recurrent (wrt $|.|$).   □

Whilst this definition now admits a simple termination proof of example 10 using the level mapping of that example, it is not hard to construct examples where it is inadequate.

Example 11. Consider the following program

c_1 p([]).
c_2 p([H|T]) ← q([H, H|T]), p(T).

c_3 q([]).
c_4 q([H|T]) ← q(T).

To prove that the above program is semi-recurrent requires the following unnatural level mapping: $|p(x)| = |x|_{\text{length}} + 1$ and $q(x)| = |x|_{\text{length}}$.   □

It seems that very little has actually been gained from this revised definition of recurrency which still insists that there is not an increase from the level of the head to the level of all body atoms. In fact, it does not matter if the level of a non-recursive atom is greater than the level of the head provided that such an atom is bounded whenever it is selected.

To be fair, the notion of semi-recurrency was introduced to facilitate modular termination proofs and does indeed, in some cases, allow proofs to be based on simpler level mappings than those used in proofs of recurrency. In the above example, however, this is not the case.

Example 12. Reconsider the program of example 11. According to the methodology of [3] a modular termination proof can be constructed in a bottom-up fashion on the recursive cliques of the predicate dependency graph. First q is proven to be (semi) recurrent wrt $|.|_q$ defined by

$$|q(x)|_q = |x|_{\text{length}}$$

Second, p is proven to be (semi) recurrent wrt $|.|_p$ defined by

$$|p(x)|_p = |x|_{\text{length}} \quad |q(x)|_p = 0$$

The final step in the construction requires the derivation of a level mapping $|.|'$ such that

$$|p([t_1|t_2])|' \geq |q([t_1, t_1|t_2])|_q \quad \text{and} \quad |p([t_1|t_2])|' \geq |p(t_2)|'$$

for all ground terms t_1 and t_2. Providing the level mapping $|.|'$ exists, theorem 4.9 of [3] can be used to conclude that the program is semi-recurrent and hence terminating. In terms of automation, this existence proof is achieved through defining $|.|'$ so that the above inequalities are satisfied. However, the most likely choice of a definition for $|.|'$ is

$$|p(x)|' = |x|_{\text{length}} + 1$$

which, of course, this is no easier to derive than the original mapping $|.|$ of example 11. □

What is most conspicuous about the definition of semi-recurrency, is that the difference in levels between a non-recursive body atom and the head atom of a clause is limited to be at most zero, whereas it could be arbitrarily large, though still finite. Indeed, a simple termination proof for the program of example 11 can be obtained using a more natural level mapping if condition 2 of definition 11 is replaced by $|H\theta| + k > |B_i\theta|$ if $rel(H) \not\simeq rel(B_i)$, where k is some large constant. It is easy to prove that this revised definition of semi-recurrency is equivalent to recurrency. In addition, theorems 4.6, 4.8 and 4.9 of [3], which are used for constructing modular termination proofs, all still hold with this alternative definition.

Note that the problem with the termination proofs above arises because the atoms in the body of a clause contain extra function symbols which raise the levels of those atoms to the level of the head. Since it is fairly unlikely that such a body atom will contain, say, a million function symbols or more, by taking $k = 1000000$ the vast majority of recurrent programs which occur in practise could be proven terminating by focusing solely on their recursive structure and employing the appropriately weakened forms of the theorems of Apt and Pedreschi.

5   Semi-acceptability

Similar remarks to those of section 3 can be made about the definition of acceptability. The notion of semi-acceptability was introduced as an analogous concept to semi-recurrency for left-terminating programs.

Definition 12 (semi-acceptability [3]). Let $|.|$ be a level mapping and I an interpretation for a logic program P. A clause $c : H \leftarrow B_1, \ldots, B_n$ is semi-acceptable wrt $|.|$ and I iff

1. I is a model for c and
2. for all $i \in [1, n]$ and for every grounding substitution θ for c such that $I \models \{B_1, \ldots, B_{i-1}\}\theta$ it follows that
   (a) $|H\theta| > |B_i\theta|$ if $rel(H) \simeq rel(B_i)$,
   (b) $|H\theta| + 1 > |B_i\theta|$ if $rel(H) \not\simeq rel(B_i)$.

P is semi-acceptable (wrt $|.|$ and I) iff every clause in P is semi-acceptable (wrt $|.|$ and I). $\square$

Not surprisingly, termination proofs based on semi-acceptability suffer from similar problems to those encountered in examples 11 and 12. The definition could be adjusted in the manner prescribed above for semi-recurrency, but the result is not as satisfactory as the following example shows.

Example 13. Consider the following program

```
doubleSquare(0, []).
doubleSquare(s(X), [D|Ds]) ←
    square(X, 0, Y), doublePlus(Y, 0, D), doubleSquare(X, Ds).

square(0, Y, Y).
square(s(X), Acc, Y) ←
    doublePlus(X, s(Acc), Acc1), square(X, Acc1, Y).

doublePlus(0, X, X).
doublePlus(s(X), Y, s(s(Z))) ←
    doublePlus(X, Y, Z).
```

The function symbol s is interpreted as the successor function. Let $|0|_s = 0$ and $|s(x)|_s = 1 + |x|_s$ and I be the interpretation

$$\{\text{doublePlus}(t_1, t_2, t_3) \mid |t_3|_s = 2|t_1|_s + |t_2|_s\} \cup$$
$$\{\text{square}(t_1, t_2, t_3) \mid |t_3|_s = |t_1|_s^2 + |t_2|_s\} \cup$$
$$\{\text{doubleSquare}(t, [t_1, t_2, \ldots, 0]) \mid |t_i|_s = 2(|t|_s - i)^2\}$$

Thus, for example, the goal $\leftarrow$ doubleSquare(s(s(s(0))), L) will succeed with L = [s(s(s(s(s(s(s(s(0)))))))),s(s(0)),0]. Observe that I is a model for the program. Now let the level mapping $|.|$ be defined by

$$|\text{doubleSquare}(x, y)| = |\text{square}(x, y, z)| = |\text{doublePlus}(x, y, z)| = |x|_s$$

The predicates square and doublePlus are both semi-recurrent (and hence semi-acceptable) wrt $|.|$ and I. Now consider doubleSquare and in particular the inequality $|\text{doubleSquare}(s(X), [D|Ds])\theta| + k > |\text{doublePlus}(Y, 0, D)\theta|$ where θ is any grounding substitution. Since $I \models \text{square}(X, 0, Y)\theta$ it follows that $|Y\theta|_s = |X\theta|_s^2$, hence there exists no k for which $1 + |X\theta|_s + k > |Y\theta|_s$ always holds. There-fore the inequality $|\mathsf{doubleSquare}(\mathsf{s}(X), [D|Ds])\theta| + k = 1 + |X\theta|_s + k > |Y\theta|_s = |\mathsf{doublePlus}(Y, 0, D)\theta|$ cannot always hold. Hence the predicate $\mathsf{doubleSquare}$ is not semi-acceptable wrt $|.|$ and I under the revised definition suggested above even though the level mapping is natural.

It is easy to prove semi-acceptability of the program, however, wrt the level mapping $|.|'$ where $|.|'$ is defined exactly as for $|.|$ except that

$$|\mathsf{doubleSquare}(x, y)|' = |x|_s^2$$

Note that a goal is bounded wrt $|.|$ iff it is bounded wrt $|.|'$ and all such goals are left-terminating. It seems reasonable then to base a proof of termination on the former level mapping since it more closely relates to the recursion and as a result is easier to derive automatically. However, no automatic termination analysis has yet been devised which can manipulate quadratic level mappings such as $|.|_s^2$. □

Observe that the k above acts as an upper bound on the difference between the level of any body atom and the level of the head atom. Of course, this ad hoc approach falls down when there is no upper bound as in example 13.

In summary, although semi-recurrency and semi-acceptability are more flex-ible notions than their predecessors, they still enforce a dependence between the level of a head atom and the levels of non-recursive body atoms. This depen-dence is counter intuitive and forces one to use artificial level mappings to obtain termination proofs.

6   Bounded-Recurrency

Recall from section 3 that there are two conditions which must be fulfilled to ensure that a program is terminating.

1. The levels of mutually recursive calls are strictly decreasing.
2. All subcomputations are initiated from a bounded goal.

It is possible to define what constitutes a terminating program directly from these two requirements.

Definition 13 (bounded-recurrency). Let $|.|$ be a level mapping for a logic pro-gram P. A clause $c : H \leftarrow B_1, \ldots, B_n$ is bounded-recurrent (wrt $|.|$) iff for every substitution θ for c such that $H\theta$ is bounded and for all $i \in [1, n]$ it follows that

1. $B_i\theta$ is bounded and
2. $|[H\theta]| > |[B_i\theta]|$ whenever $rel(H) \simeq rel(B_i)$.

P is bounded-recurrent (wrt $|.|$) iff every clause in P is bounded-recurrent (wrt $|.|$). □

Observe that no decrease is enforced between the level of the head of a clause and the levels of the non-recursive body atoms. All that is required is that each atom is bounded whenever the head is bounded. While this is more intuitively appealing, observe that boundedness of non-recursive atoms still influences the definition of the level mapping in a non-modular way.

Example 14. Consider the following program for Curry's type assignment taken from [3].

typ_1 type(E, var(X), T) ← in(E, X, T).
typ_2 type(E, apply(M, N), T) ← type(E, M, arrow(S, T)), type(E, N, S).
typ_3 type(E, lambda(X, M), arrow(S, T)) ← type([(X, S) | E], M, T).

in_1 in([(X, T) | E], X, T).
in_2 in([(Y, S) | E], X, T) ← X ≠ Y, in(E, X, T).

One may observe that the predicate in is inductively defined over the length of its first argument which is a list. The predicate type is inductively defined on the size of its second argument which is a λ-term. As a result, one would hope to base a termination proof on the level mapping $|.|$ defined by

$$|\mathsf{in}(x, y, z)| = |x|_{\text{length}} \quad |\mathsf{type}(x, y, z)| = |y|_{\text{size}}$$

The problem, of course, is that any call type(E, var(X), t) which is bounded wrt $|.|$ can give rise to a call in(E, X, T) which is not bounded wrt $|.|$. Clearly this can lead to non-termination. Definition 13, therefore, insists that for the clause typ_1 the body atom in(E, X, T) is bounded whenever the head is. Unfortunately this entails that the level mapping must now be modified to take the first argument of type into account. This in turn leads to problems with the clause typ_3 since the first argument is increasing in the recursive call. Eventually, one arrives at a level mapping definition such as

$$|\mathsf{in}(x, y, z)|_1 = |x|_{\text{length}} \quad |\mathsf{type}(x, y, z)|_1 = |x|_{\text{length}} + 2|y|_{\text{size}}$$

which bears no immediate relation to the program structure. As a result such a mapping is likely to be difficult to derive automatically.   □

Clearly there is an interdependence between ensuring non-recursive atoms are bounded wrt $|.|$ and ensuring that the levels of recursive calls are decreasing wrt $|.|$. This plainly arises out of the use of the one level mapping. It seems therefore that the obvious way to break the dependence is to use *two* level mappings. One holds the responsibility for ensuring the recursive decrease in levels, while the other assures that non-recursive atoms are bounded. This idea is captured in the following definition.

Definition 14 (bounded-recurrency). Let $|.|_1$ and $|.|_2$ be level mappings for a logic program P. A clause $c : H \leftarrow B_1, \ldots, B_n$ is bounded-recurrent (wrt $|.|_1$ and $|.|_2$) iff for every substitution θ for c such that $H\theta$ is bounded wrt $|.|_1$ and $|.|_2$ and for all $i \in [1, n]$ it follows that

1. $B_i\theta$ is bounded wrt $|.|_1$ and $|.|_2$ and
2. $|[H\theta]|_1 > |[B_i\theta]|_1$ whenever $rel(H) \simeq rel(B_i)$.

P is bounded-recurrent (wrt $|.|_1$ and $|.|_2$) iff every clause in P is bounded-recurrent (wrt $|.|_1$ and $|.|_2$). $\qquad\square$

It is informally understood that a goal G is bounded wrt $|.|_1$ and $|.|_2$ iff G is bounded wrt $|.|_1$ and G is bounded wrt $|.|_2$. Note that, when the two level mappings coincide, that is when $|.|_1 \equiv |.|_2$, then definition 14 is equivalent to definition 13.

Example 15. Returning to the program of example 14, recall that the stumbling block in the derivation of a natural level mapping arose because any call type(E, var(X), T) which is bounded wrt $|.|$ can give rise to a call in(E, X, T) which is not bounded wrt $|.|$. At this point, one intuitively reasons that if the first argument of a call to type is a rigid list then the first argument of all subsequent calls to type will also be a rigid list. So define a second level mapping $|.|'$ by

$$|in(x, y, z)|' = |x|_{\text{length}} \quad |type(x, y, z)|' = |x|_{\text{length}}$$

The program is bounded-recurrent wrt $|.|$ and $|.|'$. Indeed, any call to type or in which is bounded wrt $|.|$ and $|.|'$ only gives rise to calls which are bounded wrt $|.|$ and $|.|'$. Combine this with the fact that recursive calls are decreasing wrt $|.|$ and termination can be proven in a very intuitive manner. Furthermore, the level mappings $|.|$ and $|.|'$ follow directly from the structure of the program, facilitating their automatic derivation. $\qquad\square$

Lemma 3 and corollary 3 below establish that bounded-recurrent programs are indeed terminating. Proof of this relies on orderings which not only take into account the levels of atoms but also their relation to each other in the predicate dependency graph. For a level mapping $|.|$ and goal $G =\leftarrow A_1, \ldots, A_n$, if G is bounded wrt $|.|$ then let $|[G]|$ denote the finite multiset of pairs $\{|\langle rel(A_1), |[A_1]|\rangle, \ldots, \langle rel(A_n), |[A_n]|\rangle|\}$. Let $\prec$ be the lexicographical ordering on $\Pi(\sqsubset) \times \mathbb{N}(<)$ and let $\prec_{mul}$ be the multiset ordering induced from $\prec$. Observe that $\prec_{mul}$ is well founded.

Lemma 3. Let $|.|_1$ and $|.|_2$ be level mappings for a logic program P. Let P be bounded-recurrent wrt $|.|_1$ and $|.|_2$ and let G be a goal which is bounded wrt $|.|_1$ and $|.|_2$. Let G' be an SLD-resolvent of G from P. Then

1. G' is bounded wrt $|.|_1$ and $|.|_2$,
2. $|[G']|_1 \prec_{mul} |[G]|_1$, and
3. every SLD-derivation of $P \cup \{\leftarrow G\}$ is finite.

Proof. Assume A_j is the selected literal in $G =\leftarrow A_1, \ldots, A_m$ and the used clause is $c : H \leftarrow B_1, \ldots, B_n$ $(n \geq 0)$. Then $G' =\leftarrow (A_1, \ldots, A_{j-1}, B_1, \ldots, B_n, A_{j+1}, \ldots, A_m)\theta$ where $\theta \in mgu(A_j, H)$.

1. Since G is bounded wrt $|.|_1$ and $|.|_2$, it follows that A_k and $A_k\theta$ are bounded wrt $|.|_1$ and $|.|_2$ for all $k \in [1, m]$. In particular, $A_j\theta = H\theta$ is bounded wrt $|.|_1$ and $|.|_2$. It follows, by definition 14, that $B_i\theta$ is bounded wrt $|.|_1$ and $|.|_2$ for all $i \in [1, n]$ and hence G' is bounded wrt $|.|_1$ and $|.|_2$.
2. Moreover, $|[A_k]|_1 \geq |[A_k\theta]|_1$ for all $k \in [1, m]$ by lemma 1. Finally, for all $i \in [1, n]$
   (a) $|[A_j\theta]|_1 > |[B_i\theta]|_1$ if $rel(A_j) = rel(H) \simeq rel(B_i)$, by definition 14, and
   (b) $rel(B_i\theta) \sqsubset rel(A_j)$ otherwise.
   Hence $\langle rel(B_i\theta), |[B_i\theta]|_1 \rangle \prec \langle rel(A_j), |[A_j]|_1 \rangle$ for all $i \in [1, n]$ and also $\langle rel(A_k\theta), |[A_k\theta]|_1 \rangle \preceq \langle rel(A_k), |[A_k]|_1 \rangle$ for all $k \in [1, m]$ thereby proving $|[G']|_1 \prec_{mul} |[G]|_1$.
3. Since $\prec_{mul}$ is well-founded the result follows immediately.

Corollary 3. *Every bounded-recurrent program is terminating.*

Theorem 4. *Let $|.|_1$ and $|.|_2$ be level mappings for a logic program P. The following hold.*

1. *If P is recurrent wrt $|.|_1$ then P is bounded-recurrent wrt $|.|_1$ and $|.|_1$.*
2. *If P is bounded-recurrent wrt $|.|_1$ and $|.|_2$, then there exists a level mapping $|.|_3$ such that P is recurrent wrt $|.|_3$. Moreover, for any atom A, A is bounded wrt $|.|_3$ if A is bounded wrt $|.|_1$ and $|.|_2$.*

Proof. Let $c : H \leftarrow B_1, \ldots, B_n$ be a clause in P. Suppose P is recurrent wrt $|.|_1$. Let θ be a substitution such that $H\theta$ is bounded wrt $|.|_1$. Then $B_i\theta$ is bounded and $|[H\theta]|_1 > |[B_i\theta]|_1$ for all $i \in [1, n]$ by recurrency. The second part follows by lemma 3 and theorem 2.2 and corollary 2.2 of [5].

7   Bounded-Acceptability

The definition of bounded-recurrency is easily adapted to obtain a characterisation of left-terminating programs.

Definition 15 (bounded-acceptability). *Let $|.|_1$ and $|.|_2$ be level mappings and I an interpretation for a logic program P. A clause $c : H \leftarrow B_1, \ldots, B_n$. is bounded-acceptable (wrt $|.|_1$, $|.|_2$ and I) iff*

1. *I is a model for c and*
2. *for all $i \in [1, n]$ and for every substitution θ such that $H\theta$ is bounded wrt $|.|_1$ and $|.|_2$, $\{B_1, \ldots, B_{i-1}\}\theta$ is ground and $I \models \{B_1, \ldots, B_{i-1}\}\theta$ it follows that*
   (a) *$B_i\theta$ is bounded wrt $|.|_1$ and $|.|_2$ and*
   (b) *$|[H\theta]|_1 > |[B_i\theta]|_1$ whenever $rel(H) \simeq rel(B_i)$.*

P is bounded-acceptable (wrt $|.|_1$, $|.|_2$ and I) iff every clause in P is bounded-acceptable (wrt $|.|_1$, $|.|_2$ and I).   □

Lemma 4 asserts that every bounded-acceptable program is left-terminating. The proof of this follows along the same lines as that for acceptable programs.

Lemma 4. Let $|.|_1$ and $|.|_2$ be level mappings and I an interpretation for a program P. Let P be bounded-acceptable wrt $|.|_1$, $|.|_2$ and I, and let G be a goal which is left-bounded wrt $|.|_1$ and I and wrt $|.|_2$ and I. Let G' be an LD-resolvent of G from P. Then

1. G' is left-bounded wrt $|.|_1$ and I and wrt $|.|_2$ and I,
2. $|[G']_I|_1 \prec_{mul} |[G]_I|_1$ and
3. every LD-derivation of $P \cup \{\leftarrow G\}$ is finite.

Proof. Let $G = \leftarrow A_0, A_1, \ldots, A_m$ $(m > 0)$ and assume $c : H \leftarrow B_1, \ldots, B_n$ $(n \geq 0)$ is the program clause used. Then $G' = \leftarrow (B_1, \ldots, B_n, A_1, \ldots, A_m)\theta$ where $\theta \in mgu(A_0, H)$.

1. It is necessary to show for all $j \in [1,2]$, $i \in [1, n+m]$ that $|[G']_I^i|_j$ is finite. Firstly, for all $j \in [1,2]$, $i \in [1,n]$

$$|[G']_I^i|_j = |[\leftarrow (B_1, \ldots, B_n, A_1, \ldots, A_m)\theta]_I^i|_j$$
$$= \left\{ |B_i\theta\phi|_j \middle| \begin{array}{l} \phi \text{ grounds } G' \\ I \models \{B_1, \ldots, B_{i-1}\}\theta\phi \end{array} \right\}$$
$$= \left\{ |B_i\theta\phi\sigma|_j \middle| \begin{array}{l} \phi \text{ grounds } \{B_1, \ldots, B_{i-1}\}\theta \\ I \models \{B_1, \ldots, B_{i-1}\}\theta\phi \\ \sigma \text{ grounds } B_i\theta\phi \end{array} \right\}$$

Now by definition 15, for all $i \in [1,n]$, for every substitution ϕ such that $H\theta\phi$ is bounded wrt $|.|_1$ and $|.|_2$, $\{B_1, \ldots, B_{i-1}\}\theta\phi$ is ground and $I \models \{B_1, \ldots, B_{i-1}\}\theta\phi$

(a) $B_i\theta\phi$ is bounded wrt $|.|_1$ and $|.|_2$ and

(b) $|[H\theta\phi]|_1 > |[B_i\theta\phi]|_1$ whenever $rel(H) \simeq rel(B_i)$.

Hence, $|[G']_I^i|_j$ is finite for all $i \in [1,n]$, $j \in [1,2]$. Now for all $j \in [1,2]$, $k \in [1,m]$

$$|[G']_I^{n+k}|_j = |[\leftarrow (B_1, \ldots, B_n, A_1, \ldots, A_m)\theta]_I^{n+k}|_j$$
$$= \left\{ |A_k\theta\varphi|_j \middle| \begin{array}{l} \varphi \text{ grounds } G' \\ I \models \{B_1, \ldots, B_n, A_1, \ldots, A_{k-1}\}\theta\varphi \end{array} \right\}$$
$$\subseteq \left\{ |A_k\theta\varphi|_j \middle| \begin{array}{l} \phi \text{ grounds } \{H, A_1, \ldots, A_m\}\theta \\ I \models \{H, A_1, \ldots, A_{k-1}\}\theta\varphi \end{array} \right\}$$
$$= |[\leftarrow (A_0, A_1, \ldots, A_m)\theta]_I^{k+1}|_j$$
$$\subseteq |[\leftarrow (A_0, A_1, \ldots, A_m)]_I^{k+1}|_j$$

Since G is left-bounded wrt $|.|_1$ and I, and wrt $|.|_2$ and I, then $|[G']_I^{n+k}|_j$ is finite for all $k \in [1,m]$, $j \in [1,2]$.

2. It follows directly that for all $k \in [1, m]$, $j \in [1, 2]$, $\max |[G']_I^{n+k}|_j \leq \max$ $|[G]_I^{k+1}|_j$ and for all $i \in [1, n]$, whenever $rel(A_0) = rel(H) \simeq rel(B_i)$

$$
\begin{aligned}
\max |[G']_I^i|_1 &< \max\{|H\theta\phi|_1 \mid \phi \text{ grounds } H\theta\} \\
&= \max\{|A_0\theta\phi|_1 \mid \phi \text{ grounds } A_0\theta\} \\
&= \max |[\leftarrow A_0\theta]_I^1|_1 \\
&\leq \max |[\leftarrow A_0]_I^1|_1 \\
&= \max |[G]_I^1|_1
\end{aligned}
$$

Hence $\langle rel(B_i\theta), \max |[G']_I^i|_1 \rangle \prec \langle rel(A_0), \max |[G]_I^1|_1 \rangle$ for all $i \in [1, n]$ and $\langle rel(A_k\theta), \max |[G']_I^{n+k}|_1 \rangle \preceq \langle rel(A_k), \max |[G]_I^{k+1}|_1 \rangle$ for all $k \in [1, m]$ thereby proving $|[G']_I|_1 \prec_{mul} |[G]_I|_1$.

3. Since $\prec_{mul}$ is well-founded the result follows immediately.

Corollary 4. Every bounded-acceptable program is left-terminating.

Theorem 5. Let $|.|_1$ and $|.|_2$ be level mappings and I an interpretation for a program P. The following hold.

1. If P is acceptable wrt $|.|_1$ then P is bounded-acceptable wrt $|.|_1$ and $|.|_1$.
2. If P is bounded-acceptable wrt $|.|_1$ and $|.|_2$, then there exists a level mapping $|.|_3$ such that P is acceptable wrt $|.|_3$. Moreover, for any atom A, A is bounded wrt $|.|_3$ if A is bounded wrt $|.|_1$ and $|.|_2$. ☐

Proof. Let $c : H \leftarrow B_1, \ldots, B_n$ be a clause in P. Suppose P is acceptable wrt $|.|_1$. Then I is a model for c. Let θ be a substitution such that $H\theta$ is bounded wrt $|.|_1$, $\{B_1, \ldots, B_{i-1}\}\theta$ is ground and $I \models \{B_1, \ldots, B_{i-1}\}\theta$. Then $B_i\theta$ is bounded wrt $|.|_1$ and $|[H\theta]|_1 > |[B_i\theta]|_1$ by acceptability and lemma 2. The second part follows by lemma 4 and theorem 4.18 of [2]. ☐

Note that the proof of theorem 5, like that for theorem 4, does not need to directly specify the relationship between $|.|_1$, $|.|_2$ and $|.|_3$ (though it would be interestingly to understand this connection).

8 Discussion

The concept of bounded-acceptability proposed here is quite similar to that of rigid-acceptability defined by [13,16]. This latter notion forms the basis of a practical, demand-driven termination analysis. The analysis is essentially top-down, attempting to prove termination for a set of queries S. An important step in the analysis is the calculation of the call set $Call(P, S)$, the set of all calls which may occur during the derivation of an atom in S. The analysis focuses on the recursive components to derive a level mapping $|.|$, enforcing boundedness of sub-computations by imposing a rigidity constraint on the call set. That is, during the derivation of $|.|$, every atom in $Call(P, S)$ is required to be rigid wrt $|.|$.

For program specialisation, and partial deduction in particular, it is more useful to derive sufficient termination conditions for individual predicates rather than proving that a given top-level goal will terminate [10]. The reason is that the overall computation is unlikely to be left-terminating but some sub-computations probably will be. The required conditions can be derived in a bottom-up manner on the strongly connected components of the predicate dependency graph. The notion of bounded-acceptability lends itself naturally to this process.

In [14], the analysis of [13] is adapted to obtain the above mentioned conditions. It attempts to derive for each predicate a maximal set S of left-terminating queries. Essentially, this amounts to deriving a level mapping $|.|$ which defines S, in that an atom A is in S if and only if A is bounded wrt $|.|$. However, an important step is omitted from the paper, and the set S may contain queries which are not left-terminating. The level mapping $|.|$ is derived by only considering the recursive components of the program and thus corresponds to the level mapping $|.|_1$ in the definition of bounded-acceptability. Sub-computations are no longer guaranteed to start from bounded goals since no rigidity constraint is placed on the level mapping during its derivation as in [13]: specifically, this is because the set $Call(P, S)$ is unknown since S is unknown (the idea after all being to derive S), and as a result no rigidity constraint can be imposed on $Call(P, S)$. Hence, in relation to the current work, the missing step is the derivation of the second level mapping $|.|_2$. The maximal set $S' \subseteq S$ of left-terminating queries then, contains only those atoms which are bounded wrt $|.|_1$ and $|.|_2$. Note that $|.|_2$ can be derived entirely independently of $|.|_1$, in the sense that there is never any need to alter the definition of $|.|_1$ in order to obtain a definition of $|.|_2$ which can be used to prove bounded-acceptability. Thus the notion of bounded-acceptability allows the set S' to be easily constructed from S without requiring any change to the method of [14].

Recently, Bossi *et al* [6] have developed an entirely modular approach to termination in which acceptability is proven on a module-by-module basis by choosing a natural level mapping that focuses solely on the predicates defined within the module. The key concept is strong boundedness. A query to a program that is defined over n modules $R_1, \ldots, R_n$ is said to be strongly bounded if each call to a predicate that is defined in module R_i is bounded with respect to the level mapping for that module $|.|_i$. A sufficient condition for left-termination of a strongly bounded query is for each module R_i to be acceptable with respect to its own level mapping $|.|_i$ and a model of the whole program. Observe, however, that strong boundedness is a property of derivations rather than a model. The authors, however, argue that the approach is still attractive because strong boundedness can be verified by approximating call-patterns by goal-dependent abstract interpretation [8]. Moreover, well-moded [17] and well-typed logic programs [7] are in some sense well-behaved with respect to strong boundedness and thereby provide another route for asserting strong boundedness. This work is applicable to general logic programs and therefore generalises the modular termination proofs for well-moded definite programs originally proposed in [18]. By way of contrast, the concept of bounded-acceptability paper does rely on either call-pattern approximation or the program being well-moded or well-typed.

In summary, the notions of bounded-recurrency and bounded-acceptability enable a more mechanistic approach to be taken to the construction of level mappings since these concepts finesse some of the complications that arise in the construction of classic termination proofs. Level mappings that directly relate to the recursive structure of the program, as well as being more intuitive for a human, are bound to be easier to synthesise for a machine.

Acknowledgements This work was supported, in part, by the EPSRC studentship 93315269; in fact much of this paper is adapted from chapters 3 and 6 of [22]. The work has benefited for useful discussions with Danny De Schreye and Fred Mesnard. The authors gratefully acknowledge Nuffield grant SCI/180/94/417/G and EPSRC grant GR/MO8769 for funding their collaboration.

References

1. K. R. Apt and M. Bezem. Acyclic Programs. *New Generation Computing*, 9(3/4):335–364, 1991.
2. K. R. Apt and D. Pedreschi. Reasoning about Termination of Pure Prolog Programs. *Information and Computation*, 106(1):109–157, 1993.
3. K. R. Apt and D. Pedreschi. Modular Termination Proofs for Logic and Pure Prolog programs. In G. Levi, editor, *Advances in Logic Programming Theory*, pages 183–229. Oxford University Press, 1994. Also available as technical report CS-R9316 from Centrum voor Wiskunde en Informatica, CWI, Amesterdam.
4. M. Bezem. Characterizing Termination of Logic Programs with Level Mappings. In E. L. Lusk and R. A. Overbeek, editors, *North American Conference on Logic Programming*, pages 69–80. MIT Press, 1989.
5. M. Bezem. Strong Termination of Logic Programs. *The Journal of Logic Programming*, 15(1&2):79–97, 1993.
6. A. Bossi, N. Cocco, S. Etalle, and S. Rossi. On Modular Termination Proofs of General Logic Programs. *Theory and Practice of Logic Programming*, 2(3):263–291, 2002.
7. F. Bronsard, T. K. Lakshman, and U. S. Reddy. A Framework of Directionality for Proving Termination of Logic Programs. In K. R. Apt, editor, *Joint International Conference and Symposium on Logic Programming*, pages 321–335. MIT Press, 1992.
8. M. Bruynooghe. A Practical Framework for the Abstract Interpretation of Logic Programs. *The Journal of Logic Programming*, 10(1/2/3&4):91–124, 1991.
9. M. Bruynooghe, M. Codish, S. Genaim, and W. Vanhoof. Reuse of Results in Termination Analysis of Typed Logic Programs. In M. V. Hermenegildo and G. Puebla, editors, *Static Analysis Symposium*, number 2477 in Lecture Notes in Computer Science, pages 477–492. Springer-Verlag, 2002.
10. M. Bruynooghe, M. Leuchel, and K. F. Sagonas. A Polyvariant Binding-time Analysis for Off-line Partial Deduction. In C. Hankin, editor, *European Symposium on Programming*, volume 1381 of *Lecture Notes in Computer Science*, pages 27–41. Springer-Verlag, 1998.
11. L. Cavedon. Continuity, consistency, and completeness properties of logic programs. In G. Levi and M. Martelli, editors, *International Conference on Logic Programming*, pages 571–584. MIT Press, 1989.

12. D. De Schreye, K. Verschaetse, and M. Bruynooghe. A Framework for Analysing the Termination of Definite Logic Programs with Respect to Call Patterns. In *International Conference on Fifth Generation Computer Systems*, pages 481–488. IOS Press, 1992.

13. S. Decorte and D. De Schreye. Demand-driven and constraint-based automatic left-termination analysis of logic programs. In L. Naish, editor, *International Conference on Logic Programming*, pages 78–92. MIT Press, 1997.

14. S. Decorte and D. De Schreye. Termination analysis: Some practical properties of the Norm and Level Mapping Space. In J. Jaffar, editor, *Joint International Conference and Symposium on Logic Programming*, pages 235–249. MIT Press, 1998.

15. S. Decorte, D. De Schreye, and M. Fabris. Automatic Inference of Norms: A Missing Link in Automatic Termination Analysis. In D. Miller, editor, *International Logic Programming Symposium*, pages 420–436. MIT Press, 1993.

16. S. Decorte, D. De Schreye, and H. Vandecasteele. Constraint-based Termination Analysis of Logic Programs. *ACM Transactions on Programming Languages and Systems*, 21(6):1137–1195, 1999.

17. P. Dembiński and J. Maluszyński. And-Parallelism with Intelligent Backtracking for Annotated Logic Programs. In *Symposium on Logic Programming*, pages 29–38. IEEE Press, 1985.

18. S. Etalle, A. Bossi, and N. Cocco. Termination of Well-Moded Programs. *The Journal of Logic Programming*, 38(2):243–257, 1999.

19. S. Genaim, M. Codish, J. P. Gallagher, and V. Lagoon. Combining Norms to Prove Termination. In A. Cortesi, editor, *Verification, Model Checking and Abstract Interpretation*, number 2294 in Lecture Notes in Computer Science, pages 126–138. Springer-Verlag, 2002.

20. V. Lagoon, F. Mesnard, and P. Stuckey. Termination Analysis with Types is More Accurate. In C. Palamidessi, editor, *International Conference on Logic Programming*, Lecture Notes in Computer Science. Springer-Verlag, 2003.

21. J. Lloyd. *Foundations of Logic Programming*. Springer-Verlag, 1987.

22. J. C. Martin. *Judgement Day: Terminating Logic Programs*. PhD thesis, Department of Electronics and Computer Science, University of Southampton, 2000.

23. J. C. Martin, A. King, and P. Soper. Typed Norms for Typed Logic Programs. In J. Gallagher, editor, *Logic Program Synthesis and Transformation (Selected Papers)*, volume 1207 of *Lecture Notes in Computer Science*, pages 224–238. Springer-Verlag, 1997.

24. J. C. Martin and M. Leuschel. Sonic Partial Deduction. In D. Bjørner, M. Broy, and A. V. Zamulin, editors, *Third International Andrei Ershov Memorial Conference*, volume 1755 of *Lecture Notes in Computer Science*, pages 101–112, 1999.

25. D. Pedreschi and S. Ruggieri. Verification of Logic Programs. *The Journal of Logic Programming*, 39(1-3):125–176, 1999.

26. J. Van Leeuwen, editor. *Handbook of Theoretical Computer Science: Volume B*. Elsevier, 1990.

27. W. Vanhoof and M. Bruynooghe. When Size Does Matter. In A. Pettorossi, editor, *Logic Based Program Synthesis and Transformation (Selected Papers)*, volume 2372 of *Lecture Notes in Computer Science*, pages 129–147, 2001.

28. S. Verbaeten, D. De Schreye, and K. F. Sagonas. Termination Proofs for Logic Programs with Tabling. *ACM Transactions on Computational Logic*, 2(1):57–92, 2001.

Proving Termination for Logic Programs by the Query-Mapping Pairs Approach

Naomi Lindenstrauss[1], Yehoshua Sagiv[1], and Alexander Serebrenik[2]

[1] School of Computer Science and Engineering, The Hebrew University
Jerusalem 91904, Israel
{naomil,sagiv}@cs.huji.ac.il
[2] École Polytechnique (STIX), 91128 Palaiseau Cedex, France
Alexander.Serebrenik@stix.polytecnique.fr

Abstract. This paper describes a method for proving termination of queries to logic programs based on abstract interpretation. The method uses query-mapping pairs to abstract the relation between calls in the LD-tree associated with the program and query. Any well founded partial order for terms can be used to prove the termination. The ideas of the query-mapping pairs approach have been implemented in SICStus Prolog in a system called *TermiLog*, which is available on the web. Given a program and query pattern the system either answers that the query terminates or that there *may* be non-termination. The advantages of the method are its conceptual simplicity and the fact that it does not impose any restrictions on the programs.

1 Introduction

In this paper we describe a method for proving termination of queries to logic programs based on abstract interpretation. The results of applying the ideas of abstract interpretation to logic programs (cf. [24]) seem to be especially elegant and useful, because we are dealing in this case with a very simple language which has only one basic construct—the clause. Termination of programs is known to be undecidable, but in the case of logic programs, which have a clearly defined formal semantics and in which the only possible cause for non-termination is infinite recursion, it is possible to prove termination automatically for a large class of programs.

Given a logic program, that is a finite set of clauses of the form

$$A :- B_1, B_2, \ldots, B_n$$

where $A, B_1, B_2, \ldots B_n$ are atoms, $n \geq 0$, and a query, which is an atom, we want to find, if possible, substitutions for the variables of the query which make it a logical consequence of the program (if there are no variables in the query we just want to show that it is a logical consequence of the program). To do so we usually use SLD-resolution to compute answers to the query (for all these notions see [1,48]).

M. Bruynooghe and K.-K. Lau (Eds.): Program Development in CL, LNCS 3049, pp. 453–498, 2004.
© Springer-Verlag Berlin Heidelberg 2004

A crucial question in this case is whether the computation terminates. The way the computation proceeds depends on the choice of the atom in the goal on which resolution is performed at each step, and on the choice of the clause with which it is resolved. Termination irrespective of which atom and clause are chosen is called *strong termination* (cf. [12]) and means that all SLD-trees constructed for the program and the query are finite. One can consider a weaker notion of termination, where one can choose any clause, but the choice of atom is determined by Prolog's computation rule: always choose the leftmost atom in a goal to resolve upon. This notion amounts to finiteness of the SLD-tree constructed according to Prolog's computation rule, which is called the LD-tree (cf. [1]). A still weaker notion is ∃-termination, where one assumes that there is at least one way to choose atoms so that for any way of choosing clauses there is termination (cf. [65,57]). All notions of termination where one can choose any clause fall in the category of *universal* termination, because one computes all answers. The weakest notion of termination is *existential termination*, which means that there either is finite failure or at least one way to choose atoms and clauses, so that there is a succesful derivation (cf. [80,8,49]).

All these kinds of termination are undecidable (this follows from the fact that the operation of a Turing machine can be described by a logic program, and the halting problem for Turing machines is undecidable). Nevertheless it is important to find sufficient conditions for termination that can be verified automatically.

We consider the second notion of termination mentioned above, namely termination of computing all answers using the leftmost computation rule of Prolog. This notion of termination is also known as LD-termination (cf. [32]). Observe, that finding all answers in finite time is essential, even if one seems to be interested in finding a single answer only. The query we solved may be backtracked into and it is crucial that there will be termination also in that case (cf. the section on 'Backwards Correctness' in [56]). Moreover, Prolog's built-in predicates *findall, setof, bagof* depend on computing all answers to the query they include.

One of the difficulties when dealing with the LD-tree for a query, given a logic program, is that infinitely many different atoms may appear as subgoals. The basic idea is to abstract this possibly infinite structure to a finite one. The query-mapping pairs method (cf. [66,44]) uses a certain kind of graphs to abstract the relation between arguments of calls in the LD-tree associated with the program and query. The method has been implemented in SICStus Prolog ([68]) in a termination analyzer called *TermiLog* (cf. [46]), which is available on the web ([74]). Given a program and query pattern the analyzer either answers that the query terminates or that there *may* be non-termination.

TermiLog was, as far as we know, the first publicly available automatic tool for proving termination of logic programs. It is based on one clear and simple idea — the notion of query-mapping pair — and the use of Ramsey's theorem. This paper presents both the theoretical framework, which can be used for any well-founded order, and its application for linear norms, as implemented in *TermiLog*. The paper is completely self-contained. For instance the instantiation analysis, which is an extension of groundness analysis, and the constraint inference are developed from the basics. The whole development of *TermiLog* was done within the framework of standard Prolog. This and the inherent simplicity of the approach make the system very flexible and various optimizations can be easily added.

The remainder of the paper is organized as follows. In Section 2 the key notion of the approach, *query-mapping pairs*, is introduced. Query-mapping pairs are defined relative to a partial mapping ϕ from terms to a strictly ordered well-founded set. Any partial mapping ϕ from terms to a strictly ordered well-founded set can be taken. In Section 3 the Basic Theorem is proved with the help of Ramsey's Theorem. From the Basic Theorem a sufficient condition for termination, formulated in terms of query-mapping pairs, is derived. An example of using the condition is given for a suitable mapping ϕ. However, in order to automate the process of proving termination, we cannot let the choice of ϕ be determined by ingenuity, but need a uniform way of constructing it. This is done by means of linear norms. Section 4, which comprises the main part of the paper, explains the theoretical foundation for the use of query-mapping pairs based on linear norms, as it is implemented in the *TermiLog* system ([74,46]). First linear norms and the more general symbolic linear norms are defined. Then the weighted rule graph that corresponds to a rule[3] of the program is defined. This graph is a main tool in the construction of query-mapping pairs and in the constraint inference (Subsection 4.7). Then it is explained how to obtain all the query-mapping pairs relevant to a program and a query by the processes of generation and composition. Next, it is explained how instantiation analysis and constraint inference, which are used in the construction of the query-mapping pairs, are performed, by a process of bottom-up abstract interpretation. We then give some information about the implementation and the experimental evaluation of the system. The paper ends with some information about related work and the development of the query-mapping pairs approach.

2   LD-Trees and Query-Mapping Pairs

To prove termination we use partial mappings from terms to strictly ordered well-founded sets. A set S is called *strictly ordered* if there is a binary relation $>$ defined on it that is transitive (i.e. if x, y, z are in S then $x > y, y > z$ implies $x > z$) and asymmetric (i.e. if x, y are in S then $x > y$ implies that $y > x$ cannot hold). Note that this also means that it cannot be reflexive. A strictly ordered set $(S, >)$ is called *well-founded* if there are no infinite sequences $x_1 > x_2 > x_3 > \ldots$ of elements of S. The way to prove termination will be to show that if there was non-termination one could produce an infinite descending sequence of elements.

We will consider partial mappings ϕ from terms to a strictly ordered well-founded set $(S, >)$. Most often this will be the set of non-negative integers with the usual order, but any other strictly ordered well-founded set can be used. We

---

[3] A rule is a clause with non-empty body.

will require these mappings to be compatible with substitutions in the sense of the following definition.

Definition 2.1 (Substitution-Compatible Mapping). *A partial mapping ϕ defined for (not necessarily all) terms is called* substitution-compatible *if whenever $\phi(T)$ is defined for a term T and θ is a substitution, then $\phi(T\theta)$ is defined too and is equal to $\phi(T)$.* [4]

We now proceed to define a relation between nodes in the LD-tree that 'call' each other.

Definition 2.2. *Let P be a program and Q be a query. Let $\leftarrow P_1, \ldots, P_m$ and $\leftarrow Q_1, \ldots, Q_m$ be nodes in the LD-tree of P and Q. We say that node $\leftarrow Q_1, \ldots, Q_n$ is a* direct offspring *of node $\leftarrow P_1, \ldots, P_m$ if P_1 has been resolved with a clause c in P and Q_1 is, up to a substitution, a body subgoal of c.*

Soppose we assign to each node in the LD-tree a unique natural number (it does not matter how, as long as there is a one-to-one correspondence between nodes and numbers), and suppose that if node (k) is resolved with the clause instance $A \leftarrow B_1, \ldots, B_n$ we add a subscript (k) to all the predicates of the atoms $B_j, 1 \leq j \leq n$. Then, if the subscript of the predicate of the first atom of node (l) is (m) this means that node (l) is a direct offspring of node (m)

Definition 2.3 (Offspring Relation and Call Branch). *We define the* offspring *relation as the non-reflexive closure of the direct offspring relation. We call a path between two nodes in the tree such that one is the offspring of the other a* call branch. [5]

Take for example the program for computing Ackermann's function with the goal ack(s(0),s(s(0)),A) :

Example 2.1.
```
(i)     ack(0,N,s(N)).
(ii)    ack(s(M),0,A) :- ack(M,s(0),A).
(iii)   ack(s(M),s(N),A) :- ack(s(M),N,A1), ack(M,A1,A).
```
□

The LD-tree is given in Figure 1. Note that the predicate of each atom in the LD-tree has a subscript that reports who is its 'parent', that is the node in the LD-tree that caused this atom to be called as the result of resolution. Node

---

[4] The reader may notice a similarity between this notion and the notion of a rigid norm (cf. for example [25]). The difference is that a norm is defined for all terms. Here the mapping is partial and a crucial part of the requirements for it to be substitution-compatible is, that it be defined for $T\theta$, for any substitution θ, if it is defined for T.

[5] There is affinity between our offspring relation and the descendant relation in [69], however the relation here is defined for nodes in the LD-tree, while the relation there is defined for atoms.

(2) and node (6) are, for instance, direct offspring of node (1), because the first atoms in their respective goals come from the body of clause (iii), with which the goal of node (1) was resolved. Node (3), for instance, is an offspring of node (1), but not a direct offspring.

$(1) \leftarrow ack(s(0), s(s(0)), A)$

$(2) \leftarrow ack_{(1)}(s(0), s(0), A1), ack_{(1)}(0, A1, A)$

$(3) \leftarrow ack_{(2)}(s(0), 0, A2), ack_{(2)}(0, A2, A1), ack_{(1)}(0, A1, A)$

$(4) \leftarrow ack_{(3)}(0, s(0), A2), ack_{(2)}(0, A2, A1), ack_{(1)}(0, A1, A)$
$\qquad \{A2 \mapsto s(s(0))\}$

$(5) \leftarrow ack_{(2)}(0, s(s(0)), A1), ack_{(1)}(0, A1, A)$
$\qquad \{A1 \mapsto s(s(s(0)))\}$

$(6) \leftarrow ack_{(1)}(0, s(s(s(0))), A)$
$\qquad \{A \mapsto s(s(s(s(0))))\}$

$(7) \leftarrow$

Fig. 1. LD-tree of ack

A graphical representation of the direct offspring relation is given in Figure 2.

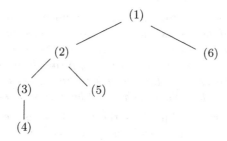

Fig. 2. The offspring relation of ack

In this example, to which we will return later, there is only one branch in the LD-tree. To give an example where the tree consists of more than one branch, take the program $pqrst$:

Example 2.2.
```
p(X) :- q(X), r(X).
p(X) :- s(X).
s(X) :- t(X).
q(a).    r(a).    t(b).
```

$\qquad \qquad \qquad \qquad \qquad \qquad \qquad \qquad \qquad \qquad \qquad \qquad \Box$

In this case the LD-tree is given in Figure 3 and a representation of the offspring relation is given in Figure 4.

$(1) \leftarrow p(X)$

$(2) \leftarrow q_{(1)}(X), r_{(1)}(X)$
$\quad \{X \mapsto a\}$

$(5) \leftarrow s_{(1)}(X)$

$(6) \leftarrow t_{(5)}(X)$

$(3) \leftarrow r_{(1)}(a)$
$\quad \{X \mapsto b\}$

$(4) \leftarrow$

$(7) \leftarrow$

Fig. 3. LD-tree of $pqrst$

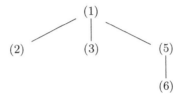

Fig. 4. The offspring relation of $pqrst$

In order to give information about call branches in the LD-tree we will use *argument mappings*, or *mappings* in short.

Definition 2.4 (Argument Mapping). *An* argument mapping *is a mixed graph, that is a graph with both arcs and edges, whose nodes correspond to argument positions of some atoms (possibly just one atom). A node corresponding to an argument position of an atom is labeled by the predicate of the atom and by the argument number. Nodes are either black or white. Nodes connected by an edge must be of the same color. Nodes connected by an arc must be black.*

The intuition behind this definition is the following: as we said in the beginning of this section we will use partial mappings ϕ from terms to a strictly ordered well-founded set. Nodes of the argument mapping correspond to arguments of atoms. The color of a node, black or white, will be used to depict whether ϕ is defined or, respectively, not known to be defined for the argument. An arc going from one node to another depicts the fact that the value of ϕ for the argument corresponding to the first node is greater than the value for the argument corresponding to the second. Nodes connected by an arc must therefore be black, because ϕ is defined for the arguments they represent. An edge can either connect two black nodes for which ϕ is defined and the values are equal, or two nodes for which the corresponding arguments are identical (and then ϕ is defined or undefined for both). Suppose we have the rule

```
p(X,Y) :- p(a,Y), q(b,X).
```

and $\phi(a) = 1$, $\phi(b) = 2$.

Then we can depict the relations between the arguments of the atoms appearing in the rule by

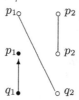

In order not to clutter the picture we will usually omit some of the labels and imply them by the layout of the graph:

One mapping may be more 'general' than another. This brings us to the definition of subsumption.

Definition 2.5 (subsumption). *Given two mappings G_1 and G_2, we say that G_1 subsumes G_2 if they have the same nodes up to color, every node that is black in G_1 is also black in G_2, and every edge or arc between nodes in G_1 also appears for the respective nodes in G_2.*

The intuition behind this definition is that we will assume that ϕ is substitution-compatible, so when we apply a substitution to an atom, the arguments for which ϕ was defined will continue to be defined and have the same value, while it may happen that ϕ will be defined for more arguments. If we have a mapping, and apply a substitution to the arguments it represents, the resulting mapping will be subsumed by the original mapping. To give an example:

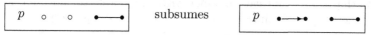

We now define *basic query-mapping pairs*. Basic query-mapping pairs give information about the size relations between the arguments of the first atoms of two nodes such that one is the direct offspring of the other.

Definition 2.6 (Basic Query-Mapping Pairs). *Let ϕ be a partial mapping from terms to a strictly ordered well-founded set $(S, >)$ that is substitution-compatible. Let a logic program and a query be given. Suppose $\leftarrow P_1, \ldots, P_m$ and $\leftarrow Q_1, \ldots, Q_n$ are two nodes in the LD-tree such that the second is a direct offspring of the first. Let θ be the composition of the substitutions along the path between these two nodes.*

A basic query-mapping pair corresponding to these two nodes consists of two parts:

- *The* query pattern, *that is a mapping whose nodes correspond to the argument positions of* $P_1 = p(t_1, \ldots, t_k)$ *and are either black, if we know that* ϕ *is defined for the corresponding argument, or white, if we don't know whether* ϕ *is defined for the corresponding argument. If we know that the value of* ϕ *is equal for the* i*'th and* j*'th arguments or that the arguments are identical, the graph will include an edge from the* i*'th to the* j*'th position. If we know that* $\phi(t_i) > \phi(t_j)$*, the graph will include an arc from the* i*'th to the* j*'th position.*
- *A mapping, whose nodes correspond to the argument positions of* $P_1\theta$ *and the argument positions of* Q_1*. Again nodes can be black or white and there can be edges and arcs between them, with the meaning as above. We call the nodes corresponding to the argument positions of* $P_1\theta$ *with the edges and arcs between them the* domain *of the mapping, and the nodes coresponding to the argument positions of* Q_1 *with the edges and arcs between them the* range *of the mapping.*

Since ϕ is assumed to be substitution-compatible, the query pattern of a query-mapping pair subsumes the domain of its mapping. Note that the information given by the query-mapping pair does not have to be complete—the important thing is that it be sound and hopefully sufficient for the proof of termination. The query describes abstractly the atom P_1. The mapping describes the relation between the atoms $P_1\theta$ and Q_1. By the time we arrive at Q_1 certain substitutions will have been applied to the variables of P_1 and we want to take them into account in order to have ϕ, which we will use to prove the termination, be defined on as many nodes as possible.

We use the following notation for the query-mapping pairs: for the query pattern we first give an atom with the predicate of P_1 and arguments b or f, depending on whether the corresponding nodes are black or white, and then a list of the edges and arcs in the form $eq(i, j)$ for an edge between the i'th and j'th argument position and $gt(i, j)$ for an arc from the i'th to the j'th argument position; for the part of the mapping we use a pictorial representation.

If we take node (1) and node (2) of the LD-tree for Ackermann's function and assume that ϕ gives for each number written in successor notation its corresponding (nonnegative) value, we get the basic query-mapping pair

If we take node (2) and its direct offspring node (3), we get the following basic query-mapping pair

Looking at each pair of nodes in the LD-tree that are direct offspring of each other is not practical, because the tree may be infinite. In our case both nodes (2) and node (3) originate from resolution with clause (iii) and their first atoms originate in the first atom of the body of the clause. So we may just look at the relation between the head and first body atom in

```
ack(s(M),s(N),A) :- ack(s(M),N,A1), ack(M,A1,A).
```

Then we get the basic query-mapping pair

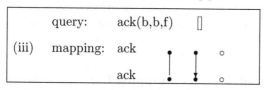

Note that this pair subsumes the previous two.

Basic query-mapping pairs express relations between first atoms of nodes that are direct offspring of each other. To express relations between first atoms of nodes that are offspring but not direct offspring of each other we compose query-mapping pairs.

We have seen that for some mappings we have defined domain and range. For such mappings we define composition.

Definition 2.7 (Composition of Mappings). *Let μ and ν be mappings with domain and range. If the range of μ and the domain of ν are labeled by the same predicate, then the composition of the mappings μ and ν, denoted $\mu \circ \nu$, is obtained by unifying each node in the range of μ with the corresponding node in the domain of ν (two nodes are corresponding if they correspond to the same argument position). When unifying two nodes, the result is a black node if at least one of the nodes is black, otherwise it is a white node. If a node becomes black, so do all nodes connected to it with an edge. The nodes of the domain of $\mu \circ \nu$ are the nodes of the domain of μ, and the nodes of the range of $\mu \circ \nu$ are the nodes of the range of ν. The edges and arcs of $\mu \circ \nu$ consist of the transitive closure of the union of the edges and arcs of μ and ν.*

The following figure shows two mappings (left) and their composition (right).

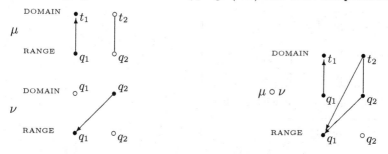

Definition 2.8 (Consistency). *A mapping is* consistent *if it has no positive cycle (a positive cycle is a cycle consisting of edges and at least one arc where all arcs are in the same direction).*

Note that a mapping that expresses relations in an LD-tree must be consistent. Indeed, assume that this is not the case, that is, there exists an inconsistent mapping expressing relations in the LD-tree. A positive cycle may only have black nodes. Because of transitivity we get that for each argument t corresponding to a node on the positive cycle we must have $\phi(t) < \phi(t)$, in contradiction to the irreflexivity of the order $<$.

Definition 2.9 (Summary). *If μ is a consistent mapping with domain and range, then the* summary *of μ consists of the nodes in the domain and range of μ and the edges and arcs between these nodes. The summary is undefined if μ is inconsistent.*

Definition 2.10 (Composition of Query-Mapping Pairs). *Let (π_1, μ_1) and (π_2, μ_2) be query-mapping pairs, such that the range of μ_1 is identical to π_2. The* composition *of (π_1, μ_1) and (π_2, μ_2) is (π_1, μ), where μ is the summary of $\mu_1 \circ \mu_2$ (and, hence, the composition is undefined if $\mu_1 \circ \mu_2$ is inconsistent).*

By composing the query-mapping pairs (i) on page 460 and (ii) on page 460 we get the query-mapping pair

query:	ack(b,b,f) [gt(2,1)]
mapping:	ack
	ack

By composing the pair (iii) on page 461 with itself we get again the pair (iii), that is, it is idempotent.

Definition 2.11. *A query-mapping pair that can be composed with itself, that is a pair in which the query is identical to the range of the mapping, is called* circular.

The pair (iii) is circular and idempotent. The following pair is circular but not idempotent:

query:	p(b,f) []
mapping:	p
	p

The result of composing it with itself is

query:	p(b,f) []
mapping:	p
	p

3   The Basic Theorems

The following theorem holds:

Theorem 3.1. *If there is an infinite branch in the LD-tree corresponding to a program and query then there is an infinite sequence of nodes $N_1, N_2, \ldots$ such that for each i, N_{i+1} is an offspring of N_i.*

Proof. Straightforward (cf. [81]).   □

Suppose we have some way to associate basic query-mapping pairs with call branches between nodes that are direct offspring of each other. Suppose that this is done in such a way that if N_2 is a direct offspring of N_1 and N_3 is a direct offspring of N_2 then the range of the mapping of the pair for N_1, N_2 is equal to the query of the pair for N_2, N_3. Then we can use composition to associate a query-mapping pair with each call branch. Note that composition of query-mapping pairs is associative. Note also that given a program there can only be a finite number of query-mapping pairs associated with it.

The finiteness of the set of query-mapping pairs allows us to use the following version of Ramsey's theorem to prove our basic theorem (cf. [29]). We will use the following notation: if M is a subset of the natural numbers $\mathcal{N}$, we will denote by $M^{[n]}$ the set of all subsets of M of cardinality n.

Theorem 3.2 (Ramsey). *Let α be a mapping from $\mathcal{N}^{[n]}$ to some finite set A. Then there is an infinite subset M of $\mathcal{N}$ such that α is constant on $M^{[n]}$.*

(Cf. [62,39]. For a short self contained proof of this version of the theorem see [10], p. 290.)

Theorem 3.3 (Basic Theorem). *Suppose the LD-tree for a program and query has an infinite branch. Suppose a substitution-compatible partial mapping ϕ from terms to a strictly ordered well-founded set is given. Suppose that basic query-mapping pairs are assigned to nodes that are direct offspring of each other in such a way that if N_2 is a direct offspring of N_1 and N_3 is a direct offspring of N_2 then the range of the mapping of the pair for N_1, N_2 is equal to the query of the pair for N_2, N_3. In this case a query-mapping pair can be assigned to each call path by composing the basic pairs along the path. Then there is a sequence of nodes $M_1, M_2, \ldots$ and a query-mapping pair (π, μ) so that for each i, M_{i+1} is an offspring of M_i, and for each j, k the query-mapping pair corresponding to the call branch from M_j to M_k is (π, μ). The pair (π, μ) can be composed with itself and is idempotent.*

Proof. By Theorem 3.1 there is an infinite sequence of nodes $N_1, N_2, \ldots$ such that for each i, N_{i+1} is an offspring of N_i. The set of query-mapping pairs that can be constructed with the predicate symbols of a program is finite. For each $i < j$ we get one query-mapping pair in this set. By using Ramsey's theorem for $n = 2$ we get that there is an infinite subsequence $N_{i_1}, N_{i_2}, \ldots$ and a unique query-mapping pair (π, μ) so that for each $k < l$ the pair assigned to the call branch from N_{i_k} to N_{i_l} is (π, μ). Clearly this pair can be composed with itself and is idempotent. To see that it is idempotent, take for example the three nodes $N_{i_1}, N_{i_2}, N_{i_3}$. The pair (π, μ) corresponds to each of the three call paths from N_{i_1} to N_{i_2}, from N_{i_2} to N_{i_3} and from N_{i_1} to N_{i_3}. Since the pair corresponding to the path from N_{i_1} to N_{i_3} is the composition of the pairs corresponding to the paths from N_{i_1} to N_{i_2} and from N_{i_2} to N_{i_3} we get the idempotence.   □

From this theorem we get the following sufficient condition for termination which is formulated in terms of query-mapping pairs.

Theorem 3.4 (Sufficient Condition for Termination). *Suppose the LD-tree for a program and query and a substitution-compatible partial mapping ϕ from terms to a strictly ordered well-founded set S are given. Consider a complete set of query-mapping pairs associated with the tree and the mapping ϕ (that is, pairs for all nodes that are direct offspring of each other and their compositions). If for every circular idempotent pair there is an arc from an argument in the domain to the corresponding argument in the range then the tree must be finite, i.e. there is termination for the query with Prolog's computation rule.*

Proof. From the previous theorem we get that if there is an infinite branch there must be an infinite sequence of nodes $N_1, N_2, \ldots$ such that the same circular idempotent pair corresponds to each pair of nodes N_i, N_{i+1}. Since every circular idempotent pair contains an arc from an argument in the domain to the corresponding argument in the range, this would imply the existence of an infinite descending sequence of ϕ values in contradiction to the assumption that S is well-founded.   □

It turns out that we do not have to construct all query-mapping pairs. Obviously it is enough to consider only pairs that may participate in the creation of a circular pair.

Definition 3.1 (Predicate Dependency Graph). *The* predicate dependency graph *of a program is a graph whose nodes are the predicates of the program and which has, for every rule $A : - B_1, \ldots, B_n$ in the program (remember that a rule is a clause with non-empty body) and every i, $1 \leq i \leq n$, an arc from the predicate of A to the predicate of B_i (cf. [58]).*

We can consider the strongly connected components of this graph. We call a strongly connected component **trivial** if it consists of a single node that has no arc going from itself to itself. It is easy to see that if the predicate dependency graph has no non-trivial strongly connected component, there can be no recursion in the program. Also the only pairs that can participate in the creation of a circular pair are those for which the predicate of the domain and the predicate of the range are in the same non-trivial strongly connected component.

Definition 3.2 (Recursive Query-Mapping Pair). *A query-mapping pair is called* recursive *if the predicates of the domain and range belong to the same strongly connected component of the predicate dependency graph.*

Theorem 3.5 (Optimization of Sufficient Condition for Termination).
Theorem 3.4 remains true if we only consider the recursive query-mapping pairs.

If we use Theorem 3.5 instead of Theorem 3.4 there will in general be fewer pairs to consider so we will get an answer more quickly.

Example 3.1. Suppose a finite directed acyclic graph is given by a set of facts of the form $arc(X, Y)$ denoting an arc going from X to Y. We can use this graph to define a relation $X > Y$ if there is a path of arcs from X to Y. This relation is clearly transitive. Because of the acyclicity of the graph, it is also asymmetric. Hence, the relation we have defined is an order. Moreover it is well-founded because of the finiteness and acyclicity of the graph. Consider the program consisting of all the facts of the form $arc(\_, \_)$ and the clauses

```
gt(X,Y)  :- arc(X,Y).
gt(X,Y)  :- arc(X,Z), gt(Z,Y).
```

and the query pattern $gt(f, f)$.

If we resolve the goal $\leftarrow gt(X, Y)$ with the second rule we get

$$\leftarrow arc(X, Z), gt(Z, Y).$$

After one more step of LD-resolution we get $\leftarrow gt(z_0, Y)$, where $\{X \rightarrow x_0, Z \rightarrow z_0\}$ is a substitution that unifies $arc(X, Z)$ with one of the facts of the program. To construct query-mapping pairs we can take as ϕ the identity mapping on the nodes of the acyclic graph with the order defined above. We get the query-mapping pair

	query:	gt(f,f)	[]
(1)	mapping:	gt	
		gt	

(Note, by the way, that in this case the query pattern and the domain are different.) Now we have a new query pattern, $gt(b, f)$, for which we get the pair

	query:	gt(b,f)	[]
(2)	mapping:	gt	
		gt	

These are the only recursive query-mapping pairs in this case (if we were considering all query-mapping pairs, not only the recursive ones, we would also have pairs with predicate gt in the domain and predicate arc in the range). The only circular pair is the second one, and it has an arc from the first argument in the domain to the first argument in the range, so we get that there is termination for the query pattern $gt(f, f)$. Note that this result is not obvious, since for graphs that are not acyclic we could get non-termination of queries matching the query pattern.   □

4   Query-Mapping Pairs Based on Linear Norms

This section explains the theoretical foundations for the implementation of the *TermiLog* system [74,46]. Since our aim is automatic termination analysis, we need a uniform method to create query-mapping pairs associated with a query and program in order to test the sufficient condition of Theorems 3.4 and 3.5. What we need is a uniform way of ordering terms. In our case, the order on terms is defined by means of linear norms.

4.1   Linear Norms and Symbolic Linear Norms

For each ground term we define a *norm,* which is a non-negative integer; note that different terms may have the same norm.

Definition 4.1 (Linear   Norms).   *A   linear   norm   of   a   ground   term* $f(T_1, \ldots T_n)$ *is defined recursively as follows*

$$\|f(T_1, \ldots T_n)\| = c + \sum_{i=1}^{n} a_i \|T_i\|$$

where c and $a_1, \ldots, a_n$ are non-negative integers that depend only on f/n. Note that the definition also applies, as a special case, to constants (which are zero-arity function symbols).

Linear norms generalize earlier norms used in automatic termination analysis. In particular, the list size of [76] and the term size of [78] are special cases of linear norms. Plümer used in his work on termination two restricted cases of linear norms. One corresponds to the case where all the a_i are equal to 1 (in [58], it is called a "linear norm") and the other corresponds to the case where each a_i is chosen to be either 0 or 1 (in [59], it is called a "semi-linear norm").

Since the terms that appear in logic programs are very often nonground, we extend the definition of a linear norm to nonground terms by denoting the norm of a variable X by X itself. Thus, a nonground term has a **Symbolic Linear Norm**, which is a linear expression with non-negative coefficients. For example, if for a function symbol f of arity 3, the a_i and c are all equal to 1, then the symbolic norm of the term $f(X, Y, X)$ is $2X + Y + 1$. We will say that a linear expression is in *normalized form* if each variable appears once in it and also the free coefficient appears at most once. So $2X + 5Y + 2$ is in normalized form, while $X + X + 3Y + 2Y + 1 + 1$ is not.

The idea of associating an integer variable with a logic variable goes back to [78]. In [71] what we call *symbolic norm* for the case of term-size is called *structural term size.* Some authors define the norm of a variable to be 0 and then use the norm only for terms that are *rigid* with respect to it (cf. [59],[25]). In our context it is more convenient to use the symbolic norm. If the symbolic norm of a term is an integer then we know that the term is rigid—its norm is a constant and cannot change by different instantiations of its variables.

Definition 4.2 (Instantiated Enough). A (possibly nonground) term is *instantiated enough* with respect to some linear norm if its symbolic norm is an integer.

Instantiated-enough terms are essentially *rigid* terms in the terminology of [59,25]; that is, terms that cannot change their sizes due to further unifications.

For terms t that are instantiated enough we will take $\phi(t) = \|t\|$. Thus terms that are instantiated enough will be mapped into the well-founded set of the non-negative integers. In this context black nodes will correspond to arguments that are instantiated enough.

As an example for a linear norm, consider the **list-size norm** defined for list terms as

$$\|[H|T]\| = 1 + \|T\|$$

that is, $c = 1$, $a_1 = 0$ and $a_2 = 1$, while for all other functors the norm is 0. In this case, the norm is a positive integer exactly for lists that have a finite positive length, regardless of whether the elements of those lists are ground or not. Thus, all finite lists are instantiated enough with respect to the list-size norm.

Another example is the **term-size norm**. It is defined for a functor f of arity n by setting each a_i to 1 and c to n. According to the term-size norm, a term is instantiated enough only if it is ground.

In our experimentation we found that in most cases the term-size norm is sufficient for showing termination. In some cases the list-size norm is needed. There were only few cases in which a general linear norm was needed. In the version of *TermiLog* on the web [74] it is only possible to use the term-size or list-size norms, while in the full version there also is a possibility for the user to define an appropriate general norm. Note also that the set of queries described by a query pattern depends on the norm, so if we prove termination of $append(b, b, f)$ with the term-size norm this means that there is termination for queries in which the first two arguments are ground, while termination with the list-size norm means that there is termination for queries whose first two arguments are lists of finite length that may contain variables.

4.2   The Weighted Rule Graph

Our first step is to construct from each rule of the program a graph, which extracts all the information about argument norms that is in the rule. This graph will be used in the construction of the query-mapping pairs. The graph will have nodes labeled by the terms that are the arguments of the atoms of the rule. For each term we will compute its symbolic linear norm, which is a linear expression in the variables of the term. As mentioned earlier we use the name of a logic variable to denote its norm. If nodes $N1$ and $N2$ are labeled by terms $T1$ and $T2$ and $\|T1\| = \|T2\|$ we will put in the graph an edge between the nodes. Otherwise we will compute the difference $\|T1\| - \|T2\|$. This difference is a linear expression. If this expression, when put into normalized form, has non-negative coefficients and a positive free coefficient (by "free coefficient" we mean the coefficient that does not precede a variable, say a_0 in $a_0 + a_1 X + a_2 Y$) this means that whenever the numeric variables will get non-negative norm values (when the respective logic variables become instantiated enough through appropriate substitutions) the expression will be a positive number. In this case we will put in the graph a *potential arc*, labeled by the normalized norm difference, from $N1$ to $N2$. We will draw potential arcs as dashed arcs.

It should be explained what potential arcs are. In the termination proof we use the fact that the order induced by the norm on terms that are instantiated enough is well-founded (recall that for such terms the norm is a non-negative integer). Once we know that the nodes connected by a potential arc are instantiated enough, we connect them with an arc. However, we will not do this when we do not know that the arguments are instantiated enough, because we want to be sure that there cannot be an infinite path consisting of arcs. Consider for example the program

```
int(0).
int(s(X)) :- int(X).
```

with the query $int(Y)$ and the term-size norm. From the rule we get the weighted rule graph

$$
\begin{array}{ll}
\text{int} & s(X) \\
 & \;\vdots\,1 \\
\text{int} & X
\end{array}
$$

However, there is an infinite derivation

$$\leftarrow int(Y)$$
$$\{Y \mapsto s(Y1)\}$$
$$\leftarrow int(Y1)$$
$$\{Y1 \mapsto s(Y2)\}$$
$$\leftarrow int(Y2)$$
$$\vdots$$

We now come to the formal definition:

Definition 4.3. *The* weighted rule graph *associated with a rule has as nodes all the argument positions of the atoms in the rule, each labeled by the term filling* *that argument position. Let N1 and N2 be any nodes in the graph, labeled by the terms T1 and T2, respectively. If $\|T1\| = \|T2\|$ then the graph will contain an edge between N1 and N2. If the normalized form of $\|T1\| - \|T2\|$ has non-negative coefficients and a positive free coefficient then the graph will contain a potential arc from N1 to N2 labeled by $\|T1\| - \|T2\|$.*

For example, using the term-size norm, we get for the rule

```
ack(s(M),s(N),A) :- ack(s(M),N,A1), ack(M,A1,A).
```

the weighted rule graph that is shown in the figure. (Note that in order not to clutter the figure, we do not usually show edges and arcs that could be deduced from other edges and arcs.)

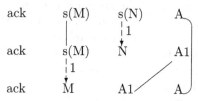

4.3   Generation of Basic Query-Mapping Pairs

To generate basic query-mapping pairs we'll use

- Results of the instantiation analysis (see Subsection 4.6).
- Results of the constraint inference (see Subsection 4.7).
- Weighted rule graphs for the rules of the program.

The instantiation analysis and constraint inference use abstract interpretation to give information about atoms that follow from the program.

Instantiation analysis tells us which instantiations we can expect in atoms that are logical consequences of a program. For instance for the Ackermann program with the term-size norm we get the instantiation patterns

$$ack(ie, ie, ie) \qquad ack(ie, nie, nie)$$

where *ie* denotes an argument that is *instantiated enough* with respect to the norm and *nie* denotes an argument that is *not instantiated enough*. The result of the instantiation analysis is a set of instantiation patterns — atoms with a predicate that is a predicate of the program and arguments that are either *ie* or *nie*. Each atom that follows logically from the program is described by one of these instantiation patterns.

Constraint inference tells us which constraints we can expect in atoms that are logical consequences of a program. For instance for the Ackermann function we get the constraints

$$constraint(ack/3, [gt(3,1), gt(3,2)]) \quad constraint(ack/3, [gt(1,2), gt(3,2)])$$

$$constraint(ack/3, [gt(3,2)])$$

(The notation $gt(i, j)$ means that the i'th argument is greater than the j'th argument.) The constraint inference gives us for each predicate of the program such a disjunction of conjunctive constraints. A conjunctive constraint has the form

$$constraint(pred/ar, list\_of\_argument\_constraints)$$

where *pred* is a predicate of the program, *ar* is its arity, and the List Of Argument Constraints contains basic constraints of the form $gt(i, j)$ or $eq(i, j)$. A disjunctive constraint for a predicate is given by a list of conjunctive constraints for the predicate. Each atom that follows logically from the program satisfies the basic constraints of one of the conjuncts of the disjunctive constraint describing its predicate. Since any atom satisfies the empty list of basic constraints, performing the constraint inference is optional — if we can prove termination without it, it usually is faster. However, there are cases in which it is impossible to prove termination without it. For each example in the tables at the end of the paper one can see whether constraint inference was used in the termination proof by observing if there is a time given in the "Constr" column. One can see that there are more examples for which it was not used. However in a case like **quicksort** we need constraint inference for *partition* to deduce that in the clause

```
quicksort([X|Xs],Ys) :- partition(Xs,X,Littles,Bigs),
                         quicksort(Littles,Ls),
                         quicksort(Bigs,Bs),
                         append(Ls,[X|Bs],Ys).
```

the norms of the local *Littles* and *Bigs* are smaller than the norm of $[X|Xs]$.

In argument mappings we only have edges and arcs and black and white nodes. In the weighted rule graph there is more information — there are weighted arcs and there are labels for the nodes. We want to deduce argument mappings from weighted graphs augmented with information about instantiations and constraints. To do so we need the following.

Definition 4.4 (Zero-Weight and Positive-Weight Paths). *When traversing a path, an edge can be traversed in both directions and its weight is zero. An arc can be traversed only in the direction of the arrow. A weighted arc with a label w can be traversed in both directions; in the direction of the arrow its weight is w and in the opposite direction its weight is $-w$. A path has a positive weight if either*

- *there is at least one arc between adjacent nodes and the normalized expression for the sum of the weights has non-negative coefficients*
  or
- *there is no arc between adjacent nodes but the normalized expression for the sum of the weights has non-negative coefficients and a positive free coefficient.*

A path has zero weight if it only has edges and weighted arcs (but no arcs) and the sum of the weights along the path is zero.

Definition 4.5 (Inferred Edges and Arcs). *Let G be an augmented weighted rule graph. We infer a new edge between nodes u and v if there is a zero-weight path between these nodes. We infer a new potential arc from node u to node v if there is a positive-weight path from u to v. This arc is a real arc if the terms labeling u and v are instantiated enough.*

If we know from the query pattern or the instantiation analysis that a certain node of the weighted rule graph is black, i.e. its label is instantiated enough, we can compute the linear norm of the label and deduce that all variables appearing in the expression for the norm are ground. By propagating this information to other labels it may be possible to deduce that they are also instantiated enough. We call this process **Inference of Black Nodes**. For example, suppose we have the rule

```
p(f(X),g(Y)) :- q(h(X,Y)).
```

and suppose we use the term-size norm. In this case the norms of the terms $f(X), g(Y), h(X, Y)$ are, respectively, $1 + X, 1 + Y, 2 + X + Y$. The weighted rule graph is:

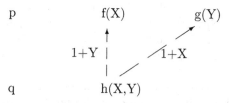

Suppose a query $p(b, b)$ is given. Then we know that X and Y must be ground and can deduce that the argument of q must be ground too, i.e. the corresponding node is black.

Suppose a query pattern Q is given. Take a rule $r : \ H : - \ S_1, \ldots, S_n$ such that the predicate of H is identical to the predicate of Q. We will describe how to *generate* a query pattern corresponding to S_i and, only if the predicates of H and S_i are in the same strongly connected component of the predicate dependency graph, a query-mapping pair corresponding to H and S_i $(1 \leq i \leq n)$. The rule r means: to prove H (that is, find substitutions for its variables so that it follows logically from the program) you have to prove $S_1, \ldots, S_n$. Since we use Prolog's computation rule we proceed from left to right. If we arrive at S_i this means that we have already proved $S_1, \ldots, S_{i-1}$, so we can use for them the results of the instantiation analysis and constraint inference. Sometimes several choices for instantiations or constraints will be possible. We will pursue all of them. So one query may generate several queries and pairs depending on the choices for rule, subgoal and the instantiations and constraints for the subgoals prededing the chosen subgoal. For each new query generated we repeat the process applied to Q.

We now outline in detail the algorithm which creates a complete set of basic query-mapping pairs, so that for each pair of nodes that are direct offspring of each other in an LD-tree for the the given program and a query that matches the query pattern Q, there is a basic query-mapping pair in the set corresponding to it.

Put **BasicPairs**= $\emptyset$, **QueryQueue**= $[Q]$.
While **QueryQueue**$\neq \emptyset$ do
{ Remove a query pattern $Q1$ from **QueryQueue** and repeat for it the following two stage process for every possibility of program rule r, index i of body atom of the rule, possible instantiation pattern and possible conjunctive constraint:
STAGE 1. Augmenting the weighted rule graph:

1. Construct the weighted rule graph G of a rule $r: \ H \ : - \ S_1, \ldots, S_n$ such that H has the same predicate as $Q1$.
2. Blacken the nodes of the head that are instantiated enough according to the query pattern, and add arcs and edges for the constraints that appear in the query pattern.
3. Propagate the information about black nodes to infer, if possible, further black nodes.
4. For each j, $1 \leq j < i$, choose an instantiation pattern, given by the instantiation analysis, that is compatible with the black nodes of S_j in the sense that if an argument in S_j is black then the corresponding argument in the instantiation pattern is ie. If a node of S_j is white and the corresponding argument in the instantiation pattern is ie, blacken that node and propagate the information.
5. In case constraint inference was performed, insert for each S_j, $1 \leq j < i$, edges and potential arcs in accordance with one of the disjuncts of the constraint inferred for its predicate. (Note that if it is possible to prove termination without using the constraint inference, it is usually preferrable to avoid it.)
6. Turn all potential arcs or potential weighted arcs to arcs, respectively weighted arcs, if their endpoints are black, i.e. instantiated enough.
7. Add to G all the inferred edges and arcs between nodes of S_i.
8. If the predicate symbols of H and S_i are in the same strongly connected component of the predicate dependency graph, add to G all the inferred edges and arcs between nodes of H and S_i.

STAGE 2: Getting a new query pattern and possibly a new query-mapping pair from the augmented weighted rule graph:

1. Convert all weighted arcs to arcs by deleting their labels.
2. Delete all nodes except those corresponding to argument positions of H and S_i.
3. Delete labels of nodes, leaving only their being black or white.
4. Delete all edges and arcs except for edges that connect existing nodes and arcs that connect existing black nodes.
5. If the predicates of H and S_i are in the same strongly connected component of the predicate dependency graph put in **BasicPairs** a query-mapping pair

for which the query is $Q1$ and the mapping is given by the nodes of H and S_i and the edges and arcs between them.

6. Generate a new query pattern with the argument positions of S_i and the edges and arcs between them. If this query pattern has not been investigated before, put it in **QueryQueue**.

}

Note that this process must terminate, because there is only a finite number of query patterns that can be formed with the predicate symbols of the program.

Let us return to the Ackermann function program in section 2 and let us use the term-size norm. The query pattern corresponding to `ack(s(0),s(s(0)),A)` is the pattern $ack(b, b, f)$ [] (note that [] denotes the empty constraint list). Using the weighted rule graph for the rule

(ii)   `ack(s(M),0,A) :- ack(M,s(0),A).`

and inserting the information from the query pattern we get the query-mapping pair (a):

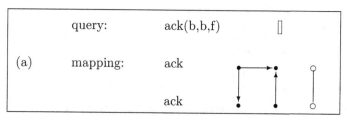

The 'new' query generated in this case is the same as the query we started with.

By the way, this is a circular idempotent pair which satisfies the condition of Theorem 3.4 — there is an arc between the first argument of the domain and the first argument of the range. If the condition had not been satisfied we could have halted — our method would not have been able to prove termination.

If we take the rule

(iii)   `ack(s(M),s(N),A) :- ack(s(M),N,A1), ack(M,A1,A).`

and augment the weighted rule graph on p. 469 with the information from the query, we get:

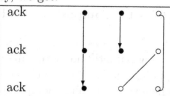

For the first subgoal of the rule we get from this graph the query-maping pair

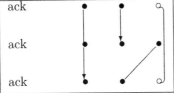

(b)   query: ack(b,b,f)   []

mapping: ack

ack

and no new query is generated.

If we do not use the results of the instantiation analysis, we would get from the graph, for the second subgoal of the rule, a new query $ack(b, f, f)$. For this query we would not have been able to prove termination because it does not terminate. However, if we use the results of the instantiation analysis, we know that there are only two possible instantiation patterns for the predicate ack :

$$ack(ie, ie, ie) \qquad ack(ie, nie, nie)$$

The only pattern that is compatible with the middle row of our graph is the first one. Using this pattern and propagating the information we get the augmented weighted rule graph

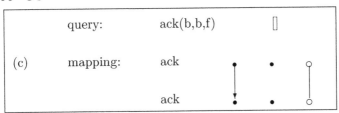

ack

ack

ack

From this graph we get for the second subgoal the old query and the query-mapping pair

(c)   query: ack(b,b,f)   []

mapping: ack

ack

No more queries or basic query-mapping pairs can be generated from the original query pattern. Now we have to use composition in order to get all possible query mapping pairs.

4.4   Creation of All Query-Mapping Pairs by Composition and the Termination Test

Now we have to *compose* the basic query-mapping pairs till no more pairs can be created. Since the number of query-mapping pairs that can be associated with a program is finite this process terminates. Whenever a circular idempotent pair is encountered we check that there is an arc from an argument in the domain to the corresponding argument in the range. If this is not so, we halt — our method cannot prove termination in this case. If all query-mapping pairs have been created, and every circular idempotent pair has an arc from an argument in the domain to the corresponding argument in the range, we know that there is termination.

In our example composition of the pairs (a) and (b) gives a new pair (d):

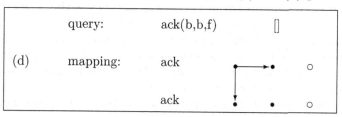

Composing the pairs (a) and (c) gives the pair (e):

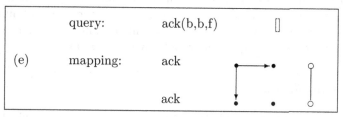

Composing the pairs (b) and (a) gives the pair (f):

No further pairs can be created by composition as the following 'multiplication table' of the pairs shows:

	a	b	c	d	e	f
a	a	d	e	d	e	d
b	f	b	f	f	f	f
c	c	f	c	f	c	f
d	d	d	d	d	d	d
e	e	d	e	d	e	d
f	f	f	f	f	f	f

In this case all the query-mapping pairs are circular and idempotent and satisfy the condition of Theorem 3.4, so we get that there is termination for the query pattern $ack(b, b, f)$.

It should be noted that by the method we outlined of generating basic query-mapping pairs and then composing them till no new pairs can be obtained, we can assign a pair to each call branch. This pair gives a not necessarily complete description of arguments that are instantiated enough and size relations between the norms of these arguments. The pair assigned to a call branch in this case depends not only on the endpoints of the branch (as was the case in the examples in Section 2), but also on the location of the branch in the tree. It is a sound approximation to the relation between the calls at the ends of the branch.

The number of query-mapping pairs that can be formed with the predicate symbols of a program is exponential in their arities, and there are cases in which the number of query-mapping pairs relevant to a program and query is large. The following result about complexity is relevant. In [41] size-change graphs are used to prove termination of functional programs. These graphs are the counterpart of our query-mapping pairs in the simpler context of functional programming, where all the problems connected with instantiation fall away. It is proved there that the analysis is PSPACE hard. However, if the maximal arity of a predicate, the maximal number of different variables in a clause and the maximal number of subgoals in a clause is limited by a relatively small number, we can expect our method to behave reasonably, as illustrated by our experiments.

4.5   Possible Optimizations

The optimization of Theorem 3.5, that only query-mapping pairs in which the predicates of the domain and range belong to the same strongly connected component of the predicate dependency graph need be considered, was implemented in the *TermiLog* system from the beginning.

Another optimization, implemented recently, is the following. Let us define

Definition 4.6 (Weaker Version). *Suppose that two query-mapping pairs P_1 and P_2 have identical queries and identical ranges of the mappings, and that every edge in P_1 is also included in P_2 and every arc in P_1 is also included in P_2. Then we will say that P_1 is a* weaker version *of P_2.*

Suppose that we discover that a query-mapping pair P_1 is a weaker version of a pair P_2. Then the pair P_2 can be discarded, since in the termination proof the weaker P_1 can be used in any place P_2 is used, and if termination can be proved, the edges and arcs of P_1 must be sufficient for the proof.

In the above example of the Ackermann function the basic query-mapping pairs are (a), (b) and (c). The pair (c) is a weaker version of the pair (a), so we need only use composition for the pairs (b) and (c). By composing (b) and (c) we get the pair (f). The pair (f) is a weaker version of the pair (c), so it is enough to consider all the compositions of (b) and (f). This does not give rise to further pairs. Since the pairs (b) and (f) satisfy the condition of Theorem 3.4 we get termination of the query pattern $ack(b, b, f)$.

4.6 Instantiation Analysis

Instantiation analysis of a given program is a preliminary step for our algorithm. We prove termination by using norm inequalities between sufficiently instantiated terms. The method used for the instantiation analysis is abstract interpretation as outlined in [24].

Definition 4.7 (Galois Connection). *Given two partially ordered sets $P^\flat(\preceq^\flat)$ and $P^\sharp(\preceq^\sharp)$ a Galois connection between them is a pair of maps*

$$\alpha : P^\flat \longrightarrow P^\sharp$$

$$\gamma : P^\sharp \longrightarrow P^\flat$$

such that
$$\forall p^\flat \in P^\flat : \forall p^\sharp \in P^\sharp : \quad \alpha(p^\flat) \preceq^\sharp p^\sharp \Longleftrightarrow p^\flat \preceq^\flat \gamma(p^\sharp)$$

Both for the instantiation analysis and the constraint inference we use the following Theorem from [24]:

Theorem 4.1 (Fixpoint Abstraction). *If $P^\flat(\preceq^\flat)$ and $P^\sharp(\preceq^\sharp)$ are complete lattices[6], there is a Galois connection between $P^\flat$ and $P^\sharp$ given by α and γ, and $F^\flat$ is a monotone map from $P^\flat$ to $P^\flat$, then*

$$\alpha(lfp(F^\flat)) \preceq^\sharp lfp(\alpha \circ F^\flat \circ \gamma).$$

Groundness analysis has been handled by several authors (cf. for example [24], [20]). Here we extend the ideas used for groundness analysis to the more general case of being instantiated enough for an arbitrary symbolic norm we have chosen. An argument is instantiated enough if its symbolic norm is an integer.

The usual Herbrand base whose atoms are all ground is not useful in this case and we have to extend it. We define a semantics which is similar, although not identical, to the c-semantics of [34,15]. As extended Herbrand base $\mathcal{B}$ we take all atoms that can be built from the constant, function, and predicate symbols of the program P and variables from an infinite set $\{X1, X2, \ldots\}$. The difference from the s-semantics and c-semantics is that there equivalence classes of atoms modulo variance are taken, while we take atoms with variables from the infinite set. The redundancy does not disturb us, since we are interested in the abstraction, which is finite. We define the immediate consequence operator T_P for any $I \subseteq \mathcal{B}$ in the following way:

$$T_P(I) = \{A \in \mathcal{B} : A \leftarrow A_1, \ldots, A_n \text{ is an instance of a clause in } P$$

$$\text{and } \{A_1, \ldots, A_n\} \subseteq I\}.$$

The least fixed point of T_P consists exactly of those elements of $\mathcal{B}$ that have an SLD-refutation with the identity substitution as computed answer. We shall call

---

[6] A complete lattice is a partially ordered set such that every subset has a least upper bound and a greatest lower bound (cf. [48]).

it $\mathcal{H}(P)$, the minimal extended Herbrand model for the program. Now consider the complete lattice $P^\flat$ of all subsets of $\mathcal{B}$, with the inclusion order. We define a Galois connection between $P^\flat$ and $P^\sharp$, the power set (i.e. the set of subsets) of the set of all atoms whose predicate symbol is one of the predicates of the program, and whose arguments are ie, representing an argument that is instantiated enough for its symbolic norm to be an integer, and nie, representing an argument which is not instantiated enough. (In the case of groundness analysis usually g for $ground$ and ng for $non - ground$ are used instead of our ie and nie.) We define

for a term T

$\quad \alpha(T) = ie \quad$ if the symbolic norm of T is an integer,

$\quad \alpha(T) = nie \quad$ otherwise,

for predicate symbol p

$\quad \alpha(p(T_1, \ldots, T_n)) = p(\alpha T_1, \ldots, \alpha T_n),$

and for a set of atoms S

$\quad \alpha(S) = \{\alpha(s) | s \in S\}.$

For $p^\sharp \in P^\sharp$ we define

$$\gamma(p^\sharp) = \{A \in \mathcal{B} : \alpha(A) \in p^\sharp\},$$

that is, $\gamma(p^\sharp)$ consists of all the atoms in $\mathcal{B}$ that have the instantiation patterns included in $p^\sharp$. These α and γ determine a Galois connection between $P^\flat$ and $P^\sharp$.

T_P is a monotone map from $P^\flat$ to $P^\flat$, hence we get from the Fixpoint Abstraction Theorem that

$$\alpha(\bigcup_{i=1}^{\infty} T_P^i(\emptyset)) \subseteq \bigcup_{i=1}^{\infty} (\alpha \circ T_P \circ \gamma)^i(\emptyset)$$

Since $P^\sharp$ is finite, the right hand side can be computed by a finite number of steps.

Define $T^\sharp = \alpha \circ T_P \circ \gamma$.

Algorithm for the Computation of the least fixed point of $T^\sharp$:

For each clause in the program, supposing it contains n different variables, we create all 2^n instances of substituting ie and nie for each of them. For each instance of a clause we then substitute for the arguments of the predicates ie or nie in accordance to whether or not they are instantiated enough for the norm (this can be decided by replacing the nie's in the clause instance with a variable, and then computing norms—the result should be ie if the computed norm is an integer and nie otherwise). This gives us the clauses of a new program, that has only ground arguments, and hence its success set is finite and can be computed as the least fixed point of the immediate consequence operator. But this is exactly the least fixed point of $T^\sharp$, because the new program describes its action on the atoms of $P^\sharp$.

Consider for example the *append* program

Example 4.1.
```
append([],X,X).
append([H|X],Y,[H|Z]) :- append(X,Y,Z).
```

□

with the term-size norm. A term is instantiated enough with respect to this norm if and only if it is ground. Hence, we use in this example g and ng instead of ie and nie. From the clause

```
append([],Y,Y).
```

we get for the new program

```
append(g,g,g).
append(g,ng,ng).
```

In the clause

```
append([H|X],Y,[H|Z]) :- append(X,Y,Z).
```

we have to substitute all 2^4 possibilities of g and ng for its variables. For instance the substitution

$$H \mapsto ng, \ X \mapsto g, \ Y \mapsto g, \ Z \mapsto g.$$

would give us

```
append([ng|g],g,[ng|g]) :- append(g,g,g).
```

which would give us the rule for $T^\sharp$

```
append(ng,g,ng) :- append(g,g,g).
```

We get

$$T^\sharp(\emptyset) = \{append(g, g, g), append(g, ng, ng)\}$$

$$T^{\sharp^2}(\emptyset) = \{append(g, g, g), append(g,ng,ng), append(ng, g,ng), append(ng,ng,ng)\}$$

$$T^{\sharp^3}(\emptyset) = T^{\sharp^2}(\emptyset) \qquad \bigcup_{i=1}^{\infty} T^{\sharp^i}(\emptyset) = T^{\sharp^2}(\emptyset)$$

On the other hand if we used the list-size norm we would get, for example, from the above rule and the substitution

$$H \mapsto nie, \ X \mapsto ie, \ Y \mapsto ie, \ Z \mapsto ie.$$

the instance

```
append([nie|ie],ie,[nie,ie]) :- append(ie,ie,ie).
```

and hence, since for the list-size norm $\|[H|T]\| = 1 + \|T\|$, the rule

```
append(ie,ie,ie) :- append(ie,ie,ie).
```

In this case

$$T^\sharp(\emptyset) = \{append(ie, ie, ie), append(ie, nie, nie)\}$$

$$\bigcup_{i=1}^{\infty} T^{\sharp^i}(\emptyset) = T^{\sharp^2}(\emptyset) = T^\sharp(\emptyset)$$

It should be noted that in the conclusion of the Fixpoint Abstraction Theorem we have *inclusion*, so this process gives us a superset of instantiations that may occur. To give an example where the inclusion is proper consider the following example:

Example 4.2.
```
p(X) :- g(X), h(X).
g(a).
h(b).
```
□

with the term-size norm. In this case we get the instantiation $p(ie)$ although there is no solution for $p(X)$.

The way we will use the instantiation analysis is as follows. Suppose we use the term-size norm and are given a subgoal to the *append* program with certain bindings, say $append(b, b, f)$, where b denotes a ground argument and f denotes an argument for which we do not know if it is ground. Then we know from the instantiation analysis what bindings cannot result for the arguments of this subgoal if it terminates successfully. For instance in the above case, we can infer that the third argument will become ground, because the only instantiation pattern in which the first two arguments are ground is $append(g, g, g)$.

4.7   The Inference of Constraints

Inference of monotonicity constraints was treated in [16] and inference of inequality constraints was treated in [17]. Monotonicity constraints have the advantage that once an atom is given, there is only a finite number of possibilities for them, but they are weak. Inequality constraints, say something like $\|arg1\| > \|arg2\| + n$ where n is a number, give more information, but there are infinitely many possibilities for them. The algorithm for constraint inference proposed here tries to get the best of both worlds—in the derivation step it uses quantitative norm computations, while its conclusions are formulated as monotonicity constraints. This enables us, for instance, to show termination of **quicksort**.

We again use abstract interpretation, only things are more complicated. $P^\flat = 2^\mathcal{B}$ and T_P are as before. The set $\mathcal{C}$ of abstractions of elements of $\mathcal{B}$ consists of mixed graphs, whose nodes are the argument positions of some predicate in the program and whose edges and arcs form a consistent set of constraints between the nodes. Such graphs can be denoted by a pair consisting of the predicate (with arity) and the list of edges and arcs. An edge connecting the i'th and j'th nodes will be given by $eq(i,j)$ if $i < j$ and by $eq(j,i)$ if $i > j$, and an arc going from the i'th node to the j'th node will be given by $gt(i,j)$ (remember that our arcs go from a node of larger norm to a node of smaller norm). We will call such graphs *conjunctive predicate constraints*.

Consider 2^C, whose elements are sets of conjunctive constraints. An element of 2^C is interpreted as the *disjunction* of the conjunctive constraints of which it consists. For $c_1, c_2 \in 2^C$ define an equivalence $c_1 \sim c_2$ iff the set of all ground atoms that satisfy a constraint in c_1 is equal to the set of all ground atoms that satisfy a constraint in c_2. For instance

$$\{(p/2, [])\} \sim \{(p/2, [gt(2,1)]), \ (p/2, [eq(1,2)]), \ (p/2, [gt(1,2)])\}$$

Let $P^\sharp = 2^C/_\sim$, that is the set of equivalence classes of elements of 2^C. For an element $c \in 2^C$ we denote by $c_\sim$ its equivalence class. As α we take the map that assigns to each atom in $\mathcal{B}$ the unique element in $\mathcal{C}$ that has the constraints that can be inferred for the atom, using the particular symbolic norm we have chosen. Given an atom $A \in \mathcal{B}$ we compute the symbolic norms of its arguments. If the predicate of A is p/n then $\alpha(A)$ will consist of the pair $(p/n, List)$, where List contains elements $eq(i,j)$ $(i < j)$ if the symbolic norm of the i'th argument of A equals the norm of its j'th argument, and contains $gt(i,j)$ if the normalized form of the difference between the norms of the i'th and j'th arguments of A, which is a linear expression in the variables, has non-negative coefficients and the constant term is positive (say something like $1 + X$ or $2 + 6X + 5Y$). Note that we assign to each atom one conjunctive predicate constraint. For instance, with the term-size or list-size norms,

$$\alpha(append([], Y, Y)) = \{(append/3, [eq(2,3)])\}$$

$$\alpha(p([H|X], X, Y, [H|Y], X)) = \{(p/5, [gt(1,2), gt(4,3), gt(1,5), eq(2,5)])\}$$

(We could have chosen another definition of α, which would have assigned to an atom in $\mathcal{B}$ a set of several elements in $\mathcal{C}$.) We extend α to a map from $2^\mathcal{B}$ to $P^\sharp$ in the obvious way.

The order in $P^\flat$ is the inclusion order. In $P^\sharp$ we define the order $p_1^\sharp \preceq^\sharp p_2^\sharp$ iff the set of all ground atoms that satisfy one of the constraints in $p_1^\sharp$ is included in the set of all ground atoms that satisfy one of the constraints in $p_2^\sharp$. For example

$$\{(p/3, [eq(1,2), gt(3,2), gt(3,1)])\}_\sim \ \preceq^\sharp \ \{(p/3, [gt(3,2)])\}_\sim$$

$$\{(p/3, [eq(1,2)]), (p/3, [gt(2,1)])\}_\sim \ \preceq^\sharp \ \{(p/3, [])\}_\sim$$

For $c \in \mathcal{C}$ we define

$$\gamma(c) = \{A \in \mathcal{B} : \{\alpha(A)\} \preceq^\sharp c\}$$

and extend the definition to $P^\sharp$ in the obvious way. It is easy to see that we get a Galois connection and hence, by the Fixpoint Abstraction Theorem, if we define $T^\sharp = \alpha \circ T_P \circ \gamma$,

$$\alpha(lfp(T_P)) \ \preceq^\sharp \ lfp(T^\sharp)$$

Now we will define an operator

$$\tau : 2^{\mathcal{C}}/_{\sim} \longrightarrow 2^{\mathcal{C}}/_{\sim}$$

that approximates $T^{\sharp}$ from above in the sense that for each $I \in P^{\sharp}$ we have $T^{\sharp}(I) \preceq^{\sharp} \tau(I)$.

Definition 4.8 (Inferred Head Constraint). *Given $I \in 2^{\mathcal{C}}$ and a weighted rule graph we insert for the nodes of each body atom in the weighted rule graph the edges and (potential) arcs of one relevant conjunctive constraint from I. With the help of the weighted rule graph we infer the edges and (potential) arcs for the nodes of the head atom. The resulting conjunctive constraint is an inferred head constraint.*

We define

$$\tau(\emptyset) = \{\alpha(F) : F \text{ is a fact of the program}\}$$

For a non-empty set $I \in 2^{\mathcal{C}}$ (actually we are dealing with equivalence classes) we define

$$\tau(I) = I \cup \{c : c \text{ is an inferred head constraint relative to } I$$

$$\text{and the weighted rule graph of some program rule}\}.$$

Since τ is monotone and $\mathcal{C}$ is finite the least fixed point of τ exists and the computation always terminates.

Algorithm for the inference of constraints—computation of the least fixed point of τ:

$$Old\_Constraints = \emptyset$$

$$New\_Generation\_Constraints = \{\alpha(F) \ : \ F \text{ is a fact of the program}\}$$

While $New\_Generation\_Constraints \neq \emptyset$ do

1. Let *Derived* be all those constraints that can be inferred by taking the weighted rule graph for some program rule and inserting constraints for the subgoals according to elements of

$$Old\_Constraints \text{ and } New\_Generation\_Constraints,$$

   taking care that at least one constraint from the latter is used.
2. $Old\_Constraints = Old\_Constraints \bigcup New\_Generation\_Constraints$
3. $New\_Generation\_Constraints = Derived - Old\_Constraints$

Return *Old_Constraints*.

For each $I \in P^{\sharp}$ we have $T^{\sharp}(I) \preceq^{\sharp} \tau(I)$, because by our methods we may not be inferring all the constraints and hence, because the least fixed points exist,

$$lfp(T^{\sharp}) \ \preceq^{\sharp} \ lfp(\tau)$$

To give an example where $T^{\sharp}(I)$ differs from $\tau(I)$ take the *append* program (Example 4.1).

$$\tau(\emptyset) = \{(append/3, [eq(2,3)])\}$$

$$T^{\sharp}(\emptyset) = \{(append/3, [eq(1,2), eq(2,3), eq(1,3)]),$$

$$(append/3, [gt(2,1), gt(3,1), eq(2,3)])\}$$

Using the Fixpoint Abstraction Theorem we get

$$\alpha(lfp(T_P)) \preceq^{\sharp} lfp(T^{\sharp}) \preceq^{\sharp} lfp(\tau)$$

This means that every atom in the success set of the program satisfies at least one of the conjunctive predicate constraints in $lfp(\tau)$.

Consider for example the *append* program (Example 4.1). Then

$$\tau(\emptyset) = \{(append/3, [eq(2,3)])\}$$

The weighted rule graph for the second clause of the program is

Putting for the body nodes (the ones with $append^{(2)}$) the one constraint we got thus far we get the constraint $(append/3, [gt(3,2)])$, so we get

$$\tau^2(\emptyset) = \{(append/3, [eq(2,3)]), (append/3, [gt(3,2)])\}$$

Applying τ to this new set we realize that no new constraint can be derived, so we have found a fixed point for τ. So we have inferred a disjunctive constraint for *append* consisting of two conjunctive constraints.

We found it advantageous to keep track of whether a constraint is obtained just once during the inference or more than once. Consider for example the program **mergesort**.

```
mergesort([],[]).
mergesort([X],[X]).
mergesort([X,Y|Xs],Ys) :- split([X,Y|Xs],X1s,X2s),
       mergesort(X1s,Y1s), mergesort(X2s,Y2s), merge(Y1s,Y2s,Ys).

split([],[],[]).
split([X|Xs],[X|Ys],Zs) :- split(Xs,Zs,Ys).

merge([],Xs,Xs).
merge(Xs,[],Xs).
merge([X|Xs],[Y|Ys],[X|Zs]) :- X=<Y, merge(Xs,[Y|Ys],Zs).
merge([X|Xs],[Y|Ys],[Y|Zs]) :- X>Y, merge([X|Xs],Ys,Zs).
```

If we try to infer constraints for the predicate *split* we get after the first application of $T^\sharp$ to $\emptyset$ the constraint $[eq(2,1), eq(3,1)]$, after a second application the constraint $[eq(2,1), gt(1,3)]$, and for all further applications only the constraint $[gt(1,2), gt(1,3)]$. The disjunction of these three constraints is not sufficient for inferring the termination of **mergesort** by the query-mapping pairs method, while the last constraint by itself is. In this case we can separate by unfolding the predicate **split** into three predicates and obtain the program **mergesort1**,

```
mergesort([],[]).
mergesort([X],[X]).
mergesort([X,Y|Xs],Ys) :- split2([X,Y|Xs],X1s,X2s),
        mergesort(X1s,Y1s), mergesort(X2s,Y2s), merge(Y1s,Y2s,Ys).

split(Xs,Ys,Zs) :- split0(Xs,Ys,Zs).
split(Xs,Ys,Zs) :- split1(Xs,Ys,Zs).
split(Xs,Ys,Zs) :- split2(Xs,Ys,Zs).

split0([],[],[]).
split1([X],[X],[]).
split2([X,Y|Xs],[X|Ys],[Y|Zs]) :- split(Xs,Ys,Zs).

merge([],Xs,Xs).
merge(Xs,[],Xs).
merge([X|Xs],[Y|s],[X|Zs]) :- X=<Y, merge(Xs,[Y|Ys],Zs).
merge([X|Xs],[Y|Ys],[Y|Zs]) :- X>Y, merge([X|Xs],Ys,Zs).
```

for which we can prove termination by the query-mapping pairs method. More details on this unfolding-based technique can be found in [47].

5   The Implementation and Experimental Evaluation

5.1   The Implementation

The *TermiLog* system [46]), is based on the approach outlined in this paper. The version available on the web ([74]) can use the term-size norm and the list-size norm. In the full version (that is an off-line version available on request) it is also possible for the user to define other linear norms. Moreover there is a possibility to handle programs that use modules. First the module is analyzed and the results are put in a file, which is then used when the program calling the module is analyzed. For handling larger programs there is an option of using a 'big version', that infers the subqueries that will be created from the original query by using only the results of the instantiation analysis, and then checking only those subqueries that have a recursive predicate.

Predefined predicates can be handled if their instantiation patterns are supplied to the system (recall that the instantiation patterns depend on the norm). In the current implementation, the instantiation patterns of most predefined predicates are already included in the system. Constraints of predefined predicates may also be included, but this is not necessary. Operator declarations that appear in a given program are asserted as facts of the system.

Control predicates have to be dealt with in a special way, since they are not part of the declarative semantics of logic programs. Cuts are simply ignored. Of course, if the semantics of cut is needed to show termination, then our system will not be able to determine that the given program terminates.

Other control predicates are handled by transforming the given program into a new program that does not have these control predicates, such that if termination can be shown for the new program, then the original program also terminates.

If a negated subgoal appears in a clause, say

```
A :-  B, C, \+D, E,F.
```

then the above clause is replaced with the following two clauses:

```
A :-  B, C, D.
A :-  B, C, E, F.
```

If several negations appear in the same clause, they can be handled by repeated application of the above transformation.

There is one point here that should be taken into account. The clause

```
A :- B, C, D
```

should not be used in the instantiation analysis and constraint inference, since for A to succeed D should fail, that is D cannot provide any bindings.

Disjunction, "if-then" and "if-then-else" are handled in an analogous way.

We will mention just one little example illustrating the usefullness of the system.

Take the following predicate *sublist*, whose intended function is to find whether one list is a sublist of another:

```
sublist(X,Y) :- append(X1,X,X2), append(X2,X3,Y).
append([],X,X).
append([H|X],Y,[H|Z]) :- append(X,Y,Z).
```

This is probably the most natural way to express the *sublist* relation (cf. [77]). However, if the query pattern $sublist(b, b)$ is given, our system will say that there may be non-termination because the first *append* gets the binding $append(f, b, f)$, and indeed a query like $sublist([1], [2, 3])$ does not terminate.

If we switch the subgoals (as it is done in [73])

```
sublist(X,Y) :- append(X2,X3,Y), append(X1,X,X2).
```

our system shows that the query $sublist(b, b)$ terminates.

This example shows how a user who writes a program according to the logic of a problem without thinking about the execution mechanism of Prolog can benefit from our system. This is especially true for predicates that succeed on the first call but go into an infinite loop when backtracked into. Switching the order of the subgoals does not change the logic of the program, but it may, as it does in this example, improve the termination behaviour.

5.2 Comparison with Other Automatic Approaches to Termination Analysis

When our system was developed, the CLP(R) package of SICStus Prolog [68] was not yet available, so the constraints we inferred, within the framework of standard Prolog, were only equality or monotonicity relations between arguments (this is in contrast with later systems like *TerminWeb* and *cTI*, that use CLP(R)). Therefore our system cannot handle the following program from [58]:

```
perm([],[]).
perm(L,[H|T]) :- append(V,[H|U],L),
                 append(V,U,W),
                 perm(W,T).
append([],Y,Y).
append([H|X],Y,[H|Z]) :- append(X,Y,Z).
```

The query $perm(b, f)$ terminates for this program, but our system cannot show termination. To prove termination we need the fact that for *append* the sum of the term-sizes of the first and second arguments equals the term-size of the third.

We can transform the definition of append to a form in which our system, which only infers term-size equality for arguments, will be able to infer the above linear equality:

```
perm([],[]).
perm(L,[H|T]) :- append1(p(V,[H|U]),s(s(L))),
                 append1(p(V,U),s(s(W))),
                 perm(W,T).
append1(p([],Y),s(s(Y))).
append1(p([H|X],Y),s(s([H|Z]))) :- append1(p(X,Y),s(s(Z))).
```

(The functors p and s are used so that, for atoms with predicate *append1* in the success set, the norms of the two arguments will be equal.) For the transformed program, which is clearly equivalent to the original one, our system easily proves termination of $perm(b, f)$.

In [9] argument size relationships are inferred with CLP(R). In *TerminWeb*'s old version (cf. [23]) ideas similar to our query-mapping pairs method are augmented with the analysis of [9], so termination of the example can be proved. It also can be proved with *cTI*.

cTI is a bottom-up constraint-based inference tool for Prolog (cf. [51,50]). This tool is goal independent — it infers sufficient universal left-termination conditions for all the predicates in the given program (the recent implementation of *TerminWeb* does so too — cf. [37]). The new version of *cTI*, that uses the Parma Polyhedra Library (cf. [7]), is very efficient. However, it cannot prove termination for the program *vangelder* with query $q(b, b)$ (see Table 4), which *TermiLog* can do. *cTI* uses the term-size norm only (but as we have seen this is the most useful of the linear norms).

In contrast with the termination inference systems, *TermiLog* is goal directed, and in case it suspects non-termination it produces to the user the circular idempotent query-mapping pair that did not satisfy the termination test, thus showing him which predicate he should suspect.

The constraint based approach [27] is implemented but not publicly available. It starts with a general level mapping and general linear norm and infers the coefficients. This is efficient when it can be done but may run into trouble when there are nested expressions (because then we get products of the coefficients). It cannot handle the program of Ackermann's function (that *TermiLog* can handle) because in that case we need argument-by-argument comparisons instead of weighted sums.

The following two termination analyzers fall in a slightly different category, as both of them impose requirements on the logic programs handled.

TALP ([55]) is a publicly available tool that proves termination of logic programs by transforming them into term-rewriting systems. It requires the program and query to be well-moded. This requirement follows from the fact that term-rewriting systems have a clear distinction between input and output. This strongly differs from logic programs, where the same predicate can be used in different modes.

The compiler of the Mercury programming language contains a termination checker. This is described in [72] and its times are compared to *TermiLog*'s times for the benchmarks in our tables. The Mercury termination checker is usually faster than *TermiLog*, but one must remember that in Mercury the text of the program being checked contains mode informations as part of the language requirements. Another termination checker for Mercury is described in [35].

5.3 Experimental Evaluation

The technique presented here was implemented in the *TermiLog* system [46]. The system has been implemented in SICStus Prolog [68].

The 1996 version of the system has been applied to well over 100 logic programs, some quite long. The detailed experimental results can be found in [43,45]. It should be noted that the times for the system as it was written in 1996 are now an order of magnitude faster because of improvements in computers and in SICStus Prolog.

We now improved the efficiency of the system in two ways:

1. Instead of checking for the presence of a forward positive cycle in circular pairs (as was done in the old version) we now only check for an arc between

corresponding arguments in circular idempotent pairs. It turns out that this not only adds to the efficiency of the system but also to its power (cf. [29]).

2. We implemented the optimization of Section 4.5.

We tested the improved system on the benchmarks we had and the results are reported here. First, classical benchmarks for termination of symbolic computations were studied. Tables 1 and 2 summarise the performance of the system on the programming examples of [5,30], and [58]. Next (Table 3), we applied our technique to study termination of benchmarks that were originally used for study of parallelism in logic programming [18,36,53,19]. Benchmarks in this collection go back to Ramkumar and Kalé [61] (*occur*), Santos-Costa et al. [67] (*zebra*), Tick [75] (*bid*) and Warren (*palin, qplan, warplan*). A complete description of this collection may be found in [53]. Finally (Table 4), we have collected a number of programs from different sources, including Prolog textbooks [1,73] and research papers [2,4,77,83,82]. Termination of most of the examples considered, with clearly indicated exceptions such as *serialize*, was established by using the term-size norm. Note also that there are cases in which we can establish termination of a query pattern both with the term-size norm and the list-size norm. Since being instantiated enough depends on the norm, the kind of queries corresponding to a query pattern will depend in these cases on the norm.

Note that all the benchmarks referred to in the tables are available, in compressed and uncompressed form, on the homepage [42].

In the tables the following abbreviations are used:

- *Ref* denotes a reference to the paper from which the program is taken.
- *F* and *R* denote, respectively, the numbers of facts and rules in the program.
- *Inst, Constr* and *Prs* denote, respectively, the times in seconds for the instantiation analysis, constraint inference and construction of pairs. Since constraint inference is an optional step the corresponding column is often empty, meaning that it has not been applied. Observe that for some examples the time needed to perform the corresponding step of the analysis was too small to be measured exactly. These cases are indicated by 0.00.
- *Pr#* is the number of query-mapping pairs constructed.
- *A* is the answer given by the system. It is either *T*, meaning that queries matching the query pattern terminate, or *N*, meaning that there *may* be queries having this pattern that don't terminate. For *N* we add an indication if there really is non-termination, denoted by *N+*, or if there is termination and the system is not strong enough to see it, denoted by *N−*.
- *Rem* means a remark. For remarks we use the following abbreviations:
  - *..._mod* means the module feature was used for the named file.
  - *after 4.7 transf* in the *mergesort* example means that the transformation outlined at the end of Subsection 4.7 was used.
  - *mem* means that there are memory problems when trying to handle the program.
  - *big* means that we used the version for big programs. If the big version has been used, measurements in the *Constr*-column present time spent on subquery generation and constraint inference.

Table 1. Examples from [5,30]

Program	F R Query	Inst	Constr	Prs	Pr#	A	Rem
		Examples of [5]					
append	1 1 app(b,f,f)	0.00		0.01	1	T	
	app(f,f,b)			0.01	1	T	
curry	1 4 type(b,b,f)	0.03		0.36	15	T	
	general norm: list-size for lists,						
	term-size otherwise						
dc_schema	0 2 dcsolve(b,f)	0.01		0.03	1	T	using *dc_mod*
fold	2 1 fold(b,b,f)	0.00		0.02	1	T	
gtsolve	0 1 gtsolve(b,f)	0.00		0.00	0	T	using *gt_mod*
list	1 1 list(b)	0.00		0.00	1	T	
lte	2 2 goal	0.00		0.01	2	T	
map	2 1 map(b,f)	0.00		0.01	1	T	
member	1 1 member(f,b)	0.00		0.01	1	T	
mergesort	5 4 mergesort(b,f)					N-	
mergesort	5 4 mergesort(b,f)			0.90	9	T	after 4.7 transf
naive_rev	2 2 reverse(b,f)	0.00		0.01	2	T	
ordered	2 1 ordered(b)	0.00		0.01	1	T	
overlap	1 3 overlap(b,b)	0.00		0.01	2	T	
permutation	2 2 perm(b,f)	0.01	0.11			N-	
quicksort	3 4 qs(b,f)	0.01	5.23	5.06	6	T	
select	1 1 select(f,b,f)	0.00		0.01	1	T	
subset	2 2 subset(b,b)	0.00		0.02	2	T	
	subset(f,b)					N+	
sum	1 1 sum(f,b,f)	0.00		0.01	1	T	
	sum(f,f,b)			0.01	1	T	
		Examples of [30]					
append	1 1 append(b,f,f)	0.00		0.01	1	T	
	append(f,f,b)			0.01	1	T	
	append(f,b,f)					N+	
bool	2 4 dis(b)	0.00		0.02	5	T	
	con(b)			0.02	5	T	
duplicate	1 1 duplicate(b,f)	0.00		0.00	1	T	
merge	2 2 merge(b,b,f)	0.00		0.06	3	T	
permute	2 2 permute(b,f)	0.01	0.02	0.01	2	T	
reverse	1 1 reverse(b,f,b)	0.00		0.01	1	T	
sum	1 1 sum(b,b,f)	0.00		0.02	1	T	

- *no rec* means that there is no recursion in the program. Termination can be, therefore, established trivially.
- *cannot* means that it is clear our methods cannot handle the program. For instance, this is the case if the benchmark reads input and, hence, its termination depends on the presence of the end-of-file. Another case is programs that include *assert*.

Table 2. Examples from [58]

Program	Ref	F	R	Query	Inst	Constr	Prs	Pr#	A
append	1.1	1	1	append(b,f,f)	0.00		0.01	1	T
				append(f,f,b)			0.01	1	T
perm	1.2	2	2	perm(b,f)	0.01	0.11			N-
perm_t		2	2	perm(b,f)	0.02	0.03	0.04	3	T
transitivity	2.3.1	2	1	p(f,b)	0.00				N+
1el_list	3.5.6	3	2	p(f)	0.00				N+
append3	4.0.1	1	2	append3(b,b,b,f)	0.01		0.01	1	T
				append3(f,b,b,b)					N+
merge	4.4.3	2	2	merge(b,b,f)	0.00		0.07	3	T
perm_a	4.4.6a	3	2	perm(b,f)	0.00		0.02	2	T
arithmetic	4.5.2	1	4	s(b,f)	0.00				N+
loops	4.5.3a	1	1	p(b)	0.00				N+
	4.5.3b	2	1	goal≡p(X),q(X)	0.00				N+
	4.5.3c	2	1	goal≡p(X),q(X)	0.00				N+
turing	5.2.2	1	6	turing(b,b,b,f)	0.52				N+
quicksort	6.1.1	3	4	qsort(b,f)	0.01	5.38	5.84	6	T
mult	7.2.9	2	2	mult(b,b,f)	0.01		0.02	2	T
reach1	7.6.2a	1	3	reach(b,b,b)	0.01				N+
reach2	7.6.2b	1	3	reach(b,b,b,b)	0.01				N-
reach3	7.6.2c	2	4	reach(b,b,b,b)	0.01	0.09	0.23	6	T
mergesort1	8.2.1	5	4	mergesort(b,f)					N-
mergesort1	8.2.1	5	4	mergesort(b,f)		after 4.7 transf	0.90	9	T
mergesort2	8.2.1a	5	4	mergesort(b,f)	0.02	0.79	0.52	6	T
mergesort_t		6	7	mergesort(b,f)	0.04	0.53	0.15	9	T
minsort	8.3.1	4	6	minsort(b,f)	0.01	0.15			N-
minsort1	8.3.1a	3	6	minsort(b,f)	0.00	0.09	0.11	5	T
evenodd	8.4.1	1	2	even(b)	0.00		0.01	4	T
				odd(b)			0.01	4	T
parser	8.4.2	3	6	e(b,f)	0.00	0.03	0.10	14	T

- *succ* means transformation of integers to successor notation was applied.
- = means that the equalities elimination transformation was used. This transformation performs the unifications given by equalities like $X = Expression$ and thus reduces the number of variables. The *zebra* example shows how useful it can be. In this example the number of variables in the first clause is reduced from 25 to 15, thus speeding up the analysis very much. However, the transformation is not safe, as the following example shows:

```
p(X) :- loop(X), X=a.
loop(b) :- loop(b).
```

Here $p(X)$ does not terminate, while after the transformation it does. In the full system the user can apply this transformation on his own responsibility.

Table 3. Examples from [18]

Prog	F	R	Query	Inst	Constr	Prs	Pr#	A	Rem
aiakl	3	10	init_vars(b,b,f,f)	0.27		24.11	215	T	
ann	101	76	go(b)	84.43				N+	
bid	24	26	bid(b,f,f,f)	0.7		0.37	7	T	
boyer	63	73	tautology(b)	0.23				N-	
browse	4	25	main	2.25				N-	
deriv	2	16	d(b,b,f)	0.03		0.23	1	T	
fib_t	2	4	fib(b,f)	0.00		0.06	4	T	succ
grammar	12	4						T	no rec
hanoiapp_suc	2	2	shanoi(b,b,b,b,f)	0.06		0.72	7	T	succ
mmatrix	7	8	mmultiply(b,b,f)	0.02		0.04	3	T	
			trans_m(b,f)					N+	
money	6	8	money(f,f,f,	0.35	0.93	0.85	2	T	
			f,f,f,f)		0.63+0.02	0.02	2	T	big
occur	3	6	occurall(b,b,f)	0.01		0.06	3	T	
peephole	72	62	popt1(b,f)						mem
progeom	4	14	pds(b,f)	0.08	5.1			N	
qplan	63	85	qplan(b,f)	73.26				N	
qsortapp	3	4	qsort(b,f)	0.01	5.55	4.97	6	T	
query	50	2						T	no rec
rdtok	7	48							cannot
read	15	73							cannot
serialize	5	9	serialize0(b,f)	0.04	2.87	2.64	8	T	

general norm: term-size except
$$\|pair(X,Y)\| = 1 + \|X\|$$

Prog	F	R	Query	Inst	Constr	Prs	Pr#	A	Rem
tak	0	3							cannot
tictactoe	26	43							cannot
warplan	43	55							mem
zebra	14	4	zebra(f,f,f,f,f,f,f)	1440	5.36+0.01	0.02	4	T	big
				0.96	9.57	0.76	2	T	=
					0.68+0.01	0.03	2	T	= and big
zebra.pt	2	3	houses(f)	0.00	0.02	0.03	2	T	

Tests were performed on Intel®Pentium®4 with 1.60GHz CPU and 260Mb memory, running 2.4.20-pre11 Linux, using SICStus Prolog Version 3.10.0.

6   Related Work and Conclusion

In the context of logic languages the ability to program declaratively increases the danger of non-termination. Therefore, termination analysis received considerable attention in logic programming. In our work we have considered universal termination of logic programs with respect to the left-to-right selection rule of

Table 4. Examples from [45]

Program	Ref	F	R	Query	Inst	Constr	Prs	Pr#	A
ack	[73]	1	2	ack(b,b,f)	0.00		0.05	3	T
arit_exp	[82]	0	6	e(b)	0.01		0.05	12	T
associative		1	3	normal_form(b,f)	0.01	0.03	0.02	2	T
general norm: term-size except $\|op(X,Y)\| = 1 + 2\|X\| + \|Y\|$									
blocks	[54]	12	5	tower(b,b,b,f)	0.02	0.13			N+
credit	[73] 21.1/2	33	24	credit(b,f)	0.06		1.12	4	T
deep_rev		1	3	deep(b,f)	0.00		0.07	7	T
game	[4]	0	1	win(b)	0.00		0.01	1	T
				Using *game_mod*					
huffman		2	8	huffman(b,f)	0.12	0.09	0.07	2	T
				code(b,f,f)			0.01	1	T
p	[21]	1	2	p	0.01				N+
pql		2	2	p(b,f)	0.01	0.02	0.21	13	T
				q(b,f)		0.02	0.24	14	T
				q(f,b)			0.17	9	T
				p(f,b)					N+
				q(f,f)					N+
queens	[21]	4	5	queens(b,f)	0.01	0.21	0.38	4	T
sicstus1	[68]	3	4	concatenate(b,f,f)	0.00		0.01	1	T
				concatenate(f,f,b)			0.01	1	T
				member(f,b)			0.01	1	T
				reverse(b,f)			0.03	1	T
				concatenate(f,b,f)					N+
				member(b,f)					N+
				reverse(f,b)					N+
sicstus2	[68]	4	2	descendant(b,b)	0.00				N+
sicstus3	[68]	2	7	put_assoc(b,b,b,f)	0.14		0.61	9	T
				get_assoc(b,b,f)			0.26	8	T
sicstus4	[68]	0	7	d(b,b,f)	0.01		0.18	1	T
sublist	[77]	1	2	sublist(b,b)	0.01				N+
vangelder	[79]	1	10	q(b,b)	0.00		8.92	153	T
yale_s_p	[2]	2	3	holds(b,b)	0.00		0.48	9	T
				holds(f,b)			0.82	18	T
				holds(b,f)					N+

Prolog. Early works on termination made no assumptions on the selection rule, that is, required termination with respect to all possible selection rules [11,2,12]. However, this notion of termination turned out to be very restrictive—the majority of real-world programs turn out to be non-terminating with respect to it. Thus, most of the authors studied termination with respect to some subset of selection rules. The most popular selection rule is left-to-right, as adopted by most of the Prolog implementations. Termination with respect to non-standard selection rules was considered, for instance, in [3,38,57,65,69,70].

Roughly, the existing work on termination analysis proceeded along three important lines: providing necessary and sufficient conditions of termination [27,14], providing sufficient (but not necessary) conditions for termination that can be verified automatically [37,41,52] and proving decidability or undecidability results for special classes of programs [13,33,64]. Our work is clearly situated in the second group: the condition presented in Theorems 3.4 and 3.5 implies termination and can be verified automatically.

While considering sufficient conditions for termination found in the literature one can distinguish between *transformational* [63,6,40,55] and *direct* approaches [23,27,52]. A transformational approach first transforms the logic program into an "equivalent" term-rewrite system (or, in some cases, into an equivalent functional program). Here, equivalence means that, at the very least, the termination of the term-rewrite system should imply the termination of the logic program, for some predefined collection of queries. The approach of Arts [6] is exceptional in the sense that the termination of the logic program is concluded from a weaker property of *single-redex normalisation* of the term-rewrite system. Direct approaches, including our work, do not include such a transformation, but prove the termination directly on the basis of the logic program. Unlike the transformational approaches they usually do not put restrictions on the programs. Another advantage of the direct approaches is that the termination proof can be presented to the user in terms of the original program. In the case of the transformational approach the user does not necessarily understand the language of the transformed object.

The direct approaches can be classified as *local* and *global*. For local approaches termination is implied by the fact that for each loop there exists a decreasing function (cf. [29,22]). Global approaches require the existence of a function that decreases along all possible loops in the program (cf. [27]). Correctness of the local approaches is based on Ramsey's Theorem. Our approach is clearly local. This also means that *TermiLog* can be used not only to prove termination but also to provide a user with the reason why non-termination is suspected.

The query-mapping pairs approach originated in the algorithm of [66]. The original algorithm of [66] was based on an abstraction of a logic program as a datalog program with relations that could be infinite (this type of abstraction was proposed in [60]). The problem with this type of abstraction is that it loses too much valuable information about the original logic program and, in particular, one has to assume that every variable in the head of a rule also appears in the body. In the present approach logic programs are handled directly, so all the information incorporated in them can be used. There are no restrictions whatsoever on the logic programs considered. Moreover, the termination condition in [66,43,44], which was formulated in terms of circular variants with positive forward cycle, is replaced here, with the help of Ramsey's Theorem, by a much simpler condition which gives a stronger termination theorem (cf. [29]).

As far as the power of the approach is concerned one has to remember that termination is undecidable, so one cannot expect too much. It is rather surprising for how many programs the system is applicable. An interesting fact that emerges from the experimentation is that in most cases the use of the the the term-size norm suffices and it is not necessary to use more sophisticated norms. The PSPACE hardness result of [41] applies to *TemiLog*'s analysis. Going over the different parts of the system one can see that if the maximal arity of a predicate, the maximal number of different variables in a clause and the maximal number of subgoals in a clause is limited by a relatively small number, one can expect our method to behave reasonably, as illustrated by the experiments. There are cases in which a linear norm is not sufficient for proving termination. For every linear norm a ground term is instantiated enough. In [29] an example is given of a program such that queries of the form $d(ground, free)$ terminate, but this cannot be proved by any linear norm. There are cases, where the differentiation between arguments that are instantiated enough and those that are not, is not enough. We can use the query-mapping pairs as before with the only difference that we will abstract nodes not to just black and white ones but to a larger, though finite, set. For instance, if we have a program

```
p(1) :- p(1).
p(0).    p(2).
```

and take the term-size norm and a query $p(b)$, the query-mapping pair algorithm will say that there may be non-termination. However, we can use the abstractions $1, g, f$, where g means any ground term that is not 1 and f means any term, and apply the above algorithm, with the only difference being in the unification of the abstractions (both when applying the instantiation pattern of the query and when composing query-mapping pairs). In the present case g and 1 will not unify, so we will be able to prove that $p(g)$ terminates.

Acknowledgements

We are grateful to the referees for their careful reading.

References

1. K. R. Apt. *From Logic Programming to Prolog.* Prentice Hall, 1997.
2. K. R. Apt and M. Bezem. Acyclic Programs. *New Generation Computing*, 9:335-363, 1991.
3. K. R. Apt and I. Luitjes. Verification of logic programs with delay declarations. In V. S. Alagar and M. Nivat, editors, *Algebraic Methodology and software Technology, 4th International Conference*, 1995, *Lecture Notes in Computer Science*, Vol. 936, 66-90, Springer Verlag, 1995.
4. K. R. Apt and D. Pedreschi. Reasoning about Termination of Pure Prolog Programs. *Information and Computation*, 106:109-157, 1993.

5. K. R. Apt and D. Pedreschi. Modular Termination Proofs for Logic and Pure Prolog Programs. In *Advances in Logic Programming Theory*, 183-229, Oxford University Press, 1994.
6. T. Arts. *Automatically proving termination and innermost normalisation of term rewriting systems*. PhD thesis, Universiteit Utrecht, 1997.
7. R. Bagnara, E. Ricci, E. Zaffanella and P. M. Hill. Possibly not closed convex polyhedra and the Parma Polyhedra Library. In *Static Analysis: Proceedings of the 9th International Symposium*, M. V. Hermenegildo and G. Puebla, eds., LNCS, Vol. 2477, 213–229, Springer Verlag, 2002.
8. M. Baudinet. Proving termination properties of Prolog programs: a semantic approach. *Journal of Logic Programming*, 14:1-29, 1992.
9. F. Benoy and A. King. Inferring argument size relationships with CLPR(R). *International Workshop on Logic Program Synthesis and Transformation* (LOPSTR'96), 1996, 204-223.
10. Y. Benyamini and J. Lindenstrauss. *Geometric Nonlinear Functional Analysis, Vol. 1*. AMS Colloquium Publications Vol. 48. Providence, Rhode Island, 2000.
11. M. Bezem. Characterizing termination of logic programs with level mappings. In E. L. Lusk and R.A. Overbeek, editors, *Logic Programming, Proceedings of the North American Conference 1989*, 69-80, MIT Press, 1989.
12. M. Bezem. Strong termination of logic programs. *J. Logic Programming*, 15:79-97, 1993.
13. E. Börger. Unsolvable decision problems for Prolog programs. In E. Börger, ed., *Computation Theory and Logic, Lecture Notes in Computer Science*, Vol. 270, 37-48, Springer Verlag, 1987.
14. A. Bossi, N. Cocco, S. Etalle and S. Rossi. On modular termination proofs of general logic programs. *Theory and Practice of Logic Programming*, 2(3):263-291, 2002.
15. A. Bossi, M. Gabrielli, G. Levi, M. Martelli. The s-semantics approach: theory and Applications. *J. Logic Programming*, 19/20:149-198, 1994.
16. A. Brodsky and Y. Sagiv. Inference of monotonicity constraints in Datalog programs. *Proceedings of the Eighth ACM SIGACT-SIGART-SIGMOD Symposium on Principles of Database Systems*, 1989, 190-199.
17. A. Brodsky and Y. Sagiv. Inference of inequality constraints in logic programs. *Proceedings of the Tenth ACM SIGACT-SIGART-SIGMOD Symposium on Principles of Database Systems*, 1991, 227-240.
18. F. Bueno, M. García de la Banda and M. Hermenegildo. Effectiveness of Global Analysis in Strict Independence-Based Automatic Program Parallelization. *International Symposium on Logic Programming*, 320-336. MIT Press, 1994.
19. M. Codish, M. Bruynooghe, M. J. García de la Banda, and M. V. Hermenegildo. Exploiting Goal Independence in the Analysis of Logic Programs. *Journal of Logic Programming*, 32(3):247–262, 1997.
20. M. Codish and B. Demoen. Analyzing Logic Programs using "Prop"-ositional Logic Programs and a Magic Wand. *Proceedings International Logic Programming Symposium*, Vancouver, 1993.
21. M. Codish and B. Demoen. Collection of benchmarks.
22. M. Codish, S. Genaim, M. Bruynooghe, J. Gallagher and W. Vanhoof. One Loop at a Time. *6th International Workshop on Termination*, 2003.
23. M. Codish and C. Taboch. A semantic basis for termination analysis of logic programs. *Journal of Logic Programming 41*, 1, 103-123.
24. P. Cousot and R. Cousot. Abstract interpretation and application to logic programs. *J. Logic Programming*, 13:103-179, 1992.

25. S. Decorte and D. De Schreye. Automatic Inference of Norms: a Missing Link in Automatic Termination Analysis. *Logic Programming: Proceedings of the 1993 International Symposium*, ed. D. Miller. MIT Press, 1993.

26. S. Decorte and D. De Schreye. Demand-driven and constraint-based automatic left-termination analysis for Logic Programs. *Proceedings of the 1997 International Conference on Logic Programming*. MIT Press, 1997.

27. D. Decorte, D. De Schreye and H. Vandecasteele. Constraint-based termination analysis of logic programs. *ACM TOPLAS*, 21(6):1137-1195, 1999.

28. N. Dershowitz. Orderings for term-rewriting systems. *Theoretical Computer Science*, 17:279-301, 1982.

29. N. Dershowitz, N. Lindenstrauss, Y. Sagiv and A. Serebrenik. A general framework for automatic termination analysis of logic programs. *Applicable Algebra in Engineering, Communication and Computing*, 12, 1-2, 2001.

30. D. De Schreye and S. Decorte. Termination of Logic Programs: the Never-Ending Story. *J. Logic Programming*, 19/20:199-260, 1994.

31. D. De Schreye and A. Serebrenik. Acceptability with general orderings. *Computational Logic. Logic Programming and Beyond. Essays in Honour of Robert A. Kowalski, Part I. Lecture Notes in Computer Science*, Vol. 2407, 187-210, Springer Verlag, 2002.

32. D. De Schreye, K. Verschaetse and M. Bruynooghe. A framework for analyzing the termination of definite logic programs with respect to call patterns. *Proc. of the Int. Conf. on Fifth Generation Computer Systems*, 481-488. IOS Press, 1992.

33. P. Devienne, P. Lebègue and J. C. Routier. Halting problem of one binary Horn clause is undecidable. STACS 93, *Lecture Notes in Computer Science*, Vol. 665, 48-57, Springer Verlag, 1993.

34. M. Falaschi, G. Levi and C. Palamidessi. Declarative modeling of the operational behavior of logic languages. *Theoretical Computer Science*, 69:289-318, 1989.

35. J. Fischer. Termination analysis for Mercury using convex constraints. Master's thesis, University of Melbourne, Department of Computer Science and Software Engineering, 2002.

36. M. J. García de la Banda, K. Mariott, P. Stuckey, and H. Søndergaard. Differential methods in logic programming analysis. *Journal of Logic Programming*, 35(1):1–38, April 1998.

37. S. Genaim and M. Codish. Inferring termination conditions for logic programs using backwards analysis. *Logic for Programming, Artificial Intelligence and Reasoning, 8th International Proceedings, Lecture Notes in Computer Science*, Vol. 2250, 685-694, Springer Verlag, 2001.

38. R. Gori. An abstract interpretation approach to termination of logic programs. *Logic for Programming and Automated Reasoning, 7th International Conference, Springer Lecture Notes in Computer science*, Vol. 1955, 362-380, Springer Verlag, 2000.

39. R. L. Graham. *Rudiments of Ramsey theory*. Number 45 in regional conference series in mathematics. American Mathematical Society,1980.

40. M. Krishna Rao, D. Kapur and R. Shyamansundar. Transformational methology for proving termination of logic programs. *Journal of Logic Programming*, 34:1-41, 1998.

41. C. S. Lee, N. D. Jones and A. M. Ben-Amram. The Size-Change Principle for Program Termination. *ACM Symposium on Principles of Programming Languages 2001*, 81-92.

42. N. Lindenstrauss. Homepage: http://www.cs.huji.ac.il/~naomil/

43. N. Lindenstrauss and Y. Sagiv. Checking Termination of Queries to Logic Programs, 1996. http://www.cs.huji.ac.il/~naomil/
44. N. Lindenstrauss and Y. Sagiv. Automatic Termination Analysis of Logic Programs. In *Proceedings of the 14th International Conference on Logic Programming*, ed. L. Naish, MIT Press, 1997, 63-77.
45. N. Lindenstrauss and Y. Sagiv. Automatic Termination Analysis of Logic Programs — version with Appendix. http://www.cs.huji.ac.il/~naomil/
46. N. Lindenstrauss, Y. Sagiv and A. Serebrenik. *TermiLog*: A System for Checking Termination of Queries to Logic Programs. In *Computer Aided Verification, 9th International Conference*, ed. O. Grumbach, LNCS 1254, 63–77, Springer Verlag, 1997.
47. N. Lindenstrauss, Y. Sagiv and A. Serebrenik. Unfolding the Mystery of *Mergesort*. In *Proceedings of the 7th International Workshop on Logic Program Synthesis and Transformation*, ed. N. Fuchs, LNCS 1463, 206–225, Springer Verlag, 1998.
48. J. W. Lloyd. *Foundations of Logic Programming*. Springer Verlag, second edition, 1987.
49. M. Marchiori. Proving existential termination of normal logic programs. In M. Wirsing and M. Nivat, eds., *Proceedings of the 5th International Conference on Algebraic Methodology and Software Technology, Lecture Notes in Computer Science*, Vol. 1101, 375-390, Springer Verlag, 1996.
50. F. Mesnard and R. Bagnara. cTI: A constraint-based termination inference tool for ISO-Prolog. *TPLP*, to appear, 2004.
51. F. Mesnard and U. Neumerkel. Applying static analysis techniques for inferring termination conditions of logic programs. In *Static Analysis, 8th International Symposium*, LNCS, Vol. 2126, 93–110, Springer Verlag, 2001.
52. F. Mesnard and S. Ruggieri. On proving left termination of constraint logic programs. *ACM Transactions on Computational Logic*, 4(2):207-259, 2003.
53. K. Muthukumar, F. Bueno, M. J. García de la Banda, and M. V. Hermenegildo. Automatic compile-time parallelization of logic programs for restricted, goal level, independent and parallelism. *Journal of Logic Programming*, 38(2):165–218, February 1999.
54. N. J. Nilsson. *Principles of Artificial Intelligence*. Tioga Publishing Company, 1980.
55. E. Ohlebusch, C. Claves and C. Marché. TALP: A tool for the termination analysis of logic programs. *11th International Conference on Rewriting Techniques and Applications, Lecture Notes in Computer Science*, Vol. 1833, 270-273, Springer Verlag, 2000.
56. R. A. O'Keefe. *The Craft of Prolog*. MIT Press, 1990.
57. D. Pedreschi, S. Ruggieri and J.-G. Smaus. Classes of terminating logic programs. *Theory and Practice of Logic Programming*, 2(3):369-418, 2002.
58. L. Plümer. *Termination Proofs for Logic Programs*. Springer Verlag, LNAI 446, 1990.
59. L. Plümer. Automatic Termination Proofs for Prolog Programs Operating on Nonground Terms. In *International Logic Programming Symposium*. MIT Press, 1991.
60. R. Ramakrishnan, F. Bancilhon, and A. Silberschatz. Safety of recursive Horn clauses with infinite relations. In *Proceedings of the ACM SIGACT-SIGMOD-SIGART Symposium on Principles of Database Systems*, 1987.
61. B. Ramkumar and L. V. Kalé. Compiled execution of the reduce-OR process model on multiprocessors. In E. L. Lusk and R. A. Overbeek, editors, *Logic Programming, Proceedings of the North American Conference*, pages 313–331. MIT Press, 1989.

62. F. P. Ramsey. On a Problem of Formal Logic. Proc. of London Math. Soc., 30:264-286, 1928.

63. U. S. Reddy. Transformation of logic programs into functional programs. In *Proceedings of the 1984 International Conference on Logic Programming*, 187–196, IEEE-CS, 1984.

64. S. Ruggieri. Decidability of logic program semantics and application to testing. *Journal of Logic Programming*, 46(1-2):103-137, 2000.

65. S. Ruggieri. ∃-universal termination of logic programs. *Theoretical Computer Science*, 254(1-2):273-296,2001.

66. Y. Sagiv. A termination test for logic programs. In *International Logic Programming Symposium*. MIT Press, 1991.

67. V. Santos Costa, D. H. D. Warren, and R. Yang. Andorra-I: A parallel Prolog system that transparently exploits both And- and Or-parallelism. In *Proceedings of the Third ACM SIGPLAN Symposium on Principles & Practice of Parallel Programming (PPOPP)*, pages 83–93. ACM Press, 1991.

68. *SICStus Prolog User's Manual*. Swedish Institute of Computer Science.

69. J.-G. Smaus. *Modes and Types in Logic Programming*. PhD thesis,University of Kent at Canterbury, 1999.

70. J.-G. Smaus. Proving termination of input-consuming logic programs. In D. De Schreye, ed., *Proceedings of the International Conference on Logic Programming*, pages 335–349. MIT Press, 1999.

71. K. Sohn and A. Van Gelder. Termination Detection in Logic Programs using Argument Sizes. *Proceedings of the Tenth ACM SIGACT-SIGART-SIGMOD Symposium on Principles of Database Systems*, 1991, 216–226.

72. C. Speirs, Z. Somogyi and H. Søndergaard. Termination Analysis for Mercury. In *Proc. of the 1997 Intl. Symp. on Static Analysis*, P. van Hentenrick, ed., LNCS, Vol. 1302, 157–171, Springer Verlag.

73. L. Sterling and E. Shapiro. *The Art of Prolog*. MIT Press, 1986.

74. TermiLog. http://www.cs.huji.ac.il/~naomil/termilog.php

75. E. Tick and C. Banerjee. Performance evaluation of Monaco compiler and runtime kernel. In D. S. Warren, editor, *Logic Programming, Proceedings of the Tenth International Conference on Logic Programming*, pages 757–773, 1993.

76. J. D. Ullman and A. Van Gelder. Efficient tests for top-down termination of logical rules. JACM 35:2(1988), 345-373.

77. M. H. Van Emden. An Interpretation Algorithm for Prolog Programs. In *Implementations of Prolog*, ed. J. A. Campbell, 1984.

78. A. Van Gelder. Deriving constraints among argument sizes in logic programs. *Annals of Mathematics and Artificial Intelligence*, 3:361–392, 1991.

79. A. Van Gelder. Personal communication.

80. T. Vasak and J. Potter. Characterisation of terminating logic programs. In *Proceedings of the 1986 Symposium on Logic Programming*, 140–147, 1986.

81. K. Verschaetse. Static termination analysis for definite Horn clause programs. PhD thesis, Department of Computer Science, K. U. Leuven, Belgium, 1992.

82. K. Verschaetse, S. Decorte, and D. De Schreye. Automatic Termination Analysis. *LOPSTR*, 1992, 168-183.

83. K. Verschaetse and D. De Schreye. Deriving Termination Proofs for Logic Programs, using Abstract Procedures. In *Proc. of the 8th ICLP*, 301-315, 1991.

Herbrand Constraints in HAL

Bart Demoen[1], María García de la Banda[2], Warwick Harvey[2], Kim Marriott[2], David Overton[2], and Peter J. Stuckey[3]

[1] Department of Computer Science, Catholic University Leuven, Belgium
Bart.Demoen@cs.kuleuven.ac.be
[2] School of Computer Science & Software Engineering, Monash University, Australia
{maria,wharvey,marriott,dmo}@mail.csse.monash.edu.au
[3] Department of Computer Science & Software Engineering,
University of Melbourne, Australia
pjs@cs.mu.oz.au

Abstract. Mercury is a logic programming language that is considerably faster than traditional Prolog implementations, but lacks support for full unification. HAL is a new constraint logic programming language specifically designed to support the construction of and experimentation with constraint solvers, and which compiles to Mercury. In this paper we describe the HAL Herbrand constraint solver and show how by using PARMA bindings, rather than the standard WAM representation, we can implement a solver that is compatible with Mercury's term representation. This allows HAL to make use of Mercury's more efficient procedures for handling ground terms, and thus achieve Mercury-like efficiency while supporting full unification. An important feature of HAL is its support for user-extensible dynamic scheduling since this facilitates the creation of propagation-based constraint solvers. We have therefore designed the HAL Herbrand constraint solver to support dynamic scheduling. We provide experiments to illustrate the efficiency of the resulting system, and systematically compare the effect of different declarations such as type, mode and determinism on the resulting code.

1 Introduction

The logic programming language Mercury [11] is considerably faster than traditional Prolog implementations for two main reasons. First, Mercury requires the programmer to provide type, mode and determinism declarations and information from these is used to generate efficient target code. Types allow a compact representation for terms, modes guide reordering of literals and multivariant specialization, and determinism is used to remove the overhead of unnecessary choice point creation. The second main reason for Mercury's efficiency is that variables can only be *ground* (i.e., bound to a ground term) or *new* (i.e., first time seen by the compiler and thus unbound and unaliased). Since neither aliased variables nor partially instantiated structures are allowed, Mercury does not need to support full unification; only assignment, construction, deconstruction and equality testing for ground terms are required. Furthermore, it does not need to

M. Bruynooghe and K.-K. Lau (Eds.): Program Development in CL, LNCS 3049, pp. 499–538, 2004.
© Springer-Verlag Berlin Heidelberg 2004

perform trailing, a technique that allows an execution to continue computation from a previous program state by logging information about prior states during forward computation and using it to restore the states again during backtracking. Trailing usually means recording the state of unbound variables right before they become aliased or bound. Since Mercury's new variables have no run-time representation they do not need to be trailed.

This paper investigates whether it is possible to have Mercury-like efficiency, yet still support true logical variables. In order to do so we describe our experiences with HAL, a new constraint logic programming language that compiles to Mercury so as to leverage from Mercury's sophisticated compilation techniques. Like Mercury, HAL requires the programmer to provide type, mode and determinism declarations. Unlike Mercury, HAL was specifically designed to support the construction of and experimentation with constraint solvers [2].

In particular, HAL includes a built-in Herbrand constraint solver that provides full unification (without the occurs check), thus supporting logical variables. The Herbrand solver uses PARMA bindings [12] rather than the standard variable representation used in the WAM [1,14]. PARMA bindings represent equivalence of variables by keeping all equivalent variables in a cycle, as opposed to WAM bindings which implement a union-find style equivalence class. The use of PARMA bindings allows the solver to use essentially the same term representation for ground terms as does Mercury (see Section 4.4). This is important because it allows the HAL compiler to replace calls to the Herbrand constraint solver by calls to Mercury's more efficient term manipulation routines whenever ground terms are being manipulated.[4]

An important feature of HAL is its use of type classes to distinguish between solver and non-solver types (i.e., types with an associated solver and types without) and for the hierarchical organisation of constraint solvers. Type classes allow a clean separation between a constraint solver's interface and its implementation, thus supporting experimentation with different solvers. We detail how HAL's Herbrand constraint solver fits into this hierarchy.

Another important feature of HAL is its support for user-extensible dynamic scheduling, that is intended to support communication between solvers and construction of efficient propagation-based solvers. We have therefore designed the HAL Herbrand constraint solver to support dynamic scheduling. Here we detail how this has been achieved with a PARMA-binding based solver. Again type classes allow us to distinguish between solvers that support dynamic scheduling and those that do not.

The HAL programmer may specify for a particular constructor type t whether t requires a Herbrand constraint solver (i.e. must support full unification) and, if so, whether this solver should support dynamic scheduling. The HAL compiler will then automatically generate an appropriate instance of the Herbrand solver for t. By requiring that constructor types that need a solver must be specified, HAL can simplify the representation, analysis and compilation of constructors types that do not need a solver.

---

[4] Actually, as long as the term is "sufficiently" instantiated.

The results of our empirical evaluation of HAL and its Herbrand solver are very promising since they show that HAL is capable of using information from type, mode and determinism declarations, as well as information about which types require true constraint solving and dynamic scheduling, to significantly reduce the overhead of Herbrand constraint solving. In particular they show that, with appropriate declarations, HAL is almost as fast as Mercury (the extra overhead is mainly due to support for trailing), yet allows true logical variables. And while without declarations its efficiency is about half that of SICStus Prolog, with declarations it is an order of magnitude faster.

The experiments are also designed to systematically evaluate the effect of each kind of declaration (type, mode, determinism, need to support full-unification and dynamic scheduling) on the efficiency of HAL programs so as to determine where this speedup is coming from. This is possible since, as HAL provides full unification and a "constrained" mode, all versions are legitimate HAL programs. Our results suggest that mode declarations have the most impact on execution speed, while determinism declarations provide only moderate speedup. Also, although type declarations can also provide speedup, the use of polymorphic types can actually lead to slowdown. The overhead of unnecessary support for delay is noticeable but small.

The remainder of the chapter is organized as follows. In Section 2 we first introduce the HAL language by means of a simple example, and then examine the different declarations in some detail. Section 3 provides the general design of HAL's Herbrand solvers in terms of their interface and associated predicates, while Section 4 details their actual implementation. Next, we examine how dynamic scheduling is defined in HAL in Section 5 before detailing how we implement dynamic scheduling for Herbrand solvers in Section 6. We give our empirical evaluation in Section 7, discuss related work in Section 8, and conclude in Section 9.

2   The HAL Language

This section provides a brief overview of the HAL language, concentrating on its support for Herbrand constraints; for more details see [2]. The basic HAL syntax follows the standard Constraint Logic Programming (CLP) syntax, with variables, rules and predicates defined as usual (see, e.g., [10] for an introduction to CLP). The module system in HAL is similar to that of Mercury. A module is defined in a file, it imports the modules it uses and has export annotations on the declarations for the objects that it wishes to be visible to those importing it. Selective importation is also possible.

The core language supports integer, float, character, and string data types plus polymorphic constructor types (such as lists) based on these base types. However, this support is limited to assignment, testing for equality, and construction and deconstruction of ground terms. More sophisticated manipulation is available by importing (or building) a constraint solver for each of the types involved.

As a simple example, the following program is a HAL version of the Towers of Hanoi benchmark which uses difference lists to build the list of moves.

```
:- module hanoi.                                                    (L1)
:- import int.                                                      (L2)

:- export typedef tower    -> (a ; b ; c).                          (L3)
:- export typedef pair(T) -> (T - T).                               (L4)
:- export typedef move     = pair(tower).                           (L5)
:- export typedef list(T) -> ([] ; [T|list(T)]) deriving herbrand.  (L6)

:- export pred hanoi(int,list(move)).                               (L7)
:-         mode hanoi(in ,no) is semidet.                           (L8)
hanoi(N,M) :- hanoi2(N,a,b,c,M-[]).                                 (L9)

:- pred hanoi2(int,tower,tower,tower,pair(list(move))).            (L10)
:- mode hanoi2(in ,in    ,in    ,in    ,oo) is semidet.            (L11)
hanoi2(N,A,B,C,M-Tail) :-
    ( N = 1 ->
        M = [A-C|Tail]
    ;   N > 1,
        N1 is N - 1,
        hanoi2(N1,A,C,B,M-Tail1),
        Tail1 = [A-C|Tail2],
        hanoi2(N1,B,A,C,Tail2-Tail)
    ).
```

The first line $(L1)$ states that the file defines the module hanoi. Line $(L2)$ imports the standard library module int which provides (ground) arithmetic and comparison predicates for the type int. Lines $(L3)$, $(L4)$, $(L5)$ and $(L6)$ define constructor types used in and exported by this module. The type tower gives the names of the towers, pair defines a polymorphic pairing type, move defines a move as a pair of towers using a type equivalence, and list defines polymorphic lists. The type declaration for lists contains the directive deriving herbrand indicating to the HAL compiler to generate an instance of the Herbrand constraint solver for list types.

Line $(L7)$ declares that this module exports the predicate hanoi/2 which has two arguments, an int and a list of moves. This is the *type* declaration for hanoi/2.

Line $(L8)$ is an example of a *mode of usage* declaration. The predicate hanoi/2's first argument has mode in meaning that it will already be ground (i.e., bound to a ground term) when called, the second argument has mode no meaning that it will be new (i.e., never seen before) on calling and old (i.e., possibly "constrained") on return.[5] The second part of the declaration "is semidet" is a determinism statement. It indicates that hanoi/2 either succeeds with ex-

---

[5] We could have given the mode out which means that the list will be ground on return, but HAL's mode checker is not yet powerful enough to confirm this.

actly one answer or fails. In general, predicates may have more than one mode of usage declaration.

The rest of the file contains the rules defining `hanoi/2` and declarations and rules for the auxiliary predicate `hanoi2/5` (here the mode `oo` means the argument is possibly "constrained" on both call and return).

2.1 Declarations

As we can see from the above example, HAL allows programmers to annotate predicate definitions with type, mode, determinism declarations (modelled on those of Mercury). Like Mercury, it also provides purity declarations and type classes. Here we examine these issues in more detail.

Type Declarations: Type declarations detail the representation format of a variable or argument. Types are defined using (polymorphic) regular tree type statements such as those shown in ($L3$)–($L6$). As another example, the statement

```
:- typedef tree(K,I) -> (item(K,I) ; node(tree(K,I),K,tree(K,I)).
```

defines the type constructor `tree/2` for binary keyed tree types with key type K and item type I. The definition states that type constructor `tree/2` has two functors: `item/2`, which represents a leaf node and is used to store an item with its key, and `node/3`, which represents an internal binary tree node and is a used to store a key (for directing the search) and the two subtrees.

Equivalence types are also allowed. For example, the statement

```
:- typedef move = pair(tower).
```

defines the type constructor `move/0` as an equivalent name for type constructor `pair/1` with type constructor `tower/0` as argument. Note that the right-hand side of an equivalence type is only allowed to contain type constructors not functors.

Ad-hoc overloading of predicates and functions is allowed, although the definitions for different type signatures must appear in different modules. For example, in the module `hanoi` the binary function "-" is overloaded and may mean either integer subtraction or difference list pairing. Overloading is important in CLP languages since it allows the programmer to overload the standard arithmetic operators and relations (including equality) for different types, allowing a natural syntax in different constraint domains.

Mode Declarations: Mode declarations specify how execution of a predicate modifies the "instantiation state" of its arguments. A mode is associated with each argument of a predicate and has the form $Inst_1 \to Inst_2$ where $Inst_1$ describes the input instantiation state of the argument and $Inst_2$ describes the output instantiation state. Arguments of unknown structure (i.e., those associated with a variable type) can only have one of the *base* instantiation states:

new, old or ground. We say that program variable X is new if it has not been
seen by its associated constraint solver (if one exists), old if it has, and ground
if X has a known fixed value.

The *base* modes are mappings from one base instantiation to another: we use
two letter codes (oo, no, og, gg, ng) based on the first letter of the instantiation,
e.g. ng is new→ground. The standard modes in and out are synonyms for gg
and ng, respectively.

For terms with known structure, such as a list of moves, more complex instantiation states (lying between old and ground) may be used to describe the
state. An example is

```
:- instdef bound_difflist -> bound(old - old).
```

which defines an instantiation state in which the difference list pair is certainly
constructed, but the elements in the pair may still be unbound variables. Note
that the bound keyword may be dropped from the definition since this is HAL's
default.

Fully understanding the above instantiation definition is more complex than
it may first appear, since this requires combining the instantiation with the type.
This is because the actual meaning of old for a program variable X depends
on whether its constructor type t is a solver-type or not. If t is a solver type,
it indicates that X might be possibly unbound. If it is not, X must be bound.
This applies recursively to all types associated to the arguments of the term to
which X is bound (if any). This allows the base instantiation old to be used as
a shorthand for the most general instantiation state of an initialized (i.e., not
new) program variable.

For example, in the instantiation bound_difflist the base instantiation old
is used for variables with type list(move) (or, equivalently,
list(pair(tower))). Thus, it is actually a shorthand for the instantiation

```
:- instdef old_list_of_move -> ifbound([] ; [old_move|old_list_of_move]).
:- instdef old_move -> bound(old_tower-old_tower).
:- instdef old_tower -> bound(a; b; c).
```

which indicates that a variable with instantiation old_list_of_move may be
unbound (since it is enclosed by the ifbound keyword), but, if bound, it is
either bound to an empty list or to a list with a bound move in the head, and a
tail with the same instantiation state. Note that old means bound for the pair
and tower constructor types since they are not solver types. [6]

It is important to note that HAL does not allow nesting of the base instantiation new within a structure, i.e., all arguments in the structure must already
be either ground or old. As we will see later, this ensures that all subparts of a
data structure properly exist on the heap.

Instantiation declarations can be parametric in their instantiation variables.
For example, the instantiation definition

---

[6] The ifbound form of instantiation definition is not available to the programmer,
and is only generated internally by translation from old. This is because arbitrary
ifbound instantiations are not checkable without sophisticated sharing analysis.

```
:- instdef bound_list(I) -> bound([] ; [ I | bound_list(I) ]).
```

defines lists whose skeleton is fixed, and whose elements have instantiation I.

As we have seen, instantiations in HAL can be quite powerful. However, defining such instantiations can also be laborious, especially since they are often type specific. Fortunately, being able to use old as a shorthand for the most general instantiation state of any type as illustrated above, means the user rarely needs to define such instantiations.

Finally, modes can be defined using statements of the form $Inst_1 \rightarrow Inst_2$ where, as indicated before, $Inst_1$ describes the input instantiation state and $Inst_2$ describes the output instantiation state. Equivalence modes are also allowed. Examples are

```
:- modedef in(I) -> (I -> I).
:- modedef in = in(ground).
:- modedef out(I) -> (new -> I).
:- modedef out = out(ground).
:- modedef new2old_list_of_move = out(old_list_of_move).
```

Note that mode definitions can be parametric, i.e., contain instantiation variables such as I above. This is, however, not the case for predicate mode declarations which cannot contain variables. For more details about mode and instantiations in HAL the reader is referred to [4].

Determinism Declarations: Determinism declarations detail how many answers a predicate may have. HAL uses the Mercury hierarchy: nondet means any number of solutions; multi at least one solution; semidet at most one solution; det exactly one solution. The determinism erroneous indicates a run-time error, while failure indicates the predicate always fails.

Type Class Declarations: HAL also provides type class and class instance declarations based on those of Mercury [7]. Type classes support *constrained* polymorphism by allowing the programmer to write code that relies on parametric types having certain associated predicates and functions. In particular, a class provides a name for a set of types (which are parameters to the type class) for which certain predicates and/or functions (called the *methods*) are defined, and which form its interface.

For example, one of the most important built-in type classes in HAL is

```
:- class eq(T) where [
      pred T = T,
      mode oo = oo is semidet ].
```

which defines types T that support equality testing, i.e., for which an implementation of the method =/2 for mode of usage oo = oo exists. Note however that, like Mercury, all types in HAL have an associated "equality" for modes in=out and `out=in`, which correspond to assignment, construction or deconstruction, and which are implemented using specialised built-in procedures rather than implementation of the more general `=/2` method.

Instances of the `eq/1` class can be specified, for example, by the declaration

```
:- instance eq(pair(T)) <= eq(T) where [
            pred(=/2) is pair_1_SolveEqual ].
```

which declares the type `pair(T)` to be an instance of the `eq/1` type class, as long as T is also an instance of the class, and as long as there exists a predicate called `pair_1_SolveEqual` which appropriately implements the `=/2` method for type `pair(T)`. Most types support testing for equality, the main exception being for types with higher-order subtypes. Therefore, HAL automatically generates instances of `eq/1` (including the predicates implementing the `=/2` method) for all constructor types (such as `pair/1`) which do not contain higher-order subtypes and for which the programmer has not already declared an instance, thus removing this burden from the programmer.

One major motivation for providing type classes in HAL is that they provide a natural way of specifying a constraint solver's interface and allow us to naturally capture the notion of a type having an associated constraint solver: It is a type for which there is a method for initialising variables and a method for defining true equality. Thus, the built-in `solver/1` type class is defined by:

```
:- class solver(T) <= eq(T) where [
            pred init(T),
            mode init(no) is det ].
```

The above declaration indicates that the `solver/1` type class provides initialisation method `init/1`. The class definition also indicates that `solver/1` is a subclass of `eq/1` and, thus, any instance of `solver/1` must also be an instance of `eq/1`. Therefore, for type T to be in the `solver/1` type class, there must exist predicates implementing the methods `init/1` and `=/2` for this type with mode and determinism as shown. The HAL compiler automatically inserts calls to `init/1` to initialize new variables and may generate calls to `=/2` because of normalization.

Purity Declarations: Purity declarations [3] capture whether a predicate is impure (affects or is affected by the computation state), or **pure** (otherwise). By default predicates are pure. Any predicate that uses an impure predicate must have its predicate declaration annotated as either **impure** (so that it is also impure) or **trust pure** (so that even though it uses impure predicates it is considered pure). Calls to pure predicates can be reordered by the HAL compiler during mode analysis but predicate calls are never reordered past an impure predicate call.

Combined Declarations: For predicates with only one mode, HAL, as Mercury, provides syntax for combining all declarations into a single line. For example, lines ($L7$) and ($L8$) in the `hanoi` example can be expressed as

```
:- export pred hanoi(int::in, list(move)::no) is semidet.
```

We will often use this compact form in the sequel.

3   Herbrand Constraint Solvers

Term manipulation is at the core of any logic programming language. As indicated previously, the HAL base language only provides limited operations for dealing with terms, corresponding to those supported by Mercury. If the programmer wishes to make use of more complex constraint solving for terms of some type t, then they must explicitly declare that they wish to use a Herbrand constraint solver for t.

This is achieved by adding the annotation `deriving herbrand` to the type definition. The HAL compiler will then automatically generate a Herbrand constraint solver for that constructor type. In order to do this, the compiler makes use of the following predicates and type classes defined in the system module:

```
:- export pred herbrand_init(T::no) is det.
```

```
:- class herbrand(T) <= solver(T) where [].
```

```
:- export impure pred var(T::oo) <= herbrand(T) is semidet.
:- export impure pred nonvar(T::oo) <= herbrand(T) is semidet.
:- export impure pred ===(T::oo,T::oo) <= herbrand(T) is semidet.
```

The first predicate implements the init/1 method for any Herbrand type declared as instance of the `solver/1` class. The herbrand/1 type class will be used to identify the set of Herbrand types, i.e., the constructor types which support full unification (since every instance of herbrand(T) must also be an instance of solver(T)), and a number of non-logical operations commonly used in Prolog style programming such as var/1, nonvar/1, and ===/2. The last three predicates implement such non-logical operations for any Herbrand type. Predicates nonvar/1 and var/1 can be used to test if a Herbrand variable is bound or not, respectively. Predicate ===/2 succeeds only if both arguments are identical unbound Herbrand variables.[7] Note that we could have included these predicates as methods in the herbrand/1 class instead of simply adding the class constraint herbrand(T) to their predicate type declaration. However, since the implementation of such methods will be identical for all types in the class, that would only complicate matters.

As mentioned before, the HAL compiler automatically generates a Herbrand constraint solver for any constructor type annotated with `deriving herbrand`.

---

[7] ===/2 is analogous to Prolog ==/2 but only succeeds if both arguments are unbound variables. Determining if two non-variable arguments are identical in HAL would require recursively traversing and comparing the sub-terms in the arguments. Hence, every subtype of the term would require the ability to test equivalence. Simply testing if two variables are identical only depends on the topmost type constructor.

In doing this the compiler generates appropriate instances for the `herbrand/1`, `solver/1` and `eq/1` classes. For example, in the `hanoi` module, since the types (`move`, `tower` and `pair`) are only manipulated when bound and, therefore, do not require the full power of unification, these types were not annotated with `deriving herbrand`. On the other hand, since the program uses difference lists, a Herbrand constraint solver is needed for the list type. Hence, the list type is defined as

```
:- typedef list(T) -> ([] ; [T | list(T)]) deriving herbrand.
```

The HAL compiler will then automatically generate the following declarations:

```
:- instance eq(list(T)) <= eq(T) where [
          pred(=/2) is list_1_SolveEqual ].

:- instance solver(list(T)) <= eq(T) where [
          pred(init/1) is system:herbrand_init ].

:- instance herbrand(list(T)) <= eq(T).
```

plus the definition of the predicate `list_1_SolveEqual` which implements unification specialised for the list data type as the general `=/2` method for lists. Exactly how this is done will be discussed in detail in the following section. Note that `herbrand_init/1`, implementing the `init/1` method, is already defined in the `system` module.

The reader might be wondering why there is a need for the programmer to distinguish types for which Herbrand solving is supported from those for which it is not, since one could have simply defined all constructor types as Herbrand types, provided full unification for them, and then relied on the compiler to replace calls to the Herbrand solver by more efficient calls to the term assignment, construction, etc, procedures provided by Mercury. The main reason to separate the types is one of efficiency. The problem is that the compiler is not always capable of detecting whether a more efficient procedure can be used since to do so requires examining reordering of literals. Another reason is that a slightly more compact representation can be used for non-Herbrand terms since there is no need to have a tag for the case where the term is a variable. Separating the types means that these overheads will always be avoided in the case of the far more common non-Herbrand types.

The above decision improves efficiency at the cost of code duplication. For example, since the type of lists with associated Herbrand solving support is different from that of lists without support, HAL needs to provide two library modules, one for each type. Furthermore, terms of one type cannot be unified with those of the other type.

4   Implementing Herbrand Constraint Solving

In this section we describe how Herbrand constraint solvers are implemented in HAL. We start by briefly introducing the WAM and Mercury approaches to term representation and manipulation, as well as describing the PARMA binding scheme of Taylor. Then we show how the PARMA binding scheme is used to implement Herbrand constraint solvers in HAL.

4.1   Term Representation and Manipulation in the WAM

The Warren Abstract Machine (WAM) [14,1] forms the basis of most modern Prolog implementations. Terms are stored on a heap,[8] which is an array of data cells. A cell is usually broken into two parts: a tag and a reference pointer. The most important tag values are REF (a variable reference), ATM (an atomic object, i.e., a non-variable term with arity 0), and STR (a structure, i.e., a non-variable term with one or more arguments). An unbound variable (on the heap) is represented by a cell with a REF tag and a pointer to itself. An atom is represented by a cell with tag ATM and a pointer into the atom table. The structure $f(t_1, \ldots, t_n)$ is represented by a STR tagged pointer to a contiguous sequence of $n+1$ cells. The first cell contains the functor f and the arity n, and the next n cells hold the representations of t_1, ..., t_n. For example, a possible heap representation of the term $f(h(X), Y, a, Z)$ is shown in Figure 1.

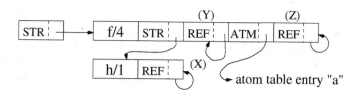

Fig. 1. WAM heap representation of $f(h(X), Y, a, Z)$.

The native representation of base types such as integers and floats (usually) uses the entire cell. WAM implementations either treat them as atoms, wrap them in a special functor, or assign tag values for the types and use the remaining bits to store the data.

Unification of two objects on the heap proceeds as follows. First, both objects are dereferenced. That is, their reference chain is followed until either a non-REF tag or a self reference is found. If at least one of the dereferenced objects is a self reference (i.e. an unbound variable) that object is modified to point to the other object. Otherwise, the tags of the dereferenced objects are checked for equality. In the case of an ATM tag, they are checked to see they have the same atom table entry. In the case of a STR tag, the functor and arity are checked for equality, and, if they are equal, the corresponding arguments are unified.

For example, consider the heap state of Figure 1. If we first unify Y with the heap variable Z and then with another heap variable V, we obtain the heap

---

[8] For simplicity, we ignore stack variables.

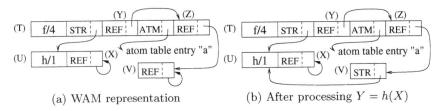

(a) WAM representation   (b) After processing $Y = h(X)$

Fig. 2. WAM term and variable binding schemes

shown in Figure 2(a). If we then unify Y with $h(X)$ we obtain the heap shown in Figure 2(b). Notice how reference chains can exist throughout the heap.

The address of any pointer variable modified by unification is (conditionally) placed in the trail. Since the modified variable is always a self reference, its previous state can be restored from this information alone.

4.2   Term Representation and Manipulation in PARMA

In the PARMA system [12], Taylor introduced a new technique for handling variables that avoided the need for dereferencing (potentially long) chains when checking whether an object is bound or not. A non-aliased non-bound (i.e. free) variable on the heap is still represented as a self-reference as in the WAM. The difference occurs when two free variables are unified. Rather than pointing one at the other, as in the WAM, a cycle of bindings is created. In general n variables which are aliased are represented by n cells forming a cycle. When one of the variables is equated to a non-variable all variables in the cycle are changed to direct (tagged) pointers to this structure and changes are trailed.

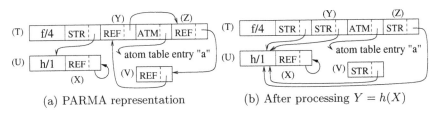

(a) PARMA representation   (b) After processing $Y = h(X)$

Fig. 3. PARMA term and variable binding schemes

For example, the PARMA heap structures corresponding to Figures 2(a) and (b) are shown in Figures 3(a) and (b), respectively.

The PARMA scheme for variable representation has the advantage that dereferencing of bound terms on the heap is never required. However, it has three potential disadvantages:

(a) Checking if two unbound variables are equivalent is more involved, and is required for variable-variable binding. Essentially, each variable's cycle of aliased variables may need to be traversed. Furthermore, trailing of each variable requires two words (the variable's position and its old value).

(b) When instantiating a variable cycle (conditional) trailing must occur for each cell in the cycle (rather than one as for the WAM). Also, as before, the trail requires two words.

(c) When creating a structure that will hold a copy of an already existing unbound variable, the cycle of variables grows, and trailing potentially occurs.

However, the impact of each of these factors is dependent on the length of the cycles that are manipulated. Since, as we shall see, cycles rarely grow beyond length one (a self pointer), the overhead involved is limited, although not completely eliminated (particularly in the case of trailing overhead).

It is important to note that only heap variables can be placed in a variable's alias cycle. An unbound initialized variable on the stack or in a register points into a cycle on the heap. If this cycle is then bound, the stack or register variable becomes a pointer to a bound object. This means that when accessing data through a stack variable or register, the PARMA scheme sometimes requires a single step dereference.

4.3 Term Representation and Manipulation in Mercury

Types in HAL with no solver attached are identical to Mercury types. In this section we explain Mercury's approach to type representation and manipulation.

Recall that variables in Mercury can only be either **new** (which means they do not have a representation) or **ground**. Thus, there is no need for the REF tagged references used in the WAM. This combined with the fact that types are always known at compile time, allows Mercury to use a compact type-specific representation for terms in which tags are used instead to distinguish among the different type functors defined for the type. Hence, an object of a base type, like an integer, is free to use its entire cell to store its value. For more details see [11]. As an example, consider the Mercury type for lists:[9]

```
:- typedef list(T) -> ([] ; [T | list(T)] ).
```

Given a term of type `list(T)` there are only two possibilities for its (top-level) value, it is either nil "`[]`" or cons "`[|]`". Mercury reserves one tag value (NIL) for nil, and one (CONS) for cons. Since the nil reference does not need any further information the pointer part is 0. A cons structure is simply two contiguous cells: the first is a representation of the first element (e.g. a tagged pointer or a 32 bit int) and the second is a reference to the rest of the list.

Assuming 32 bit words and aligned addressing, the low two bits of a pointer are zero. In Mercury these bits are used for storing the tag values, hence four different tags are available. For types with more than four functors, the representation is modified. Since for a constant functor (such as NIL) the remaining part of the cell is unused, the remaining 30 bits can be used to store different

---

[9] For uniformity we use HAL syntax rather than that of Mercury.

constant functors. For types with more non-constant functors than remaining tags, the Mercury representation uses an extra cell to store the identity of the extra functors, much like the WAM representation (although the arity of the functor does not need to be stored since the type information gives this). In what follows, we will ignore this for simplicity.

Mercury performs program normalization, so that only two forms of equations are directly supported: $X = Y$ and $X = f(A_1, \ldots, A_n)$ for each functor f where $A_1, \ldots, A_n$ are distinct variables.

As mentioned before, equations of the form $X = Y$ are only valid in three modes: in = out, out = in, and in = in. For the first two modes, the ground variable is copied into the new. For the third mode a procedure to check that the two terms are identical is called. Mercury automatically generates a specialized procedure (which we shall refer to as unify_gg) that does this for each type.

The equation $X = f(A_1, \ldots, A_n)$ is only valid in two modes: out = in (i.e., X is new and A_1, ..., A_n are all ground) and in = out (i.e., X is ground and each A_1, ..., A_n is new). In the first case a contiguous block of n cells is allocated, the values of A_1, ..., A_n are copied into these cells, and X is set to a pointer to this block with an appropriate tag. In the second case, after testing that X is bound to the appropriate type functor, the values in the contiguous block of n cells that it points to are copied into A_1, ..., A_n. The case where some of A_1, ..., A_n are new and some ground (e.g. A_4) is handled by replacing each such variable in the equation by a new variable (e.g. A_4') and a following equation (e.g. $A_4' = A_4$).

As an example, consider how Mercury will (attempt to) compile the equation, $T = f(h(1), Y, a, Y)$ where Y and T are new. First, it is normalized to give the equations $X = 1, U = h(X), S = a, Z = Y, T = f(U, Y, S, Z)$. The first three equations can be compiled to "construct" variables X, U and S, respectively. The two remaining equations cannot be compiled since they do not satisfy one of the above modes. If later in the goal Y is given a ground value by literal l, then these two equations can be reordered after l and compiled to construct Z and T.

4.4   Term Representation and Manipulation in HAL

Since HAL is compiled into Mercury, it makes considerable sense for HAL to use as far as possible Mercury's basic term manipulation functions even for types that sometimes require full unification. The idea is that, when possible, term equations should be compiled into Mercury's basic term manipulations (assignment, construction, deconstruction, and equality testing) rather than calling the more expensive unification solving method. However for this to be possible, terms in HAL must use a term representation which is compatible with that of Mercury.

HAL employs the PARMA approach to variable binding with the Mercury term representation scheme. The main reason for using the PARMA approach, rather than that of the WAM, is that when a term structure becomes ground in the PARMA scheme it has no reference chains within it. Hence, once it is ground it becomes a legitimate Mercury term. Furthermore, even when a term is only partially bound, the HAL compiler can (mis)use the efficient Mercury operations to manipulate the bound part of the term, since they will still give the desired behaviour. In order to do this, HAL reserves the tag 0 in all Herbrand solver types for use as the REF tag. This means that instead of the four tags generally available for representing a type in Mercury there are only three available for a solver type.

For example, given the type declarations:

```
:- typedef erk -> (f(erk, erk, atm, erk) ; h(erk); g) deriving herbrand.
:- typedef atm -> (a ; b ; c ; d ; e).
```

the HAL representation of the term $T = f(h(X), Y, a, Z)$ is shown in Figure 4.

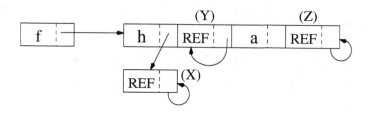

Fig. 4. HAL heap representation of $f(h(X), Y, a, Z)$.

Dereferencing: As in the PARMA system, only heap variables can be placed in a variable's alias cycle. Thus, a stack variable or a register must be a pointer somewhere into the cycle. As a result, when accessing data through a stack variable or register, HAL sometimes requires a single step dereference. Consider the following goal, where all variables are initially **new**:

```
init(Z), X = Z, X = [a], X = [A|B].
```

Figure 5 illustrates the changes to the heap and the registers holding X and Z during the execution of the first 3 atoms in the goal. Note that (due to the way Mercury handles registers) X and Z remain as pointers to the instantiated list rather than being updated to its value (what it points at on the heap). Before the execution of the atom X = [A|B] we must perform a one step dereference so that we can handle the equation simply as a Mercury deconstruct.

HAL produces Mercury code that maintains the assumption that:

- an **old** Herbrand object may need to be dereferenced.
- a **bound** Herbrand object is already dereferenced.

To do so, explicit dereferencing instructions are added to the output Mercury code, that create a new dereferenced version of a variable. Such dereferencing

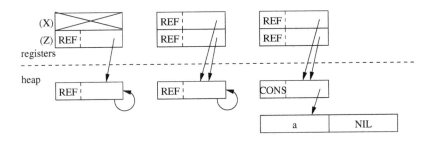

Fig. 5. Register and heap representation for each stage of `init(Z)`, `X=Z`, `X=[a]`.

instructions are only required to be added to the user's code when the compiler detects that the instantiation state of a variable changes from `old` to some bound instantiation. For example, the goal above is translated to Mercury code of the form

```
init(Z), X = Z, X = [a], X_Derefd = deref(X), X_Derefd = [A|B].
```

The `deref` pseudo-C code simply returns the value pointed to by its argument if this is not a variable[10]

```
deref(X) {
    if (derefd_var(X) && !derefd_var(*X)) return *X;
    return X; }
```

The code `derefd_var` to check whether a pointer is a variable pointer is simply

```
derefd_var(X) { return (tag(X) == REF); }
```

The code `var` to check whether an arbitrary `old` term is a variable must do the one step dereference. It is defined as follows:

```
var(X) { return (derefd_var(X) && derefd_var(*X)); }
```

The code for `nonvar` simply uses `var`.

```
nonvar(X) { return !var(X); }
```

Unification: HAL, as Mercury, normalizes programs so that only two forms of equations arise: $X = Y$ and $X = f(A_1, \ldots, A_p)$ (where each A_i is a distinct variable). The compiler translates these equations into calls to appropriate Mercury and C code to implement the PARMA variable scheme as follows.

Consider an equation of the form $X = Y$. For modes `in` = `out`, `out` = `in`, and `in` = `in` we simply call the Mercury's more efficient procedures.[11] If one

---

[10] Importantly the code does not return the next address in a variable chain, but the original address. This will be required later for correctness of dynamic scheduling.

[11] For `in` = `in`, this is correct only if X and Y contain no non-Herbrand solver types. For the purposes of this paper we will ignore this.

of the variables is new and the other one is old, we can simply assign the old variable to the new. This is identical to what Mercury does for this case (with the understanding that old is interpreted as ground) and we can therefore again use Mercury's procedure. When both X and Y are new an initialization init(Y) is added beforehand. The initialization allocates a new cell on the heap, makes it a self-pointer and returns a reference to this cell in Y. This makes Y old and the previous case applies. The (psuedo-C) code for init is simply

```
init(X) { X = top_of_heap++; *X = X; }
```

The only remaining case, where both X and Y are old, requires true unification. We replace the equation with a call to the Herbrand unification procedure unify_oo, which is automatically generated by the HAL compiler for the solver type t of X and Y. A simplified version of the code for unify_oo is shown in Figure 6. In the actual code (which is specialised for each type rather than being polymorphic) the calls to nonvar and deref are folded into one call.

```
:- pred unify_oo(T,T) <= herbrand(T).
:- mode unify_oo(oo,oo) is semidet.
unify_oo(X,Y) :-
    (nonvar(X) ->
        (nonvar(Y) ->
            unify_val_val(deref(X),deref(Y))
        ;   unify_var_val(Y,deref(X)))
    ;   (nonvar(Y) ->
            unify_var_val(X,deref(Y))
        ;   unify_var_var(X,Y))).
```

Fig. 6. HAL code for equating two old objects of type T.

The procedure unify_val_val is similar to Mercury's procedure unify_gg except it calls unify_oo on arguments of unified terms rather than unify_gg. It assumes that its arguments are dereferenced. For example, unify_val_val and unify_gg for list types are shown in Figure 7. In practice the final calls to unify_oo and unify_gg would be specialized since we know they apply to list arguments (and thus we know the name of the predicate which implements the method).

The procedure unify_var_val in Figure 8 unifies a variable and a nonvariable. This means modifying all the variables in the cycle to directly refer to the non-variable, and trailing the changes. The procedure assumes the second argument is dereferenced.

The procedure unify_var_var shown in Figure 9 unifies two variables. This means checking that the variables are not already the same, and then joining the cycles together, trailing the change. Note that, unlike the case for the WAM, the code for unifying two variables is symmetric, treating each variable the same

```
:- pred unify_gg(list(T),list(T)) <= eq(T).
:- mode unify_gg(in,in) is semidet.
unify_gg([],[]).
unify_gg([X|Xs], [Y|Ys]) :-
      unify_gg(X,Y),
      unify_gg(Xs,Ys).

:- instdef nonvar_list -> bound([]; [old|old]).
:- pred unify_val_val(list(T),list(T)) <= eq(T).
:- mode unify_val_val(in(nonvar_list),in(nonvar_list)) is semidet.
unify_val_val([],[]).
unify_val_val([X|Xs], [Y|Ys]) :-
      unify_oo(X,Y),
      unify_oo(Xs,Ys).
```

Fig. 7. HAL code for equating two nonvariable objects of type $list(T)$.

```
unify_var_val(X,Y) {
   QueryX = X;
   repeat
      {  Next = *QueryX;
         trail(QueryX);         /* trail chain pointer */
         *QueryX = Y;           /* replace by value */
         QueryX = Next; }
   until (QueryX == X) }
```

Fig. 8. Pseudo-C code for HAL unification of a variable and value

```
unify_var_var(X,Y) {
   QueryX = *X;
   QueryY = *Y;
   while (QueryX != Y && QueryY != X)    /* while equality not found */
      if (QueryX != X && QueryY != Y) {  /* if loops unfinished */
         QueryX = *QueryX;               /* advance */
         QueryY = *QueryY;
      } else {
         trail(X); trail(Y);             /* else trail X and Y */
         Tmp = *X; *X = *Y; *Y = Tmp;    /* merge chains */
         break; } }                      /* and finish */
```

Fig. 9. Pseudo-C code for HAL unification of two variables

way. Also note that the algorithm traverses the two cycles in parallel stopping when the shortest cycle has been completed.

Processing an equation of the form $X = f(A_1, \ldots, A_p)$ is more complicated since we may have to create objects on the heap. First, let us consider the simple case when X is bound, then the case when X is new, and finally the most complex case: when X is old.

The easiest case for handling an equation of the form $X = f(A_1, \ldots, A_p)$ occurs when X is known to be bound and $A_1, \ldots, A_p$ are new. This is simply left to Mercury. If one (or more) of $A_1, \ldots, A_p$ are not new, they are replaced by new variables and equations as in the Mercury case.

The second case, when X is new, will require the construction of a new structure on the heap. For this to happen, and since arguments within a structure are not allowed to be new in HAL, each variable A_i with instantiation new must first be initialised. If the type of the variable is known at compile time to be a Herbrand type or other solver type, initialisation is not a problem. If, however, the type is known to be neither Herbrand nor any other solver-type, a compile-time error can be issued. Finally, if the type of the variable is not known at compile-time (i.e., it is a variable type), we must call a general initialisation procedure that decides what to call at run-time and can result in a run-time error if the type ends up not being a solver type. This would be simple if one could at run-time check whether a variable has a type which is an instance of certain type class (such as `herbrand/1` or `solver/1`). However, this is not yet possible in Mercury. Thus, in order to support this and other type-related queries, HAL defines the following internal type class:

```
:- class hal_type_info(T) where [
        pred maybe_init(T::no) is det,
        pred is_type_herbrand(T::oo) is semidet,
        pred is_type_solver(T::oo) is semidet].
```

where `maybe_init/1` initialises the variable in the heap if this is needed before performing a construction, `is_type_herbrand` succeeds if the type is Herbrand, and `is_type_solver` succeeds if the type is a non-Herbrand solver-type. HAL will also automatically create an instance of `hal_type_info/1` for every user-defined type t as follows. If t is neither Herbrand nor a solver type, the instance is:

```
:- instance hal_type_info(t) where [
        pred(maybe_init) is error,
        pred(is_type_herbrand) is fail,
        pred(is_type_solver) is fail].
```

where `error` will issue a run-time error, and `fail` will always fails. If t is not a Herbrand but a solver type, the instance is:

```
:- instance hal_type_info(t) where [
        pred(maybe_init) is init,
        pred(is_type_herbrand) is fail,
        pred(is_type_solver) is true].
```

where `init` is the predicate appearing in the `solver(t)` as the implementation of method `init/1`, `true` always succeeds and `fail` always fails. Finally, if t is a Herbrand type, the instance is:

```
:- instance hal_type_info(t) where [
            pred(maybe_init) is dummy_init,
            pred(is_type_herbrand) is true,
            pred(is_type_solver) is fail].
```

where dummy_init does nothing (as we will see, Herbrand variables do not require initialisation before a construction), and true and fail are as before.

Using the above predicates, the construction of term $X = f(A_1, \ldots, A_p)$ can be done as follows. Let us assume that all variables have variable type, variables $A_{o_1}, \ldots, A_{o_m}$ are old while $A_{n_1}, \ldots, A_{n_l}$ are new. Then, the translation to Mercury is essentially:

```
maybe_init(A_{n_1}), ..., maybe_init(A_{n_l}),
X = f(A_1, ..., A_p),
(is_type_herbrand(A_{n_1}) -> A_{n_1} = init_heap(X,n_1 - 1) ; true),
...,
(is_type_herbrand(A_{n_l}) -> A_{n_l} = init_heap(X,n_l - 1) ; true),
(is_type_herbrand(A_{o_1}) -> fix_copy(X,o_1 - 1) ; true),
...,
(is_type_herbrand(A_{o_m}) -> fix_copy(X,o_m - 1) ; true)
```

where the method maybe_init is first used to initialise all non-Herbrand new variables. Once this is done, the construction can be scheduled as a Mercury construct. Then, is_type_herbrand is used to perform a run-time check to see if the actual type of the arguments is a herbrand type and, if so, call specialised code to appropriately initialise the argument. This is done by the $\texttt{init\_heap}(X, i)$ function, which creates a self reference in the ith slot of the heap region pointed to by X and returns it. Note that indices for slots on the heap start from 0 and, therefore, we must use $\texttt{init\_heap}(\texttt{X}, n_j - 1)$ rather than $\texttt{init\_heap}(\texttt{X}, n_j)$. The function is defined as:

```
init_heap(X,i) { return X[i] = &(X[i]); }
```

Note that init_heap is effectively a specialized version of init/1 for the PARMA representation of variables inside data structures.

Finally, each old herbrand argument A_{o_k} was copied by Mercury into the new heap structure. For cases where this simple copy may not have achieved the desired result we need to call $\texttt{fix\_copy}(X, o_k - 1)$. If A_{o_k} was an unbound variable, the copy performed by Mercury results in a reference to the cycle in the o_k^{th} cell rather than the o_k^{th} cell being placed in the cycle. Thus, fix_copy needs to add the o_k^{th} cell into the cycle. If A_{o_k} is bound but not dereferenced (this can happen for stack and register variables), fix_copy must replace the contents of the o_k^{th} cell by what it refers to. The procedure is defined as:

```
fix_copy(X,i) {
    AXi = &(X[i]); Xi = X[i];
    if (derefd_var(Xi))
        if (derefd_var(*Xi)) { trail(Xi); *AXi = *Xi; *Xi = AXi }
        else *AXi = *Xi; }
```

If, as it is usually the case, the types are known at compile time the generated code can be (and is) simplified enormously. Knowing the type allows the run-time type checks to be eliminated and the code simplified appropriately.

For example, consider the construction of $T = f(U, V, S, Z)$ where T and Z are **new**, U is known to be bound (to $h(X)$), S is known to be bound (to a), and V is **old** (and part of a cycle). In this case we know the type of all arguments completely. The generated code is

```
maybe_init(Z),       %% Noop as Z is Herbrand
T = f(U,V,S,Z),      %% Mercury construct
Z = init_heap(T,3),%% initialize Z
fix_copy(T,1)        %% fix V
```

After executing the Mercury construction $T = f(U, V, S, Z)$ the heap is as shown in Figure 10(a). Applying `init_heap(T,3)` and `fix_copy(T,1)` gives the heap shown in Figure 10(b).

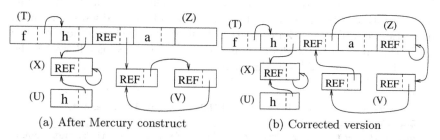

(a) After Mercury construct   (b) Corrected version

Fig. 10. Adapting Mercury's term construction for Herbrand terms

To illustrate polymorphic code, consider the literal $X = [A|Y]$ where both X and Y have type `list(T)`, A has type `T`, X is **new** and both A and Y are **old**. The construction code is shown below:

```
X = [A|Y]                %% Mercury construct
(is_type_herbrand(A) ->  %% if A is a term solver type
     fix_copy(X,0) ; true),  %% fix A
fix_copy(X,1)            %% fix Y
```

The third and final case handles the equation $X = f(A_1, \ldots, A_p)$ when X is **old**. The generated code checks if X is bound in which case it treats the equation as if it were the deconstruction $X = f(B_1, \ldots, B_p)$ followed by equations $A_i = B_i$. Otherwise, X is a variable and the code constructs the term $f(A_1, \ldots, A_p)$ on the heap[12] and then equates X to this term using `unify_var_val`.

Consider again the literal $X = [A|Y]$ where both X and Y have type `list(T)` and A has type `T`, this time with A **new** and both X and Y **old**. The generated code has the form

---

[12] Depending on whether arguments are solver types or not this may not be possible, causing a run-time error.

```
(nonvar(X) ->                          %% deconstruct
      Xd = deref(X),
      Xd = [An|Yn],                    %% Mercury deconstruct
      A = An,                          %% copy operation (A is new)
      unify_oo(Y,Yn)                   %% arbitrary unification
;                                      %% construct
      maybe_init(A),                   %% possible initialization of A
      X = [A|Y],                       %% Mercury construct
      (is_type_herbrand(A) ->          %% if A is a term solver type
            A = init_heap(X,0) ; true), %% fix A
      fix_copy(X,1))                   %% fix Y
```

Again a run-time error can occur if X is a variable, since the call to maybe_init will raise an exception if A does not have a solver type.

4.5   Implementation of herbrand/1 Methods

Supporting the methods in the herbrand type class is straightforward once the representation of terms is decided. We have already defined var/1 and nonvar/1 in Section 4.4. The ===/2 predicate only needs to check whether two variables are in the same reference chain. This can be implemented as follows (cf. the code for unifying two variables in Figure 9).

```
===(X,Y) {
    if (!var(X) || !var(Y)) return FALSE; /* not both vars */
    QueryX = *X; QueryY = *Y;
    while (QueryX != Y && QueryY != X)    /* while equality not found */
        if (QueryX != X && QueryY != Y) { /* if neither loop finished */
            QueryX = *QueryX;             /* advance */
            QueryY = *QueryY;
        } else
            return FALSE;                 /* not identical */
    return TRUE; }
```

5   Dynamic Scheduling

Most modern logic programming languages allow predicates or goals to delay until a particular condition (such as becoming bound or being unified with another variable) is satisfied. Usually they are implemented by hooks in the unification algorithm using attributed variables [6]. SISCtus Prolog provides the ability to suspend a goal until a term is instantiated, ground or two terms are either identical or definitely not identical, and conjunctions and disjunctions of these. ECL^{i}PS^e provides the ability to suspend a goal until a term is bound to a variable or instantiated, and provides a user extensible hook (constrained) which is used to indicate any change made to a variable by a constraint solver. In HAL, dynamic scheduling hooks (we call them delay conditions) are implemented by individual constraint solvers, and are completely extensible.

In the remainder of this section we describe the general dynamic scheduling mechanisms of HAL, and how Herbrand solvers fit into this scheme. In the next section we discuss how this is implemented.

5.1 Dynamic Scheduling in HAL

The HAL language provides a form of more "persistent" dynamic scheduling designed specifically to support constraint solving. A delay construct is of the form

$$cond_1 \texttt{ ==> } goal_1 \mid \cdots \mid cond_n \texttt{ ==> } goal_n$$

where the goal $goal_i$ will be executed *every time* the delay condition $cond_i$ is satisfied. This is useful, for example, if the delay condition is satisfied every time the lower bound of a solver variable has changed. Delayed goals may also contain calls to the special predicate `kill/0`. When this is executed, all delayed goals in the immediate surrounding delay construct are killed; that is, will never be executed again.

The delay construct of HAL is designed to be extensible, so that programmers can build constraint solvers that support delay. In order to do so, one must create an instance of the `delay` type class defined as follows:

```
:- class delay(D,I) <= delay_id(I) where [
        pred delay(D, I, pred),
        mode delay(oo, in, in(pred is semidet)) is semidet ].
:- class delay_id(I) where [
        impure pred get_id(I::out) is det,
        impure pred kill(I::in) is det ].
```

where type I represents the unique identifier (id) of each delay construct, type D represents the supported delay conditions (such as `bound(X)` in the case of the Herbrand solver), `delay/3` takes a delay condition, an id and a goal,[13] and stores the information in order to execute the goal whenever the delay condition holds, `get_id/1` returns an unused id, and `kill/1` causes all goals delayed for the input id to no longer wake up.

The HAL compiler translates each delay construct into the base delay methods provided by the classes as follows. Consider the generic delay construct shown above. This construct is translated into:

$$\texttt{get\_id(Id), delay}(cond_1,\texttt{Id},goal_1'), \ldots, \texttt{delay}(cond_n,\texttt{Id},goal_n')$$

where each call to `kill/0` in $goal_i$ is replaced by a call to `kill(Id)` in $goal_i'$. The separation of the delay type class into two parts allows different solver types

---

[13] To simplify analysis, each $goal_i$ must be **semidet** and may not change the instantiation state of variables. As a result, the possibility of delayed code waking up can be ignored during mode and determinism checking since such code can never change the current instantiation or determinacy.

to share delay ids. Thus, we can build delay constructs which involve conditions belonging to more than one solver as long as they use a common delay id.

As mentioned above, a constraint solver supporting dynamic scheduling must declare an instance of the `delay/2` type class. In order to do so it needs to

- define a type D expressing the kinds of allowable delay conditions;
- define a type I for representing identities (ids) for delay constructs;
- define the predicate `get_id/1` which returns a new unused delay id;
- define the predicate `kill/1` which causes all delaying code with the input delay id to no longer wake up (and hence effectively be removed from the solver); and
- define the predicate `delay/3` which takes a delay condition, delay id and a goal, and stores the information in order to execute the goal when the delay condition holds.

If the programmer uses the annotation `deriving delay` instead of using `deriving herbrand` when defining a constructor type t, the compiler will automatically generate a Herbrand constraint solver for t that supports delay. As we will see later, the reason to distinguish between Herbrand solvers that support delay and those which do not is a matter of efficiency: the implementation of delay for Herbrand solvers introduces an overhead that HAL programmers might wish to avoid when support for dynamic scheduling is not needed.

In order to generate a Herbrand solver that supports delay, the HAL compiler makes use of the following types, classes, instances and predicates defined in the system module:

```
:- export_abstract typedef herbrand_delay_id = int.
:- export typedef delay_cond(T) -> (bound(T) ; touched(T)).

:- export class herbrand_delay(T) <= herbrand(T) where [].
:- export instance delay_id(herbrand_delay_id).
:- export instance delay(delay_cond(T),herbrand_delay_id) <=
                    herbrand_delay(T).

:- export impure pred get_id(herbrand_delay_id).
:-              mode get_id(out) is det.

:- export impure pred kill(herbrand_delay_id).
:-              mode kill(in) is det.

:- export pred delay(delay_cond(T),herbrand_delay_id, pred) <=
                    herbrand_delay(T).
:-        mode delay(oo, in, in(pred is semidet)) is semidet.
```

The module defines the type `herbrand_delay_id` as an integer and abstractly exports it (i.e. the type is visible from outside but its particular definition is not). It also exports the type `delay_cond(T)` which defines the delay conditions supported for a herbrand variable of type T: bound(X) will succeed whenever variable X becomes bound, while touched(X) will succeed whenever variable X becomes bound or aliased to another variable *which also has associated delayed goals*. While the bound(X) condition will succeed at most once, the touched(X) condition may succeed more than once. Note that touched(X) does not wake when X is bound to a variable without any associated delayed goals since such a unification does not change the "meaning" of the constraint store.[14]

The purpose of the herbrand_delay/1 class is simply to record which Herbrand types support delay. The rest of the module exports the instances of classes delay_id/1 and delay/2 which will be used by all Herbrand constraint solvers that support delay, and the predicates which implement the associated methods. All Herbrand solvers which support delay will use the common delay conditions bound(X) and touched(X), the common delay id type herbrand_delay_id, and its system-defined instance of delay_id. Note, however, that herbrand_delay_id can also be used by user-defined solvers.

Based on the above types and classes, the only difference at compile-time between a type defined as deriving herbrand and one defined as deriving delay is that, for the latter, the HAL compiler automatically generates an instance of the herbrand_delay/1 class, in addition to those of herbrand/1, solver/1, and eq/1 classes which are generated for both types.

As an example of the use of delay, the following code shows (part of) a simple Boolean constraint solver which is implemented using Herbrand constraint solving.

```
:- export typedef boolv -> ( f ; t ) deriving delay.
:- export pred and(boolv::oo,boolv::oo,boolv::oo) is semidet.
and(X,Y,Z) :-
  ( bound(X) ==> kill, (X = f -> Z = f ; Y = Z)
  | bound(Y) ==> kill, (Y = f -> Z = f ; X = Z)
  | bound(Z) ==> kill, (Z = t -> X = t, Y = t ; notboth(X,Y))).
:- export trust pure pred notboth(boolv::oo,boolv::oo) is semidet.
notboth(X,Y) :-
  ( bound(X) ==> kill, (X = t -> Y = f ; true)
  | bound(Y) ==> kill, (Y = t -> X = f ; true)
  | touched(X) ==> (X === Y -> kill, X = f ; true)
  | touched(Y) ==> (X === Y -> kill, X = f ; true)).
```

The constructor type boolv is used to represent Booleans. Since the type is defined as deriving delay, the compiler will automatically generate instances of the classes herbrand_delay/1, herbrand/1, solver/1 and eq/1. Thus old variables of this type are allowed and represent unknown Boolean values.

The Boolean constraint solver defines two constraints: and(X,Y,Z) which implements the formula $X \wedge Y \leftrightarrow Z$, and notboth(X,Y), which implements the formula $\neg X \vee \neg Y$. Both constraints are defined using dynamic scheduled code. The code for and(X,Y,Z) delays until one of its arguments is bound (which for

---

[14] This is analogous to the case of unifying an attributed variable to a non-attributed variable.

this type is equivalent to ground), and then executes once (it is immediately killed on wake up). If either X or Y is bound the constraint is solved. If Z is bound to f the constraint notboth(X,Y) is created. Note that we could also have made use of touched delay conditions in the definition of and.

The code for notboth(X,Y) delays until either X or Y is bound in which case the constraint is enforced, or if X or Y is touched (bound or unified with a different variable which also has delayed code). In the second case if X and Y are identical (===), the delay construct is killed and both are set to *false* (the only way to satisfy the constraint), otherwise the construct remains. This illustrates how delayed code can be executed multiple times. Note that notboth/2 uses the impure predicate "===," however, since the actions of notboth as seen from the outside are pure, we use a trust pure declaration for the constraint.

To illustrate how dynamic scheduling works, consider the execution of goal:

```
and(A,B,C), and(A,C,D), and(A,E,F), D = f, C = G, A = E, B = t.
```

where all variables are assumed to have just been initialised. Initially all three and constraints delay. When the constraint D = f is executed, and(A,C,D) wakes up, kills its delay construct and calls notboth(A,C) which delays. When C = G is executed, no delayed goal wakes up since there is nothing delaying on G. When A = E is executed, notboth(A,C) wakes (since A is touched) but since A === C fails the wake up does nothing. Executing B = t wakes and(A,B,C), kills its delay construct and adds the constraint A = C. This wakes notboth(A,C) since it causes a touched event on A (and C), finds that they are identical, kills its delay construct and sets both A (and C through the equality) to f. This wakes and(A,E,F) which kills its delay construct and sets F to f. The solution gives $A = C = D = E = F = G = f$ and $B = t$.

Currently HAL only supports simple delay conditions, rather than conjunctions or disjunctions of delay conditions. For example, it would be convenient to replace the last two lines of constraint notboth(X,Y) by the single line

```
(touched(X);touched(Y)) ==> (X === Y -> kill, X = f ; true)
```

These more complex delay conditions are not directly supported by HAL yet, but can be implemented by straightforward program transformation.

6   Implementing Dynamic Scheduling

In this section we begin by discussing the usual approach to implementing dynamic scheduling for Herbrand constraints in the WAM, and then consider how it is implemented in HAL.

6.1   Implementing Dynamic Scheduling in the WAM

Most Prolog systems, including SICStus Prolog and ECL^{i}PS^e, support dynamic scheduling based on Herbrand constraint solving using attributed variables [6]. For simplicity we shall illustrate the delay mechanism assuming a single (delay)

attribute, and only explain waking up when a variable is bound to a non-variable using the builtin `freeze` which corresponds to the delay condition **bound**. See also the section on Attributed Variables in [5] for a more detailed explanation.

Essentially a new kind of variable is introduced, which we will represent using the tag ATT. An attributed variable is stored in two contiguous data cells. The first cell acts like a variable, while the second cell is used to store the attributes of the variable, which for our purposes is a list of goals to be executed when the variable is bound to a non-variable.

The goal `freeze(X,G)` thus creates a new attributed variable Y with attribute [G], and then unifies it with X.

Unification is extended to deal with attributed variables as follows. When an attributed variable X is unified with a non-variable term, then all the delayed goals in the delay attribute of X are executed. If an attributed variable X is unified with another attributed variable Y, then the two lists of delayed goals are concatenated, and the resulting list replaces that of the variable which will be pointed at after unification.

For example, consider the goal

```
G = write(X), freeze(X,G), H = write(g(Y)), freeze(Y,H), X = Y, X = f(Z).
```

After the first four literals are executed, the heap holds the two attributed variables X and Y with their delayed goals, as shown on the left of Figure 11. During the unification of X and Y the two lists are appended replacing the attribute of Y, and X is pointed at Y, resulting in the heap state in the middle of Figure 11. When X is bound to `f(Z)` it is first dereferenced to obtain Y, the goal list [G,H] is remembered for execution, and Y pointed to `f(Z)`. The heap state is now as in the right of Figure 11. The delayed goals are then executed, causing `f(Z)g(f(Z))` to be printed (although the other order `g(f(Z))f(Z)` is equally probable in practice).

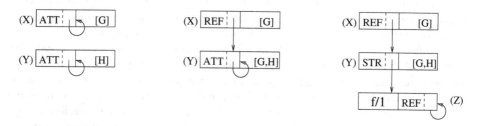

Fig. 11. WAM heap representation for dynamically scheduled goals and after executing each literal X = Y, X = f(Z).

Prolog systems typically include a global register for holding all the delayed goals scheduled. The goals in this register are executed only at certain points in the code, typically just before a predicate call is made.

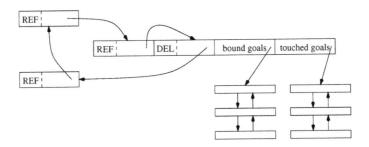

Fig. 12. A delay node within an alias cycle.

6.2   Implementing Dynamic Scheduling in HAL

As we saw in Section 5.1, each delay construct is converted by the compiler to a more low-level set of delay primitives: get_id/1, kill/1 and delay/3. In the following subsections we will explain how the procedures get_id/1, kill/1 and delay/3 are implemented for Herbrand solvers.

6.3   Storing Dynamically Scheduled Goals

Herbrand delay conditions bound(X) and touched(X) are associated with variable X by placing an entry in the alias cycle associated with X. Since each entry in the alias cycle must be a variable, they all have a variable tag (REF). Thus, we can use any other tag (which is already used by the type) to represent a delay node (DEL). We use tag 1.

A delay node is stored as four consecutive heap cells as shown in Figure 12. These four components are: a dummy variable node which points to the next component, the DEL tagged delay node pointing to the next variable in the alias chain, a pointer to the doubly linked list of goals to be woken on a bound event, and a pointer to the doubly linked list of goals to be woken on a touched event. The system maintains at most one delay node in any alias cycle. The apparently unnecessary extra (dummy) variable node allows us to ensure that we never encounter the DEL tagged node in a context where it might be confused with the usual functor that uses tag 1. In particular, fix_copy performs a one step dereference on things which appear to be variables; we need to make sure it doesn't encounter a delay node at that point or it will mistake it for a bound term. Note that this also means that we should take care when dereferencing a variable, since if we store the resultant address we may have a direct pointer to the dummy node, which if dereferenced will incorrectly appear to be a bound term.

Adding a dynamically scheduled goal to the alias cycle is straightforward. We search the alias cycle for a delay node; if there isn't one we create a new empty one and place it in the cycle. We then add the goal to the appropriate doubly linked list of goals (depending on the delay condition). Note that if the variable is already bound, then the goal is simply executed immediately.

6.4   Modifying Unification for Delay

For `herbrand_delay` types we need to modify the code for manipulating variables in order to recognize when a delay condition has been satisfied. When unifying an alias cycle with a structure we know that both `bound(X)` and `touched(X)` for any variable X in the chain is satisfied. Thus, we need to adjust the `unify_var_val/2` algorithm to detect whether a delay node appears in the chain and, if so, execute both lists of delayed goals. The code is shown in Figure 13 (cf. the original code in Figure 8). If we detect that the next item in the chain has a DEL tag then we are currently looking at the dummy variable in the chain, and the next element is the delay node. We record this and skip past the delay node. Otherwise we proceed as usual. If after traversing the chain we have detected a delay node, we execute both lists of delayed goals.

```
unify_var_val(X,Y) {
    QueryX = X;
    DelayNode = null;
    repeat {
        Next = *QueryX;
        if (tag(*Next) != REF) {          /* Found delay node */
            DelayNode = Next;              /* save in DelayNode */
            QueryX = (strip_tag(*Next));   /* continue */
        } else {
            trail(QueryX);
            *QueryX = Y;
            QueryX = Next;
        } }
    until (QueryX == X)
    if (DelayedNode) {
        execute_delayed_goals(*(DelayNode+1)); /* execute bound goals */
        execute_delayed_goals(*(DelayNode+2)); /* execute touched goals */
    } }
```

Fig. 13. Pseudo-C code for HAL unification of a variable and value supporting delay

Unifying two alias cycles is more complex, as shown in Figure 14. If only one variable chain contains a delay node, we proceed as in Figure 9. If both contain a delay node, then we need to merge their delay nodes, and also wake up goals with a touched delay condition. Note that we have to be careful not to insert an extra node in between the first two elements (the cycle elements) of a delay node.

If the variables are the same we immediately return, otherwise we look through the X cycle until we either find Y (in which case we return), or find a delay node, or complete the cycle. We then look through the Y cycle until we either find X, in which case we return, or find a delay node or complete the

```
unify_var_var(X,Y) {
  if (X == Y) return;                    /* shortcut return */
  QueryX = X;
  DelayNodeX = null;
  repeat {                               /* search for delay node in X */
    NextX = *QueryX;
    if (NextX == Y) return;              /* shortcut return */
    if (tag(*NextX) != REF) {            /* found delay node */
      DelayNodeX = NextX;
      break; }
    QueryX = NextX; }
  until (QueryX == X);
  if (DelayNodeX == null) {              /* no delay in X, just unify */
    NextY = *Y;                          /* search for insert place */
    if (tag(*NextY) != REF) {            /* found delay node */
      DelayNodeY = NextY;
      trail(X); trail(DelayNodeY);       /* add X to cycle for Y */
      Tmp = strip_tag(*DelayNodeY);      /* after Ys delay node */
      *DelayNodeY = add_tag(DEL,*X);
      *X = Tmp;
    } else {                             /* otherwise Y not dummy node */
      trail(X); trail(Y);
      Tmp = *X; *X = *Y; *Y = Tmp; }
    return; }
  QueryY = Y;
  DelayNodeY = null;
  repeat {                               /* search for delay node in Y */
    NextY = *QueryY;
    if (NextY == X) return;              /* shortcut return */
    if (tag(*NextY) != REF) {            /* found delay node */
      DelayNodeY = NextY;
      break; }
    QueryY = NextY; }
  until (QueryY == Y);
  if (DelayNodeY == null) {              /* add Y to cycle for X */
    trail(Y); trail(DelayNodeX);         /* after Xs delay node */
    Tmp = strip_tag(*DelayNodeX);
    *DelayNodeX = add_tag(DEL,*Y);
    *Y = Tmp;
  } else if (DelayNodeY == DelayNodeX)   /* same variable */
    return;
  else {
    merge_delay_goals(DelayNodeX, DelayNodeY); /* merge into X delay */
    trail(QueryY); trail(DelayNodeX);
    *QueryY = strip_tag(*DelayNodeX);
    *DelayNodeX = *DelayNodeY;
    execute_delayed_goals(*(DelayNodeX+2)); /* execute touched goals */
  } }
```

Fig. 14. Pseudo-C code for HAL unification of two variables supporting delay

cycle. If we found no delay nodes, we proceed as before. If we find one delay node, we insert the other chain just after the delay node. If we find two delay nodes, we merge the lists of delayed goals into the delay node for X (using merge_delay_goals) and then insert the the X cycle just after the dummy node in the cycle of Y, stripping out the rest of the delay node.[15]

We now illustrate the execution of the same goal, as previously considered for the usual Prolog approach

```
G = write(X), freeze(X,G), H = write(g(Y)), freeze(Y,H), X = Y, X = f(Z).
freeze(X,G) :- (bound(X) ==> call(G)).
```

After the first four literals are executed the heap holds the two attributed variables X and Y and their delay nodes which contain the delayed goals, as shown on the top of Figure 15. During the unification of X and Y the two lists are appended and the cycles are merged, eliminating the delay node of Y, resulting in the heap state in the middle of Figure 15. When X is bound to f(Z) the goal list [G,H] is remembered for execution, and every (non-delay) element in the cycle for X is pointed to f(Z). The heap state is now as shown in the bottom of Figure 15. The delayed goals are then executed, causing f(Z)g(f(Z)) to be printed.

As we can see, the heap usage performed by the HAL representation is more complicated than that of the corresponding WAM representation. Note also that the addition of delay for a solver type potentially slows down all unifications for that type since we may need to search both alias cycles to determine if we have delay nodes in them. That is why HAL requires the user to explicitly indicate whether a Herbrand type requires support for delay, so that it can generate calls to the more efficient versions of unify_var_val and unify_var_var where possible.

6.5   Killing Dynamically Scheduled Code

Because the dynamically scheduled code is potentially executed multiple times, the delay constructs need to be explicitly killed when they are no longer needed. As we have seen before, for Herbrand constructs the herband_delay_id type is an integer and the get_id predicate is thus implemented using a global integer counter. The ability to kill dynamically scheduled code is managed by associating with each herband_delay_id the list of delayed goal nodes that make up the construct. The kill/1 predicate simply traverses this list removing each delayed goal node from the doubly linked list in which it occurs.

7   Evaluation

Our empirical evaluation has three aims. The first is to compare the performance of HAL and its Herbrand solver with a state-of-the-art Prolog implementation,

---

[15] Actually by keeping track of the previous pointers we can avoid using the dummy node for Y, unless the delay nodes are the first things we encounter in both chains.

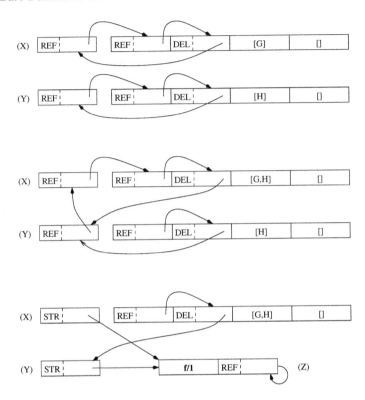

Fig. 15. HAL heap representation for dynamically scheduled goals and after executing each literal X = Y, X = f(Z).

SICStus Prolog. The second is to investigate the impact of each kind of declaration on efficiency. The third is to compare HAL with Mercury so as to determine the overhead introduced by the run-time support for Herbrand solving.

To achieve the first aim we take a number of Prolog benchmarks[16] and compare them with the equivalent HAL programs. In order to build these equivalent programs we must first transform built-ins not present in HAL (such as cut) into their HAL equivalents (such as if-then-else). Also, although Prolog does not have type, mode and determinism declarations, the current HAL compiler requires them. We solve this problem by defining a "universal" constructor type for the HAL program which contains all functors occurring in the program and declaring this type to be a Herbrand solver type supporting dynamic scheduling by using `deriving delay`.

Note that all integers, floats, chars and strings in the original Prolog program must be wrapped in the HAL program, and each wrapping functor must appear in the "universal" constructor type. Finally, all predicate arguments are declared

---

to have this type and mode oo, and all predicates are declared to have determinism **nondet**. Most of these tasks are done automatically by a pre-processor.

For example, for the original **hanoi** Prolog program (the code in Section 2 minus the declarations), the preprocessor will add the declarations

```
:- typedef htype -> (int(int) ; float(float) ; a ; b ; c ; []
                     ; [htype|htype] ; mv(htype,htype) ; htype-htype )
                     deriving delay.
:- pred hanoi(htype,htype).
:- mode hanoi(oo,oo) is nondet.
:- pred hanoi2(htype,htype,htype,htype,htype).
:- mode hanoi2(oo,oo,oo,oo,oo) is nondet.
```

The preprocessor will also replace the three occurrences of 1 in the program text by int(1), and will create predicates for the wrapped versions of >, is and function -.

To achieve our second aim of investigating the impact of each kind of declaration on efficiency, we take these Prolog-equivalent HAL programs and progressively transform them as follows.

- The first step is to add precise type information, i.e., to add the required type definitions and acccurate predicate type declarations. All types must still be declared as Herbrand solver types supporting delay since the associated terms may sometimes be treated as logical variables. This also implies that we must continue to wrap integers and other primitive types since they may be placed in data structures or equated before they are fixed.
- The second step is to remove the support for dynamic scheduling for those Herbrand solver types upon which nothing is delayed. We simply replace the directive **deriving delay** by the directive **deriving herbrand** wherever possible.
- The third step adds accurate mode declarations. Types which are never associated with the **old** instantiation need not be declared as Herbrand solver types (i.e. their **deriving herbrand** directive is removed) and, in the case of the primitive types, such types can have their wrapping removed.
- In the fourth and last step precise determinism declarations are added.

We then evaluate the efficiency of the programs obtained at each step.

Our third and final aim is to compare the efficiency of HAL and Mercury to determine the overhead introduced by the run-time support for HAL, i.e., the overhead introduced by trailing, the reserved REF tag used for solver-types, extra type classes, predicate renamings, etc. In order to do so we took the program resulting from compiling the HAL program obtained in the fourth step above, and modified it by using the Mercury libraries (instead of HAL ones), eliminating any unification-related code (which was actually dead-code anyway), and eliminating any predicate renaming introduced due to the use of type classes, etc. The resulting program was then compiled using two different compilation grades of Mercury: one that does not provide trailing and one that does. Both grades also avoid reserving the extra REF tag for solver-types, but are otherwise equivalent to the Mercury grade used for compiling the HAL programs. Note that since Mercury does not provide full unification, we could only do this for benchmarks with no remaining herbrand types.

All timings are in seconds on a dual Pentium II-400MHz with 632M of RAM running Linux 2.2.9. We have turned garbage collection off in all three systems: SICStus Prolog 3.8.6 (compact code), Mercury (release-of-the-day 2003-08-09 version), and HAL.

We have used a subset of the standard Prolog benchmarks: aiakl, boyer, deriv, fib, mmatrix, serialize, tak, warplan, hanoi and qsort. The last two are shown in two forms, one using "normal" lists and append/3, the other using difference lists. The reason for choosing these benchmarks is that they did not require extensive changes to the original Prolog benchmarks[17] and hence the comparison is fairer. To this we added two HAL benchmarks using delay, both based around Boolean constraint solving. The first bqueens is the classic n-queens problem, the second nono is a nonogram solver.[18]

Benchmark	Preds	Lits	OSICS	SICS	None	T	TS	TSM	TSMD	Merc+tr	Merc
aiakl	7	21	0.09	0.08	0.39	0.94	0.97	0.02	0.03	0.03	0.01
boyer	14	124	1.79	0.51	2.36	2.00	2.23	0.11	0.05	0.08	0.02
bqueens	23	99	—	73.38	4.86	5.04	5.04	4.77	4.73	—	—
deriv	1	33	1.54	2.41	5.02	4.88	4.08	0.83	0.68	0.69	0.15
fib	1	6	1.20	1.21	0.36	0.33	0.27	0.02	0.02	0.01	0.01
hanoiapp	2	7	2.57	2.61	6.30	14.36	13.77	0.64	0.32	0.27	0.19
hanoidiff	2	6	1.81	1.75	0.54	0.73	0.74	0.66	0.63	—	—
mmatrix	3	7	1.26	1.26	1.22	2.96	2.35	0.10	0.05	0.04	0.01
nono	30	181	—	16.35	11.21	17.56	17.56	2.12	2.08	—	—
qsortapp	3	10	2.94	1.60	5.14	10.13	10.10	0.51	0.22	0.21	0.11
qsortdiff	3	10	2.91	1.64	5.22	9.92	10.06	0.53	0.24	—	—
serialize	5	19	1.41	1.36	2.30	2.56	2.83	0.63	0.46	—	—
tak	1	9	0.49	0.60	0.90	0.76	0.68	0.08	0.06	0.05	0.01
warplan	25	88	0.51	0.60	2.12	1.14	1.06	0.40	0.32	—	—
Average				1.16	0.77	0.77	1.04	8.61	1.38	1.11	2.72

Table 1. Execution times in seconds

Table 1 provides the execution time for the benchmarks. The second and third columns of Table 1 detail the benchmark sizes (number of predicates and

---

[17] aiakl, deriv, qsort, serialize and tak only required replacement of cuts by if-then-else while warplan also needed to transform the \+ built-in into an if-then-else and include a well-typed version of univ for warplan. The only exception is boyer, for which the starting point was a restricted Mercury version, rather than the Prolog one.

[18] See e.g. http://www.puzzlemuseum.com/griddler/griddler.htm

literals before normalization, excluding dead code and the query). Subsequent columns give the execution time for:

- the original program run with SICStus Prolog (OSICS),
- the modified Prolog program run with SICStus Prolog (SICS),
- the Prolog-equivalent HAL program (obtained with the preprocessor) which containts no precise declarations (None),
- with precise type declarations (T),
- with precise type declarations and scheduling information (i.e. replacing `deriving delay` by `deriving herbrand` wherever possible) (TS),
- with precise type declarations, scheduling information, and mode declarations (TSM),
- with precise type declarations, scheduling information, and mode and determinism declarations (TSMD),
- this last version run with Mercury (if possible) compiled with trailing support (Merc+tr),
- the same Mercury version without trailing support (Merc).

The last row of the table contains the geometric mean speed ratio between the preceeding column and the current column. For example, programs in the TSM column are, on average, 8.61 times as fast as the corresponding program in the TS column.

The benchmarks `nono` and `bqueens` use dynamic scheduling code which is required to be `semidet`. Hence, we required some modification of the original code to ensure that the determinism was checkable by the compiler for versions before TSMD.

In general, the original and modified SICStus programs have similar speed. `deriv` slows down because of loss of indexing caused by the introduction of if-then-elses, while the two versions of quick sort improve because a badly placed cut in the original program is replaced by a more efficient if-then-else.

The Prolog-equivalent HAL versions are mostly slower than the modified SICStus versions. Slow-down occurs in `aiakl`, `boyer` and `warplan` because no indexing is currently available for possibly unbound input arguments. Surprising speed-up occurs for `fib` and `hanoidiff`; we suspect because of Mercury's handling of recursion. For the benchmarks with delay, since the scheduling strategies are impossible to make the same, the comparison is rather meaningless.

Generally, adding precise type information leads to a slow down (on average 0.77 times as fast). For the version with no information, we used a monomorphic "universal" type which included all the functors in the program. For the version with type information, we use the polymorphic types where appropriate. The slow down is due to the use of polymorphic unification predicates. The compiler could remove this cost by providing type specialized versions of these predicates (indeed if we use only non-polymorphic types the relative performance is 1.33 in favour of types). The programs `fib` and `tak` do not use polymorphic types and therefore do not incur this cost. We see improvements for both of these benchmarks. For `warplan` we gain a large improvement because it allows a type specialized version of univ to be used.

Adding precise scheduling information provides a modest improvement for most of the benchmarks (average 1.04 times). It provides no improvement for bqueens and nono, both of which make extensive use of dynamic scheduling.

Adding mode declarations provides the most speed-up (on average 8.61 times). This is because it allows calls to the Herbrand solver to be replaced by calls to Mercury's specialized term manipulation operations and also allows indexing. Interestingly bqueens obtains no speedup since the bulk of the time is in the search, using the dynamic scheduling, and this is unchanged. For nono the dynamic scheduled code is itself complex, and so benefits from mode information.

Determinism declarations also lead to significant speed-up (on average 1.38 times). Again the benchmarks with dynamic scheduling are the least affected, since the search dominates.

The times given in final three columns of Table 1 are too small to make a meaningful comparison. For that reason, Table 2 shows the execution times for 100 repeats of each benchmark. We omit bqueens, hanoidiff, nono, qsortdiff, serialize and warplan since their final HAL versions still need herbrand types.

Benchmark	TSMD	Merc+tr	Merc
aiakl	4.85	4.3	3.55
boyer	9.37	10.53	9.97
deriv	79.73	76.02	35.52
fib	2.61	2.61	1.17
hanoiapp	40.07	40.15	34.78
mmatrix	5.27	4.99	4.99
qsortapp	32.79	33.25	24.23
tak	6.06	6.35	4.2
Average		1.01	1.40

Table 2. Execution times in seconds for 100 repeats

The HAL version running with precise declarations is very similar to the Mercury version with trailing support. When we compile the Mercury version without trailing support we see an improvement of 1.4 times on average.

We have also investigated the effect of the declarations on memory usage. Table 3 shows the trail usage for each benchmark, whereas Table 4 shows heap usage. The size of the trail is mostly affected by the presence or absence of precise mode declarations. Adding precise mode declarations greatly reduces trail size — only those benchmarks with Herbrand solver types may need to use the trail.

In many cases, adding precise type definitions causes a significant increase in heap usage. This is due to the use of polymorphic data types. The unification predicates for such types construct data structures for run time type information on the heap, and the affected benchmarks make many calls to these predicates.

Adding precise modes causes a significant reduction in heap size for most benchmarks. This is mainly because most of the calls to the unification predicates

Benchmark	None	TS	TSM	TSMD	Merc
aiakl	3637	2641	0	0	0
boyer	4904	4904	0	0	0
bqueens	3562	3581	3446	3446	—
deriv	40530	40530	0	0	0
fib	1897	1897	0	0	0
hanoiapp	72704	72704	0	0	0
hanoidiff	7168	7168	6144	6144	—
mmatrix	7970	7970	0	0	0
nono	953	953	307	307	—
qsortapp	51449	51449	0	0	0
qsortdiff	51126	51126	352	352	—
serialize	17244	17244	1552	1552	—
tak	5173	5173	0	0	0
warplan	34	34	2	2	—

Table 3. Memory usage in Kbytes for the Trail

Benchmark	None	TS	TSM	TSMD	Merc
aiakl	2712	38498	1231	1231	1231
boyer	5948	5950	3561	3561	3561
bqueens	81074	641074	101074	101074	—
deriv	27712	27712	24949	24949	24949
fib	2371	2371	0	0	0
hanoiapp	41472	438783	37888	36864	36864
hanoidiff	6656	20480	57344	57344	—
mmatrix	19610	47659	79	79	79
nono	641082	641074	641082	641082	—
qsortapp	25842	269666	25607	25490	25490
qsortdiff	25446	261314	28317	28317	—
serialize	8928	90622	8331	8331	—
tak	5173	5173	0	0	0
warplan	23	22	18	18	—

Table 4. Memory usage in Kbytes for the Heap

can be removed. It is also no longer necessary to box primitive types, such as
ints and floats. For example, without such boxing fib and tak use no heap
space at all.

Finally, we have investigated the size of the alias cycles constructed using
PARMA bindings. The results are shown in Table 5. Virtually all cycles have
length one immediately before being bound to a non-variable term. Only four
benchmarks, bqueens, deriv, warplan and serialize, have a maximum cycle
length of more than two (154, 129, 4 and 18 respectively). The cycles disappear
for deriv with mode information. The percentage of non unit cycles dramatically

Benchmark	None	TS	TSM	TSMD
aiakl	<1 (2)	0 (1)	0 (1)	0 (1)
boyer	<1 (2)	<1 (2)	0 (1)	0 (1)
bqueens	80 (154)	85 (154)	100 (154)	100 (154)
deriv	<1 (129)	<1 (129)	0 (1)	0 (1)
fib	0 (1)	0 (1)	0 (1)	0 (1)
hanoiapp	0 (1)	0 (1)	0 (1)	0 (1)
hanoidiff	25 (2)	25 (2)	100 (2)	100 (2)
mmatrix	<1 (2)	0 (1)	0 (1)	0 (1)
qsortapp	0 (1)	0 (1)	0 (1)	0 (1)
qsortdiff	<1 (2)	<1 (2)	100 (2)	100 (2)
serialize	1 (18)	1 (18)	100 (18)	100 (18)
tak	0 (1)	0 (1)	0 (1)	0 (1)
warplan	<1 (4)	1 (4)	99 (4)	99 (4)

Table 5. Percentage of chains with more than one element, and maximum chain

increases for `hanoidiff`, `qsortdiff`, `serialize` and `warplan` with the addition of mode information. However, this is not because the number of non unit cycles has increaseed but, rather, because the number of unit cycles is reduced to zero (and thus all cycles are non unit cycles). This is due to the addition of mode information which allows us to remove the `deriving herbrand` declarations for some types, thus avoiding the use of PARMA chains when binding variables of those types.

8   Related Work

As far as we know, HAL is the first logic programming implementation to use the PARMA variable representation and binding scheme since it was introduced in [12]. We note that [8] discusses in detail the differences between the PARMA and WAM schemes. However, there seems to be no compelling reason to prefer one over the other; in fact, artificial examples can be constructed for which each scheme easily outperforms the other. There has been some earlier work on the impact of type, mode and determinism information on the performance of Prolog, but the results are quite uneven. In [9], information about type, mode and determinism is used to (manually) generate better code. Its results show up to a factor of two speedup for mode information, and the same result for type information. [13] describes Aquarius, a Prolog system in which compile-time analysis information (including type, mode and determinism information) is used for optimizing the execution. In its results, analysis information had a relatively low impact on speed: on average about 50% for small programs without built-ins (for `tak` 300%) and about 12% for larger programs with built-ins (for `boyer` only 3%). Finally, in the context of the PARMA system, [12] also reports on speedup obtained from information provided by compile time analysis. Its results are highly benchmark dependent, with only 10% speed up for `boyer` but a factor of 8 for `nrev`.

It is difficult to directly compare our results (from Section 7) with those found for Aquarius and PARMA. One problem is the differences between the underlying abstract machines and the optimizations performed by each compiler. For instance, Mercury performs particular optimizations like specializing the tags per type, the use of a separate stacks for deterministic and nondeterministic predicates and a middle-recursion optimization, which are not found in PARMA or Aquarius. On the other hand, Mercury lacks real last call optimization. However, in accord with our findings, for all systems mode information gives greater speedups than type information. Another problem is that their information is obtained from compile time analysis, rather than from programmer declarations. We suspect that compile time analysis is not powerful enough to find accurate information about the larger benchmarks, while in our experiments the programmer provides this information. This would explain why our performance improvements are more uniform (and larger) across all benchmarks, regardless of size.

9   Conclusions

Our empirical evaluation of HAL is very pleasing. It demonstrates that it is possible to combine Mercury-like efficiency for ground data structure manipulation with Prolog-style logical variables by using PARMA bindings to ensure that the representation for terms used by HAL's Herbrand solver is consistent with that used by Mercury for ground terms. This means that the compiler is free to use the more efficient Mercury term manipulation operations whenever this is possible.

There are however a number of ways to improve HAL's Herbrand constraint solving which we shall investigate. These include better tracking of where one-step dereferencing may be (or rather, is not) required, and more specialized cases for equality and indexing for old terms.

Prolog-like programs written in HAL run somewhat slower than in SICStus, in part because there is no term indexing for possibly unbound instantiations. However, once declarations are provided the programs run an order of magnitude faster. (Much of this arises from the sophisticated compilation techniques used by the underlying Mercury compiler.) Our results show that the biggest performance improvement arises from mode declarations while type and determinism declarations give moderate speed improvement. All declarations reduce the space requirements.

It should be remembered that declarations are not only useful for improving efficiency. They also allow compile time checking to improve program robustness, help program debugging and facilitate integration with foreign language procedures.

Acknowledgements

Many people have helped in the development of HAL. In particular, we would like to thank the Mercury development team, especially Fergus Henderson and Zoltan Somogyi, who have helped us with many modifications to the Mercury system to support HAL. We would also like to thank David G. Jeffery, Nick Nethercote and Peter Schachte.

References

1. H. Aït-Kaci. *Warren's Abstract Machine*. MIT Press, 1991.
2. B. Demoen, M. García de la Banda, W. Harvey, K. Marriott, and P.J. Stuckey. An overview of HAL. In J. Jaffar, editor, *Proceedings of the Fourth International Conference on Principles and Practices of Constraint Programming*, LNCS, pages 174–188. Springer-Verlag, October 1999.
3. T. Dowd, P. Schachte, F. Henderson, and Z. Somogyi. Using impurity to create declarative interfaces in Mercury. Technical Report 2000/17, Department of Computer Science, University of Melbourne, 2000.
   http://www.cs.mu.oz.au/research/mercury/information/papers.html.
4. M. García de la Banda, P.J. Stuckey, W. Harvey, and K. Marriott. Mode checking in HAL. In J. LLoyd et al., editor, *Proceedings of the First International Conference on Computational Logic*, LNCS 1861, pages 1270–1284. Springer-Verlag, July 2000.
5. Programming Systems Group. *SICStus Prolog User's Manual*, release 3.11.0 edition, 2003.
6. C. Holzbaur. Metastructures vs. attributed variables in the context of extensible unification. In *Proceedings of the International Symposium on Programming Language Implementation and Logic Programming*, number 631 in LNCS, pages 260–268. Springer-Verlag, 1992.
7. D. Jeffery, F. Henderson, and Z. Somogyi. Type classes in mercury. Technical Report Technical Report 98/13, Department of Computer Science, University of Melbourne, Melbourne, Australia, 1998.
8. T. Lindgren, P. Mildner, and J. Bevemyr. On Taylor's scheme for unbound variables. Technical report, UPMAIL, October 1995.
9. A. Mariën, G. Janssens, A. Mulkers, and M. Bruynooghe. The impact of abstract interpretation: an experiment in code generation. In *Proc. of the ICLP89*, pages 33–47, 1989.
10. K. Marriott and P.J. Stuckey. *Programming with Constraints: an Introduction*. MIT Press, 1998.
11. Z. Somogyi, F. Henderson, and T. Conway. The execution algorithm of Mercury: an efficient purely declarative logic programming language. *Journal of Logic Programming*, 29:17–64, 1996.
12. A. Taylor. PARMA–bridging the performance gap between imperative and logic programming. *Journal of Logic Programming*, 29(1–3), 1996.
13. P. Van Roy. Can Logic Programming Execute as Fast as Imperative Programming? Report 90/600, UCB/CSD, Berkeley, California 94720, Dec 1990.
14. D. H. D. Warren. An abstract Prolog instruction set. Technical Report 309, SRI International, Menlo Park, U.S.A., Oct. 1983.

Author Index

Lecture Notes in Computer Science

For information about Vols. 1–2997

please contact your bookseller or Springer-Verlag

Vol. 3045: A. Laganà, M.L. Gavrilova, V. Kumar, Y. Mun, C.K. Tan, O. Gervasi (Eds.), Computational Science and Its Applications – ICCSA 2004. LIII, 1040 pages. 2004.

Vol. 3044: A. Laganà, M.L. Gavrilova, V. Kumar, Y. Mun, C.K. Tan, O. Gervasi (Eds.), Computational Science and Its Applications – ICCSA 2004. LIII, 1140 pages. 2004.

Vol. 3043: A. Laganà, M.L. Gavrilova, V. Kumar, Y. Mun, C.K. Tan, O. Gervasi (Eds.), Computational Science and Its Applications – ICCSA 2004. LIII, 1180 pages. 2004.

Vol. 3042: N. Mitrou, K. Kontovasilis, G.N. Rouskas, I. Iliadis, L. Merakos (Eds.), NETWORKING 2004, Networking Technologies, Services, and Protocols; Performance of Computer and Communication Networks; Mobile and Wireless Communications. XXXIII, 1519 pages. 2004.

Vol. 3040: R. Conejo, M. Urretavizcaya, J.-L. Pérez-de-la-Cruz (Eds.), Current Topics in Artificial Intelligence. XIV, 689 pages. 2004. (Subseries LNAI).

Vol. 3039: M. Bubak, G.D.v. Albada, P.M. Sloot, J.J. Dongarra (Eds.), Computational Science - ICCS 2004. LXVI, 1271 pages. 2004.

Vol. 3038: M. Bubak, G.D.v. Albada, P.M. Sloot, J.J. Dongarra (Eds.), Computational Science - ICCS 2004. LXVI, 1311 pages. 2004.

Vol. 3037: M. Bubak, G.D.v. Albada, P.M. Sloot, J.J. Dongarra (Eds.), Computational Science - ICCS 2004. LXVI, 745 pages. 2004.

Vol. 3036: M. Bubak, G.D.v. Albada, P.M. Sloot, J.J. Dongarra (Eds.), Computational Science - ICCS 2004. LXVI, 713 pages. 2004.

Vol. 3035: M.A. Wimmer (Ed.), Knowledge Management in Electronic Government. XII, 326 pages. 2004. (Subseries LNAI).

Vol. 3034: J. Favela, E. Menasalvas, E. Chávez (Eds.), Advances in Web Intelligence. XIII, 227 pages. 2004. (Subseries LNAI).

Vol. 3033: M. Li, X.-H. Sun, Q. Deng, J. Ni (Eds.), Grid and Cooperative Computing. XXXVIII, 1076 pages. 2004.

Vol. 3032: M. Li, X.-H. Sun, Q. Deng, J. Ni (Eds.), Grid and Cooperative Computing. XXXVII, 1112 pages. 2004.

Vol. 3031: A. Butz, A. Krüger, P. Olivier (Eds.), Smart Graphics. X, 165 pages. 2004.

Vol. 3030: P. Giorgini, B. Henderson-Sellers, M. Winikoff (Eds.), Agent-Oriented Information Systems. XIV, 207 pages. 2004. (Subseries LNAI).

Vol. 3029: B. Orchard, C. Yang, M. Ali (Eds.), Innovations in Applied Artificial Intelligence. XXI, 1272 pages. 2004. (Subseries LNAI).

Vol. 3028: D. Neuenschwander, Probabilistic and Statistical Methods in Cryptology. X, 158 pages. 2004.

Vol. 3027: C. Cachin, J. Camenisch (Eds.), Advances in Cryptology - EUROCRYPT 2004. XI, 628 pages. 2004.

Vol. 3026: C. Ramamoorthy, R. Lee, K.W. Lee (Eds.), Software Engineering Research and Applications. XV, 377 pages. 2004.

Vol. 3025: G.A. Vouros, T. Panayiotopoulos (Eds.), Methods and Applications of Artificial Intelligence. XV, 546 pages. 2004. (Subseries LNAI).

Vol. 3024: T. Pajdla, J. Matas (Eds.), Computer Vision - ECCV 2004. XXVIII, 621 pages. 2004.

Vol. 3023: T. Pajdla, J. Matas (Eds.), Computer Vision - ECCV 2004. XXVIII, 611 pages. 2004.

Vol. 3022: T. Pajdla, J. Matas (Eds.), Computer Vision - ECCV 2004. XXVIII, 621 pages. 2004.

Vol. 3021: T. Pajdla, J. Matas (Eds.), Computer Vision - ECCV 2004. XXVIII, 633 pages. 2004.

Vol. 3019: R. Wyrzykowski, J.J. Dongarra, M. Paprzycki, J. Wasniewski (Eds.), Parallel Processing and Applied Mathematics. XIX, 1174 pages. 2004.

Vol. 3018: M. Bruynooghe (Ed.), Logic Based Program Synthesis and Transformation. X, 233 pages. 2004.

Vol. 3016: C. Lengauer, D. Batory, C. Consel, M. Odersky (Eds.), Domain-Specific Program Generation. XII, 325 pages. 2004.

Vol. 3015: C. Barakat, I. Pratt (Eds.), Passive and Active Network Measurement. XI, 300 pages. 2004.

Vol. 3014: F. van der Linden (Ed.), Software Product-Family Engineering. IX, 486 pages. 2004.

Vol. 3012: K. Kurumatani, S.-H. Chen, A. Ohuchi (Eds.), Multi-Agnets for Mass User Support. X, 217 pages. 2004. (Subseries LNAI).

Vol. 3011: J.-C. Régin, M. Rueher (Eds.), Integration of AI and OR Techniques in Constraint Programming for Combinatorial Optimization Problems. XI, 415 pages. 2004.

Vol. 3010: K.R. Apt, F. Fages, F. Rossi, P. Szeredi, J. Váncza (Eds.), Recent Advances in Constraints. VIII, 285 pages. 2004. (Subseries LNAI).

Vol. 3009: F. Bomarius, H. Iida (Eds.), Product Focused Software Process Improvement. XIV, 584 pages. 2004.

Vol. 3008: S. Heuel, Uncertain Projective Geometry. XVII, 205 pages. 2004.

Vol. 3007: J.X. Yu, X. Lin, H. Lu, Y. Zhang (Eds.), Advanced Web Technologies and Applications. XXII, 936 pages. 2004.

Vol. 3006: M. Matsui, R. Zuccherato (Eds.), Selected Areas in Cryptography. XI, 361 pages. 2004.

Vol. 3005: G.R. Raidl, S. Cagnoni, J. Branke, D.W. Corne, R. Drechsler, Y. Jin, C.G. Johnson, P. Machado, E. Marchiori, F. Rothlauf, G.D. Smith, G. Squillero (Eds.), Applications of Evolutionary Computing. XVII, 562 pages. 2004.

Vol. 3004: J. Gottlieb, G.R. Raidl (Eds.), Evolutionary Computation in Combinatorial Optimization. X, 241 pages. 2004.

Vol. 3003: M. Keijzer, U.-M. O'Reilly, S.M. Lucas, E. Costa, T. Soule (Eds.), Genetic Programming. XI, 410 pages. 2004.

Vol. 3002: D.L. Hicks (Ed.), Metainformatics. X, 213 pages. 2004.

Vol. 3001: A. Ferscha, F. Mattern (Eds.), Pervasive Computing. XVII, 358 pages. 2004.

Vol. 2999: E.A. Boiten, J. Derrick, G. Smith (Eds.), Integrated Formal Methods. XI, 541 pages. 2004.

Vol. 2998: Y. Kameyama, P.J. Stuckey (Eds.), Functional and Logic Programming. X, 307 pages. 2004.